THE SUPREME COURT AND THE FOURTH AMENDMENT'S EXCLUSIONARY RULE

The Supreme Court and the Fourth Amendment's Exclusionary Rule

Tracey Maclin

OXFORD
UNIVERSITY PRESS

OXFORD
UNIVERSITY PRESS

Oxford University Press is a department of the University of Oxford. It furthers the University's objective of excellence in research, scholarship, and education by publishing worldwide.

Oxford New York
Auckland Cape Town Dar es Salaam Hong Kong Karachi Kuala Lumpur Madrid
Melbourne Mexico City Nairobi New Delhi Shanghai Taipei Toronto

With offices in
Argentina Austria Brazil Chile Czech Republic France Greece Guatemala Hungary
Italy Japan Poland Portugal Singapore South Korea Switzerland Thailand
Turkey Ukraine Vietnam

Published in the United States of America by
Oxford University Press
198 Madison Avenue, New York, NY 10016

Library of Congress Cataloging-in-Publication Data

Maclin, Tracey.
The Supreme Court and the Fourth Amendment's exclusionary rule / Tracey Maclin.
p. cm.
Includes bibliographical references and index.
ISBN 978-0-19-979547-5 ((hardback) : alk. paper)
1. Exclusionary rule (Evidence)—United States. 2. Searches and seizures—United States.
3. United States. Constitution. 4th Amendment. 4. United States. Supreme Court. I. Title.
KF9662.M25 2012
347.73'62—dc23
2012014688

9 8 7 6 5 4 3 2

Printed in the United States of America on acid-free paper

Note to Readers
This publication is designed to provide accurate and authoritative information in regard to the subject matter covered. It is based upon sources believed to be accurate and reliable and is intended to be current as of the time it was written. It is sold with the understanding that the publisher is not engaged in rendering legal, accounting, or other professional services. If legal advice or other expert assistance is required, the services of a competent professional person should be sought. Also, to confirm that the information has not been affected or changed by recent developments, traditional legal research techniques should be used, including checking primary sources where appropriate.

(Based on the Declaration of Principles jointly adopted by a Committee of the American Bar Association and a Committee of Publishers and Associations.)

For Karen Tosh

Contents

Acknowledgments

THERE ARE SEVERAL individuals who helped me complete this book. First, I want to thank several of my colleagues at Boston University School of Law. My original plan was to write a book about the Fourth Amendment. I had a ninety-page draft on the exclusionary rule, which I envisioned as the first chapter of the book. After I presented this draft at a law school workshop, two colleagues, James Fleming and Larry Yackle, convinced me that I should focus solely on the exclusionary rule. This advice was perfect. Thanks also to Ward Farnsworth, Andrew Kull, Gary Lawson, and William Ryckman who read and commented on drafts of the initial chapters.

Special appreciation goes to Yale Kamisar who read and commented on drafts of the first four chapters. As always, I greatly benefited from Yale's insights. During the summer of 2011, Al Alschuler read drafts of chapters 1 through 6. Al's comments and critique were invaluable. Al's precise legal analysis persuaded me to rewrite parts of these chapters. John C. Jeffries, Jr. read a draft of chapter 4. Dean Jeffries's comments sharpened my understanding of Justice Lewis Powell's views on the Fourth Amendment's exclusionary rule.

Thanks also to several Boston University School of Law students who assisted me during the preparation of this book. They include Alexander Barrett, Jesse Boodoo, Andrew Churella, Darren Goldman, Todd Marabella, Carlos Maycotte, Negar Mortazavi, Jennifer Rader, Elizabeth Rossi, and Carrie Turner. Special thanks to Julia Mirabella, Kelsey Kingsbery, and Diana Nevins. Julia's legal analysis, editing, and organizational skills were extraordinarily helpful at a crucial time. During the final stages of the project, Kelsey and Diana provided superior editing of the text and checking of footnotes. I could not have completed the book without the support of these three individuals.

Rachel Ortiz, who is now the Assistant Dean for Library and Information Services at Roger Williams University School of Law, and Stefanie Weigmann, who is the Assistant Director for Research, Faculty Services, and Educational Technology at Boston University School of Law, were extremely helpful locating documents and helping me navigate the archives of retired justices. Del Dickson helped decipher the handwriting of William J. Brennan, Jr. and William Douglas. Jeffrey M. Flannery, the head of reference at the Manuscript Division of the Library of Congress, and John Jacob, Special Collections law librarian and archivist of the Lewis F. Powell, Jr. Papers at Washington and Lee University School of Law, were extremely helpful and patient with my many requests and questions. Stephen Wermiel helped me gain access to Justice Brennan's case histories. Dean Larry Sager expedited my access to Tom Clark's papers at the Tarlton Law Library at the University of Texas School of Law. Rod Smolla, the former Dean of Washington and Lee University School of Law and now President of Furman University, made my trips to study the Powell papers efficient and productive. Also, I want to thank Joseph Lipsitt for his financial support of my scholarship, and Robert Smith for his support given through the David Saul Smith Award Fund for Excellence in Legal Scholarship, which provided a generous financial grant supporting this project.

Thanks to Floyd Abrams and Judge Boyce F. Martin, Jr. for their confidence in my legal skills when I was a "legal pup." Finally, I thank my parents, Murray Maclin and the late Gertrude Maclin, for their lifelong support.

Introduction

MOST AMERICANS UNDERSTAND that police need a search warrant before they can forcibly enter a person's home. And many also know that a person cannot be arbitrarily arrested. These legal protections derive from the Fourth Amendment. But what does the Constitution require when the police violate a person's Fourth Amendment rights and discover incriminating evidence hidden in a bedroom closet or inside the trunk of a car? There is no easy answer. In fact, this question has divided the justices of the Supreme Court for over half a century.

The Fourth Amendment, which protects people against unreasonable governmental searches and seizures, is the most litigated constitutional provision in the nation's courts. Judges throughout the country decide more search and seizure issues than they do questions concerning the First Amendment, the Equal Protection Clause of the Fourteenth Amendment, or the Commerce Clause contained in Article I of the Constitution. Most frequently, judges are determining whether the police conducted an unconstitutional search or seizure before obtaining incriminating evidence against a person. If the incriminating evidence was, in fact, obtained as a result of a Fourth Amendment violation, the legal principle that prohibits admission of such evidence in a criminal trial is known as the exclusionary rule. As Wayne LaFave, the greatest scholar on the Fourth Amendment in American history, has observed: "It is primarily because of the exclusionary rule that courts are called upon to meet the seemingly unceasing challenge of marking the dimensions of the protections flowing from the Fourth Amendment."[1] This book explores the

[1] 1 WAYNE R. LAFAVE, SEARCH AND SEIZURE: A TREATISE ON THE FOURTH AMENDMENT, §1.1(a), at 5 (4th ed. 2004).

origins, development, and controversy surrounding the Fourth Amendment's exclusionary rule in the Supreme Court.

Stanford Law Professor John Kaplan once remarked that it "is difficult to state the exclusionary rule with great precision."[2] For the first half-century of its existence, the rule was an essential aspect of the protection provided by the Fourth Amendment. Approaching the midpoint of the twentieth century, the Court viewed the exclusionary rule as absolute: whenever federal officers obtained evidence by violating the Fourth Amendment rights of an individual, that evidence was inadmissible against that individual in a federal prosecution. At this point, however, the exclusionary rule was limited to federal prosecutions as the Fourth Amendment did not yet apply to searches and seizures by state law enforcement officers.

Because the exclusionary rule requires the suppression of relevant and highly probative evidence of a person's guilt, the rule has been highly controversial, on and off the Court. In 1926, while he was then a judge on the New York Court of Appeals, Benjamin Cardozo succinctly summarized the problem with the rule with his memorable remark: "The criminal is to go free because the constable has blundered."[3] In 1949, however, the Court, in an opinion authored by Felix Frankfurter, abandoned the position that the exclusionary rule was part and parcel of the Fourth Amendment. And by the mid-1970s, the Burger Court jettisoned the view that the exclusionary rule is a personal right; rather, the Court explained that the rule is a judicially created remedy to deter police violations of the Fourth Amendment.

Opponents of the rule have insisted that exclusion imposes huge costs on society in the form of lost convictions and overly lenient plea bargains for criminals subjected to illegal searches and seizures. Critics of the exclusionary rule also contend that suppression of evidence is not only bad policy but an unwarranted remedy because exclusion is neither mandated by the text of the Fourth Amendment nor any other provision of the Constitution. Finally, critics argue that because judges, like most people, are opposed to excluding relevant evidence, the exclusionary rule encourages judges to reject Fourth Amendment claims. When this happens, critics say that the rule results in narrowing the scope of Fourth Amendment protection for everyone.

On the other side of the debate, those who defend exclusion maintain that such criticisms are misdirected. Defenders note that the exclusionary rule does not restrict the powers of the police; the Fourth Amendment does. As retired Justice Potter Stewart observed in a 1983 speech: "Much of the criticism leveled at the exclusionary rule is misdirected . . . . [C]ritics sometimes fail to acknowledge that, in many instances, the same extremely relevant evidence would not have been obtained had the police officer complied with the commands of the fourth amendment in the first place."[4] Put differently,

[2] John Kaplan, *The Limits of the Exclusionary Rule*, 26 Stan. L. Rev. 1027, 1029 (1974).

[3] People v. Defore, 150 N.E. 585, 587 (N.Y. 1926).

[4] Potter Stewart, *The Road to* Mapp v. Ohio *and Beyond: The Origins, Development and Future of the Exclusionary Rule in Search-and-Seizure Cases*, 83 Colum. L. Rev. 1365, 1392 (1983) (footnotes omitted).

the costs incurred in the form of lost convictions and lenient guilty pleas that critics bemoan are not imposed by the exclusionary rule, but by the Fourth Amendment itself.[5] The exclusionary rule, in other words, reminds society of the price we pay for having the Fourth Amendment.[6]

Although scholars have refuted claims that the exclusionary rule prevents the successful prosecution of large numbers of violent offenders,[7] the perception persists that the exclusionary rule "handcuffs" the police and enables the release of violent criminals. In theory, the rule requires the suppression of illegally acquired evidence. In practice, though, the exclusionary rule hardly functions as the absolute bar to the admission of such evidence as originally intended. As this book demonstrates, over the last forty years, the ascendency of a Republican and conservative Court has taken much of the "bite" out of the rule. By 1986, the Burger Court had created so many exceptions to the rule and ways for police and prosecutors to avoid suppression, that one scholar commented that the rule had been converted into "chicken broth."[8] Since then, the Rehnquist and Roberts Courts have continued to restrict the scope and application of the rule.

As governor of New York, Charles Evans Hughes, in a 1907 speech in Elmira, New York, stated: "We are under a Constitution, but the Constitution is what the judges say it is . . . ."[9] This observation certainly rings true for the Court's exclusionary rule jurisprudence. The justices determine the meaning of the Constitution, and in this context, the

---

[5] *See* Albert W. Alschuler, *Fourth Amendment Remedies: The Current Understanding*, *in* THE BILL OF RIGHTS: ORIGINAL MEANING AND CURRENT UNDERSTANDING 197, 199 (Eugene W. Hickok, Jr. ed., 1999) ("The framers of the Fourth Amendment were willing to incur substantial law-enforcement costs, including the failure to punish some murderers, to preserve our freedom from unreasonable searches and seizures.").

[6] *Cf.* Kaplan, *supra* note 2, at 1037 (stating that the exclusionary rule "flaunts before us the costs we must pay for fourth amendment guarantees," and "rubs our noses in it"); Carol S. Steiker, *Second Thoughts About First Principles*, 107 HARV. L. REV. 820, 848 (1994) ("Despite its many flaws, the exclusionary rule is, I am convinced, the best we can realistically do."); William J. Stuntz, *The Virtues and Vices of the Exclusionary Rule*, 20 HARV. J.L. & PUB. POL'Y 443, 444 (1997) ("The exclusionary rule is, by a wide margin, the best legal tool available for regulating the police. But it distorts the rest of the criminal justice system."). In a book published book shortly after his death, Bill Stuntz takes a harsher view of exclusion. WILLIAM J. STUNTZ, THE COLLAPSE OF AMERICAN CRIMINAL JUSTICE 216-227 (2011) (criticizing the Warren Court's decision to impose the exclusionary rule on the states, and arguing that the Court should have ordered another remedy for police violations of the Fourth Amendment: "institutional injunctions—orders compelling police departments whose officers frequently violate search and seizure law to adopt better procedures").

[7] *See, e.g.*, Thomas Y. Davies, *A Hard Look at What We Know (and Still Need to Learn) About the "Costs" of the Exclusionary Rule: The NIJ Study and Other Studies of "Lost" Arrests*, 1983 AM. B. FOUND. RES. J. 611, 680 (1983) (finding that the "most striking feature of the data is the concentration of illegal searches in drug arrests (and possibly weapons possession arrests) and the extremely small effects in arrest for other offenses, including violent crimes").

[8] Steven Duke, *Making* Leon *Worse*, 95 YALE L.J. 1405, 1414 (1986).

[9] Charles Evan Hughes, Speech before the Elmira Chamber of Commerce (May 3, 1907), *in* ADDRESSES AND PAPERS OF CHARLES EVANS HUGHES: GOVERNOR OF NEW YORK, 1906–1908, at 133, 139 (1908) ("We are under a Constitution, but the Constitution is what the judges say it is, and the judiciary is the safeguard of our liberty and of our property under the Constitution."). Hughes was later appointed to the Court, and became Chief Justice of the United States in 1930.

meaning of the exclusionary rule. And their explanations of the rule's meaning and role, as expressed in the seminal exclusionary rule cases, were in large measure prompted by the judicial politics of certain members of the Court. Felix Frankfurter, one of the key protagonists in the development (and downfall) of the exclusionary rule, once said: "The history of the Supreme Court is not the history of an abstraction, but the analysis of individuals acting as a Court who make decisions and lay down doctrines."[10] Frankfurter's statement accurately captures the history and development of the exclusionary rule in the second half of the twentieth century.

This book examines the evolution of the exclusionary rule by analyzing the actions, thoughts, and motivations of the justices when deciding suppression cases. Supreme Court practitioners and scholars know that the Court's published opinions do not always divulge what the justices actually thought about a case. As one observer of the Court has noted, the justices do not "necessarily explain their decisions fully or candidly." Often, the opinions "do not reveal what the justices really thought about a case; at best, they provide *clues* as to their thoughts and preferences."[11] Put another way, the opinions announced in the Court's official reporter represent the "justifications" the Court provides for a given decision. The Court's opinions, however, often do not reveal the "motivations" behind the results announced by the Court.[12] In describing the justifications and motivations behind the Court's exclusionary rule cases, I rely heavily on archival materials taken from the private papers of retired justices.[13] The briefs filed by lawyers, the conference notes of the justices, correspondence among the justices and their law clerks, and draft opinions tell much of the story regarding the Court's motivations. Through these sources and an analysis of the cases themselves, this book reveals how the justices' thoughts and motivations have shaped the Court's exclusionary rule decisions, and thus shaped the protection provided by the Fourth Amendment.

---

[10] Felix Frankfurter, Letter to Stanley Reed (Apr. 13, 1939), Frankfurter Papers, Library of Congress, *quoted in* Bernard Schwartz, The Ascent of Pragmatism: The Burger Court in Action 2 (1990).

[11] The Supreme Court in Conference (1940–1985): The Private Decisions Behind Nearly 300 Supreme Court decisions xxiv (Del Dickson ed., 2001).

[12] *Cf.* Thomas Y. Davies, *An Account of* Mapp v. Ohio *That Misses the Larger Exclusionary Rule Story*, 4 Ohio St. J. Crim. L. 619, 630 n.36 (2007) (book review).

[13] Regarding my quotation of the justices' conference notes, I followed the lead of Del Dickson in his extraordinary and informative book, *The Supreme Court in Conference (1940–1985)*. *See* Dickson, *supra* note 11. I added punctuation and "nonessential" words to provide a natural flow of the justices' conversations. As Professor Dickson did in his book, I added no new sentences or thoughts, and my quotations of the conference notes "contain only what the Justices themselves reported. If it was not reasonably clear what a Justice meant by a particular comment or sentence fragment, then the passage was either omitted or left verbatim." *Id.* at xix.

1 The Fourth Amendment Means that Illegally Acquired Evidence "shall not be used at all"

THE FOURTH AMENDMENT to the United States Constitution protects individuals against unreasonable governmental searches and seizures. Although an important provision of the Bill of Rights and considered the fundamental law of the land, the protection provided by the Fourth Amendment is illusory. If police are determined to search a car or detain a person, no one can stop them.[1] Robert Jackson, a former Solicitor General and one of the nation's more conservative and respected Supreme Court justices, once observed that the right secured by the Fourth Amendment "is one of the most difficult to protect. Since the officers are themselves the chief invaders, there is no enforcement outside of court."[2] In 1949, Jackson remarked that there were "many unlawful searches of homes and automobiles of innocent people which turn up nothing incriminating, in which no arrest is made, about which courts do nothing, and about which we never hear."[3]

When law enforcement officials obtain evidence against a person in violation of the Fourth Amendment, the legal principle that prohibits the admission of that evidence in a criminal trial is known as the exclusionary rule. According to its numerous

[1] Yale Kamisar, *Does (Did) (Should) the Exclusionary Rule Rest on a "Principled Basis" Rather Than an "Empirical Proposition"?*, 16 CREIGHTON L. REV. 565, 568 (1983) [hereinafter Kamisar, *Principled Basis*] ("As a practical matter, nobody can stop the police from carrying out a search or seizure, if they are unwilling to be stopped, not even a lawyer.").

[2] Brinegar v. United States, 338 U.S. 160, 181 (1949) (Jackson, J., dissenting).

[3] *Id.*

critics, both on and off the Supreme Court, the Fourth Amendment exclusionary rule is severely flawed. Because the exclusionary rule suppresses the truth regarding a defendant's criminal conduct, critics argue it imposes enormous costs on society in the form of lost convictions and the acceptance of lenient plea bargains. Opponents also contend that the exclusionary rule neither deters police misconduct nor provides a remedy to innocent persons subjected to unconstitutional police intrusions.[4] Some critics argue the rule "encourages" certain types of illegal police conduct.[5] Thus, from these perspectives, the only function served by the rule is to provide a windfall to guilty defendants. Opponents further contend that the rule is an "awkward and embarrassing remedy" because exclusion is not mandated by the text of the Fourth Amendment or any other provision of the Constitution.[6] Last, detractors of court-ordered exclusion submit that a "powerful, unthinking emotional attachment" to the exclusionary rule prevents the development of a rational alternative sanction.[7] For these reasons, Chief Justice Warren Burger once described the rule as "one of the great hoaxes on the public" created by the Court.[8] Others have argued that the rule should be abolished.[9]

Although a reader of the Court's modern exclusionary rule decisions would never know it, widespread criticism of the rule is a relatively recent phenomenon.[10] In fact,

---

[4] *See, e.g.*, Christopher Slobogin, *Why Liberals Should Chuck the Exclusionary Rule*, 1999 U. ILL. L. REV. 363, 368–92. *See generally* Dallin H. Oaks, *Studying the Exclusionary Rule in Search and Seizure*, 37 U. CHI. L. REV. 665, 709 (1970) (concluding that there is no empirical proof that the rule deters illegal searches and seizures, but also noting that his findings "obviously fall short of an empirical substantiation or refutation of the deterrent effect of the exclusionary rule").

[5] STEVEN R. SCHLESINGER, EXCLUSIONARY INJUSTICE: THE PROBLEM OF ILLEGALLY OBTAINED EVIDENCE 57 (1977); Oaks, *supra* note 4, at 739 n.220.

[6] Akhil Reed Amar, *Fourth Amendment First Principles*, 107 HARV. L. REV. 757, 785 (1994). Referring to the exclusionary rule, Judge Malcolm Wilkey once said: "This rule of evidence did not come from on high. It's man-made, not God-given. . . . It's not even in the Constitution." *Task Force on Violent Crime: Public Hearing Before the Attorney General* 34–35 (1983) (statement of Hon. Malcolm R. Wilkey, J., United States Court of Appeals for the District of Columbia Circuit), *quoted in* Charles McC. Mathias, Jr., *The Exclusionary Rule Revisited*, 28 LOY. L. REV. 1, 7 (1982).

[7] Malcolm Richard Wilkey, *The Exclusionary Rule: Why Suppress Valid Evidence?* 62 JUDICATURE 214, 217 (1978). Judge Wilkey's assessment of the rule echoed Wigmore's early twentieth-century appraisal of the rule: "All this is misguided sentimentality. For the sake of indirectly and contingently protecting the Fourth Amendment, [the exclusionary rule] appears indifferent to the direct and immediate result, viz., of making Justice inefficient, and of coddling the criminal classes of the population." 4 JOHN HENRY WIGMORE, A TREATISE ON THE ANGLO-AMERICAN SYSTEM OF EVIDENCE IN TRIALS AT COMMON LAW § 2184, at 637 (2d ed. 1923). Wigmore predicted: "Some day, no doubt, we shall emerge from this quaint method of enforcing the law. . . . It will be abandoned only as the judiciary rises into a more appropriate conception of its powers and a less mechanical idea of justice." *Id.* at 639.

[8] Warren Burger, Letter to Lewis Powell on *Wolff v. Rice* and *Stone v. Powell* (June 16, 1976), Lewis F. Powell, Jr. Papers, Washington and Lee University School of Law, Box 30.

[9] *See* SCHLESINGER, *supra* note 5, at 5–7, 71–92; MALCOLM RICHARD WILKEY, ENFORCING THE FOURTH AMENDMENT BY ALTERNATIVES TO THE EXCLUSIONARY RULE (1982); Amar, *supra* note 6, at 811–16; Steven R. Schlesinger, *It is Time to Abolish the Exclusionary Rule*, WALL ST. J., Sept. 10, 1981, at 24.

[10] *Cf.* JAMES J. TOMKOVICZ, CONSTITUTIONAL EXCLUSION: THE RULES, RIGHTS, AND REMEDIES THAT STRIKE THE BALANCE BETWEEN FREEDOM AND ORDER 58 (2011) (explaining that "[a]t its birth," *Weeks*

the term "exclusionary rule" did not appear in the Court's criminal procedure rulings until 1949.[11] In the late nineteenth century and the early part of the twentieth, the Court did not employ the phrase "exclusionary rule," "suppression doctrine," or other idiom to describe the constitutional bar on the use of unlawfully secured evidence in federal criminal proceedings. Rather, the Court explained that when evidence is obtained in violation of a defendant's Fourth Amendment rights, that evidence simply cannot be used at trial. The prohibition on the admission of illegally obtained evidence was a constitutional right belonging to the citizen. Two cases decided during this period, *Boyd v. United States*[12] and *Weeks v. United States*,[13] established the foundation for what would become the rule that individuals were entitled to keep illegally acquired evidence out of criminal proceedings.

Boyd v. United States was the first time that the Court ruled that evidence procured through a Fourth Amendment violation could not be used in a criminal proceeding.[14] A federal forfeiture proceeding was begun after customs officials seized thirty-five cases of plate glass belonging to an importing company owned by Edward and George Boyd. The glass was seized because the Boyds allegedly failed to pay customs duties. Pursuant to an 1874 federal tax statute, the district court issued an order requiring the Boyds to produce the invoice for the glass. Under the statute, failure to comply with the order meant the government's allegations would be taken as confessed. The Boyds complied with the order but argued that compelled production of incriminating evidence violated their rights under the Self-Incrimination Clause of the Fifth Amendment. The

---

v. United States, 232 U.S. 383 (1914), the Court's first decision relying solely on the Fourth Amendment as a basis for exclusion, was "remarkably uncontroversial"). To be sure, when they were announced, the Court's initial rulings regarding exclusion were subject to criticism. The eminent evidence scholar John Henry Wigmore was an early and influential critic of the rule. *See* John H. Wigmore, *Using Evidence Obtained by Illegal Search and Seizure*, 8 A.B.A. J. 479 (1922) [hereinafter Wigmore, *Using Evidence*]. One early twentieth-century supporter of the rule acknowledged that exclusion was a disputed issue among state courts and that the "violent criticism of the legal principles announced in the *Weeks* case has made the [exclusion] doctrine a virtual battle-ground." Thomas E. Atkinson, *Prohibition and the Doctrine of the* Weeks *Case*, 23 MICH. L. REV. 748, 749 (1925). Wigmore's scholarship opposing the rule is skillfully critiqued in Roger Roots, *The Originalist Case for the Fourth Amendment Exclusionary Rule*, 45 GONZ. L. REV. 1, 55–64 (2010) (concluding that the cases cited by Wigmore do not prove that "exclusion was a radical departure from the settled law of the late nineteenth century, but that the law governing illegally seized physical evidence was unsettled and developing during the period").

11 Kamisar, *Principled Basis*, *supra* note 1, at 590 n.162 (explaining that Justice Hugo Black popularized the term "exclusionary rule" in a 1949 ruling).

12 116 U.S. 616 (1886).

13 232 U.S. 383 (1914).

14 Most scholarly discussions of the exclusionary rule begin with an analysis of *Boyd*. *See, e.g.*, JACOB W. LANDYNSKI, SEARCH AND SEIZURE AND THE SUPREME COURT: A STUDY IN CONSTITUTIONAL INTERPRETATION 49–61 (1966); BRADFORD P. WILSON, ENFORCING THE FOURTH AMENDMENT: A JURISPRUDENTIAL HISTORY 45–55 (1986). For an interesting report on the factual background of *Boyd*, see SAMUEL DASH, THE INTRUDERS: UNREASONABLE SEARCHES AND SEIZURES FROM KING JOHN TO JOHN ASHCROFT 48–53 (2004).

trial court rejected the claim. When the government offered the invoice at the forfeiture proceeding, the Boyds renewed their Fifth Amendment objection. The court again overruled the objection, the jury found for the United States, and the forfeiture of the plate glass was granted.

On appeal to the Court, the Boyds argued that the court order violated both the Fourth and Fifth Amendments. The government replied that the Fourth Amendment was not implicated because the order did not authorize a search or seizure of books or papers, but simply required the defendants to produce them. The Court, however, ruled in favor of the Boyds. It concluded the statute authorizing the court order was unconstitutional because the order violated the Fourth and Fifth Amendment rights of the Boyds. Thus, the Court ruled that the invoice was inadmissible against the Boyds, and the forfeiture proceeding itself was unconstitutional.[15]

Writing for the Court, Justice Bradley agreed that no search or seizure was authorized by the court order. Because failure to comply with the order meant that the government's allegations would be taken as proven, however, Bradley found that the order was "tantamount to compelling" production of the invoice.[16] Bradley then reasoned that a compulsory production of a person's papers triggered Fourth Amendment protection "because it is a material ingredient, and effects the sole object and purpose of search and seizure."[17] And the court order was "unreasonable" under the Fourth Amendment because it sought private papers, which Bradley distinguished from a search seeking stolen goods or contraband.[18]

After deciding that the court order violated the Fourth Amendment, Bradley then addressed the Fifth Amendment's Self-Incrimination Clause. Bradley envisioned an "intimate relation between" the Fourth and Fifth Amendments.[19]

> They throw great light on each other. For the "unreasonable searches and seizures" condemned in the Fourth Amendment are almost always made for the purpose of compelling a man to give evidence against himself, which in criminal cases is condemned in the Fifth Amendment; and compelling a man "in a criminal case to be a witness against himself," which is condemned in the Fifth Amendment, throws light on the question as to what is an "unreasonable search and seizure" within the

---

15 *Boyd*, 116 U.S. at 638 ("We think that the notice to produce the invoice in this case, the order by virtue of which it was issued, and the law which authorized the order, were unconstitutional and void, and that the inspection by the district attorney of said invoice, when produced in obedience to said notice, and its admission in evidence by the court, were erroneous and unconstitutional proceedings.").

16 *Id.* at 621–22.

17 *Id.* at 622.

18 *Id.* at 621–22, 623 ("The search for and seizure of stolen or forfeited goods, or goods liable to duties and concealed to avoid the payment thereof, are totally different things from a search for and seizure of a man's private books and papers for the purpose of obtaining information therein contained, or of using them as evidence against him.").

19 *Id.* at 633.

meaning of the Fourth Amendment. And we have been unable to perceive that the seizure of a man's private books and papers to be used in evidence against him is substantially different from compelling him to be a witness against himself.[20]

After discerning this nexus between the Amendments, Bradley found that admission of the invoice at the forfeiture proceeding violated the Fifth Amendment, as well as the Fourth Amendment. He explained that compelling the owner of goods that are the subject of a forfeiture proceeding to produce his own private books and papers "is compelling him to be a witness against himself, within the meaning of the Fifth Amendment to the Constitution, and is the equivalent of a search and seizure—and an unreasonable search and seizure—within the meaning of the Fourth Amendment."[21] Thus, the court order requiring the production of the invoice was unconstitutional, and admitting the invoice as evidence in the forfeiture hearing was error and resulted in an unconstitutional proceeding.[22]

Practically speaking, *Boyd* created "the rule that evidence obtained in violation of a person's rights under the Fourth Amendment may not under the Fifth Amendment be validly received against him in any criminal prosecution in a federal court."[23] To be sure, the facts in *Boyd* did not look like a Framing-era search or seizure. The Framers opposed the use of general warrants and writs of assistance that authorized the search of homes and businesses without probable cause that untaxed goods would be found inside.[24] Furthermore, even if one stretches the meaning of the Fourth Amendment to encompass a court order for production of the invoice, the order surely did not involve an *unreasonable* search or seizure. There was good reason to believe the Boyds possessed the invoice, and the order particularly described the object of the governmental intrusion. Under modern constitutional standards, therefore, any search or seizure encompassed by the order was reasonable. Put simply, the order was not a fishing expedition to look for incriminating evidence against the Boyds.

Under the legal norms of the late nineteenth century, however, the *Boyd* Court found that the governmental seizure of private papers violated the Fourth Amendment. Because private papers were afforded absolute protection from forcible or compulsory governmental seizure, the court order for the invoice constituted an unreasonable seizure. In reaching this conclusion, Bradley's opinion in *Boyd* relied heavily on Lord Camden's well-known 1765 ruling, *Entick v. Carrington*.[25]

---

20 *Id.*

21 *Id.* at 634–35.

22 *Id.* at 638.

23 Edward S. Corwin, *The Supreme Court's Construction of the Self-Incrimination Clause*, 29 MICH. L. REV. 191, 203 (1930).

24 The most informative analyses of the history of the Fourth Amendment are found in WILLIAM J. CUDDIHY, THE FOURTH AMENDMENT: ORIGINS AND ORIGINAL MEANING 602–1791 (2009) and Thomas Y. Davies, *Recovering the Original Fourth Amendment*, 98 MICH. L. REV. 547 (1999).

25 (1765) 95 Eng. Rep. 807 (K.B.); 19 How. St. Tri. 1029.

In 1762, the British Crown accused John Entick, a publisher, of involvement with several seditious publications. The British Secretary of State, Lord Halifax, issued a warrant for Entick's arrest and the seizure of his papers. After his release from custody, Entick sued the officials who searched his home and seized his papers. Lord Camden upheld the award of money damages to Entick and rejected the government's argument that the search warrant was a valid means of "detecting offenders by discovering evidence."[26] The search was illegal, according to Lord Camden, because "our law has provided no paper-search in these cases to help forward the conviction .... It is very certain that the law obligeth no man to accuse himself; because the necessary means of compelling self-accusation, falling upon the innocent as well as the guilty, would be both cruel and unjust; and it should seem, that search for evidence is disallowed upon the same principle."[27] This portion of *Entick* became known as the "mere evidence" rule. At the time of *Entick*, governmental officials had no free-standing authority to seize evidence—even with a valid warrant. Instead, the government's power to search and seize was restricted to property to which the government had a superior claim. For example, searches for stolen goods, items subject to unpaid taxes, or contraband materials were permissible. But "it was not enough that the purpose of the search and seizure was to obtain evidence for the apprehension or conviction of a criminal."[28] Put another way, *Entick* appeared to rule that the common law did not allow "the use of search warrants to obtain evidence of crime."[29]

Boyd embraced *Entick*'s common-law principle that mere evidence could not be the target of a governmental search or seizure and consequently transformed it into a constitutional mandate. Bradley wrote that the principles announced in *Entick* "affect the very essence of constitutional liberty and security."[30] According to Bradley, those principles go beyond the facts of *Entick* and apply to "all invasions" by the government "of the sanctity of a man's home and the privacies of life."[31] Having already distinguished a government search for stolen goods or contraband, Bradley explained that a search for *private property* was an entirely different matter.

> It is not the breaking of his doors, and the rummaging of his drawers, that constitutes the essence of the offence; but it is the invasion of his indefeasible right of personal security, personal liberty and private property, where that right has never been forfeited by his conviction of some public offence,—it is the invasion of this sacred right which underlies and constitutes the essence of Lord Camden's

---

26 *Id.* at 1073.

27 *Id.*

28 1 WAYNE R. LAFAVE, SEARCH AND SEIZURE: A TREATISE ON THE FOURTH AMENDMENT § 2.6(d), at 703 (4th ed. 2004).

29 TELFORD TAYLOR, TWO STUDIES IN CONSTITUTIONAL INTERPRETATION: SEARCH, SEIZURE, AND SURVEILLANCE AND FAIR TRIAL AND FREE PRESS 53 (1969).

30 Boyd v. United States, 116 U.S. 616, 630 (1886).

31 *Id.*

judgment. . . . [A]ny forcible and compulsory extortion of a man's own testimony or of his private papers to be used as evidence to convict him of crime or to forfeit his goods, is within the condemnation of that judgment. In this regard the Fourth and Fifth Amendments run almost into each other.[32]

At bottom, *Boyd* seemed to declare a "categorical" Fourth Amendment rule that forbade the government from searching for or seizing private property, "particularly private papers, in which it had no possessory or other property interest, even when it could assert a rational basis for the intrusion."[33] The government could seize the fruits of crime, instrumentalities of crime, and contraband items because individuals had no right to possess such things. Correspondingly, the government could not seize a person's bloody shirt because it was his shirt, nor could the government seize a person's private papers because they were his papers. To be sure, under the legal principles of that era, the court order to produce the invoice violated the Fifth Amendment's Self-Incrimination Clause, as Justice Miller's concurrence recognized, because the Boyds were compelled to produce incriminating evidence.[34] Thus, it was through a merger or linkage of the Fourth and Fifth Amendments that the *Boyd* Court required exclusion of relevant evidentiary papers in a quasi-criminal proceeding.

Although many of the constitutional principles announced in *Boyd* have been overturned by the modern Court,[35] liberals view *Boyd*'s existence as important because "it was part of the process through which the Fourth Amendment, by means of the exclusionary rule, has become more than a dead letter in the federal courts."[36]

---

[32] *Id.*

[33] Morgan Cloud, *The Fourth Amendment During the* Lochner *Era: Privacy, Property, and Liberty in Constitutional Theory*, 48 STAN. L. REV. 555, 579 (1996) [hereinafter Cloud, *Fourth Amendment and* Lochner]. Bill Stuntz described *Boyd* as "a radical decision, though not in terms of its effect on ordinary criminal cases." William J. Stuntz, *The Substantive Origins of Criminal Procedure*, 105 YALE L.J. 393, 423 (1995) (explaining the impact *Boyd*'s reasoning might have had on the emerging regulatory state: "If people could not be forced to disclose records because they might have violated a record-keeping rule, the government could not *have* record-keeping rules, at least not meaningful ones. And if requiring the keeping of records was impermissible, a good deal of regulation would be, in practical terms, impermissible as well. . . . People like [the Boyds] were, potentially, immune from a great deal of compelled disclosure, and consequently exempt from a great deal of government regulation.").

[34] *See Boyd*, 116 U.S. at 639 (Miller, J., concurring).

[35] During the conference discussion of *United States v. Ortiz*, 422 U.S. 891 (1975), Chief Justice Burger told his colleagues, "A lot of *Boyd v. United States* is a lot of unmitigated nonsense." THE SUPREME COURT IN CONFERENCE (1940–1985): THE PRIVATE DISCUSSIONS BEHIND NEARLY 300 SUPREME COURT DECISIONS 468 (Del Dickson ed., 2001).

[36] Abel v. United States, 362 U.S. 217, 255 (1960) (Brennan, J., dissenting). For a valuable discussion and analysis of *Boyd*, see, for example, Note, *Formalism, Legal Realism, and Constitutionally Protected Privacy Under the Fourth and Fifth Amendments*, 90 HARV. L. REV. 945 (1977) [hereinafter Note, *Formalism*]; Note, *The Life and Times of* Boyd v. United States (1886–1976), 76 MICH. L. REV. 184 (1977), and see also LANDYNSKI, *supra* note 14, at 49–61.

Boyd remains relevant, according to one contemporary scholar, not only because it established the foundations of the exclusionary rule,[37] but more important, because *Boyd*'s conclusion that the Fourth and Fifth Amendments run together "to create a zone of individual privacy protected from government intrusions maximized individual freedom at the expense of government power."[38] Interestingly, both proponents and opponents of the exclusionary rule agree that the result in *Boyd* rested on constitutional principles.[39] Even fierce critics of the Fourth Amendment's exclusionary rule acknowledge the constitutional foundation of *Boyd* and do not characterize its holding as a judicially created "rule of evidence" or based on the Court's supervisory authority over the federal judiciary.[40]

The Court's next significant exclusionary rule decision diverged from *Boyd*'s reliance on a link between the Fourth and Fifth Amendments. In *Weeks v. United States*, the justices unanimously held that private papers obtained through an unconstitutional search and seizure could not be used in a criminal prosecution.[41] Unlike *Boyd*, *Weeks* concluded that the Fourth Amendment alone forbade the admission of illegally obtained evidence in a federal prosecution.

Fremont Weeks was a delivery clerk for the Adams Express Company at Union Station in Kansas City, Missouri. His job provided frequent contacts with express messengers for other companies and train crews. Weeks utilized these connections to send lottery coupons of the International Mining & Investment Company of San Domingo to investors. On December 21, 1911, while Weeks was at work, a local police officer searched his home

---

[37] Cloud, *Fourth Amendment and* Lochner, *supra* note 33, at 581 ("[*Boyd*] suggested a broad exclusionary rule: Even lawful means, including valid search warrants and subpoenas, could not justify compulsory production or seizure of any private property unless the government could establish that it had some property interest in the item. [*Boyd*] also suggested a more specific exclusionary rule: The government could not search for and seize—directly or indirectly—private papers, even if it used otherwise lawful means.").

[38] *Id.* at 576.

[39] *See, e.g.*, Olmstead v. United States, 277 U.S. 438, 473–79 (1928) (Brandeis, J., dissenting); McNabb v. United States, 318 U.S. 332, 339 (1942) (majority opinion of Frankfurter, J.) (citing *Boyd* and *Weeks* for the proposition that "a conviction in the federal courts, the foundation of which is evidence obtained in disregard of liberties deemed fundamental by the Constitution, cannot stand"); *see also* Note, *Formalism*, *supra* note 36, at 956 (observing that the *Boyd* Court "viewed the remedy of exclusion and return [of private papers] as an essential part of the citizen's constitutional right").

[40] *See, e.g.*, Linkletter v. Walker, 381 U.S. 618, 649 (1965) (Black, J., dissenting) (commenting that "[b]oth the majority and the concurring members of the *Boyd* Court seemed to believe they were construing the Constitution" when fashioning the exclusionary rule). John Henry Wigmore, however, was critical of both *Boyd* and the notion that the Fourth Amendment required the exclusion of relevant evidence unlawfully obtained by federal officials. Writing in the first part of the twentieth century, Wigmore argued the Self-Incrimination Clause of the Fifth Amendment was triggered only where the government compelled a defendant to produce "testimonial" conduct or to "extract from the person's own lips an admission of his guilt." 4 WIGMORE, *supra* note 7, § 2263, at 863–64. Regarding *Boyd*, Wigmore rejected the view that the Fifth Amendment prohibited the search and seizure of private papers. Wigmore called this legal theory a "dangerous heresy." *id.* § 2264, at 867. The modern Court would eventually agree with Wigmore's interpretation of the Fifth Amendment.

[41] Weeks v. United States, 232 U.S. 383 (1914).

without a warrant and seized various documents. These documents were then given to the United States Marshal. Weeks was arrested by local police officers, and a second warrantless search of his home occurred later the same day. During the second search, the federal Marshal accompanied the police to look for additional evidence. The Marshal's search revealed additional private papers and letters that were found in the drawers of a chiffonier in Weeks's bedroom. The United States Attorney's Office received all of these documents and later charged Weeks with unlawfully using the mail to transport lottery tickets.

After the searches of Weeks's home and before the start of his trial, Weeks petitioned the federal district court for the return of the papers, claiming that the searches violated his Fourth and Fifth Amendment rights under the Constitution. The trial court partially granted the request but refused to return the papers that were relevant to the charges against Weeks. At the trial, Weeks again moved to bar the admission of the papers taken by the federal Marshal, which showed his use of the mail to ship lottery coupons. The trial judge denied the motion, and Weeks was convicted.

In the Court, there was no dispute that the federal Marshal's warrantless search was illegal.[42] Because the search was unconstitutional, Weeks argued that the trial court committed error by refusing his request for the return of his property and papers, and permitting their use at the trial. Weeks claimed that the refusal to return the papers and the use of these materials as evidence violated his Fourth and Fifth Amendment rights. Interestingly, Weeks's brief to the Court acknowledged that it was "necessary to give a liberal interpretation to the Fourth Amendment" in *Boyd* because "according to the strict letter of the law, there was no actual search and seizure" in that case.[43] Nonetheless, Weeks repeatedly cited *Boyd* in his brief and argued that *Boyd* controlled his case.[44]

Although there is no hint of this in Weeks's brief, *Boyd*'s fusion of the Fourth and Fifth Amendments to produce an exclusionary sanction was a problematic constitutional analysis.[45] There was nothing inherently wrong with Bradley's conclusion that the court order to the Boyds to produce papers constituted a "search" under the Fourth Amendment. The order was akin to a subpoena, and twenty years after *Boyd*, the Court declared that a grand jury subpoena "for the production of books and papers may constitute an unreasonable search and seizure within the Fourth Amendment."[46] While the order for the invoice in *Boyd* may have been a search, it was not an "unreasonable search" (at least under modern doctrine) because it sought specific papers.[47]

---

[42] *Id.* at 393 ("The United States Marshal could only have invaded the house of the accused when armed with a warrant issued as required by the Constitution.... Instead, he acted without sanction of law....").

[43] Brief for Plaintiff in Error at 34–35, *Weeks*, 232 U.S. 383 (No. 461).

[44] *Id.* at 32–34.

[45] *See, e.g.*, Yale Kamisar, Wolf *and* Lustig *Ten Years Later: Illegal State Evidence in State and Federal Courts*, 43 MINN. L. REV. 1083, 1088 n.16 (1959); *see also* Kamisar, *Principled Basis*, *supra* note 1, at 601 n.219.

[46] Hale v. Henkel, 201 U.S. 43, 76 (1906).

[47] *See* LANDYNSKI, *supra* note 14, at 60 ("The judicial order for the Boyd papers was not a general warrant for a 'fishing expedition,' as in the *Entick* case, but a writ authorized by Congress ordering production of

But there is a more fundamental problem with *Boyd*'s constitutional theory for the exclusionary rule. The essential problem with the union-of-the-amendments-requires-exclusion theory is that the typical unconstitutional search and seizure fails to produce compelled testimony from the victim of the illegal police conduct. In *Weeks*, for example, no government compulsion required Weeks to create or produce the documents illegally seized from his home. And in modern cases, when police illegally search a car or home and seize drugs or a weapon, there is no compelled testimony required from the victim of the unconstitutional search. Even where an illegal wiretap results in the seizure of a defendant's words, there is no Fifth Amendment violation.[48] As Jacob Landynski has described it, the amendments "are complementary, not duplicates."[49] The Fourth Amendment protects privacy and possessory interests against unreasonable governmental intrusions, while the Fifth Amendment protects against governmental compulsion to provide incriminating testimonial evidence. Indeed, within a few years of the *Boyd* ruling, the Court itself recognized that "the Fourth and Fifth Amendments a[re] quite distinct, hav[e] different histories, and perform[] separate functions."[50] Ultimately, *Boyd* reached the right result for the wrong reasons. "There was no need for the Court to press the Fourth Amendment into service in order to protect the Boyds from the consequences of the forced production of their papers."[51] The Court could have ruled in favor of the Boyds by finding that the subpoena to produce the invoice violated the Fifth Amendment.

Perhaps recognizing the problems with *Boyd*'s linkage theory, at one point, Weeks's brief did suggest that the Fourth Amendment violation itself required reversal of his conviction.[52] To support this claim, Weeks argued that when the Framers outlawed unreasonable searches and seizures, "they prohibited whatever was necessary to make the prohibition effective; they restricted the right to do, by indirection, that which could not be done directly."[53] Thus, according to Weeks's brief, if an officer of the court, for example, a federal Marshal, does "in violation of the Constitution, what the court could not itself do, that is, if the court by indirection does what it could not do directly, it follows that if the decision in the one instance be invalid so is it in the other."[54] Therefore, Weeks

specific documents.... The protection of the Fourth Amendment is extended equally to 'persons, houses, papers and effects'; the amendment does not appear to endow papers with any special sanctity.").

48 *Cf.* Olmstead v. United States, 277 U.S. 438, 462 (1928) ("There is no room in the present case for applying the Fifth Amendment unless the Fourth Amendment was first violated. There was no evidence of compulsion to induce the defendants to talk over their many telephones. They were continually and voluntarily transacting business without knowledge of the interception. Our consideration must be confined to the Fourth Amendment.").

49 Landynski, *supra* note 14, at 59.

50 *Hale*, 201 U.S. at 72.

51 Landynski, *supra* note 14, at 55.

52 Brief for Plaintiff in Error, *supra* note 43, at 47, 55.

53 *Id.* at 46.

54 *Id.*

contended: "[I]t is apparent that the [Fourth] Amendment . . . prohibit[s] the use of the evidence procured by an unlawful search and seizure, even [if] the [Fifth] Amendment did not exist."[55]

In contrast to Weeks's sixty-seven-page brief, the Solicitor General's argument for the government was a mere two pages long. His point was succinct, if not informative: the Court's precedents established that the retention of private papers and their admission in evidence did not violate either the Fourth or Fifth Amendments.[56] Remarkably, the government's brief did not cite *Boyd*.

Significantly, Justice Day's opinion for a unanimous Court ignored Weeks's claim that the admission of the incriminating evidence at trial violated the Fifth Amendment. Instead, Day concentrated on the Fourth Amendment.[57] Focusing on whether the Fourth Amendment alone mandated reversal of the conviction was a subtle, but noteworthy, departure from the constitutional framework announced in *Boyd*. In *Boyd*, Bradley found an "intimate relation" between the Fourth and Fifth Amendments that prohibited the admission of evidence obtained through an unlawful search or seizure.[58] But the linkage theory did not elucidate the meaning of the Fourth Amendment, nor did it explain why exclusion was constitutionally required when evidence was acquired through an unreasonable search or seizure.[59] Departing from *Boyd*'s merger theory, *Weeks* held that the Fourth Amendment itself protected against the use of evidence secured through an illegal search or seizure.

Day begins his analysis in *Weeks* by emphasizing the obligations that the Fourth Amendment imposes on federal judges. The Amendment, he tells us, puts federal judges and executive branch officials "under limitations and restraints as to the exercise of [their] power and authority, and to forever secure the people, their persons, houses, papers and effects against all unreasonable searches and seizures under the guise of law."[60] Day notes that the Amendment does not distinguish between persons "accused of crime or not," and he states that those entrusted with the administration of federal law enforcement have a "duty" to give the Amendment force and effect.[61] Finally, Day acknowledges the

---

55 *Id.* at 47.

56 Brief for the United States, Weeks v. United States, 232 U.S. 383 (1914) (No. 461).

57 *Weeks*, 232 U.S. at 389 ("We shall deal with the Fourth Amendment . . . .").

58 Boyd v. United States, 116 U.S. 616, 633 (1886).

59 *Cf.* Dash, *supra* note 14, at 55–56 (explaining that Bradley's merger theory "could only lead to confusion over search and seizure law," and that the *Boyd* opinion "would have been more consistent with history and a clearer guide to government agents" if Bradley had relied on the Fifth Amendment alone); Thomas S. Schrock & Robert C. Welsh, *Up from* Calandra*: The Exclusionary Rule as a Constitutional Requirement*, 59 Minn. L. Rev. 251, 283 n.97 (1974) [hereinafter Schrock & Welsh, *Up from* Calandra] (observing that "Bradley does a great and revolutionary thing by getting courts to think about the exclusion of seized evidence; but in the very same motion he ties the fourth amendment so closely to the fifth, that, with the notable exception of *Weeks* and its progeny, judges have refrained from asking the fourth amendment to perform exclusionary labors single-handedly" (citation omitted)).

60 *Weeks*, 232 U.S. at 391–92.

61 *Id.* at 392.

"tendency" among federal executive branch officials "to obtain conviction by means of unlawful seizures and enforced confessions."[62] Such illegal practices, he explains, "should find no sanction in the judgments of the courts which are charged at all times with the support of the Constitution and to which people of all conditions have a right to appeal for the maintenance of such fundamental rights."[63]

A few points are worth highlighting. First, Day makes clear that the Fourth Amendment imposes obligations on federal judges "in the exercise of their power and authority."[64] Second, he rejects the notion that guilty defendants are unworthy of the Amendment's protection; instead, federal judges, who are an integral part of the federal law enforcement system, have a "duty" to give "force and effect" to the rights secured by the Amendment to both innocent and guilty persons.[65] Finally, Day takes a practical approach to the realities of law enforcement. While recognizing the tendency of federal officers to violate the Fourth Amendment, Day states that such practices should find no approval in the federal courts because federal judges are responsible for upholding the "Constitution," and "people of all conditions" have a right to appeal to judges for the maintenance of their fundamental rights.[66]

Turning to Weeks's specific claim, Day explains that the case is not merely a legal dispute between Weeks and the federal Marshal. Rather, the case involves "the right of the court" to retain for evidentiary purposes papers unlawfully seized from Weeks's home.[67] The consequence of admitting such evidence for Weeks's Fourth Amendment rights was plain:

> If letters and private documents can thus be seized and held and used in evidence against a citizen accused of an offense, the protection of the Fourth Amendment declaring his right to be secure against such searches and seizures is of no value, and, so far as those thus placed are concerned, might as well be stricken from the Constitution.[68]

For Day and the rest of the justices, the choice for the judiciary—whether to retain and admit the incriminating evidence against Weeks, or to return the documents to the defendant—was clear. The trial court had no discretion to admit the illegally seized papers; the documents should have been returned. Otherwise, a contrary result "would be to affirm by judicial decision a manifest neglect if not an open defiance of

---

[62] *Id.*
[63] *Id.*
[64] *Id.*
[65] *Id.*
[66] *Id.*
[67] *Id.* at 393.
[68] *Id.*

the prohibitions of the Constitution, intended for the protection of the people against such unauthorized action."[69]

When trying to decipher whether the *Weeks* Court viewed exclusion of illegally obtained evidence as a command of the Constitution, or merely a judicially created rule of evidence, certain passages of Day's opinion are enlightening. For example, his statements that allowing the use of illegally obtained evidence in a criminal prosecution meant that the Fourth Amendment had "no value" for Weeks, and sanctioning such a proceeding would amount to "a manifest neglect if not an open defiance of the prohibitions of the Constitution."[70] Fifty years later, in an unpublished essay, Justice Felix Frankfurter wrote: "Surely any practice which makes a constitutional provision of 'no value' is forbidden by that provision."[71] Day also emphasized that the fruits of illegal searches should have no part in the judgments of the courts because judges are "charged at all times with the support of the Constitution."[72]

But equally illuminating is what the *Weeks* Court did *not* say. As Yale Kamisar, the nation's preeminent constitutional criminal procedure scholar, has explained, the *Weeks* opinion never describes exclusion of illegally obtained evidence as a "remedy."[73] There is no mention of the effectiveness of exclusion versus the effectiveness of tort remedies, internal police self-discipline, or other remedial options. Moreover, there is no talk of barring the use of unlawfully obtained evidence as a form of "deterrence" for police illegality,[74] discussion of the Court's "supervisory authority" over the federal judicial system,[75] or any statements indicating that the Court considered its holding a "rule of evidence."[76] Instead, the *Weeks* Court relied upon "the protection of the Fourth Amendment" when it concluded that the papers illegally obtained from Weeks's home had to be returned and could not be admitted in the prosecution against him.[77] As Justice Black, a fierce critic of the Fourth Amendment exclusionary rule, would later conclude, *Weeks* held that "the

---

69 *Id.* at 394.

70 *Id.* at 393–94.

71 Felix Frankfurter, A Dialogue 7 (undated) (unpublished essay), Felix Frankfurter Papers, Harvard Law School Library, Box 152.

72 *Weeks*, 232 U.S. at 392.

73 Kamisar, *Principled Basis*, *supra* note 1, at 598.

74 *See* Arval A. Morris, *The Exclusionary Rule, Deterrence, and Posner's Economic Analysis of Law*, 57 WASH. L. REV. 647, 649 (1982); *see also* Francis A. Allen, *The Judicial Quest for Penal Justice: The Warren Court and the Criminal Cases*, 1975 U. ILL. L.F. 518, 536 n.90 (explaining that the *Weeks* opinion "contains no language that expressly justifies the [exclusionary] rule by reference to a supposed deterrent effect on police officials"); James L. Oakes, *The Proper Role of the Federal Courts in Enforcing the Bill of Rights*, 54 N.Y.U. L. REV. 911, 935–36 (1979).

75 Schrock & Welsh, *Up from* Calandra, *supra* note 59, at 281–82.

76 Lane V. Sunderland, *The Exclusionary Rule: A Requirement of Constitutional Principle*, 69 J. CRIM. L. & CRIMINOLOGY 141, 143 (1978); *see also* Schrock & Welsh, *Up from* Calandra, *supra* note 59, at 281–82, 296–307.

77 *Weeks*, 232 U.S. at 393.

Fourth Amendment itself barred admission of evidence seized in violation of the Fourth Amendment."[78]

Day's authorship of *Weeks* provides another reason to believe that the *Weeks* Court viewed exclusion as compelled by the Constitution rather than a judge-made rule of evidence. Day certainly understood the common-law rule that trial courts normally do not examine the manner in which competent evidence is offered in court. Under the common law, a dispute over the manner or legality in which a witness obtained competent evidence was considered a "collateral issue" that should not divert a trial judge while presiding over a criminal proceeding.[79] In 1922, John Henry Wigmore neatly summarized the common law: "[T]he admissibility of evidence [in a criminal prosecution] is not affected by the illegality of the means through which the party has been enabled to obtain the evidence."[80] Today, the common-law competent evidence rule might be called an "evidence-laundering" or "don't ask, don't tell" rule. If the judge does not allow defense counsel to ask the police officer about how the evidence was obtained, the officer will not tell how he got it.[81]

Ten years prior to *Weeks*, Day relied, in large part, on this common-law rule to dismiss a defendant's constitutional challenge to the admission of incriminating evidence at his criminal trial. In *Adams v. New York*,[82] state officials, while executing a search warrant for gambling paraphernalia—policy slips—at Adams's office, also seized other private papers that identified Adams's handwriting on gambling materials and demonstrated his possession of such materials.

During his gambling prosecution, Adams unsuccessfully objected that the admission of testimony concerning the private papers violated his rights under the Fourth and Fifth Amendments. The New York courts rejected his claim, citing the common-law rule

[78] Coolidge v. New Hampshire, 403 U.S. 443, 497 (1971) (Black, J., concurring and dissenting).

[79] *See* 1 SIMON GREENLEAF, A TREATISE ON THE LAW OF EVIDENCE § 254a, at 302 (Boston, Charles C. Little & James Brown, 2d ed. 1844) ("[T]hough papers and other subjects of evidence may have been illegally taken from the possession of the party against whom they are offered or otherwise unlawfully obtained, this is no valid objection to their admissibility if they are pertinent to the issue. The Court will not take notice how they were obtained, whether lawfully or unlawfully, nor will it form an issue to determine that question."), *cited in* Adams v. New York, 192 U.S. 585, 594-95 (1904); Commonwealth v. Dana, 43 Mass. (2 Met.) 329, 337 (1841) ("When papers are offered in evidence, the court can take no notice how they were obtained, whether lawfully or unlawfully; nor would they form a collateral issue to determine that question."). Professor Davies contends that "[c]ontrary to the claim of the Massachusetts judges [in *Dana*], th[e collateral issue doctrine] was not a settled rule at common law, but was actually a novel creation." Thomas Y. Davies, *An Account of* Mapp v. Ohio *That Misses the Larger Exclusionary Rule Story*, 4 OHIO ST. J. CRIM. L. 619, 624 n.17 (2007) (book review) [hereinafter Davies, *Book Review*] (citation omitted); *see also* Davies, *supra* note 24, at 664 n.318 (1999).

[80] Wigmore, *Using Evidence*, *supra* note 10, at 479.

[81] Yale Kamisar deserves the credit for describing how the common-law competent evidence rule functions like an "evidence-laundering" or "don't ask, don't tell" rule. Telephone Conversation with Yale Kamisar, Professor, University of Michigan Law School (July 27, 2009).

[82] 192 U.S. 585 (1904).

on competent evidence.[83] When Adams's case came to the Court, Day first explained that the *admission* of the private papers as evidence did not violate Adams's Fourth or Fifth Amendment rights.[84] When *Adams* was decided, the Fourth Amendment was not binding on state officials, so there was no need for Day to address whether the search and seizure itself violated the Amendment.[85] Instead, the lion's share of his opinion was devoted to establishing that "the weight of authority as well as reason limits the inquiry [of courts] to the competency of the proffered testimony, and the courts do not stop to inquire as to the means by which the evidence was obtained."[86]

Ten years later in his *Weeks* opinion, Day's explanation of how the Fourth Amendment impacted the common-law competent evidence rule is hardly flawless, nor particularly convincing. In *Weeks*, Day asserts that *Adams* provides no authority for the admission of the incriminating papers at Weeks's prosecution.[87] The result in *Adams*, according to Day, rested on two grounds. First, the seizure of the private papers was incidental to a lawful search for the gambling paraphernalia—i.e., policy slips.[88] Second, *Adams* relied on the "doctrine that a collateral issue will not be raised to ascertain the source from which testimony, competent in a criminal case, comes."[89] By contrast, in *Weeks*, the search and seizure were admittedly illegal, and Weeks had twice moved to have his papers returned before the commencement of his prosecution. Thus, according to Day's opinion in *Weeks*, it was "evident" that *Adams* did not control the situation where a defendant makes a motion *before* trial "for the return of papers seized in violation of the Constitutional Amendment."[90]

Shortly after *Weeks* was announced, the nation's leading evidence scholar, John Henry Wigmore, complained that "the principle of the *Adams* case is squarely repudiated" by *Weeks*. He noted: "[A] defendant cannot turn a collateral fact into a material fact by merely making a formal motion before trial, instead of waiting till the offer of

---

83 *See* People v. Adams, 176 N.Y. 351, 358 (1903) ("The underlying principle obviously is that the court, when engaged in trying a criminal cause, will not take notice of the manner in which witnesses have possessed themselves of papers, or other articles of personal property, which are material and properly offered in evidence.").

84 Day stated: "We think there was no violation of the constitutional guaranty of privilege from unlawful search or seizure in the *admission of this testimony*. Nor do we think the accused was compelled to incriminate himself . . . . He was not compelled to testify concerning the papers or make any admission about them." *Adams*, 192 U.S. at 597-98 (emphasis added).

85 At the start of his opinion, Day cautioned that the Court did "not feel called upon to discuss" whether the Fourth and Fifth Amendments were binding on the states through the Fourteenth Amendment. *Id.* at 594; *see also* Marron v. United States, 275 U.S. 192, 198 (1927) ("[*Adams*] did not decide whether the seizure violated the Fourth Amendment. It decided that the admission in evidence of the private papers did not infringe the Fourth or Fifth Amendments.").

86 *Adams*, 192 U.S. at 594.

87 United States v. Weeks, 232 U.S. 383, 396 (1914).

88 *Id.*

89 *Id.*

90 *Id.*

evidence. . . . The point is that the fact of eligibility of method in obtaining evidential materials is a collateral fact; and all the motions in the world will not make it anything else."[91] As one lower federal court judge noted, *Weeks* never "explained how a defendant can turn a collateral fact into a material fact merely by making a formal motion before trial."[92] Nevertheless, this same judge recognized that *Weeks* required reversal of a conviction where evidence was admitted at trial that had been obtained in violation of the defendant's Fourth Amendment rights.[93] Admittedly, *Weeks* does not discuss, let alone discard, the competent evidence rule. The implication of *Weeks*'s holding, however, was manifest: the protection provided by the Fourth Amendment now trumped the common-law rule on competent evidence. *Weeks*'s harshest contemporaneous critic, Professor Wigmore, acknowledges as much.[94] Even Justice Frankfurter, who later would insist that *Weeks*'s exclusionary rule was not constitutionally based, recognized the point of *Weeks*. Almost thirty years later, Frankfurter remarked that the principle established in *Weeks*, contrary to the prevailing rule of many states, "renders evidence obtained through an improper search inadmissible no matter how relevant."[95]

---

[91] John Henry Wigmore, *Evidence-Fourth Amendment—Documents Illegally Seized*, 9 ILL. L. REV. 43 (1915).

[92] Flagg v. United States, 233 F. 481, 487 (2d Cir. 1916) (Veeder, J.).

[93] *Id.*

[94] *See* Wigmore, *Using Evidence*, *supra* note 10, at 482 ("[T]he essential fallacy of Weeks v. United States and its successors is that it virtually creates a novel exception, where the Fourth Amendment is involved, to the fundamental principle . . . that *an illegality in the mode of procuring evidence is no ground for excluding it*. The doctrine of such an exception rests on a reverence for the Fourth Amendment so deep and cogent that its violation will be taken notice of, at any cost of other justice, and even in the most indirect way." (citation omitted)); *cf.* DASH, *supra* note 14, at 62 (discussing the common-law rule on competent evidence and then stating that *Weeks* "announce[s] a new rule of exclusion from the trial of evidence obtained by an unlawful search and seizure"); Emmerich Handler, *The Fourth Amendment, Federalism, and Mr. Justice Frankfurter*, 8 SYRACUSE L. REV. 166, 172 (1957) (commenting that it "was not *Weeks*, but the fourth amendment, that had theretofore been held to make the exception to the common-law rule").

Of course, it was *Boyd*, rather than *Weeks*, that created the original exception to the common-law rule on admissibility. *See* LANDYNSKI, *supra* note 14, at 60 (explaining that *Boyd* "was, in effect, discarding the common-law rule of admissibility and requiring exclusion of the fruits of illegal searches from *all* criminal trials"); Cloud, *Fourth Amendment and* Lochner, *supra* note 33, at 590 (stating that *Boyd* established the foundations of the exclusionary rule thirty years before *Weeks*). Professor Donald Dripps provides a persuasive explanation for what he calls the "flip-flop" between *Adams* and *Weeks*: "*Adams* was a state case, in which the defendant claimed that the Fourteenth Amendment applied the Fourth to the states. Reversing the conviction would have required the *Mapp* [*v. Ohio*, 367 U.S. 643 (1961)] holding fifty-eight years early. In *Weeks*, the Court carefully distinguished the evidence seized by the local police in the initial search from the evidence seized later by the U.S. Marshal. . . . Thus the *Weeks* Court gave a negative answer to the incorporation question reserved in *Adams*; the Fourth Amendment holding of *Adams* was effectively overruled." DONALD A. DRIPPS, ABOUT GUILT AND INNOCENCE: THE ORIGINS, DEVELOPMENT, AND FUTURE OF CONSTITUTIONAL CRIMINAL PROCEDURE 16–17 (2003). *But cf.* Cloud, *Fourth Amendment and* Lochner, *supra* note 33, at 583–84 (explaining that rather than overruling *Boyd*, the *Adams* Court distinguished *Boyd* by noting that the search of Adams's office involved a search warrant, and not a judicial subpoena compelling individuals to produce their own records that were potentially incriminating).

[95] Harris v. United States, 331 U.S. 145, 159 (1947) (Frankfurter, J., dissenting).

Although *Boyd* ruled that exclusion of unconstitutionally obtained property was required by a merger of the Fourth and Fifth Amendments, *Weeks* determined that exclusion was an essential element of the Fourth Amendment alone—at least with respect to private papers. Fundamentally, *Weeks* established a Fourth Amendment right to exclusion.[96] But *Weeks* did retain one aspect of *Boyd*. Both rulings recognized that the admission of illegally acquired evidence tainted the respective judicial proceedings. *Weeks*'s holding was summarized near the end of Day's opinion. Day's language paralleled the language used by Bradley in *Boyd*. In *Boyd*, Bradley found that the court order to produce the invoice was "unconstitutional and void," and the federal prosecutor's inspection of the invoice and its admission as evidence by the court "were erroneous" and rendered the proceeding "unconstitutional."[97] In *Weeks*, a federal Marshal had obtained papers "in direct violation of the constitutional rights" of Weeks.[98] Because Weeks had made a timely request for the return of the papers, refusing that request constituted "a denial of the constitutional rights of the accused."[99] Therefore, "holding [the papers] and permitting their use upon the trial" was "prejudicial error."[100]

Weeks can be interpreted narrowly, and some modern justices and scholars have done so. They argue that *Weeks*'s exclusionary rule is based on property rights. For example, Bradford Wilson contends that exclusion in *Weeks* was driven by a concern for protecting property rights. Wilson has emphasized the importance of Weeks's application to the lower

---

[96] Schrock & Welsh, *Up from* Calandra, *supra* note 59, at 282 ("Justice Day recognized a personal fourth amendment right to exclusion."); Daniel J. Meltzer, *Deterring Constitutional Violations by Law Enforcement Officials: Plaintiffs and Defendants as Private Attorneys General*, 88 COLUM. L. REV. 247, 268 (1988) (explaining that *Weeks* "was based on the defendant's personal right to exclusion"); Note, *Formalism*, *supra* note 36, at 958 (stating that in *Weeks* "[e]xclusion was a personal constitutional right of the accused rather than a judge-fashioned remedy subject to the discretion of the court") (footnote omitted). For a critique of the theory that the Fourth Amendment affords a personal right to exclusion, see Donald Dripps, *Living With* Leon, 95 YALE L.J. 906, 918–22 (1986). One academic critic of exclusion contends that "*Weeks* is not an exclusionary rule case." Gerard V. Bradley, *Present at the Creation? A Critical Guide to* Weeks v. United States *and its Progeny*, 30 ST. LOUIS U. L.J. 1031, 1035 (1986). According to Professor Bradley, the result in *Weeks* was inspired by *Marbury v. Madison*, 5 U.S. (1 Cranch) 137 (1803). Bradley, *supra*, at 1066–67. Bradley states that at the time of *Weeks*, a trespass lawsuit against a United States Marshal was unlikely to succeed. *Id.* at 1066. Because Weeks was "practically without recourse" for the illegal search of his home, *id.*, Professor Bradley writes that *Marbury* mandated that the Court provide a remedy. "The *Weeks* rule—that upon a pretrial motion for return of property illegally seized, a court *must* order restitution, even if the government is thereby deprived of its use at a subsequent trial—was produced by the familiar judicial obligation to provide a remedy for every legal injury." *Id.* at 1035 (footnote omitted). Professor Bradley also asserts that none of the Court's rulings between *Weeks* and 1949 support a personal right to exclusion based on *Weeks*. *Id.* at 1073–86.

[97] Boyd v. United States, 116 U.S. 616, 638 (1886).

[98] United States v. Weeks, 232 U.S. 383, 393 (1914).

[99] *Id.* at 398.

[100] *Id.* Professor Tom Davies has explained that "the logic of exclusion" was first raised in *Boyd* and solidified in *Weeks*. According to Davies, "the logic of exclusion as set out in *Weeks* is merely the logic of nullity—if a government search violated the Constitution, the search would be a legal nullity, so a court could have no authority to recognize the results of such a search." Davies, *Book Review*, *supra* note 79, at 623.

court to return his letters and the court's refusal to do so, stating that the "applications constituted the central factor upon which the Supreme Court's decision rested, and are the key to recognizing that the foundation of the constitutional ruling in *Weeks* is the defendant's right to property."[101] Similarly, Professor Chris Slobogin contends that *Weeks* "justified suppression on the simple ground that, because the letters had been obtained in violation of the Fourth Amendment and the defendant had made 'seasonable application' for their return, the government could not retain them."[102] Finally, in a speech given after he left the Court, Potter Stewart explained that the exclusionary rule announced in *Weeks* was "a by-product of the fourth amendment's mandate that the government return wrongfully seized property; therefore, the rule could be operative only with property—once again, such as papers or books—that people are entitled to own, and not with contraband."[103] Stewart, moreover, disagrees that *Weeks* stands for the proposition that the Fourth Amendment grants a personal right to exclude unconstitutionally obtained evidence. Stewart contended that the "constitutional right Justice Day referred to in the *Weeks* case was not a right to have illegally obtained evidence excluded; it was the right to the *return* of illegally seized property."[104] Thus, Stewart stated that "*Weeks* offers little real support for the argument that the exclusionary rule is directly mandated by the Constitution."[105]

A contrary view of *Weeks* can be gleaned from several passages in the opinion. First, the Court acknowledged early in its opinion that Weeks was assigning error to the trial court's refusal to "return . . . his property, *and* in permitting the papers to be *used at the trial*."[106] Further, the *Weeks* Court characterized the case as involving the authority of a court "in a criminal prosecution to retain for the *purposes of evidence* the letters and correspondence of the accused" seized in violation of his constitutional rights.[107] More important, when describing the consequences of the unlawful search and seizure, Day did not merely refer to the right to the return of illegally seized property. Rather, he was thinking about a constitutional right of exclusion in a criminal prosecution. Thus, he noted that if the government can seize a person's private letters and documents and use them as evidence against

---

101 Wilson, *supra* note 14, at 60.

102 Slobogin, *supra* note 4, at 427–28; *see also* Amar, *supra* note 6, at 787–89 (characterizing *Boyd*, *Weeks*, and other Supreme Court Fourth Amendment precedents in the 1920s as the product of "*Lochner*-era property worship."); *cf.* James Boyd White, *Forgotten Points in the "Exclusionary Rule" Debate*, 81 Mich. L. Rev. 1273, 1279 (1983) (stating the rule of exclusion developed in *Boyd* and its progeny "was simply an automatic consequence of the . . . view that one's property was immune from seizure; in such cases exclusion is built into the fourth amendment itself"). Amar's reference to *Lochner* refers to *Lochner v. New York*, 198 U.S. 45 (1905), which invalidated, under the Fourteenth Amendment Due Process Clause, a New York law that restricted the number of hours bakery employees could work. *Lochner* held that the law violated the employer's "right to contract."

103 Potter Stewart, *The Road to* Mapp v. Ohio *and Beyond: The Origins, Development and Future of the Exclusionary Rule in Search-and-Seizure Cases*, 83 Colum. L. Rev. 1365, 1375 (1983).

104 *Id.* at 1381 (emphasis added).

105 *Id.*

106 Weeks v. United States, 232 U.S. 383, 389 (1914) (emphasis added).

107 *Id.* at 393 (emphasis added).

him in a criminal trial, "the protection of the Fourth Amendment declaring his right to be secure against such searches and seizures is of no value, and, so far as those thus placed are concerned, might as well be stricken from the Constitution."[108]

Those who view *Weeks* narrowly reason that the Court declared only a right to exclude evidence the government had no right to possess in the first place—evidence that should have been returned to the defendant. According to this view, the logic behind the rule was simple: if the government had no right to possess a defendant's papers because they were obtained pursuant to an unconstitutional search and should be returned to the defendant, the government should not be allowed to use those papers as evidence in a criminal prosecution. But *Weeks* did not, under this view, announce a right to exclude evidence that the government could properly keep even after an unconstitutional search and seizure—fruits of crime, instrumentalities of crime, forfeited items, or contraband. Those who take a broader view of *Weeks* insist that Day's opinion declared a personal right to exclude all evidence obtained in violation of the Fourth Amendment.

In the end, *Weeks* undoubtedly established an exclusionary rule. The scope of the rule, however, was unclear. What *Weeks* did not resolve (or at least did not clearly resolve) was whether exclusion was mandated by the Fourth Amendment when the government could properly possess evidence—contraband whiskey or stolen property—that was obtained through an unconstitutional search and seizure. The answer to that question would come later.

In the meantime, there was another question that seemed to linger in the aftermath of *Weeks*—the continuing validity of the common-law competent evidence rule. If *Weeks* left any doubts about whether the Fourth Amendment trumped the common-law rule on incriminating evidence, those doubts were eliminated after Justice Holmes announced his opinion in *Silverthorne Lumber Co. v. United States*.[109] While a federal grand jury was investigating schemes to defraud the government, federal law enforcement agents arrested Frederick W. Silverthorne, the president of the Silverthorne Lumber Company; and his father, Asa K. Silverthorne, the company's general manager, for conspiracy to defraud the federal government. While the Silverthornes were being detained, federal officials delivered a subpoena *duces tecum* to the company, and then immediately and "without a shadow of authority" conducted "a clean sweep of all the books, papers and documents" of the company.[110] The seized materials were delivered to the United States

[108] *Id.* At the time *Weeks* was decided, many lower federal courts understood that *Weeks* stood for more than the narrow proposition that property must be returned to a defendant upon timely motion before trial. The lower court rulings demonstrated the courts' understanding that *Weeks* required the reversal of convictions when illegally obtained evidence was admitted at trial. *See* Crank v. United States, 61 F.2d 981, 985 (8th Cir. 1932); Watson v. United States, 6 F.2d 870, 871 (3d Cir. 1925); Legman v. United States, 295 F. 474, 478–79 (3d Cir. 1924); Flagg v. United States, 233 F. 481 (2d Cir. 1916); *cf.* Bush v. United States, 269 F. 455, 457–58 (W.D.N.Y. 1920) (quashing indictment based on illegally seized evidence).

[109] 251 U.S. 385 (1920).

[110] *Id.* at 390.

Attorney's Office and shown to the grand jury. The federal prosecutor's office also photographed and made copies of the materials. Within days of the federal search, the company petitioned the federal district court for the return of its papers.

The district court found that the government had unlawfully seized the materials. The court ordered the return of the original materials to the company, but it impounded the photographs and copies made of the original materials. The Silverthornes were indicted for conspiracy to defraud the United States government. The federal prosecutor issued six new subpoenas requesting many of the same materials that had been seized during the prior illegal search, which the company subsequently refused to produce. Finally, the district court held the Silverthornes and the company in contempt for refusing to comply with the new subpoenas.

The Silverthornes appealed the contempt order to the Court, and in their briefs highlighted the practical effect of a government victory:

> Illegal searches and seizures will then be made whenever a prosecuting officer desires information in the possession of any individual or corporation; the evidence thereby obtained will be examined and photographed; the documents will then be formally returned, but their production will be immediately secured by means of a subpoena *duces tecum* fully naming and identifying them.[111]

The defendants argued that the constitutional holding of *Weeks* "indisputably provides that documents illegally seized" shall not "be used in evidence against the person whose constitutional rights have been violated."[112] Thus, according to the defendants, if the government prevails, "nothing of substance"[113] was determined in *Weeks,* and "the constitutional guaranty against unreasonable searches and seizures will have been rendered practically futile as to both individuals and corporations."[114]

Interestingly, in his brief for the government, the Solicitor General did not refute the practical consequences described by the defendants if the Court upheld the government's position. While condemning the initial illegal search and seizure of the company's papers, the government denied that such illegal action "should forever prevent the United States from securing by legal process relevant testimony to a violation of its laws where no right under the fifth amendment can be successfully set up."[115] *Weeks*, according to the Solicitor General, was a case

> where the trial court should have refused to retain custody of the papers, not because of anything connected with the original unlawful seizure, but because of

---

[111] Brief in Opposition to Motion of Defendant-In-Error to Dismiss or Affirm at 11, *Silverthorne Lumber*, 251 U.S. 385 (No. 996).

[112] *Id.*

[113] Brief on Behalf of the Plaintiffs-in-Error at 43, *Silverthorne Lumber*, 251 U.S. 385 (No. 358).

[114] Brief in Opposition to Motion of Defendant-In-Error to Dismiss or Affirm, *supra* note 111, at 20.

[115] Brief on Behalf of the United States at 47–48, *Silverthorne Lumber*, 251 U.S. 385 (No. 358).

the defendant's claim of immunity under the fifth amendment, the papers being the private papers of an individual seized at his residence.[116]

According to the Solicitor General, the constitutional evil in *Weeks* was that the failure to return the papers "amounted to the issuance by the court of a *subpoena duces tecum* for them, or to an impounding order, and hence to compulsory process for their production as testimony."[117] By the government's lights, Weeks's conviction was reversed due to the failure to return the papers "and not because of their reception as evidence."[118] Put simply, the constitutional ruling declared in *Weeks* rested on Fifth Amendment concerns and was not intended to remedy violations of the Fourth Amendment.

As was his style, Holmes's reaction to the government's arguments was laconic. As Holmes saw it, the government's argument was that the Fourth Amendment protects a citizen's "physical possession [of papers] but not any advantages that the Government can gain over the object of its pursuit by doing the forbidden act."[119] Not only was the government's interpretation of *Weeks* "not the law," but the logic of the government's position "reduces the Fourth Amendment to a form of words."[120]

Holmes also dismissed the government's reliance on the common-law rule forbidding inquiry into the manner in which competent evidence is secured. *Weeks*, Holmes explained, had displaced the common-law rule and effectively overruled *Adams v. New York*.[121]

---

[116] *Id.* at 24.

[117] *Id.* at 51 (citation omitted).

[118] *Id.*

[119] *Silverthorne Lumber*, 251 U.S. at 391.

[120] *Id.* at 391–92.

[121] *Id.* at 392 ("The numerous decisions, like *Adams v. New York*, . . . holding that a collateral inquiry into the mode in which evidence has been got will not be allowed when the question is raised for the first time at the trial, are no authority in the present proceeding, as is explained in *Weeks v. United States* . . . ."). Five years later, Holmes was more emphatic. In his dissent in *Olmstead*, he stated that the common-law rule on the admission of illegally obtained evidence had been "overthrown" by *Weeks*. Olmstead v. United States, 277 U.S. 438, 470–71 (1928) (Holmes, J., dissenting). Potter Stewart took a contrary view of Holmes's treatment of the common-law rule. In a speech he delivered after he retired from the Court, Stewart asserted that in *Silverthorne Lumber* Holmes "offered no explanation for why the evidence could not be admitted under the *Adams* decision; the Court's opinion simply stated that the *Weeks* case was controlling." Stewart, *supra* note 103, at 1376. While Stewart may have disagreed with Holmes's theory for exclusion, *see id.* at 1382–83 (explaining his disagreement with Holmes), it is inaccurate to say that Holmes "offered no explanation" for why the competent evidence rule of the common law was not controlling in *Silverthorne Lumber*. The evidence seized in *Silverthorne Lumber* could not be used because it was secured in violation of the Fourth Amendment. That was what *Weeks* had established. While Holmes could have been more explicit in *Silverthorne Lumber*, his dissent in *Olmstead* eliminated all remaining doubts that the competent evidence rule was "overthrown by *Weeks*." *Olmstead*, 277 U.S. at 470–71 (Holmes, J., dissenting) ("I am aware of the often-repeated statement that in a criminal proceeding the court will not take notice of the manner in which papers offered in evidence have been obtained. But that somewhat rudimentary mode of disposing of the question has been overthrown by *Weeks v. United States* . . . and the cases that have followed it."). For Holmes, exclusion was a constitutional right belonging to the victim of an illegal search and seizure. *See* Dodge v. United States, 272 U.S. 530, 532 (1926) (explaining, in dicta, that if "the

Tellingly, Holmes cited a lower court ruling, *Flagg v. United States*,[122] which, according to Holmes, "stated satisfactorily" *Weeks*'s impact on *Adams*.[123] That lower court decision concluded that *Weeks* required exclusion at trial of the fruits of an illegal search. Returning the original papers to the defendant "did not cure the original trespass," and was "an idle ceremony" that did not remedy the violation of a defendant's Fourth Amendment rights.[124]

Finally, Holmes adopted a plain meaning interpretation of the Fourth Amendment. He stated: "The essence of a provision forbidding the acquisition of evidence in a certain way is that not merely evidence so acquired shall not be used before the Court but that it shall not be used at all."[125] Modern justices would interpret this passage to mean that Holmes was merely announcing an exclusionary rule for derivative evidence. Although this interpretation is not technically wrong, it does not fully capture Holmes's interpretation of the Amendment. Holmes's language conveyed a more direct, two-fold meaning. First, when the government violates the Amendment, evidence obtained through that violation "shall not be used before the Court." Second, the government cannot use evidence that is derivative of its unconstitutional conduct either. In Holmes's view, the first point was obvious. The second point, if not obvious before *Silverthorne Lumber* was decided, was now clear. As in *Weeks*, there was no reference or mention of an "exclusionary rule" in *Silverthorne Lumber*. The legal prohibition on the use of unlawfully obtained evidence came from the Fourth Amendment itself.

Notably, Holmes's opinion in *Silverthorne Lumber*, like Day's opinion in *Weeks*, did not invoke the Fifth Amendment's Self-Incrimination Clause as justification for reversing the lower court's judgment. It was enough that the challenged evidence was obtained pursuant to an unconstitutional search and seizure. Among the justices of his era, not only was Holmes's interpretation of the Fourth Amendment and *Weeks* unquestioned, it was confirmed in *Olmstead v. United States*, when Chief Justice Taft stated: "The striking outcome of the *Weeks* case and those which followed it was the sweeping declaration that the Fourth Amendment, although not referring to or limiting the use of evidence in courts, really forbade its introduction if obtained by government officers through a violation of the Amendment."[126] Last, unlike in *Boyd* and *Weeks*, Holmes did not reverse the

search and seizure are unlawful as invading personal rights secured by the Constitution those rights would be infringed yet further if the evidence were allowed to be used").

122 233 F. 481 (2d Cir. 1916).

123 *Silverthorne Lumber*, 251 U.S. at 392.

124 *Flagg*, 233 F. at 486.

125 *Silverthorne Lumber*, 251 U.S. at 392.

126 *Olmstead*, 277 U.S. at 462; *cf.* Gouled v. United States, 255 U.S. 298, 312-13 (1921) (finding first a violation of the Fourth Amendment and a violation of the Fifth Amendment because the illegally obtained evidence was admitted at trial, and then explaining that it is the duty of trial judges to entertain an objection to the admission of evidence or "a motion for their *exclusion*," even where such a motion to return the papers has been denied before trial; "A rule of practice [(the common-law rule)] must not be allowed for any technical reason to prevail over a *constitutional right*.") (emphasis added). To be sure, Taft's opinion in *Olmstead*

contempt order against the Silverthornes because the government had no right to possess the papers it had subpoenaed. Instead, he focused on the legality of the government's initial intrusion. As Professor Morgan Cloud has observed, the result in *Silverthorne Lumber* "did not turn on whether the disputed documents were contraband, instrumentalities or evidence of criminal activity, or required records. The outcome depended upon the legitimacy of the means used by the government."[127] While Holmes did not reject the property-based focus of *Boyd* and *Weeks,* "he did not embrace it."[128]

It soon became apparent that the Court's view of the exclusionary rule was absolute.[129] One month after announcing *Silverthorne Lumber*, the Court decided *Gouled v. United States*.[130] In that case, Gouled raised Fourth and Fifth Amendment challenges to the admissibility in his fraud prosecution of certain contracts that had been surreptitiously taken from his office by a government informant. The Court ruled in favor of Gouled. Among other things, *Gouled* made crystal clear what *Boyd* seemed to establish, namely, that the Fourth Amendment barred the use of search warrants "as a means of gaining access to a man's house or office and papers solely for the purpose of making search to secure evidence to be used against him in a criminal or penal proceeding."[131] The Court ruled that a lawful warrant permitted the search and seizure of papers only when the government has "a primary right" in the property to be seized, or a "right to the possession of it," or when "a valid exercise of the police power renders possession of the property by the accused unlawful and provides that it may be taken."[132]

But *Gouled* went a step further by explaining that there "is no special sanctity in papers, as distinguished from other forms of property, to render them immune from search and seizure."[133] In other words, papers, like other types of property, could be subject to seizure pursuant to a valid warrant, but only if the government could assert a superior claim to the paper. The effect of the Court's holding was significant: law enforcement officials

dilutes his earlier description of *Weeks* when, in a later passage, he states that *Weeks* and its progeny "established as the law for the federal courts, that the protection of the Fourth Amendment would be much impaired, unless it was held that not only was the official violator of the rights under the Amendment subject to action at the suit of the injured defendant, but also that the evidence thereby obtained could not be received." *Olmstead*, 277 U.S. at 463. This subsequent account suggests that *Weeks*'s exclusionary rule was a product of the Court's supervisory authority over the lower federal courts. The modern Court has made the same suggestion. *See* United States v. Williams, 504 U.S. 36, 45–46 (1992). The problem with this interpretation is that there is nothing in either *Weeks* or *Silverthorne Lumber* that supports Taft's supposition that exclusion was the product of the Court's supervisory authority.

127 Cloud, *Fourth Amendment and* Lochner, *supra* note 33, at 607.

128 *Id.* at 608.

129 *Cf.* Stewart, *supra* note 103, at 1376 (acknowledging that the rulings in *Silverthorne Lumber* and *Gouled* "went far towards converting the limited rules of the *Boyd* and *Weeks* cases into a full-blown rule of exclusion at federal trials").

130 255 U.S. 298 (1921), *overruled by* Warden v. Hayden, 387 U.S. 294 (1967).

131 *Gouled*, 255 U.S. at 309.

132 *Id.*

133 *Id.*

could not utilize lawful searches to secure "mere evidence" to facilitate the conviction of criminal suspects.

For good measure, *Gouled* also declared that the common-law competent evidence rule could not prevent a criminal defendant from invoking his right to exclude unlawfully obtained evidence. "A rule of practice," the Court emphasized, "must not be allowed for any technical reason to prevail over a constitutional right."[134] And in a companion case to *Gouled*, the Court, without elaboration, appeared to address the issue that *Weeks* had not definitively resolved: whether the Fourth Amendment's exclusionary rule conferred a right to exclude *all* evidence, such as contraband whiskey, that the government could properly seize. In *Amos v. United States*,[135] the Court ruled that a warrantless search of Amos's home and a "store" within the curtilage of the home was unconstitutional. As a result, the seizure of untaxed whiskey was inadmissible at Amos's federal prosecution.[136]

Four years later, a unanimous Court in *Agnello v. United States*,[137] without citing *Amos*, left no doubt that the scope of the exclusionary rule extended to the suppression of contraband, and it also rejected the government's argument that there should be an impeachment exception to the rule. In *Agnello*, federal revenue officers observed Frank Agnello hand cocaine to a government informant inside the informant's home. The officers then entered the home and arrested Agnello. After searching Agnello, officers discovered more cocaine in his pockets. The officers then took Agnello to his home and searched it without a warrant. They discovered a can of cocaine in his bedroom.

At Agnello's trial for conspiracy to violate federal narcotics laws, the government offered the can of cocaine found in Agnello's bedroom as part of its case-in-chief. The trial court, however, excluded it because the search of Agnello's home violated the Fourth Amendment. In his defense, Agnello testified on direct that he had never spoken about cocaine with any of his codefendants. On cross-examination, Agnello denied he had ever possessed cocaine. The prosecution then produced the can of cocaine and asked Agnello whether he had ever seen it. Agnello denied that he had seen the can or that it was found in his bedroom. On cross-examination, as a means of impeaching Agnello's credibility, the prosecution presented the officers' testimony that the can had been seized from Agnello's bedroom. The jury found Agnello and his codefendants guilty.

When Agnello appealed his conviction to the Court, the government offered the Court an escape hatch from the strictures of the exclusionary rule. The government's brief argued that the illegally obtained evidence was admissible for rebuttal purposes

---

134 *Id.* at 313.

135 255 U.S. 313 (1921).

136 *Id.* at 316–17. Interestingly, at his trial, Amos made a motion for the return of the whiskey and the exclusion of the whiskey and the government agents' testimony related to the seized whiskey.

137 269 U.S. 20 (1925).

because Agnello had impliedly waived his Fourth Amendment right to exclusion by committing perjury:

> It was only when the defendant . . . on the witness stand, resorted to obvious falsehoods, testifying that he did not know that he was carrying narcotics on the night of the arrest, that he had never seen narcotics before, and that he had never seen the can of cocaine [] until the trial—it was only then, in rebuttal of these statements, that the Government was permitted to give evidence that the can had been found in his room. The evidence of the search was used only as a medium of discrediting the witness, and was not used in any way either as a direct part of the Government's main case, or as an indirect clue toward obtaining other evidence.[138]

A unanimous Court reversed Agnello's conviction and rejected the government's attempt to create an impeachment exception to the exclusionary rule. According to the Court, the government's argument that the illegally acquired evidence was merely used for rebuttal purposes was "without merit."[139] Citing Holmes's statement in *Silverthorne Lumber* that unconstitutionally seized evidence "'shall not be used at all,'"[140] the Court explained in dicta that Agnello "did nothing to waive his constitutional protection or to justify cross-examination" regarding the illegally seized evidence.[141] *Agnello* also demonstrated that the common-law competent evidence rule was no obstacle to enforcing the Fourth Amendment, even in a case where a defendant could have, but for obvious reasons chose not to seek, the return of evidence illegally seized from his home. More important, *Agnello* made clear that the principle of exclusion announced in *Weeks* extended beyond the remedy of exclusion and return of private papers. Whereas *Weeks* and *Silverthorne Lumber* applied the exclusionary rule to bar the government's use of private papers illegally seized from the defendants, *Agnello* allowed an obvious perjurer to invoke the rule to prohibit the introduction of testimony concerning the defendant's possession of contraband and to bar the prosecution from impeaching the defendant's credibility.

Despite the reasoning and results in *Weeks* and *Silverthorne Lumber*, from time to time in the first half of the twentieth century, lower federal courts continued to rely upon the common-law rule when deciding defense motions to exclude evidence obtained in violation of the Fourth Amendment.[142] At the same time, when defendants in federal prosecutions sought to exclude evidence obtained by an unreasonable search

---

138 Brief on Behalf of the United States at 17-18, *Agnello*, 269 U.S. 20 (No. 45) (citation omitted).

139 *Agnello*, 269 U.S. at 35.

140 *Id.* at 35 (quoting Silverthorne Lumber Co. v. United States, 251 U.S. 385, 392 (1920)).

141 *Id.*

142 *See, e.g.*, MacDaniel v. United States, 294 F. 769, 771–72 (6th Cir. 1924); Rice v. United States, 251 F. 778, 780–81 (1st Cir. 1918); Lyman v. United States, 241 F. 945, 948 (9th Cir. 1917); United States v. O'Dowd, 273 F. 600, 602–03 (N.D. Ohio 1921).

and seizure, they invoked the protections of both the Fourth and Fifth Amendments.[143] If such a case reached the Court, sometimes, but not always, the Court would cite the Fifth Amendment when ruling that evidence obtained from an unreasonable search and seizure should have been excluded at trial.

For example, before rejecting the government's effort to create an impeachment exception to the exclusionary rule, *Agnello* stated that it is "well settled that, when properly invoked, the Fifth Amendment protects every person from incrimination by the use of evidence obtained through search or seizure made in violation of his rights under the Fourth Amendment."[144] While such references to the Fifth Amendment were not unusual, there is no evidence that the Court intended such brief statements as departures from or repudiations of the *Weeks-Silverthorne Lumber* analysis. Indeed, it is important to understand that in the period between *Silverthorne Lumber* and *Wolf v. Colorado*, the Court "had little to say about the rationale of the exclusionary rule and absolutely nothing to say about the relative merits of the exclusionary rule and alternative methods of enforcing the fourth amendment."[145] For the remainder of the first half of the twentieth century, in federal cases the Court did not deviate from Holmes's conclusion that evidence secured in violation of the Fourth Amendment "shall not be used at all."[146]

---

[143] *See, e.g.*, Garske v. United States, 1 F.2d 620 (8th Cir. 1924); Legman v. United States, 295 F. 474 (3d Cir. 1924); Murby v. United States, 293 F. 849 (1st Cir. 1923).

[144] *Agnello*, 269 U.S. at 33–34; *see also* United States v. Lefkowitz, 285 U.S. 452, 467 (1932) (finding that if a search or seizure is unreasonable, the search or seizure violates the defendant's "rights under the Fourth and Fifth Amendments"); Marron v. United States, 275 U.S. 192, 194 (1927) ("It has long been settled that the Fifth Amendment protects every person against incrimination by the use of evidence obtained through search or seizure made in violation of his rights under the Fourth Amendment."). In *Gouled v. United States*, 255 U.S. 298 (1921), the Court relied on *Boyd* when it ruled that a violation of the Fifth Amendment occurs when evidence obtained from an unreasonable search and seizure is admitted in a criminal prosecution. According to *Gouled*: "In practice the result is the same to one accused of crime, whether he be obliged to supply evidence against himself or whether such evidence be obtained by an illegal search of his premises and seizure of his private papers. In either case he is the unwilling source of the evidence, and the Fifth Amendment forbids that he shall be compelled to be a witness against himself in a criminal case." *Id.* at 306. Professor Francis A. Allen has stated that in all the cases following *Weeks* (and before *Wolf v. Colorado*, 338 U.S. 25 (1949)) where the Court had occasion to explain the legal basis of the exclusionary rule, "heavy reliance is placed upon the 'intimate relation' between the Fourth and Fifth Amendments," and it is "clear that the exclusionary rule is conceived as deriving in some manner and in some degree from the privilege against self-incrimination." Francis A. Allen, *The* Wolf *Case: Search and Seizure, Federalism, and the Civil Liberties*, 45 ILL. L. REV. 1, 15 (1950) [hereinafter Allen, *The* Wolf *Case*]; *see also* Bradley, *supra* note 96, at 1082. Professor Allen's description does not account for *Silverthorne Lumber*, which does not mention, let alone place "heavy reliance" upon, the Fifth Amendment as justification for exclusion. It should also be noted that the Court decided nearly a dozen cases between 1927 and 1949, the year *Wolf* was decided, which relied solely on the Fourth Amendment as justification for reversing convictions based on evidence obtained from illegal searches and seizures. *United States v. Di Re*, 332 U.S. 581 (1948), was the last pre-*Wolf* case where the Court, without mentioning the Fifth Amendment or the exclusionary rule, reversed the defendant's conviction because it was based on evidence obtained from an unreasonable search and seizure.

[145] Kamisar, *Principled Basis*, *supra* note 1, at 601.

[146] Silverthorne Lumber Co. v. United States, 251 U.S. 385, 392 (1920).

In an article published in 1950, Professor Francis Allen, an astute observer of the Court's criminal procedure rulings, commented that the scope of the exclusionary rule had not been given a broad reading. He explained that, as then defined, the rule "does not operate in every case to exclude even in the federal courts the use of evidence seized in violation of constitutional commands."[147] Allen noted three limitations on the scope of the rule. First, it does not apply when evidence is obtained in violation of the Fourth Amendment rights of a third party. Second, it does not apply when state officers, acting without the participation or involvement of federal officers, illegally obtain evidence in violation of the defendant's rights. Finally, the rule is inapplicable when evidence has been illegally obtained by a private individual without the involvement of federal officials.[148]

Although Professor Allen accurately describes the law as it existed in 1950, these three limitations on the scope of the exclusionary rule do not tell us very much about the Court's thinking on the rule. First, the standing limitation identified by Professor Allen was a product of the lower federal courts, not the Court. And while the Court did recognize in dicta that the lower federal courts "in numerous cases, and with unanimity, have denied standing to one not the victim of an unconstitutional search and seizure to object to the introduction in evidence of that which was seized,"[149] at least three justices, including Frankfurter, stated that these rulings on standing were "hard to square with" *Silverthorne Lumber*'s explanation of the exclusionary rule.[150]

Second, the fact that the Court did not apply the exclusionary rule in cases where federal prosecutors presented evidence illegally seized by state officers—the so-called "silver platter" cases—also reveals very little about the Court's logic behind the rule. The first case to approve this practice was *Weeks*, and the subsequent cases following it do not discuss the rationale or basis for the exclusionary rule itself.[151] In fact, in one of those cases, *Byars v. United States*, dicta from a unanimous Court endorsed a broad reading of the exclusionary rule. *Byars* stated: "[T]he doctrine has never been recognized by this Court, nor can it be tolerated under our constitutional system, that evidences of crime discovered by a federal officer in making a search without lawful warrant may be used against the victim of the unlawful search where a timely challenge has been interposed."[152] The results in the "silver platter" cases did not indicate disapproval of the exclusionary rule or suggest a restriction on the scope of the rule, but turned on

---

147 Allen, *The* Wolf *Case*, *supra* note 144, at 21.

148 *Id.* at 21–22.

149 Goldstein v. United States, 316 U.S. 114, 121 (1942).

150 *Id.* at 127 (Murphy, J., dissenting); *see also id.* at 128 n.4 ("It is evident that to allow the Government to use evidence obtained in violation of the Fourth Amendment against parties not victims of the unconstitutional search and seizure is to allow the Government to profit by its wrong and to reduce in large measure the protection of the Amendment.").

151 *See, e.g.*, Lustig v. United States, 338 U.S. 74 (1949); Byars v. United States, 273 U.S. 28 (1927).

152 *Byars*, 273 U.S. at 29–30.

the legal principle that the Fourth Amendment did not apply to searches and seizures conducted by state officers.

Finally, the result in *Burdeau v. McDowell*,[153] which upheld the admission into evidence in a criminal proceeding of papers stolen by private individuals, without government involvement, does not illuminate the Court's thinking on the exclusionary rule. *Burdeau* merely held that constitutional protections are not implicated when private parties give stolen items to a prosecutor. Authored by Day, *Burdeau* simply stands for the proposition that the Constitution does not apply to the action of private individuals.

In any event, the Court's understanding of the exclusionary rule would soon change with the announcement of *Wolf v. Colorado*.[154]

---

[153] 256 U.S. 465 (1921).

[154] 338 U.S. 25 (1949).

2 The Influence of Felix Frankfurter

THE EFFECT OF *Weeks* and *Silverthorne Lumber* was that evidence obtained from an unreasonable search and seizure could not be used in a federal prosecution. This judgment—that the exclusionary rule is part and parcel of the protection provided by the Fourth Amendment—would go unchallenged for nearly thirty years. The *Weeks-Silverthorne Lumber* interpretation of the amendment, however, vanished with the 1949 ruling in *Wolf v. Colorado*.[1] Felix Frankfurter's opinion in *Wolf* is a focal case for myriad reasons, not the least being that after *Wolf*, a majority of the Court would never again embrace the *Weeks-Silverthorne Lumber* conclusion that the Fourth Amendment mandates the exclusion of evidence acquired through unreasonable searches and seizures.

The conventional understanding of *Wolf* is that the Court unanimously ruled that the Fourth Amendment was applicable to the states through the Fourteenth Amendment's Due Process Clause. A majority of the Court also held, however, that Due Process does not require state courts to exclude evidence that would be inadmissible in federal court because it was obtained in violation of the Fourth Amendment. Three justices—Douglas, Murphy, and Rutledge—dissented from this latter holding. The dissenters believed that unlawfully acquired evidence had to be excluded from state prosecutions; otherwise, there would be no effective remedy for Fourth Amendment violations.[2] In a separate dissenting opinion, Rutledge made clear his view that the result in *Wolf* could not be squared with the *Weeks-Silverthorne Lumber* interpretation of the Amendment: "The

---

[1] 338 U.S. 25 (1949).

[2] *See, e.g, id.* at 40 (Douglas, J., dissenting).

view that the Fourth Amendment itself forbids the introduction of evidence illegally obtained in federal prosecutions is one of long standing and firmly established."[3]

Although the conventional view of *Wolf* has endured among many commentators and justices,[4] an accurate description of what happened in *Wolf* requires more elaboration. Further detail is necessary because while *Wolf* refused to impose the Fourth Amendment rule of exclusion (what Frankfurter referred to as "the *Weeks* doctrine") on the states as a matter of constitutional law, what Frankfurter said about the Fourth Amendment's applicability to the states is not nearly as clear as judges and commentators thought when *Wolf* was decided. Looking backward, we can now see that Frankfurter did not intend to make the Amendment binding on the states. That result would occur twelve years later, with Frankfurter dissenting, when *Mapp v. Ohio* was decided.

The traditional understanding of *Wolf*'s holding, moreover, does not capture the significance of *Wolf*. The result and logic of *Wolf* are important for at least three reasons. First, *Wolf*'s holding—that the exclusionary rule does not apply to the states—marked the first occasion where the Court uncoupled the exclusionary rule and the Fourth Amendment. The result in *Wolf* taught future justices that they had discretion to decide not only the scope of the rule, but also whether the rule would even apply in cases where police violate the amendment. This aspect of *Wolf* is important because the Burger and Rehnquist Courts would follow this approach in their decisions narrowing the rule's application.

Wolf's mode of analysis is crucial for another reason, closely related to the first. By separating—or "driving a wedge between the fourth amendment and the exclusionary rule"[5]—the *Wolf* Court not only showed future justices how to restrict the exclusionary rule without appearing to abolish the rule itself, it also "planted the seeds of destruction

---

[3] *Id.* at 48 (Rutledge, J., dissenting).

[4] *See, e.g.*, Vern Countryman, The Judicial Record of Justice William O. Douglas 203 (1974); Fred P. Graham, The Self-Inflicted Wound 39 (1970); Carolyn N. Long, Mapp v. Ohio: Guarding Against Unreasonable Searches and Seizures 48 (2006); Francis A. Allen, *Federalism and the Fourth Amendment: A Requiem for* Wolf, 1961 Sup. Ct. Rev. 1, 3. Even some members of the modern Court have embraced the conventional view of *Wolf* long after it was clear that *Wolf* did not apply the Fourth Amendment to the states. *See, e.g.*, United States v. Leon, 468 U.S. 897, 939 (1984) (Brennan, J., dissenting); California v. Minjares, 443 U.S. 916, 921 (1979) (Rehnquist, J., dissenting) (stating that *Wolf* "held that the Fourth Amendment was applicable to the States by incorporation through the Fourteenth Amendment"); Mapp v. Ohio, 367 U.S. 643, 655 (1961) (explaining that "the Fourth Amendment's right of privacy has been declared enforceable against the States through the Due Process Clause of the Fourteenth [Amendment]," and that "the Court held in *Wolf* that the Amendment was applicable to the States through the Due Process Clause").

[5] William J. Mertens & Silas Wasserstrom, *The Good Faith Exception to the Exclusionary Rule: Deregulating the Police and Derailing the Law*, 70 Geo. L.J. 365, 380 (1981); *see also* Potter Stewart, *The Road to* Mapp v. Ohio *and Beyond: The Origins, Development and Future of the Exclusionary Rule in Search-and-Seizure Cases*, 83 Colum. L. Rev. 1365, 1378 (1983) (explaining that *Wolf* "for the first time explicitly treated the question of whether to exclude illegally obtained evidence as a matter of *remedies*, separate from the *right* secured by the fourth amendment").

for the exclusionary rule—in federal as well as state cases."[6] *Wolf*'s analysis of the exclusionary rule would soon influence how the Court would apply the rule in federal cases, a result one could not predict upon reading the *Wolf* opinion. *Wolf*'s way of thinking about whether exclusion is mandated by the Constitution, although rejected temporarily by *Mapp*, would soon return as the analytical framework favored by the Burger and Rehnquist Courts for restricting the exclusionary rule in all prosecutions.

Finally, it is important to understand precisely what *Wolf*'s "other" holding said. In addition to ruling that the Due Process Clause does not require state courts to exclude evidence obtained by unreasonable searches and seizures, Frankfurter's opinion for the *Wolf* majority also stated that "[t]he security of one's privacy against arbitrary intrusions by the police—which is at the core of the Fourth Amendment—is basic to a free society," and thus, is enforceable against the states through the Due Process Clause.[7] Although not immediately apparent, this second holding would become just as controversial as *Wolf*'s decisive holding that the exclusionary rule is not applicable to the states. Indeed, the realization that *Wolf*'s holding did not apply the Fourth Amendment to the states provided additional motivation for the Warren Court to overrule *Wolf* in *Mapp v. Ohio.*

I. Before *Wolf*: Frankfurter, the Fourth Amendment, and Exclusion

Frankfurter's opinion in *Wolf* certainly deserves the attention and scrutiny that it has received for over a half century. *Wolf* was one of Frankfurter's "most prized—and scorned opinions"[8] and "one of the cornerstones of the Frankfurter juristic edifice."[9] Frankfurter's authorship of *Wolf* is fascinating. On the one hand, "[n]o member of the Court has more vigorously defended the protections of the Fourth Amendment against encroachment by police officials or has with more eloquence urged the value of those provisions in the maintenance of the free society."[10] According to another scholar, "Frankfurter always considered himself something of an expert on the Fourth Amendment."[11] Two years before *Wolf* was decided, Frankfurter described himself to his colleagues as fanatical about the Fourth Amendment: "I am nuts about it because there is no provision of the

6 Yale Kamisar, *Does (Did) (Should) The Exclusionary Rule Rest on a "Principled Basis" Rather Than an "Empirical Proposition"?*, 16 Creighton L. Rev. 565, 616 (1983) [hereinafter Kamisar, *Principled Basis*].

7 *Wolf*, 338 U.S. at 27–28.

8 Tinsley E. Yarbrough, John Marshall Harlan: Great Dissenter of the Warren Court 271 (1992).

9 Bernard Schwartz, Super Chief: Earl Warren and His Supreme Court—A Judicial Biography 391 (1983).

10 Francis A. Allen, *The* Wolf *Case: Search and Seizure, Federalism, and the Civil Liberties*, 45 Ill. L. Rev. 1, 6–7 (1950).

11 Melvin I. Urofsky, Felix Frankfurter: Judicial Restraint and Individual Liberties 157 (1991) [hereinafter Urofsky, Felix Frankfurter].

Constitution more important to be nuts about. There is nothing more important in the Bill of Rights than search and seizure."[12] Ten years later, in a letter to Chief Justice Earl Warren, Frankfurter confessed his devotion to the Fourth Amendment when he wrote: "To the extent that I am charged, not by you, with being 'a nut' on the subject of the 'knock at the door,' I am ready to plead guilty."[13] Indeed, some of the most memorable statements written in the United States Reports about the Fourth Amendment have been authored, fittingly in dissenting opinions, by Frankfurter.[14] One justice, however, was not impressed with Frankfurter's dedication to the Fourth Amendment. To his colleague, Hugo Black, "it was a term of scorn when he called someone a 'search and seizure liberal,' meaning a Justice like Frankfurter who went all out on search and seizure issues but did not support a Communist's claim of free speech."[15]

While Frankfurter was passionate about the Fourth Amendment, at the same time, he was also a firm advocate of judicial restraint, federalism, and the notion that the Due Process Clause of the Fourteenth Amendment is not "shorthand for the first eight

---

[12] Frank Murphy, Conference Notes on *Harris v. United States* (undated), Frank Murphy Papers, Library of Congress, Manuscript Division, Reel 135. In a subsequent letter to Murphy after the Court upheld the search in *Harris*, Frankfurter explained why the Court must be vigilant in protecting Fourth Amendment rights: "That provision of the Bill of Rights calls for more alert enforcement by this Court, not because it is more important say than the First Amendment but because it is much more likely to be lost in the shuffle—to be encroached upon by a case like the *Harris* case in a short-sighted desire to protect society against crime." Felix Frankfurter, Letter to Frank Murphy (Feb. 15, 1947), Murphy Papers, Reel 135.

[13] Felix Frankfurter, Letter to Earl Warren 3 (Apr. 19, 1957), Frankfurter Papers, Box 92.

[14] The old saw that hard cases make bad law has its basis in experience. But petty cases are even more calculated to make bad law. The impact of a sordid little case is apt to obscure the implications of the generalization to which the case gives rise. Only thus can I account for a disregard of the history embedded in the Fourth Amendment and the great place which belongs to that Amendment in the body of our liberties as recognized and applied by unanimous decisions over a long stretch of the Court's history. It is a fair summary of history to say that the safeguards of liberty have frequently been forged in controversies involving not very nice people. And so, while we are concerned here with a shabby defrauder, we must deal with his case in the context of what are really the great themes expressed by the Fourth Amendment.

United States v. Rabinowitz, 339 U.S. 56, 68–69 (1950) (Frankfurter, J., dissenting).

> [I]t is precisely because the appeal to the Fourth Amendment is so often made by dubious characters that its infringements call for alert and strenuous resistance. Freedom of speech, of the press, of religion, easily summon powerful support against encroachment. The prohibition against unreasonable search and seizure is normally invoked by those accused of crime, and criminals have few friends. The implications of such encroachment, however, reach far beyond the thief or the blackmarketeer. I cannot give legal sanction to what was done in this case without accepting the implications of such a decision for the future, implications which portend serious threats against precious aspects of our traditional freedom.

Harris v. United States, 331 U.S. 145, 156–57 (1947) (Frankfurter, J., dissenting).

> It is not only under Nazi rule that police excesses are inimical to freedom. It is easy to make light of insistence on scrupulous regard for the safeguards of civil liberties when invoked on behalf of the unworthy. It is too easy. History bears testimony that by such disregard are the rights of liberty extinguished, heedlessly at first, then stealthily, and brazenly in the end.

Davis v. United States, 328 U.S. 582, 597 (1946) (Frankfurter, J., dissenting).

[15] Joseph P. Lash, From the Diaries of Felix Frankfurter 81 (1975).

amendments of the Constitution and thereby incorporates them."[16] In contrast to Black, who believed that all of the Bill of Rights applied to the states through the Due Process Clause, Frankfurter was convinced that the history of the Fourteenth Amendment "obligated the Court only to impose standards of procedural fairness on state courts through the due process clause, and not the full substantive guarantees of the Bill of Rights."[17] According to Frankfurter, judges inherently knew what Due Process meant. One scholar aptly described Frankfurter's philosophy on Due Process: "[O]ne need not incorporate [the Bill of Rights]; the due process clause by itself is a sufficient limit on state abuse; judges 'know' what is fundamentally fair and what is not; judges have the power and duty to pronounce what is fair and what offends that fairness."[18] Another scholar observed that Frankfurter's "understanding of due process was founded on an image of judges as the quintessential experts, capable of understanding and discerning the core principles that united a progressive, democratic state."[19] But, as this same scholar has also observed, Frankfurter's judicial philosophy "rested upon a contradiction." Frankfurter wanted to limit the "judicial subjectivity and lawmaking of an earlier era while at the same time avoiding inflexible, absolute standards designed to control that same subjectivity." Frankfurter's "model of constitutional decision making sought to free judges from inflexible standards that would restrict judicial judgment." Put differently, Frankfurter's constitutional jurisprudence "did not seek to prevent judicial enforcement of principle; it did, however, seek to make the choice of principle as well as the means and extent of enforcement a matter of enlightened judicial judgment."[20] *Wolf* reveals that the conservative characteristics of Frankfurter's judicial philosophy trumped his passion for enforcing the Fourth Amendment.

When Frankfurter joined the Court on January 30, 1939, there were no exceptions to the exclusionary rule. And his opinions prior to *Wolf* did not hint at what was to come. Less than a year after taking his seat on the Court, Frankfurter wrote *Nardone v. United States II*.[21] In the first *Nardone* case, the Court ruled evidence obtained from a wiretap in violation of the Communications Act of 1934 was inadmissible in a federal prosecution.[22] The issue in *Nardone II* was whether derivative evidence from an illegal wiretap was also inadmissible. Concluding that derivative evidence had to be excluded, Frankfurter reasoned that admitting such evidence would defeat the policy that compelled *Nardone*

---

16 Wolf v. Colorado, 338 U.S. 25, 26 (1949).

17 James F. Simon, The Antagonists: Hugo Black, Felix Frankfurter and Civil Liberties in Modern America 175 (1989).

18 Urofsky, Felix Frankfurter, *supra* note 11, at 152; *see generally* Melvin I. Urofsky, Division and Discord: The Supreme Court Under Stone and Vinson, 1941–1953, at 213–40 (1997) [hereinafter Urofsky, Division and Discord].

19 Mark Silverstein, Constitutional Faiths: Felix Frankfurter, Hugo Black, and the Process of Judicial Decision Making 149 (1984).

20 *Id.* at 128–29.

21 Nardone v. United States (*Nardone II*), 308 U.S. 338 (1939).

22 Nardone v. United States (*Nardone I*), 302 U.S. 379 (1937).

I. He explained: "To forbid the direct use" of illegal wiretap evidence "but to put no curb on their full indirect use would only invite the very methods deemed 'inconsistent with ethical standards and destructive of personal liberty.'"[23] Frankfurter declared that Holmes's view of the Fourth Amendment and exclusion—evidence obtained in violation of the amendment "shall not be used at all"—was "pertinent here."[24]

Significantly, exclusion in both of the *Nardone* cases was based on the Court's supervisory power over the federal judiciary, and not the Fourth Amendment. Although Frankfurter was not interpreting the Fourth Amendment in *Nardone II*, the Court's prior Fourth Amendment rulings seemed to influence his analysis. Indeed, although it was unnecessary to decide the case, Frankfurter elaborated on what Holmes meant in *Silverthorne Lumber* when Holmes said, in dicta, that the Fourth Amendment does not require excluding evidence "gained from an independent source."[25] According to Frankfurter, it was a "matter of good sense" that the connection between an illegal search and the evidence proffered by the government at trial "may have become so attenuated as to dissipate the taint."[26] Therefore, once the defendant shows that a substantial portion of the case against him was "fruit of the poisonous tree," the government must be given the chance to show that its proof had an "independent origin."[27] Thus were born the concept of "fruit of the poisonous tree" and the doctrine of "attenuation," both of which would play a major role in the Court's exclusionary rule cases of the late twentieth century. Although *Nardone II* was decided when *Weeks* and *Silverthorne Lumber* reigned, Frankfurter "did not explain why or how the admission of attenuated evidence was consistent with the personal entitlement to exclude both direct and indirect products of illegalities."[28]

In 1943, six years before *Wolf*, Frankfurter wrote *McNabb v. United States*,[29] which ruled that confessions obtained by federal law enforcement officials after several days of interrogation were inadmissible in a federal murder prosecution. The defendants argued their confessions were inadmissible under the Fifth Amendment. But Frankfurter avoided the constitutional claim. Again relying on the Court's supervisory powers, he held that the confessions had to be excluded because the defendants had not been, as required by federal law, promptly taken to a magistrate after their arrests. "Plainly, a conviction resting on evidence secured through such a flagrant disregard of the procedure which Congress

---

[23] *Nardone II*, 308 U.S. at 340 (quoting *Nardone I*, 302 U.S. at 383). As others have explained, this "forward looking, consequentialist rationale is now called 'deterrence,' although [Frankfurter] did not employ that term in 1939." Silas Wasserstrom & William J. Mertens, *The Exclusionary Rule on the Scaffold: But Was It a Fair Trial?*, 22 Am. Crim. L. Rev. 85, 142-43 (1984).

[24] *Nardone II*, 308 U.S. at 340.

[25] Silverthorne Lumber Co. v. United States, 251 U.S.385, 392 (1920).

[26] *Nardone II*, 308 U.S. at 341.

[27] *Id.*

[28] James J. Tomkovicz, Constitutional Exclusion: The Rules, Rights, and Remedies that Strike the Balance Between Freedom and Order 102 n.238 (2011).

[29] 318 U.S. 332 (1943).

has commanded cannot be allowed to stand without making the courts themselves accomplices in willful disobedience of law."[30] Although no federal statute mandated the suppression of the confessions, the absence of an explicit statutory exclusionary rule did not deter Frankfurter: to "permit such evidence to be made the basis of a conviction in the federal courts would stultify the policy which Congress has enacted into law."[31]

Interestingly, there is not a word in either of the *Nardone* cases or *McNabb* questioning the wisdom of *Weeks* or the view that the exclusionary rule is part and parcel of the Fourth Amendment itself. To be sure, *Nardone II* and *McNabb* were based on the Court's supervisory power, and not on the Fourth or Fifth Amendments. But as Yale Kamisar recognized over fifty years ago, Frankfurter's views in these cases about "applying and implementing the rights of the accused generally, whether or not such rights are grounded in the Constitution" are hard to reconcile with his later opinion in *Wolf* that the exclusionary rule is not inherent in the Fourth Amendment.[32]

Moreover, Frankfurter's vote in a third case, *Goldstein v. United States*,[33] is also hard to square with the subsequent ruling in *Wolf*. The issue in *Goldstein* concerned whether the exclusionary rule of the *Nardone* cases could be invoked by a defendant who was not a party to an illegally intercepted communication. In deciding this issue, the *Goldstein* Court reaffirmed *Weeks*'s reading of the Fourth Amendment and its exclusionary rule: "It has long been settled that evidence obtained in violation of the prohibition of the Fourth Amendment cannot be used in a prosecution against the victim of the unlawful search and seizure if he makes timely objection."[34] As in the *Nardone* cases and *McNabb*, *Goldstein*'s holding rested upon the Court's supervisory power. Nonetheless, the *Goldstein* majority relied in large part on the fact that the lower federal courts had unanimously denied standing to a third party who was not the victim of an unconstitutional search or seizure.[35] The *Goldstein* Court applied this practice of denying standing to third parties to violations of the Communications Act of 1934.

Justice Murphy, joined by Chief Justice Stone and Frankfurter, dissented in *Goldstein*. While Murphy did not challenge the majority's reaffirmation of *Weeks*, he did contend that the results and reasoning in the *Nardone* cases dictated that a third party be afforded standing to suppress evidence derived from an illegal wiretap.[36] Murphy argued it was "a complete *non sequitur* to conclude" that only a party to the communication had

---

30 *Id.* at 345.

31 *Id.* For an informative examination of the Court's supervisory power cases, *see* Sara Sun Beale, *Reconsidering Supervisory Power in Criminal Cases: Constitutional and Statutory Limits on the Authority of the Federal Courts*, 84 COLUM. L. REV. 1433 (1984).

32 Yale Kamisar, Wolf *and* Lustig *Ten Years Later: Illegal State Evidence in State and Federal Courts*, 43 MINN. L. REV. 1083, 1124 (1959) [hereinafter Kamisar, Wolf *and* Lustig]; *see also* Kamisar, *Principled Basis*, *supra* note 6, at 616 n.296.

33 316 U.S. 114 (1942).

34 *Id.* at 120.

35 *Id.* at 121.

36 *Id.* at 126 (Murphy, J., dissenting).

standing to object to the use of the illegal wiretap; withholding standing to a third party, he argued, would defeat the policy and purpose of the statute.[37] According to Murphy, the exclusionary rule announced in the *Nardone* cases was designed to implement "the Congressional command that society shall not be plagued with such practices as wiretapping."[38] Interestingly, Murphy thought the lower court cases denying standing to third parties who were not themselves victims of unreasonable searches or seizure were "hard to square" with Holmes's interpretation of the Fourth Amendment in *Silverthorne Lumber*.[39] Denying standing to third parties would "allow the Government to profit by its wrong and to reduce in large measure the protection of the Amendment."[40] Murphy also cited *Weeks* for the principle that evidence obtained in violation of federal law by federal agents was inadmissible in federal prosecutions.[41]

Putting aside the Court's disagreement over whether third parties had standing to suppress evidence obtained in violation of the Communications Act, the majority and dissenting opinions in *Goldstein* reveal unanimity among the justices on the meaning of *Weeks*; namely, all evidence—not just private papers—obtained in violation of the Fourth Amendment could not be used against the victim of an unconstitutional search. When explaining the holding and meaning of *Weeks*, neither the majority nor dissenting opinion in *Goldstein* questioned the principle that exclusion was mandated by the Fourth Amendment itself. This unanimous view of the Fourth Amendment's exclusionary rule would be drastically altered by Frankfurter's opinion in *Wolf*.[42]

Frankfurter played a prominent role in changing the Court's jurisprudence on the exclusionary rule. In the view of its critics, the exclusionary rule is objectionable because it acts as a hard-and-fast windfall to criminals. It has been suggested that Frankfurter opposed absolute and immutable principles.[43] Although Frankfurter was a self-described "nut" about the Fourth Amendment, his fervor did not extend to the exclusionary rule. Indeed, Frankfurter's description of the rule in *Wolf* would have a lasting impact on the Court. Put simply, unlike his hero Holmes, who saw the rule as inherent in the Fourth Amendment, Frankfurter viewed the rule as judge-made law, a mere rule of evidence, subject to the discretion of judges who knew when it should and should not be applied.

---

37 *Id.* at 126–27.

38 *Id.* at 127.

39 *Id.*

40 *Id.* at 127 n.4.

41 *Id.* at 128.

42 Two years before *Wolf* was decided, in a dissenting opinion in *Harris v. United States*, 331 U.S. 145 (1947), Frankfurter was circumspect in his description of the Fourth Amendment's exclusionary rule. Rather than describe exclusion as inherent in the Amendment, he stated that "the federal rule" established in *Weeks*, "as against the rule prevailing in many states," barred the admissibility of evidence no matter how relevant. *Id.* at 159 (Frankfurter, J., dissenting). And he explained that *Boyd* "gave legal effect to the broad historic policy underlying" the Amendment, and that *Boyd* provided the guide to interpreting the Amendment "to which the Court has most frequently recurred." *Id.* at 160 (Frankfurter, J., dissenting).

43 *See* SILVERSTEIN, *supra* note 19, at 128-29.

A. The Background of Wolf

Curiously, Frankfurter's opinion in *Wolf* omits the facts. Julius A. Wolf was a Denver, Colorado, physician and surgeon whose practice "consisted principally in the treatment of diseases of women, obstetrics, and pelvic and abdominal surgery."[44] The local prosecutor's office suspected that Dr. Wolf was performing illegal abortions. Without judicial authorization, investigators for the prosecutor went to Wolf's office, arrested him, searched his office, and seized patient appointment books and records. The seized materials revealed the identities of female patients, who were later summoned and interrogated by investigators regarding Dr. Wolf's medical practices. The documents seized during the raid were later admitted at Wolf's prosecution for conspiracy to commit abortion. Wolf was convicted, and the Colorado Supreme Court affirmed the conviction, though it all but conceded that the warrantless search and seizure of Wolf's office violated the Colorado Constitution.

The procedural history of *Wolf* in the Court is not widely known, and the backstage proceedings reveal a division among the justices regarding the exclusionary rule that would persist into the twenty-first century. The Court initially decided not to review Wolf's case. Wolf's petition for a writ of certiorari, which is a request that the Court review a case, was filed on February 14, 1948. On March 27, Black, Murphy, and Rutledge voted to hear the case, but six justices, including William Douglas, opposed reviewing the case.[45] Interestingly, Frankfurter, who voted against granting Wolf's petition for certiorari, told his colleagues that "he [did] not know what he would decide on the merits."[46] By April 5, the Court had decided to deny the writ.

In response to the denial of certiorari, Rutledge prepared a dissent that was never published. Rutledge described the Court's refusal to hear the case as "[completely] indefensible."[47] He also addressed the apparent reason for not reviewing the case:

> Perhaps some of my brethren . . . rely on a tortuous distinction between a right to be protected against unlawful search and seizure carrying with it a right of redress against the offending officers, which they would hold to be incorporated in the concept of due process, and the right to have evidence obtained in violation of constitutional guarantees suppressed, which they feel is not protected by the Fourteenth Amendment.[48]

---

[44] Wolf v. People, 187 P.2d 926, 927 (Col. 1947) (en banc).

[45] Felix Frankfurter, Docket Sheet on *Wolf v. Colorado* (undated),Frankfurter Papers, Box 31.

[46] *Id.*; *see also* Jan Palmer, The Vinson Court Era: The Supreme Court's Conference Votes 230 (1990) (stating the original denial of certiorari in *Wolf* occurred on April 2, 1948).

[47] Wiley Rutledge, Unpublished Dissent on *Wolf v. Colorado* 1 (undated) (brackets in original), Wiley Rutledge Papers, Library of Congress, Manuscript Division, Box 163.

[48] *Id.* at 3.

Rutledge found such a distinction "renders the protection of the Fourth Amendment illusory" and could not be reconciled with *Weeks*.[49]

Despite the earlier vote to deny certiorari, *Wolf* remained on the Court's agenda. Frankfurter's docket sheet notes that on April 21, Douglas was "firm and sharp in voting 'NO'" on reviewing the case.[50] Then, on April 24, Frankfurter writes that "Douglas changed vote."[51] Two days later, the Court officially decided to review Wolf's case. After oral argument, the Court's conference discussion forecast the influential role that Black would have on the development of the exclusionary rule. The discussion also showed that Black could never make up his mind on why he opposed the rule. Black initially voted to "reverse" the judgment of the Colorado Supreme Court, maintaining that the "14th takes in 4th."[52] But by the end of the discussion, Black decided to "pass" and was "waiting to see what the 4th amendment means in the federal constitution."[53]

In the period between the conference discussion and the Court's announcement of *Wolf*, Black would have an opportunity to expound on the exclusionary rule, albeit in a context dramatically different from the facts in *Wolf*. Almost six weeks before *Wolf* was decided, Black spoke for a unanimous Court in *United States v. Wallace & Tiernan Co.*[54] A subpoena was served on a corporation requiring the production of documents for a federal grand jury's investigation. The documents were produced, and the grand jury returned an indictment against the corporation and others. Because women had been excluded from the grand jury, an illegally comprised grand jury issued the subpoena. This, a federal district court concluded, rendered the otherwise valid subpoena an unconstitutional search and seizure, and the court consequently dismissed the indictment.

Black's opinion reversed this ruling because the exclusion of women was not a sufficient reason to bar the government from using the subpoenaed documents.[55] Referring

---

[49] *Id.*

[50] Frankfurter, Docket Sheet on *Wolf v. Colorado*, *supra* note 45.

[51] *Id.*

[52] Wiley Rutledge, Conference Notes on *Wolf v. Colorado* (Oct. 23, 1948), Rutledge Papers, Box 173. Rutledge's conference notes were written on the back pages of a bench memo prepared in *Wolf*.

[53] *Id.* Douglas' docket sheet on *Wolf* also notes "pass" next to Black's name regarding his vote on the merits. William Douglas, Docket Sheet on *Wolf v. Colorado* (voted on Oct. 23, 1948), William Douglas Papers, Library of Congress, Manuscript Division, Box 1121. Douglas's conference notes on *Wolf* record a slightly different version of Black's comments. According to Douglas, Black told his colleagues that reversal was required based on the "constitutional scope of the Fourth Amendment, as construed by the Court." Black also stated that "if" the Fourth Amendment "has the exclusionary evidence penalty, then it should apply in state courts, whatever view of due process is taken—the Fourth Amendment in its full scope is the law of each state." William Douglas, Conference Notes on *Wolf v. Colorado* (Oct. 23, 1948), Douglas Papers, Box 176; *see also* THE SUPREME COURT IN CONFERENCE (1940–1985): THE PRIVATE DISCUSSIONS BEHIND NEARLY 300 SUPREME COURT DECISIONS 476-78 (Del Dickson ed., 2001). As recorded by Douglas, Black's comments indicate a tentative inclination to see the exclusionary rule as mandated by the Fourth Amendment itself.

[54] 336 U.S. 793 (1949).

[55] *Id.* at 800.

to what he called "the *Silverthorne* rule" or "the *Silverthorne* exclusionary rule," Black wrote that it "is an extraordinary sanction, judicially imposed, to limit searches and seizures to those conducted in strict compliance with the commands of the Fourth Amendment."[56] Although his rationale is not apparent, it seems that Black thought that exclusion served no purpose in this context because there was no Fourth Amendment violation. Alternatively, Black may have believed there was only a technical infraction of the Constitution. While *Wallace & Tiernan Co.* was never cited by the Court in another exclusionary rule case, Black's views on exclusion would play an important role in the subsequent development and eventual demise of the rule.[57]

The conference discussion in *Wolf* also previewed Frankfurter's thinking about the case. Notwithstanding his earlier uncertainty on how he would vote on the merits, Frankfurter voted to affirm the judgment of the Colorado Supreme Court. Frankfurter told his colleagues, "Due process is due process. That's that—*not* the 1st, or 5th or 4th amendments."[58] In other words, for Frankfurter, at issue in *Wolf* was whether the search of Dr. Wolf's office violated the dictates of Due Process, not whether the intrusion violated the Fourth Amendment. Frankfurter stated he would hold that Due Process forbids the police the "right to do anything they please," but that the facts in *Wolf* had not risen to such a level.[59] Frankfurter also told his colleagues that Congress "might" overrule the *Weeks* case.[60] The issue of the Court overruling *Weeks*, let alone Congress doing so, had not been raised in the parties' briefs. In fact, the brief of the Attorney General of Colorado conceded that, in federal cases "there is no argument that evidence, if it has been illegally seized, is not admissible."[61] But Frankfurter told his colleagues that the remedy of excluding testimony secured by an illegal search and seizure "is *not* part of 4th

---

[56] *Id.* at 796-98.

[57] It is difficult to assess the long-term impact of Black's analysis of the exclusionary rule in *Wallace & Tiernan Co.* On the one hand, *Wallace & Tiernan Co.* "marks the first time the Court indicated that the exclusionary rule is based on a 'deterrence' rationale and the first time it suggested that the rule may not be a command of the fourth amendment." Kamisar, *Principled Basis*, *supra* note 6, at 604. Both of these points became (and remain) central arguments of justices and others who oppose exclusion. On the other hand, *Wallace & Tiernan Co.* "seems to have vanished without a trace." *Id.* at 605. As Professor Kamisar observes, neither Black nor any other justice "ever cited the case in any of the opinions in *Wolf* or in *Mapp*. Nor has [it] once been cited, let alone quoted, in any search and seizure case decided by the Burger Court." *Id.* The apparent disappearance of *Wallace & Tiernan Co.* may be due to Black's repeated references to "the *Silverthorne* exclusionary rule" and "the *Silverthorne* rule," or because the facts in *Wallace & Tiernan Co.* did not involve an actual violation of the Fourth Amendment. *Id.* at 605. When *Wallace & Tiernan Co.* was pending, Murphy, a strong supporter of the exclusionary rule, wrote to Black that he agreed with a draft opinion circulated to the Court. Murphy told Black that it "would be completely out of harmony" with the rationale of the Fourth Amendment and the Court's cases interpreting the Amendment to affirm the lower court's judgment, "for the violation was only a technical one." Frank Murphy, Letter to Hugo Black (undated), Murphy Papers, *Wallace & Tiernan Co.* File.

[58] Rutledge, Conference Notes on *Wolf v. Colorado*, *supra* note 52.

[59] *Id.*

[60] *Id.*

[61] Brief of Respondent at 23, Wolf v. Colorado, 338 U.S. 25 (1949) (Nos. 17, 18).

Amendment."[62] Three days later, on October 25, Frankfurter was assigned to write *Wolf*, along with *Lustig v. United States*, which was argued on the same day as *Wolf*.[63]

In his opinion for the Court, Frankfurter never says the search of Dr. Wolf's office was unconstitutional.[64] Instead, Frankfurter finesses the point by assuming, without admitting the assumption, that the search violated the Fourth Amendment.[65] In other words, Frankfurter brushes past the question whether the search violated the Fourth Amendment in order to decide the issue of exclusion. That the search may have hypothetically violated the Fourth Amendment, however, did not resolve the issue of whether Wolf's conviction should have been reversed, like Weeks's federal conviction had been. The crucial issue, according to Frankfurter, was whether Wolf's state court conviction violated the Due Process Clause of the Fourteenth Amendment solely because evidence was admitted at his trial that would have been inadmissible in a federal prosecution under *Weeks*'s holding. In resolving this question, Frankfurter's ruling is traditionally read to contain two grounds: *Wolf* ruled the Fourth Amendment was enforceable against the states through the Due Process Clause but also ruled that in a state prosecution, Due Process "does not forbid the admission of evidence obtained by an unreasonable search and seizure."[66] In other words, the second grounds meant that *Weeks*'s prohibition on the admission of evidence obtained through an unconstitutional search was not applicable to the states.

Wolf's holding that the states are free to admit evidence obtained from unconstitutional searches in criminal trials has rightly generated much attention and commentary. For purposes of this book, it is crucial to highlight Frankfurter's (and Black's) treatment of *Weeks*. Not only does Frankfurter remove the constitutional foundation of *Weeks*'s holding that evidence obtained in violation of the Fourth Amendment cannot be used at trial, he also questions the legitimacy of the exclusionary rule itself. By separating the exclusionary rule and the Fourth Amendment, doubting the rule's legitimacy, and declaring deterrence as the purpose for the rule, Frankfurter set the terms for future debate on the merits of the rule. Not surprisingly, Frankfurter's critique of the rule also

---

62 Rutledge, Conference Notes on *Wolf v. Colorado*, *supra* note 52.

63 Wiley Rutledge, Assignment Sheet (Oct. 25, 1948), Rutledge Papers, Box 167. *Lustig v. United States*, 338 U.S. 74 (1949), was another "silver platter" case. It ruled that evidence obtained during an illegal search of the defendant's hotel room was inadmissible in a federal prosecution for counterfeiting; although the local police initiated the illegal search, a federal agent who was later called to the scene participated in the search because he played a "vital" role in evaluating the significance of the seized evidence for federal counterfeiting violations. *Id.* at 79–80.

64 Tom Davies makes this precise point. He further explains, Frankfurter's opinion "clearly did not treat the search by state officers as a violation of the Fourteenth Amendment Due Process Clause; indeed, if the Court had concluded that the search violated the Due Process Clause, it would have ordered the prosecution to be dismissed." Thomas Y. Davies, *An Account of* Mapp v. Ohio *That Misses the Larger Exclusionary Rule Story*, 4 Ohio St. J. Crim. L. 619, 626 n. 24 (2007) (book review) [hereinafter Davies, *Book Review*].

65 *See id.* ("Frankfurter's opinion assumed *hypothetically* that the search would have violated the Fourth Amendment *if* the Fourth Amendment applied" to this case.).

66 *Wolf*, 338 U.S. at 33.

provides the analytical blueprint used by the conservative justices of the Burger and Rehnquist Courts to purge the exclusionary rule in federal and state cases.

II. Rewriting *Weeks*'s Holding

Frankfurter's uncoupling of the rule and the Fourth Amendment begins with his description of *Weeks*'s holding. The differences between *Weeks*'s holding and Frankfurter's description of it are striking. Recall that Day summarized *Weeks*'s holding near the end of his opinion when he explained a federal officer had obtained papers "in direct violation of the constitutional rights" of Weeks.[67] Because Weeks had made a timely request for the return of the papers, refusing that request constituted "a denial of the constitutional rights of the accused."[68] Therefore, "holding [the papers] and permitting their use upon the trial" was "prejudicial error."[69]

Also, in concluding that exclusion was constitutionally mandated, it did not matter to the *Weeks* Court that the text of the Fourth Amendment said nothing, positive or negative, about the use or exclusion of relevant evidence. Furthermore, *Weeks* did not characterize its holding as a rule of evidence. To the contrary, as Holmes, who was a member of the *Weeks* Court, would later recognize, the effect of *Weeks* was to repeal the common-law competent evidence rule. Nor did it matter to the result in *Weeks* that criminals would be the beneficiaries of its holding. Finally, there was no statement in *Weeks* that the purpose of the rule was to deter future unconstitutional searches and seizures by federal officers.

In *Wolf*, Frankfurter writes that *Weeks*'s holding "was not derived from the explicit requirements of the Fourth Amendment."[70] Instead, he asserts, "The decision was a matter of judicial implication."[71] After noting that many states rejected exclusion as a matter of state law, Frankfurter observes "the exclusion of evidence is a remedy which directly serves only to protect those upon whose person or premises something incriminating has been found."[72] Whereas *Weeks* never mentions deterrence as a basis for exclusion, *Wolf* injects deterrence into the calculus for determining whether exclusion is the appropriate remedy for a Fourth Amendment violation.[73] But Frankfurter left no doubt that he did not view deterrence as a persuasive basis for imposing exclusion on the states.[74] He

---

67 Weeks v. United States, 232 U.S. 383, 398 (1914).

68 *Id.*

69 *Id.*

70 *Wolf*, 338 U.S. at 28.

71 *Id.*

72 *Id.* at 30–31.

73 *See id.* at 31.

74 Mertens & Wasserstrom, *supra* note 5, at 379 (explaining that *Wolf* was responsible for injecting "the instrumental rationale of deterrence of police misconduct into its discussion of the exclusionary rule. At the same time, however, it made clear that it did not view this rationale as compelling." (footnote omitted)).

observed the Court "cannot brush aside the experience of States which deem the incidence of [unlawful] conduct by the police too slight to call for a deterrent remedy not by way of disciplinary measures but by overriding the relevant rules of evidence."[75]

Finally, and perhaps most significantly, Frankfurter's analysis of *Weeks* gratuitously raises an issue that had never been broached by the Court. He notes that while the Court has "interpreted the Fourth Amendment to forbid the admission of [unlawfully obtained] evidence, a different question would be presented if Congress under its legislative powers were to pass a statute purporting to negate the *Weeks* doctrine."[76] According to Frankfurter, the Court was "forced" to adopt the federal exclusionary rule because Congress had not acted on the issue.[77] Black's concurring opinion agrees with Frankfurter's conclusion that exclusion is not derived from the Constitution. But Black goes a step further when he asserts that he "agree[s] with what appears to be a plain implication of the Court's opinion that the federal exclusionary rule is not a command of the Fourth Amendment but a judicially created rule of evidence which Congress might negate."[78]

These passages about Congress's authority to negate *Weeks* do more than raise academic questions. The confluence of these statements—that the exclusionary rule is a "matter of judicial implication," which functions as a "rule of evidence;" that the rule's deterrent purpose was not sufficient to justify exclusion; that the Court had been "forced" to adopt the rule; and that Congress might override the rule—is a not-so-subtle

---

[75] *Wolf*, 338 U.S. at 31–32.

[76] *Id.* at 33.

[77] *Id.*

[78] *Id.* at 39–40 (Black, J., concurring). Black's understanding of *Weeks*, Frankfurter's opinion in *Wolf*, and the Framers' intentions regarding exclusion of unconstitutionally obtained evidence is revealed in a hand-written draft of Black's *Wolf* concurrence. In a section that was crossed out and would not appear in his published opinion, Black wrote:

> The framers of the Constitution could easily have used language barring introduction of evidence obtained by unreasonable searches [and] seizures. They did not. They simply outlined the guarantee of unreasonable searches [and] seizures [and] left to the legislative process the responsibility for choosing means to enforce the Amendment. Congress has not chosen to select the exclusionary evidence rule as a means to enforce the amendment. In 1914 this Court did adopt the exclusionary rule for federal courts in *Weeks v. United States*. Whether there should be such a rigid exclusionary rule, is as the Court says, a question on which men may reasonably differ. I do not here question the wisdom of the rule nor challenge the power of the Court to declare it. But I think the Court should make clear the plain implications of its opinion namely, that the exclusionary rule is a judicial creation on the legislative level, not a constitutional command. I say that the Court impliedly treats the rule as below the constitutional level, because the opinion indicates that Congress could "negate" it. Of course, Congress could not "negate" the rule if it is a part of the Fourth Amendment, whether there "explicitly" or by "judicial implication." See *McNabb v. United States*.

Hugo Black, Hand-Written Draft of Concurrence in *Wolf v. Colorado* 1–2 (undated), Hugo Lafayette Black Papers, Library of Congress, Manuscript Division, Box 302. Significantly, Black does not mention the Fifth Amendment or *Boyd*, in either his handwritten draft or his final opinion, as a basis for excluding unconstitutionally obtained evidence.

invitation to either Congress or a future group of justices to overturn the constitutional principle announced in *Weeks*. Moreover, no precedent, or even dicta from Court precedents, backed any of these statements. Frankfurter and Black were adopting a novel view of the Fourth Amendment. Both omitted from their respective opinions that neither *Weeks* nor *Silverthorne Lumber*, nor any other Fourth Amendment ruling of the Court prior to *Wolf*, had suggested the federal exclusionary remedy was a "rule of evidence." Both justices also neglected to mention that never before had the Court spoken of being "forced" to create the rule because of congressional inaction on the issue nor had the Court indicated that Congress had the authority to negate the rule.[79]

The traditional understanding of *Wolf* declares that the case merely held that the Due Process Clause does not impose on the states the federal rule barring the use of evidence obtained from a Fourth Amendment violation. This understanding, while technically correct as a matter of law, nevertheless ignores the logic and impact of *Wolf*. While acknowledging that *Weeks*'s holding has been "frequently applied" and claiming that the Court was "stoutly adher[ing] to it,"[80] in reality, Frankfurter was rewriting *Weeks* and undermining the constitutional principle it announced. *Wolf* removed the constitutional basis of the rule by uncoupling the exclusion doctrine from the Fourth Amendment. At the same time, Frankfurter also questioned the exclusionary rule's legitimacy and effectiveness, and invited Congress or a subsequent Court to override the rule in a future case.

III. Applying the Due Process Clause to Arbitrary Police Intrusions, But Not Applying the Fourth Amendment to the States

Felix Frankfurter was known as "a believer in the power of words, gracefully arranged and forcefully expressed."[81] In *Wolf*, Frankfurter wrote:

> The security of one's privacy against arbitrary intrusion by the police—which is at the core of the Fourth Amendment—is basic to a free society. It is therefore implicit in "the concept of ordered liberty" and as such enforceable against the States through the Due Process Clause.[82]

Despite his reputation as a master of the English language, what Frankfurter meant by this prose has been debated by justices and scholars for a half-century.

---

79 *See* Kamisar, *Principled Basis*, *supra* note 6, at 617 n.296.

80 *Wolf*, 338 U.S. at 28.

81 Bruce Allen Murphy, The Brandeis/Frankfurter Connection: The Secret Political Activities of Two Supreme Court Justices 253 (1982).

82 *Wolf*, 338 U.S. at 27–28.

The established view of this passage maintains that Frankfurter ruled that the Fourth Amendment was applicable to the states via the Fourteenth Amendment's Due Process Clause. That was also the view held by the concurring and dissenting opinions in *Wolf*. For example, Black stated that he "agree[d] with the conclusion of the Court that the Fourth Amendment's prohibition of 'unreasonable searches and seizures' is enforceable against the states."[83] And the dissenting justices read Frankfurter's opinion as applying the amendment to the states.[84] Concededly, Frankfurter states that the "security of one's privacy against arbitrary intrusion by the police—which is at the core of the Fourth Amendment—is basic to a free society." Therefore, he continues, "It is . . . enforceable against the States through the Due Process Clause." Finally, a few lines later, Frankfurter states that if a state were to "affirmatively" sanction arbitrary police intrusions, "it would run counter to the guaranty of the Fourteenth Amendment."[85]

When analyzing this part of *Wolf*, it is critical to understand that Frankfurter never writes that the "Fourth Amendment" applies to the states. He only says that "one's privacy against arbitrary intrusion by the police" is protected by the Due Process Clause.[86] Thus, when read precisely, this part of Frankfurter's opinion only supports the view that the "Due Process Clause included some 'core' protection of privacy that overlapped with some of the broader protection afforded by the Fourth Amendment." It does not, however, support the view, either explicitly or otherwise, that "the Due Process Clause required the states to afford as strong a protection of privacy as the Fourth Amendment required of the federal government."[87] In fact, in a critical sentence sometimes overlooked

[83] *Id.* at 39 (Black, J., concurring).

[84] *See id.* at 41 (Murphy, J., dissenting) ("Of course I agree with the Court that the Fourteenth Amendment prohibits activities which are proscribed by the search and seizure clause of the Fourth Amendment."); *id.* at 47 (Rutledge, J., dissenting) ("I welcome the fact that the Court . . . today finds the substance of the Fourth Amendment 'to be implicit in the concept of ordered liberty, and thus, through the Fourteenth Amendment, . . . valid as against the states.'" (second ellipsis in original) (citation omitted)).

[85] *Id.* at 27-28 (majority opinion).

[86] *Id.* at 27.

[87] Davies, *Book Review*, *supra* note 64, at 626 n.24. Black's concurring opinion in *Wolf* appears to acknowledge Frankfurter's sleight of hand as well. He noted: "It is not amiss to repeat my belief that the Fourteenth Amendment was intended to make the Fourth Amendment in its *entirety* applicable to the states." *Wolf*, 338 U.S. at 40 (Black, J., concurring) (emphasis added). Legal scholars have been debating this aspect of *Wolf* for many years. *Compare* Mertens & Wasserstrom, *supra* note 5, at 379 n.60 ("The Court did not incorporate at once the whole of the fourth amendment into the fourteenth amendment. The Court in *Wolf* took the first step. The range of the fourth amendment interests encompassed by *Wolf* remained unclear, however, until the Court ruled in *Ker v. California*, 374 U.S. 23 (1963), that the fourth amendment applied with full force to the states, and that the constitutional standards governing federal officials also apply to state officials. Until it extended the exclusionary rule to the states in *Mapp v. Ohio*, 367 U.S. 643 (1961), there were simply no cases requiring the Court to elucidate just what constraints the fourth amendment imposed on state officials through the fourteenth amendment."), *with* Yale Kamisar, Mapp v. Ohio*: The First Shot Fired in the Warren Court's Criminal Procedure "Revolution," in* CRIMINAL PROCEDURE STORIES 45, 63–64 (Carol S. Steiker ed., 2006) (pointing out that although Frankfurter does not "address the question explicitly," he "seemed to equate the *substantive* protection against unreasonable searches and seizures provided by the Fourteenth Amendment with the specific guarantees of the Fourth. He seemed to

by scholars, Frankfurter juxtaposes "protection against arbitrary intrusion by the police" against exclusion of evidence "obtained by an unreasonable search and seizure."[88]

Why are these verbal niceties significant? And why is it important to clarify that *Wolf* did not apply the Fourth Amendment—rather than some smaller "core" interest of "privacy" barring arbitrary intrusions affirmatively sanctioned by the state—to the states? Professor Tom Davies has suggested that the "conventional misreading" of *Wolf*, which Davies contends surfaced in the 1960 ruling in *Elkins v. United States*,[89] has not been accidental. The traditional understanding that *Wolf* applied the Fourth Amendment to the states has allowed the justices in subsequent cases "to dodge the need to explain *why* the Fourth Amendment was incorporated in the Fourteenth Amendment Due Process Clause."[90] As a result, even today "there is no explanation of the incorporation of the Fourth Amendment into the Fourteenth in the Supreme Court opinions."[91]

But there are other reasons why it is important to read Frankfurter's words precisely and to understand the significance of not applying the Fourth Amendment to the states, as opposed to some "core" element of privacy. For starters, *Wolf* does not define what constitutes "the security of one's privacy," nor does it identify what counts as an "arbitrary intrusion" by state police officers. After all, one could reasonably ask why the warrantless search and seizure of Dr. Wolf's office did not infringe the "core" of the privacy interest that Frankfurter said was "basic to a free society." Surely, if federal officers had conducted this raid, their actions would have violated the Fourth Amendment. But that is the point. Frankfurter was not applying the Fourth Amendment to the states; he was interpreting the Due Process Clause to decide whether state officials conducted an arbitrary police intrusion. Frankfurter did not view the police conduct in *Wolf* as an arbitrary invasion of privacy. And he certainly was not prepared to overturn a state court's judgment that Wolf's conviction was not a deprivation of due process of law.[92]

---

say that even though the Fourteenth Amendment does *not require the exclusion* of the resulting evidence, the Amendment is violated when state police conduct *any* unreasonable search and seizure." (footnote omitted)); *see also* Kamisar, Wolf *and* Lustig, *supra* note 32, at 1101–08.

[88] *Wolf*, 338 U.S. at 28. The full sentence states: "But the immediate question is whether the basic right to protection against arbitrary intrusion by the police demands the exclusion of logically relevant evidence obtained by an unreasonable search and seizure because, in a federal prosecution for a federal crime, it would be excluded." *Id.*

[89] 364 U.S. 206 (1960).

[90] Davies, *Book Review*, *supra* note 64, at 626 n.24.

[91] *Id.*

[92] What Frankfurter wrote in another incorporation case, Adamson v. California, 332 U.S. 46 (1947), partially explains why he affirmed Wolf's conviction. In *Adamson*, a majority of the Court rejected the defendant's claim that the Fifth Amendment privilege against self-incrimination applied to the States. Agreeing with that result, Frankfurter wrote: "[T]he issue is not whether an infraction of one of the specific provisions of the first eight Amendments is disclosed by the record. The relevant question is whether the criminal proceedings which resulted in conviction deprived the accused of the due process of law. . . . The judicial judgment in applying the Due Process Clause must move within the limits of accepted notions of justice and is not to be based upon the idiosyncrasies of a merely personal judgment. The fact that judges among

The elusiveness of Frankfurter's language regarding whether the Fourth Amendment actually applied to the states is not merely an academic concern. It soon became apparent that under *Wolf*'s reasoning, state police officers were allowed to conduct searches and secure incriminating evidence admissible in state criminal proceedings, where identical searches by federal officers would result in the exclusion of evidence and the automatic reversal of convictions obtained in federal cases. Thus, the constitutional validity of identical police behavior would turn on the status of the officer conducting the search and seizure. Soon, a majority of the justices also recognized that Frankfurter's Due Process analysis encouraged uncertain and subjective judgments regarding the legality of state police searches and seizures. Equally important, *Wolf* left state law enforcement officials free to infringe basic Fourth Amendment protections and to use the fruits of those intrusions to help convict individuals. Within a short period of time, three cases—an obscure case from New Jersey and two controversial cases from California—showed that, despite the conventional view that the Fourth Amendment was enforceable against the states, local police were ignoring the amendment, and the justices were not applying Fourth Amendment principles in cases involving illegal searches and seizures by local police.

Wolf's impact, however, would not be confined to state cases. Frankfurter's attitude toward the exclusionary rule also influenced how the justices applied the rule in federal cases. In *Walder v. United States*,[93] the Court, in an opinion written by Frankfurter, adopted the first exception to the exclusionary rule and thus permitted the use of evidence illegally acquired by federal officials despite Holmes's admonition that the essence of the Fourth Amendment—"forbidding the acquisition of evidence in a certain way"—meant that evidence so acquired "shall not be used at all." And in *Jones v. United States*,[94] the Court, in another Frankfurter opinion, embraced the standing limitation, which requires a defendant to prove the government violated *his* Fourth Amendment rights before invoking the exclusionary rule. Consequently, Frankfurter's way of thinking about exclusion would predominate until the summer of 1960, when two other dynamics combined to effect a historic change in the nation's constitutional criminal procedure rules. The first was Justice Tom Clark's frustration with *Wolf*. The second was the subtle acknowledgment by four justices—Chief Justice Warren and Justices Black, Douglas, and Brennan—that *Wolf*, in truth, had not applied the Fourth Amendment to the states. Within a year, these four justices would join Clark to overrule *Wolf*.

---

themselves may differ whether in a particular case a trial offends accepted notions of justice is not disproof that general rather than idiosyncratic standards are applied. An important safeguard against such merely individual judgment is an alert deference to the judgment of the State court under review." *Id.* at 67–68 (Frankfurter, J., concurring).

93 347 U.S. 62 (1954).

94 362 U.S. 257 (1960).

A. Stefanelli v. Minard

Almost six months after *Wolf* was announced, local and county police officers illegally entered and searched George Stefanelli's East Orange, New Jersey, home. The officers seized evidence of unlawful bookmaking. Four months later, Newark, New Jersey, police conducted an unlawful search of the premises occupied by Jerry Malanga, Joseph Maglione, and Frank D'Innocenzio. Police arrested the men and seized evidence related to bookmaking. After the four were indicted, lawsuits were filed in federal court seeking to enjoin the use of the bookmaking evidence in the upcoming state prosecutions. New Jersey law allowed the admission of unlawfully obtained evidence in criminal trials, and the defendants argued that a federal civil rights statute authorized equitable relief in cases where state officials had violated an individual's constitutional rights. The lower federal courts refused to intervene in the state proceedings, and the defendants appealed to the Court.

Wolf was a major topic of the Court's conference discussion in *Stefanelli v. Minard*. The discussion also obliquely revealed that the Fourth Amendment was not on the minds of the justices. Chief Justice Fred Vinson told his colleagues that it would be "bad" to split a criminal proceeding into two proceedings.[95] He voted to affirm and stated that *Wolf* controlled.[96] Black spoke next and seemed to forget what he wrote in his separate opinion in *Wolf*. Black stated that his vote depended on the meaning of *Wolf*. "If *Wolf* comes from the Constitution, the Fourth Amendment applies to the states—and the *Weeks* exclusionary rule would then apply to the states. If the Fourth Amendment does not apply to the states it should not apply in this injunctive manner."[97] Black then remarked that federal courts "should not sit in review of evidence going into state courts" and agreed with the Chief Justice's view that criminal trials should not be divided between two courts.[98] At the end of his remarks, Black voted to pass, but stated that he was inclined to the view that the federal civil rights statute "should not be applied."[99]

Stanley Reed also voted to affirm because the federal statute authorized an equitable proceeding, and the facts called for a discretionary power of an equity court.[100] As to *Wolf* and the exclusionary rule, Reed thought *Wolf* applied the Fourth Amendment to the states but that the exclusionary rule is an "evidentiary rule," not a "constitutional" mandate.[101] Reed conceded that *Weeks* "may indicate a contrary" view, but that *Olmstead* was "favorable" to his construction of the rule.[102]

---

95 William Douglas, Conference Notes on *Stefanelli v. Minard* (Oct. 20, 1951), Douglas Papers, Box 1121.

96 *Id.*

97 *Id.*

98 *Id.*

99 *Id.*

100 *Id.*

101 Tom Clark, Conference Notes on *Stefanelli v. Minard* (undated), Tom C. Clark Papers, Tarlton Law Library, University of Texas at Austin, Box B146.

102 *Id.*

Frankfurter began his remarks with a familiar theme: the Fourteenth Amendment does not incorporate the Fourth Amendment or any of the first eight amendments of the Bill of Rights. For Frankfurter, *Wolf* did not resolve the question the Court had to decide. "The question before us is the right to obtain an injunction to hold the arm of the State from using the fruit of an illegal search."[103] Frankfurter closed his comments by asking, "Does the Civil Rights Act cover this situation?"[104]

Douglas voted to reverse.[105] Justice Robert Jackson, like the others, thought an equitable remedy "would be bad" and "cannot be enforced this way."[106] Justice Harold Burton said he "agrees with *Weeks* and *Wolf*."[107] He continued: "Congress could negate the *Weeks* doctrine or impose it on the states. Congress could enjoin a threatened seizure by state officers. But this act does not go far enough to reach this conduct."[108] Burton believed that Congress "has not said in the act that the state official can be enjoined. State officials were using the evidence as state law permitted."[109] Finally, Clark also felt the federal act should not be applied in these circumstances, but Clark told his colleagues they should be "realistic about" *Wolf*.[110] He stated, "*Weeks* should apply to the states."[111]

In light of the views expressed during the conference, it is not surprising that the defendants in *Stefanelli* did not prevail in the Court. Frankfurter's opinion held that "federal courts should refuse to intervene in State criminal proceedings to suppress the use of evidence even when claimed to have been secured by unlawful search and seizure."[112] Rather than concluding that the federal civil rights statute did not authorize the defendants' claim, Frankfurter based his ruling on the same federalism concerns that animated *Wolf*'s conclusion that the exclusionary rule should not be imposed on the states. Regarding *Wolf* itself, Frankfurter made clear that *Wolf*'s holding was based on the Due Process Clause and not the Fourth Amendment.[113] In *Stefanelli*, Frankfurter saw no violation of Due Process. The facts showed no irreparable injury demanding the attention of the federal judiciary: "At worst, the evidence sought to be suppressed may provide the basis for conviction of the petitioners in the New Jersey courts."[114] But *Wolf*,

---

103 *Id.*

104 *Id.*

105 William Douglas, Docket Sheet on *Stefanelli v. Minard* (assigned on Oct.23, 1951), Douglas Papers, Box 1121.

106 Clark, Conference Notes on *Stefanelli v. Minard*, *supra* note 101. Justice Douglas's conference notes record Jackson saying that "nothing would hurt state courts more than this intrusion by federal courts—this power would destroy state justice." Douglas, Conference Notes on *Stefanelli v. Minard*, *supra* note 95.

107 Douglas, Conference Notes on *Stefanelli v. Minard*, *supra* note 95.

108 *Id.*

109 *Id.*

110 *Id.*

111 *Id.*

112 Stefanelli v. Minard, 342 U.S. 117, 120 (1951).

113 *Id.* at 119.

114 *Id.* at 122.

Frankfurter explained, had already held that such a conviction "would not deprive them of due process of law."[115]

In other words, it did not matter that the conduct of the New Jersey officers, if committed by federal law enforcement officers, violated the Fourth Amendment. As the conference discussion disclosed, in *Stefanelli*, Fourth Amendment concerns were not in play. To be sure, the actions of the New Jersey officers were subject to the restraints of the Fourteenth Amendment's Due Process Clause. But *Wolf* established that a garden-variety or ordinary violation of the Fourth Amendment and the admission of its fruits in a state prosecution did not violate Due Process. Without explaining why, Black and Clark concurred in the result. Only Douglas dissented in *Stefanelli*, noting that the Court's holding made "the Fourth Amendment an empty and hollow guarantee so far as state prosecutions are concerned."[116]

B. Rochin v. California

Sometime during the morning of July 1, 1949, sheriff officers of the County of Los Angeles entered the home of Antonio Rochin without permission and forcibly opened the door of his bedroom. Inside they found Rochin sitting on the bed partially dressed and his wife lying in the bed. The officers also saw two capsules on a nightstand. After Rochin put the capsules in his mouth, a struggle ensued. The officers then took Rochin to a hospital where a "stomach pump" was performed without his consent, inducing Rochin to vomit. The capsules were found in Rochin's vomit. The capsules contained morphine, and Rochin was convicted of unlawful possession of morphine.

Rochin appealed his conviction, contending that the police conduct and the admission of the morphine capsules at trial violated his constitutional rights, including those under the Fourth Amendment. The state appellate court did not deny that the police violated Rochin's Fourth Amendment rights; it nonetheless affirmed his conviction based upon previous rulings of the California Supreme Court that held that the admission of illegally obtained evidence did not infringe Due Process when such evidence does not affect the fairness or impartiality of the trial. Although affirming Rochin's conviction, the California appellate court was troubled enough by the facts to take the unusual step of condemning police behavior that resulted in the capture and conviction of a guilty individual. The court stated the officers "were guilty of unlawfully breaking into and entering defendant's room and were guilty of unlawfully assaulting and battering defendant while in the room," and one officer was "guilty of unlawfully assaulting, battering, torturing and falsely imprisoning the defendant at the alleged hospital."[117] One judge on the court also commented that "this case reveals a shocking series of violations of constitutional rights."[118] The California

[115] *Id.* at 120–22.

[116] *Id.* at 125 (Douglas, J., dissenting).

[117] People v. Rochin, 225 P.2d 1, 3 (Cal. Dist. Ct. App. 1950).

[118] *Id.* at 3 (Vallée, J., concurring).

Supreme Court declined to review the case despite the forceful dissent of two justices, one of whom asked: "Could any one imagine [the right of privacy] being any more ruthlessly violated under a totalitarian regime than it was in the case at bar?"[119]

Rochin v. California and *Stefanelli* were discussed in the same conference. Unlike the dialogue in *Stefanelli*, however, *Wolf* was not the focus in *Rochin*. Vinson began the discussion by noting that the coerced confessions cases were not relevant here. Vinson said coerced confessions are excluded as evidence because "a man under pain will tell a lie," and the "evidence is apt to be untrustworthy."[120] But here "the capsules were seen and known."[121] Vinson voted to affirm.[122] Black voted to reverse.[123] Reed stated that although the case troubled him and "makes him puke," he voted to affirm because there is "only a search of the person."[124] Reed noted that police "can use force to search pockets" and "can use force here."[125]

After declaring that the "case makes him puke" as well, Frankfurter disputed Vinson's claim that the coerced confession rule rested on "a test of trustworthiness alone."[126] According to Frankfurter, the confession rule rested on "decency."[127] Frankfurter declared the search of Rochin "violates due process."[128] Jackson voted for reversal but told his colleagues the case presented difficulties because it also implicated the government's authority to take blood samples, lie detectors, and physical examinations.[129] Burton commented that there are "borderline questions" and "reasonable and unreasonable use of force."[130] This case, according to Burton, "is in the latter category." Clark voted to reverse.[131] Thus, at the end of the *Rochin* conference, only Vinson and Reed had voted to affirm Rochin's conviction.[132] When *Rochin* was announced, however, both Vinson and Reed had changed their minds.[133]

---

119 People v. Rochin, 225 P.2d 913, 914 (Cal. 1951) (Carter, J., dissenting).

120 William Douglas, Conference Notes on *Rochin v. California* (Oct. 20, 1951), Douglas Papers, Box 1121.

121 *Id.*

122 William Douglas, Docket Sheet on *Rochin v. California* (assigned on Oct. 23, 1951), Douglas Papers, Box 1121.

123 *Id.*

124 Douglas, Conference Notes on *Rochin v. California*, *supra* note 120.

125 *Id.*

126 *Id.*

127 *Id.*

128 *Id.*

129 *Id.*

130 *Id.*

131 *Id.*

132 *See* PALMER, *supra* note 46, at 325.

133 Vinson's decision to join Frankfurter's opinion in *Rochin* may have been influenced by a letter Frankfurter sent Vinson. After informing Vinson that Justices Reed and Burton had joined Frankfurter's opinion, Frankfurter told Vinson that he "deeply" cared about the result in *Rochin*. Frankfurter's feelings were motivated by his anti-incorporation views: "I do think it profoundly important that we should express in some such way as I have tried to do what kind of an instrument the Due Process Clause is against the States, thereby restating the conception of the Due Process Clause which this Court has enforced ever since the

The California courts upheld Rochin's conviction because admission of the morphine capsules did not impair the fairness of the trial proceedings and thus did not violate the Due Process Clause.[134] In reversing that result, Frankfurter's opinion for the Court took a different view of the requirements of Due Process. His opinion, however, was more noteworthy for what it did not say about the Fourth Amendment. After explaining that the Due Process Clause requires judges to evaluate the whole course of a criminal proceeding to determine whether it "offend[s] those canons of decency and fairness which express the notions of justice of English-speaking peoples,"[135] Frankfurter concluded that the police conduct in *Rochin* "shocks the conscience" and was "bound to offend even hardened sensibilities."[136] The behavior of the police was "too close to the rack and the screw to permit of constitutional differentiation."[137] Allowing the conviction to stand "would be to afford brutality the cloak of law."[138] It was sufficient that Rochin's conviction "ha[d] been obtained by *methods* that offend the Due Process Clause,"[139] and thus, required reversal.

Frankfurter's silence on the Fourth Amendment seemed more significant and informative than his vague description of what Due Process imposed on the states. Rochin had consistently argued throughout his appeals that the Fourth Amendment barred the admission of the morphine capsules. By most measures, the police intrusion in *Rochin* was comparable to, if not more offensive than, the arbitrary invasion of privacy that Frankfurter condemned in *Wolf* where he stated that "[t]he knock at the door, whether by day or by night, as a prelude to a search, without authority of law but solely on the authority of the police" was "inconsistent with the conception of human rights enshrined in the history and the basic constitutional documents of English-speaking peoples."[140]

Indeed, the facts of *Rochin* seemed tailor-made for Frankfurter to say that this is what the *Wolf* Court envisioned when it spoke of police behavior that violated the "core" of the Fourth Amendment. Or, Frankfurter could have said about the facts in *Rochin* that this type of egregious Fourth Amendment violation also violates Due Process and thus requires exclusion of the illegally acquired evidence. Despite the outrageous nature of the police conduct, Frankfurter never expresses an opinion on whether the search and seizure of Rochin violated the Fourth Amendment, or the "core" privacy interest that *Wolf* said was enforceable against the states. In fact, his *Rochin* opinion never mentions *Wolf*. In

---

Fourteenth Amendment was adopted, and rejecting the notion that that clause is a handbag for the eight original Amendments. . . . In short, if you gather that I deem the *Rochin* case important, you will be just 100% correct." Felix Frankfurter, Letter to Fred Vinson (Nov. 29, 1951), Felix Frankfurter Papers, Reel 4, Frame 675.

134 *See* People v. Rochin, 225 P.2d 1, 3 (Cal. Dist. Ct. App. 1950).

135 Rochin v. California, 342 U.S. 165, 169 (1952).

136 *Id.* at 172.

137 *Id.*

138 *Id.* at 173.

139 *Id.* at 174 (emphasis added).

140 Wolf v. Colorado, 338 U.S. 25, 28 (1949).

1952, these omissions were further proof, although more proof seemed unnecessary after *Wolf*, that a violation of the Fourth Amendment alone would not prompt the Court to reverse a state court conviction based on the admission of unlawfully obtained evidence.

* * *

President Harry Truman appointed Tom Clark as his second attorney general in 1945 to succeed Francis Biddle. When Frank Murphy died in 1949, Truman named Clark to fill Murphy's seat on the Court. According to one source, Truman put Clark on the Court "at the urging of Chief Justice Vinson, who wanted a colleague who would support his point of view."[141] During his first few years on the Court, Clark's voting habits leaned toward law enforcement interests. Before Earl Warren was named Chief Justice in October 1953, "Clark rejected civil liberties claims 75 percent of the time, a little below Vinson's rate of 83 percent, and was a strong supporter of the government position in the Cold War cases that came before the high court."[142] After five years on the Court, Clark voted for the government in nearly every Fourth Amendment case.[143] Notably, Clark refused to join Douglas's dissents in *Stefanelli* and *Schwartz v. Texas*[144] and Douglas's separate opinion in *Rochin*, wherein Douglas criticized *Wolf*. Indeed, in 1957, Clark reaffirmed *Wolf* while rejecting a defendant's claim that evidence obtained from an involuntary blood test was inadmissible at his state manslaughter trial. Clark explained that *Wolf* established that the fruits of a Fourth Amendment violation are admissible in state prosecutions.[145] Almost two years after *Rochin* was decided, Clark, newly appointed Chief Justice Earl Warren, and the rest of the Court would be asked to create the first exception to *Weeks*'s exclusionary rule in *Walder v. United States*.[146]

In 1950, federal officers arrested Sam Walder on narcotics charges. Although no evidence was found on Walder, the officers drove Walder to his home and searched it without probable cause or a warrant. Inside the home, the officers found a one-ounce capsule of heroin. Although Walder was indicted, a federal district court dismissed the charges after ruling that the search of Walder's home was unconstitutional.

A year later, Walder again faced federal narcotics charges. This time, the government presented testimony of federal officers and informants who stated that Walder had sold drugs to the informants. Walder was the only defense witness and denied that he had ever sold or given anyone narcotics. Walder said one of the informants owed him money and attributed his incriminating testimony to his desire to get even with him.

---

141 Harold F. Gosnell, Truman's Crises: A Political Biography of Harry S. Truman 419 (1980).

142 Urofsky, Division and Discord, *supra* note 18, at 155.

143 One case in which Clark did vote for the defendant was *United States v. Jeffers*, 342 U.S. 48 (1951).

144 344 U.S. 199 (1952).

145 Breithaupt v. Abram, 352 U.S. 432 (1957).

146 347 U.S. 62 (1954). For an excellent analysis and discussion of *Walder* and the Court's impeachment cases, see James L. Kainen, *The Impeachment Exception to the Exclusionary Rules: Policies, Principles, and Politics*, 44 Stan. L. Rev. 1301 (1992).

On cross-examination, the prosecutor asked Walder whether he had ever "had anything to do with narcotics," which Walder denied.[147] Over the objection of defense counsel, the prosecutor then asked Walder whether federal officers had taken heroin from his home a year earlier. After Walder denied the accusation, on rebuttal and solely for the purpose of impeaching Walder's credibility, the prosecutor presented the testimony of one of the officers who had seized heroin from Walder's home a year earlier. Walder was convicted.

When Walder sought reversal of his conviction, the Court appointed Paul Porter of the prestigious Washington, D.C., law firm Arnold, Fortas & Porter to represent him. The government urged the Court not to review the case, contending that *Agnello* permitted the use of unconstitutionally acquired evidence for impeachment purposes where the government did not attempt to introduce the fruit of an illegal search directly into evidence. In a memo designed to help his boss decide whether to hear the case, one of Clark's law clerks wrote that *Agnello* and *Walder* were hard to distinguish: "Here, as [in *Agnello*], the testimony on direct was that the defendant had never seen or handled narcotics. Here, as [in *Agnello*], evidence gained by an illegal search was offered to rebut that assertion."[148]

The justices did vote to hear Walder's appeal, and Paul Porter's argument on behalf of Walder was straightforward: there was no principled distinction between *Agnello* and *Walder*.[149] The government, by contrast, argued that *Agnello* implicitly recognized that if a defendant's direct testimony "opened the door" to questioning about evidence that had been illegally seized, cross-examination and the use of that evidence might be permissible.[150] Porter, however, told the Court that Walder had opened the door no wider than did Agnello, who denied on direct examination that he had ever talked with any of his codefendants about cocaine.[151] Porter's brief reminded the Court that the government offered the same implied waiver argument in *Agnello*, and there was no new reason for accepting the argument that *Agnello* had already rejected.[152] Moreover, Porter urged that unconstitutionally seized evidence "is just as inadmissible on rebuttal as it is on the prosecution's case in chief."[153] There were no exceptions to the exclusionary rule, "no matter how extreme the invitation by the defendant or how special the case."[154]

The Solicitor General's brief did not challenge Porter's assertion that there were no exceptions to the exclusionary rule. The government did, however, describe the rule differently from Porter. Whereas Porter described the rule in constitutional terms, the

---

147 United States v. Walder, 201 F.2d 715, 716 (8th Cir. 1953).

148 Law Clerk, Memorandum on *Walder v. United States* 5 (undated), Clark Papers, Box B152.

149 Brief for Petitioner at 8, Walder v. United States, 347 U.S. 62 (1954) (No. 121).

150 Brief for the United States at 28, *Walder*, 347 U.S. 62 (No. 121).

151 Brief for Petitioner, *supra* note 149, at 8.

152 *Id.* at 8 n.4.

153 *Id.* at 8–9.

154 *Id.* at 9.

government told the Court that application of the rule was a matter of "policy."[155] The point of the rule, according to the government, is to deter unconstitutional searches and seizures. The rule is "the result of the careful balancing" of social interests.[156] And, therefore, the government explained, "the rule cannot be absolute."[157] Citing *Wolf*, the government asserted that the remedy provided by the rule "is not an essential ingredient of the right of privacy."[158]

Chief Justice Warren began the conference discussion of *Walder* by asking whether the exclusionary rule should extend so "that one who benefits from it should be able to commit perjury without being impeached."[159] Warren stated that carrying the rule that far "would degrade the courts."[160] Warren voted to affirm Walder's conviction.[161] Black voted to reverse.[162] Reed voted to affirm, explaining that when the "accused tries to bring the evidence in . . . you should have the right to impeach."[163] Frankfurter spoke next and asked, "why I must draw from the *Weeks* doctrine by reversing here—a defendant cannot trade on this doctrine and have its advantage" to lie.[164] Frankfurter voted to affirm.[165]

Douglas voted to reverse and told his colleagues "the *Weeks* rule lets off lots of criminals. This was a violation of the Fourth Amendment rule and I'd apply *Weeks*."[166] Jackson followed Douglas and stated that *Silverthorne Lumber* ruled that "no evidence of this type is admissible. But here only one person could get this evidence in and that was the defendant. Where he uses it then the rule folds."[167] Jackson added that "if we reverse we would make *Weeks* look foolish."[168] Jackson voted to affirm.[169] Burton voted to reverse based on *Agnello*, though he noted that if Walder "were indicted for perjury the evidence would be admissible."[170] Clark voted to affirm,[171] and Sherman Minton ended the discussion by stating that he "would apply *Weeks* all the way."[172] Thus, at the end of the Conference, the justices voted five to four to affirm Walder's conviction.

---

155 Brief for the United States, *supra* note 150, at 23.
156 *Id.* at 24.
157 *Id.*
158 *Id.*
159 William Douglas, Conference Notes on *Walder v. United States* (Dec. 5, 1953), Douglas Papers, Box 1147.
160 *Id.*
161 *Id.*
162 *Id.*
163 *Id.*
164 Tom Clark, Conference Notes on *Walder v. United States* (undated), Clark Papers, Box B152.
165 *Id.*
166 *Id.*
167 *Id.*
168 Douglas, Conference Notes on *Walder v. United States*, *supra* note 159.
169 *Id.*
170 *Id.*
171 *Id.*
172 Clark, Conference Notes on *Walder v. United States*, *supra* note 164.

After Frankfurter's first draft of *Walder* arrived in Clark's chambers, one of Clark's law clerks wrote a memo to Clark criticizing Frankfurter's reasoning. He told Clark that Holmes's admonition in *Silverthorne Lumber* that illegally seized evidence "shall not be used at all" meant that Walder's conviction required reversal.[173] Apart from that, the clerk argued Frankfurter's draft had avoided the crucial issue presented in *Walder*, namely, whether permitting the use of illegally seized evidence, even for impeachment purposes, encourages federal officers to conduct unlawful searches. Such a result, the clerk asserted, could not be reconciled with the "sole justification for the *Weeks* exclusionary rule," which was deterrence of illegal searches and seizures.[174] The clerk wrote that "a forthright [analysis] of the issue demands that this point be treated; if [Frankfurter] does not do it, the 4 dissenters certainly will anyway."[175] On the top of Frankfurter's draft, the clerk suggested that Clark "hold off" joining Frankfurter's opinion until seeing the dissent.

Interestingly, there was no dissenting opinion in *Walder*. Although four justices voted against the government in the conference discussion, when *Walder* was announced on February 1, 1954, only Black and Douglas dissented, and they did so without comment. Thus, none of the justices publicly contested Frankfurter's analysis in *Walder*. Without saying so explicitly, Frankfurter created the first exception to the exclusionary rule and Holmes's principle that illegally seized evidence "shall not be used at all." Although the factual differences between *Agnello* and *Walder* were trivial, that aspect of Frankfurter's opinion would also go unchallenged. Finally, none of the justices called attention to the fact that allowing the use of unconstitutionally acquired evidence, even for impeachment purposes, was inconsistent with the deterrence rationale behind the exclusionary rule, which Frankfurter had announced in *Wolf* and reaffirmed in *Walder*.

C. Irvine v. California

Exactly seventeen months to the day Los Angeles County sheriff officers illegally invaded Antonio Rochin's home and subjected him to physical violence, Los Angeles police officers illegally entered Patrick Irvine's home. They suspected that Irvine was engaged in illegal bookmaking but lacked proof. Despite a lack of evidence, the Los Angeles Chief of Police, who was acting with the knowledge of the Los Angeles County District Attorney, authorized officers to break into Irvine's home to install a concealed microphone to record evidence of potential wrongdoing. After the first intrusion, police covertly entered Irvine's house twice more, placing the microphone in his bedroom and eventually in a closet "where the device remained until its purpose of enabling the officers to overhear incriminating statements was accomplished."[176] Evidence obtained from the microphone helped convict Irvine of violating California gambling laws.

---

[173] Law Clerk, Memorandum to Tom Clark on *Walder v. United States* 1 (undated), Clark Papers, Box A30.

[174] *Id.* at 2.

[175] *Id.*

[176] Irvine v. California, 347 U.S. 128, 131 (1954).

The conference discussion in *Irvine* was led by newly appointed Chief Justice Earl Warren. Once again, *Wolf* dominated the conversation. The Chief Justice asked, "shall we rely on *Wolf*," or "does the conduct rise to the indecency of *Rochin*?"[177] Warren told his colleagues that they "should consider whether the state encourages this type of conduct."[178] Warren, a former Attorney General and Governor of California, asserted that the police conduct here "has slipped in" and told the justices that in California "we do not permit wiretapping at all."[179] Warren said that the police behavior "does not outrage my sense of decency."[180] Warren also stated that "he would not alter *Wolf*."[181] Warren voted to affirm.[182] Black passed, and Reed agreed with the Chief Justice to affirm.[183]

Frankfurter spoke next and voted for reversal, "though adhering to *Wolf*."[184] He declared that "*Rochin* governs"[185] and stated that "in *Weeks* this court said the only way to deter illegal searches and seizures was to make it unprofitable to so obtain the evidence. But it is inescapable that we must take each case by itself."[186] Douglas told his colleagues that "what Felix Frankfurter says is enough for me"[187] and voted to reverse. Jackson opposed Frankfurter's position that the Court had to resolve these cases one by one. "If you take each case by itself you cannot give the rule necessary for law enforcement."[188] While Jackson said the facts were "bad," he asked whether the break-in was "any worse than other cases we have ok'd."[189] He also noted that the Court has ruled that "a state may adopt its own rule of evidence."[190] Finally, Jackson remarked "this offends me worse than *Rochin*—I don't want people breaking into my house," but we "must concede the state has some latitude."[191] Jackson voted to affirm but noted that he was "doubtful" about his decision.[192]

Burton thought the police conduct "too shocking a practice."[193] *Rochin* was "different—doing it in office, etc ok but can't go for home."[194] Burton voted to reverse. Clark, on the other hand, said, "*Wolf* governs—we should stick by it as long as it's on the

---

177 Tom Clark, Conference Notes on *Irvine v. California* (undated), Clark Papers, Box 151.

178 *Id.*

179 *Id.*

180 *Id.*

181 William Douglas, Conference Notes on *Irvine v. California* (Dec. 5, 1953), Douglas Papers, Box 1121.

182 *Id.*

183 *Id.*

184 *Id.*

185 *Id.*

186 Clark, Conference Notes on *Irvine v. California*, *supra* note 177.

187 *Id.*

188 Douglas, Conference Notes on *Irvine v. California*, *supra* note 181.

189 Clark, Conference Notes on *Irvine v. California*, *supra* note 177.

190 *Id.*

191 *Id.*

192 *Id.* Jackson's own docket sheet for *Irvine* has written next to his initials: "Have to stand by *Wolf*." Robert Jackson, Docket Sheet on *Irvine v. California* (voted on Dec. 5, 1953), Robert Houghwout Jackson Papers, Library of Congress, Manuscript Division, Box 185.

193 Douglas, Conference Notes on *Irvine v. California*, *supra* note 181.

194 Clark, Conference Notes on *Irvine v. California*, *supra* note 177.

books—*Rochin* whittled *Wolf*."[195] Clark said he "does not like *Wolf* but he stands by it." Presumably referring to the exclusionary rule, Clark described it as "a mere rule of evidence."[196] Finally, Minton stated that he "would adhere to *Wolf*."[197] He explained: there is "a lot of difference between forcing a key in a lock and forcing a pump into a stomach."[198] Minton voted to affirm.

At the end of the conference discussion, there were five votes to affirm Irvine's conviction, three votes to reverse, and one "pass."[199] But the conference discussion on *Irvine* would be the beginning, not the end, of an extended dialogue between the justices on their views of the exclusionary rule and the meaning and scope of *Wolf*. Twelve days after the conference, Frankfurter circulated a memorandum, which described *Weeks*'s exclusionary rule as based on deterrence. "The philosophy of the rule is that it is more important to hold law officers to the observance of constitutional safeguards by making their unlawfulness unprofitable in securing convictions, than it is to admit all evidence bearing on the accused's guilt or innocence, however obtained."[200] Frankfurter explained that *Wolf* "held that the absolute rule of *Weeks* was not to be deemed part of the concept of due process."[201] But *Wolf* and Frankfurter's understanding of Due Process did not give the states carte blanche to decide what evidence is admissible in a criminal trial.[202]

Frankfurter noted that the Court had overturned more than a dozen state convictions "based on evidence obtained under circumstances which offended the implications of the Due Process Clause, although unquestionably the evidence was intrinsically relevant and not to be rejected because untrustworthy."[203] (Frankfurter did not acknowledge that all but one of the cases he relied upon involved coerced confessions. The sole exception was *Rochin*.) Furthermore, according to Frankfurter's memo, *Wolf* did not govern in *Irvine* because *Wolf* "was limited to the bare legal question whether evidence that would have been excluded from a federal trial must, *for that reason alone*, be excluded from a state trial."[204] By contrast, in *Irvine*, the justices had to resolve "whether all the attendant circumstances whereby the police officers obtained the evidence leading to a conviction were, as in *Rochin*, such as to offend 'a sense of justice.'"[205] Deciding that question, Frankfurter declared, "lies in the domain of judgment—a matter of degree."[206]

---

195 Douglas, Conference Notes on *Irvine v. California*, *supra* note 181.

196 *Id.*

197 *Id.*

198 *Id.*

199 Robert Jackson, Docket Sheet on *Irvine v. California*, *supra* note 192. Justice Black voted "pass." *Id.*

200 Felix Frankfurter, Memorandum on *Irvine v. California* 1 (circulated Dec. 17, 1953), Clark Papers, Box A28.

201 *Id.*

202 *Id.* at 1–2.

203 *Id.* at 2.

204 *Id.* at 3.

205 *Id.* (quoting Brown v. Mississippi, 297 U.S. 278, 285-86 (1936)).

206 *Id.* at 4.

Twelve days later, Frankfurter sent Clark a letter expanding on the themes contained in his memorandum. The letter noted Clark's readiness to overrule *Wolf*, but if that could not be done, Clark would apply *Wolf* to affirm Irvine's conviction.[207] Frankfurter insisted, however, that *Irvine* is not precisely *Wolf* and explained why *Wolf* should not be read as a Fourth Amendment ruling after all. He stressed that the *Wolf* decision held only that "a State conviction is not invalidated under the Fourteenth Amendment *merely* because some evidence in a State court would have to be excluded by virtue of the Fourth Amendment in a Federal prosecution and by reason of that fact would invalidate a Federal conviction."[208] The controlling factor in *Irvine* and *Rochin* was that "there was conduct by the police in obtaining this evidence which went way beyond merely not having a search warrant for the assailed evidence."[209] Frankfurter acknowledged that one could extend *Wolf* to the generalization "that so long as evidence is relevant, no matter how it was obtained is immaterial so far as the due process clause of the Fourteenth Amendment is concerned."[210] "But that is not what *Wolf* decided."[211]

Eight days after Clark received Frankfurter's letter, Jackson, who was assigned to write the Court's opinion in *Irvine*, circulated a draft directly challenging both Frankfurter's conception of what Due Process mandated and his view of *Wolf*.[212] Significantly, Jackson conceded Irvine's Fourth Amendment rights had been violated; indeed, he was astonished by the police conduct: "That officers of the law will break and enter a home, secrete such a device, even in a bedroom, and listen to the conversation of the occupants for over a month would be almost incredible if it were not admitted."[213] Unlike Frankfurter's opinions in *Wolf* and *Rochin*, Jackson exhibited no reticence in concluding that the police conduct violated the Fourth Amendment. In fact, in a passage that would appear in the final opinion, Jackson wrote: "Few police measures have come to our attention that more flagrantly, deliberately, and persistently violated the fundamental principle declared by the Fourth Amendment."[214]

But this extreme conduct did not justify reversing Irvine's conviction. Jackson explained that *Wolf* "stopped short of absorbing into the Fourteenth Amendment as constitutional limitations on the states the body of subsidiary procedural and evidentiary doctrines developed by the federal courts."[215] Evidence secured from an illegal search "is not inherently incredible like that turned out by coercing a confession," and

---

207 Felix Frankfurter, Letter to Tom Clark on *Irvine v. California* 1 (Dec. 29, 1953), Clark Papers, Box A28.

208 *Id.*

209 *Id.*

210 *Id.*

211 *Id.*

212 Robert Jackson, Draft of *Irvine v. California* (Jan. 6, 1954), Clark Papers, Box A28.

213 *Id.* at 5. This language would also appear in the published opinion of *Irvine*. *See* Irvine v. California, 347 U.S. 128, 132 (1954).

214 Jackson, Draft of *Irvine v. California*, *supra* note 212, at 4; *see also Irvine*, 347 U.S. at 132.

215 Jackson, Draft of *Irvine v. California*, *supra* note 212, at 4.

may yield "the most reliable evidence" of a defendant's guilt.[216] "Hence it was within the province of state law to say whether such illegally obtained evidence should be admitted."[217] In other words, *Wolf*, according to Jackson, afforded the states discretion to decide whether evidence obtained from an unreasonable search or seizure is admissible in a state prosecution. The remarkable thing about Jackson's *Irvine* draft was that it never cited, let alone discussed or distinguished, *Rochin*. As one of Clark's law clerks described, Jackson's draft opinion was affirming Irvine's conviction by ruling that "evidence obtained by unreasonable search and seizure is never inadmissible on due process grounds in a state court."[218]

Within a month, Jackson circulated another draft of *Irvine*, which Warren, Reed, and Minton now joined. Although this draft contained most of what was eventually published in the official version of *Irvine*, there were several significant changes. First, Jackson omitted the sentence that "it was within the province of state law to say whether such illegally obtained evidence should be admitted." Second, he distinguished *Rochin* from the facts in *Irvine*. *Rochin*, Jackson now stated, "presented an element totally lacking here—coercion . . . applied by a physical assault upon [the] person to compel submission to the use of a stomach pump."[219] These changes represented a modest retreat from the initial draft, which had effectively given the states a free hand to admit evidence secured by illegal searches, no matter how shocking the intrusion. By acknowledging and distinguishing *Rochin*, Jackson was drawing a constitutional line around the admission of evidence obtained from physically violent searches.

Jackson's other two changes may have been directed at Clark, who indicated in conference a desire to overrule *Wolf*. Jackson wrote: "We think the *Wolf* decision should not be overruled, for the reasons so persuasively stated therein."[220] Finally, Jackson questioned the wisdom of applying substantive Fourth Amendment standards and *Weeks*'s exclusionary rule to searches and seizures conducted by state officers. He observed that the Court and individual justices "have wavered considerably" over the meaning of the Fourth Amendment, and applying *Weeks*'s evidentiary rule of exclusion "before the states have had adequate opportunity to adopt or reject the rule would be an unwarranted use of federal power."[221]

On the same day that Jackson circulated his updated draft to the Court, Clark circulated a concurring opinion. Only a page long, this opinion was essentially the same as the one Clark delivered in *Irvine*. Clark joined the judgment affirming Irvine's conviction, but he commented that had he been a member of the Court when *Wolf* was decided, he

---

216 *Id.*

217 *Id.*

218 Law Clerk, Memorandum to Tom Clark on *Irvine v. California* 1 (undated), Clark Papers, Box A28.

219 Robert Jackson, Draft Opinion of *Irvine v. California* 5 (re-circulated Feb. 4, 1954), Clark Papers, Box A28.

220 *Id.* at 6.

221 *Id.*

would have applied *Weeks* to the states.[222] Instead of dissenting, however, Clark took the position that "adherence to the tenor of [*Wolf*] may bring needed converts to the cause for its extinction."[223]

Clark's dissatisfaction with *Wolf* was known to his colleagues since at least the *Stefanelli* conference. What his colleagues may not have known was the depth of his views. One member of the Court, however, was well aware of Clark's sentiments. During the deliberations in *Irvine*, Clark worked on a memorandum that was shown only to Jackson. This memorandum, which had the look and tone of a separate opinion, demonstrated that not only was Clark prepared to overrule *Wolf* but also that he read *Weeks* the way Holmes read *Weeks*.[224] When compared with Clark's 1961 opinion in *Mapp v. Ohio*, the *Irvine* memo is a remarkable document. As chapter 3 will reveal, Clark's opinion in *Mapp* relies upon an amalgam of constitutional and policy-based arguments to justify imposing the exclusionary rule on the states, including *Boyd*'s "linkage" theory that the Fourth and Fifth Amendments combine to require exclusion of unlawfully seized evidence. By contrast, his *Irvine* memo reveals that in 1953 Clark had concluded that the Fourth Amendment itself provided a constitutional right to exclusion.

The first pages of Clark's memo present the choice between Jackson's view of Due Process, which provides "*carte blanche* for the states in the realm of unconstitutional search and seizure";[225] and Frankfurter's view, which adopts a case-by-case approach for determining when a police search violates Due Process. Jackson's view was unacceptable to Clark because, *inter alia*, it "overrules *Rochin, sub silentio*."[226] Frankfurter's approach, on the other hand, engendered different problems. Under Frankfurter's theory, "it is impossible to predict how brazen the invasion of the intimate privacies of one's home has to be in order for it to shock itself into the protective arms of the Constitution."[227] As a practical matter, Clark believed that Frankfurter's model meant that "when five Justices are sufficiently revolted by local police action then a conviction is overturned and a guilty man goes free," which explains the result in *Rochin*.[228] Seeking an alternative to these positions, Clark thought overruling *Wolf* was a better choice. But before explaining why *Wolf* was wrongly decided, Clark offers a rebuttal to *Wolf*'s defenders. Interestingly, this dissection of *Wolf* does not appear in the *Mapp* opinion.

Starting with the premise that "[a]pparently all agree" that *Wolf* made the Fourth Amendment applicable to the states, Clark notes that *Wolf*'s defenders contend that the

---

222 Tom Clark, Draft of Concurring Opinion on *Irvine v. California* 1 (circulated Feb. 4, 1954), Clark Papers, Box A28.

223 *Id.* at 2.

224 Tom Clark, Memorandum on *Irvine v. California* (undated) [hereinafter Clark, Memorandum on *Irvine v. California*], Clark Papers, Box A28.

225 *Id.* at 2.

226 *Id.*

227 *Id.*

228 *Id.* at 3.

amendment "forbids the illegal 'taking' of evidence but not its 'use' at trial."[229] Clark replies that a constitutional distinction between "taking" and "using" illegally obtained evidence has never been employed by the Court.[230] In fact, "[t]his 'taking-use' dichotomy seems to be an ad hoc proposition good only for the *Wolf* case."[231] The Due Process cases addressing the admissibility of coerced confessions at criminal trials did not rely upon this distinction.[232] Nor did this legal theory appear in *Rochin*, which heavily relied on the coerced confession cases in finding that Rochin's conviction violated Due Process. Indeed, Clark pointedly observes this "taking" versus "use" distinction does not appear in Frankfurter's memorandum in *Irvine*, which declared: "'The protection of the Fourteenth Amendment may be invoked by the victim of an unfair trial—and a trial is unfair if its result was obtained by *methods* which our standards for criminal justice find offensive.'"[233] As Clark read the Court's precedents, "[t]he unbroken thread running through the cases—except for *Wolf*—is that if the 'taking' is bad, the 'use' is forbidden."[234]

After explaining why the "taking-use" dichotomy established in *Wolf* was not supported by prior rulings, Clark then explains why *Wolf* was wrong as a matter of constitutional law. In his view, "the fundamental error in *Wolf* was its failure to recognize the constitutional imperative in the language of *Weeks v. United States*."[235] Here, Clark quotes the passage from *Weeks* that stated that if illegally seized documents can be used in evidence against the victim of an illegal search, the protection of the Fourth Amendment "is of no value" and "might as well be stricken from the Constitution."[236] Clark saw this

---

229 *Id.*

230 *Id.* at 3–4.

231 *Id.* at 3.

232 In an earlier version of the draft, Clark states that "there is no suggestion of this ["taking-use" dichotomy] in the *Weeks* decision or its progeny while members of the *Weeks* Court were still sitting." Tom Clark, Work Sheet for Revision of First Draft of Memorandum on *Irvine v. California* 9 (undated) [hereinafter Clark, Work Sheet on *Irvine v. California*], Clark Papers, Box A28. This sentence is omitted in the draft sent to Jackson. The earlier version of the draft also provided a longer explanation of why "the dichotomy is alien to this Court's analysis of other cases where due process is used to challenge state convictions." *Id.* Clark explained:

> Coerced confession cases provide a good example. There the due process test is formulated in terms of whether there has been a fair trial. As this Court stated in Lisenba v. California, 314 U.S. 219, 236–37 (1941): "Such unfairness [as is sufficient to involve a denial of due process] exists when a coerced confession is *used* as a means of obtaining a verdict of guilty." (Emphasis supplied.) In other words, the *use* of evidence *obtained by an unfair method* is a denial of due process, not merely the *taking*. In the words of Chief Justice Hughes, speaking for a unanimous Court in *Brown v. Mississippi*, 297 U.S. 278, 286 (1936): "It would be difficult to conceive of *methods* more revolting to the sense of justice than those taken to procure the confessions of these petitioners, and the *use* of the confessions thus obtained as the basis for conviction and sentence was a clear denial of due process." (Emphasis supplied.)

Id. (alteration in original). This section was also omitted from the draft sent to Jackson.

233 Clark, Memorandum on *Irvine v. California*, *supra* note 224, at 5.

234 *Id.*

235 *Id.*

236 *Id.* at 5-6 (quoting Weeks v. United States, 232 U.S. 383, 393-94 (1914)).

passage as the "heart of the Court's rationale in *Weeks*." Clark maintains that Justice Day "intended that the exclusionary rule be an essential part of the constitutional safeguards against unreasonable searches and seizures."[237] Clark writes that Holmes's opinion in *Silverthorne Lumber* followed this view of *Weeks* and quotes a passage from *Gouled v. United States*, which stated that the common-law competent evidence rule "must not be allowed for any technical reason to prevail over a constitutional right." According to Clark, "The only *constitutional* right that could have been referred to by that statement" in *Gouled* "is the constitutional right of an individual not to have unlawfully seized evidence admitted against him at trial."[238] Clark also highlights a passage from *Byars v. United States* that stated that "the doctrine has never been recognized by this Court, *nor can it be tolerated under our constitutional system*, that evidences of crime discovered by a federal officer in making a search without lawful warrant may be used against the victim of the unlawful search where a timely challenge has been interposed."[239]

Clark ended his memorandum by observing: "If the Fourth Amendment ban against unreasonable searches and seizures by federal officers necessitates exclusion of unlawfully seized evidence from federal trials, *a fortiori*, the Fourteenth Amendment's ban against such seizures by state officers requires exclusion of tainted evidence from state trials."[240] Overruling *Wolf* would be consistent with "the long line of federal cases since *Weeks*" and would "dissipate the confusion now existing in our cases as to the protection the states must afford this important constitutional right of each of our citizens."[241]

Clark's *Irvine* memo was never published in the Court's official reporter. And despite the intensity with which he expressed his views in the memo, Clark concurred in the judgment affirming Irvine's conviction. Clark, however, did not join Jackson's plurality opinion that concluded that *Wolf* controlled the outcome in *Irvine*, and that the exclusionary rule was not compelled by the Constitution. Jackson's opinion maintained that *Rochin* was not an obstacle to affirming Irvine's conviction. Certainly, both Rochin and Irvine had been subjected to illegal searches. But it was clear to Jackson that the result in *Rochin* did not turn on the illegal search, because the *Rochin* Court "studiously avoided it and never once mentioned the *Wolf* case. Obviously, [the *Rochin*] Court thought that illegal search and seizure alone did not call for reversal."[242] Instead, *Rochin* turned on the presence of police coercion. Thus, *Rochin* was distinguishable because however "obnoxious" the facts were in *Irvine*, they did not "involve coercion, violence or brutality to the person, but rather a trespass to property, plus eavesdropping."[243]

---

237 Clark, Work Sheet on *Irvine v. California*, *supra* note 232, at 5.

238 *Id.* at 5-6.

239 *Id.* at 6; *see also* Byars v. United States, 273 U.S. 28, 29–30 (1927).

240 Clark, Memorandum on *Irvine v. California*, *supra* note 224, at 7.

241 *Id.* at 7-8.

242 Irvine v. California, 347 U.S. 128, 133 (1954) (Jackson, J.).

243 *Id.*

As noted, Jackson was also unwilling to overrule *Wolf*. Nor was he disposed to "make inroads upon *Wolf*" by limiting its reach to "searches and seizures which produce on our minds a mild shock, while if the shock is more serious, the states must exclude the evidence or we will reverse the conviction."[244] As he stated in the conference discussion, Jackson saw no benefit in a rule that distinguished illegal searches and seizures based on the type of shock produced on the judicial mind. Such a constitutional rule would "introduce vague and subjective distinctions," and be "so indefinite that no state court could know what it should rule in order to keep its processes on solid constitutional ground."[245]

While the above reasoning was sufficient to decide Irvine's case and nothing about the case required discussion of the federal exclusionary rule, Jackson's opinion nevertheless offered several critical comments about the federal rule. First, despite what was said and done in *Weeks*, *Silverthorne Lumber*, and *Agnello*, Jackson asserted that application of the federal exclusionary rule "is left largely to our discretion," because the admissibility of evidence is controlled by common-law principles.[246] Just as Frankfurter did in *Wolf*, Jackson made no effort to prove that the exclusion remedy recognized in *Weeks* and *Silverthorne Lumber* lacked a constitutional foundation. He simply assumed that *Weeks* and *Silverthorne Lumber* announced a rule of evidence.

Jackson also expressed doubts about the effectiveness of the exclusionary rule. While acknowledging the lack of empirical evidence regarding the "actual experience" under the rule, Jackson insisted that the Court's own cases showed that application of the rule had not eliminated illegal intrusions by federal officers.[247] He also opined that someone like Irvine invokes the rule "only to set aside his own conviction of crime."[248] At the same time, the "disciplinary or educational effect of the court's releasing the defendant for police misbehavior is so indirect as to be no more than a mild deterrent at best."[249]

Although these critical comments were unnecessary to decide *Irvine*, perhaps Jackson offered them as a way of bolstering *Wolf*, which may have been, in Jackson's mind, in need of supporters. As we will soon see, Earl Warren, who was appointed in 1953, a few months

244 *Id.* at 133–34.

245 *Id.* at 134. Clark's concurring opinion in *Irvine* was even more critical of Frankfurter's "shock the conscience" standard for judging the constitutionality of police searches. Clark noted that a case-by-case rule of law "makes for such uncertainty and unpredictability that it would be impossible to foretell—other than by guesswork—just how brazen the invasion of the intimate privacies of one's home must be in order to shock itself into the protective arms of the Constitution." *Id.* at 138 (Clark, J., concurring). In Clark's view, the "practical result" of Frankfurter's standard "is simply that when five Justices are sufficiently revolted by local police action, a conviction is overturned and a guilty man may go free." *Id.* Such a rule of law may "vindicate the abstract principle of due process, but . . . do[es] not shape the conduct of local police one whit." *Id.*

246 *Id.* at 134–35 (Jackson, J.).

247 *Id.* at 135.

248 *Id.* at 136.

249 *Id.* at 136–37.

before *Irvine* was argued, would eventually join the "liberals" on the Court who favored overruling *Wolf.* But before Warren became an opponent of *Wolf,* he was generally a supporter of the government in many criminal law and criminal procedure cases.[250] Indeed, in the *Irvine* conference, Warren stated, "I would not alter *Wolf,*" and he cast an important, if not the deciding, vote to uphold Irvine's conviction.[251] Warren assigned the case to Jackson because he was impressed by Jackson's presentation at the Court's conference on *Irvine.*[252]

At the end of his opinion, Jackson urged the Justice Department to commence a federal criminal prosecution against the California police officers "if an unconstitutional wrong" had been committed against Irvine.[253] Every member of the Court, except Warren, refused to join Jackson's recommendation for a federal prosecution. Warren later learned that no federal prosecution was brought. Although Warren may not have known it, the officers were not prosecuted because they "'were acting under orders of the Chief of Police, who in turn was acting with the full knowledge of the local District Attorney.'"[254] The failure to bring a federal prosecution "must have been a revelation" for Warren,[255] a long-time prosecutor, before becoming Chief Justice of the United States. "The failure of the executive branch to act to enforce the law and Irvine's rights had a profound effect on Earl Warren's views about the need for a remedy—like exclusion—that could be enforced by judges engaged in the process of constitutional judicial review."[256]

In the final analysis, it did not matter to the five justices who voted to affirm that Irvine "would not be getting a new trial, even though every member of the Court believed that his constitutional rights had been massively violated."[257] *Irvine* demonstrated that the Fourth Amendment, despite the traditional understanding of *Wolf,* did not protect against unreasonable searches and seizures by state police. Reversal of a state conviction was constitutionally required—by the Due Process Clause—only if incriminating evidence was obtained by physical violence to the defendant. Indeed, the result in *Irvine,* when combined with *Wolf,* stunningly showed that state officers could violate the Fourth Amendment as a routine matter without consequence. As Yale Kamisar

---

[250] G. EDWARD WHITE, EARL WARREN: A PUBLIC LIFE 181 (1982) (commenting that in his early years on the Court, Warren "consistently supported the government in criminal law and procedures" cases).

[251] Douglas, Conference Notes on *Irvine v. California*, *supra* note 181.

[252] SCHWARTZ, *supra* note 9, at 136.

[253] *Irvine*, 347 U.S. at 137.

[254] Note, *State Police, Unconstitutionally Obtained Evidence and Section 242 of the Civil Rights Statute*, 7 STAN. L. REV. 76, 94 n.75 (1954) (quoting Letter from Warren Oleny III, Assistant United States Attorney General (Feb. 15, 1955) (on file with the Stanford Law Review)).

[255] SCHWARTZ, *supra* note 9, at 137.

[256] Morgan Cloud, *Rights Without Remedies: The Court That Cried* "Wolf," 77 MISS. L.J. 467, 497 (2007); *see also* WHITE, *supra* note 250, at 266 (explaining that after *Irvine*, Warren would "not rely on other branches of government to remedy abuses that came to the Court's attention. After *Irvine*, Warren rarely sustained a conviction that he thought had been unfairly obtained and never relied on law enforcement bodies to discipline themselves."). Seven years later Warren voted to overrule *Wolf.*

[257] Dennis D. Dorin, *Marshaling* Mapp: *Justice Tom Clark's Role in* Mapp v. Ohio's *Extension of the Exclusionary Rule to State Searches and Seizures*, 52 CASE W. RES. L. REV. 401, 411 (2001).

explained, after *Wolf* ruled that "not all police misconduct which violates the protection against search and seizure *necessarily* vitiates a subsequent conviction," *Irvine* applied *Wolf* such that, absent physical brutality to the accused, "all police misconduct which violates the protection against search and seizure—no matter how 'deliberate' or 'flagrant' or 'obnoxious' or 'incredible'—*necessarily does not* vitiate the conviction."[258]

D. Standing to Invoke the Exclusionary Rule

In *Wolf*, Frankfurter introduces deterrence as the primary, if not only, rationale for the exclusionary rule. Ten years later, in *Walder*, Frankfurter writes, this time in a federal case, that the purpose of suppression was to deter illegal searches and seizures. In *Irvine*, although Jackson questions the effectiveness of the rule as a deterrent, he does not deny that the purpose of the exclusionary rule was to deter unlawful police intrusions. Thus, by 1960, deterrence was the raison d'être for the exclusionary rule.

At the same time, the lower federal courts had unanimously ruled that a defendant could invoke the exclusionary rule only when the police violated *his* Fourth Amendment rights. Thus, a defendant lacked "standing" to challenge the admission of evidence that was seized in violation of the Fourth Amendment rights of a third party. The standing limitation is justified by an understanding that because the Fourth Amendment affords a personal right, only the individual whose right was violated should be allowed to object to the admission of unlawfully seized evidence. Put another way, if the exclusionary rule is designed to place the victim of an illegal search in the position he would have occupied if no unlawful search had occurred, then if a defendant's own Fourth Amendment rights were not violated, the judiciary does not owe him a constitutional remedy. The standing limitation was also thought to be supported by *Boyd*'s "linkage" theory of exclusion, which found that the Fourth and Fifth Amendments combine to require suppression of illegally acquired evidence. Under this view, restricting invocation of the rule to "search victims makes sense because the evil to be remedied is the combination of intrusion plus incrimination, not incrimination alone."[259]

Although the Court had yet to explicitly address the standing issue, in 1942, in *Goldstein v. United States*,[260] the Court appeared to endorse the standing limitation in a case involving the Federal Communications Act of 1934, which barred the interception and divulging of telephone conversations. *Goldstein* observed that no lower court had afforded standing to a party to object to the admission of evidence seized in violation of the Fourth Amendment rights of a third party.[261] Interestingly, the dissenters in *Goldstein*, which included Frankfurter, argued that the standing limitation announced

---

258 Kamisar, Wolf *and* Lustig, *supra* note 32, at 1113.

259 Note, *Standing to Object to an Unreasonable Search and Seizure*, 34 U. CHI. L. REV. 342, 348 (1967); *see also* Comment, *Judicial Control of Illegal Search and Seizure*, 58 YALE L.J. 144, 156 (1948).

260 316 U.S. 114 (1942).

261 *Id.* at 121.

by the lower courts was "hard to square" with the holding of *Silverthorne Lumber*,[262] which ruled that unconstitutionally obtained evidence "shall not be used at all."

From one perspective, the dissenters' skepticism toward the standing limitation seemed well grounded. After all, if the exclusionary rule is a right inherent in the Fourth Amendment, as *Weeks* held, why limit invocation of the rule to victims of illegal intrusions? The amendment protects a right—the "right of the people" to be secure from unreasonable searches and seizures—and is designed to bar the government from infringing that right. "It is a general prohibition, a fundamental part of the constitutional compact, the observance of which is essential to the welfare of all persons."[263] Accordingly, as Justice Abe Fortas would later contend, "any defendant against whom illegally acquired evidence is offered, whether or not it was obtained in violation of his right to privacy, may have the evidence excluded."[264] But Fortas's conception of universal standing had its own theoretical flaw if it meant that a criminal—a burglar, for example—had the right to suppress evidence because his criminal behavior, robbing a private home, was discovered by an illegal police entry into the crime victim's home.

Furthermore, even assuming that the exclusionary rule is not a direct command of the Fourth Amendment itself, the standing limitation was inconsistent with the deterrent purpose of the rule. In 1955, the California Supreme Court recognized this point and eliminated the standing requirement in California courts. Writing for a unanimous court, Justice Roger Traynor concluded that the standing limitation "virtually invites law enforcement officers to violate the rights of third parties and to trade the escape of a criminal whose rights are violated for the conviction of others by the use of the evidence illegally obtained against them."[265] Traynor also observed, citing *Walder* for support, that the Supreme Court "has clearly recognized that the purpose of the exclusionary rule is not to provide redress or punishment for a past wrong, but to deter lawless enforcement of the law."[266] Finally, Traynor explained, "since all of the reasons that compelled us to adopt the exclusionary rule are applicable whenever evidence is obtained in violation of constitutional guarantees, such evidence is inadmissible whether or not it was obtained in violation of the particular defendant's constitutional rights."[267] Indeed, by 1960, many academic commentators, taking the Court at its word when it said that the exclusionary rule was designed to deter unconstitutional searches and seizures, asserted that the standing requirement was irreconcilable with the general deterrence theory of the rule and called for its abolishment.[268]

---

262 *Id.* at 127–28 (Murphy, J., dissenting).

263 Alderman v. United States, 394 U.S. 165, 205 (1969) (Fortas, J., concurring in part and dissenting in part).

264 *Id.* at 205–06.

265 People v. Martin, 290 P.2d 855, 857 (Cal. 1955).

266 *Id.*

267 *Id.*

268 *See, e.g.*, Albert R. Beisel, Jr., Control Over Illegal Enforcement of the Criminal Law: Role of the Supreme Court 18 (1955); Francis A. Allen, *The* Wolf *Case: Search and Seizure,*

So matters stood when *Jones v. United States*[269] arrived at the Court. Cecil Jones was arrested after federal narcotics officers executed a search warrant for the apartment where Jones had been staying. The apartment belonged to a friend of Jones, and the friend had given Jones permission to use the apartment. The officers found narcotics in a bird's nest in the awning of the apartment. Prior to trial, Jones moved to suppress the narcotics, claiming that the warrant had been issued without a sufficient showing of probable cause. The government challenged Jones's standing to make the motion because he alleged neither ownership of the narcotics nor a property interest in the apartment. At best, Jones was a mere guest or invitee in the apartment, which was an insufficient basis to challenge the search. In response, Jones testified that he had been given a key to the apartment and used it to enter the apartment on the day of the search and arrest. He also stated that his home was elsewhere, and that he had some clothes in the apartment and had slept there "maybe a night" while his friend was out of town.[270] The district court denied Jones's suppression motion, the evidence was admitted, and Jones was convicted.

In the Court, one of the lawyers representing Jones was University of Pennsylvania Law Professor Louis Henkin, a former Frankfurter law clerk. Henkin's brief tracked Frankfurter's views on the exclusionary rule. The brief asserted that the standing requirement was inconsistent with the spirit and goal of *Weeks*, which was to deter illegal searches and seizures.[271] The brief acknowledged a possible basis for the standing limitation: the exclusionary rule of *Weeks* is remedial only, "i.e., designed to restore the constitutional rights of the defendant violated by the unlawful search and seizure."[272] If that was the correct interpretation of the exclusionary rule, then the standing rule was appropriate.[273] But the brief explained that subsequent rulings, including *Walder*, showed that the exclusionary rule served other purposes beyond remedying the constitutional rights of an aggrieved search victim. Those additional purposes were deterrence and protecting the integrity of the judicial process.[274] Accordingly, the brief stated that "deterrence against violating constitutional rights will be stronger if the police are barred from using the evidence against anyone, rather than only against the direct victim of the search."[275]

Federalism, and the Civil Liberties, 45 ILL. L. REV. 1, 22 (1950); Comment, *Judicial Control*, *supra* note 259, at 158. Many years later, in a provocative article, Professor Sherry Colb would argue that "standing doctrine is not simply *in tension* with the goals of the exclusionary rule, but that, properly applied with the *ex post* perspective that defines Fourth Amendment standing, the doctrine altogether *precludes* the assertion of Fourth Amendment rights by any defendant bringing a suppression motion at his or her criminal trial." Sherry F. Colb, *Standing Room Only: Why Fourth Amendment Exclusion and Standing Can No Longer Logically Coexist*, 28 CARDOZO L. REV. 1663, 1666-67 (2007).

269 362 U.S. 257 (1960).

270 *Id.* at 259.

271 Brief for Petitioner at 17, *Jones* 362 U.S. 257 (No. 69).

272 *Id.* at 23.

273 *Id.*

274 *Id.* at 23–24.

275 *Id.* at 25.

The brief also argued that even assuming that a defendant must have "standing" to invoke the exclusionary rule, the facts showed Jones had sufficient standing to contest the search because he was lawfully in possession and control of the apartment.[276] Moreover, the brief contended the government was being duplicitous. When a person is charged with "possession" of narcotics, "the prosecution ought not to be able both to insist that defendant possessed the narcotics in its effort to convict him of crime and at the same time challenge his right to suppress on the ground that he did not have or claim possession."[277] Allowing the government to maintain such contradictory positions would undermine a defendant's Fourth and Fifth Amendment rights.

The government's brief did not dispute Jones's claim that the purpose of exclusion is to deter federal officers from violating the Fourth Amendment. However, the government insisted that the standing requirement rests upon "sound considerations of public policy."[278] The exclusionary rule, the government explained, was an exception to the common-law competent evidence rule.[279] And the rule was designed to protect a personal right. Therefore, the government argued, it "follows from the personal nature of the underlying right protected that only a person whose rights have been infringed is eligible to invoke the rule, and to enjoy the immunity it confers."[280]

The government also maintained that Jones's failure to claim either possession of the drugs or a substantial possessory interest in the premises searched prevented him from challenging the legality of the search. Recognizing that such an allegation might also convict as it confers standing, the government argued that because Jones's suppression motion did not claim any interest in the seized property or the searched premises, his case did not raise the issue of whether a defendant's incriminating statement claiming possession of contraband could be introduced against him at trial.

The conference discussion in *Jones* indicates that all of the justices, except Clark, thought Jones had sufficient standing to challenge the search. Interestingly, however, none of the justices mentioned the conflict between the standing requirement and the prevailing view that exclusion was designed to deter unconstitutional searches and seizures. Warren stated that Jones had standing and "had sufficient occupancy to complain of an invasion of privacy. You can't prosecute for possession and then say he has no claim to the premises. His privacy was invaded regardless of his tenancy . . . ."[281] Black and Frankfurter agreed with Warren on the standing point.[282] While Douglas voted to reverse Jones's conviction, Clark voted to affirm the conviction.[283] Clark thought that

---

[276] *Id.* at 18.

[277] *Id.*

[278] Brief for the United States at 22, *Jones*, 362 U.S. 257 (No. 69).

[279] *Id.* at 13–14.

[280] *Id.* at 22.

[281] William Douglas, Conference Notes on *Jones v. United States* (Jan. 22, 1960), Douglas Papers, Box 1255.

[282] *Id.*

[283] *Id.*

the Court should not discuss the standing issue, but if it did, he thought Jones lacked standing. He noted, "all the Court of Appeals are against it. A defendant has to lay a foundation that he was in possession."[284]

Justice Harlan spoke next and stated: "In a possessory case where you are charged with possession you have standing."[285] And Harlan thought that Jones "had enough relation to the premises to claim possession."[286] Justice Brennan also believed that Jones's relation to the premises was sufficient to confer standing.[287] Justice Whittaker likewise thought "there would be standing in a possession case. Showing possession shows status to suppress."[288] Justice Stewart similarly believed that Jones had "enough connection with the property to give standing."[289] Stewart also thought there "is standing in this possession case."[290] Finally, Frankfurter ended the discussion by observing that he "prefers to find standing in relation to the premises rather than on the basis of the nature of the crime," and noted that a "majority seems to be that way."[291]

Frankfurter was assigned to write the opinion in *Jones*, and his analysis began with an endorsement of the standing limitation. Without acknowledging *Silverthorne Lumber*'s rule that illegally obtained evidence "shall not be used at all" and his earlier agreement with the conclusion that the standing limitation was "hard to square" with *Silverthorne Lumber*, Frankfurter explained that a "party will not be heard to claim a constitutional protection unless he 'belongs to the class for whose sake the constitutional protection is given.'"[292] He also reaffirmed that the purpose of the exclusionary rule is deterrence of illegal searches and seizures. Exclusion, he wrote, "is a means for making effective the protection of privacy."[293] Thus, according to *Jones*, it is ordinarily proper to require a defendant seeking to invoke the exclusionary rule to show that he was "the victim of an invasion of privacy."[294]

Frankfurter did not address Jones's claim that deterrence would be strengthened by scrapping the standing limitation. Rather than address the conflict between the standing limitation and deterrence theory, it was enough for Frankfurter and the rest of the justices that the government's charge that Jones possessed narcotics eliminated the requirement that a suppression motion allege an interest in the premises searched or the property seized. "The possession on the basis of which petitioner is to be and was convicted suffices to give him standing."[295] Alternatively, the Court concluded that the

284 *Id.*
285 *Id.*
286 *Id.*
287 *Id.*
288 *Id.*
289 *Id.*
290 *Id.*
291 *Id.*
292 Jones v. United States, 362 U.S. 257, 261 (1960) (quoting Hatch v. Richardson, 204 U.S. 152, 160 (1907)).
293 *Id.*
294 *Id.*
295 *Id.* at 264.

facts showed that Jones's legitimate presence on the premises conferred sufficient standing for him to contest the legality of the search. *Jones* held that effective law enforcement would not be hampered by recognizing the rule that "anyone legitimately on premises where a search occurs may challenge its legality by way of a motion to suppress, when its fruits are proposed to be used against him."[296]

Jones thus confirmed what the lower courts and legal commentators already knew. Without saying so explicitly, the Court had transformed the meaning and purpose of the Fourth Amendment's exclusionary rule. Under *Weeks* and its immediate progeny, exclusion was a right inherent in the Fourth Amendment. *Wolf* adopted a different interpretation of the exclusionary rule. By 1960, *Wolf*'s way of thinking about the rule had extended beyond state cases. Even in federal cases like *Walder* and *Jones*, Frankfurter's perspective on exclusion controlled. Although the Court continued to suppress illegally obtained evidence in most federal cases, the rule was no longer the absolute bar against the admission of unconstitutionally seized evidence that it was in *Agnello*. Frankfurter's view that the primary purpose of the rule was deterrence now eclipsed the *Weeks-Silverthorne Lumber* interpretation that the rule was a personal right of the defendant.

E. The Lead-In to Mapp v. Ohio

While *Jones* demonstrated that Frankfurter's way of thinking about the exclusionary rule remained persuasive among most of the justices, there was another facet of Frankfurter's jurisprudence that was beginning to falter. That other aspect concerned the Fourth Amendment's applicability to searches and seizures by state police officers. After *Wolf* was decided in 1949, judges and law enforcement officials pretended that the Fourth Amendment controlled state police intrusions. The facts in scores of cases, however, including *Stefanelli*, *Rochin*, and *Irvine*, revealed that in many states police officers were ignoring Fourth Amendment principles. Two cases in the October 1959 Term forced the Court to confront the fact that *Wolf* had not applied the Fourth Amendment to the states.

In one case, *Elkins v. United States*,[297] speaking for the majority, Stewart continued to embrace the legal fiction that *Wolf* made the Fourth Amendment controlling on state searches. Stewart probably did not believe what he wrote in *Elkins*. A year earlier, in *Frank v. Maryland*,[298] Stewart stated in conference that the "Fourteenth Amendment, not the Fourth Amendment," controlled the constitutionality of searches conducted by state officers.[299] And in that conference, Stewart acknowledged what others had been

---

296 *Id.* at 267.

297 364 U.S. 206 (1960).

298 359 U.S. 360 (1959).

299 William Douglas, Conference Notes on *Frank v. Maryland* (Mar. 6, 1959), Douglas Papers, Box 1210.

unwilling to acknowledge, namely, that *Wolf* did not apply the Fourth Amendment to the states. Stewart observed that "while the core of the Fourth Amendment is carried over, it's not all carried over."[300]

Notwithstanding these earlier statements, Stewart's opinion in *Elkins* claimed that the Fourth Amendment governed state searches. Not surprisingly, Frankfurter's dissent in *Elkins* challenged this statement and explained that *Wolf* held that only the "'core of the Fourth Amendment,' not the Amendment itself, is enforceable against the States."[301] Perhaps, because the *Elkins* majority was determined to keep evidence unlawfully obtained by state officers out of federal prosecutions, it refused to accept the reality that the Due Process Clause, as applied by *Wolf*, barred only a few truly outrageous police intrusions by state officials, like the type of intrusion in *Rochin*.

Yet, on the same day the Court decided *Elkins*, it also decided *Eaton v. Price*.[302] In *Eaton*, four justices from the *Elkins* majority acknowledged that *Wolf* had allowed the Court to apply a "watered-down, subjective version" of the Fourth Amendment in state cases.[303] The tension between these two conflicting views of *Wolf* would be settled within a year with the ruling in *Mapp v. Ohio*, which would finally establish that the Fourth Amendment itself and its exclusionary rule did apply to the states.

* * *

The issue in *Elkins v. United States* was whether evidence obtained by state officers from an unreasonable search and seizure, without involvement of federal officials, was admissible against the victim of the search in a federal prosecution. Elkins and his codefendants were convicted in federal court of intercepting and divulging telephone communications, a violation of federal law. Evidence that had been illegally obtained by Oregon police officers was proffered at the trial. The federal district court assumed the evidence was obtained pursuant to an unconstitutional search, but admitted it anyway, because there was no proof federal officials knew of the search.

As far back as *Weeks*, the Court ruled evidence from an unconstitutional state search was admissible in federal court. Because the Fourth Amendment did not apply to state actors, a federal prosecutor was free to use such evidence. As one of Frankfurter's law clerks described the situation in a memo about *Elkins*, *Weeks*'s failure to cite the Fourteenth Amendment indicated that the Court "did not then conceive that an unreasonable search by state officials amounted to a violation of the Constitution."[304] Or, as Frankfurter himself summarized the point several years earlier, the Fourth Amendment only controls searches involving or encouraged by federal officials; "it is not a search

---

300 *Id.*

301 *Elkins*, 364 U.S. at 238 (Frankfurter, J., dissenting).

302 364 U.S. 263 (1960) (per curiam). In *Eaton*, the justices divided four to four, affirming the ruling below. Brennan wrote a separate opinion expressing his views on the merits of the case.

303 *Id.* at 275 (Brennan, J.).

304 Law Clerk, Memorandum to Felix Frankfurter on *Elkins v. United States* (undated), Frankfurter Papers, Box 116.

by a federal official if evidence secured by state authorities is turned over to the federal authorities on a silver platter."[305]

Elkins was an important and controversial case, and the divisions among the justices were evident at their conference. Warren stated he would "abolish the 'silver platter' rule."[306] Warren was against deciding any constitutional issues presented in the case, including the continuing validity of *Wolf*.[307] Warren wanted to base the ruling on the Court's supervisory authority over the lower federal courts.[308] Black stated that he considered the "silver platter" doctrine "a rule of evidence under our supervisory power unless Congress says to the contrary."[309] He also noted that "where evidence is taken in a manner which if taken by federal officers would be unconstitutional, it should not be used in a federal prosecution."[310]

Frankfurter spoke next, and his comments laid bare his views of the exclusionary rule. Referring to the evidence seized by Oregon police officials, Frankfurter remarked that "this is concededly relevant testimony and the exclusion of such testimony must have a strong underpinning before we can deny its use to prove truth. Federalism compounds the difficulty."[311] Frankfurter envisioned four grounds for exclusion: constitutional, statutory, the Court's supervisory power, and comity between the federal and state courts.[312] On the constitutional point, Frankfurter made plain that the Fourth Amendment did not mandate the federal exclusionary rule and that *Wolf* did not apply the Fourth Amendment to the states: "*Weeks* is surely a rule of evidence only. *Wolf* means that what was done here did not violate the Constitution."[313] He continued by noting that "what was done doesn't violate the U.S. Constitution. Coerced confessions may be court outlawed but not illegally obtained evidence as here."[314]

There was no statutory basis for excluding the evidence, which left only the Court's supervisory power or comity concerns as grounds for exclusion. Frankfurter told his colleagues that he would "not reject the 'silver platter doctrine,' though he is sorry he ever used the phrase."[315] He also ridiculed the idea that exclusion would have a deterrent effect on state police officers:

> Most cops aren't brazen but honestly mistaken. So its screwy to forbid federal courts to use relevant evidence as a means of keeping state cops law abiding. . . . On

---

305 Lustig v. United States, 338 U.S. 74, 78–79 (1949).

306 William Douglas, Conference Notes on *Elkins v. United States* (Apr. 1, 1960), Douglas Papers, Box 1215.

307 *Id.*

308 *Id.*

309 William J. Brennan, Jr., Conference Notes on *Elkins v. United States* (undated), William J. Brennan, Jr. Papers, Library of Congress, Manuscript Division, Box I: 28.

310 Douglas, Conference Notes on *Elkins v. United States*, *supra* note 306.

311 Brennan, Conference Notes on *Elkins v. United States*, *supra* note 309.

312 *Id.*

313 *Id.*

314 *Id.*

315 Douglas, Conference Notes on *Elkins v. United States*, *supra* note 306.

> the other hand, there are things that go too far. *Burdeau v. McDowell* is a specific case of stolen stuff received from a thief. If it's unseemly and shabby it's out. This means dealing with cases individually of course, but we can't help that. To that extent, I would make inroads on the silver platter doctrine. I wouldn't jettison.[316]

Frankfurter voted to affirm.[317]

Douglas spoke next and voted to reverse. Douglas stated that if the state court determines that the search was illegal, the federal court should not admit the evidence.[318] Clark voted to affirm and said he would not change the "silver platter" doctrine. "Law enforcement is in the hands of local authorities. Most local officers take the evidence over to federal officers—that is the practice and should be followed. There is no real abuse in the field—very few cases. State officers are most useful in producing evidence for the federal courts."[319] Harlan spoke next and voted to affirm: "It would be a step backwards to abandon the 'silver platter' rule."[320]

Brennan voted to reverse. He thought it was "immaterial that there have been any state proceedings—this is a federal proceeding. Even if there had been no challenge in state courts, the evidence should not be admitted." Brennan added that the "*Weeks* rule is the only means of giving real effect to the Fourth Amendment."[321] Whittaker spoke after Brennan and stated, "originally he would have thought the exclusionary rule was not evidentiary but constitutional."[322] But he "would not make unlawful state action invalid for federal crimes."[323] At the same time, referring to *Rochin v. California*, Whittaker said, "any conduct by state officers which if done by federal officers would be 'shocking' should be excluded."[324] Stewart expressed his agreement with Brennan's position that the Court should "not look at all to see what a state court has done—federal standards should apply."[325] Stewart's conception of the exclusionary rule "would exclude evidence seized by state officers if it would have been illegal if seized by federal officers."[326] Stewart voted to reverse. Warren ended the conference discussion by noting his agreement with Stewart and Brennan.[327] Thus the justices voted five to four to overrule the "silver platter" doctrine.

Stewart was assigned to write *Elkins*, and his second draft, citing *Wolf*, explicitly stated that the exclusionary rule was a "rule of evidence" and not "a constitutional

---

316 Brennan, Conference Notes on *Elkins v. United States*, *supra* note 309.

317 *Id.*

318 *Id.*

319 Douglas, Conference Notes on *Elkins v. United States*, *supra* note 306.

320 *Id.*

321 *Id.*

322 *Id.*

323 *Id.*

324 *Id.*

325 *Id.*

326 *Id.*

327 *Id.*

command."[328] This statement prompted objections from Douglas and Brennan, who separately wrote Stewart. Douglas told Stewart he had a "contrary" view; Douglas thought exclusion was "inherent in the constitutional command" of the Fourth Amendment.[329] Brennan had a similar concern but was less sure of his position than Douglas. Brennan told Stewart, "I'd feel better if there was left a little more open the question whether the *Weeks* rule is an imperative of the Fourth Amendment."[330] Brennan acknowledged that Black and Clark had previously indicated that "the *Weeks* rule is not immune from congressional alteration."[331] Brennan worried that Stewart's statement might be used in the future "as a square dictum that Congress could change the exclusionary rule as to federal seizures under the Fourth Amendment."[332] This, of course, was the very thing that Frankfurter and Black discussed in *Wolf* and the position favored by Black and (ironically, in light of his unpublished *Irvine* memo) Clark in *Elkins*.[333] Interestingly and without explaining his reasoning, Brennan then stated, "I grant that Congress' power is probably clear as to state seizures, but I am not so sure as to federal seizures."[334] Brennan's letter continued: "Would you think well of a footnote to the effect that 'We leave open the question whether the rule of exclusion within the *Weeks* area itself is an imperative of the Fourth Amendment, or a rule of evidence, which Congress is competent to change, designed to effectuate the constitutional command.'"[335] Stewart responded to Douglas's and Brennan's concerns by explaining that his next draft eliminated "all discussion of what the Constitution might or might not require" regarding the exclusionary rule.[336]

---

328 Potter Stewart, Second Draft of *Elkins v. United States* 11 (circulated May 20, 1960), Clark Papers, Box A95. The draft stated: "We assume . . . that though the right of privacy from unreasonable search and seizure is protected by the Fourth and Fourteenth Amendments, the Constitution itself does not require that this protection be effectuated by suppressing all evidence unlawfully obtained." *Id.*

329 William Douglas, Letter to Potter Stewart on *Elkins v. United States* (May 20, 1960), Potter Stewart Papers, Yale University Library, Manuscripts and Archives, Box 5.

330 William J. Brennan, Jr., Letter to Potter Stewart on *Elkins v. United States* 1-2 (May 23, 1960), Stewart Papers, Box 5.

331 *Id.* at 2.

332 *Id.*

333 In an article published after he retired from the Court, Stewart related that while his original draft in *Elkins* bothered Douglas and Brennan, "Justice Black, on the other hand, expressed agreement with what I had written." Stewart, *supra* note 5, at 1379. Before *Mapp* was decided, Black was not the only justice who believed that Congress could repeal the exclusionary rule even in federal cases. Although he would later author *Mapp*, ten years earlier in *United States v. Jeffers*, 342 U.S. 48 (1951), Clark wrote that the congressional enactment of forfeiture laws was not intended "to abolish the exclusionary rule formulated by the courts in furtherance of the high purposes of the Fourth Amendment." *Id.* at 54. As Clark would subsequently recognize when he started to write *Mapp*, this language from *Jeffers* suggested that the exclusionary rule was judicially created and that Congress could repeal it. *See* Dorin, *supra* note 257, at 417–18; LONG, *supra* note 4, at 88. Clark's view of the rule announced in *Jeffers* was also in contrast with his description of the rule outlined in his unpublished memo in *Irvine*.

334 Brennan, Letter to Potter Stewart on *Elkins v. United States*, *supra* note 330, at 2.

335 *Id.*

336 Potter Stewart, Letter to William J. Brennan, Jr. on *Elkins v. United States* (May 31, 1960), Stewart Papers, Box 5.

Stewart's published opinion in *Elkins* did omit all discussion of whether the Fourth Amendment mandated the exclusionary rule. Although *Elkins* passed on the question that *Wolf* negatively answered when Frankfurter wrote that *Weeks*'s exclusionary rule was a judge-made rule of evidence, ironically, *Elkins* relied on another aspect of *Wolf* to overrule the "silver platter" doctrine. *Elkins* explained that *Wolf* had destroyed the constitutional underpinnings of the "silver platter" doctrine. According to Stewart, after *Wolf* made the Fourth Amendment enforceable against the states, logic dictated abolishment of the "silver platter" doctrine and excluding evidence obtained from unreasonable state searches in federal prosecutions. "For surely no distinction can logically be drawn between evidence obtained in violation of the Fourth Amendment and that obtained in violation of the Fourteenth."[337] The Constitution is violated in both cases, and the identity of the officer certainly makes no difference to the person whose rights have been violated. There was no reason for federal courts, Stewart explained, "to differentiate between unconstitutionally seized evidence upon so arbitrary a basis."[338] Thus, *Elkins* held that if state police obtain evidence from an illegal search, that evidence is inadmissible in a federal trial.[339] When determining the constitutionality of a state search, a federal judge should independently determine whether the state intrusion violated the Fourth Amendment.[340]

Frankfurter's dissent in *Elkins* directly challenged the premise of Stewart's holding. Stewart read *Wolf* to prohibit unreasonable searches and seizures by state officials. But Stewart was wrong, Frankfurter maintained, because the Court had never applied the Fourth Amendment to state searches and seizures. Stewart's analysis ignored what *Wolf* stated. Frankfurter explained that *Wolf* held "that only what was characterized as the 'core of the Fourth Amendment,' not the Amendment itself, is enforceable against the States, [and] ... what was said in *Wolf* was said with reference to the Due Process Clause of the Fourteenth Amendment, and not with reference to the specific guarantees of the Fourth Amendment."[341] Frankfurter's dissent in *Elkins* also emphasized, as did *Wolf* and *Irvine*, that the "scope and effect" of the Fourth and Fourteenth Amendments could not be equated.[342] "The identity of the protection of the Due Process Clause against arbitrary searches with the scope of protection of the Fourth Amendment is something [that the *Elkins* majority] assumes for the first time today."[343] Moreover, *Wolf*'s distinction, Frankfurter explained, not only distinguished how "the Fourteenth Amendment is to be enforced against state officials from how the Fourth is to be enforced against federal

337 Elkins v. United States, 364 U.S. 206, 215 (1960).

338 *Id.*

339 *Id.* at 223.

340 *Id.* at 223–24.

341 *Id.* at 237–38 (Frankfurter, J., dissenting).

342 *Id.* at 238.

343 *Id.* at 239–40.

officers," but the logic of that distinction also dictated "that the remedies under the two Amendments are not the same."[344]

While Frankfurter's dissent in *Elkins* explained why the conventional view of *Wolf*—which Stewart had embraced—was mistaken, an unpublished paper he circulated criticizing *Elkins* provided a more insightful and revealing view of Frankfurter's thinking in *Wolf*. Entitled "*A Dialogue*," this essay portrayed a Socratic exchange between a "doctor" and "student" discussing the Court's search and seizure cases.[345] Several familiar aspects of Frankfurter's search and seizure jurisprudence pervade the essay, including the principle that *Wolf* did not make the Fourth Amendment enforceable against the states. Thus, when the doctor asks whether *Wolf* applied the amendment to the states, the student replies:

> *Wolf* makes clear that the Fourth Amendment as part of the Bill of Rights is not part of, or incorporated in, the Due Process Clause of the Fourteenth Amendment. . . . *Wolf* nowhere indicates or intimates that the very specific provisions of the Fourth Amendment, to wit, unreasonable search and seizure, are carried over into the Fourteenth Amendment. On the contrary, *Wolf* was careful to use very different language conveying very different concepts and presumably implying very different legal consequences to restrictions in this field upon federal authorities as compared with restrictions upon State authorities.[346]

A second aspect of Frankfurter's search and seizure philosophy was the distinction he made between "an arbitrary intrusion by the police" and an "unreasonable search and seizure." The Due Process Clause not only prohibits the former, but it also bars the admission of evidence obtained by an arbitrary invasion of privacy in a state prosecution. This explains Frankfurter's analysis in *Rochin*. On the other hand, police conduct that fell short of an arbitrary intrusion—for example, a mere illegal search or seizure, like the police conduct in *Wolf*—did not violate the Due Process Clause, according to Frankfurter. Consequently, he believed that the Due Process Clause did not require state courts to exclude evidence secured by an unreasonable search conducted by state law enforcement. By contrast, the Fourth Amendment, in Frankfurter's eyes, meant that federal officials could not conduct unreasonable searches and use the fruits of such searches to secure a federal conviction, subject, of course, to the impeachment exception

344 *Id.* at 240.

345 Felix Frankfurter, A Dialogue (undated) [hereinafter Frankfurter, A Dialogue] (unpublished essay), Frankfurter Papers, Box 152. Frankfurter's law clerk, Anthony Amsterdam, originally drafted *A Dialogue*. In an undated letter, Frankfurter thanks Amsterdam for "both the form and substance" of the paper. Felix Frankfurter, Letter to Anthony Amsterdam (undated), Frankfurter Papers, Box 152, Reel 77, Frames 585-86.

346 Frankfurter, A Dialogue, *supra* note 345, at 4.

created in *Walder* and the standing limitation announced in *Jones*, both authored by Frankfurter.

Reflecting Frankfurter's views, the student explains that under *Wolf*, Due Process provides a right of privacy "against 'arbitrary intrusion by the police,'" and a right "against a State's affirmatively sanctioning [arbitrary] police incursion."[347] *Wolf*, the student continues, juxtaposed the "'protection against arbitrary intrusion by the police'" against "'exclusion of evidence obtained by an unreasonable search and seizure.'"[348] Thus, the concept of "affirmative sanction of arbitrary intrusion by the police is a very different thing from the niceties of questions [the Court confronts] . . . when dealing with what is and what is not an unreasonable search and seizure [under the Fourth Amendment]."[349]

It is not surprising to learn that Frankfurter opposed applying the Fourth Amendment against the states and that he differentiated between what the Due Process Clause and the Fourth Amendment protected. These were familiar themes in his jurisprudence.[350] There is, however, one surprising theme that surfaces in *A Dialogue*. Recall in *Wolf*, Frankfurter described the exclusionary rule of *Weeks* as not derived from the Amendment itself, but rather as "a matter of judicial implication."[351] In *A Dialogue*, Frankfurter describes *Weeks* very differently. When the doctor asks whether the exclusionary rule of *Weeks* is "a constitutional doctrine" or a rule derived from the Court's supervisory power, the student observes:

> Perhaps the shortest way to answer your question is to say that *Weeks* was decided in 1914, and not until Justice Black's concurring opinion in *Wolf* thirty-four years later did anyone make the suggestion that the exclusionary rule in *Weeks* was not a constitutional consequence of the Fourth Amendment but rather an application of the [Court's supervisory authority]. . . . *Weeks* said that not to exclude the evidence in that case would make the Fourth Amendment's protection of no value; that, so far as the defendant was concerned, the Amendment "might as well be stricken from the Constitution." Surely any practice which makes a constitutional provision of "no value" is forbidden by that provision. In short, the exclusionary rule of *Weeks* for me is like the exclusionary rule barring coerced testimony concededly truthful.[352]

This passage means that the Constitution requires the exclusionary rule. But Frankfurter did not believe it. Indeed, he said the opposite a few months earlier when he told his

347 *Id.*

348 *Id.*

349 *Id.* at 4–5.

350 Frankfurter's view that the Fourteenth Amendment's Due Process Clause did not "incorporate" the Bill of Rights and make them fully applicable to the states was set out in his concurring opinion in *Adamson v. California*, 332 U.S. 46, 62–65 (1947) (Frankfurter, J., concurring).

351 Wolf v. Colorado, 338 U.S. 25, 28 (1949).

352 Frankfurter, A Dialogue, *supra* note 345, at 6–7 (citation omitted).

colleagues during the *Elkins* conference that "*Weeks* is surely a rule of evidence only." Similarly, in a later unpublished paper which, unlike the informal style of *A Dialogue*, had the look and style of an academic article, Frankfurter refers to *Weeks*'s exclusionary rule as "a deterrent sanction selected" by the Court "in the exercise of its supervisory powers."[353] Finally, in his dissent in *Elkins*, Frankfurter unequivocally stated: "The underlying assumption on which the exclusionary rule of *Weeks* rests is that barring evidence illegally secured will have an inhibiting, one hopes civilizing, influence upon law officers."[354] And he followed that assertion with the further claim that "the exertion of controlling pressures upon the police is admittedly the only justification for any exclusionary rule."[355]

A Dialogue highlighted the divergent views of *Wolf* that Stewart and Frankfurter espoused in *Elkins*. Stewart insisted that *Wolf* had applied the Fourth Amendment to the states, while Frankfurter vehemently disagreed. Despite these conflicting positions, *Elkins* also showed that Stewart and Frankfurter could occupy common ground on the exclusionary rule. *Elkins*'s holding to overrule the "silver platter" doctrine was not based upon the Constitution, but on the Court's supervisory power over the administration of criminal proceedings in the federal courts. Although Stewart's opinion in *Elkins* did not discuss or question the validity of *Wolf*'s holding that the exclusionary rule did not apply to the states, he did describe the "basic postulate" of the rule.[356] Without citing *Weeks*, *Silverthorne Lumber*, or any other majority opinion of the Court, Stewart observed: "The rule is calculated to prevent, not to repair. Its purpose is to deter—to compel

---

353 Felix Frankfurter, *"Incorporation" of the Fourth into the Fourteenth Amendment?*, at 11 (undated) [hereinafter Frankfurter, *"Incorporation"*] (unpublished essay), Frankfurter Papers, Box 168. Interestingly, in an April 19, 1957, letter to Warren, Frankfurter called *Weeks* and *Silverthorne Lumber* "among the most important decisions" decided by the Court in the field of civil liberties. Frankfurter, Letter to Earl Warren, *supra* note 13, at 2. In that letter, Frankfurter described how his view of the Fourth Amendment differed from Black's:

> The fact of the matter is that from the time I came on the Court there has been a deep cleavage of view regarding the Fourth Amendment between Black and myself. On more than one occasion, he expressed hostility to the *Silverthorne* decision and readiness to overrule it; and for him the *Weeks* decision merely stands for a judicially created rule of evidence. For me, *Silverthorne* and *Weeks* are among the most important decisions of this Court in the domain of civil liberties. You will therefore, I hope, appreciate why I cannot be a party to a point of view with which I deeply disagree, namely, the subordination of the commands of the Fourth Amendment to a mere judge-made rule, particularly considering a series of decision [sic] since I have been here that have from my point of view flouted the commands of the Fourth Amendment.

Id. Frankfurter's letter was prompted by the consideration of a federal search incident to arrest case, *Kremen v. United States*, 353 U.S. 346 (1957) (per curiam). His comments about *Weeks* should be read in the context of a federal case, and do not suggest that his views on *Weeks* with respect to a state search and seizure had changed.

354 Elkins v. United States, 364 U.S. 206, 241 (1960) (Frankfurter, J., dissenting).

355 *Id.*

356 *Id.* at 217 (majority opinion).

respect for the constitutional guaranty in the only effectively available way—by removing the incentive to disregard it."[357] Frankfurter could not have said it better. In fact, Stewart's characterization of the rule's purpose mirrored Frankfurter's description, provided in his *Elkins* dissent, that deterrence of illegal police searches was the "underlying assumption" of *Weeks* and the "only justification for any exclusionary rule."[358]

* * *

While *Elkins* insisted that *Wolf* made the Fourth Amendment applicable to the states, four justices from the *Elkins* majority seemed no longer willing to ignore the obvious: since *Wolf*, the Court was using two different constitutional standards to judge the validity of searches and seizures—one standard for intrusions conducted by federal officers and another standard for intrusions by state officers. In an obscure case entitled *Ohio ex rel. Eaton v. Price*,[359] decided on the same day as *Elkins*, Brennan, joined by Warren, Black, and Douglas, did what Stewart was unwilling to do in *Elkins*—concede that the Court was not applying the Fourth Amendment to determine the constitutionality of searches and seizures conducted by state officers.

Eaton was a four-to-four per curiam ruling, with Stewart not participating because his father had sat as a judge in the decision below. *Eaton* affirmed an Ohio Supreme Court decision upholding the constitutionality of a Dayton ordinance authorizing suspicionless administrative searches of private homes by city housing inspectors. A year before, when the Court noted probable jurisdiction in *Eaton*,[360] four justices, led by Frankfurter, published their view that *Frank v. Maryland* controlled the outcome in *Eaton*.[361] *Frank v. Maryland*[362] was a contentious five-to-four ruling authored by Frankfurter, which held that a warrantless administrative search by a Baltimore housing inspector did not violate the Due Process Clause of the Fourteenth Amendment.

In *Eaton*, Brennan, writing for himself and three other justices, observed that it has "now become clear that the *Frank* decision may have turned in substantial part on the positing of a distinction between the affirmative guaranty of privacy against official incursion raised by the Fourth Amendment against federal action, and that raised by the Due Process of the Fourteenth Amendment against state action."[363] Pointedly noting Frankfurter's dissent in *Elkins*, Brennan observed that "[i]t is now clear that part of the [*Frank* majority] does not subscribe" to the view that *Wolf* made the Fourth Amendment applicable to the states.[364] Without citing examples, Brennan hinted that prior to *Elkins*, the Court had

---

357 *Id.* Stewart cited a New Jersey Supreme Court case, *Eleuteri v. Richman*, 141 A.2d 46, 50 (N.J. 1958), to support his statement on the exclusionary rule's purpose. *Elkins*, 364 U.S. at 217.

358 *Elkins*, 364 U.S. at 241 (Frankfurter, J., dissenting).

359 364 U.S. 263 (1960).

360 Ohio *ex rel.* Eaton v. Price, 360 U.S. 246 (1959) (per curiam).

361 *See id.* at 248 (separate memorandum of Frankfurter, J.). Clark, Harlan, and Whittaker joined Frankfurter's memorandum in *Eaton*.

362 359 U.S. 360 (1959).

363 *Eaton*, 364 U.S. at 274.

364 *Id.*

not been applying the Fourth Amendment to state searches and seizures. As he put it, using the Due Process Clause to decide the constitutionality of searches and seizures conducted by state officers "is not a license to the judiciary to administer a watered-down, subjective version of the individual guarantees of the Bill of Rights when state cases come before us."[365]

But that is exactly what the Court had done in *Wolf*, *Irvine*, and *Frank*, and Brennan had proof from his participation in *Frank*. After *Frank* was argued, all of the justices except Douglas agreed to affirm the Maryland court decision upholding Frank's conviction and twenty-dollar fine for refusing an inspection of his home without a search warrant after a housing inspector discovered rodent infestation on the property.[366] As noted above, during the *Frank* conference, Stewart reminded his colleagues that because this was a state case, the Fourteenth Amendment controlled, "not the Fourth." And echoing what Frankfurter held in *Wolf*, Stewart stated that "while the core of the Fourth Amendment is carried over, it's not all carried over." *Frank* was assigned to Frankfurter, and the drafts he circulated were "essentially the same as the final opinion that he delivered" for the Court.[367] Frankfurter's opinion in *Frank* was a replay of his Due Process analysis, the same legal theory that supported his opinions for the Court in *Wolf* and *Rochin*, and his dissent in *Irvine*.

After receiving Frankfurter's second draft, Brennan circulated a short concurrence emphasizing that the Court was not abandoning the principle that the "'Due Process Clause of the Fourteenth Amendment enjoins upon the States the guarantees of privacy embodied in the Fourth Amendment.'"[368] Brennan also explained that he was concurring in Frankfurter's opinion because it "demonstrates to me that enforcement of the demand [by the housing inspector] made upon [Frank] does not amount to enforcing an unreasonable search."[369]

Frankfurter responded to Brennan's proposed concurrence with a "Dear Bill" letter that stated: "[I]t would be a wrong way of getting at our problem in the *Frank* case to determine whether it would or wouldn't constitute a violation of the Fourth Amendment and from that conclude that, therefore, it does or doesn't violate the Fourteenth Amendment."[370] Frankfurter maintained that his mode of analysis is to "derive the protection of privacy that the Fourteenth Amendment accords, not from the Fourth Amendment, but from the Fourteenth Amendment, though it turn[s] out to

---

365 *Id.* at 275.

366 Douglas's conference notes for *Frank* list only himself as voting for reversal. William Douglas, Conference Notes on *Frank v. Maryland* (Mar. 6, 1959), Douglas Papers, Box 1210.

367 SCHWARTZ, *supra* note 9, at 327.

368 William J. Brennan, Jr., Draft of Concurring Opinion on *Frank v. Maryland* (Apr. 16, 1959), Clark Papers, Box A84.

369 *Id.*

370 Felix Frankfurter, Letter to William J. Brennan, Jr. on *Frank v. Maryland* 1 (Apr. 16, 1959), Stewart Papers, Box 163; Frankfurter Papers, Box 109.

be the same as that which for federal situations is covered by the Fourth Amendment." Thus, he deemed it "a wrong analysis" to determine whether the search of Frank's home constituted an "unreasonable search under the Fourth Amendment." The last paragraph of Frankfurter's letter to Brennan insisted that he did not "'retreat' from what [he] said in *Wolf* one infinitesimal iota." And he closed the letter by explaining:

> I simply do not have to lift myself by the Fourth Amendment in order to apply the Fourteenth Amendment. But I can't imagine how any fair reading of my opinion would lead anybody to think that I would regard the search made of [Frank's] premises here a violation of the Fourth Amendment were the case to arise under federal law.[371]

Undeniably, Frankfurter's opinion in *Frank* was not a "retreat" from *Wolf. Frank* was consistent with its author's anti-incorporation views, and thus it did not apply the Fourth Amendment to housing inspections conducted by state officials. At the same time, Frankfurter's claim to Brennan that the "protection of privacy" afforded by his Due Process analysis "turn[s] out to be the same as that which for federal situations is covered by the Fourth Amendment" was not supported by the Court's cases, as illustrated by the results in *Wolf, Irvine*, and *Frank*.

Furthermore, Frankfurter did not believe that the protection of privacy guaranteed by the Due Process Clause was the equivalent of the constitutional protection secured by the Fourth Amendment. In his view, Due Process only reached shocking or aggravated intrusions of privacy; by contrast, a Fourth Amendment violation did not require outrageous police conduct. In an unpublished article written after *Mapp v. Ohio* was decided, Frankfurter wrote that *Boyd v. United States* stood for the rule that "the introduction in a federal court of evidence procured by a 'bare' search and seizure was then and there a violation of the Fourth Amendment, one necessitating exclusion of the evidence."[372] This rule, according to Frankfurter, was "far from a holding that the fruits of a 'bare' search and seizure by state officers must be excluded by state courts."[373] And in the Socratic exchange portrayed in his *A Dialogue*, the "student" explains why the Due Process Clause does not render unconstitutional the same conduct that is rendered unconstitutional by the Fourth Amendment: "Surely, 'arbitrary intrusion by the police' is something much more obviously drastic, some obviously different kind of an intrusion by the police, than a five-to-four determination whether there was or wasn't an unreasonable search and seizure."[374]

---

371 *Id.* at 2.

372 Frankfurter, *"Incorporation," supra* note 353, at 7.

373 *Id.*

374 Frankfurter, A Dialogue, *supra* note 345, at 6.

If Frankfurter's hypothetical "student" surely knew that under the Court's precedents, the privacy afforded by the Due Process Clause was less protective against state police searches than the constitutional protection secured by the Fourth Amendment, Brennan also knew it. After receiving Frankfurter's "Dear Bill" letter, Brennan decided to join Douglas's dissent in *Frank*, which argued that city housing inspections were subject to the full protections of the Fourth Amendment, including the warrant requirement.[375] Eventually, Warren and Black would also switch their votes to join Douglas's dissent. At one point, Douglas's dissent persuaded Whittaker to change his vote, which gave Douglas a majority to declare that Frank's conviction for refusing to permit a warrantless search of his home violated the Fourth Amendment. "When the final vote on [*Frank*] was taken," however, "Whittaker switched again and Frankfurter delivered his opinion for a five-man Court."[376] Interestingly, Whittaker filed a brief concurrence in *Frank*. Citing *Wolf*, he noted: "The core of the Fourth Amendment prohibiting unreasonable searches applies to the States through the Due Process Clause of the Fourteenth Amendment."[377] Whittaker also observed that enforcement of the police demand to search Frank's home was not "an unreasonable search within the meaning of the Fourth and Fourteenth Amendments. "[378] Evidently, Whittaker, like Stewart in *Elkins*, embraced the conventional view of *Wolf*.

Thus, by the close of the 1959 Term, Frankfurter's view of the exclusionary rule, as announced in *Wolf*, remained predominate. But the other element of *Wolf* that was so important to Frankfurter—that the Fourth Amendment did not control the constitutionality of searches and seizures by state officers—was slowly losing its grip on a majority of the justices. Brennan's opinion in *Eaton* demonstrated that four of the justices were no longer willing to deny the obvious—that *Wolf* did not make the Fourth Amendment binding on the states. In the next Term, Clark, normally an ally of Frankfurter, would author the opinion, *Mapp v. Ohio*, which unexpectedly overruled *Wolf*.

---

375 SCHWARTZ, *supra* note 9, at 327–28 ("The Douglas dissent was an eloquent assertion of the need to hold administrative inspections, as well as police searches, to the warrant requirement of the Fourth Amendment.").

376 *Id.* at 328.

377 Frank v. Maryland, 359 U.S. 360, 373 (1959) (Whittaker, J., concurring).

378 *Id.* at 374.

3 The Warren Court on Exclusion: *Mapp v. Ohio*, then Retreat

FOR NEARLY EVERYONE, the ruling in *Mapp v. Ohio* was stunning.[1] In his review of the 1960 Court Term for the *New York Times*, Anthony Lewis described the result in *Mapp* "as the most sweeping restriction ever put on state criminal procedure by a single Supreme Court decision."[2] A young Philadelphia Assistant District Attorney, Arlen Specter, wrote that *Mapp* "revolutionized" police practices and prosecution procedures, and that it was "the most significant event in criminal law since the adoption of the fourteenth amendment."[3] Specter observed that the initial reaction to *Mapp* in the Pennsylvania courts "was one of dismay," with one trial judge describing *Mapp* "as a 'hurricane' which 'swept over our fair land.'"[4] A high-ranking New York City police official had a similar reaction:

> The *Mapp* case was a shock to us. We had to reorganize our thinking, frankly. Before this, nobody bothered to take out search warrants. Although the U.S. Constitution requires warrants in most cases, the U.S. Supreme Court had ruled

---

[1] 367 U.S. 643 (1961).

[2] Anthony Lewis, *Term of Supreme Court Marked By 2 Blows Dealt to U.S. Reds*, N.Y. TIMES, June 25, 1961, at 43.

[3] Arlen Specter, Mapp v. Ohio*: Pandora's Problems for the Prosecutor*, 111 U. PA. L. REV. 4, 4 (1962).

[4] *Id.*

that evidence obtained without a warrant—illegally if you will—was admissible in state courts. So the feeling was, why bother?[5]

These descriptions of and reactions to *Mapp* are a little puzzling. After all, *Mapp* did not impose any restrictions on the police. By overruling *Wolf*'s second holding regarding the exclusionary rule, *Mapp* simply held that evidence obtained in violation of a defendant's Fourth Amendment rights was inadmissible in a state prosecution. But *Wolf*'s first holding, according to almost everyone who had read the case, had already made the Fourth Amendment binding on state officials. Consequently, after *Wolf*, state and local police were theoretically compelled to comply with the Amendment's restrictions. If this were true, why then was *Mapp* so "revolutionary" and "shocking," and why was it received with "dismay" by trial judges, prosecutors, and the police? All *Mapp* did was rule that Fourth Amendment violations have legal consequences at subsequent prosecutions. The ruling itself neither extended the scope of the Fourth Amendment, nor did it impose any new restrictions on police search and seizure practices. It simply made the Fourth Amendment relevant in state criminal prosecutions.

The truth of the matter was that *Mapp* was a "shock" and caused "dismay" in state law enforcement circles because police had been routinely ignoring the Fourth Amendment. As Arlen Specter and other law enforcement officials admitted, before *Mapp*, police officers "for years had presented their evidence in court without any regard to how it had been obtained."[6] As Specter observed, prior to *Mapp*, the feeling among local police, prosecutors, and judges was that it "is more important to convict the guilty than to prevent the unconstitutional search and seizure of the innocent which is only unpleasant."[7] Practically speaking, the result in *Mapp* posed serious problems for prosecutions involving unconstitutional searches and seizures. Although police officials knew that they were supposed to respect the constitutional rights of citizens, failing to do so was inconsequential in many states because illegally obtained evidence was admissible in criminal cases. In almost half the states, including California, New York, and Pennsylvania, it was routine procedure to admit evidence obtained from illegal police searches.[8] For example, in Los Angeles, neither the district attorney's office nor the Los Angeles Police

---

5 Sidney E. Zion, *Detectives Get a Course in Law*, N.Y. TIMES, Apr. 28, 1965, at 50, *quoted in* Yale Kamisar, *The Exclusionary Rule in Historical Perspective: The Struggle to Make the Fourth Amendment More Than 'An Empty Blessing,'* 62 JUDICATURE 337, 349–50 (1979).

6 Specter, *supra* note 3, at 5.

7 *Id.* at 41.

8 *See* Roger J. Traynor, Mapp v. Ohio *at Large in the Fifty States*, 1962 DUKE L.J. 319, 321–22 (1962) (noting that as a justice on the California Supreme Court, his "misgivings about [admitting illegally obtained evidence] grew as [he] observed that time after time it was being offered and admitted as a routine procedure. It became impossible to ignore the corollary that illegal searches and seizures were also a routine procedure subject to no effective deterrent; else how could illegally obtained evidence come into court with such regularity? It was one thing to condone an occasional constable's blunder, to accept his illegally obtained evidence so that the guilty would not go free. It was quite another to condone a steady course of illegal police

Department "paid any attention" to Fourth Amendment rules until the exclusionary rule was applied to the states.[9] *Mapp* created immediate difficulties for long-standing police practices nationwide. Indeed, many police officials "reacted as if the Fourth Amendment or its state constitutional counterpart had just been adopted."[10]

From a theoretical and evolutionary perspective, *Mapp* was also an extremely important case. Since the 1930s, a majority of the Court had consistently rejected Black's position that the Due Process Clause of the Fourteenth Amendment made the original Bill of Rights binding on the states. During this period, Frankfurter fought hardest among the justices in opposing "incorporation" of the Bill of Rights into the Due Process Clause. *Wolf*, of course, was one of Frankfurter's cornerstone decisions reflecting his anti-incorporation views. But *Mapp* marked the beginning of the end of Frankfurter's dominance on the issue of incorporating the Bill of Rights' criminal procedure guarantees.

Mapp was the first decision to interpret the Due Process Clause to impose on the states the same substantive constitutional criminal procedure standards that are imposed on the federal government. Once the Warren Court took this significant step, it "signaled the beginning of a due process revolution that was to transform the rules of state law enforcement and criminal procedure and provoke the [ ] protest [of the late 1960's] that the Supreme Court [was] coddling criminals and handcuffing the police."[11] After *Mapp* finally applied the Fourth Amendment to the states, the Court would inevitably also make the Self-Incrimination Clause of the Fifth Amendment and the Right to Counsel Clause of the Sixth Amendment applicable to the states. Ultimately, the Warren Court would "bring almost the entire range of state police action within the detailed control of the Federal judiciary."[12] In fact, within three years of the *Mapp* decision, the Fifth Amendment's privilege against self-incrimination and the right to counsel guaranteed by the Sixth Amendment were made binding on the states.[13]

As important as *Mapp* was in 1961, it would meet its demise less than two decades after it was decided with the judicial retrenchment of the conservative justices of the Burger and Rehnquist Courts. Conceivably, *Mapp*'s downfall was preordained in light of the justices appointed by Presidents Richard Nixon, Ronald Reagan, George Bush, and George W. Bush. But Clark's opinion in *Mapp* also contained the seeds for its own destruction. *Mapp* was an easy target for the Burger and Rehnquist Courts because the

---

procedures that deliberately and flagrantly violated the Constitution of the United States as well as the state constitution.").

[9] John Kaplan, *The Limits of the Exclusionary Rule*, 26 STAN. L. REV. 1027, 1034 (1974).

[10] Yale Kamisar, Mapp v. Ohio*: The First Shot Fired in the Warren Court's Criminal Procedure "Revolution," in* CRIMINAL PROCEDURE STORIES 45, 76 (Carol S. Steiker ed., 2006) [hereinafter Kamisar, *First Shot Fired*].

[11] FRED P. GRAHAM, THE SELF-INFLICTED WOUND 28 (1970).

[12] *Id.* at 48.

[13] *See* Gideon v. Wainwright, 372 U.S. 335 (1963) (holding that the Sixth Amendment's Right to Counsel Clause applies to the states); *see also* Malloy v. Hogan, 378 U.S. 1 (1964) (applying the Fifth Amendment's Self-Incrimination Clause to the states).

opinion was a mixture of constitutional principles and policy arguments. In contrast to the single-meaning focus of *Weeks*, Clark's opinion in *Mapp* sought to justify the exclusionary rule from a variety of judicial perspectives—some of which were unpersuasive. Equally relevant to *Mapp*'s downfall was Black's influence on Clark's opinion and the separate opinion he authored, which professed agreement with Clark's opinion and judgment. As later justices would recognize, Black articulated a constitutional basis for the exclusionary rule that was out of sync with the thrust of Clark's opinion, and constitutionally unsound in its own right. Ultimately, Black's contribution to *Mapp* would do more harm than good for *Mapp*'s long-term survival.

* * *

The scene for what would later become the nation's most famous search and seizure case began on May 23, 1957. Cleveland police received an anonymous tip that a suspect wanted in the bombing of Don King's residence was hiding in the home of Dollree Mapp. The police were also told that "policy paraphernalia" connected to illegal gambling was in Mapp's home. Three officers arrived at the house and demanded entry. Mapp, however, on the advice of her lawyer refused entry until the police displayed a search warrant. The police waited outside of the home, and a few hours later more officers joined the scene. The officers again demanded entry. Eventually, the police forced open a back door. After the officers gained entry, Mapp's lawyer arrived, but the police would not allow him to see Mapp or enter the house.[14]

Once the police were inside her home, Mapp again demanded to see a search warrant. One of the officers showed Mapp a piece of paper alleged to be a warrant. Mapp grabbed the paper and "placed it in her bosom."[15] A tussle ensued in which the police sought to recover the "warrant." After the officers retrieved the paper, they handcuffed Mapp and conducted a top-to-bottom search of her home. The search revealed four books: *Affairs of a Troubadour, Little Darlings, London Stage Affairs*, and *Memories of a Hotel Man*; and a hand-drawn picture,[16] all of which were allegedly obscene.

Mapp was charged under a statute that criminalized the knowing possession of obscenity. At her trial, the state failed to produce a search warrant. Nevertheless, Mapp was convicted and sentenced to prison because Ohio courts permitted the admission of illegally obtained evidence as a matter of state law. The Ohio Supreme Court affirmed the conviction, albeit noting that "[t]here is, in the record, considerable doubt as to whether there ever was any warrant for the search of the defendant's home," and notwithstanding the fact that the conviction was based upon evidence obtained by an unlawful search of Mapp's home.[17]

---

[14] *See* CAROLYN N. LONG, *Mapp v. Ohio*: GUARDING AGAINST UNREASONABLE SEARCHES AND SEIZURES 5–9 (2006); *see also* PRISCILLA H. MACHADO ZOTTI, INJUSTICE FOR ALL: *Mapp vs. Ohio* AND THE FOURTH AMENDMENT 16–23 (2005).

[15] Mapp v. Ohio, 367 U.S. 643, 644 (1961).

[16] *See* Potter Stewart, *The Road to* Mapp v. Ohio *and Beyond: The Origins, Development and Future of the Exclusionary Rule in Search-and-Seizure Cases*, 83 COLUM. L. REV. 1365, 1367 (1983).

[17] State v. Mapp, 166 N.E.2d 387, 389 (Ohio 1960).

At the Court, *Mapp v. Ohio* was initially an obscenity case. During their conference discussion, the justices unanimously agreed that the Ohio statute criminalizing the mere knowing possession of obscenity violated the Free Speech Clause of the First Amendment.[18] But the discussion also revealed that four members of the Court—Warren, Douglas, Clark, and Brennan—wanted to use the case to overrule *Wolf*.[19]

Clark was assigned to write *Mapp*, and his initial handwritten draft rejected Mapp's Fourth Amendment claim and resolved the case on Free Speech grounds.[20] But Clark eventually changed his mind, deciding instead to treat *Mapp* as a search-and-seizure case.[21] But *Mapp* was no ordinary Fourth Amendment case because Clark would have

---

[18] William Douglas, Conference Notes on *Mapp v. Ohio* (Mar. 31, 1961), Douglas Papers, Box 1254. Douglas's docket sheet for *Mapp* records a unanimous vote in favor reversing the judgment below. William Douglas, Docket Sheet on *Mapp v. Ohio* (voted on Mar. 31, 1961), Douglas Papers, Box 1121.

[19] William Douglas, Conference Notes on *Mapp v. Ohio*, *supra* note 18. The subject of overruling *Wolf* was raised during the oral argument in *Mapp*. Participating as amicus curiae, counsel for the American Civil Liberties Union asked the Court to "re-examine" *Wolf*. Transcript of Oral Argument at 13, *Mapp*, 367 U.S. 643 (No. 236). When the subject of overruling *Wolf* was raised with Mapp's lawyer, his answers revealed that he was not well versed with *Wolf* or the Court's other precedents addressing the applicability of the exclusionary rule in state cases. *See id.* at 8–9 (in response to the question of whether he was asking the Court to overrule *Wolf*, stating: "No, I don't believe we are."); *see also id.* at 43 (when asked whether Mapp's case came within the doctrine of *Rochin*, stating "I don't have all of the facts [of that] case").

[20] Tom C. Clark, Handwritten Draft of *Mapp v. Ohio* (undated), Clark Papers, Box A115.

[21] There are several accounts of what precipitated *Mapp*'s transformation. According to Bernard Schwartz, after the conference on *Mapp*, Black, Clark, and Brennan met in the elevator, and Clark asked his colleagues "'wouldn't this be a good case to apply the exclusionary rule and do what *Wolf* didn't do?'" BERNARD SCHWARTZ, SUPER CHIEF: EARL WARREN AND HIS SUPREME COURT—A JUDICIAL BIOGRAPHY 393 (1983). Potter Stewart relies on Schwartz's account in his article about *Mapp*, which was written after he retired from the Court. *See* Stewart, *supra* note 16, at 1368. Roger Newman's biography of Black provides a slightly different version of events. Newman reports that after the elevator meeting, Warren suggested to Black that he should write the opinion reversing *Wolf*, to which Black replied, "'I don't want to. Somebody else should.'" Later, Clark was assigned *Mapp*. ROGER K. NEWMAN, HUGO BLACK: A BIOGRAPHY 555 (1994). Another biographer of Warren, Ed Cray, writes that Warren, Douglas and Brennan went to see Black after the conference on *Mapp*, and convinced Black to join them in overruling *Wolf*. ED CRAY, CHIEF JUSTICE: A BIOGRAPHY OF EARL WARREN 374–75 (1997).

Mapp was argued on March 29, 1961, and the conference was held on March 31. Douglas, Conference Notes on *Mapp v. Ohio*, *supra* note 18. Clark's first draft opinion treating the case as a Fourth Amendment ruling was sent to Black on April 22. Tom Clark, Letter to Hugo Black (Apr. 22, 1961), Clark Papers, Box A115.

According to a recent biography of Judge Richard Arnold, who clerked for Brennan during the Term that *Mapp* was decided: "The most important development was Black's decision on the Fourth Amendment question." POLLY J. PRICE, JUDGE RICHARD S. ARNOLD: A LEGACY OF JUSTICE ON THE FEDERAL BENCH 53 (2009). According to Arnold's biographer, "Brennan made it a regular practice to discuss with his clerks the results of the Friday conferences." *Id.* And Arnold kept a personal diary that reported Brennan's recollections. According to Arnold's diary, sometime after the first conference on *Mapp*, "Black [came] in to see [Brennan] before lunch. He has decided to go along with overruling of *Wolf* in *Mapp*. He had just talked an hour with Clark—is convinced that the Fourth Amendment is an empty guarantee without the exclusionary rule. He told Clark he would join him if his opinion applied the Fourth Amendment to the states, as such, as a specific of the Bill of Rights." *Id.* Arnold's diary also reports that the Court held at least three conferences on *Mapp*. In a subsequent conference, "Frankfurter became violent. He shook, almost cried—it

to reconceptualize the Court's view of exclusion. Because he was determined to overrule *Wolf*'s holding that the exclusionary rule did not apply to the states, Clark would have to establish that the rule was rooted in the Constitution.

Yale Kamisar rightly states that the "whole thrust" of Part I of Clark's opinion in *Mapp* was intended to establish that the exclusionary rule "is not a 'mere rule of evidence' or an exercise of the Court's supervisory powers over federal criminal justice, but a command of the Constitution."[22] At the same time, Kamisar also acknowledges that Clark's analysis in *Mapp* was confusing and unfocused because he sought to advance "as many reasons for the exclusionary rule as he could find, whether constitutional or pragmatic."[23]

One of the more perplexing aspects of *Mapp* was Clark's reliance on *Boyd v. United States* for the conclusion that the exclusionary rule is constitutionally binding on the states. Clark begins addressing the merits in *Mapp* by asserting that *Boyd* considered the Fourth and Fifth Amendments "as running 'almost into each other'" as protection against government invasions of privacy.[24] And later in his opinion, Clark quotes *Boyd* for the proposition that the Fourth and Fifth Amendments "do enjoy an 'intimate relation' in their perpetuation" of principles of civil liberties.[25] Reasoning that if a coerced confession is inadmissible in a criminal trial despite its reliability and relevance to the defendant's guilt, it would be inconsistent not to apply a similar rule of exclusion to "what is tantamount to coerced testimony by way of unconstitutional seizure of goods, papers, effects, documents, etc."[26] He states that the Fourth and Fifth Amendments are "complementary to, although not dependent upon, that of the other in its sphere of influence—the very least that together they assure in either sphere is that no man is to be convicted on unconstitutional evidence."[27]

It was surprising to see citations and references to the Fifth Amendment in a case that did not involve compelled testimony. And there was little reason to predict that Clark would rely on the Fifth Amendment to support imposing the exclusionary rule on the states. Prior to *Mapp*, Clark was known as a law-and-order justice. He had always opposed applying the criminal procedure provisions of the Bill of Rights to the states, and was a reliable supporter of Frankfurter's anti-incorporation position. In fact, three years after *Mapp*, Clark dissented when the Court ruled that the Self-Incrimination Clause applied to the states.[28]

---

is 'a death blow for federalism.' [Frankfurter] demanded reargument—which was voted down, five to four." *Id.* at 54. At the final conference, "Frankfurter sa[id] *Mapp* is the worst tragedy since *Dred Scott.*" *Id.* at 55.

[22] Yale Kamisar, *Does (Did) (Should) the Exclusionary Rule Rest on a "Principled Basis" Rather than an "Empirical Proposition"?*, 16 CREIGHTON L. REV. 565, 624 (1983) [hereinafter Kamisar, *Principled Basis*].

[23] *Id.* at 622–23; *see also* Larry Yackle, *The Burger Court and the Fourth Amendment*, 26 U. KAN. L. REV. 335, 418 (1978) (commenting that *Mapp* "ultimately fastened the exclusionary rule on the states in reliance upon *all* the rationales thus far proposed").

[24] *Mapp*, 367 U.S. at 646.

[25] *Id.* at 657 (footnote omitted).

[26] *Id.* at 656.

[27] *Id.* at 657.

[28] Malloy v. Hogan, 378 U.S. 1, 14–33 (1964) (Harlan, J., dissenting).

When Clark began writing *Mapp*, he avoided reliance on the Fifth Amendment. In an early draft, one of Clark's law clerks crossed out a quote from *Boyd* that stated that "any forcible and compulsory extortion of a man's own testimony or of his private papers to be used as evidence to convict him of crime or to forfeit his goods" was to be condemned.[29] In the margin, the law clerk wrote, "This raises [Fourth and Fifth] Amendments interrelation aspect which you want to avoid."[30] This quote was omitted from the April 22, 1961, draft that was sent only to Black.[31] Although the April 22 draft does quote *Boyd*, it omits any reference to the Fifth Amendment as a basis for excluding evidence obtained from an illegal search and seizure. Clark sent an additional draft to Black a few days later, again omitting any citation to or reliance on the Fifth Amendment.[32] The first references to the Fifth Amendment appear in an April 27 draft, which has on the top of the draft the handwritten inscription "TCC draft after OK from HLB."[33] This draft also contains the observation that illegally seized evidence is "tantamount to coerced testimony."[34] All of these references to the Fifth Amendment would appear in the final version of *Mapp*.

Clark's decision to include *Boyd* and the Fifth Amendment in his *Mapp* opinion was strategic: to obtain Black's vote. After the conference discussion of *Mapp*, four justices were ready to overrule *Wolf*, but a fifth vote was needed. Black expressed a willingness to overrule *Wolf* and make the exclusionary rule applicable to the states, but was unwilling to do it based on the Fourth Amendment alone.[35] Ever since his well-known dissent in 1947 in *Adamson v. California*,[36] Black had consistently taken the position that the Self-Incrimination Clause and the rest of the Bill of Rights were binding on the states. Two years later, in *Wolf*, Black concluded that the Fourth Amendment was enforceable against the states, but he did not read the Amendment to require the states to exclude evidence obtained from unreasonable searches and seizures. Eleven years later, in *Mapp*, Black had not wavered; he maintained that the Fourth Amendment did not constitutionally impose an exclusionary rule on the states. Black was willing, on the other hand, to use *Mapp* as the vehicle to make the Fifth Amendment binding on the states—his long-standing objective expressed in his *Adamson* dissent.

---

29 Tom Clark, Draft of *Mapp v. Ohio* 9 (undated), Clark Papers, Box A115.

30 *Id.*

31 Tom Clark, Draft of *Mapp v. Ohio* (Apr. 22, 1961), Clark Papers, Box A115. Dennis Dorin states that the April 22 and April 25 drafts "would go only to Black." Dennis D. Dorin, *Marshaling* Mapp*: Justice Tom Clark's Role in* Mapp v. Ohio*'s Extension of the Exclusionary Rule to State Searches and Seizures*, 52 CASE W. RES. L. REV. 401, 415 (2001); *see also* LONG, *supra* note 14, at 88 ("The first draft of Clark's *Mapp* opinion was sent only to Black on April 22, 1961.").

32 Tom Clark, Draft of *Mapp v. Ohio* (Apr. 25, 1961), Clark Papers, Box A115.

33 Tom Clark, Draft of *Mapp v. Ohio* 3, 14 (Apr. 27, 1961), Clark Papers, Box A115.

34 *Id.* at 14. On the back of the last page of this draft, Clark writes that "*Boyd* did something else it showed the inseparable connection between 4th and 5th—same as if compelled against 5th—the philosophy is same in relation to the conduct." *Id.* at 18.

35 *See* NEWMAN, *supra* note 21, at 555.

36 332 U.S. 46, 68 (1947) (Black, J., dissenting).

Sometime in early June of 1961, after Clark had circulated a printed draft of *Mapp* to the rest of the Court, Black sent Clark a typed draft of a concurring opinion that stated: "As I understand the Court's opinion in this case, we . . . now definitely hold that the Fifth Amendment's protection against enforced self-incrimination and the Fourth Amendment's protections against unreasonable searches and seizures have both been extended to the states through the Fourteenth Amendment."[37] On June 6, Clark replied that he did not intend for *Mapp* to apply the Fifth Amendment to the states. Clark explained to Black: "While I am personally satisfied that the Fourth Amendment, standing alone, is sufficient authority for a constitutional rule of exclusion, I drew upon the Fifth Amendment for analogous support of that conclusion, finding no reason in law to distinguish between coerced real evidence and coerced verbal evidence when both are secured prior to trial by methods which offend the Constitution."[38] Clark also reminded Black that "[t]estimonial compulsion at trial is, of course, not involved in this case."[39]

Two days later, and then again on June 12, Black circulated to the full Court printed drafts of his concurrence that omitted the previous reference to *Mapp* extending the Fifth Amendment to the states.[40] In place of that language, Black wrote that he understood *Mapp* as adopting *Boyd*'s "constitutional doctrine" that holds that the Fourth and Fifth Amendments "are of vital importance in our constitutional scheme of liberty and that both are entitled to a liberal rather than a niggardly interpretation."[41] Black closed his opinion by saying that he accepted the "*Boyd* doctrine as controlling in this state case" and that he was joining "the Court's judgment and opinion which are in accordance with that constitutional doctrine."[42] Black never retreated from his belief that the Fourth Amendment was an inadequate basis for enforcing the exclusionary rule against the states. During the deliberations in *Mapp*, however, Black convinced himself that a merger of the Fourth and Fifth Amendments—*Boyd*'s theory of exclusion—justified the same. Black agreed to provide the fifth vote to overrule *Mapp*'s conviction and make the exclusionary rule binding on the states. But, as future rulings would reveal, the price for Black's vote was to compromise *Mapp*'s constitutional status.

Clark's use of *Boyd* and the Fifth Amendment were not the only noteworthy features of *Mapp* that would eventually loom large when the Burger and Rehnquist Courts confronted the exclusionary rule. Another example was Clark's description of the federal exclusionary rule. He explains—using a "paraphrase" from *Wolf*—that *Weeks* was the first time the Court held the Fourth Amendment barred the use of evidence obtained

---

37 Hugo Black, Draft Opinion of *Mapp v. Ohio* 5–6 (June 6, 1961), Black Papers, Box 349.

38 Tom Clark, Letter to Hugo Black on *Mapp v. Ohio* (June 6, 1961), Clark Papers, Box A115 (citation omitted).

39 *Id.*

40 Hugo Black, Draft of Concurring Opinion in *Mapp v. Ohio* (June 8, 1961), Clark Papers, Box A115; Hugo Black, Draft of Concurring Opinion in *Mapp v. Ohio* (June 12, 1961), Clark Papers, Box A115.

41 Hugo Black, Draft of Concurring Opinion in *Mapp v. Ohio* (June 12, 1961), *supra* note 40, at 6.

42 *Id.*

from an illegal search and seizure. And since *Wolf*, according to Clark, the Court has "required of federal law officers a strict adherence to that command which this Court has held to be a clear, specific, and constitutionally required—even if *judicially implied*—deterrent safeguard without insistence upon which the Fourth Amendment would have been reduced to 'a form of words.'"[43]

Part II of *Mapp* sought to demonstrate that the trend among the states in rejecting the exclusionary rule had slowed, if not reversed, since *Wolf* was decided, and that certain "factual considerations" that *Wolf* had relied upon, such as the "silver platter" doctrine and strict requirements of standing to challenge the use of illegally acquired evidence, were no longer controlling on the constitutional question of whether the rule applied to the states.[44] Parts III and IV sought to prove that the exclusionary rule was "an essential part of the right to privacy."[45] Clark maintains that if the right of privacy was binding on the states, as *Wolf* ruled, it was incumbent upon the Court to also make the exclusionary rule binding on the states. "Since the Fourth Amendment's right of privacy has been declared enforceable against the States through the Due Process Clause of the Fourteenth, it is enforceable against them by the same sanction of exclusion as is used against the Federal Government."[46] Without exclusion, the right of privacy would be worthless: "To hold otherwise is to grant the right but in reality to withhold its privilege and enjoyment."[47]

Clark eliminated all doubt that *Mapp*'s holding rested on the Constitution when he wrote "all evidence obtained by searches and seizures in violation of the Constitution is, by that same authority, inadmissible in a state court."[48] He also devoted several lines to explaining why the exclusionary rule was "constitutionally necessary," "an essential ingredient of the right newly recognized by . . . *Wolf*," and why "*Wolf* could not consistently tolerate denial of its most important constitutional privilege." Ironically, Clark follows all of this by quoting *Elkins*—a case that deliberately avoided addressing the constitutional basis of the exclusion doctrine—to establish that the purpose of the rule "'is to deter—to compel respect for the constitutional guaranty in the only effectively available way—by removing the incentive to disregard it.'"[49]

After arguing in the previous sections of his opinion that the rule was compelled by the "logical dictate of prior cases," in the final section of *Mapp*, Clark endeavors to show why the rule "also makes very good sense."[50] Here, Clark pens the well-known line

---

[43] Mapp v. Ohio, 367 U.S. 643, 648 (1961) (emphasis added) (quoting Silverthorne Lumber Co. v. United States, 251 U.S. 385, 392 (1920).

[44] *Id.* at 653.

[45] *Id.* at 656.

[46] *Id.*

[47] *Id.*

[48] *Id.* at 655.

[49] *Id.* at 655–56 (quoting Elkins v. United States, 364 U.S. 206, 217 (1960)).

[50] *Id.* at 657.

that "[t]here is no war between the Constitution and common sense."[51] In response to Cardozo's famous epigram that "'[t]he criminal is to go free because the constable has blundered,'" Clark retorts that "the imperative of judicial integrity" must be considered as well.[52] Without explaining in detail why admitting evidence obtained from illegal searches would undermine the integrity of judges or the judicial process, Clark simply offers that if the criminal must go free, "it is the law that sets him free."[53] But Clark was unwilling to assume that the exclusionary rule actually "fetters law enforcement."[54] He notes that the federal courts and federal law enforcement agencies like the Federal Bureau of Investigation have lived with the rule for nearly half a century without any untoward consequences.[55] And he closes with the view that the rule grants to the citizen "no more than that which the Constitution guarantees him, to the police officer no less than that to which honest law enforcement is entitled, and, to the courts, that judicial integrity so necessary in the true administration of justice."[56]

The Problems with Mapp v. Ohio

Mapp was an easy target for its critics. To begin with, although Clark unambiguously states that the exclusionary rule announced in *Weeks* "is of constitutional origin,"[57] a reader of *Mapp* might be hard pressed to explain why. Clark begins his constitutional analysis by referencing *Boyd*, emphasizing the "'the intimate relation'" between the Fourth and Fifth Amendments in protecting civil liberties and stating that "together" the amendments assure that no person is to be convicted on unconstitutional evidence. In doing so, Clark fosters the impression that the exclusionary rule is compelled either by a linkage of the Fourth and Fifth Amendments or because evidence obtained from an illegal search is the constitutional equivalent of coerced testimony.

The appearance and prominence of *Boyd* and the Fifth Amendment, particularly in a case that involved no compelled self-incrimination, legitimately begs the question, why are Fifth Amendment concerns being interjected into a Fourth Amendment case? Certainly the reasoning of *Weeks* did not compel Clark to utilize *Boyd*. *Weeks*, like *Mapp*, was a straight Fourth Amendment case that ignored the Fifth Amendment claim raised by Weeks when it ruled that exclusion was constitutionally required when federal officers violate the Fourth Amendment. Moreover, by the time that *Mapp* was decided, the validity of *Boyd*'s linking the Fourth and Fifth Amendments as a basis for exclusion had been subjected to harsh criticism, if not wholly rejected. The typical illegal search

[51] *Id.*
[52] *Id.* at 659.
[53] *Id.*
[54] *Id.*
[55] *Id.* at 659–60.
[56] *Id.* at 660.
[57] *Id.* at 649.

and seizure produces physical evidence—narcotics, contraband, or weapons—that is not protected by the Self-Incrimination Clause. That clause only protects against "testimonial compulsion." In other words, the Fifth Amendment only bars evidence compelled from the mind of the suspect. While the facts in *Boyd* did raise a Fifth Amendment issue, and thus was clearly distinguishable from *Mapp*, Clark would not try to differentiate the cases.[58] In fact, he was determined to utilize *Boyd*; his use of *Boyd* was calculated to secure Black's vote.[59]

Another aspect of *Mapp* that would undermine the *Weeks-Silverthorne Lumber* view of exclusion were paradoxical statements by Clark that were later used by conservative members of the Burger and Rehnquist Courts to bolster their arguments that the exclusionary rule was not mandated by the Constitution. The first such statement was Clark's observation that the rule was "a clear, specific, and constitutionally required—even if judicially implied—deterrent safeguard without insistence upon which the Fourth Amendment would have been reduced to 'a form of words.'"[60] Legally speaking, this passage "is incorrigibly ambiguous, mixing in about equal portions vague constitutional references, deterrence rationale, and empirical generalization."[61] Equally important, the assertion that the rule is a "constitutionally required—even if *judicially implied*—deterrent safeguard" suggested that Clark had not closely scrutinized the language of rulings adverse to *Mapp*. The notion that exclusion of unlawfully obtained evidence was a judicially implied remedy designed to deter illegal searches, and not a command of the Constitution, did not come from *Weeks* or *Silverthorne Lumber*. Rather, Black first suggested this position in *Wallace & Tiernan Co.*[62] Two months later, in *Wolf*, Frankfurter

---

[58] Dorin, *supra* note 31, at 418 ("[Clark] would not attempt to ignore or distinguish *Boyd*. Nor would he dream of arguing that the Fourth and Fifth Amendments together comprised a doctrinal basis for an extension of the exclusion doctrine to the states.").

[59] *Id.* (describing how Clark attempted to "employ just enough of *Boyd*'s language to tempt Black" into joining his opinion). Clark's determined use of *Boyd* was somewhat ironic. His law clerks had warned him about the implications of using *Boyd*'s merger of the Fourth and Fifth Amendments. "[I]t could be inferred that if evidence were not seized in violation of the Fifth Amendment, as it was not in the *Mapp* case, it would be admissible." *Id.* Finally, because of the need to secure Black's vote, which required invocation of *Boyd* and the Fifth Amendment, Clark could not rely on the analytical model contained in his unpublished draft opinion in *Irvine*, which focused solely on *Weeks* and the Fourth Amendment.

[60] *Mapp*, 367 U.S. at 648 (quoting Silverthorne Lumber Co. v. United States, 251 U.S. 385, 392 (1920)).

[61] Thomas S. Schrock & Robert C. Welsh, *Up from* Calandra*: The Exclusionary Rule as a Constitutional Requirement*, 59 MINN. L. REV. 251, 319 (1974). The authors rightly noted that Clark's statement "does not make clear whether the exclusionary rule is constitutionally required as such or is required only because it is a deterrent. Nor does he make clear whether, if it is constitutionally required as a deterrent, it is required because of its deterrent *intention*, or because it actually *works* as a deterrent. If the exclusionary rule is constitutionally mandated as, but only as, an *actual* deterrent, Justice Clark does not vouchsafe the constitutional theory that would make a requirement of the fourth amendment depend on this kind of contingency." *Id.*

[62] United States v. Wallace & Tiernan Co., 336 U.S. 793, 796 (1949) ("[The exclusionary rule] is an extraordinary sanction, judicially imposed, to limit searches and seizures to those conducted in strict compliance with the commands of the Fourth Amendment.").

wrote that *Week*'s exclusionary rule "was not derived from the explicit requirements of the Fourth Amendment," but instead was "a matter of judicial implication."[63] And whereas neither *Weeks* nor *Silverthorne Lumber* ever mentions deterrence as a basis for the rule, *Wolf* asserts that deterrence is the only legitimate basis for exclusion.[64]

In the contentious setting of the Court's exclusionary rule cases, the phrase "judicially implied," like the expression "judicially imposed" or "judicially created," carried a negative connotation. Such phrases arose in opinions that concluded the Court lacked a constitutional basis for a particular ruling.[65] Similarly, prior to *Mapp*, opponents of the exclusionary rule, like Frankfurter and Black, questioned the constitutional legitimacy of the rule, because the text of the Fourth Amendment did not require exclusion. Of course, this criticism of the exclusionary rule conflicted with Frankfurter's own critique of a textual approach to constitutional decision making,[66] and Black's subsequent admission that *Boyd*'s exclusionary doctrine was "not required by the express language of the Constitution strictly construed."[67] More important, this complaint about *Weeks* and *Mapp* ignores the fact that an overwhelming majority of constitutional rulings announced by the Court are a matter of judicial implication, including one of the most famous, *Marbury v. Madison*, which was the first time the Court invalidated an act of Congress. *Marbury* expressly embraced the power to review and invalidate legislative acts, a power not found in the text of the Constitution.[68]

---

63 Wolf v. Colorado, 338 U.S. 25, 28 (1949).

64 *Id.* at 31–32.

65 *See* United States v. Rabinowitz, 339 U.S. 56, 66–67 (1950) (Black, J., dissenting); *Wallace & Tiernan Co.*, 336 U.S. at 796; *Wolf*, 338 U.S. at 39–40 (Black, J., concurring).

66 *See* SCHWARTZ, *supra* note 21, at 46 ("To Frankfurter, Black's absolutist approach had no legitimate place in constitutional jurisprudence."). In a letter to Warren in 1957, Frankfurter wrote: "We get into a lot of trouble by talking about the plain and unequivocal language of the First Amendment in its provision about 'abridging the freedom of speech.' . . . The Constitution after all is not a verbal marionette in which one takes the words with literalness." *Id.* (quoting Felix Frankfurter, Letter to Earl Warren (May 27, 1957), John Marshall Harlan Papers, Mudd Manuscript Library, Princeton University).

67 Mapp v. Ohio, 367 U.S. 643, 662 (1961) (Black, J., concurring); *see also* Schmerber v. California, 384 U.S. 757, 776 (1966) (Black, J., dissenting) (conceding that *Boyd*'s interpretation "was not completely supported by the literal language of the Fifth Amendment").

68 Marbury v. Madison, 5 U.S. (1 Cranch) 137 (1803); *see* Kamisar, *Principled Basis*, *supra* note 22, at 581–89 (explaining that much of constitutional law does not derive from the text of the Constitution, but is instead judge-made law); *see also*, Schrock & Welsh, *supra* note 61, at 350, 351 n.251 (arguing that "exclusionary rule" is just a term signifying that judges "practice constitutionalism and show their fidelity to the rule of law by observing the fourth amendment," and that those who oppose exclusion because the text of the Fourth Amendment omits such a remedy assume "the absurdity that conduct challenged under *any* clause of the Constitution must be impervious to judicial review unless there is a proviso attached to that clause authorizing the Court to invalidate or nullify governmental conduct in violation of it"). One might say that *Marbury* itself supports imposition of the exclusionary rule because it established the proposition that the judiciary should provide "a remedy for the violation of a vested legal right." *See* William Michael Treanor, *The Story of* Marbury v. Madison: *Judicial Authority and Political Struggle*, *in* FEDERAL COURTS STORIES 29, 56 (Vicki C. Jackson & Judith Resnik eds., 2010) (quoting *Marbury*, 5 U.S. at 163).

Strictly speaking, the text of the Fourth Amendment says nothing positive or negative about exclusion or the award of money damages as a consequence for its violation. Even Wigmore, who opposed exclusion at the time *Weeks* was announced, acknowledged that his preferred remedies for Fourth Amendment violations—a civil action by the citizen whose rights were violated and criminal contempt against the offending officer—had to be inferred from the text of the amendment.[69] In fact, because the text of the amendment has nothing to say about the consequences of an unreasonable search or seizure, the Frankfurter-Black interpretation that permits the use of illegally obtained evidence in criminal prosecutions and leaves victims of illegal police intrusions to other remedies is "no less 'creative' or 'judge-made' than the view of the *Weeks* Court."[70]

Like most provisions in the Bill of Rights, the text of the Fourth Amendment provides a right without specifying *any* remedy. The Constitution does not tell judges how these rights should be enforced or "how violations should be remedied."[71] Interestingly, conservative critics of the exclusionary rule and *Mapp* do not describe Holmes's holding in *Silverthorne Lumber* that derivative evidence of a Fourth Amendment violation must be excluded as a judicially created remedy or judge-made law. Holmes's ruling was based on the premise that the Framers did not intend the Fourth Amendment to be a dead letter—as Holmes put it—"a form of words."[72] If Holmes was right, if the Framers did not intend for the Fourth Amendment to be reduced to a form of words, they intended for the judiciary to provide or infer a remedy when the right was violated. As James Madison told the First Congress on June 8, 1789:

> If [the Bill of Rights] are incorporated into the Constitution, independent tribunals of justice will consider themselves in a peculiar manner the guardians of those rights; they will be an impenetrable bulwark against every assumption of power in the Legislative or Executive; they will be naturally led to resist every encroachment upon rights expressly stipulated for in the Constitution by the declaration of rights.[73]

---

[69] John H. Wigmore, *Using Evidence Obtained By Illegal Search And Seizure*, 8 A.B.A. J. 479, 481 (1922). Wigmore argued that the "object of the amendment was to protect the citizen from domestic disturbance by the disorderly intrusion of irresponsible administrative officials. It expressly forbids such official misconduct, and it *implies* both a civil action by the citizen thus disturbed and a process of criminal contempt against the offending officials." *Id.* (emphasis added). Interestingly, Wigmore rejected the claim made by modern critics of the exclusionary rule who insist that *Weeks* only recognized a right to have papers and property returned to the victim of an unreasonable search. According to Wigmore, "no such consequence is implied in the Fourth Amendment." *Id.*

[70] Kamisar, *Principled Basis*, *supra* note 22, at 585.

[71] Stewart, *supra* note 16, at 1383.

[72] Silverthorne Lumber Co. v. United States, 251 U.S. 385, 392 (1920).

[73] 1 Annals of Cong. 439 (1789).

The best that can be said about Clark's description of the exclusionary rule as a "constitutionally required—even if judicially implied—deterrent safeguard" is that it is an awkward way of saying what Holmes said in *Silverthorne Lumber*.

The Fourth Amendment's silence concerning remedies naturally prompts the question, "*what* remedy should the judiciary adopt for violations?" Opponents of exclusion are quick to assert that the remedy for an unreasonable search or seizure is the remedy available during the Framing era: a civil trespass lawsuit against the officer who committed the tort.[74] But under that remedy, if a jury found that an officer conducted an unlawful search or seizure, the officer was liable, and the jury had the discretion to award large damages.[75] Although this remedy was used in the Framing era, the Warren Court eliminated that option in *Pierson v. Ray* when it ruled that police officers have qualified immunity under the federal civil rights statute, 42 U.S.C. § 1983, when they act in good faith and with probable cause when making an arrest under a state law they mistakenly believe is valid.[76]

Professor Al Alschuler has observed that the Warren Court approved qualified immunity for police officers, "not because §1983 incorporated a well understood historical practice, but because qualified immunity seemed like a good idea at the time."[77] Warren wrote in *Pierson*: "A policeman's lot is not so unhappy that he must choose between being charged with dereliction of duty if he does not arrest when he has probable cause, and being mulcted in damages if he does."[78] As Alschuler notes, those who favor an "originalist" interpretation of the Constitution or who seek to "restore the remedial regime favored by the Framers of the Fourth Amendment" would not have approved the result in *Pierson*.[79] Yet, restrictions on the scope of §1983 lawsuits and the "whole-cloth invention of qualified immunity for police officers has met with the whole-hearted approval [of the conservative justices] of the Burger, Rehnquist, and Roberts Courts."[80] Thus, if

---

[74] *See, e.g.*, Akhil Reed Amar, *Fourth Amendment First Principles*, 107 Harv. L. Rev. 757, 786–87 (1994); Bradford P. Wilson, *The Fourth Amendment as More Than a Form of Words: The View from the Founding*, *in* The Bill of Rights: Original Meaning and Current Understanding 151, 153–58 (Eugene W. Hickok, Jr. ed., 1991).

[75] For a fuller description of Framing-era arrest and search standards, see Thomas Y. Davies, *How the Post-Framing Adoption of the Bare-Probable-Cause Standard Drastically Expanded Government Arrest and Search Power*, Law & Contemp. Probs., Summer 2010, at 1, 8–24.

[76] Pierson v. Ray, 386 U.S. 547 (1967).

[77] Albert W. Alschuler, Herring v. United States*: A Minnow or a Shark?*, 7 Ohio St. J. Crim. L. 463, 506 (2009) [hereinafter Alschuler, *A Minnow or a Shark?*].

[78] *Pierson*, 386 U.S. at 555.

[79] Alschuler, *A Minnow or a Shark?*, *supra* note 77, at 506.

[80] *Id.* In another article, Professor Alschuler explains that restoring to the victims of unconstitutional searches and seizures the type of damages lawsuit available during the Framing era "would bring much valuable law enforcement to a halt." Albert W. Alschuler, *The Exclusionary Rule and Causation:* Hudson v. Michigan *and Its Ancestors*, 93 Iowa L. Rev. 1741, 1771 (2008) [hereinafter Alschuler, *Causation*]. That type of damages action "could lead officers to play it safer than they should. As long as an [arrest or search] conceivably might be held illegal, an officer faced with the prospect of damage liability would have little to gain and much to lose by making it." *Id.* at 1771–72; *see also* William J. Stuntz, *The Virtues and Vices of the*

the implied remedy for Fourth Amendment violations is not to be the one utilized in the eighteenth century, what other remedy should the Court impose? In *Mapp*, Clark concluded that the best option, in fact, the only option, was the implied remedy of exclusion. Why exclusion? Because the experience of states operating without a suppression remedy demonstrated that "other remedies have been worthless and futile."[81]

In any event, Clark's statement in *Mapp* that the rule is constitutionally required as a judicially created deterrent safeguard was a concession that the rule was not based on the text of the Constitution. This admission bolstered opponents' claims that *Mapp* was not justified by a strict interpretation of the Constitution, and that it did not announce a personal constitutional right of exclusion. Instead, according to critics of the rule, the exclusionary rule was, at best, a judicially imposed remedy to deter unlawful behavior, or, at worst, judicial "legislation."

While Clark's characterization of the exclusionary rule as "judicially implied" certainly did not strengthen the rule's constitutional status, his explanation of the rule's purpose, "'to deter—to compel respect for the constitutional guaranty in the only effectively available way—by removing the incentive to disregard it,'"[82] would be most damaging to *Mapp*'s constitutional standing. Interestingly, Clark inserted this statement late in the drafting process of *Mapp*.[83] Peculiarly situated after Clark's explanation that, *inter alia*, the rule was "an essential part of the right to privacy" and that exclusion was the "most important constitutional privilege" of the right of privacy,[84] this statement was truly puzzling. On its face, the statement added nothing to *Mapp*'s holding; not only was it obiter dicta, it was taken from a case, *Elkins v. United States*,[85] which expressly avoided discussing the constitutional basis of the exclusionary rule. Further, this statement was unnecessary to link *Mapp* with the constitutional heritage of *Weeks* and its progeny. Most important, there was "no suggestion in *Weeks* or the search and seizure cases decided during the next thirty-five years that the exclusionary rule's *survival* depended on proof that it was significantly affecting police behavior."[86]

Exclusionary Rule, 20 HARV. J.L. & PUB. POL'Y 443, 445 (1997) (explaining that damages lawsuits against officers may overdeter police: "If an officer faces serious loss whenever he makes a bad arrest, he will make fewer bad arrests, but also many fewer good ones. The same is true, only more so, if the law threatens the officer with jail for constitutional violations.").

81 Mapp v. Ohio, 367 U.S. 643, 652 (1961); *see* Kamisar, *Principled Basis*, *supra* note 22, at 612 & n.276 (noting that Fourth Amendment abuse was "widespread" prior to *Mapp v. Ohio*); *id.* at 617 (pointing to the "woeful inadequac[ies] of tort remedies, criminal prosecutions and internal police discipline as checks on police misconduct").

82 *Mapp*, 367 U.S. at 656 (quoting Elkins v. United States, 364 U.S. 206, 217 (1960).

83 *See* Dorin, *supra* note 31, at 431 (explaining that the writing of *Mapp* had undergone several drafts, and that by the first week of June 1961, Clark's opinion would go through two more circulations to the Court; it was during those circulations that Clark added the "statement that the main purpose of exclusion was the deterrence of illegal police actions").

84 *Mapp*, 367 U.S. at 656.

85 364 U.S. 206, 217 (1960).

86 Kamisar, *First Shot Fired*, *supra* note 10, at 55.

Clark's statement about deterrence was designed to counter *Wolf*'s earlier claim that suppression was not an effective deterrent against illegal searches. To be sure, Clark merely said the "purpose" of exclusion was to deter unlawful searches and seizures; he never said that deterrence is the sole or only purpose for exclusion. Yet, the seed was planted. By trying to defeat Frankfurter with the same argument Frankfurter had wielded against exclusion, Clark constructed the exclusionary rule's eventual demise. Asserting that suppression deters future misconduct by the police is a difficult task because, as the Court recognized in *Elkins*, the proponent of exclusion has to prove a negative or non-event.[87]

Moreover, describing the rule as a deterrent was a strategic and linguistic mistake. As many scholars would later explain, the exclusionary rule does not and never will "deter" police unlawful behavior in the same way that the criminal law deters illegal behavior by civilians. Demonstratively, "[t]he rule does not inflict a 'punishment' on police who violated the fourth amendment; exclusion of the evidence does not leave the police in a worse position than if they had never violated the Constitution in the first place."[88] Rather than punish or deter police, the point of the exclusionary rule is to influence police conduct. The rule provides a "disincentive"—a mechanism of "eliminating significant incentives for making illegal searches, at least where the police contemplate prosecution and conviction."[89]

What Clark should have said in *Mapp* was that without the exclusionary rule, there would be no Fourth Amendment law. In the absence of suppression, police would continue to perform unconstitutional searches and seizures as they did in *Stefanelli*, *Rochin*, *Irvine*, and in other nonexclusion states. Although imposing the exclusionary rule on the states would not guarantee the end of police misconduct, without the rule, as the facts in *Mapp* dramatically demonstrated, police had little to lose and much to gain by conducting an illegal search. The aftermath of *Mapp* clearly indicates that imposition of the rule did have a positive impact on state police officials.[90] And if exclusion is necessary to prevent the Fourth Amendment from becoming a dead letter because it is the only effective remedy, a judge could certainly conclude that exclusion is necessary for that reason as well. But it was a fatal error to suggest that the constitutional justification for the exclusionary rule turned on proof that the rule would deter illegal searches. Once *Mapp* determined that the Constitution demands exclusion and reversal of a criminal conviction, little more needed to be said about the "purpose" for the Court's result. As Holmes put it in *Silverthorne Lumber*: "The essence of a provision forbidding the acquisition of

---

[87] *Elkins*, 364 U.S. at 218; *see also* Arval A. Morris, *The Exclusionary Rule, Deterrence and Posner's Economic Analysis of Law*, 57 WASH. L. REV. 647, 653 (1982) ("Police compliance with the exclusionary rule produces a non-event which is not directly observable—it consists of *not* conducting an illegal search.").

[88] Kamisar, *Principled Basis*, *supra* note 22, at 597 n.204; *see also* Anthony G. Amsterdam, *Perspectives on the Fourth Amendment*, 58 MINN. L. REV. 349, 431–32 (1974).

[89] Kamisar, *Principled Basis*, *supra* note 22, at 597 n.204.

[90] 1 WAYNE R. LAFAVE, SEARCH AND SEIZURE: A TREATISE ON THE FOURTH AMENDMENT § 1.2(b), at 33-34 (4th ed. 2004); Donald Dripps, *Living with* Leon, 95 YALE L.J. 906, 927–28 (1986); Kamisar, *Principled Basis*, *supra* note 22, at 618–20.

evidence in a certain way is that . . . evidence so acquired shall not be used before the Court."[91] Holmes did not identify a deterrent or any other "purpose" for exclusion;[92] it was enough that the Constitution itself demanded the result. Exclusion was a constitutional right of the defendant. But Clark's opinion did not have the focus or clarity of *Silverthorne Lumber*, and the Burger and Rehnquist Courts would use his description on the purpose of the rule as a bludgeon to destroy the constitutional foundation of *Mapp*.

Clark's final basis for the exclusionary rule was "'the imperative of judicial integrity.'"[93] Like the description of the rule's purpose, this statement on judicial integrity came from Stewart's opinion in *Elkins*. But the concept of judicial integrity as a basis for exclusion had been previously articulated in the dissents of Brandeis and Holmes in *Olmstead*.[94] In *Mapp*, Clark maintained that the need for judicial integrity was a counterweight to the concern that the exclusionary rule frees guilty persons because of mistakes by police officers. Clark wrote that the use of illegally obtained evidence in a criminal prosecution—what he called an "ignoble shortcut to conviction"—undermines the citizenry's faith in their government and "tends to destroy the entire system of constitutional restraints on which the liberties of the people rest."[95]

There are myriad reasons why the conservative justices of the Burger and Rehnquist Courts would reject judicial integrity as justification for the exclusionary rule. While Clark could not be expected to provide a meticulous theoretical framework for this concept in *Mapp*, one explanation for the judicial integrity rationale is that judges should "avoid the taint of partnership in official lawlessness and of assuring the people—all potential victims of unlawful government conduct—that the government would not profit from its lawless behavior, thus minimizing the risk of seriously undermining popular trust in government."[96] Put simply, the preservation of judicial integrity—indeed, the

---

[91] Silverthorne Lumber Co. v. United States, 251 U.S. 385, 392 (1920).

[92] *Cf.* Schrock & Welsh, *supra* note 61, at 320 n.167 (noting that *Silverthorne Lumber* "leaves absolutely no doubt about Holmes's meaning," and there is "no mention in [*Silverthorne Lumber*] of deterrence of executive misconduct").

[93] Mapp v. Ohio, 367 U.S. 643, 659 (1961) (quoting Elkins v. United States, 364 U.S. 206, 222 (1960)).

[94] *See* Olmstead v. United States, 277 U.S. 438, 470 (1928) (Holmes, J., dissenting) ("We have to choose, and for my part I think it a less evil that some criminals should escape than that the Government should play an ignoble part."); *id.* at 484–85 (Brandeis, J., dissenting) ("But the objection that the plaintiff comes with unclean hands will be taken by the court itself. . . . The court protects itself." (footnote omitted)). Because the *Olmstead* Court did not find a violation of the Constitution in that case, the dissents of Holmes and Brandeis were not "predicated on a constitutional exclusionary right, and therefore had to be predicated on judicial integrity or some other supervisory power rationale standing alone. Brandeis and Holmes perceived such a necessity because they were on the losing side of a controversy over whether the fourth amendment applied at all to wiretapping. As they understood the effect of their defeat on the coverage point, it precluded them from making constitutional arguments for exclusion because the *Olmstead* majority had held that there was no constitutional violation in the procurement." Schrock & Welsh, *supra* note 61, at 282 (footnote omitted).

[95] *Mapp*, 367 U.S. at 660.

[96] United States v. Calandra, 414 U.S. 338, 357 (1974) (Brennan, J., dissenting).

"preservation of legality"—ought to be sufficient reason for excluding illegally acquired evidence.[97] But this is not a universal truth. The conservative justices of the Burger and Rehnquist Courts could reasonably determine that allowing the admission of reliable evidence, highly probative of a defendant's guilt, does not stain the integrity of judges or impugn the administration of the criminal justice system. Arguably, admitting such evidence is exactly what judges should be doing in criminal trials because the admission of such evidence promotes the ultimate goal of the system of identifying guilty individuals. Indeed, this was the view offered by a federal appellate judge named Warren Burger in 1964 when he observed that the exclusionary rule "unhappily brings to the public gaze a spectacle repugnant to all decent people—the frustration of justice."[98]

There is another aspect of Clark's discussion of judicial integrity that led to the dismantling of the exclusionary rule. By asserting that the need for judicial integrity was "another consideration" in analyzing the rule's utility,[99] Clark conceivably rendered the judicial integrity rationale just another factor to weigh—like the concern over releasing guilty criminals—in a judicial balancing process for determining the applicability of the rule in a given situation. In fairness to Clark, a neutral reading of *Mapp* would not conclude that Clark had employed such a balancing model to reach the judgment that the exclusionary rule was binding on the states. But the conservative justices of the Burger and Rehnquist Courts rarely, if ever, read *Mapp* dispassionately. They interpreted *Mapp* to match their own views about the Fourth Amendment and exclusion. If judicial integrity was just one of many factors to be weighed in an ad hoc balancing formula for determining the exclusionary rule's expediency, the conservative justices had more than enough leeway to ignore or discount this factor when deciding future exclusionary rule cases.

When read as a whole, and considered in conjunction with the controversy generated by the cases from *Wolf* to *Eaton*, *Mapp* sent an unmistakable signal: the Fourth Amendment was now actually binding on the states, and the Court was ready to reverse state convictions based on evidence obtained from unreasonable searches and seizures. But the signal sent by *Mapp* would be relatively fleeting. By the mid-1970s, a majority of the Burger Court adopted a very different view of the case. *Mapp*'s holding that the exclusionary rule was constitutionally compelled was transformed to the considerably weaker proposition that the rule is a not a constitutional right of the defendant, but rather a judicially created remedy designed to deter unreasonable searches and seizures by police officers. And whether the rule would apply in a given situation would turn on an ad hoc balancing formula.

* * *

---

97 J. Patrick Green, Stone v. Powell*: The Hermeneutics of the Burger Court*, 10 CREIGHTON L. REV. 655, 659 n.20 (1977).

98 Warren E. Burger, *Who Will Watch the Watchman?*, 14 AM. U. L. REV. 1, 12 (1964).

99 *Mapp*, 367 U.S. at 659.

Before finishing our discussion of *Mapp*, Black's influence on the case must be highlighted. Bernard Schwartz once wrote that "if impact on the law is a hallmark of the outstanding judge, few occupants of the bench have been more outstanding than Black."[100] Black's impact on *Mapp* was indisputable and significant. Without Black's vote, there would not have been a majority to overrule *Wolf*'s holding that the exclusionary rule was not binding on the states. Moreover, Clark injected *Boyd* and the Fifth Amendment into *Mapp* in order to secure Black's vote. No other justice in the *Mapp* majority thought exclusion should rest upon a merger of the Fourth and Fifth Amendments. Only Black advocated this position. In the long run, however, Black's influence on Clark contributed to the demise of *Mapp*.

It is more than a little ironic that Black would control the outcome in what many consider to be the most important Fourth Amendment case decided by the Court. As a general matter, Black had an extremely narrow view of the Fourth Amendment.[101] And while his position on the exclusionary rule was unpredictable,[102] he never endorsed the view that the Fourth Amendment itself required exclusion of evidence obtained from an unreasonable search and seizure. In *Wolf*, Frankfurter refused to construe the Fourteenth Amendment's Due Process Clause to make exclusion binding on the states because of federalism concerns. But he insisted that the Court was "stoutly adher[ing] to" *Weeks*'s exclusionary rule in federal cases.[103] Black, on the other hand, bluntly stated that "the federal exclusionary rule is not a command of the Fourth Amendment but is a judicially created rule of evidence which Congress might negate."[104]

Three years later, Black reiterated his view that the federal exclusion doctrine "is not a constitutional command, but rather an evidentiary policy adopted by this Court in the exercise of its supervisory powers over federal courts."[105] Thus, continued application of the rule, Black maintained, "presents no more than a question of what is wise judicial policy."[106] No wonder Frankfurter told Warren in a 1957 letter that there was "a deep cleavage of view regarding the Fourth Amendment between Black and myself."

---

100 Schwartz, *supra* note 21, at 48.

101 Jacob W. Landynski, *In Search of Justice Black's Fourth Amendment*, 45 Fordham L. Rev. 453, 454 (1976) ("Black as a rule construed the fourth amendment in as restrictive a manner as any other justice in the modern history of the Court."); *see also* Newman, *supra* note 21, at 372 (quoting one of Black's former law clerks that Black's concurring opinion in *Wolf* "'may well be the most restrictive interpretation of the Fourth Amendment by any Justice in the Court's history'").

102 Landynski, *supra* note 101, at 478 (explaining that during his time on the Court, "Black had taken nearly every possible position on the [exclusionary] rule's derivation: that it was required by the fifth amendment; that it was required by the fourth and fifth amendments in combination; or conversely, that it was not required at all by the Constitution. Every position, that is, except that most consonant with his general approach to search and seizure interpretation: that the rule is required, or at any rate authorized, by the fourth amendment alone").

103 Wolf v. Colorado, 338 U.S. 25, 28 (1949).

104 *Id.* at 39–40 (Black, J., concurring).

105 United States v. Rabinowitz, 339 U.S. 56, 67 (1950) (Black, J., dissenting).

106 *Id.*

Frankfurter thought that Black was hostile to *Silverthorne Lumber* and wanted to overrule it, and that Black viewed *Weeks* merely as a "judicially created rule of evidence." By contrast, Frankfurter told Warren that he believed that "*Silverthorne* and *Weeks* are among the most important decisions of this Court in the domain of civil liberties."[107]

In the 1940s, Black opposed constitutional status for the exclusionary rule—in both federal and state cases—because the Constitution did not explicitly provide for suppressing evidence unlawfully obtained. In *Mapp*, he repeated his position that "the Fourth Amendment, standing alone" does not justify exclusion, because it does not "contain any provision expressly precluding" the use of illegally seized evidence.[108] Nevertheless, Black determined that "a constitutional basis emerges which not only justifies but actually requires the exclusionary rule."[109]

What provision in the Constitution *actually requires* the exclusionary rule? Black turned to the legal theory that supported *Boyd*'s holding. He explained that the "close interrelationship between the Fourth and Fifth Amendments" required exclusion.[110] Of course, in *Wolf*, Black ignored *Boyd* and the "close interrelationship" between the Amendments. And in *Mapp* he acknowledged that *Boyd*'s exclusion doctrine was "not required by the express language of the Constitution strictly construed."[111] Ultimately, Black believed that exclusion was mandated by the Constitution because the Bill of Rights "should be liberally construed."[112]

It is hard to defend Black's legal analysis in *Mapp*. His use of *Boyd* to impose exclusion on the states is even less convincing than is Clark's use of *Boyd*. Although Black did not directly acknowledge it, the foundation of his *Mapp* opinion was the Fifth Amendment's Self-Incrimination Clause. But the Fifth Amendment was irrelevant in *Mapp*. While the defendants in *Boyd* possessed a viable self-incrimination claim, the facts in *Mapp* in no way involved compelled testimony of the defendant. Similarly, Black's conclusion that the "close interrelationship" between the Fourth and Fifth Amendments demands exclusion

---

107 Felix Frankfurter, Letter to Earl Warren 2 (Apr. 19, 1957), Frankfurter Papers, Box 92.

108 Mapp v. Ohio, 367 U.S. 643, 661 (1961) (Black, J., concurring).

109 *Id.* at 662.

110 *Id.*

111 *Id.*

112 *Id.* at 663 (quoting Boyd v. United States, 116 U.S. 616, 635 (1886)); *see also* One 1958 Plymouth Sedan v. Pennsylvania, 380 U.S. 693, 704–05 (1965) (Black, J., concurring). In *Plymouth Sedan*, Black explained the basis for his vote in *Mapp* was *not* grounded on the text of the Constitution, but instead on an "interpretive principle":

> It was because of the Court's reliance on the *Boyd* doctrine—which held that the Fourth and Fifth Amendments *together* barred use of unreasonably seized evidence—that I joined the Court's opinion in *Mapp*. . . . I recognize that this interpretation was reached in *Boyd* on the principle that "constitutional provisions for the security of person and property should be liberally construed." . . . But that interpretive principle, I think, is a desirable one if our Constitution is to be given its proper place in our Government.

Id. (quoting *Boyd*, 116 U.S. at 635).

is unpersuasive. This theory suggests that a successful suppression motion requires proof of both an unreasonable search or seizure *and* coerced testimony. Therefore, the "close interrelationship" theory appears inapplicable to typical unlawful search or seizure cases like *Mapp* where there is no compelled incrimination. Despite this discrepancy, Black does not even attempt to explain why the facts in *Mapp* involved a nexus or "interrelationship" between the Fourth and Fifth Amendments.

Finally, Black seems almost fickle in his methodology for determining whether the exclusionary rule merits constitutional standing. In *Wolf*, he states that the Fourth Amendment provides no textual support for the rule, and in *Mapp* he makes the rule binding on the states while acknowledging that the text of the Constitution, strictly construed, does not support this result. Six years later in a case challenging New York's wiretap statute, Black says the rule rests on the supervisory power of the Court over the lower federal courts.[113] This type of on-and-off textualism is hardly a principled approach to deciding constitutional issues. Someone who reads Black's opinion in *Mapp* might wonder "why Black was satisfied in basing the exclusionary rule on a 'liberal' rendering of the fifth amendment while requiring nothing less than an 'express' provision in order to locate the rule in the fourth amendment; why, in short, the fifth amendment, liberally construed, 'requires' the exclusionary rule, while the fourth amendment, in the absence of an express provision, does not even 'justify' it."[114]

In the final analysis, Black's legal reasoning in *Mapp* is unconvincing and mistaken.[115] His insistence on interjecting the Fifth Amendment into a case that involved no testimonial compulsion undermined the legal standing of *Mapp* in two ways. First, in order to secure Black's vote and agreement to join the majority's opinion, Clark appeared to make the Fifth Amendment a noteworthy, if not an essential, part of *Mapp*'s holding. Critics of the exclusionary rule would later point to Clark's reliance on the Fifth Amendment as a reason to discount the legal analysis in *Mapp*. Second, it was evident that the premise of Black's opinion in *Mapp* rested on the Fifth Amendment.[116] Clark's opinion in *Mapp*,

---

113 Berger v. New York, 388 U.S. 41, 76 (1967) (Black, J., dissenting).

114 Landynski, *supra* note 101, at 470.

115 On the theory that the Fourth and Fifth Amendments combine to require exclusion, Professor Lucas Powe has commented that only Black "could have concocted and believed such a preposterous theory." LUCAS A. POWE, JR., THE WARREN COURT AND AMERICAN POLITICS 196–97 (2000). But Powe explains that this theory was an "essential step to [Black's] objective of having all of the Bill of Rights apply exactly to the states as it did to the federal government." *Id.* at 197. Professor Kamisar thinks Powe's criticism is too harsh, but agrees that "Black's theory of the exclusionary rule is badly flawed and . . . nobody subscribes to it today." Kamisar, *First Shot Fired*, *supra* note 10, at 52.

116 *See Mapp*, 367 U.S. at 664 (Black, J., concurring). Ten years later, Black claimed that his vote in *Mapp* rested solely on the Fifth Amendment. He disavowed reliance on the Fourth Amendment and argued that only the Fifth Amendment provides a legitimate basis for the exclusionary rule. *See* Coolidge v. New Hampshire, 403 U.S. 443, 497–99 (1971) (Black, J., concurring in part and dissenting in part):

> The truth is that the source of the exclusionary rule simply cannot be found in the Fourth Amendment. That Amendment did not when adopted, and does not now, contain any constitutional rule barring

however, was ultimately grounded on the Fourth Amendment. Therefore, Black's views on exclusion were out of sync with the primary thrust of Clark's opinion. Opponents of the exclusionary rule would exploit this dichotomy and argue that the legal reasoning of *Mapp* was never endorsed by a majority of the Court, and thus, should not be afforded the respect normally given to the Court's precedents.

Mapp launched a controversial and exciting period of constitutional criminal procedure doctrine. The ruling in *Mapp* not only overruled *Wolf*, but also brought the Court full circle back to *Weeks* and beyond. While *Weeks* concluded that unconstitutionally seized evidence was inadmissible in federal cases, it also ruled that the Fourth Amendment did not apply to searches and seizures by state officials.[117] By overruling *Wolf*, *Mapp* embraced *Weeks*'s conclusion that the exclusionary rule was a command of the Constitution. But *Mapp* also extended *Weeks*. By reversing a state conviction because it was based on evidence obtained from an unreasonable search and seizure, *Mapp* did what the Court had never done before: demonstrate that the Fourth Amendment actually applies to the states.

For a brief period of time, *Mapp* was a revolutionary decision. But *Mapp* did not end, as one scholar predicted, the half-century debate on the exclusionary rule among the justices.[118] The conservative justices of the Burger and Rehnquist Courts would revoke *Mapp*'s status as constitutional law. But *Mapp* was also partly responsible for its own downfall. Clark's opinion did not speak with the clarity of Holmes's opinion in *Silverthorne Lumber*, nor did it contain the single-minded focus of *Weeks*. Ironically, *Mapp* did not maintain the concentration of Clark's memorandum in *Irvine*. In the *Irvine* memo, there was no reliance on *Boyd* or the Fifth Amendment. There was no description of the exclusionary rule as a judicially implied remedy. Nor was there any

---

> the admission of illegally seized evidence. . . . The Fifth Amendment in and of itself directly and explicitly commands its own exclusionary rule—a defendant cannot be compelled to give evidence against himself. Absent congressional action taken pursuant to the Fourth Amendment, if evidence is to be excluded, it must be under the Fifth Amendment, not the Fourth. . . . [T]hat was the thrust of my concurring opinion in *Mapp*.

Id. at 497–98. Black went on to explain that the evidence seized in *Mapp* was excluded not by the Fourth Amendment which contains no exclusionary rule, but by the Fifth Amendment which does. The introduction of such evidence compels a man to be a witness against himself, and evidence so compelled must be excluded under the Fifth Amendment, not because the Court says so, but because the Fifth Amendment commands it. *Id.* at 498.

Professor Chris Slobogin has rightly characterized a Fifth Amendment theory of exclusion as "largely incoherent." Christopher Slobogin, *Why Liberals Should Chuck the Exclusionary Rule*, 1999 U. ILL. L. REV. 363, 367. According to Black's biographer, by 1971, Black "was ready to abandon" the exclusionary rule. NEWMAN, *supra* note 21, at 604. *But cf.* BOB WOODWARD & SCOTT ARMSTRONG, THE BRETHREN: INSIDE THE SUPREME COURT 113–17 (1979) (explaining that although Black told Harlan sometime in the early part of 1971 that he was "rethinking" his position on the rule, by June, 1971, Black refused to vote to overrule *Mapp*).

117 Weeks v. United States, 232 U.S. 383, 398 (1914).

118 Francis A. Allen, *Federalism and the Fourth Amendment: A Requiem for* Wolf, 1961 SUP. CT. REV. 1, 48.

suggestion that the rule was necessary to deter unconstitutional police searches and seizures. Instead, Clark grounded his *Irvine* memo on the principle that exclusion was the "constitutional right of an individual not to have unlawfully seized evidence admitted against him at trial." According to the *Irvine* memo, the exclusionary rule embodied an "important constitutional right of each of our citizens" that the states were required to protect. In other words, if Clark had written *Mapp* based on the reasoning of his *Irvine* memo, *Mapp* would not have been the easy target it became and might not have lent itself so readily to disintegration by future justices hostile to exclusion.

* * *

In the period between *Mapp* and the formation of the Burger Court, the justices of the Warren Court seemed reluctant to embrace the *Weeks-Silverthorne* view that the exclusionary rule was part and parcel of the constitutional protection provided by the Fourth Amendment. Indeed, in several key cases decided during this period, the Warren Court not only embraced aspects of *Mapp* that suggested that the rule was not required by the Fourth Amendment, but also, and more significantly, it never recognized exclusion as a constitutional right of the victim of an unreasonable search or seizure.

In the aftermath of *Mapp*, the Court's initial references to the exclusionary rule lent credence to the claims of *Mapp*'s critics that the Fifth Amendment had played an important part in the outcome of that case. In two cases decided within three years of *Mapp*, the Court reaffirmed the notion that exclusion was the product of a merger of the Fourth and Fifth Amendments.[119] Ironically, the holdings in both cases did not involve the exclusionary rule. A third case, which did involve the rule, revealed that Clark was willing to disown his reliance on the Fifth Amendment in *Mapp*, and that Black remained committed to the notion that the Fourth Amendment alone did not require exclusion.[120] Thus, the two key players responsible for *Mapp* still had not settled their differences over the meaning of that case.

Ker v. California[121] was the first post-*Mapp* case that required the justices to decide whether the constitutionality of state searches and seizures were to be evaluated by the same standard used to assess federal searches and seizures, or whether the states were free to apply their own standards of "reasonableness." This issue was not resolved in *Mapp* because the Ohio courts conceded that the search of Dollree Mapp's home was illegal, leaving the Court only to decide whether the exclusionary rule applied to evidence discovered by the search. By contrast, in *Ker*, the California state courts determined the entry and search of Ker's home, which resulted in the discovery of illegal narcotics, was lawful because the police had probable cause to arrest Ker.

Based on what was said at the conference in *Ker*, it appeared that some of the justices were still debating whether the Fourth Amendment applied to the states. Clark told his

[119] *See* Malloy v. Hogan, 378 U.S. 1, 8 (1964); Ker v. California, 374 U.S. 23, 30 (1963).

[120] One 1958 Plymouth Sedan v. Pennsylvania, 380 U.S. 693 (1965).

[121] 374 U.S. 23 (1963).

colleagues that "*Mapp* makes each case turn on its facts, though the rule is federal."[122] Harlan, on the other hand, insisted that *Mapp* had not changed the standard for determining whether a state search was unconstitutional.[123] Ironically, Harlan cited Clark to support his view: "*Mapp*—as Tom Clark says—does not adopt federal standards across the board."[124] Harlan noted that if this were a federal case, he did not know how he would vote, but "by state standards there is nothing wrong here."[125] Brennan thought that *Mapp* made federal standards controlling. He stated the "same basic fundamentals would reach the states under *Mapp*."[126]

Stewart asked: "Does *Mapp* apply federal Fourth Amendment standards to the states?"[127] Apparently forgetting that in *Elkins* he wrote that "the Federal Constitution, by virtue of the Fourteenth Amendment, prohibits unreasonable searches and seizures by state officers,"[128] Stewart now commented that he "did not think *Mapp* made the Fourth Amendment applicable to the states—California is free to develop its own ground rules so far as it is not an unreasonable search."[129] By contrast, Goldberg told his colleagues that he "thought *Mapp* incorporated the fourth amendment." Black then asserted that "*Mapp* held that the fourth and fifth amendments applied to the states."[130] Clark closed the discussion by noting that his "views are the same as Hugo Black's, except on the Fifth Amendment."[131]

After the conference voted to affirm Ker's conviction, Clark was assigned the opinion. As Clark began writing his opinion, his characterization of *Mapp*'s holding was transformed as a result of Black's input. In his first two circulations of *Ker*, Clark explained that exclusion was mandated by the Fourth Amendment itself. He wrote, "We held in *Mapp* ... 'that all evidence obtained by searches and seizures in violation of the Constitution is, by that same authority, inadmissible in a state court.'"[132] Not surprisingly, Black was not satisfied with this description of *Mapp*. Twelve days later, Clark sent Black a third draft. Attached to this draft was a handwritten note from Clark drawing Black's attention to a new footnote.[133] The footnote acknowledged Black's conclusion in *Mapp*, "'that when the Fourth Amendment's ban against unreasonable searches and seizures is considered together with the Fifth Amendment's ban against

---

[122] William Douglas, Conference Notes on *Ker v. California* (Dec. 14, 1962), Douglas Papers, Box 1281.

[123] *Id.*

[124] *Id.*

[125] *Id.*

[126] *Id.*

[127] *Id.*

[128] Elkins v. United States, 364 U.S. 206, 213 (1960).

[129] Douglas, Conference Notes on *Ker v. California*, *supra* note 122.

[130] *Id.*

[131] *Id.*

[132] Tom Clark, Second Draft Opinion of *Ker v. California* 6 (Apr. 12, 1963), Clark Papers, Box A139 (quoting Mapp v. Ohio, 367 U.S. 643, 655 (1960)).

[133] Tom Clark, Letter to Hugo Black (Apr. 24, 1963), Clark Papers, Box A139.

compelled self-incrimination, a constitutional basis emerges which not only justifies but actually requires the exclusionary rule.'"[134]

But merely recognizing Black's conclusion in a footnote was apparently not enough. Eventually, in the fifth draft of *Ker*, Clark replaced the footnote with a more prominent attribution to *Boyd*'s and the Fifth Amendment's impact on *Mapp*'s holding. Thus, Clark wrote "In *Mapp v. Ohio*, we followed *Boyd v. United States*, which held that the Fourth Amendment, implemented by the self-incrimination clause of the Fifth, forbids the Federal Government to convict a man of crime by using testimony or papers obtained from him by unreasonable searches and seizures as defined in the Fourth Amendment."[135] This description of *Mapp* would appear in the final version of *Ker*.[136]

In a second case, Brennan was even more explicit in describing the role the Fifth Amendment played in *Mapp*. *Malloy v. Hogan* addressed whether the Fifth Amendment's Self-Incrimination Clause was enforceable against the states. Brennan explained that *Mapp*'s holding supported the Court's conclusion that the Self-Incrimination Clause was enforceable against the states. He described *Mapp* as holding that "the Fifth Amendment privilege against self-incrimination implemented the Fourth Amendment in [cases involving evidence obtained by an unreasonable search and seizure], and that the two guarantees of personal security conjoined in the Fourteenth Amendment to make the exclusionary rule obligatory upon the States."[137] Brennan also wrote that *Mapp* had "relied upon the great case" of *Boyd*,[138] and that *Mapp*'s reliance on *Boyd* repudiated the theory of the privilege "as a mere rule of evidence 'best defended not as an unchangeable principle of universal justice, but as a law proved by experience to be expedient.'"[139]

Finally, in *One 1958 Plymouth Sedan v. Pennsylvania*,[140] which was decided less than a year after *Malloy*, the Court addressed whether the exclusionary rule applied in a state forfeiture proceeding when the forfeiture of an automobile depended on the admission of evidence obtained in violation of the Fourth Amendment. The focus of the discussion at the conference was whether there was probable cause to stop the suspected vehicle. Five justices voted to reverse the forfeiture order due to a lack of probable cause. Tellingly, there was no discussion on whether *Mapp* should apply to forfeiture proceedings. The underlying assumption seemed to be that if the Fourth Amendment applied to forfeiture proceedings, then, of course, *Mapp* prohibited the states from forfeiting a vehicle that had been stopped in violation of the Fourth Amendment. No opposition was recorded when both Warren and Stewart, who voted differently on the probable

---

[134] *Id.* at 7 n.5 (quoting *Mapp*, 367 U.S. at 662 (Black, J., concurring)).

[135] Tom Clark, Fifth Draft Opinion of *Ker v. California* 6–7 (undated), Clark Papers, Box A139 (citations and footnotes omitted).

[136] Ker v. California, 374 U.S. 23, 30 (1963).

[137] Malloy v. Hogan, 378 U.S. 1, 8 (1964).

[138] *Id.*

[139] *Id.* at 9 (quoting Twining v. New Jersey, 211 U.S. 78, 113 (1908)).

[140] 380 U.S. 693 (1965).

cause issue, stated that the "Fourth Amendment should apply to a forfeiture case as well as to a criminal case."[141]

After the conference, Goldberg circulated a draft opinion that contained a footnote acknowledging that *Mapp* had relied upon *Boyd*'s statement that the Fourth and Fifth Amendments should be considered "as running 'almost into each other.'"[142] Clark sent Goldberg a note requesting that the footnote be omitted.[143] Repudiating what he wrote in *Mapp*, Clark told Goldberg that "the only one *depending* on the 5th in *Mapp* was Hugo."[144] Clark, moreover, felt that Goldberg's footnote "enlarges" what had been said in *Mapp*, and he reminded Goldberg that *Mapp* described the Fourth and Fifth Amendments "as only having 'a close connection.'"[145]

The final version of *Plymouth Sedan* deleted the footnote. Goldberg characterized exclusion of unlawfully acquired evidence as "the constitutional exclusionary rule enunciated" in *Weeks* and *Mapp*, and held that "the constitutional exclusionary rule" does apply to a forfeiture proceeding.[146] Significantly, Goldberg's opinion never cites the Fifth Amendment or analogizes evidence obtained from an illegal seizure to compelled testimony. By contrast, Black explained why his vote in *Plymouth Sedan* and *Mapp* did depend on the Fifth Amendment: "It was because of the Court's reliance on the *Boyd* doctrine—which held that the Fourth and Fifth Amendments *together* barred use of unreasonably seized evidence—that I joined the Court's opinion in Mapp."[147]

Ker, *Malloy*, and *Plymouth Sedan* show that the argument started in *Wolf* over the exclusionary rule's constitutional status had never really ended; *Mapp* certainly had not quieted the debate. These three cases of the early 1960s, however, did not alter the meaning or scope of *Mapp*. Nor did these cases directly challenge the *Weeks-Silverthorne Lumber* view that exclusion was required by the Constitution. But the next significant exclusionary rule case, *Linkletter v. Walker*,[148] would be a different matter. Announced a little over a month after *Plymouth Sedan*, *Linkletter* rejected the *Weeks-Silverthorne Lumber* view that exclusion was compelled by the Fourth Amendment. Looking back, it is now clear that *Linkletter* reconstructed the foundation upon which the exclusionary rule rested.

* * *

[141] William Douglas, Conference Notes on *One 1958 Plymouth Sedan v. Pennsylvania* (Apr. 2, 1965), Douglas Papers, Box 1333.

[142] Arthur Goldberg, Second Draft Opinion of *One 1958 Plymouth Sedan v. Pennsylvania* 6 n.6 (Apr. 10, 1965), Clark Papers, Box A177.

[143] Tom Clark, Letter to Arthur Goldberg on *One 1958 Plymouth Sedan v. Pennsylvania* (Apr. 13, 1965), Clark Papers, Box A177.

[144] *Id.*

[145] *Id.*

[146] One 1958 Plymouth Sedan v. Pennsylvania, 380 U.S. 693, 696 (1965).

[147] *Id.* at 704 (Black, J., concurring).

[148] 381 U.S. 618 (1965).

While *Ker v. California* was pending, a petition for a writ of certiorari arrived in a case that resembled the facts in *Wolf*.[149] California law enforcement officers suspected that Ruth Bawden was facilitating illegal abortions. Police entered her home without a warrant and seized documents that were later admitted at her prosecution for abortion and conspiracy to commit abortion. Bawden was convicted, and her petition claimed that the search and seizure violated the Constitution. One of Justice Clark's law clerks sent him a bench memo suggesting that, in light of *Ker*'s pendency, the Court might want to wait on deciding *Bawden* "since it comes up on *Mapp* grounds." On the top of that memo, Clark wrote: "Let's see what happens. I want to go slow on *Mapp* for awhile."[150]

Whatever hesitation Clark had about confronting *Mapp* in 1962, it disappeared three years later when he was assigned to write the Court's opinion in *Linkletter v. Walker*. At issue was whether the "exclusionary principle" announced in *Mapp* applies to state court convictions that had become final before *Mapp* was decided.[151]

The substance of the conference discussion in *Linkletter* was quite different from the discussion in *Plymouth Sedan*. In the latter case, there was no talk of the exclusionary rule not applying to forfeiture proceedings. Nor was there a discussion about whether applying the exclusionary rule to a forfeiture proceeding promoted the purpose behind the rule. Finally, the justices did not discuss whether application of the rule would affect the "fairness" of the forfeiture proceeding. Instead, all of the justices appeared to agree that if the Fourth Amendment applied to forfeiture proceedings, so did the exclusionary rule. Three years later, the conference discussion in *Linkletter* had a very different focus.

Warren began the discussion by noting that the case "greatly bothered him" because he had "always been against deciding constitutional questions" prospectively.[152] But this case was different from other cases, such as *Gideon v. Wainwright*,[153] which held that indigent criminal defendants are entitled to free legal counsel, where the Court had applied new constitutional rulings retroactively because "under those conditions a fair trial was not possible—that's not true here to the same extent."[154] Rather than voting, however, Warren initially passed.[155] Black spoke next and made clear that his vote did not depend on how many defendants might be released from jail: "If we hold something unconstitutional then it should apply wherever and however."[156] Black stated a failure to

---

[149] People v. Bawden, 25 Cal. Rptr. 368 (1962).

[150] Martin J. Flynn, Bench Memorandum on *Bawden v. California* (Mar. 27, 1963), Clark Papers, Box B190. The Court ultimately decided not to review the case. *See* Bawden v. California, 372 U.S. 959 (1963).

[151] *Linkletter*, 381 U.S. 618, 622 (1965). Because *Mapp* had already been applied to cases still pending on direct review, the *Linkletter* Court found, without discussion, that *Mapp* applied to cases still on direct review at the time *Mapp* was announced. *See* Johnson v. New Jersey, 384 U.S. 719, 732 (1966).

[152] William Douglas, Conference Notes on *Linkletter v. Walker* (Mar. 12, 1965), Douglas Papers, Box 1332.

[153] 372 U.S. 335 (1963).

[154] Douglas, Conference Notes on *Linkletter v. Walker*, *supra* note 152.

[155] *Id.*

[156] *Id.*

apply *Mapp* retroactively meant that defendants "in jail today are suffering a penalty" that others similarly situated would not suffer.[157] Black told his colleagues that it "makes no difference to him how many may be freed" by applying *Mapp* retroactively.[158]

Clark agreed that this was a different situation from applying *Gideon* retroactively because "we did not overrule a principle as we did in *Mapp*."[159] Clark noted that *Gideon* "involved 'fair trial' procedures."[160] In contrast, "the purpose of the *Mapp* rule was to be a deterrent on police rather than the vehicle for a fair trial."[161] Thus, Clark was "inclined to make the exclusionary rule prospective only."[162] Black, speaking out of turn, countered Clark's remarks by noting that "Fourth Amendment questions are relevant to fair trials."[163] Harlan agreed with Clark that the reversal in *Mapp* "does not go to the essence of a fair trial like *Gideon* did."[164]

Brennan spoke next and stated that "this case has given him great trouble."[165] The dilemma for Brennan was that if "*Mapp* says *Wolf* was wrong—why can I apply *Gideon* retroactively, but not *Mapp*?"[166] Brennan would vote against retroactive application of *Mapp* and explained that his voted turned on "what affects a 'fair trial.'"[167] He distinguished the Court's earlier decisions on racial discrimination, coerced confession, and the right to counsel cases because the constitutional violations in those cases go to a "basic infirmity in the trial itself."[168] Stewart also was unwilling to apply *Mapp* retroactively. He thought there were "vast differences between this case and *Gideon*" because the latter case "went to what was a fair trial—this does not."[169] Stewart opined that "*Mapp* was a rule to deter police and had nothing to do with a fair trial."[170] Goldberg stated that he agreed with Clark.[171] By the end of the conference discussion, seven justices voted against applying *Mapp* retroactively; only Black and Douglas thought that *Mapp* should apply retroactively.

As in *Mapp* and *Ker*, Clark was assigned to write the opinion for the *Linkletter* majority. Like his opinion in *Mapp*, certain aspects of Clark's opinion in *Linkletter* significantly

---

157 *Id.*

158 *Id.*

159 *Id.* Of course, *Gideon* did overrule the "principle" announced in *Betts v. Brady*, 316 U.S. 455 (1942), which held that the Sixth Amendment Right to Counsel Clause is not a fundamental right that must made available in every state prosecution, no matter what the circumstances.

160 Douglas, Conference Notes on *Linkletter v. Walker*, *supra* note 152.

161 *Id.*

162 *Id.*

163 *Id.*

164 *Id.*

165 *Id.*

166 *Id.*

167 *Id.*

168 *Id.*

169 *Id.*

170 *Id.*

171 *Id.*

undermine the constitutional standing of not only *Mapp*, but the exclusionary rule itself. Indeed, the mode of analysis in *Linkletter* was reminiscent of Frankfurter's view of exclusion. The most striking aspect of *Linkletter* is that deterrence again becomes the raison d'être for the exclusionary rule. Clark asserts that *Mapp* and the Court's other cases in this area determined that the rule is a "deterrent safeguard necessary to the enforcement" of the Fourth Amendment.[172] He cites *Silverthorne Lumber* to support that assertion,[173] but there is not a word in *Silverthorne Lumber* that describes the rule in this manner. Clark then says that the "prime purpose" of *Mapp* was the enforcement of the Fourth Amendment "through the inclusion of the exclusionary rule within its rights."[174] He maintains that *Mapp* found that exclusion was the "only effective deterrent" to illegal police conduct.[175] Indeed, Clark explains, "all of the cases since *Wolf* requiring the exclusion of illegal evidence have been based on the necessity for an effective deterrent to illegal police action."[176] As two commentators have noted: "In light of [Clark's] own opinion in *Mapp*, this [description of *Mapp*] is patently false. But it served its purpose."[177] It put to rest "the short-lived attempt to ground the exclusionary rule in a 'logically and constitutionally necessary' deduction from a fourth amendment 'right to privacy.'"[178] After *Linkletter*, the rule would forever be viewed by a majority of the Court as a deterrent-based remedy, and not mandated by the Constitution itself.

The other facet of *Linkletter* that was entirely different from *Weeks* and *Silverthorne Lumber* (and even *Mapp*) was the adoption and application of a balancing formula for determining *Mapp*'s retroactivity. Significantly, a balancing test was required neither by precedent nor by the issue being decided. Clark concedes that the Court's prior cases had always applied newly announced constitutional holdings retroactively.[179] But he insists that "the Constitution neither prohibits nor requires retrospective effect,"[180] and states, without explanation, that a balancing model "is particularly correct with reference to the Fourth Amendment's prohibitions as to unreasonable searches and seizures."[181] Accordingly, Clark explains that whether *Mapp* would be applied retroactively turned

---

[172] Linkletter v. Walker, 381 U.S. 618, 635 (1965).

[173] *Id.*

[174] *Id.* at 636.

[175] *Id.*

[176] *Id.* at 636–37. Six months after *Linkletter* was decided, the Court decided *Tehan v. United States ex rel. Shott*, 382 U.S. 406 (1966). *Tehan* addressed the retroactivity of *Griffin v. California*, 380 U.S. 609 (1965), which ruled that adverse comment by a judge or prosecutor on the defendant's failure to testify in a state criminal case violates the Fifth Amendment privilege against self-incrimination. In ruling that *Griffin* does not apply retroactively, *Tehan* reaffirmed that the "prime purpose of the rule of *Mapp*" was deterrence. *See Tehan*, 382 U.S. at 413.

[177] Steven R. Schlesinger & Bradford Wilson, *Property, Privacy and Deterrence: The Exclusionary Rule in Search of a Rationale*, 18 DUQ. L. REV. 225, 237 (1980).

[178] *Id.*

[179] *Linkletter*, 381 U.S. at 628.

[180] *Id.* at 629.

[181] *Id.*

on a three-prong test: "the purpose of the *Mapp* rule; the reliance placed on the *Wolf* doctrine; and the effect on the administration of justice of a retrospective application of *Mapp*."[182]

The adoption of a balancing test to determine the retroactivity of a newly announced interpretation of the Bill of Rights was unprecedented; in fact, the "Court's practice *always* had been to apply new constitutional decisions retroactively and *never* did a majority opinion even consider that something less would be permissible."[183] But *Linkletter* neglected that long-standing practice and marked a fundamental change in the law.[184] Furthermore, the manner in which Clark applies his novel balancing test suggests that a majority of the Warren Court was still unsettled about the purpose of the exclusionary rule. And even if the *Linkletter* Court was not having second thoughts about the purpose and wisdom of exclusion, it certainly was not applying the same analysis utilized in *Weeks*, *Silverthorne Lumber*, and *Mapp*.

For example, to bolster his conclusion that deterrence of police misconduct was the primary purpose behind *Mapp*, Clark introduces a concern that had not been discussed in *Mapp* and had not played a prominent role in previous exclusionary rule cases. Essentially, Clark contends that because the facts of an illegal search cannot be reversed, exclusion serves no legitimate interest other than deterrence.[185] But retrospective application of the exclusionary rule cannot deter, according to Clark, because the unlawful police action prior to *Mapp* "has already occurred and will not be corrected by releasing the prisoners involved," and the "ruptured privacy" suffered by the victims of unreasonable searches and seizures "cannot be restored"; "Reparation comes too late."[186]

Concededly, giving *Mapp* retrospective effect would not undo or fix the warrantless search of Victor Linkletter's home. However, Clark fails to recognize, or at least acknowledge in his opinion, that this shortcoming of exclusion exists in every case. Suppressing reliable evidence never undoes police misconduct that has already occurred. Nor does exclusion ever repair the victims' "ruptured privacy." Clark's reasoning, thus, would support overruling *Mapp*—and *Weeks*.

Regarding the second prong of his test, Clark observes that the states had "relied on *Wolf* and followed its command."[187] Exactly what type of "reliance" interest Clark had in mind here is unclear. After all, *Wolf* did not authorize the warrantless search of Linkletter's home. On the contrary, according to the conventional understanding at the

---

[182] *Id.* at 636.

[183] James B. Haddad, *"Retroactivity Should Be Rethought": A Call for the End of the* Linkletter *Doctrine*, 60 J. Crim. L. Criminology & Police Sci. 417, 425 (1969).

[184] Subsequent to *Linkletter*, in *Griffith v. Kentucky*, 479 U.S. 314 (1987), the Court held that "new" rulings in criminal cases would be applied retroactively to all lower court rulings "pending on direct review or not yet final" at the time the new rule was announced. *Id.* at 328.

[185] *Linkletter*, 381 U.S. at 636–37.

[186] *Id.* at 637.

[187] *Id.*

time, *Wolf* had made the Fourth Amendment binding on the states, which meant that the police should have procured a warrant before entering Linkletter's home. Perhaps the reliance interest Clark had in mind is that state prosecutors and judges could have relied upon *Wolf* to forgo establishing a record showing the lawfulness of searches and seizures because, after *Wolf*, the admission of evidence did not turn on the validity of the search or seizure. In other words, after *Wolf*, state prosecutors and judges could legitimately choose not to bother taking the time and effort to prove the constitutional validity of a particular search since there was no federal requirement to demonstrate the lawfulness of the police action in order to admit the fruits of the search.

On the other hand, where a search or seizure was plainly illegal, like the search of Linkletter's home, the state's claim of "reliance" is hardly compelling. In that situation, the argument for prospective-only application of *Mapp* "was simply a request that the States be permitted to keep the fruits of the conduct which was unlawful even by the standards prevailing when it occurred."[188] Why the Court should recognize the states' interest in using the fruits of illegal searches is not self-evident, particularly in light of *Mapp*. The tacit motivation of the Court was that it did not want to order new trials for lots of prison inmates, especially when there was a good chance that new convictions or plea bargains would be difficult to secure.

Last, Clark addresses the third factor in his balancing test—the "effect on the administration of justice of a retrospective application of *Mapp*."[189] Here, Clark sounds more like Frankfurter and Black than Day or Holmes. Clark finds that allowing already convicted prisoners to invoke the exclusionary rule—which he calls "an extraordinary procedural weapon that has no bearing on guilt"—would "seriously disrupt the administration of justice."[190] He points out that "there is no likelihood of unreliability or coercion present in a search-and-seizure case."[191] Nor was there anything shocking about admitting the evidence found in Linkletter's home; rather than being abhorrent, "the use in state trials of illegally seized evidence had been specifically authorized" by *Wolf*.[192] Clark also states that "the fairness of [Linkletter's] trial is not under attack."[193] Rather, Linkletter only attacked the "admissibility of evidence, the reliability and relevancy of which is not questioned."[194]

It is doubtful that Clark's views on the Fourth Amendment and exclusion had fundamentally changed in the four years between *Mapp* and *Linkletter*. Although Clark would not admit it in *Linkletter*, what drove the result in that case was the concern that retrospective application of *Mapp* would produce a "jail break" for defendants convicted on

---

188 Haddad, *supra* note 183, at 435 n.173.

189 *Linkletter*, 381 U.S. at 636.

190 *Id.* at 637–38.

191 *Id.* at 638.

192 *Id.*

193 *Id.* at 639.

194 *Id.*

the basis of unconstitutionally obtained evidence in state prosecutions. Indeed, the fear of the chaos caused by retrospective application was initially debated during the deliberations of *Mapp*. In a letter to Clark, Harlan complained that overruling *Wolf* would, *inter alia*, lead to "a jail delivery of uncertain, but obviously serious, proportions" for state prisoners convicted under trials that permitted the admission of illegally acquired evidence.[195] In a letter rebutting Harlan's various concerns about reversing *Wolf*, Clark told Harlan that a "jail delivery" was unlikely because "relatively few" defendants had objected to the admission of unlawfully seized evidence at their trials.[196] Such an objection, Clark insisted, would be necessary for state prisoners to successfully attack their convictions in collateral proceedings.[197]

Of course, Linkletter's lawyer had not raised such an objection, and Clark correctly predicted that objections to the admission of illegally seized evidence in state prosecutions would be rare. Thus, the real motivation behind the result in *Linkletter* was not constitutional principle, but the fear of too much justice if *Mapp* was given retroactive application. Instead of frankly acknowledging this concern, Clark's opinion in *Linkletter* obscured the point by attacking the shortcomings of the exclusionary rule.

Ironically, Black's dissent in *Linkletter* revealed how far Clark's opinion had departed from *Mapp*. The "different treatment of Miss Mapp and Linkletter points up at once the arbitrary and discriminatory nature of the judicial contrivance utilized here to break the promise of *Mapp* by keeping all people in jail who are unfortunate enough to have had their unconstitutional convictions affirmed" before *Mapp* was decided.[198] Acknowledging that there might be circumstances where a change in the law might justify prospective-only application of a new constitutional principle, for Black, *Linkletter* was not such a case: "No such unjust consequences to Linkletter, however, can possibly result here by giving him and others like him the benefit of a changed constitutional interpretation where he is languishing in jail on the basis of evidence concededly used unconstitutionally to convict him."[199] Nor did Louisiana have any vested interest that should be recognized by the Court in order to keep Linkletter in jail.[200]

Finally, Black observed that the deterrence rationale that justified *Linkletter*'s holding was flatly inconsistent with *Mapp*'s constitutional holding: "I have read and reread the *Mapp* opinion but have been unable to find one word in it to indicate that the exclusionary search and seizure rule should be limited on the basis that it was intended to do nothing in the world except to deter officers of the law."[201] But by relying on deterrence as the basis for the exclusionary rule, Clark transformed exclusion from a

---

195 John Harlan, Letter to Tom Clark on *Mapp v. Ohio* 2 (May 1, 1961), Clark Papers, Box A115.

196 Tom Clark, Letter to John Harlan on *Mapp v. Ohio* 1 (May 4, 1961), Clark Papers, Box A115.

197 *Id.*

198 *Linkletter*, 381 U.S. at 641 (Black, J., dissenting).

199 *Id.* at 645.

200 *Id.*

201 *Id.* at 649.

constitutional mandate to a rule based upon its ability to deter police misconduct. Indeed, Clark's opinion in *Linkletter* was a major retreat from *Mapp. Linkletter* did more to undermine the theory of exclusion set out in *Weeks* and *Silverthorne Lumber* than did *Mapp*. Liberal legal scholars and the press are quick to blame the Burger and Rehnquist Courts for dismantling the exclusionary rule. But *Linkletter* did much of the dismantling long before the Burger and Rehnquist Courts came on the scene.

While the result in *Linkletter* may not have surprised some legal scholars, the importance of the case is best measured in the way *Linkletter* "affected the future of the exclusionary rule."[202] Subsequent cases showed that the *Linkletter* Court's way of looking at the exclusionary rule would not only become the approach favored by the Burger and Rehnquist Courts, but would also remain the way that the Warren Court viewed the rule. In fact, during the final two Terms of Warren's tenure as Chief Justice, the Warren Court continued to view exclusion as a deterrent-based remedy. More important, a majority of the justices on the Warren Court never took the position that the rule was a constitutional right of victims of unreasonable searches and seizures.

The best evidence of the Warren Court's unwillingness to embrace exclusion as a constitutional right can be seen in what was *not* said about the exclusionary rule in *Terry v. Ohio*.[203] At issue in *Terry* was whether an officer violated the Fourth Amendment when he stopped and frisked individuals for weapons who were suspected of being armed and dangerous. Writing for all of the justices except Douglas, Warren ruled that a stop and frisk on evidence short of probable cause for an arrest did not violate the Fourth Amendment. Before reaching this conclusion, the Chief Justice penned several lines about the exclusionary rule, all of which were dicta, but nonetheless illuminate how the justices' thinking about the rule had evolved since *Mapp*.

Warren began his discussion of the exclusionary rule with the observation that "[e]ver since its inception," the rule has been recognized "as a principal mode of discouraging lawless police conduct."[204] Thus, "its major thrust is a deterrent one."[205] The other vital function served by the rule was "'the imperative of judicial integrity.'"[206] These were the only purposes for the rule acknowledged by Warren. But Warren's comments about the rule did not end here. He also voiced concerns about exclusion that had previously been articulated only by opponents of the rule. For example, Warren opined that the exclusionary rule has limitations "as a tool of judicial control," noting that the rule cannot

---

202 Kamisar, *Principled Basis*, *supra* note 22, at 633 ("How the *Linkletter* Court looked back on the exclusionary rule is not as important as how it looked forward. Whatever one thinks of the manner in which *Linkletter* read *Mapp* and the *Weeks* line of cases, one must consider the way it has affected the future of the exclusionary rule."). Kamisar was one of the legal scholars who was not surprised by the result in *Linkletter*. *See id.* at 628. Interestingly, after he retired from the Court, Stewart characterized *Linkletter* as a "relatively uncontroversial" ruling. Stewart, *supra* note 16, at 1389.

203 392 U.S. 1 (1968).

204 *Id.* at 12.

205 *Id.*

206 *Id.*

deter Fourth Amendment violations where the police are uninterested in prosecutions or concerned with promoting interests unrelated to prosecution.[207] Further, Warren remarked that the exclusion of evidence at criminal trials will not stop the "wholesale harassment" of certain individuals by the police.[208] "Yet a rigid and unthinking application of the exclusionary rule, in futile protest against practices which it can never be used effectively to control, may exact a high toll in human injury and frustration of efforts to prevent crime."[209]

To be sure, Warren did not sever the exclusionary rule from the Fourth Amendment, as the Burger Court would eventually do. On the contrary, Warren recognized that as a practical matter, the legality of a police search was intertwined with the issue of exclusion,[210] and that a judicial decision to admit evidence in a criminal trial "has the necessary effect of legitimizing the conduct which produced the evidence, while an application of the exclusionary rule withholds the constitutional imprimatur."[211] Warren also warned that judges retain their traditional responsibility "to guard against police conduct which is overbearing or harassing, or which trenches upon personal security without the objective evidentiary justification which the Constitution requires."[212] When such conduct occurs, Warren explained, judges must condemn it, and the fruits of illegal police behavior "must be excluded from evidence in criminal trials."[213] Warren closed his discussion by noting that the Court did not intend to discourage the use of other remedies that can more effectively deal with certain police misconduct.[214]

Warren's description of the exclusionary rule reiterated *Linkletter*'s view that the rule is primarily designed to deter. It is notable, however, that in this rather "abstract discussion" of the limits of the exclusionary rule,[215] Warren never refers to the rule as part of the constitutional protections provided by the Fourth Amendment itself. One could argue that the failure to describe the rule as a constitutional right was unnecessary since *Terry* rejected the defendants' Fourth Amendment arguments. But that benign view of Warren's comments misses the point. Warren's comments were intended to signal that there was only so much the Court could do about police harassment of minority citizens. During the initial drafting of the *Terry* opinion, Warren had originally included this

---

207 *Id.* at 13.

208 The individuals Warren had in mind were African-Americans. *See id.* at 14–15.

209 *Id.* at 15.

210 *Id.* at 12.

211 *Id.* at 13.

212 *Id.* at 15.

213 *Id.*

214 *Id.*

215 This is how Fortas characterized Warren's discussion. Abe Fortas, Handwritten Letter to Earl Warren (undated), Earl Warren Papers, Library of Congress, Manuscript Division, Box 624. Fortas's letter acknowledged "that the exclusionary rule does not and cannot effectively deal with all abuses of police power," but he questioned whether "the detailed description of what the cops can get away with may not incite them to greater use of the latitude described" in Warren's opinion. *Id.*

discussion in a footnote, but Brennan suggested putting this "very important point" in the text of the *Terry* opinion.[216] Brennan told Warren: "Now that the Court is rejecting the extreme position that an officer may stop a citizen only if he has probable cause to arrest him, critics of polic[e] abuses ought to be told that that they should turn to other agencies of government for the cure."[217]

Of course, if the justices believed that the rule was required by the Constitution, centuries of legal rulings established that the judicial branch was the proper forum for protecting a constitutional right. *Terry*, however, revealed that the justices were less sanguine about the rule than they were in *Mapp*.[218] The nation experienced tumultuous events between *Mapp* and *Terry*. Perhaps the liberal justices of the Court were worn out after the political assassinations, rising crime rates, racial tensions exposed by the civil rights struggle, and Richard Nixon's political rhetoric against the Warren Court during the 1968 Presidential campaign.[219] The 1960s were a controversial decade, on and off the Court. In *Mapp*, the Court imposed the exclusionary rule on the states, because the Court would "no longer permit [the Fourth Amendment] to be revocable at the whim of any police officer who, in the name of law enforcement itself, chooses to suspend its enjoyment."[220] Seven years later in *Terry*, the Court adopted the view that even in cases where police violate the Fourth Amendment, "a stern refusal by th[e] Court to condone such activity does not necessarily render it responsive to the exclusionary rule."[221]

Nearly nine months after announcing *Terry*—on March 24, 1969—the Court decided *Kaufman v. United States*[222] and *Desist v. United States*.[223] *Kaufman* addressed whether federal prisoners can bring Fourth Amendment claims under the federal habeas corpus statute. The vast majority of the federal courts of appeals, including the Eighth Circuit, which decided against Kaufman's petition, had ruled that search and seizure

---

216 William J. Brennan, Jr., Letter to Earl Warren 5–6 (Jan. 30, 1968), Warren Papers, Box 624.

217 *Id.*

218 *See* Yale Kamisar, *The Warren Court and Criminal Justice: A Quarter-Century Retrospective*, 31 TULSA L.J. 1, 5 (1995) (explaining *Terry* as an example of the Warren Court's "change in tone and attitude," and that the Court was "a good deal less exuberant about the exclusionary rule" in 1968).

219 Although *Terry* was decided on June 10, 1968, several months before Richard Nixon became the Republican party's nominee for president, Nixon had already been linking the Court with the rising crime rates the nation was experiencing and claiming that decisions like *Miranda v. Arizona*, 384 U.S. 436 (1966), and *Escobedo v. Illinois*, 378 U.S. 478 (1964), were impeding law enforcement activities. *See, e.g., Nixon Urges Wiretaps, Easier Confession Rules to Fight Crime*, BOS. GLOBE, May 9, 1968, at 16 (reporting on a press release from the Nixon campaign in which the candidate argues that rulings like *Miranda* and *Escobedo* were "'seriously ham-stringing the peace forces in our society and strengthening the criminal forces'"). On May 30, 1968, eleven days before *Terry* was announced, Nixon told a Dallas audience that the Court's criminal procedure rulings had a given a "green light" to the "criminal elements" of society, and that recent Court decisions were largely responsible for the rise in crime rates. *Nixon Links Court to Rise in Crime*, N.Y. TIMES, May 31, 1968, at 18.

220 Mapp v. Ohio, 367 U.S. 643, 660 (1961).

221 Terry v. Ohio, 392 U.S. 1, 14 (1968).

222 394 U.S. 217 (1969).

223 394 U.S. 244 (1969).

claims should be heard on direct appeals and not litigated in collateral proceedings.[224] The government argued that Fourth Amendment claims should be barred from federal collateral review because, unlike other constitutional claims that were reviewable in a federal habeas petition, the use of evidence from an illegal search does not undermine the integrity of the truth-finding process at trial.[225] Moreover, the government contended, the exclusionary rule is designed to deter, and invoking the rule during collateral proceedings would have slight deterrent impact on police illegality.[226]

The conference discussion in *Kaufman* followed along familiar lines except for the fact that Douglas voted to dismiss the case.[227] According to Brennan's private papers, Douglas's vote was based on the belief that Kaufman's Fourth Amendment claim was "totally frivolous."[228] Stewart was also willing to dismiss the case. Additionally, Stewart told his colleagues that the "exclusionary rule is not a constitutional rule. *Mapp* says it is and therefore the Eighth Circuit is wrong" in saying that exclusionary rule challenges can never be raised in a federal habeas proceeding.[229] Justice Byron White also thought that the lower court ruling precluding Fourth Amendment claims in federal collateral proceedings was "not sound."[230] After the conference, four justices voted to vacate the lower court ruling (Brennan, Stewart, White, and Fortas), three voted to affirm (Warren, Black, and Harlan), and Douglas voted to dismiss the case.[231]

Brennan was assigned the *Kaufman* opinion, and he ruled that search and seizure claims could be raised in federal habeas proceedings. Brennan cryptically explained that the "availability of post-conviction relief serves significantly to secure the integrity of proceedings at or before trial and on appeal."[232] And such relief "contributes to the present vitality of all constitutional rights whether or not they bear on the integrity of the fact-finding process."[233] Because the case involved the interpretation of a federal statute,

---

224 For example, in *Springer v. United States*, 340 F.2d 950, 951 (8th Cir. 1965), the Eighth Circuit stated that "it is settled that the question whether evidence was seized illegally ordinarily may not be successfully raised in a proceeding which constitutes a collateral attack on the sentence, but must be presented in the appeal from the conviction." *See also* Warren v. United States, 311 F.2d 673, 675 (8th Cir. 1963) (same). In both *Springer* and *Warren*, Judge Harry Blackmun sat as a member of the Eighth Circuit panel of judges. Interestingly, Blackmun authored the Eighth Circuit ruling affirming Kaufman's conviction, *see* Kaufman v. United States, 350 F.2d 408 (8th Cir. 1965), but that opinion did not address Kaufman's Fourth Amendment claim, *Kaufman*, 394 U.S. at 220 n.3.

225 Brief for the United States at 29–30, *Kaufman*, 394 U.S. 217 (No. 53).

226 *Id.* at 30–32.

227 William Douglas, Conference Notes on *Kaufman v. United States* (Nov. 22, 1968), Douglas Papers, Box 1432.

228 William J. Brennan, Jr., Case Histories, October Term, 1968, at x (undated), Brennan Papers, Box II: 6.

229 Douglas, Conference Notes on *Kaufman v. United States*, *supra* note 227.

230 *Id.*

231 *Id.* Brennan's Case Histories for *Kaufman* state that the conference vote "was seven to vacate and one (Justice Douglas) to dismiss." Brennan, Case Histories, *supra* note 228, at x. Thurgood Marshall did not participate in *Kaufman*.

232 Kaufman v. United States, 394 U.S. 217, 229 (1969).

233 *Id.*

Brennan's opinion for the majority did not discuss the exclusionary rule or *Mapp* in any substantive manner. Brennan's sole reference to the exclusionary rule was in response to Black's dissent.[234]

The premise of Black's dissent was that the availability of federal collateral review should largely turn on whether the petitioner raised a claim of innocence.[235] According to Black, Fourth Amendment claims are different from other constitutional rights because the evidence seized is trustworthy and "establishes beyond virtually any shadow of a doubt that the defendant is guilty."[236] Thus, search and seizure claims should "correspond" to the purpose behind the exclusionary rule.[237] Ignoring or forgetting the premise of his *Linkletter* dissent where he argued that there was not one word in *Mapp* that suggested that the exclusionary rule was based on a deterrence theory; in *Kaufman*, Black maintained the only purpose behind the rule was deterrence. Indeed, Black chided the majority for making "no effort to justify its result in terms of the long-recognized deterrent purpose of the exclusionary rule."[238] And he asserted, without mentioning *Mapp*, that the results in *Elkins* and *Linkletter* revealed that the only purpose served by exclusion was deterrence, and that those cases had not recognized a "personal right" to exclude unconstitutionally obtained evidence.[239]

Brennan's reply to Black's dissent was subtle but telling. Black had questioned, as Brennan acknowledged, "the propriety of the exclusionary rule itself."[240] But Black also insisted that the Court's prior cases held that the rule was not a personal right of the defendant. While Brennan defended the rule, he did not challenge or refute Black's latter claim. Brennan did not describe exclusion as a constitutional right of the victim of an unreasonable search or seizure. Instead, he noted that invocation of the rule was not intended to turn on the possibility of a defendant's innocence.[241] Exclusion of illegally secured evidence, Brennan explained, "is deemed necessary to protect the *right of all citizens*, not merely the citizen on trial, to be secure against unreasonable searches and seizures."[242]

Although Brennan's *Kaufman* opinion was unwilling to challenge Black's characterization of the exclusionary rule, Fortas drafted a concurring opinion that directly confronted Black's view of the rule. Describing the Fourth Amendment as a "fundamental guaranty of liberty," Fortas observed that the right "is not qualified by the proposition that it exists only where its violation affects the 'integrity of the fact-finding process'

---

234 *Id.*

235 *Id.* at 232–33 (Black, J., dissenting).

236 *Id.* at 237.

237 *Id.* at 237–38.

238 *Id.* at 239.

239 *Id.* at 239–40.

240 *Id.* at 229 (majority opinion).

241 *Id.*

242 *Id.* (emphasis added).

of a trial."[243] According to Fortas, if the Amendment is violated, a person "can compel the State or the Federal Government to disgorge the fruits of its violation, totally apart from any criminal proceedings, or from any question of his guilt or innocence."[244] Fortas also rebutted Black's claim that the purpose behind exclusion was deterrence of illegal searches. Deterrence is not "the sole or primary reason for saying to the officials of the state that they may not use the fruits of their violation of a person's Fourth Amendment rights. The basic reason is not deterrence of a violation of a right. It is to vindicate the right itself, whether or not vindication also operates to deter."[245] For Fortas, "at stake here is a principle—that a man's person is sacred, that his home is his castle—and not a tactic in the struggle to persuade the police to be law abiding."[246]

While Fortas's concurrence in *Kaufman* was never published, it starkly reveals the differences between Fortas and the other justices who signed Brennan's *Kaufman* opinion. Whereas Fortas saw exclusion as a personal constitutional right of the defendant, *Kaufman* characterized exclusion as necessary to protect the rights of all citizens, which is a subtle way of saying that exclusion is designed to deter. Fortas's unpublished opinion also highlights that a majority of the Warren Court was unwilling, eight years after *Mapp* was decided, to ground the exclusionary rule in the Fourth Amendment itself.

On the same day the Court decided *Kaufman*, it also announced *Desist v. United States*.[247] Because *Desist* was another retroactivity case, the Court applied *Linkletter*'s three-part test for determining the retroactivity of a new Fourth Amendment holding. Although *Desist* did not change the law, it is an important case for understanding the Court's thinking on the exclusionary rule because it was written by Stewart, a key swing justice on both the Warren and Burger Courts. In *Mapp*, Stewart did not express his views on exclusion because he felt that the Court had decided an issue not properly before it. Based on Stewart's published statements as a retired justice,[248] Professor Kamisar has commented that had the *Mapp* Court ordered reargument in that case, or simply waited for another state case presenting the exclusionary rule issue, Stewart probably would have provided a fifth vote for imposing the exclusionary rule on the states based on the Fourth Amendment alone.[249] Had Stewart voted for exclusion, "Justice

[243] Abe Fortas, Draft of Concurring Opinion in *Kaufman v. United States* 5-6 (undated), Brennan Papers, Box I: 187.

[244] *Id.* at 6.

[245] *Id.* at 7.

[246] *Id.* at 8. Ultimately, Fortas withdrew his separate concurrence and joined Brennan's majority without comment.

[247] 394 U.S. 244 (1969).

[248] In 1983, Stewart described his thinking about the exclusionary rule when *Elkins* and *Mapp* were decided: "I believed then, and I believe now, that the exclusionary rule *is* constitutionally required, not as a 'right' explicitly incorporated in the fourth amendment's prohibitions, but as a remedy necessary to ensure that those prohibitions are observed in fact.... I agree with [*Mapp*'s] conclusion that the exclusionary rule *is* necessary to keep the right of privacy secured by the fourth amendment from 'remain[ing] an empty promise.'" Stewart, *supra* note 16, at 1389 (second alteration in original) (quoting Mapp v. Ohio, 367 U.S. 643, 660 (1961)).

[249] Kamisar, *First Shot Fired*, *supra* note 10, at 53.

Clark probably would not have needed Justice Black's vote nor have had to put up with Black's Fifth Amendment theory of the exclusionary rule."[250]

While Stewart's writings as a retired justice demonstrate that he had reached the conclusion that the exclusionary rule is "constitutionally required, not as a 'right,' ... but as a remedy,"[251] his comments during conference discussions suggest that Stewart never fully accepted the view that exclusion was a constitutionally required remedy. His statement in the *Kaufman* conference and his draft opinion in *Elkins* reveal that Stewart saw the rule as not required by the Constitution, but rather as a judge-made rule of evidence. Similarly, in 1972, when the Court was deciding whether President Nixon had the inherent authority to employ warrantless wiretaps in domestic security cases,[252] Stewart told his colleagues in the conference discussion "If *Weeks* were overruled, we would have no problem."[253] Although cryptic, this statement does not suggest that Stewart saw exclusion as a right inherent in the Fourth Amendment. And his opinion in *Desist* confirms that Stewart did not view the exclusionary rule as part and parcel of the Fourth Amendment.

Desist addressed whether *Katz v. United States*[254] would apply retroactively. Also authored by Stewart, *Katz* held that electronic wiretapping of a telephone conversation constitutes a search within the meaning of the Fourth Amendment. As Wayne LaFave has explained, the theory behind *Linkletter*'s view of the retroactivity of new search and seizure rulings is that the primary purpose of the exclusionary rule is deterrence, and "no deterrence will be gained by excluding evidence obtained by police conduct which fully comported with the decisions of the Supreme Court at the time that conduct occurred."[255] And the most important factor of *Linkletter*'s three-prong balancing test is the "purpose" prong, which asks what purpose is served by the new constitutional principle. When this logic is applied to whether *Mapp* should be given retroactive treatment, the result in *Linkletter* is understandable because there is little deterrence to be gained from excluding evidence in cases where the police had previously operated under a regime where illegally acquired evidence was admissible at trial. This logic, however, does not automatically dictate that *Katz* should be denied retroactive application. Yet, in *Desist*, Stewart explains that the purpose prong of *Linkletter* "strongly supports prospectivity for a decision amplifying the evidentiary exclusionary rule."[256] He then reaffirms *Linkletter*'s conclusion that the purpose of *Mapp* was strictly deterrence.[257] This is all that Stewart says about the purpose of *Katz*.

---

250 *Id.*

251 Stewart, *supra* note 16, at 1389.

252 United States v. U.S. District Court, 407 U.S. 297 (1972).

253 Lewis Powell, Conference Notes on *United States v. U.S. District Court* (undated), Powell Papers, Box 2.

254 389 U.S. 347 (1967).

255 6 LaFave, *supra* note 90, § 11.5(a), at 385.

256 Desist v. United States, 394 U.S. 244, 249 (1969).

257 *Id.*

Stewart's explanation for prospective-only application of *Katz* raises several questions. First, by characterizing exclusion as "the evidentiary exclusionary rule" and calling it the "court-made exclusionary rule,"[258] Stewart appears to be reopening the debate that *Mapp* had resolved, namely, whether the rule is compelled by the Fourth Amendment. *Mapp*, of course, concluded that the exclusionary rule was mandated by the Constitution. Moreover, Stewart's application of *Linkletter*'s "purpose" prong is bewildering. *Katz* concerned the scope of the Fourth Amendment; it sought to clarify the Court's prior rulings addressing whether electronic surveillance triggered the Amendment's protection.[259] The "purpose" of *Katz* was to provide constitutional protection to a person's private telephone conversations. *Katz* did not consider or discuss the exclusionary rule. Nevertheless, Stewart links the purpose behind *Katz* with purpose of the exclusionary rule. By so doing, *Desist* implies, incorrectly, that all Fourth Amendment rulings are ultimately about deterrence of police misconduct.

In his last footnote in *Desist*, Stewart replies to the argument that he has confused the substance of the Fourth Amendment with the intent of the exclusionary rule.[260] Fortas's dissent in *Desist* charged that the majority denies "the benefit of a fundamental constitutional provision, and not merely of court-made rules implementing a constitutional mandate."[261] Stewart countered that he was doing no more than what was done in *Linkletter*—namely, weighing the expediency of applying the exclusionary rule in a particular setting. Thus, Stewart explained that the Court was simply declining "to extend the court-made exclusionary rule to cases in which its deterrent purpose would not be served. The exclusionary rule 'has no bearing on guilt' or 'the fairness of the trial.'"[262]

Stewart's approach to the exclusionary rule in *Desist* was puzzling in light of the different purposes behind *Mapp* and *Katz*. The upshot of *Desist* was to link the retroactivity of new Fourth Amendment rulings with the purpose of the exclusionary rule. By contrast, White's discussion of the rule in *Alderman v. United States*,[263] the last important Warren Court decision on the rule, was unequivocal. The defendants in *Alderman* had been convicted in three separate prosecutions. Subsequently, it was learned that the government might have illegally wiretapped conversations involving the defendants. Before

---

258 *Id.* at 254 n.24.

259 *See* David A. Sklansky, Katz v. United States*: The Limits of Aphorism*, in CRIMINAL PROCEDURE STORIES 223, 226–36 (Carol S. Steiker ed., 2006).

260 *Desist*, 394 U.S. at 254 n.24.

261 *Id.* at 271 (Fortas, J., dissenting).

262 *Id.* at 254 n.24 (majority opinion).

263 394 U.S. 165 (1969). Besides the Fourth Amendment issues it addressed, *Alderman* was important because of the controversy that surrounded the case after it was decided. SCHWARTZ, *supra* note 21, at 749. According to Warren and other members of the Court, the result in *Alderman* prompted a deliberate effort by the Nixon Administration's Department of Justice "'to surreptitiously influence the action of [the Court].'" *Id.* (alteration in original) (quoting EARL WARREN, THE MEMOIRS OF EARL WARREN 337 (1977)); *see also* MICHAL R. BELKNAP, THE SUPREME COURT UNDER EARL WARREN 1953–1969, at 301–302 (2005).

deciding what procedures were required to determine whether any of the government's evidence supporting the convictions was the fruit of the unlawful wiretaps, the Court addressed the separate question of the defendants' standing to challenge the use of illegal wiretap evidence at their prosecutions.

The defendants argued that they had a right to exclude any evidence proffered by the prosecution if the evidence was the product of an illegal wiretap, "regardless of whose Fourth Amendment rights the surveillance violated."[264] Alternatively, they contended that if illegally acquired wiretap evidence is inadmissible against one defendant or conspirator, it is also inadmissible against a fellow codefendant or coconspirator.[265] White's opinion for the Court rejected both arguments. Only Fortas and Douglas dissented.

Alderman held that a defendant may not challenge the admission of evidence obtained in violation of the Fourth Amendment rights of another person. On a first read, this holding was uncontroversial and should have been expected. One year before *Mapp*, a unanimous Court had stated in *Jones v. United States* that a defendant who challenges the legality of a search must show that "he himself was the victim of an invasion of privacy."[266] Moreover, as far back as 1942, the Court cited with approval the unanimous view of the lower federal courts that a defendant in a criminal case could object to the introduction of illegally seized evidence only when his own Fourth Amendment rights had been violated.[267] As White explained in *Alderman*, prior rulings established "the general rule that Fourth Amendment rights are personal rights which, like some other constitutional rights, may not be vicariously asserted."[268]

On the other hand, if the Fourth Amendment itself compels the exclusionary rule, as *Mapp* held, then, as Fortas observed in his separate opinion in *Alderman*, "there is no basis for confining its invocation to persons whose right of privacy has been violated by an illegal search."[269] The Amendment places restrictions on the government at large. It is "a fundamental part of the constitutional compact, the observance of which is essential to the welfare of all persons."[270] This view of the Fourth Amendment and its exclusionary sanction supports the conclusion that "any defendant against whom illegally acquired evidence is offered, whether or not it was obtained in violation of his right to privacy, may have the evidence excluded."[271] This argument, one would think, might have persuaded liberal members of the *Alderman* Court like Warren, Brennan, and Marshall. But it did not. Only Fortas and Douglas were prepared to allow defendants to challenge the admission of evidence unlawfully obtained from third parties.

264 *Alderman*, 394 U.S. at 171.

265 *Id.*

266 Jones v. United States, 362 U.S. 257, 261 (1960).

267 Goldstein v. United States, 316 U.S. 114, 121 (1942).

268 *Alderman*, 394 U.S. at 174.

269 *Id.* at 205 (Fortas, J., concurring in part and dissenting in part).

270 *Id.*

271 *Id.* at 205–06.

While *Alderman* revealed that a substantial majority of the Warren Court would not extend the logic of *Mapp* to defendants who had not been the victims of Fourth Amendment violations, it also demonstrated that the meaning of *Mapp* had permanently changed. To be sure, *Alderman* did not characterize the exclusionary rule as "a judicially created remedy,"[272] or uncouple the rule from the Fourth Amendment itself, as the Burger Court subsequently did to restrict the rule's scope.[273] White's opinion in *Alderman* appeared to treat the rule as a constitutional requirement of the Fourth Amendment. White stated that "there is a substantial difference for *constitutional* purposes between preventing the incrimination of a defendant through the very evidence illegally seized from him and suppressing evidence on the motion of a party who cannot claim this predicate for exclusion."[274]

But *Alderman* did reaffirm and solidify what *Linkletter* said about the exclusionary rule, and in the process showed how nimble the Court was in shifting from theory to theory to justify its exclusionary rule decisions. Quoting *Linkletter* and *Elkins*, but not *Mapp*, White acknowledged the deterrent purpose of exclusion.[275] Doubtlessly recognizing that the standing limitation was inconsistent with the instrumental view of the rule endorsed by *Elkins* and *Linkletter*,[276] White explained that the Court had never endorsed the position that "anything which deters illegal searches is thereby commanded by the Fourth Amendment."[277] In other words, even though the Court had justified exclusion under an instrumental theory of deterrence, *Alderman*'s holding was based on the personal right theory of exclusion announced in *Weeks* and implicitly disavowed by *Wolf* and *Linkletter*. *Alderman* exercised a prerogative that the Court would repeat in the future: "The Court shifts to whichever reason for exclusion gives it a reason not to exclude."[278]

Equally important, White signaled that future applications of the exclusionary rule would turn on an amorphous balancing test.[279] Adopting a balancing formula for determining the

[272] United States v. Calandra, 414 U.S. 338, 348 (1974).

[273] United States v. Leon, 468 U.S. 897, 906 (1984) ("Whether the exclusionary sanction is appropriately imposed in a particular case, our decisions make clear, is 'an issue separate from the question whether the Fourth Amendment rights of the party seeking to invoke the rule were violated by police conduct.'").

[274] *See Alderman*, 394 U.S. at 174 (emphasis added); *see also id.* at 175–76 (stating that while Congress or state legislatures may extend the exclusionary rule and provide that tainted evidence is inadmissible against anyone for any purpose, "for *constitutional* purposes, we are not now inclined to expand the existing rule that unlawful wiretapping or eavesdropping, whether deliberate or negligent, can produce nothing usable against the person aggrieved by the invasion" (emphasis added)).

[275] *Id.* at 174.

[276] Both before and after *Alderman*, scholars have recognized the tension between the standing requirement and the exclusionary rule's focus on deterring the police. *See, e.g.*, Joshua Dressler & Alan C. Michaels, 1 Understanding Criminal Procedure 345–46 (4th ed. 2006); Sherry F. Colb, *Standing Room Only: Why Fourth Amendment Exclusion and Standing Can No Longer Logically Coexist*, 28 Cardozo L. Rev. 1663 (2007).

[277] *Alderman*, 394 U.S. at 174.

[278] Alschuler, *Causation*, *supra* note 80, at 1756.

[279] *Alderman*, 394 U.S. at 174–75. White stated: "The deterrent values of preventing the incrimination of those whose rights the police have violated have been considered sufficient to justify the suppression of

utilization of the rule in a particular setting was consistent with *Linkletter* but at odds with *Mapp*. As noted earlier, *Mapp* eschewed a balancing test and rested the exclusionary rule on the Fourth Amendment itself. By embracing a vague balancing formula, *Alderman* was a significant alteration of the reasoning of *Mapp*. It also suggested that future applications of the exclusionary rule would turn, not on a neutral legal principle, but instead on the attitudes of the justices toward the Fourth Amendment and the exclusionary rule itself.

* * *

The reasoning and results in *Linkletter* and the cases that followed it demonstrated the Warren Court's unwillingness to extend the exclusionary rule beyond the boundaries established in *Mapp*. Perhaps because the liberal justices were concerned about the political fallout of applying the exclusionary rule retroactively, or because some justices concluded that retrospective application of *Mapp* might preclude future progressive results,[280] *Linkletter*'s holding prevented the "jail delivery" that Harlan predicted when *Mapp* was under consideration in the Court.[281] But a desire to preempt a massive jailbreak does not explain Warren's narrow description of the interests served by the exclusionary rule and his cautious comments about the rule's effectiveness in *Terry*. Nor does the "jailbreak" theory rationalize *Alderman*'s characterization of the exclusionary rule. In the post-*Mapp* era, the Warren Court altered the foundation of the exclusionary rule; exclusion was grounded on a deterrence model. This was a significant change from the premise of *Mapp*. In fact, it was a return to Frankfurter's view of the exclusionary rule. Having finally decided to overrule *Wolf* in a revolutionary ruling that no one predicted, by the end of the 1960s, the justices had started a slow, but discernible, retreat from the implications and principles contained in *Mapp*. That retreat would gain greater momentum with the appointment and confirmation of Warren Burger as the next Chief Justice of the United States.

---

probative evidence even though the case against the defendant is weakened or destroyed. We adhere to that judgment. But we are not convinced that the additional benefits of extending the exclusionary rule to other defendants would justify further encroachment upon the public interest in prosecuting those accused of crime and having them acquitted or convicted on the basis of all the evidence which exposes the truth." *Id.* Professor Meltzer has observed that although *Alderman* "purported to consider the [issue of standing to invoke the exclusionary rule] in light of the deterrent rationale," White's opinion "was purely conclusory." Daniel J. Meltzer, *Deterring Constitutional Violations by Law Enforcement Officials: Plaintiffs and Defendants as Private Attorneys General*, 88 COLUM. L. REV. 247, 275 (1988).

280 *See* Haddad, *supra* note 183, at 439 (explaining that liberal justices like Warren and Brennan recognize that prospective-only application of criminal procedure rulings "permits them to engage in what they sincerely believe is the necessary task of their Court: the upgrading of the safeguards for citizens confronted by the criminal process, particularly state court defendants, in areas where history, they believe, teaches that lower courts, and particularly state courts, simply will not take action"); *see also* POWE, *supra* note 115, at 426–27 ("Warren, Brennan, and Fortas voted for nonretroactivity because it freed them to do good. They understood that if the criminal procedure rules were retroactive, then there would be a huge backlash against the changes and the Court. Making the decisions nonretroactive muted that backlash.").

281 Harlan, Letter to Tom Clark on *Mapp v. Ohio*, *supra* note 195.

4 The Burger Court: Uncoupling the Exclusionary Rule from the Constitution

IN ONE OF the last Fourth Amendment opinions of the Warren Court, the Court stated: "Our decisions recognize no exception to the rule that illegally seized evidence is inadmissible at trial, however relevant and trustworthy the seized evidence may be as an item of proof."[1] One month later, President Richard Nixon nominated Warren E. Burger as Earl Warren's replacement as Chief Justice of the United States. Within the next three years, President Nixon would appoint three more justices, none of whom were considered supporters of the Fourth Amendment's exclusionary rule. With the ascendancy of the Burger Court, the scope of the exclusionary rule predictably experienced significant curtailment. But why the Court did not abolish the rule outright remains a perplexing question. Certainly, eliminating the exclusionary rule was one of the goals of Chief Justice Warren Burger.

As a judge on the federal Court of Appeals for the District of Columbia, Warren Burger had a reputation as a "law and order" jurist. Appointed by President Eisenhower in 1956, Judge Burger often dissented from the criminal procedure rulings announced by his more liberal colleagues. Off the bench, Burger was an outspoken critic of Warren Court rulings that he felt tipped the scales of justice to unduly favor criminal defendants. On May 21, 1967, Burger delivered the commencement address at Ripon College. Burger told his audience that one of the negative aspects of the American criminal

[1] Davis v. Mississippi, 394 U.S. 721, 724 (1969).

justice system was that "[w]e afford the accused more procedural protections, such as the exclusion and suppression of evidence and the dismissal of cases for irregularities in the arrests or searches, than under any other system."[2] Burger's speech was later reprinted in the *U.S. News & World Report* and caught the eye of a Republican politician.[3] In his memoirs, Richard Nixon recalled that he was impressed with the speech "on the role of law and order in society."[4] Nixon used several themes from the speech during his 1968 presidential campaign.[5] Although the Ripon College speech did not dwell on the evils of the exclusionary rule, three years earlier, Burger discussed the rule in a lecture at the Washington College of Law at American University entitled, "*Who Will Watch the Watchman?*"[6] This talk revealed Burger's utmost antipathy toward the exclusionary rule.

Observing that the exclusionary rule had no roots in the common law of England, Burger remarked that suppression of illegally obtained evidence was as "indigenous to America as tobacco," and had "flourished almost with the vigor of the cigarette industry."[7] He acknowledged that earlier exclusionary rule precedents, such as *Boyd v. United States*[8] and *Weeks v. United States*[9] had built the rule upon a constitutional foundation, and that it was not "until many years later [that] we find utterances about supervisory powers of appellate courts, police discipline, deterrence of illegal police conduct to prevent polluting the stream of justice, or a basic unfairness of using illegally acquired evidence" as justifications for exclusion.[10] Indeed, regarding *Weeks*, Burger noted that the "idea of deterrence may be lurking between the lines of the opinion but is not expressed."[11]

By the mid-1960s, however, Burger explained that the Court had settled upon deterrence of illegal searches and seizures as the principal basis for exclusion. Though Burger provided his audience no empirical proof that the rule failed to deter, he believed the deterrence rationale was a chimera. He stated, "the notion that suppression of evidence in a given case effectively deters the future action of the particular policeman or of policemen generally was never more than wishful thinking on the part of the courts."[12] He was also convinced that suppression undermined enforcement of the criminal law, threatened public safety, and "brings to the public gaze a spectacle repugnant to all decent

---

2 Warren E. Burger, *Paradoxes in the Administration of Criminal Justice*, 58 J. CRIM. L. CRIMINOLOGY & POLICE SCI. 428, 429 (1967).

3 RICHARD NIXON, THE MEMOIRS OF RICHARD NIXON 420 (1978).

4 *Id.*

5 *Id.*

6 Warren E. Burger, *Who Will Watch the Watchman?*, 14 AM. U. L. REV. 1 (1964) [hereinafter Burger, *Watchman*].

7 *Id.* at 1 (footnote omitted).

8 116 U.S. 616 (1886).

9 232 U.S. 383 (1914).

10 Burger, *Watchman*, *supra* note 6, at 4–5.

11 *Id.* at 5.

12 *Id.* at 12.

people—the frustration of justice."[13] Burger urged society to "recognize suppression as an essential tool to implement the Constitution and nothing more, and that other and different means of deterrence must be devised."[14]

Perhaps because he recognized that the Court's precedents established that the exclusionary rule was constitutionally required, or perhaps because he recognized the direction of the political winds on the Court, Burger did not propose eliminating the rule. Instead, he suggested the creation of independent review boards to investigate complaints of illegal police conduct as supplements to the rule.[15] But he left no doubt about his own view of exclusion and his belief that the time had arrived for society to reexamine the rule. Exclusion of evidence was "a necessary evil and hardly more than a manifestation of sterile judicial indignation," and Burger questioned whether "any community is entitled to call itself an 'organized society' if it can find no way to solve this problem except by suppression of truth in the search for truth."[16] Although few people would have predicted it in 1964, in a few years Burger would occupy the center chair on the Court and be uniquely positioned to affect not only the scope of the exclusionary rule but also whether the rule would survive.

When President Nixon chose Warren Burger to succeed Chief Justice Earl Warren, Nixon told reporters that he selected Burger because Burger agreed with his view that judges should strictly interpret the Constitution. Nixon also noted that Burger shared his belief that the Warren Court had gone too far in expanding the rights of criminal suspects and defendants.[17] Nixon's sense of Burger's legal instincts was dead on as Burger "came to the Court with an agenda that included a massive dismantling of the jurisprudential edifice erected by the Warren Court, particularly in the field of criminal justice."[18]

It did not take long for Burger to begin undermining the foundations of the exclusionary rule. Burger's first move came in a *Miranda* interrogation case, *Harris v. New York*.[19] At issue was whether a statement obtained in violation of *Miranda* could be used to impeach a defendant's credibility at trial. Harris was charged with selling heroin to an undercover officer. When he took the stand, Harris admitted selling the contents of a glassine bag but testified it was baking powder. On cross-examination, the prosecutor asked Harris about statements that he had made while under arrest, but without the benefit of full *Miranda* warnings. These statements partially contradicted Harris's direct testimony. Harris stated he could not remember all of his statements. The prosecutor was allowed to impeach Harris's credibility by reading to the

[13] *Id.*
[14] *Id.* at 13.
[15] *Id.* at 16-23.
[16] *Id.* at 23.
[17] Robert B. Semple Jr., *Nixon Influenced by Fortas Affair in Court Choices*, N.Y. Times, May 23, 1969, at 1.
[18] Bernard Schwartz, The Ascent of Pragmatism: The Burger Court in Action 7 (1990).
[19] 401 U.S. 222 (1971).

jury Harris's post-arrest statements. Harris was convicted of selling narcotics, and the New York courts ruled that the incriminating statements could be considered by the jury in judging Harris's credibility but not as evidence of his guilt.

As Brennan would describe the process, when it arrived at the Court, *Harris* "slip[ped] by everyone."[20] The conference vote was unanimous against Harris, and Burger assigned the case to himself. Burger's first circulation stated that Frankfurter's opinion in *Walder v. United States*, which had created an impeachment exception for evidence obtained from an unlawful search regarding a collateral matter, "is dispositive" on the issue of whether illegally obtained evidence was admissible for impeachment purposes.[21] Within a few days, however, Black, Douglas, and Brennan wrote Burger to register disagreement with this conclusion.[22] In particular, Brennan told Burger that he read *Walder* "to imply that the defendant's testimony at trial merely denying the elements of the charged crime cannot be impeached by illegally obtained evidence."[23] Brennan told Burger that he was changing his vote and would soon circulate a draft dissent, in which he described *Walder* as a case involving impeachment using collateral evidence unrelated to the charges at trial.

Burger then circulated another opinion, which became the final opinion in *Harris* and was joined by four other justices. Burger conceded that *Walder* involved impeachment concerning collateral matters, whereas Harris was impeached with evidence directly bearing on the crimes charged.[24] But Burger was "not persuaded that there is a difference in principle" between the two cases.[25] What was important to Burger was that impeachment of Harris's credibility "provided valuable aid to the jury," and that aid should not be lost because of the "speculative possibility that impermissible police conduct will be encouraged thereby."[26] While Burger was willing to assume a deterrent effect from exclusion, he concluded that "sufficient deterrence" was achieved when illegally acquired evidence is barred from proving a defendant's guilt.[27]

The effect of *Harris* was plain: it expanded the scope of *Walder*'s arguably narrow ruling that permitted a prosecutor to impeach a defendant's credibility with unconstitutionally acquired evidence related to collateral matters. After *Harris*, prosecutors could

---

20 William J. Brennan, Jr., Case Histories, October Term, 1970, at XVII (undated) [hereinafter Brennan, Case Histories O.T. 1970], Brennan Papers, Box II: 6.

21 Warren Burger, Memorandum to the Conference on *Harris v. New York* 4 (Jan. 4, 1971), Harlan Papers, Box 432.

22 *See* Hugo Black, Letter to Warren Burger on *Harris v. New York* (Jan. 5, 1971), Harlan Papers, Box 432; William J. Brennan, Jr., Letter to Warren Burger on *Harris v. New York* (Jan. 6, 1971), Harlan Papers, Box 432; William Douglas, Letter to Warren Burger on *Harris v. New York* (Jan. 5, 1971), Harlan Papers, Box 432.

23 Brennan, Letter to Warren Burger on *Harris v. New York*, *supra* note 22.

24 Warren Burger, Third Draft of *Harris v. New York* 4 (Feb. 5, 1971), Harlan Papers, Box 432.

25 *Id.*

26 *Id.*

27 *Id.*

also impeach a defendant's credibility with tainted evidence that was directly related to his guilt, which was forbidden under *Agnello v. United States*, which many years earlier had rejected the government's claim that illegally acquired evidence was admissible for rebuttal purposes when a defendant testified falsely on direct examination. The continuing validity of *Agnello* was unknown because it was neither cited nor discussed by Burger.[28]

Harris established Burger's opposition to the principle that illegally obtained evidence should remain untouchable by the judiciary. By contrast, Brennan thought it "monstrous" that the Court would assist police who violate *Miranda* and complained that *Harris* "goes far toward undoing much of the progress made in conforming police methods to the Constitution."[29] Two well-known law professors insisted that *Harris* had overruled *Agnello v. United States sub silentio*.[30] The result in *Harris* was a harbinger of things to come. Looking back at the breadth of the Burger Court's criminal procedure jurisprudence, *Harris* is a foundational case. During the early years of the Burger Court, however, only a handful scholars and lawyers would have cited *Harris* as the initial step in the dismantling of the exclusionary rule. Burger's opinions and conference commentary in four search-and-seizure cases decided in the same Term as *Harris*, however, offered explicit proof that he was eager and determined to abolish the exclusionary rule.

* * *

Harold Whiteley was arrested by Laramie, Wyoming, police officers after the state police radio network announced a bulletin that an arrest warrant for burglary charges had been issued for Whiteley and another man. A search of Whiteley's car revealed evidence related to the burglary. It was later determined that the arrest warrant was based on a tip that failed to establish probable cause. Whiteley argued that the evidence discovered in his car had to be suppressed because the warrant was not supported by probable cause, and the Laramie officers had no independent grounds for the arrest or search since they were relying on the radio bulletin announcing the existence of the warrant. The Wyoming courts and two federal habeas courts rejected Whiteley's claim and affirmed his conviction.

The Court initially denied Whiteley's petition for writ of certiorari. White, however, circulated a dissent that explained why Whiteley's arrest was unconstitutional.[31] According to White, it was not necessary that the Laramie police know the facts justifying the arrest. But if the arresting officers themselves did not have probable cause,

---

28 In a penetrating and comprehensive article on the impeachment exception, one scholar argues that *Harris* "dealt a severe blow to *Agnello*." James L. Kainen, *The Impeachment Exception to the Exclusionary Rules: Policies, Principles, and Politics*, 44 STAN. L. REV. 1301, 1307 (1992).

29 Harris v. New York, 401 U.S. 222, 232 (1971) (Brennan, J., dissenting).

30 Alan M. Dershowitz & John Hart Ely, Comment, Harris v. New York*: Some Anxious Observations on the Candor and Logic of the Emerging Nixon Majority*, 80 YALE L.J. 1198, 1213 (1971).

31 Byron White, Dissent from Denial of Certiorari in *Whiteley v. Warden* (recirculated Apr. 21, 1970), Harlan Papers, Box 430.

the warrant itself needed to be supported by probable cause. White observed that the Laramie police

> should not be criticized, punished, or held civilly liable for making the arrest on the basis of the police broadcast. But the good faith of the arresting officer did not make the arrest constitutional. Inadequate cause does not become adequate probable cause when an arrest order is passed from one police officer to another either by word of mouth or by radio.[32]

Shortly after White circulated his dissent, Douglas and Marshall joined it. Soon, Harlan was also on board and stated that White's dissent had convinced him to change his vote to review the case.[33]

Because of White's proposed dissent, *Whiteley v. Warden* was restored to the docket. Although neither litigant in *Whiteley* addressed the exclusionary rule nor proposed overruling *Mapp v. Ohio* in their briefs or during oral argument, both topics were raised in the *Whiteley* conference. Burger began the discussion by noting that the case turns on whether the sheriff who obtained the warrant had a right to arrest Whiteley. If the sheriff had "no such right, then he could give it to no one else."[34] Burger then shifted grounds and stated that "we should put an end to the exclusionary rule."[35] And he closed his remarks by saying, "I'd overrule *Mapp* and *Weeks*."[36] Burger voted to affirm Whiteley's conviction.[37] Black also voted to affirm and Douglas passed.[38] Harlan stated that he "would overrule *Mapp* if a Court can be mustered for it."[39] Harlan explained that he would "have trouble doing the same with *Weeks* since that deals with our supervisory power."[40] If the Court was not prepared to overrule *Mapp*, Harlan thought there was no probable cause for the arrest, and the state "can't bootstrap probable cause by a radio broadcast."[41] Stewart stated that he agreed "with everything that John Harlan has said."[42] White spoke next and stated that he "would not overrule *Mapp* or *Weeks*."[43] Blackmun closed the discussion by noting that "this case really gets down to whether we should overrule *Mapp*."[44]

---

32 *Id.* at 2.

33 John Harlan, Memorandum to the Conference on *Whiteley v. Warden* (Apr. 21, 1970), Harlan Papers, Box 430.

34 William Douglas, Conference Notes on *Whiteley v. Warden* (Jan. 15, 1971), Douglas Papers, Box 1490.

35 *Id.*

36 William J. Brennan, Jr., Conference Notes on *Whiteley v. Warden* (undated) [hereinafter Brennan, *Whiteley* Conference Notes], Brennan Papers, Box I: 228.

37 Douglas, Conference Notes on *Whiteley v. Warden*, *supra* note 34.

38 *Id.*

39 Brennan, *Whiteley* Conference Notes, *supra* note 36.

40 *Id.*

41 *Id.*

42 *Id.*

43 *Id.*

44 *Id.*

Despite Burger's call to use *Whiteley* as the vehicle to repeal the exclusionary rule, Harlan's opinion for the Court simply reversed Whiteley's conviction. Harlan explained that when police officers are asked to assist other officers in executing an arrest warrant, police "are entitled to assume that the officers requesting aid offered the magistrate the information requisite to support an independent judicial assessment of probable cause."[45] But if the requesting officers themselves did not possess probable cause to obtain a warrant, "an otherwise illegal arrest cannot be insulated from challenge by the decision of the instigating officer to rely on fellow officers to make the arrest."[46] Although four justices indicated in conference their willingness to consider overruling *Mapp*, Harlan's opinion gave no indication that the Court was deeply divided over the exclusionary rule. He succinctly noted that because Whiteley's arrest violated the Fourth Amendment, *Mapp* required that the evidence secured from that arrest should have been excluded from Whiteley's trial.[47] That was all *Whiteley* had to say about the exclusionary rule.

Like Harlan's opinion in *Whiteley*, the published opinion in *Williams v. United States*[48] provides no hint that the case and its companion case, *Elkanich v. United States*, involved another skirmish over the exclusionary rule. The issue in *Williams* was whether a recent search incident to arrest ruling, *Chimel v. California*,[49] should apply retroactively or in post-conviction collateral proceedings. Two years earlier, *Chimel* drastically reduced the authority of police to search the premises of persons arrested inside their homes or offices.[50]

Brennan's private papers explain that after the conference vote in *Williams*, the "Chief Justice, sensing a strong majority and some dissatisfaction with *Mapp* and *Chimel*, initially assigned the opinions to himself, apparently with some hope of mustering a Court to overrule one or both of those decisions."[51] But Burger evidently changed his mind, and the cases were assigned to White, who stated at the conference that he "wouldn't apply the exclusionary rule retroactively since it doesn't further deterrence objectively."[52]

At the start of the Burger Court, White's view of the exclusionary rule was difficult to determine. Although he joined the Warren Court shortly after *Mapp* was decided, conventional wisdom had it that White opposed the exclusionary rule.[53] In August of 1966, White gave a speech to the National District Attorneys Association Foundation

---

45 Whiteley v. Warden, 401 U.S. 560, 568 (1971).

46 *Id.*

47 *Id.* at 568-69.

48 401 U.S. 646 (1971).

49 395 U.S. 752 (1969).

50 *Id.*

51 Brennan, Case Histories O.T. 1970, *supra* note 20, at XLII-XLIII.

52 William J. Brennan, Jr., Conference Notes on *Williams v. United States* (undated), Brennan Papers, Box I: 228.

53 *See* DENNIS J. HUTCHINSON, THE MAN WHO ONCE WAS WHIZZER WHITE: A PORTRAIT OF JUSTICE BYRON R. WHITE 344–45 (1998).

that seemed circumspect toward *Mapp*.[54] According to a newspaper account, White told his audience that neither the text nor the history of the Fourth Amendment "requires or even strongly suggests that illegally seized evidence is inadmissible in the court of a criminal trial. But neither do they preclude such a holding."[55] White also observed that rulings like *Mapp* and *Miranda* involve important public policy questions "which must be decided in terms of the long-range aims of the community."[56]

During the final Term of the Warren Court, White authored a majority opinion that sent mixed signals about the rule. In *Alderman*, he seemed to treat the rule as a constitutional requirement, but he also wrote that the sole purpose of the rule was deterrence of illegal intrusions. In the final years of the Burger Court, White's opinions would clearly demonstrate that he no longer viewed exclusion as mandated by the Fourth Amendment itself. But in the early 1970s, White's view of the rule was apparently still evolving. And as far as eliminating exclusion as a remedy, White stated in the *Whiteley* conference that he opposed overruling either *Weeks* or *Mapp*.[57]

An exchange between Brennan and White regarding White's description of the rule's purpose in *Williams* reveals White's ambivalence toward the rule at the time. According to Brennan's private papers, White's first draft of *Williams* was sent to Brennan "privately for a looksee before circulation" to the other justices.[58] The draft substantially tracked White's final opinion as published. Regarding suppression, the draft "justified the exclusion of illegally seized evidence solely upon the grounds of deterrence."[59] Brennan later notified White that he would write a separate opinion in *Williams* because of his strong feeling that "the exclusionary rule was not fashioned merely as a deterrent against improper police conduct but is actually an essential element of the protection of privacy secured by the Fourth Amendment."[60] White, "somewhat surprisingly," told Brennan "that he might well be happy to change his opinion" in order to secure Brennan's vote. In the meantime, White would circulate his draft to the other justices.[61]

When White's first draft had trouble obtaining five votes to rule that *Chimel* did not apply retroactively, White sought Brennan's help. According to Brennan's records, White called him "in something of a fit of depression, predicting that chaos over the retroactivity decisions might lead to the overruling of *Mapp*."[62] White also suggested that he might try revising his opinion to satisfy Brennan's view, "specifically by incorporating in the opinion a firm justification of the exclusionary rule as necessary not to deter police

---

54 *Id.* at 345.

55 *Id.*

56 John Kokish, *DAs Hear Justice White*, DENVER POST, Aug. 18, 1966, at 3. Professor Dennis Hutchinson, a former law clerk to White, interpreted White's speech as critical of *Mapp*. *See* HUTCHINSON, *supra* note 53, at 345.

57 Brennan, *Whiteley* Conference Notes, *supra* note 36.

58 Brennan, Case Histories O.T. 1970, *supra* note 20, at XLIII.

59 *Id.*

60 William J. Brennan, Jr., Letter to Byron White (Feb. 5, 1971), Brennan Papers, Box I: 237.

61 Brennan, Case Histories O.T. 1970, *supra* note 20, at XLIII.

62 *Id.* at XLIV.

conduct, but to vindicate the individual's interest in privacy." Brennan was "stunned but delighted" and said he was happy to join that opinion.[63] But Brennan never got the chance because White "never mentioned the matter again and made no such changes."[64] Looking back, it is difficult to imagine why White would have thought that he could have mustered five votes for an opinion containing such a description of the exclusionary rule. As will be seen shortly, Burger and Blackmun, who eventually joined White's plurality opinion in *Williams*, would never have joined an opinion that suggested that the exclusionary rule was a constitutional right of the defendant.

When the dust settled in *Williams*, White's discussion of *Mapp* and the exclusionary rule was consistent with what was said previously in *Linkletter* and *Alderman*: the exclusionary rule was designed "to deter official invasions of individual privacy protected by the Fourth Amendment."[65] And the deterrent purpose of the rule would only have been marginally served by extending the holding of *Chimel* retroactively to searches conducted before *Chimel* was decided.[66] Although he agreed with the result, Brennan's separate concurrence in *Williams* observed that exclusion of evidence acquired in violation of the Fourth Amendment "is required not merely in hope of deterring unconstitutional searches in the future, but in order to vindicate the right of privacy guaranteed by the Fourth Amendment."[67]

While the reasoning and results in *Whiteley* and *Williams* did little to accomplish Burger's objective of repealing or sharply restricting the exclusionary rule, Burger's efforts in *Bivens v. Six Unknown Named Agents of Federal Bureau of Narcotics*[68] and *Coolidge v. New Hampshire*[69] would eventually produce greater dividends toward his goal. Looking back, it is ironic that *Bivens* and *Coolidge* sparked efforts on and off the Court to reconsider or abolish the exclusionary rule since neither case addressed the rule. That fact, however, did not discourage or prevent Burger from making the exclusionary rule an issue in both cases.

On November 26, 1965, federal agents entered Webster Bivens's apartment and arrested him for narcotics violations. Bivens later alleged that the agents entered his home without an arrest warrant; threatened to arrest his wife and children, who were present during the raid; and that the agents searched the entire premises without a search warrant. He also alleged that he was taken to the federal courthouse in Brooklyn, where he was interrogated, booked, and subjected to a strip search. Nineteen months later, Bivens filed a pro se lawsuit against the agents, which the lower federal courts dismissed for failure to state a cause of action.[70]

---

63 *Id.*

64 *Id.*

65 Williams v. United States, 401 U.S. 646, 653 (1971).

66 *Id.* at 658–59.

67 *Id.* at 663 (Brennan, J., concurring).

68 403 U.S. 388 (1971).

69 403 U.S. 443 (1971).

70 *See* James E. Pfander, *The Story of Bivens v. Six Unknown Named Agents of the Federal Bureau of Narcotics*, *in* FEDERAL COURTS STORIES 275, 280-83 (Vicki C. Jackson & Judith Resnik eds., 2010).

Bivens presented the issue raised but left undecided twenty-five years earlier in *Bell v. Hood*[71]: does the Fourth Amendment provide for an implied cause of action for damages to the victim of an illegal search and seizure? But the justices were considering other issues as well in *Bivens*. Toward the end of the oral argument in *Bivens*, counsel for Bivens was asked a series of questions about Congress's power to reverse a ruling in favor of his client.[72] Counsel told the justices that Congress lacked such power because a ruling in favor of Bivens would be based on the Fourth Amendment, and a statute attempting to reverse the Court's judgment "would be a derogation of the Fourth Amendment."[73] Counsel was then asked whether Congress could repeal the exclusionary rule.[74] Without answering the question directly, counsel suggested that the inadequacy of civil remedies influenced the result in *Mapp*.[75] Finally, Burger asked counsel: "[I]f you prevail here the logic of the progress of events might lead the Court to be invited to reconsider, at least the full force of the exclusionary rule."[76] Counsel replied: "It certainly might."[77] Three days later at the conference on *Bivens*, Burger told his colleagues that the lower court should be affirmed, but he agreed that a ruling in favor of Bivens would be "a good first step toward abolishing the exclusionary rule."[78]

Ultimately, *Bivens* ruled that the Fourth Amendment did provide a cause of action for damages for victims of unconstitutional searches and seizures. Brennan's opinion for the Court conceded that the text of the amendment "does not in so many words provide for its enforcement by an award of money damages for the consequences of its violation."[79] But the text of the Amendment does not provide for the exclusionary rule either. Rather than rely on the text of the Amendment, Brennan asked whether Bivens was entitled to redress his injury in federal court.[80] The answer to that question, Brennan concluded, was found in the often-quoted words of Chief Justice John Marshall in *Marbury v. Madison*: "'The very essence of civil liberty certainly consists in the right of every individual to claim the protection of the laws, whenever he receives an injury.'"[81]

Burger's dissent in *Bivens* never engages the issue addressed by the Court; instead, it is more of a dissent to *Weeks* and *Mapp*. He repeats the themes of his American University

---

71 327 U.S. 678 (1946).

72 Transcript of Oral Argument at 41–42, *Bivens*, 403 U.S. 388 (No. 301).

73 *Id.* at 41, 42.

74 *Id.* at 43.

75 *Id.*

76 *Id.* at 43–44.

77 *Id.* at 44.

78 William J. Brennan, Jr., Conference Notes on *Bivens v. Six Unknown Named Agents of Federal Bureau of Narcotics* (undated), Brennan Papers, Box I: 228; *see also* THE SUPREME COURT IN CONFERENCE (1940–1985): THE PRIVATE DISCUSSIONS BEHIND NEARLY 300 SUPREME COURT DECISIONS 487 (Del Dickson ed., 2001).

79 *Bivens*, 403 U.S. at 396.

80 *Id.* at 397.

81 *Id.* (quoting Marbury v. Madison, 5 U.S. (1 Cranch) 137, 163 (1803)).

speech: the belief that exclusion of reliable evidence will deter future police misconduct is "a wistful dream."[82] Burger also asserts in his dissent that suppressing truthful evidence "has set guilty criminals free."[83] And the Court has been properly criticized "for clinging to an unworkable and irrational concept of law."[84]

Again, as in his American University speech, Burger did not propose abandoning the exclusionary rule "until some meaningful alternative can be developed."[85] He recognized that eliminating the rule entirely could raise "new problems," especially if police officials were given the impression "that all constitutional restraints on police had somehow been removed—that an open season on 'criminals' had been declared."[86] Because American society had relied upon the rule as the exclusive remedy for unlawful searches and searches, Burger lamented that "we are in a situation akin to the narcotics addict whose dependence on drugs precludes any drastic or immediate withdrawal of the supposed prop, regardless of how futile its continued use may be."[87] Burger called on Congress to develop an administrative or quasi-judicial remedy to provide compensation for victims of illegal searches and seizures. Burger ended his dissent with the observation that "the time has come to re-examine the scope of the exclusionary rule and consider at least some narrowing of its thrust so as to eliminate the anomalies it has produced."[88]

Bivens was an odd case for Burger's attack on the exclusionary rule since it did not involve the exclusion of illegally acquired evidence at a criminal prosecution. *Coolidge v. New Hampshire*,[89] on the other hand, was just the type of case that critics of the rule point to when they speak of the objectionable costs imposed by the rule. *Coolidge* involved the gruesome murder of fourteen-year-old Paula Mason, who was lured from her home to a babysitting job on January 13, 1964. Several days later, her body was found on the side of a road with her throat slashed and a gunshot wound to the head.

After Edward Coolidge's murder conviction was upheld by the New Hampshire Supreme Court, the Court was confronted with a series of search and seizure questions, none of which involved the exclusionary rule. According to someone who was present, the most electrifying moment during the *Coolidge* oral argument came when Stewart smiled and looked at counsel for Coolidge, the former Solicitor General and then-Harvard Law Professor Archibald Cox, and asked whether his entire argument "depends upon the continuing validity of the exclusionary rules."[90] Cox paused, looked

---

82 *Id.* at 415 (Burger, C.J., dissenting).

83 *Id.* at 418.

84 *Id.* at 420.

85 *Id.*

86 *Id.* at 420–21.

87 *Id.* at 421.

88 *Id.* at 424.

89 403 U.S. 443 (1971).

90 Telephone Interview with David H. Souter, retired Associate Justice, Supreme Court of the United States (June 24, 2010); *see also* Transcript of Oral Argument at 7, *Coolidge*, 403 U.S. 443 (No. 323).

at Stewart, returned the smile and said, "Oh, yes. I assume that and—if I may."[91] Cox then immediately began discussing the facts of the case. This was the only reference to the exclusionary rule during oral argument.[92]

At the *Coolidge* conference, Douglas, Harlan, Brennan, Stewart, and Marshall favored the reversal of Coolidge's conviction.[93] Burger, Black, White, and Blackmun wanted to affirm the conviction. Harlan was the swing vote. According to one report, Harlan stated at the *Coolidge* conference that he would not join the Burger group unless they were willing to overrule *Mapp*. Black, however, refused to do so.[94] After the conference discussion, Harlan switched sides and joined the Burger group. But after Stewart added ten pages to his opinion to accommodate him, Harlan ultimately joined Stewart's plurality opinion reversing Coolidge's conviction.[95] When the case was announced, five separate opinions would be filed, spanning eighty-four pages.

In the lead-up to the *Coolidge* opinions, Blackmun sent Black a letter indicating his willingness to join Black's dissenting opinion, including Black's discussion of the exclusionary rule.[96] One month later, Burger sent Blackmun a short letter questioning whether Blackmun really wanted to join Black's analysis of the exclusionary rule. Burger's letter noted that Black's "opinion 'fudges' considerably but I think it must be read as embedding the [Fifth] Amendment Exclusionary Rule via [the Fourth] Amendment."[97] Burger's letter apparently prompted Blackmun to change his mind, because the next day Blackmun wrote Black a letter that stated, "Because I am not now prepared to commit myself to the exclusionary rule, even by the Fifth Amendment, I must withdraw my earlier-indicated complete assent to your opinion."[98] Blackmun requested that Black add to the end of his opinion a note indicating Blackmun's view that "'the Fourth Amendment supports no exclusionary rule.'"[99]

Four days before *Coolidge* and *Bivens* were announced, White sent a memo to his colleagues offering the Court the opportunity to abandon *Mapp*. White observed that "[w]ith the publication of *Coolidge* and *Bivens*, four justices [Burger, Harlan, Black, and Blackmun] will have stated for the record their dissatisfaction with *Mapp v. Ohio*

---

91 Transcript of Oral Argument, *supra* note 90, at 7.

92 *Id.*; *see* also Telephone Interview with David H. Souter, *supra* note 90.

93 William J. Brennan, Jr., Conference Notes on *Coolidge v. New Hampshire* (undated), Brennan Papers, Box I: 228; William Douglas, Conference Notes on *Coolidge v. New Hampshire* (undated), Douglas Papers, Box 1491.

94 Bob Woodward & Scott Armstrong, The Brethren: Inside the Supreme Court 117 (1979).

95 Potter Stewart, Memorandum to William Douglas, William J. Brennan, Jr. and Thurgood Marshall on *Coolidge v. New Hampshire* (June 2, 1971), Brennan Papers, Box I: 244; *see* Coolidge v. New Hampshire, 403 U.S. 443, 473-84 (1971). Pages 473-84 of the opinion is the section Stewart added to obtain Harlan's vote.

96 Harry Blackmun, Letter to Hugo Black (May 4, 1971), Harry A. Blackmun Papers, Library of Congress, Manuscript Division, Box 128.

97 Warren Burger, Letter to Harry Blackmun (June 15, 1971), Blackmun Papers, Box 128.

98 Harry Blackmun, Letter to Hugo Black (June 16, 1971), Black Papers, Box 403.

99 *Id.*

insofar as the exclusionary rule is based on the Fourth Amendment."[100] White's memo was unwilling to "presume" Stewart's views, but he noted that Stewart had not joined *Mapp*.[101] White stated, "our struggles of this term suggest at least a reexamination of the premise that gave rise to them. My present view is that the exclusionary rule should at least be narrowed."[102] Finally, White suggested that the Court consider reargument in *Coolidge* "limited to the single question whether *Mapp v. Ohio* should be overruled."[103] Burger immediately replied to White's memo. While agreeing "with much of what" White had said, Burger thought that "to accommodate varying views," the Court should pose the reargument questions as follows: First, "Should *Mapp v. Ohio* be overruled"; and second, "If *Mapp v. Ohio* is not overruled should the scope of the Exclusionary Rule be narrowed so as to relate its application to the nature of the violation."[104] The response to White's memo came at the next conference. Harlan, who held the decisive vote in *Coolidge*, thought that "*Coolidge* was not the case on which to modify the rule. The facts were hopelessly convoluted. [We] should get rid of the Coolidge case and find a better test."[105]

When *Coolidge* was finally announced, Burger's brief opinion appeared inconsequential. Exploiting the fact that Coolidge's crime was a particularly heinous murder, he opined that the case "illustrates graphically the monstrous price we pay for the exclusionary rule in which we seem to have imprisoned ourselves."[106] But Burger took a step he had avoided taking in *Bivens* and in his American University speech, where he claimed that he was unwilling to abandon the rule until a meaningful substitute was available. In *Coolidge*, Burger aligned himself with Black's view of exclusion, except for "the proposition that the Fifth Amendment requires the exclusion of evidence seized in violation of the Fourth Amendment."[107] Black, of course, never believed that the Fourth Amendment required exclusion, and he reaffirmed that view in *Coolidge* when he noted: "The truth is that the source of the exclusionary rule simply cannot be found in the Fourth Amendment. That Amendment did not when adopted, and does not now, contain any constitutional rule barring the admission of illegally seized evidence."[108] Black

---

100 Byron White, Memorandum to the Conference on *Coolidge v. New Hampshire* (June 17, 1971), Blackmun Papers, Box 128.

101 *Id.* Apparently, Stewart's attitude toward exclusion was unknown even to his colleagues. A few years earlier, Stewart joined Black's dissent in *Mancusi v. DeForte*, 392 U.S. 364 (1968), wherein Black stated: "The exclusionary rule . . . has had only a precarious tenure in this Court." *Id.* at 373 (Black, J., dissenting).

102 White, Memorandum to the Conference on *Coolidge*, *supra* note 100.

103 *Id.*

104 Warren Burger, Letter to Byron White on *Coolidge v. New Hampshire* (June 17, 1971), Blackmun Papers, Box 128.

105 Woodward & Armstrong, *supra* note 94, at 119.

106 Coolidge v. New Hampshire, 403 U.S. 443, 493 (1971) (Burger, C.J., dissenting in part and concurring in part).

107 *Id.* at 492–93.

108 *Id.* at 497 (Black, J., concurring and dissenting).

saw exclusion as a by-product of merging the Fourth and Fifth Amendments. By aligning himself with Black's views except for Black's merger theory, Burger was, in effect, calling for the repeal of the Fourth Amendment's exclusionary rule. But this time, Burger had others supporting him.

Harlan's separate opinion in *Coolidge* also called for overruling *Mapp*.[109] Harlan had dissented in *Mapp* and never reconciled himself with the correctness of *Mapp*. Additionally, Blackmun registered his view that the Fourth Amendment did not support an exclusionary rule. These views, of course, did not go unnoticed. One month after *Coolidge* was announced, the Assistant Attorney General for New Hampshire, David H. Souter, petitioned the Court for a rehearing in *Coolidge*, specifically requesting that *Mapp* be overruled.[110] Souter had attended the oral argument in *Coolidge* for his boss, Warren Rudman, and viewed Stewart's question about the exclusionary rule during oral argument as an opening that should have been pursued by the state. The petition for rehearing was a belated attempt to address Stewart's question. The Court, however, denied the petition.[111] Thus, while the Court did not use *Coolidge* as the vehicle for reexamining *Mapp*, it was clear to everyone that a reevaluation of *Mapp* would come soon; in fact, a series of events would accelerate and expand the Court's opportunities to overrule, if not significantly limit, the scope of the exclusionary rule.

On October 21, 1971, President Nixon surprised the nation with two unexpected nominees—Lewis F. Powell, Jr. and William H. Rehnquist—to fill the vacancies on the Court created by Black's and Harlan's retirements. The President told the nation that Powell and Rehnquist were selected because they shared his conservative judicial philosophy: "I believe some court decisions have gone too far in the past in weakening the peace forces as against the criminal forces in our society. . . . I believe the peace forces must not be denied the legal tools they need to protect the innocent from criminal elements."[112] William Rehnquist was thought to oppose the exclusionary rule even more strongly than either Black or Harlan. Powell's views regarding exclusion were less known.

A few weeks later, the state of California asked the Court to review a case, *California v. Krivda*,[113] concerning whether the warrantless seizure of garbage left for collection at the curbside of a private home violates the Fourth Amendment. California officials also asked the Court to decide whether application of the exclusionary rule was constitutionally compelled under the circumstances of the case. On the latter issue, the California Attorney General admitted that Burger's dissent in *Bivens* had prompted the state to challenge the continued validity of the rule in the California Supreme Court.[114] Even

---

109 *Id.* at 490 (Harlan, J., concurring).

110 Petition of the State of New Hampshire for Rehearing, *Coolidge*, 403 U.S. 443 (No. 323).

111 Coolidge v. New Hampshire, 404 U.S. 874 (1971) (mem.).

112 *Remaking the Supreme Court: Nixon Sets a Pattern*, U.S. News & World Rep., Nov. 1, 1971, at 15, 16.

113 409 U.S. 33 (1972) (per curiam).

114 Petitioner's Opening Brief at 39–41, *Krivda*, 409 U.S. 33 (No. 71-651).

though the California Supreme Court did not address the question, California urged the Court to decide the exclusionary rule issue, believing that the Court's new membership presented an opportunity to dismantle, or at the very least, limit the scope of the rule.[115]

With Powell and Rehnquist now sitting on the bench, the Court agreed to review *Krivda* on April 3, 1972.[116] At one point in his brief, the California Attorney General went for the kill: "Even in the absence of a substitute remedy, it is difficult to comprehend the wisdom of retaining a rule which benefits only the guilty victim of an unlawful search. The absence of equal protection for the innocent victim is perhaps the best argument for an abandonment of the rule."[117] Short of pressing for a complete repeal, California's brief urged the Court to limit the rule to flagrant or deliberate violations of the Fourth Amendment. The brief argued that "when it appears to the police officer that it is sufficiently probable that the action he intends to take does not violate Fourth Amendment rights, the exclusionary rule should not be applied."[118] As things turned out, however, *Krivda* was not an appropriate case to address the continuing validity of the exclusionary rule. The justices unanimously agreed that it was unclear from the record whether the ruling of the California Supreme Court was based on the Fourth Amendment or upon California's Constitution or both. Consequently, the case was remanded back to the state court.[119]

In the meantime, a high-ranking official of the Nixon Administration's Department of Justice, Henry E. Petersen, endorsed what he called the "strong movement which seeks modification or abolishment" of the exclusionary rule.[120] On August 13, 1972, Petersen, then chief of the Criminal Division of the Justice Department, told a group of lawyers attending an American Bar Association meeting that he had "reached the conclusion that in its present form the exclusionary rule has not served a useful purpose, in that it has failed to discourage police officers from conducting unreasonable searches and seizures."[121] Petersen repeated Burger's criticism articulated in his *Bivens* dissent, when Petersen noted "society has a right to expect judges to exercise their discretion in cases where police error is shown in the acquisition of evidence."[122]

---

115 *Id.* at 42.

116 People v. Krivda, 486 P.2d 1262 (Cal. 1971), *cert. granted*, 405 U.S. 1039 (1972) (No. 71-651).

117 Petitioner's Opening Brief, *supra* note 114, at 42.

118 *Id.* at 51.

119 *Krivda*, 409 U.S. at 35.

120 Henry E. Petersen, Assistant Attorney General, Dep't of Justice, Address before the Section of Bar Activities Award of Merit Luncheon, American Bar Association Convention 3 (Aug. 13, 1972).

121 *Id.* at 4.

122 *Id.* In his *Bivens* dissent, Burger wrote: "I submit that society has at least as much right to expect rationally graded responses from judges in place of the universal 'capital punishment' we inflict on all evidence when police error is shown in its acquisition." Bivens v. Six Unknown Named Agents of Federal Bureau of Narcotics, 403 U.S. 388, 419 (1971) (Burger, C.J., dissenting).

Four months later, the Justice Department petitioned the Court to review a case, *United States v. Robinson*,[123] which presented the question whether the exclusionary rule requires the suppression of evidence obtained from a search incident to a lawful arrest and pursuant to a police regulation requiring such searches. The Department's petition noted that a recent draft proposal of the American Law Institute's Model Code of Prearraignment Procedure had proposed limiting application of the exclusionary rule to cases where courts determine that the police conduct constituted a "substantial" or flagrant violation of the Fourth Amendment.[124] This, of course, was the same argument that the California Attorney General made in *Krivda*.

Thus, by the close of the October 1971 Term, Burger had made headway toward eliminating the exclusionary rule. State prosecutors had gotten the message that the Court was open to arguments for restricting the rule. Additionally, the Justice Department, through the arguments proffered by the Solicitor General—known in Court circles as "the Tenth Justice"—would soon direct its prestige and legal acumen toward efforts opposing the rule.

Furthermore, Burger's *Bivens* dissent was especially influential in permanently shifting the terms of the debate over the exclusionary rule. Capitalizing on various Warren Court rulings that identified the rule's deterrent purpose, Burger and other critics of the rule were now insisting that deterrence was the sole basis for the rule and that the rule failed to deter police illegality.[125] On this front, Burger's efforts were assisted by an influential law review article authored by Professor Dallin Oaks.[126] Oaks's article, which was funded by a grant from the Law Enforcement Assistance Administration, an arm of the Justice Department,[127] concluded that there was no empirical evidence that the exclusionary rule deterred illegal searches and seizures.[128] For several years, opponents of the rule, on and off the Court, frequently cited Oaks's article for the proposition that the exclusionary rule did not deter Fourth Amendment violations. Often, however, those who cited Oaks omitted his own acknowledgement that his findings "obviously fall short of an empirical substantiation or *refutation* of the deterrent effect of the exclusionary rule,"[129] and his concession that the rule "should not be abolished until there is

---

[123] 414 U.S. 218 (1973).

[124] Petition for a Writ of Certiorari at 21, *Robinson*, 414 U.S. 218 (No. 72-936).

[125] *See* John P. MacKenzie, *Critics Fight Rule on Illegal Evidence*, WASH. POST, July 30, 1972, at A4.

[126] Dallin H. Oaks, *Studying the Exclusionary Rule in Search and Seizure*, 37 U. CHI. L. REV. 665 (1970). Oaks's article was cited by Burger and Harlan in *Coolidge*, and by Burger in *Bivens*. Eventually, Oaks's article became very popular among some of the justices. As of 2008, it had been cited fourteen times by the Court. *See* Albert W. Alschuler, Studying the Exclusionary Rule*: An Empirical Classic*, 75 U. CHI. L. REV. 1365, 1365-66 (2008).

[127] MacKenzie, *supra* note 125; *see* Critique, *On the Limitations of Empirical Evaluations of the Exclusionary Rule: A Critique of the Spiotto Research and* United States v. Calandra, 69 NW. U. L. REV. 740, 741 (1974) [hereinafter Critique, *On the Limitations*]. This Northwestern Law Review article was written by Tom Davies when he was a law student. As a law professor, Davies would continue to write influential articles on the exclusionary rule and the Fourth Amendment generally.

[128] *See generally* Oaks, *supra* note 126.

[129] *Id.* at 709 (emphasis added).

something to take its place . . . ."[130] Nevertheless, "[b]y portraying the exclusionary rule as a pragmatic social policy, rather than as a necessary adjunct to basic constitutional principles," opponents of exclusion had redefined the terms of future debate over the rule.[131] Also relevant, some members of the Court saw *Weeks*'s holding as based on the Court's supervisory power over the federal judiciary, which diminished its precedential value to insignificant terms. Finally, and most important, inside the Court, a majority of the justices were ready to restrict the scope of the exclusionary rule. Whether a majority favored outright repeal of the rule was unknown at this point.

* * *

Except for his age, 62-year-old Lewis F. Powell, Jr. was Richard Nixon's ideal candidate for a seat on the Court. Nixon wanted a Southerner, and Powell was from Virginia. Nixon also wanted a person who shared his "conservative" judicial philosophy. Powell's speeches certainly identified him as a conservative critic of the Warren Court. Further, Nixon and his advisors believed that Powell was a "law-and-order" conservative.[132] Prior to his nomination, Powell had not amassed the paper trail that Warren Burger had accumulated in opposing the exclusionary rule. But after he took his seat on the High Court, Powell, like Burger, moved quickly to restrict application of the rule and undermine its constitutional status.

After *Krivda* turned out to be an unsuitable case for curtailing the exclusionary rule, the Court's next opportunity to constrict the rule came in *Schneckloth v. Bustamonte*,[133] a consent search case out of California. *Krivda* was still pending before the Court when the California Attorney General asked the Court to review *Bustamonte*. As he had done in *Krivda*, the California Attorney General again posed an exclusionary rule question for the Court's consideration, namely, whether state prisoners, when challenging their convictions in federal habeas corpus proceedings, should be allowed to claim that unconstitutionally obtained evidence was admitted against them at trial.[134]

This was an aggressive legal maneuver because two years earlier, *Kaufman v. United States*[135] had ruled that federal prisoners could raise Fourth Amendment claims to challenge their convictions under the companion provision of federal law that state prisoners

---

130 *Id.* at 756. Opponents of exclusion also failed to acknowledge Oaks's criticism of Frankfurter's opinion in *Wolf v. Colorado*. Oaks observed that the "salient defect" of *Wolf* was "the difficulty of persuading anyone that the guarantees of the fourth amendment were seriously intended and important when there was no sanction whatever for their violation." *Id.* at 711. Finally, in a "Postscript" section of his article, Oaks recognized two vital functions served by the rule: "If constitutional rights are to be anything more than pious pronouncements, then some measurable consequence must be attached to their violation. It would be intolerable if the guarantee against unreasonable search and seizure could be violated without practical consequence." *Id.* at 756. The second advantage of the rule—"entirely apart from any direct deterrent effect"—according to Oaks, "is that it provides an occasion for judicial review, and it gives credibility to the constitutional guarantees." *Id.*

131 Critique, *On the Limitations*, *supra* note 127, at 776.

132 John W. Dean, The Rehnquist Choice 16 (2001).

133 412 U.S. 218 (1973).

134 Petition for a Writ of Certiorari at 2, *Bustamonte*, 412 U.S. 218 (No. 71-732).

135 394 U.S. 217 (1969).

utilized to challenge their convictions in federal court. Moreover, *Kaufman* seemed to already answer the question that California was asking the Court to decide when it stated: "Our decisions leave no doubt that the federal habeas remedy extends to state prisoners alleging that unconstitutionally obtained evidence was admitted against them at trial."[136] If federal prisoners could raise search and seizure claims in federal post-conviction proceedings and if the exclusionary rule was compelled by the Fourth Amendment, there was no principled reason why state prisoners could not invoke the same statute to raise the same claims in the same federal courthouses. The only thing that had changed in the two years since *Kaufman* was decided was the Court's membership. In essence, the California Attorney General was asking the Nixon appointees to join with Stewart, who had dissented in *Kaufman*, to overrule *Kaufman*.

Before the conference discussion on *Bustamonte*, Harry Blackmun, Nixon's second appointee to the Court, transcribed his views of the case. Although Blackmun became the hero of many liberals for his authorship of *Roe v. Wade*,[137] which recognized a woman's right to an abortion, Blackmun was no "liberal" regarding the exclusionary rule. In his memo on *Bustamonte*, Blackmun wrote, "There is much to be said in favor of overruling *Kaufman* and its basic case, *Fay v. Noia*."[138] *Fay* held that federal courts were free to adjudicate a state prisoner's federal habeas petition even though the prisoner had failed to appeal his conviction in state court, unless the prisoner deliberately bypassed the state courts for tactical reasons.[139] Blackmun doubted his colleagues' awareness of state judges' resentment of the Court's "interference" with the states' criminal process, stating: "There has been a constantly developing imposition upon the states of requirements that were not originally urged. I have in mind such things as representation by counsel, representative juries and [the] *Bivens* rationale."[140]

Blackmun then mulled over the exclusionary rule and whether to overrule *Kaufman*. He noted that "stakes are higher in habeas than on direct review," because "the prospects of successful reprosecution are much slimmer" for defendants who succeed in overturning their convictions. Blackmun observed that this problem "becomes particularly acute

---

[136] *Id.* at 225; *see also* Petition for a Writ of Certiorari, *supra* note 134, at 15.

[137] 410 U.S. 113 (1973). On Blackmun's status as a "liberal icon," see TINSLEY E. YARBROUGH, HARRY A. BLACKMUN: THE OUTSIDER JUSTICE 249–88 (2008), and compare LINDA GREENHOUSE, BECOMING JUSTICE BLACKMUN: HARRY BLACKMUN'S SUPREME COURT JOURNEY 207 (2005) (explaining that Blackmun's "identification with *Roe v. Wade* had long bestowed on him the mantle of champion not only of abortion rights but women's rights in general. . . . To those who lionized him late in his career, his presence in the place of honor on their podiums and at their testimonial dinners may have seemed inevitable, but it was not.").

[138] Harry Blackmun, Internal Memorandum 71-732 on *Schneckloth v. Bustamonte* 1 (Sept. 29, 1972) [hereinafter Blackmun, *Bustamonte* Internal Memo], Blackmun Papers, Box 156.

[139] Fay v. Noia, 372 U.S. 391 (1963). *Fay* was overruled in *Coleman v. Thompson*, 501 U.S. 722 (1991). *See* Larry Yackle, *The Story of* Fay v. Noia*: Another Case About Another Federalism*, *in* FEDERAL COURTS STORIES 191 (Vicki C. Jackson & Judith Resnik eds., 2010).

[140] Blackmun, *Bustamonte* Internal Memo, *supra* note 138, at 1.

when the exclusionary rule is in play."[141] Blackmun wrote, "there is no empirical data whatsoever that is supportive of the rule's effectiveness," and the rule protects "only the guilty and not the innocent."[142] He closed his memo by observing: "[T]he Court has gone too far on Federal habeas in state cases. I could resolve the problem by a lower standard of review of state cases. If this is impossible, I vote to overrule *Kaufman* or even to do away with the exclusionary rule."[143]

The conference discussion of *Bustamonte* revealed that the Nixon appointees were ready to dispatch *Kaufman*, and Rehnquist offered the analytical framework for overruling it. Brennan, the author of *Kaufman*, stated that he would not overrule *Kaufman* and explained that *Kaufman* was "both a constitutional and a statutory interpretation case."[144] When it was his turn to speak, Rehnquist stated that the Court had "mangled" the federal habeas corpus statute.[145] He continued: "The exclusionary rule is not mandated by the Constitution—look at *Harris*[*v. New York*]. It follows from that case to say that the exclusionary rule is not required by the Constitution. I would reverse *Kaufman* and overrule the constitutional aspect of *Kaufman*."[146]

While the Nixon appointees indicated their readiness to overrule *Kaufman*, they lacked a fifth vote because Stewart and White were unwilling to do so, at least not yet. Stewart simply stated that he "would not reach the *Kaufman* issue."[147] By contrast, White seemed conflicted about what to do with the exclusionary rule. White had originally joined the *Kaufman* majority opinion. During the *Bustamonte* conference, White stated that he was "unwilling to act piecemeal on the *Kaufman* issue,"[148] suggesting that if a majority of the Court was ready to bar Fourth Amendment challenges by both federal and state prisoners, he might be ready to overrule *Kaufman*. Also, White said he "would vote to modify *Mapp*."[149] If read narrowly, however, *Mapp* did not control because it applied the exclusionary rule to state criminal trials; *Bustamonte*, by contrast, involved whether the rule could be invoked in federal collateral proceedings for state prisoners. White, however, saw "little difference between direct and collateral attacks" by defendants invoking the exclusionary rule.[150] *Bustamonte* was assigned to Stewart.

After the conference, Powell began working on an opinion that would be a first step toward undermining, if not overruling, *Kaufman*. Rehnquist sent Powell a

---

141 *Id.* at 2.

142 *Id.*

143 *Id.* at 4.

144 Lewis Powell, Conference Notes on *Schneckloth v. Bustamonte* (Oct. 11, 1972) [hereinafter Powell, *Bustamonte* Conference Notes], Powell Papers, Box 6.

145 Dickson, *supra* note 78, at 456.

146 *Id.*

147 Powell, *Bustamonte* Conference Notes, *supra* note 144.

148 *Id.*

149 *Id.*

150 *Id.* Douglas's conference notes record White as saying: "I will stand by *Kaufman*, but I would re-do and reformulate *Mapp*." *See* Del Dickson, *supra* note 78, at 456.

letter elaborating on Rehnquist's comments and Brennan's interpretation of *Kaufman*. Rehnquist explained that *Kaufman* essentially decided two points: First, *Weeks*'s exclusionary rule "requires, as a matter of constitutional law, that a judgment of conviction be set aside even after it has become final if evidence adduced at the trial was obtained in violation of the Fourth Amendment."[151] Second, Fourth Amendment claims can be raised under the federal habeas statute.[152] On the statutory point, Rehnquist argued that while the original 1867 federal statute had been distorted by Court rulings, "it would take still further distortion on our part to say that there is an implied exception for search and seizure cases from the general rule that claims of constitutional deprivation may be litigated in federal habeas."[153] Thus, Rehnquist concluded that overruling the statutory element of *Kaufman* was not "a particularly appealing course."[154]

Rehnquist, however, thought that the constitutional holding of *Kaufman* was wrong in light of the Court's rulings in *Walder v. United States* and *Harris*. According to Rehnquist, Frankfurter's opinion in *Walder* "establishes the proposition that the Fourth Amendment does not automatically require exclusion of all illegally seized evidence, but that the policy behind the exclusionary rule must be weighed against competing policies."[155] And though *Harris* "was undoubtedly something of an expansion" of *Walder*, it "offers further support for the proposition that the exclusionary rule of *Weeks* is not an inexorable command, but merely a constitutional policy that may be counterbalanced by the need for effective determination of guilt or innocence at a trial."[156] Rehnquist thought "*Walder* and *Harris* could be logically extended here to hold that while the *Weeks* rule requiring exclusion of evidence is constitutionally mandated on direct appeal from the conviction, it is not so mandated when collateral attack of a final judgment is involved."[157]

Rehnquist acknowledged that the distinction between direct appeal and collateral attack was not fully supported by the deterrence theory behind the rule.[158] But he had an answer for that point, and it came from Clark's opinion in *Linkletter*. *Linkletter* held that *Mapp* would not apply retroactively, in part, because the use of illegally obtained evidence did not taint the fairness of a criminal prosecution, and retrospective application could not be expected to deter police conduct that occurred before *Mapp* was decided. For Rehnquist, this rationale also justified denying state prisoners the opportunity to invoke the rule in federal habeas proceedings. The failure to apply the exclusionary rule at Bustamonte's trial did not undermine the fact-finding process, and the

---

151 William Rehnquist, Letter to Lewis Powell 1 (Nov. 6, 1972), Powell Papers, Box 6.

152 *Id.*

153 *Id.* at 2.

154 *Id.*

155 *Id.*

156 *Id.* at 3.

157 *Id.*

158 *Id.* at 4.

deterrent impact loses its constitutional "steam" when a defendant invokes the rule in a collateral proceeding that occurs years after the trial.[159] Powell was apparently impressed with Rehnquist's analysis because he put check marks and asterisks beside Rehnquist's comments on *Walder*, and he underlined and wrote "use" besides Rehnquist's comments on *Harris*.[160]

While Powell would eventually incorporate Rehnquist's analysis in his *Bustamonte* opinion, Powell knew that Burger and Rehnquist's support would not be enough to reverse *Kaufman* or to dismantle the exclusionary rule itself. He would need Stewart's and White's votes to achieve either result. To ascertain Stewarts's thoughts, Powell sent Stewart a letter that revealed his own "tentative thoughts" on the best way to arrange a full dress review of the exclusionary rule.[161]

From several conversations with Stewart, Powell knew that Stewart was "leaning toward the view" that *Kaufman* went too far, but Stewart was reluctant to reverse *Kaufman* unless White "was willing to join us."[162] Powell recalled from the *Bustamonte* conference that White "would go further and reconsider the full sweep of *Mapp* but is hesitant about what he regards as a 'piecemeal' approach."[163] Powell opined that "*Mapp* opened new frontiers not required by the Constitution" or the federal habeas statute.[164] Recognizing "there may be some merit in taking one step at a time," Powell preferred "that we take the first one in *Bustamonte*."[165] Thus, Powell informed Stewart that he had prepared a concurring opinion in the event that Stewart's opinion in *Bustamonte* did not address the *Kaufman* issue.[166]

Powell's letter added that "recent developments" on the Court's docket could provide the vehicle for "a broad reconsideration of the scope of the [exclusionary] rule."[167] Here, Powell referred to the federal government's suggestion in *United States v. Robinson* that the Court significantly narrow the scope of the rule. Because *Robinson* was a federal case, it would allow the Court to reconsider *Weeks*, which Powell described as "an older and arguably more solidly based precedent than *Mapp*."[168] Two state cases on the docket, *Gustafson v. Florida* and *Cady v. Dombrowski*, would permit reconsideration of *Mapp*. Powell conceded none of these cases by themselves were "particularly attractive" for a major review of the exclusionary rule.[169] But, he suggested, "one possibility would be, if

---

159 *Id.*

160 *See generally id.*

161 Lewis Powell, Letter to Potter Stewart (Mar. 1, 1973), Powell Papers, Box 6.

162 *Id.* at 1.

163 *Id.*

164 *Id.*

165 *Id.*

166 *Id.*

167 *Id.*

168 *Id.* at 2.

169 *Id. Gustafson v. Florida*, 414 U.S. 260 (1973), and *Cady v. Dombrowski*, 413 U.S. 433 (1973), were decided without addressing the exclusionary rule.

five of us agreed, to carry all of these cases over to the next term for a full dress reconsideration of the scope and extent of the exclusionary rule."[170] Powell closed his letter to Stewart by noting, "These are tentative thoughts only."[171] His letter was not sent to the other justices because he had "discussed [the] subject only in the most cursory manner with one or two other justices," and asked, "In short, what do you think?"[172]

Neither Powell's nor Stewart's papers disclose Stewart's reaction to Powell's letter. Ultimately, Stewart's *Bustamonte* opinion did not reach the *Kaufman* issue. Blackmun's brief concurrence indicated his disapproval of *Kaufman* and his agreement "with nearly all" of Powell's "detailed and persuasive" opinion.[173] But Blackmun refrained from joining Powell's opinion, because there was no need to decide the *Kaufman* issue once the Court determined that the search of the car in which Bustamonte was riding was constitutional.[174] Powell's opinion, which Burger and Rehnquist joined, proposed a significant rollback of federal judges' power to adjudicate Fourth Amendment claims in habeas corpus proceedings. Unless a state prisoner's search and seizure claim related to his innocence, federal judges should be confined to determining solely whether the "defendant was provided a fair opportunity in the state courts to raise and have adjudicated [his] Fourth Amendment claim."[175]

On the exclusionary rule itself, Powell made no attempt to address what the Court said in *Weeks*. Instead, Powell observed that the rule "has occasioned much criticism" and said the purpose for the rule is to deter illegal searches and seizures by the police.[176] Citing Oaks's article, he noted the efficacy of the deterrent function has been seriously questioned.[177] Following the tack suggested by Rehnquist's letter, Powell pointed to *Linkletter* and *Walder* as examples of the "pragmatic approach" utilized by the Court to determine the applicability of the exclusionary rule in a given context.[178] *Walder*, in particular, Powell wrote, "revealed most pointedly that the policies behind the exclusionary rule are neither absolute nor all-encompassing, but rather must be weighed and balanced against a competing and more compelling policy, namely the need for effective determination of truth at trial."[179] Curiously, Powell included a footnote in which he explained that his mentioning of the exclusionary rule controversy was "not to suggest here its total abandonment (certainly not in the absence of some other deterrent to deviant police conduct) but rather to emphasize its precarious and undemonstrated basis, especially

---

170 Lewis Powell, Letter to Potter Stewart, *supra* note 161, at 2.

171 *Id.*

172 *Id.*

173 Schneckloth v. Bustamonte, 412 U.S. 218, 249 (1973) (Blackmun, J., concurring).

174 *Id.*

175 *Id.* at 266 (Powell, J., concurring).

176 *Id.* at 267.

177 *Id.* at 267 n.25.

178 *Id.* at 270.

179 *Id.* at 271.

when applied to a Fourth Amendment claim on federal habeas review of a state court decision."[180]

The reason for the footnote is not readily apparent. The language is reminiscent of Burger's earlier statements, professing an unwillingness to abolish the rule—at least, not yet—without an effective substitute. The comment about the rule's "precarious and undemonstrated basis," of course, is equally applicable to other contexts in which defendants invoke the rule. Perhaps the best explanation for the footnote is that it provided cover for Powell in future cases either to retain or discard the rule under a balancing analysis.

Powell's views on the exclusionary rule began to crystallize with the filings in *United States v. Robinson*.[181] At issue in *Robinson* was the validity of a search incident to the arrest of a person found driving with a revoked license. An officer discovered narcotics inside a cigarette package taken from the arrestee's pocket. The government argued that the search was constitutional, but even assuming the search was unconstitutional, the government insisted that the exclusionary rule should not apply. The government argued that because the search was designed to remove any weapons on the arrestee and was made pursuant to a police regulation requiring such searches, the exclusionary rule was inapplicable.

The Solicitor General's brief in *Robinson* was a studied endeavor to persuade the Court to restrict application of the exclusionary rule to flagrant and willful Fourth Amendment violations. While the government was careful not to call for the immediate elimination of the rule ("we do not consider it necessary in the present case to challenge its general validity"),[182] it did urge the Court "to distinguish those searches that are reasonably motivated, and are unlikely to be deterred . . . from searches that involve flagrant and willful violations."[183] The brief cited Burger's *Bivens* dissent four times. It also referenced the American Law Institute's Model Code of Prearraignment Procedure, which proposed applying the exclusionary rule, *inter alia*, according to the substantiality and flagrance of the constitutional infraction.[184] Under the multifactor criteria proposed by the ALI, the government argued that the contraband found on Robinson's person should not be suppressed because the search was compelled by standard procedures that were facially reasonable and could not be considered reckless, malicious, or willful.[185]

One of Powell's law clerks for the 1972 Term, John Jeffries, Jr., told his boss that the fate of the ALI's proposal "may well be the most important question before the Court this Term."[186] Jeffries's fifty-one page *Robinson* memorandum noted that the ALI proposal "involves a dramatic repudiation of precedent" and was "irreconcilable" with the

---

180 *Id.* at 267 n.25.

181 414 U.S. 218 (1973).

182 Brief for the United States at 39, *Robinson*, 414 U.S. 218 (No. 72-936).

183 *Id.* at 41.

184 *Id.* at 42.

185 *Id.*

186 John Calvin Jeffries Jr., Memorandum to Lewis Powell on *United States v. Robinson* 28 (Aug. 15, 1973), Powell Papers, Box 131.

view that exclusion was a constitutional right of the defendant rather than a remedy designed to protect Fourth Amendment rights generally.[187] But Jeffries opined that the problem with the "personal right" theory for exclusion was "its sheer extravagance."[188] Further, Powell's *Bustamonte* opinion contradicted the personal right theory. Jeffries wrote that if a defendant has a constitutional right to suppress evidence, that right could be invoked "in any available forum. His claim cannot logically be denied on the ground that enforcement of his rights would have only a tenuous relation to controlling police conduct."[189] Interestingly, in two places near the end of his memo, Jeffries seemed to think that his boss was disposed to abolishing the rule.[190]

Two weeks after receiving Jeffries's memorandum, which Powell described as "excellent" and "reflecting careful and thoughtful work," Powell responded with his own memorandum, which elaborated his views on exclusion far more than what his *Bustamonte* opinion revealed.[191] First, Powell conceded that he did not "regard the exclusionary rule as a constitutional right of the individual."[192] Instead, he saw it "as a remedy designed to effectuate Fourth Amendment rights which has been given a measure of constitutional status by this Court. There is nothing in the Constitution itself, its history, or the English experience from which we derived most of our concepts of personal rights of accused persons, to justify enshrining the exclusionary rule as a personal constitutional right."[193]

Next, Powell acknowledged that the Court did not yet know enough about how the rule operated "to draw many positive and final conclusions."[194] He acknowledged that the educational value of the rule has been "significant," but also stated: "I would be hard to convince that it actually deters—or indeed should deter—many of the limited searches made in good faith under the customary exigent circumstances of a warrantless search."[195]

Acknowledging that he was "keenly interested" in addressing the exclusionary rule, Powell objected to Jeffries's suggestion that the Court had only two options with respect to the exclusionary rule: "(i) retain the exclusionary rule in its full sweep, just as if it were written verbatim in the Constitution; or (ii) abandon it altogether."[196] He explained, as his *Bustamonte* opinion showed, that he was already committed to the "distinction between application of the rule at trial and on direct review, and its application in post-conviction cases."[197] Moreover, Powell disagreed with the view that the ALI proposal

[187] *Id.* at 28, 29.

[188] *Id.* at 29.

[189] *Id.* at 30.

[190] *Id.* at 41–42.

[191] Lewis Powell, Memorandum to John Calvin Jeffries, Jr. on *United States v. Robinson* (Aug. 31, 1973) [hereinafter Powell, *Robinson* Memo], Powell Papers, Box 131.

[192] *Id.* at 1.

[193] *Id.*

[194] *Id.*

[195] *Id.* at 2 (footnote omitted).

[196] *Id.* at 3.

[197] *Id.*

was tantamount to abandonment of the rule. Admitting that he was inclined to a case-by-case "balancing" of the accused's rights versus society's interests, Powell stated the ALI criteria for determining exclusion provided reasonable guidelines to the "conscientious judge."[198]

Powell also disagreed with Jeffries's conclusion that the ALI proposal would diminish the deterrent effect of the rule "precisely where it is needed most" by not requiring exclusion where police reasonably, but mistakenly, believe that their actions are consistent with Fourth Amendment precepts or where police commit minor or technical violations.[199] Powell replied that "it is unlikely that any rule, short of some drastic civil or criminal penalty on police themselves, will deter the good faith type of error which the ALI would except from the present rule."[200] He agreed that it is the "substantial" violation of Fourth Amendment rights, as identified under the ALI criteria, which must be deterred.[201] "There is less risk of serious or significant infringement of the protected privacy of law abiding citizens in the typical 'good faith error' type of case."[202]

Powell did, however, concur with Jeffries's statement that applying the exclusionary rule as a constitutional right "is unprincipled because of 'its sheer extravagance.'"[203] He shared Jeffries's view that "the suppression of evidence does not simply return the defendant to the *status quo ante*, but rather confers on him an undeserved immunity from prosecution," and wrote: "It strikes me that something is fundamentally fallacious in slavish adherence to a rule which produces such a bizarre result."[204] Significantly, neither Powell nor Jeffries addressed the fact that *Weeks* held that exclusion was a constitutional right of the defendant.

Finally, Powell signaled how he was likely to judge future cases implicating exclusion under the Fourth Amendment: "I instinctively suspect the merit of any rule that forecloses all judicial discretion and allows admittedly guilty defendants to go free—especially when there is genuine doubt as to the efficacy of the rule in accomplishing its avowed purpose."[205] But *stare decisis* mattered to Powell: "[W]e do not write on a clean slate. I would not therefore argue for the abolition of the exclusionary rule. I cannot and do not wish to ignore or overturn the entire body of case law supporting the principle or the rule."[206] Powell told Jeffries that he was seeking "a more rational position than that which has evolved from the judicial process since 1914."[207]

---

198 *Id.* at 4–5.

199 *Id.* at 5.

200 *Id.*

201 *Id.*

202 *Id.*

203 *Id.* (quoting Jeffries, Memorandum to Lewis Powell on *United States v. Robinson, supra* note 186, at 29).

204 *Id.* at 5–6.

205 *Id.* at 6–7.

206 *Id.* at 7.

207 *Id.*

As things turned out, the Court upheld the search in *Robinson*, and Rehnquist's majority opinion had no reason to address the exclusionary rule. In contrast to his actions in *Bustamonte* where Powell unnecessarily addressed the exclusionary rule, in *Robinson*, Powell remained silent on the Justice Department's proposal to restrict the rule's application to substantial or flagrant Fourth Amendment violations. Within a month, however, Powell would have another opportunity to address the rule in *United States v. Calandra*.[208] At issue in *Calandra* was whether a grand jury witness could refuse to answer questions because they were based on evidence obtained from an illegal search and seizure. This time Powell wrote for a six-to-three majority in an opinion representing a "watershed" moment in the evolution of the exclusionary rule.[209]

In December 1970, federal agents, armed with a search warrant, searched the Royal Machine & Tool Company in Cleveland, Ohio, which was owned by John Calandra. Although the agents did not find what they were seeking—evidence of illegal gambling—they did find and seize evidence suggesting that Calandra was involved in loansharking. A federal grand jury was convened and Calandra was called as a witness. After Calandra refused to testify, he was granted transactional immunity. Despite the immunity grant, Calandra refused to answer questions and moved the federal district court for suppression and return of the items seized by the agents because the warrant obtained by the agents had been issued without probable cause, and the search exceeded the scope of the warrant. The district court granted the motion and ruled that Calandra could refuse to answer any of the grand jury's questions based on the illegally seized items.

After reading the briefs, but before the oral argument in *Calandra*, Powell transcribed his "entirely preliminary" and "superficial" thoughts about the case in a "Summer Memorandum."[210] In the memo, Powell stated that he was "strongly inclined" toward the government's position "primarily because I am opposed to a further extension of the exclusionary rule."[211] Powell feared that under *Mapp*, if federal grand jury witnesses were permitted to invoke the exclusionary rule, the rule would also extend to state grand juries and to collateral proceedings in federal and state courts.[212] Powell wrote: "[U]nless and until empiric[al] evidence documents more fully than at present the efficacy of the exclusionary rule, I consider its extension in collateral proceedings [and habeas corpus proceedings] is not only a futile exercise but gravely impinges on other important interests."[213]

---

208 414 U.S. 338 (1974).

209 *See* Henry P. Monaghan, *Foreword: Constitutional Common Law*, 89 HARV. L. REV. 1, 4 (1975) (describing *Calandra* as a "watershed" case because it "cut the exclusionary rule entirely free from any personal right or necessary remedy approach, thereby removing the clearest authority for imposing the rule on the states").

210 Lewis Powell, Summer Memorandum on *United States v. Calandra* 1 (July 30, 1973), Powell Papers, Box 13.

211 *Id.* at 3.

212 *Id.*

213 *Id.*

Five months later, Powell wrote another memorandum that indicated his views from the summer had solidified. For example, echoing the logic of *Linkletter v. Walker*, Powell thought it important to emphasize that "the intrusion on [Calandra's] privacy has already occurred (and cannot be repaired)" by the exclusionary rule.[214] Powell also had come to accept the government's claim that invocation of the rule in the grand jury setting would have minimal deterrent impact: "It is quite unrealistic to assume that even the relatively sophisticated policeman would be thinking of the implications of a search and seizure with respect to a grand jury investigation."[215] Whatever deterrent impact the rule had on obtaining convictions, Powell thought, "it simply strains credulity to suggest that police conduct will be affected one way or the other by extending the Rule to grand jury proceedings."[216] Finally, Powell concluded that "the central theme" of the opinion "should be a *balancing*" of the "societal interests in safeguarding the role of grand juries against the marginal deterrent effect (if any) on police misconduct which might result from extending the Rule to grand jury proceedings."[217]

As his law clerk, John Buckley, began to revise the drafts of the *Calandra* opinion, Powell made two other important decisions. He told Buckley to keep in mind "that the Solicitor General is trying to persuade the Court to adopt the substance of the ALI formulation with respect to the exclusionary rule."[218] Powell had not yet reached a "final position" on the proposal, but he did not "want to foreclose either myself or the Court" from embracing the ALI proposal by what was written in *Calandra*.[219] Second, and more important, Powell wanted the *Calandra* opinion "to settle the question that is sometimes raised as to whether the exclusionary rule is itself a constitutional personal right."[220] Although he anticipated that "the Brennan Douglas Marshall axis will react strongly" to the formulation contained in the draft opinion, Powell himself had "no doubt" as to the correctness of his conclusion "as a matter of constitutional law."[221]

Powell's second choice, and the decision to incorporate this judgment into the final opinion, made *Calandra* a critical and evolutionary case. When *Calandra* asserted that the exclusionary rule "is a judicially created remedy designed to safeguard Fourth Amendment rights generally through its deterrent effect, rather than a personal constitutional right of the party aggrieved,"[222] the "Brennan-Douglas-Marshall axis" did react

---

[214] Lewis Powell, Memorandum to John J. Buckley on *United States. v. Calandra* 2 (Nov. 8, 1973), Powell Papers, Box 13.

[215] *Id.* at 3.

[216] *Id.* at 3–4.

[217] *Id.* at 4.

[218] Lewis Powell, Memorandum to John J. Buckley on *United States v. Calandra* 2 (Nov. 10, 1973), Powell Papers, Box 13.

[219] *Id.* at 2–3.

[220] *Id.* at 2.

[221] *Id.* at 1–2.

[222] United States v. Calandra, 414 U.S. 338, 348 (1974).

strongly. So did legal scholars.[223] The reaction occurred because *Calandra* was the first time "since the tangled constitutional debate in *Wolf* that the Court has suggested that the exclusionary rule does not function as a fundamental right of the accused."[224] And by deciding that exclusion was not a constitutional right of the defendant—not part and parcel of the Fourth Amendment's protection as *Weeks* held—both academics and the *Calandra* dissenters realized that the logic of Powell's opinion undermined the legitimacy of the exclusionary rule itself. As one legal scholar who seemed skeptical about the rule put it after *Calandra*: "As a matter of traditional constitutional theory, the significant issue is whether the Supreme Court has the authority to mandate the exclusionary rule if the rule is not a necessary corollary of a constitutional right."[225] Though Powell did not address this concern, both supporters and opponents of the rule concluded that *Calandra* marked the end of the rule's constitutional status.[226]

Besides determining that the exclusionary rule was not a constitutional right, other aspects of the *Calandra* opinion further jeopardized the future operation of the rule. For example, Powell's opinion emphasized that the constitutional "wrong" committed in the case was the illegal search and seizure of Calandra's office.[227] Grand jury questions based on the illegally seized evidence "involve no independent governmental invasion" of privacy; such questions are "only a derivative use of the product" of a past illegal intrusion,[228] and "[t]hey work no new Fourth Amendment wrong."[229] But under this logic, evidence obtained from an unconstitutional search should be admissible in any proceeding, including a trial, because the admission of the evidence "involve[s] no independent governmental invasion," is "only a derivative use of the product" of the unlawful search, and "work[s] no new Fourth Amendment wrong." This logic goes a long way toward abolishing the rule.[230]

Though some of Powell's reasoning in *Calandra* was a significant departure from the Court's past descriptions of the rule, other parts of his analysis paralleled the approach of earlier decisions. For instance, the centerpiece of *Calandra* was the balancing analysis

---

223 *See, e.g.*, Thomas S. Schrock & Robert C. Welsh, *Up from* Calandra*: The Exclusionary Rule as a Constitutional Requirement*, 59 MINN. L. REV. 251, 300–02 (1974).

224 Critique, *On the Limitations*, *supra* note 127, at 786–87.

225 Monaghan, *supra* note 209, at 6 (footnote omitted).

226 Thomas S. Schrock & Robert C. Welsh, *Reconsidering the Constitutional Common Law*, 91 HARV. L. REV. 1117, 1119 (1978); *see also* Yale Kamisar, *Does (Did) (Should) the Exclusionary Rule Rest on a "Principled Basis" Rather Than an "Empirical Proposition"?*, 16 CREIGHTON L. REV. 565, 640 (1983) [hereinafter Kamisar, *Principled Basis*]; William J. Mertens & Silas Wasserstrom, *The Good Faith Exception to the Exclusionary Rule: Deregulating the Police and Derailing the Law*, 70 GEO. L.J. 365, 385 (1981).

227 *Calandra*, 414 U.S. at 354.

228 *Id.*

229 *Id.*

230 *See* Critique, *On the Limitations*, *supra* note 127, at 780 (asking whether under *Calandra*'s logic, "*any* use of illegally obtained evidence would constitute an 'independent governmental invasion' rather than 'only a derivative use of the product of a past unlawful search,'" and observing that *Calandra*'s logic "would eliminate the exclusionary rule entirely").

Powell suggested in his memo. As explained in *Calandra*, the Court would determine whether to the extend the exclusionary rule to grand juries by "weigh[ing] the potential injury to the historic role and functions of the grand jury against the potential benefits of the rule as applied in this context."[231] Powell ultimately concludes that the potential damage to the grand jury process by invocation of the rule "outweighs" any potential deterrent benefit.[232] As support for this balancing approach, Powell cites the balancing analysis White utilized in *Alderman*, where the Court ruled defendants may not invoke the exclusionary rule to bar the admission of evidence obtained in violation of the rights of third parties.[233]

Of course, two very different legal concepts were at issue in *Alderman* and *Calandra*. *Alderman* concerned the standing of defendants to assert the constitutional rights of others. When *Alderman* held defendants who were not themselves victims of illegal searches could not invoke the exclusionary rule, the Court justified its decision not on deterrence grounds, but because the rule was considered to be a constitutional privilege possessed only by a defendant who was the victim of an illegal search. *Calandra*, by contrast, repudiated the principle that exclusion was a constitutional right. Under *Calandra*, exclusion turned on its ability to deter illegal searches.

Similarly, when confronted with the issue of whether grand juries should be free to ask questions based on unlawfully obtained evidence, Powell explains that the Court is presented with "a question, not of rights, but of remedies."[234] By formulating the question this way, Powell uncouples the exclusionary rule from the Fourth Amendment. This technique was first performed by Frankfurter in *Wolf*. One advantage of this methodology is that it advanced Powell's fierce opposition to extending the rule beyond the boundaries established in *Mapp*. As John Jeffries told Powell, if *Mapp* stood for the proposition that the exclusionary rule was an essential part of the Fourth Amendment, a person was free to assert the right in any available forum. But by divorcing the rule

---

[231] *Calandra*, 414 U.S. at 349.

[232] *Id.* at 354. Powell thought that any deterrent impact gained by extending the exclusionary rule to grand jury proceedings was "uncertain at best." *Id.* at 351. According to Powell, applying the rule to grand juries "would deter only police investigation consciously directed toward the discovery of evidence solely for use in a grand jury investigation." However, the incentive to violate the Fourth Amendment to obtain an indictment "is substantially negated by the inadmissibility of the illegally seized evidence in a subsequent criminal prosecution of the search victim," and, generally speaking, prosecutors are unlikely "to request an indictment where a conviction could not be obtained." *Id.* Powell's reasoning has been challenged. *See* Donald L. Horowitz, The Courts and Social Policy 240 (1977) (explaining that because nearly ninety percent of criminal defendants plead guilty, "indictment may be tantamount to conviction." Thus, there may be "a very strong incentive for the police to obtain evidence illegally which can be used in grand jury proceedings, even if that evidence would be inadmissible at a trial if one were ever held. . . . Because the deterrence reasoning in *Calandra* is based on the criminal trial as the implicit norm, ignoring the way in which most criminal cases are actually disposed of, the opinion takes as given a structure of police and prosecution incentives that may prove to be fictitious.").

[233] *Calandra*, 414 U.S. at 350–51.

[234] *Id.* at 354.

from the Constitution, *Calandra* eliminates the constitutional authority of the rule and leaves the Court free to decide as a matter of social policy whether to apply the rule in a particular context.

As Powell predicted, the Brennan-Douglas-Marshall axis did have a strong reaction to his opinion. Indeed, Brennan privately conceded that his dissent "was a vigorous one and strongly worded."[235] Among other things, Brennan's dissent asserted that the result in *Calandra* signaled that a majority of the Court was ready to scrap the rule altogether, because "surely they cannot believe that application of the exclusionary rule at trial furthers the goal of deterrence, but that its application in grand jury proceedings will not 'significantly' do so."[236] Brennan also challenged his colleagues' professed reliance on deterrence as justification for the rule: "Unless we are to shut our eyes to the evidence that crosses our desks every day, we must concede that official lawlessness has not abated and that no empirical data distinguishes trials from grand jury proceedings."[237]

Powell's opinion did not directly respond to these challenges other than to reaffirm that at trial, defendants are entitled "to the suppression of, not only the evidence obtained through an unlawful search and seizure, but also any derivative use of that evidence,"[238] and by observing that the Court was not considering "the extent of the rule's efficacy in criminal trials."[239] Privately, however, Powell was genuinely bothered by the tone of Brennan's dissent. According to Brennan, Powell later told him that the dissent's "reference to the Court's betrayal of constitutional principles had deeply troubled him."[240] Brennan believed his dissent had "two important effects."[241] It convinced Marshall, who had originally voted with the majority at the conference, to join Brennan's dissent.[242] Also, after Brennan circulated the first draft of his dissent to his colleagues, Stewart called Brennan "to say that, while he had joined the Court's opinion, he would not, so long as he was on the Court, participate in a total overruling of the exclusionary rule."[243]

Calandra unquestionably concluded that the exclusionary rule is not a constitutional privilege. Aspects of its reasoning also seemed to suggest that illegally acquired evidence

---

235 William J. Brennan, Jr., Case Histories, October Term, 1973 at IX (undated) [hereinafter Brennan, Case Histories O.T. 1973], Brennan Papers, Box II: 6.

236 *Calandra*, 414 U.S. at 365 (Brennan, J., dissenting).

237 *Id.*

238 *Id.* at 354 (majority opinion).

239 *Id.* at 348 n.5. In a long footnote near the end of his opinion, Powell distinguished the factual and legal proceedings surrounding *Silverthorne Lumber* from the procedural setting in *Calandra*. *See Id.* at 352 n.8. Regarding Holmes's penultimate statement in *Silverthorne Lumber* that the Fourth Amendment meant that illegally acquired evidence "shall not be used at all," Silverthorne Lumber Co. v. United States, 251 U.S. 385, 392 (1920), Powell explained that Holmes's "broad dictum" had "been substantially undermined by later cases," *Calandra*, 414 U.S. at 352 n.8.

240 Brennan, Case Histories O.T. 1973, *supra* note 235, at IX.

241 *Id.*

242 *Id.*

243 *Id.*

should be admissible in *any* proceeding, because the admission of such evidence does not constitute a new or additional Fourth Amendment violation. Powell's logic also could support the view that exclusion is always unwarranted because suppression cannot restore the privacy loss by the victim of the unlawful intrusion. But Powell did not intend for *Calandra* to be used in this way. It was his goal to focus on the application of the exclusionary rule in various contexts by balancing the costs and benefits on a case-by-case basis. Over time, Powell came to have doubts about withdrawing the exclusionary rule altogether or limiting its application only to egregious cases. The deterrent loss from either of those positions, Powell believed, would be unacceptable. But for cases like *Calandra*, Powell was confident about curtailing the rule where any marginal gain in deterrence seemed insignificant. Throughout his tenure on the Court, Powell opposed *categorical* exclusion, and the result in *Calandra* reflected that position.

Powell still accepted the exclusionary rule as "controlling law." In other words, while Powell opposed expansion of the rule, he was generally disinclined to overturn precedents applying the rule in particular contexts. His steadfastness on this point was tested in *United States v. Peltier*,[244] when Rehnquist successfully converted a routine retroactivity case into an important ruling that would significantly influence the Court's exclusionary rule jurisprudence in the future.

On February 28, 1973, Border Patrol agents stopped James Robert Peltier's vehicle and discovered two hundred and seventy pounds of marijuana in the trunk. Four months later, in *Almeida-Sanchez v. United States*,[245] the Court held that Border Patrol agents violated the Fourth Amendment when they searched a vehicle twenty-five air miles from the Mexican border without probable cause. In the court of appeals, the government conceded that the search of Peltier's vehicle violated the principle announced in *Almeida-Sanchez*, but contended that principle should not apply to searches conducted prior to the announcement of *Almeida-Sanchez*. After the appellate court rejected that argument, the Solicitor General took *Peltier* to the Court raising two points: First, *Almeida-Sanchez* should not apply retroactively; and second, the policies behind the exclusionary rule did not require suppression of the evidence seized from Peltier's vehicle.

During the *Peltier* conference, Stewart dismissed the government's retroactivity argument because the holding of *Almeida-Sanchez* was not new.[246] Relying on a seminal 1925 ruling, *Carroll v. United States*,[247] Stewart explained that there is "nothing new about the doctrine that a car may not be stopped and searched without probable cause."[248] White, on the other hand, thought that *Almeida-Sanchez* should not be applied retroactively since the officers acted under the authority of a federal statute and with the

---

244 422 U.S. 531 (1975).

245 413 U.S. 266 (1973).

246 Lewis Powell, Conference Notes on *United States v. Peltier* (Feb. 19, 1975) [hereinafter Powell, *Peltier* Conference Notes], Powell Papers, Box 24.

247 267 U.S. 132 (1925).

248 Powell, *Peltier* Conference Notes, *supra* note 246.

approval of prior decisions of the court of appeals.[249] White also stated that he was willing to say the "exclusionary rule should not apply absent a deterrence rationale."[250] In essence, White was finding that the Border Patrol agents had acted in good faith, and no deterrent interest would be served by excluding the evidence found in Peltier's trunk. Interestingly, Rehnquist observed that if the "usual retroactivity analysis is applied, Potter may be right." But Rehnquist thought that applying "exclusionary rule rationale" required reversal.[251] For his part, Powell told his colleagues that he voted for reversal and relied "heavily on my view of the exclusionary rule."[252] In the end, there were five votes for reversal.[253]

Rehnquist was assigned to write the opinion, and he circulated a draft to his colleagues on April 2, 1975, which was very similar to the published opinion in *Peltier*.[254] The specific rationale of the draft is hard to discern. Although *Peltier* came to the Court on direct review from the court of appeals, in certain places the draft treats the case as one involving the retroactivity of *Almeida-Sanchez*. In other parts of the opinion, however, the draft is written broadly and appears to be addressing the exclusionary rule itself. In fact, when describing the government's arguments, the draft states:

> The Government contends in this Court that *Almeida-Sanchez* should not be applied retroactively and second that as a matter of exclusionary rule policy the facts and circumstances surrounding the search and seizure of the evidence in this particular case do not require suppression. The two arguments are not entirely separate, but since we agree with the Government's second contention, we find it unnecessary to resolve the first.[255]

Later in the draft, Rehnquist wrote:

> If the purpose of the exclusionary rule is to deter unlawful police conduct, then evidence obtained from a search should be suppressed only if it can be said that the law enforcement officer had knowledge, or may properly be charged with knowledge, that the search was unconstitutional under the Fourth Amendment.[256]

The intent behind these statements is obvious: Rehnquist was writing the retroactivity issue out of the case and using *Peltier* as a vehicle to limit the exclusionary rule.

---

[249] *Id.*

[250] *Id.*

[251] *Id.*

[252] *Id.*

[253] *Id.*

[254] William Rehnquist, Draft of *United States v. Peltier* (circulated Apr. 2, 1975), Powell Papers, Box 24.

[255] *Id.* at 4.

[256] *Id.* at 10.

Under his analysis, the scope of the rule would be limited to instances where police had "knowledge," or could be charged with "knowledge," that their conduct violated the Fourth Amendment. In other words, the rule would not apply to good-faith violations of the Fourth Amendment. This was comparable to the proposal offered by the California Attorney General in *Krivda*, when he argued that where it appears to the police that it is sufficiently probable their actions do not violate the Fourth Amendment, the rule should not be applied. And Rehnquist's good-faith analysis was similar to what Powell would say in a concurring opinion in *Brown v. Illinois*,[257] which was decided one day after *Peltier*.

At issue in *Brown* was whether incriminating statements of a defendant, obtained by police after an illegal arrest and the provision of *Miranda* warnings, were admissible at a murder trial. The Illinois Supreme Court concluded that providing *Miranda* warnings alone was sufficient to remove the taint of the illegal arrest and permit admission of the statements obtained from the illegal arrest. The majority in *Brown*, however, ruled that while the *Miranda* warnings were an important factor in deciding whether a confession was obtained by exploitation of an illegal arrest, they were not the only factor to consider.[258] Also important were the temporal proximity of the arrest and the confession, the presence of intervening circumstances, and the purpose and flagrancy of the police misconduct.[259] Powell's concurring opinion in *Brown* viewed the case as turning on proper application of the Fourth Amendment's exclusionary rule. Believing that not all Fourth Amendment violations are the same, Powell drew a distinction between the "flagrantly abusive" and "technical" or "good-faith" violation.[260] Because the deterrent purpose of the exclusionary rule assumes that the police have engaged in deliberate or negligent misconduct, absent such behavior, Powell saw "no legitimate justification" for suppressing reliable evidence and "would consider a statement given at the station house after one has been advised of *Miranda* rights to be sufficiently removed from the immediate circumstances of the illegal arrest to justify its admission at trial."[261] Ironically, in light of his statements about "good-faith" police conduct in *Brown*, Powell was troubled by Rehnquist's actions in *Peltier*.

Powell wrote Rehnquist that the two above-quoted passages from *Peltier* could be "read as indicating a view well beyond the retroactivity issue," which Powell thought was the basis for the conference vote, "namely, that *Almeida-Sanchez* should not be applied retroactively because the deterrence policy of the exclusionary rule would not in any way be promoted."[262] Powell suggested editorial changes to both sentences that "would make it clear the *holding* of this case does not go beyond the retroactivity issue. As you

---

[257] 422 U.S. 590 (1975).

[258] *Id.* at 603.

[259] *Id.* at 603–04.

[260] *Id.* at 610–11 (Powell, J., concurring in part).

[261] *Id.* at 612.

[262] Lewis Powell, Letter to William Rehnquist 1 (Apr. 22, 1975), Powell Papers, Box 24.

know, I consider this to be the only issue before us."[263] Powell also explained that "if and when the Court is willing to reexamine the rationale of the exclusionary rule," he favored adopting the ALI proposal, which would apply the rule in cases of flagrant or deliberate violations of the Fourth Amendment.[264] Powell informed Rehnquist that he had written a brief concurrence because the two sentences "may be read to foreclose the balancing approach recommended by the ALI."[265] Powell confessed to being "quite unaccustomed . . . to being a spokesman for the exclusionary rule," but he told Rehnquist that "apart from attempting to contain or rationalize the rule on its outer perimeters (e.g., *Bustamonte* and *Calandra*), I have accepted it as presently controlling law."[266] Indeed, Powell stated he would not have "joined *Almeida-Sanchez* without thinking that the evidence there seized would be properly excluded."[267]

Rehnquist's reply to Powell's letter tacitly admitted Rehnquist's intentions to use *Peltier* as a vehicle for restricting the exclusionary rule. He informed Powell that he was unwilling to accept Powell's first suggested editorial change "*in haec verba*" because it would make *Peltier* "just another retroactivity case with no possibility of its being used at some later date in justification of a flexible application of the exclusionary rule."[268] Rehnquist did agree to alter the language of the first sentence with a change that fudged the government's arguments.[269] However, Rehnquist did not respond to Powell's suggested change for the second sentence, which limited the exclusionary rule to cases where police knew or should have known that their actions violated the Fourth Amendment. This language remained in the final opinion, and as Powell must have known at the time, Rehnquist's language planted an important seed for what would become the "good-faith" exception to the exclusionary rule. Ultimately, Powell did not file his separate opinion, and joined Rehnquist's opinion.

* * *

The Court's willingness to adopt a good-faith exception to the exclusionary rule surfaced, and then disappeared, when the Court addressed whether the rule applied in a federal civil proceeding regarding evidence that was illegally obtained by state law enforcement officers. Relying on a search warrant, Los Angeles police officer Leonard Weissman seized over four thousand dollars and other evidence of bookmaking from Max Janis. Weissman then contacted the Internal Revenue Service (IRS), and the IRS filed an assessment against Janis for unpaid wagering tax based on the evidence seized by Weissman. The IRS seized the cash taken from Janis in partial satisfaction for the tax owed by Janis. Criminal charges were also filed against Janis in state court, but a judge

---

263 *Id.* at 2.

264 *Id.* at 1.

265 *Id.* at 1–2.

266 *Id.* at 2.

267 *Id.*

268 William Rehnquist, Letter to Lewis Powell 1 (Apr. 24, 1975), Powell Papers, Box 24.

269 *Id.*

found that the search warrant used to obtain the evidence against Janis was defective because it was not supported by probable cause. Janis subsequently filed a lawsuit seeking a refund of the cash taken by the IRS. The lower federal courts ruled in favor of Janis because the evidence used as the basis for the tax assessment was obtained pursuant to the invalid warrant.[270]

Five days before the *Janis* conference, Blackmun, the eventual author of *Janis*, transcribed his views of the case. As he did in prior memos, Blackmun reaffirmed his opposition to the exclusionary rule: "By and large, I have never been in favor of the exclusionary rule. It seems to me that the legal process should be a search for truth, and that the exclusionary rule violates that precept."[271] But Blackmun also appeared to have second thoughts about what he had said about the rule a few years earlier. In *Coolidge*, Blackmun registered his view that "the Fourth Amendment supports no exclusionary rule."[272] Now, Blackmun sounded like Powell in his willingness to live with a narrowly interpreted exclusionary rule. Blackmun wrote: "I would be satisfied with holding the exclusionary rule in as narrow confines as possible. I do not wish to expand it. I am willing to accept it within reasonable degree."[273] He added: "[T]o the extent it provides a logical deterrence to illegal police action I could go along with it. Where the deterrence factor is not present I am not nearly so sure."[274]

Regarding *Janis* itself, Blackmun could "easily agree" that the rule should apply in criminal as well as civil proceedings if the IRS "made an extreme invasion" of one's home.[275] In that scenario, Blackmun explained, "the deterrence factor is fully applicable and fully at work."[276] However, in *Janis*, where the officer acted in good-faith reliance on a warrant that was later declared invalid, he saw "no deterrent effect, or at least no proper deterrent effect."[277] He was inclined to reverse, which could be done "without damaging the exclusionary rule, and then we can leave the availability of the rule in more extreme civil cases for another day."[278]

At the *Janis* conference, there was never any doubt that a majority of the Court would reject Janis's claim that the exclusionary rule should bar the IRS from using the evidence illegally seized by the Los Angeles police. The only significant question was whether the Court would issue a broad ruling saying that the rule never applies to civil proceedings. Burger voted to reverse, and urged the Court to "limit the exclusionary rule to criminal

---

270 United States v. Janis, 428 U.S. 433, 434–39 (1976).

271 Harry Blackmun, Memorandum on *United States v. Janis* 8 (Dec. 5, 1975) [hereinafter Blackmun, *Janis* Memo], Blackmun Papers, Box 219.

272 Coolidge v. New Hampshire, 403 U.S. 443, 510 (1971) (Blackmun, J., concurring and dissenting).

273 Blackmun, *Janis* Memo, *supra* note 271, at 9.

274 *Id.*

275 *Id.*

276 *Id.*

277 *Id.*

278 *Id.* at 9–10.

cases."[279] Brennan voted to affirm. Stewart stated that *Calandra* did not settle the issue because, while a grand jury can ask questions based on illegally obtained evidence, such evidence cannot be used at trial.[280] Stewart thought the case was "close and difficult."[281] White voted to reverse but had no comment.[282] Powell's conference notes record Blackmun as saying that he "would not expand" the rule and that the "exclusionary rule should not be extended to civil side,"[283] and Brennan records Blackmun saying "confine the exclusionary rule as narrowly as possible and never extend it. . . . Generally, the rule ought not be applied on the civil side unless it's an egregious case. This isn't."[284] Powell spoke next and stated that the Court "need not decide on the broadest possible ground."[285] He favored moving toward the ALI proposal.[286] He noted the "police acted in good faith and there was no deterrence effect here."[287] Powell also observed that "judicial integrity is a subordinate policy for me, but even if this had been knocking a door down by the police without collusion of the IRS, the government should have the benefit of this evidence."[288] Rehnquist then spoke and favored reversal either by saying that the "exclusionary rule doesn't apply to civil cases" or that "there was good faith" by the police.[289] For his part, Powell wanted the Court to "write narrowly."[290] He noted that the IRS was not responsible for the illegal seizure, and there was no proof of collaboration between the city police and the IRS.[291] After the conference, *Janis* was assigned to Blackmun.

As framed by Blackmun's opinion, the issue in *Janis* was whether evidence unconstitutionally seized by state police in "good faith" is inadmissible in a civil proceeding by or against the United States.[292] Although Blackmun makes the good faith of the officer an essential part of the issue, and despite prior expressions of interest in a good-faith exception by several justices, the good-faith element of *Janis* disappears from the Court's holding. As Professor Kamisar notes, *Janis* never explains what it meant by "good faith," and Blackmun's "reasoning seems to apply whether or not the state police acted in good faith."[293]

---

279 William J. Brennan, Jr., Conference Notes on *United States v. Janis* (undated) [hereinafter Brennan, *Janis* Conference Notes], Brennan Papers, Box I: 368.

280 Lewis Powell, Conference Notes on *United States v. Janis* (Dec. 10, 1975) [hereinafter Powell, *Janis* Conference Notes], Powell Papers, Box 30.

281 *Id.*

282 *Id.*

283 *Id.*

284 Brennan, *Janis* Conference Notes, *supra* note 279.

285 *Id.*

286 *Id.*

287 *Id.*

288 *Id.*

289 Powell, *Janis* Conference Notes, *supra* note 280.

290 *Id.*

291 *Id.*

292 United States v. Janis, 428 U.S. 433, 434 (1976).

293 Kamisar, *Principled Basis*, *supra* note 226, at 643 n.426.

While Blackmun does not take advantage of the facts in *Janis* to adopt a good-faith exception, he does not shy away from another controversy then brewing over the exclusionary rule. Over the years, scholars questioned whether the rule actually deters illegal searches and seizures. In his *Bivens* dissent, Burger cited Dallin Oaks's article for the proposition that there is no empirical evidence that the rule does deter.[294] Thereafter, opponents of the rule, on and off the Court, frequently cited Oaks's article when criticizing the rule, and his article was followed by other articles questioning the deterrent value of the rule. But a few scholars challenged whether Oaks and other critics of the rule had demonstrated that the rule fails to deter.[295] In *Janis*, Blackmun acknowledged this debate and concluded that "[n]o empirical researcher, proponent or opponent of the rule, has yet been able to establish with any assurance whether the rule has a deterrent effect even in the situations in which it is now applied."[296] Yet, Blackmun also reaffirmed "that the 'prime purpose' of the rule, if not the sole one," is deterrence.[297] But if there is no empirical proof on whether the exclusionary rule deters, why keep claiming that the purpose of the rule is to deter? Blackmun's less-than-satisfactory answer is that pragmatic evidence is irrelevant because whether the rule deters or not, the Court has decided that the rule should not apply to a federal civil proceeding.[298]

On the merits, Blackmun found that suppressing the evidence in the federal tax proceeding would not produce sufficient deterrence. First, he focused on the official the Court sought to deter. Here, it was the state law enforcement officer who conducted the illegal search. Blackmun explained that no additional deterrence would be gained, because suppressing the evidence in both state and federal criminal proceedings is sufficient deterrence.[299]

Furthermore, assuming exclusion deters generally, Blackmun concluded that "the additional marginal deterrence provided by forbidding a different sovereign from using the evidence in a civil proceeding surely does not outweigh the cost to society of extending the rule to that situation."[300] On the other hand, if there is no "appreciable" deterrence, then invocation of the rule is unwarranted.[301] Blackmun thus concludes, "[u]nder either assumption, therefore, the extension of the rule is unjustified."[302] For good measure, Blackmun observed that "common sense" proves that the deterrent impact of exclusion is "highly attenuated when the 'punishment' imposed upon the offending criminal

---

294 Bivens v. Six Unknown Named Agents of Federal Bureau of Narcotics, 403 U.S. 388, 416 (1971) (Burger, C.J., dissenting).

295 *See, e.g.*, Critique, *On the Limitations*, *supra* note 127; Bradley C. Canon, *Is the Exclusionary Rule in Failing Health? Some New Data and a Plea Against a Precipitous Conclusion*, 62 Ky. L.J. 681 (1974).

296 *Janis*, 428 U.S. at 452 n.22.

297 *Id.* at 446 (quoting United States v. Calandra, 414 U.S. 338, 347 (1974)).

298 *Id.* at 453–54.

299 *Id.* at 457–58.

300 *Id.* at 453–54.

301 *Id.* at 454.

302 *Id.*

enforcement officer is the removal of that evidence from a civil suit by or against a different sovereign."[303] Put simply, exclusion would have little, or no, deterrent impact, because the federal proceeding to collect the tax from Janis "falls outside the offending officer's zone of primary interest."[304]

Blackmun acknowledged Janis's argument that the lower courts had long applied the exclusionary rule to civil proceedings. But he criticized Janis for not recognizing the difference between cases where, on the one hand, the officer who committed an illegal search was an agent of the sovereign that sought to use the evidence, and, cases where, on the other hand, the offending officer has no responsibility, duty, or agreement with the sovereign seeking to use the evidence.[305] He left open whether the exclusionary rule would apply in a civil proceeding involving an intrasovereign violation.[306]

Blackmun's final comments in *Janis* indicate his own (and perhaps, in general, the Burger Court's) frustration with the exclusionary rule. He stated: "There comes a point at which courts, consistent with their duty to administer the law, cannot continue to create barriers to law enforcement in the pursuit of a supervisory role that is properly the duty of the Executive and Legislative Branches. We find ourselves at that point in this case."[307] Obviously, these comments reveal significant discontent with the rule and are reminiscent of Blackmun's view five years earlier when he stated that the Fourth Amendment did not support an exclusionary rule. These remarks also suggest that the Court saw exclusion as a rule of evidence based on the Court's supervisory powers over the federal judiciary, and not based on the Constitution. Finally, these comments imply that the Court believed elected officials, and not the judiciary, should be devising remedies for illegal searches.

Indeed, when these remarks are considered in conjunction with the *Janis* conclusion that there is no proof on whether the rule actually deters, it appears that the Court was positioning itself to abandon the rule. In spite of all of this, the *Janis* Court did not eliminate the rule, raising two essential questions: First, if there is no empirical proof that the rule actually deters illegal searches, why does the Court continue to say that the purpose of the rule is to deter? Second, and more important, if there is no proof on the deterrent impact of the rule, what is the constitutional basis for imposing the rule on the states after *Calandra* established that the rule is not a constitutional right?

While *Janis* offered no answers to these important questions, the backstage proceedings of another case, *Stone v. Powell*,[308] which was decided on the same day as *Janis*, did provide some clues as to why the Burger Court did not eliminate the exclusionary rule. *Powell* and its companion case *Wolff v. Rice* raised several questions related

303 *Id.* at 457–58.

304 *Id.* at 458.

305 *Id.* at 455.

306 *Id.* at 455 n.31.

307 *Id.* at 459.

308 428 U.S. 465 (1976).

to the exclusionary rule, including whether the purpose of the rule was served where police seize evidence in reliance upon a statute or judicial warrant that are subsequently declared unconstitutional; whether a good-faith exception should be adopted; whether the Fourth Amendment claims of a state prisoner should be cognizable under the federal habeas corpus statute; and whether *Kaufman v. United States*,[309] which held that federal prisoners could invoke the exclusionary rule on collateral attack, should be overruled. Additionally, Burger saw in *Powell* and *Rice* the opportunity to deliver a deathblow to *Mapp*, since both cases involved obviously guilty murderers raising seemingly technical Fourth Amendment arguments against good-faith police behavior. When the opinion was announced, however, the Court only decided the issue left unresolved in *Schneckloth v. Bustamonte*,[310] namely, whether a state prisoner seeking federal habeas corpus relief could claim that illegally obtained evidence had been used to convict him.

In *Bustamonte*, Powell, joined by Burger and Rehnquist, concluded that, where there is no claim bearing on innocence, a state prisoner's search or seizure challenge to his conviction should not be cognizable in federal habeas corpus proceedings where the state court provided a fair opportunity to raise and have adjudicated the Fourth Amendment claim.[311] Although he did not join Powell's opinion, Blackmun also indicated his agreement with this position.[312] With the four Nixon appointees having already stated their position on the issue, *Stone v. Powell* seemed like a sure victory for the state, especially since Stewart had dissented in *Kaufman* during the final Term of the Warren Court. But Stewart was known to oppose overruling Warren Court precedents. Along a similar vein, White had expressed in the *Bustamonte* conference his unwillingness to overrule *Kaufman* on a "piecemeal" basis,[313] and White saw little difference between invoking the exclusionary rule on direct appeal and on collateral attack.[314] Thus, it was not certain that the state would prevail on the habeas issue in *Stone v. Powell*, let alone succeed in getting the Court to overrule *Mapp*.

Lloyd Powell and David Rice were convicted murderers. Powell had participated in the robbery of a San Bernardino, California, liquor store and shot and killed the wife of the store owner when a fight between him and the owner broke out. Several hours later, Powell was arrested in Henderson, Nevada, for violating a vagrancy ordinance, and a search incident to arrest revealed the gun used in the liquor store shooting. At his trial for murder, Powell argued the discovery of the gun should be suppressed because the ordinance was unconstitutional. The trial court rejected the argument. After California state courts affirmed his conviction, Powell petitioned for federal habeas corpus relief and renewed his search and seizure claim. The Court of Appeals for the Ninth Circuit

309 394 U.S. 217 (1969).

310 412 U.S. 218 (1973).

311 *Id.* at 250 (Powell, J., concurring).

312 *Id.* at 249 (Blackmun, J., concurring).

313 Powell, *Bustamonte* Conference Notes, *supra* note 144.

314 *Id.*

ruled that the ordinance was unconstitutionally vague, Powell's arrest was illegal, and the gun should have been excluded from his trial. The appellate court explained that although exclusion of the gun would serve no deterrent purpose with regard to the officer who arrested Powell because he was enforcing the ordinance in good faith, exclusion would deter legislators from enacting unconstitutional statutes.[315]

David Rice was convicted of murder in a Nebraska state court. On August 17, 1970, an Omaha police officer was sent to a home to investigate a call regarding a woman's screaming. The officer saw a suitcase at the doorway, and as he examined it, the suitcase exploded and killed the officer. Rice and others were suspected, and the police obtained a warrant to search Rice's home. Inside Rice's home, the police found evidence that tied Rice to the explosion. The trial court denied Rice's suppression motion, Rice was convicted of murder, and the Nebraska Supreme Court affirmed his conviction. In his federal habeas corpus petition, Rice argued that the search of his home was illegal, because the affidavit in support of the warrant did not establish probable cause. The lower federal courts agreed.[316]

Before the conference on *Stone v. Powell*, both Blackmun and Powell transcribed their thoughts about the exclusionary rule and the case. Blackmun did not believe the rule was based on the Constitution. He wrote: "The exclusionary rule has always bothered me. At the time *Kaufman* was decided I felt it was wrong. The exclusionary rule can be supported on the federal side by this Court's supervisory power. It makes much less sense to apply it federally to state actions."[317] Blackmun was also skeptical that there was empirical evidence that exclusion serves a deterrent function. Using Cardozo's famous words, he inquired: "[S]hould a guilty man go free because the constable has blundered? I think he should not, but the bleeding hearts all over the country think otherwise. Always, it seems to me, they forget the victim and the inestimable cost to society in letting their hearts bleed."[318]

Anticipating that the Court would change the law, Blackmun preferred following the approach offered by Harlan's dissent in *Kaufman* (i.e., to limit invocation of the rule in habeas proceedings only where there are limited and special circumstances). But Blackmun was also willing to join the approach Powell outlined in his concurrence in *Schneckloth v. Bustamonte*, though he viewed Powell's position as "a little more extreme than the Harlan position."[319] Although Burger and Rehnquist had already indicated support for Powell's approach, Blackmun "would feel more comfortable" if Stewart and White "would be so inclined also."[320] Blackmun closed his memo by observing: "I am

---

315 Stone v. Powell, 428 U.S. 465, 469–71 (1976).

316 *Id.* at 471–74.

317 Harry Blackmun, Memorandum on *Wolff v. Rice* and *Stone v. Powell* 13 (Feb. 23, 1976), Blackmun Papers, Box 220.

318 *Id.* at 13–14.

319 *Id.* at 16.

320 *Id.* at 17.

pretty well rejecting all this pious talk about judicial integrity, the integrity of the judicial process, and effective deterrence of the brutal police. The police may be brutal at times, but this isn't the way to attack the brutality."[321]

Like Blackmun, Powell had strong views against exclusion. Reflecting on the rule, Powell observed: "[T]he argument for continuing what I deeply believe is an injustice to societal interests also seems to me to be mechanical rather than rational."[322] He described *Mapp* as "a ruling by four Justices" which applied a "rule of evidence—the Exclusionary Rule—to the states in constitutional terminology."[323] Powell noted that more recent precedents, in particular, *Calandra* and *Peltier*, "have said—in effect—that *Mapp* cannot be read as creating a personal constitutional right in the Exclusionary Rule."[324] In Powell's view, the text of the amendment did not support the rule, "and certainly nothing supports an absolute, unbending rule."[325] Powell did, however, concede "some tension" between *Mapp*'s holding and *Calandra*'s and *Peltier*'s discussions of the rule.[326] But he thought the tension could be resolved without overruling *Mapp*, and he repeated his unwillingness to repeal the rule: "May I say here that I have no disposition to abolish the Exclusionary Rule in trials and direct appeals, although I would read some rationality into the Rule."[327] According to Powell, the rule "is simply a means—one means—of implementing the constitutional protection against unreasonable searches and seizures. In effect, it is a rule of evidence—and certainly one not engraved in marble."[328] Left unexplained, however, was the basis for continued imposition of the exclusionary rule on the states if it was nothing more than a "rule of evidence."

At the conference for *Powell* and *Rice*, Burger began by proposing to either "modify or eliminate the exclusionary rule" or overrule *Kaufman v. United States*.[329] Burger stated: "I prefer option one, but I can go along with option two."[330] Burger voted to reverse both judgments.[331] Brennan voted to affirm both judgments.[332] Stewart spoke next and implied that *Mapp* was wrongly decided. Stewart said that he "would not alter the rule of *Weeks v. United States*, which I regard as a rule of evidence in federal courts."[333] Referring to one of the grounds for *Mapp*'s holding, Stewart stated: "[T]he 'imperative of judicial

---

[321] *Id.*

[322] Lewis Powell, Notes on *Stone v. Powell* 2(Feb. 27, 1976), Powell Papers, Box 30.

[323] *Id.*

[324] *Id.* at 3.

[325] *Id.*

[326] *Id.*

[327] *Id.*

[328] *Id.*

[329] William J. Brennan, Jr., Conference Notes on *Wolff v. Rice* and *Stone v. Powell* (undated), Brennan Papers, Box I: 368.

[330] *Id.*

[331] *Id.*

[332] *Id.*

[333] *Id.*

integrity' for me refers only to federal courts. So for me, *Mapp* was a thunderbolt."[334] But Stewart was not ready to vote, so he passed.[335]

White then spoke and indicated he would not overrule *Mapp*: "The exclusionary rule should be modified but not discarded. It should be sort of an immunity rule, with a good faith, objective standard."[336] Nor did White favor overruling *Kaufman*. He told his colleagues that he "joined *Kaufman*" and that it would be a mistake to have the Supreme Court as the only federal forum where Fourth Amendment claims could be raised in a post-conviction context.[337] White also noted that the federal habeas statute "hardly seems to support a construction to exclude some kinds of Fourth Amendment claims."[338] Most likely referring to the availability of post-conviction relief for federal prisoners raising Fourth Amendment claims, finally, White said, "I can't see how, if we modify the rule for states, we can fail to modify the federal rule."[339]

Marshall spoke next and surprisingly stated he was "receptive to a limitation of the exclusionary rule, if some workable plan can be devised."[340] Eventually, however, Marshall would join Brennan's dissent in *Stone v. Powell*. Blackmun stated that he would "cut the exclusionary rule back," unless there is a "blatant disregard of the rules."[341] Powell then spoke and outlined four possibilities: First, the Court could find that there is no Fourth Amendment violation in either case.[342] Second, "we could modify the exclusionary rule to except good faith violations—I would gladly join this disposition."[343] Third, the Court could view the exclusionary rule "differently on collateral attack than from direct appeal, recognizing a good faith exception at least in habeas cases."[344] Or, fourth, "we could recede from my *Bustamonte* opinion to the extent of a claim of innocence."[345]

Rehnquist said, "I could modify the exclusionary rule to an objective test of reasonableness," and noted that *Calandra* and *Peltier* had laid the "groundwork" for that result.[346] Rehnquist could also agree to bar Fourth Amendment claims on collateral attack.[347] Or, he was willing to go along with Powell's *Bustamonte* approach.[348] Stevens spoke last and said he was close to Powell's position on *Bustamonte*, "except as to the

334 *Id.*
335 *Id.*
336 *Id.*
337 *Id.*
338 *Id.*
339 *Id.*
340 *Id.*
341 *Id.*
342 *Id.*
343 *Id.*
344 *Id.*
345 *Id.*
346 *Id.*
347 *Id.*
348 *Id.*

innocence element."[349] Stevens then explained his views on the exclusionary rule: "If we rely on a deterrence rationale, we think of preventing our society from becoming a police state. I would be rigid on that score in applying the exclusionary rule in the federal area. But where you are talking about federal collateral attacks on judgments for state prisoners, deterrence simply doesn't happen."[350] Stevens also opposed a good-faith exception to the rule. Instead, he favored "a drastic distinction between direct and collateral review, where the exclusionary rule is constitutionally compelled, and leave the question of whether the state afforded a fair chance to litigate this."[351]

It is plain from the views expressed in the conference that there were not five votes to overrule *Mapp*, the result favored by Burger. Four justices (Burger, White, Powell, and Rehnquist) supported some type of good-faith exception that would be applied at trial and on direct appeal; but, as Powell explained in a later letter to Burger, Stewart and Stevens "flatly stated their unwillingness to join an opinion going so far, or expressing any dissatisfaction with the rule at trial and on direct appeal."[352] Accordingly, Powell, who was assigned to write the opinion in *Stone v. Powell*, interpreted the conference discussion as "six firm votes to dispose of these cases solely on the applicability of the exclusionary rule to Fourth Amendment issues raised on habeas corpus."[353]

Several days after the conference, Powell's law clerk, Greg Palm, sent his boss a memo proposing two options on how the opinion could be written: "(1) interpret the habeas statute to not include [Fourth Amendment] claims, or (2) re-cast the scope of the exclusionary rule not to be cognizable in habeas proceedings since the 'right of exclusion' is limited to areas where the general deterance [sic] value exceeds the costs."[354] Regarding the first option, Palm explained that one way to proceed "is simply to re-cast your *Bustamonte* opinion into a majority opinion."[355] Palm pointed out several disadvantages with this approach, including the overruling of *Kaufman*, which was only six years old; Stewart and Stevens refused to join an approach focusing on the "innocence" of the habeas petitioner, which had been Powell's focus in his *Bustamonte* concurrence; and the roots of *Kaufman* were old enough to "make it very difficult to argue that Congress has not accepted this Court's expansive view of the habeas statute."[356] Palm also noted that there is "*no* strong historical support" for barring Fourth Amendment claims under the federal habeas statute.[357]

---

349 *Id.*

350 *Id.*

351 Dickson, *supra* note 78, at 490.

352 Lewis Powell, Letter to Warren Burger 1 (June 18, 1976), Powell Papers, Box 30.

353 *Id.*

354 Greg Palm, Memorandum to Lewis Powell on *Stone v. Powell* and *Wolff v. Rice* 1 (Mar. 11, 1976), Powell Papers, Box 30.

355 *Id.*

356 *Id.*

357 *Id.* at 2.

Palm then explained that option two involved "a re-focusing of the exclusionary rule: That is, as our recent cases have demonstrated the exclusionary rule is based on the principle of deterrence."[358] Under this approach, the essential question becomes whether "the incremental value of permitting Fourth Amendment claims in habeas outweighs the cost."[359] Palm thought that this approach would be very similar to the balancing model adopted in *Calandra*.[360] The advantages of option two were "obvious": First, it avoids reinterpretation of the federal habeas statute.[361] Second, a balancing approach was used in recent cases and is "one which the Court will certainly argue from in a later case adopting the 'good faith' exception."[362] Palm parenthetically observed, "This analysis will set the stage for that opinion."[363] The problem with option two was "the tension between this view and the view of the [Fourth Amendment] advanced in certain past cases" like *Weeks* and *Mapp*.[364] But Palm thought that the tension was not a significant problem because "it is quite clear after *Calandra* and other recent opinions that general deterrence is the moving force behind the rule."[365]

Last, Palm noted other considerations in choosing between the options. Option one gave Congress the choice to "amend the statute and overrule the Court" if it was unhappy with the Court's judgment.[366] Under option two, however, "it is not clear that there would be any way Congress could force an exclusionary rule in habeas for State prisoners."[367] And option two had implications for other constitutional claims. For example, the rationale of option two "might be extended to *Miranda* warnings."[368] Palm recommended that Powell choose option two because it is "the most defensible" and it might "swing" White's vote "since he joined *Calandra*."[369] Powell approved option two but warned that "whichever route we follow, we may have some trouble—as our six votes were not all predicated on the same line of reasoning."[370]

Powell's opinion in *Stone v. Powell* relied upon and reinforced what was said about the exclusionary rule in *Calandra* and *Peltier*. Speaking generally about the rule, Powell reaffirmed that the primary justification for the rule is deterrence of illegal police searches and seizures, and that the rule is not a personal constitutional right but instead

---

358 *Id.* at 2-3.

359 *Id.* at 3.

360 *Id.*

361 *Id.*

362 *Id.*

363 *Id.*

364 *Id.*

365 *Id.*

366 *Id.*

367 *Id.*

368 *Id.*

369 *Id.*

370 Lewis Powell, Handwritten Note to Greg Palm on *Stone v. Powell* and *Wolff v. Rice* (Mar. 11, 1976), Powell Papers, Box 30.

a judicially created remedy designed to safeguard Fourth Amendment rights generally.[371] Whether the rule should apply in a particular context, he explained, turned on a "balancing" analysis.[372] With respect to the specific issue of whether a state prisoner can invoke the rule to attack his conviction in a federal habeas proceeding, Powell explained that the answer would be decided by "weighing the utility" of the rule against the costs of extending it to a collateral proceeding.[373] Powell then listed several costs—misdirecting the attention of the trial participants from the guilt or innocence of the defendant, the loss of reliable and probative evidence, and the disparity in particular cases between the error committed by the police and the windfall gained by the guilty defendant[374]—all of which are also imposed when the rule is invoked at the trial and on direct appeal. Such costs, Powell noted, "persist" when a state prisoner seeks federal habeas review.[375]

On the other hand, Powell perceived no benefits to applying the rule in habeas proceedings. He explained that the Court has "assumed" that exclusion will discourage future illegal conduct and encourage compliance with Fourth Amendment norms by police officers.[376] Powell reiterated the Court's adherence to the view that exclusion at trial and on direct appeal will promote these positive results: "But the additional contribution, if any, of the consideration of search-and-seizure claims of state prisoners on collateral review is small in relation to the costs."[377] Accordingly, Powell held that where the state has provided "an opportunity for full and fair litigation of a Fourth Amendment claim, a state prisoner may not be granted federal habeas corpus relief on the ground that evidence obtained in an unconstitutional search or seizure was introduced at his trial."[378]

Three other opinions were filed in *Stone v. Powell*. Burger's concurrence lamented the fact that the Court had not eliminated the exclusionary rule.[379] Burger had written Powell a "personal" note objecting to what he called an "endorsement" of the exclusionary rule in Powell's draft.[380] Consequently, Burger's initial draft of his concurrence refused to join Powell's opinion,[381] apparently as a protest against Powell's refusal to abolish or drastically restrict the rule. Powell was annoyed by the gesture and reminded Burger in a letter that the conference vote did not support addressing a good-faith exception as applied to trials and direct appeals.[382] Bob Woodward and Scott Armstrong wrote that

---

371 Stone v. Powell, 428 U.S. 465, 486 (1976).

372 *Id.* at 487.

373 *Id.* at 489.

374 *Id.* at 489–90.

375 *Id.* at 491.

376 *Id.* at 492.

377 *Id.* at 493.

378 *Id.* at 494 (footnote omitted).

379 *Id.* at 496 (Burger, C. J., concurring).

380 Warren Burger, Letter to Lewis Powell on *Stone v. Powell* and *Wolff v. Rice* (June 16, 1976), Powell Papers, Box 30.

381 Warren Burger, Draft Opinion on *Stone v. Powell* and *Wolff v. Rice* (June 16, 1976), Powell Papers, Box 30.

382 Lewis Powell, Letter to Warren Burger on *Stone v. Powell* and *Wolff v.* Rice (June 18, 1976), Powell Papers, Box 30.

Burger felt betrayed by Powell's failure to eliminate or modify the exclusionary rule.[383] If this is true, Burger obviously was unaware of Powell's long-standing unwillingness to scrap the rule, which dated back to *Robinson*.

While Burger was frustrated that Powell's opinion had not gone further in restricting the exclusionary rule, Brennan's dissent vigorously attacked Powell's opinion from the opposite direction.[384] Among other things, Brennan questioned Powell's reasoning, which reaffirmed the exclusionary rule at trial and on direct appeal, but barred invocation of the rule during collateral proceedings. Even accepting *Calandra*'s conclusion that the rule is not a personal right, Brennan noted that under *Mapp*, state courts have a constitutional obligation to exclude evidence obtained in violation of the Fourth Amendment.[385] And when a state court admits such evidence, "it has committed a *constitutional* error."[386] This being so, Brennan asked "what logic can support the assertion that the defendant's unconstitutional confinement obtains during the process of direct review, no matter how long that process takes, but that the unconstitutionality then suddenly dissipates at the moment the claim is asserted in a collateral attack on the conviction."[387]

White also dissented, agreeing with the substance of Brennan's argument that there is no basis for making habeas proceedings "any less available to those convicted of state crimes where they allege Fourth Amendment violations than where other constitutional issues are presented to the federal court."[388] But unlike Brennan, White was ready to limit the reach of the exclusionary rule "as presently administered" in federal and state trials.[389] Interestingly, White admitted his uncertainty on whether he would he have joined Clark's opinion in *Mapp* had he been on the Court.[390] However, as time passed, White wrote he became convinced that both *Weeks* and *Mapp* "had overshot their mark insofar as they aimed to deter lawless action" and that many applications of the exclusionary rule were "not advancing that aim in the slightest."[391] Thus, the rule was "a senseless obstacle to arriving at the truth in many criminal trials."[392] White acknowledged the many calls for repealing the rule, but he opposed overruling either *Weeks* or *Mapp*. On this point, White and Powell agreed, but White made his view public, which was something Powell never did.

White did favor, however, substantially modifying the rule in cases where police act in "good-faith belief" that their conduct "comported with existing law and having reasonable grounds for this belief."[393] In White's view, where police have acted "mistakenly,

---

383 Woodward & Armstrong, *supra* note 94, at 429–30.

384 *Stone v. Powell*, 428 U.S. at 502–36 (Brennan, J., dissenting).

385 *Id.* at 509.

386 *Id.*

387 *Id.* at 509–10 (footnote omitted).

388 *Id.* at 536 (White, J., dissenting).

389 *Id.* at 537.

390 *Id.*

391 *Id.* at 537–38.

392 *Id.* at 538.

393 *Id.*

but in good faith and on reasonable grounds, and yet the evidence they have seized is later excluded, the exclusion can have no deterrent effect."[394] Although it was not apparent at the time, White's proposal for a good-faith exception, along with Rehnquist's language from *Peltier* confining the rule to cases where police have "knowledge" that their conduct was unconstitutional, became the foundation for the good-faith exception the Court would eventually embrace.

Like *Calandra*, *Stone v. Powell* was a "watershed" decision.[395] *Stone v. Powell* overruled *Kaufman*. Although the opinion does not say so directly, *Stone v. Powell* effectively subverted the basis for *Kaufman*'s holding. Powell privately admitted as much in a memo to his law clerk when he wrote, "There is much to the view that *Kaufman* has been undercut."[396] Consequently, Fourth Amendment claims of both federal and state prisoners cannot be raised in post-conviction proceedings in federal court. And by shutting the doors of the federal courthouse to state prisoners' Fourth Amendment claims, *Stone v. Powell* created the potential to convert the exclusionary rule into a toothless admonition to state judges.[397]

At the same time, *Stone v. Powell* signaled the Burger Court's willingness to live with the exclusionary rule, for the time being, during the prosecution's case-in-chief at trial and on direct appeal. Although Burger was disappointed with this result, Burger and other opponents of the exclusionary rule still had reason to celebrate. Stewart's decision to join *Stone v. Powell* indicated a willingness to overrule a Warren Court precedent, something Stewart would have to do again in order to get a fifth vote to overrule *Mapp*. White publicly endorsed a good-faith exception. Though the public did not know it, during the *Stone v. Powell* conference, Stewart indirectly questioned the constitutional basis of both *Weeks* and *Mapp*, and Stevens expressed doubt about the deterrent impact of exclusion when the rule is invoked in post-conviction proceedings. Thus, while the exclusionary rule remained extant after *Stone v. Powell*, the rule clearly did not retain the same vigor it held when *Mapp* was announced. Burger and the other justices knew that it was only a matter of time before a good-faith exception would be adopted by the Court, which would inflict considerable and permanent damage to the rule's strength and significance.

---

394 *Id.* at 540.

395 Louis Michael Seidman, *Factual Guilt and the Burger Court: An Examination of Continuity and Change in Criminal Procedure*, 80 COLUM. L. REV. 436, 449 (1980).

396 Lewis Powell, Memorandum to Greg Palm on *Stone v. Powell* and *Wolff v. Rice* 1 (June 24, 1976), Powell Papers, Box 30.

397 Seidman, *supra* note 395, at 450 ("By closing the only effective federal forum for raising fourth amendment claims it turns the exclusionary rule into little more than a precatory suggestion to state courts and undercuts the 'dialectical federalism' at the heart of the Warren Court's strategy for vindicating constitutionally rooted claims raised in the criminal process." (footnote omitted)).

5 The Court Rushing to Limit Application of the Exclusionary Rule "somewhere, anywhere. . ."

ALTHOUGH CHIEF JUSTICE Burger did not convince his colleagues to repeal the exclusionary rule in *Stone v. Powell*, that setback did not stop him from aggressively pushing his colleagues to impose additional restrictions on the rule—if not complete abolishment. A tragic case out of Iowa, *Brewer v. Williams*,[1] gave Burger another opportunity to push his agenda to abolish the rule, albeit in a context not involving the Fourth Amendment. But as occurred in *Stone v. Powell*, where Justice Powell would not go as far as Burger wished in repealing or even substantially modifying the exclusionary rule, Powell again thwarted Burger from achieving a major victory in his fight against the rule.

Brewer v. Williams revealed that Powell, while highly critical of a mechanical application of the rule and certainly amenable to various and significant restrictions on the scope of the rule, was not an ideologue when it came to the rule and did not share all of Burger's agenda on exclusion. As his biographer put it, Powell's approach on constitutional criminal procedure issues "reflected his idea of himself as a judge. Powell did not come to the Court with an ideological agenda."[2] Despite Burger's pressure in *Williams*, this was one case where Powell would exclude evidence acquired as a result of deliberate police misconduct. As this chapter demonstrates, however, although Powell may not have been an ideologue regarding suppression, his internal memos and votes show that he strongly opposed extending the exclusionary rule beyond the boundaries established in *Mapp v. Ohio*.

---

[1] 430 U.S. 387 (1977).

[2] JOHN C. JEFFRIES, JR., JUSTICE LEWIS F. POWELL, JR. 404 (1994).

On Christmas Eve 1968, ten-year-old Pamela Powers went with her family to a YMCA in Des Moines, Iowa, to watch her brother in a wrestling match. Powers disappeared after a trip to the restroom. A search commenced and quickly focused on Robert Williams, a black resident of the YMCA and a former mental patient. Williams was seen leaving the YMCA lobby carrying clothing and a large bundle wrapped in a blanket. A teenager who helped Williams put the bundle in Williams's car later told authorities that he "saw two legs in it and they were skinny and white."[3] Williams left the scene and two days later surrendered to police in Davenport, Iowa, one hundred and sixty miles from Des Moines.

Williams was arraigned in Davenport, and his lawyers reached an "agreement" with the lead detective on the case, Captain Cletus Leaming, that Williams would not be interrogated or mistreated on the trip back to Des Moines. Despite the agreement, Leaming did question Williams. He delivered a "Christian burial speech" to Williams without Williams's lawyers present, which prompted Williams to disclose the location of the girl's body. Williams was later convicted of murder, and the Iowa courts affirmed the conviction. He filed a federal habeas corpus petition, arguing that Leaming's actions violated the Fifth and Sixth Amendments. A federal district court granted the petition, and that ruling was affirmed by the court of appeals.

When *Williams* arrived at the Court, there was no reason to view it as an exclusionary rule case. The constitutional questions focused on whether Williams's rights under *Miranda* and the Sixth Amendment right to counsel had been violated. When the justices voted to grant review, Powell wrote on his conference sheet that Stewart told his colleagues the case "does not involve the exclusionary rule."[4] Burger, however, was determined to make it an exclusionary rule case.

After oral argument, Burger told his colleagues in the conference discussion that he "would apply *Stone v. Powell*," which meant that Williams would be precluded in a federal habeas proceeding from contesting the admission of evidence that violated his right to counsel.[5] Stewart replied that he "thought that *Stone v. Powell* dealt only with Fourth Amendment" claims.[6] Powell agreed with Stewart when he said *Stone v. Powell* "didn't reach Fifth or Sixth Amendment claims, only Fourth Amendment" challenges.[7] Stevens also observed that he "would be bothered at the notion that *Stone v. Powell* might be extended here."[8] Ultimately, the justices voted five to four to affirm the court of appeals' decision to grant Williams's habeas petition.[9] Stewart was assigned the opinion.

Stewart circulated a first draft in late November 1976.[10] The draft did not mention the exclusionary rule. While this draft would undergo several stylistic and technical changes,

---

[3] *Williams*, 430 U.S. at 390.

[4] Lewis Powell, Conference Notes on *Brewer v. Williams* (Dec. 12, 1975), Powell Papers, Box 36.

[5] William J. Brennan, Jr., Conference Notes on *Brewer v. Williams* (undated), Brennan Papers, Box I: 401.

[6] *Id.*

[7] *Id.*

[8] *Id.*

[9] *Id.*

[10] Potter Stewart, First Draft of *Brewer v. Williams* (Nov. 24, 1976), Powell Papers, Box 36.

it was basically the same opinion he announced on March 23, 1977. Stewart ultimately held the Sixth Amendment was violated because Captain Leaming deliberately sought to elicit information from Williams at a time when he was entitled to counsel's assistance. Thus, neither Williams's incriminating statements made during the drive with Leaming nor any testimony describing Williams leading the police to Powers's body should have been admitted at his trial. The published opinion made no explicit mention of the exclusionary rule. A footnote at the end of the opinion did, however, allude to the possibility of admitting evidence of the body's location and of its condition at a new trial.[11]

Although Stewart's opinion never mentions the exclusionary rule, Burger's dissent was essentially a criticism of the rule. Burger complained that the exclusion of Williams's statements "interrupts what has been a more rational perception of the constitutional and social utility of excluding reliable evidence from the truth-seeking process."[12] Burger saw no reason to exclude here. Like the other dissenting justices, Burger perceived no constitutional evil in Leaming's behavior, and, even assuming a technical violation of Williams's rights, Burger found no basis for describing the detective's conduct as "egregious."[13] Burger accused the majority of ordering suppression "for no other reason than the Court's general impression that it may have a beneficial effect on future police conduct; indeed, the Court fails to say even that much in defense of its holding."[14]

For Burger, *Williams* was indistinguishable from *Stone v. Powell*. In both cases, the challenged evidence was utterly reliable, the constitutional claim supporting exclusion was irrelevant to the defendant's guilt or innocence, and allowing a habeas corpus petitioner to challenge the evidence would have minimal deterrent impact on police misconduct. According to Burger, the Court should instead mandate exclusion of probative evidence on the "basis of its benefits and costs, at least in those cases where the police conduct at issue is far from being outrageous or egregious."[15]

Burger's dissent was directed at Powell as much as it was directed at Stewart's majority opinion. Powell was the author of *Stone v. Powell*. During the deliberations on *Williams*, Burger strongly lobbied Powell to vote to extend *Stone v. Powell* to Sixth Amendment cases like *Williams*, but Powell resisted the entreaties. A frustrated Burger then attacked Powell in his dissent for voting to allow Williams to suppress evidence. But Burger knew that Powell's views on the exclusionary rule, particularly in Fourth Amendment cases, were closely aligned to his own views. In fact, after seeing a second draft of Powell's concurrence in *Williams*, Burger wrote Powell on February 10, 1976, noting that he was "happy to see that our views on the exclusionary rule mesh so closely."[16] Despite acknowledging their shared views, Burger pressed Powell to extend the reasoning of *Stone v. Powell* to Sixth Amendment cases. He told Powell that we cannot "blink the fact that

---

[11] Brewer v. Williams, 430 U.S. 387, 406 n.12 (1977).

[12] *Id.* at 421 (Burger, C.J., dissenting).

[13] *Id.* at 422.

[14] *Id.* at 422, 426.

[15] *Id.* at 427.

[16] Warren Burger, Letter to Lewis Powell 1 (Feb. 10, 1977), Powell Papers, Box 36.

the evidence sought to be suppressed in this case seems to me to fit hand in glove with your own description of why exclusion of evidence would not be appropriate here were this a Fourth Amendment case."[17]

Powell's reply letter to Burger is informative: he reminded Burger that it took "us" three years "to identify and bring to the Court just the right case to decide the issue presented in *Stone v. Powell*."[18] He explained that he had to keep his opinion in *Stone v. Powell* "sharply focused" on the Fourth Amendment in order to keep a majority of the Court.[19] In his letter, he expressed doubt that "a majority of the Court is willing at this time to extend the *Stone* line of analysis indiscriminately."[20] Powell admitted to having "misgivings" himself as to *Stone v. Powell*'s "applicability to the Sixth Amendment right to counsel."[21] Powell noted that White agreed to join *Stone v. Powell* and expressed support for the ALI modification of the exclusionary rule, which would permit the admission of illegally obtained evidence where the police act in good faith or inadvertently violate the Fourth Amendment. Powell stated, "I would join in this type of modification of the exclusionary rule."[22] But Powell thought that *Williams* was "a poor vehicle for modifying the exclusionary rule," because he had "difficulty defending the police conduct."[23] He closed his letter by observing the result in *Williams* "will not foreclose our considering a modification of the exclusionary rule in a more appropriate case."[24] And he remarked that when such a case arises, "I think you will find me a congenial spirit."[25]

Although Burger did not realize it at the time, he could claim a significant "victory" against the exclusionary rule in *Brewer v. Williams*. As noted, Stewart's initial draft made no mention of the exclusionary rule. After reading White's and Blackmun's proposed dissents, Burger wrote his colleagues to say that he would join those dissents, and he would write additionally to focus on the "irrationality" of suppressing evidence of a murder victim's body.[26] Strictly read, Stewart's draft never stated the body had to be suppressed. It ruled all evidence relating to or resulting from any statements Williams made during the ride from Davenport to Des Moines must be suppressed.[27] Stewart's final opinion, however, contained a footnote that all but encouraged the Iowa prosecutors and courts to retry Williams and permit admission of the body "on the theory that the body would have been discovered in any event, even had incriminating statements

---

17 *Id.*

18 Lewis Powell, Letter to Warren Burger 1 (Feb. 11, 1977), Powell Papers, Box 36.

19 *Id.*

20 *Id.*

21 *Id.*

22 *Id.* at 2.

23 *Id.*

24 *Id.*

25 *Id.*

26 Warren Burger, Memorandum to the Conference (Dec. 29, 1976), Powell Papers, Box 36.

27 *See* Stewart, First Draft of *Brewer v. Williams*, *supra* note 10, at 5.

not been elicited from Williams."[28] The inclusion of this footnote was not enough for Burger. He insisted that the footnote "makes clear that the Court is determined to keep the truth from the jurors pledged to find the truth."[29] Burger viewed the footnote as proposing an "unlikely theory," which "renders the prospects of doing justice in this case exceedingly remote."[30] Once again, Burger misjudged his colleagues and overplayed his hand. Seven years later, the Court, in an opinion authored by Burger, ruled that Pamela Powers's body and its condition were admissible against Williams under the theory suggested in Stewart's footnote.[31]

I. Fruit of the Poisonous Tree

Richard Nixon's 1968 presidential campaign promoted the view that the Warren Court's constitutional criminal procedure rulings "handcuffed" the police and released dangerous criminals on technicalities. Nixon's attack on the Warren Court never mentioned that the Court created the doctrine of qualified immunity for police officers who violate citizens' constitutional rights.[32] Nixon's campaign succeeded, in part, due to his caricature of the Warren Court. A complete and accurate description of the Warren Court would acknowledge that the Court's rulings were not blind to society's interest in the administration of criminal justice, and sometimes, promoted that interest at the expense of the constitutional rights of criminal defendants.[33] *Wong Sun v. United States* was such

---

[28] Brewer v. Williams, 430 U.S. 387, 406 n.12 (1977).

[29] *Id.* at 416 n.1 (Burger, C.J., dissenting).

[30] *Id.*

[31] Nix v. Williams (*Williams II*), 467 U.S. 431 (1984). *Williams II* is discussed in chapter 7.

[32] In 1967, the Court decided *Pierson v. Ray*, 386 U.S. 547 (1967). *Pierson* was a civil rights lawsuit brought by white and black clergymen against Mississippi police officers who had arrested the clergymen under a breach of the peace law for being inside a segregated bus terminal. Several years after the arrest, the breach of the peace law was declared unconstitutional. In an opinion written by Chief Justice Warren, the Court ruled that police should not be liable for acting under a statute they reasonably believe to be valid that is later held unconstitutional. Warren observed: "A policeman's lot is not so unhappy that he must choose between being charged with dereliction of duty if he does not arrest when he has probable cause, and being mulcted in damages if he does." *Id.* at 555. As Professor Al Alschuler later explained, the Warren Court granted police qualified immunity in these circumstances not because historical precedent supported such immunity, "but because qualified immunity seemed like a good idea at the time." Albert W. Alschuler, Herring v. United States*: A Minnow or a Shark*, 7 OHIO ST. J. CRIM. L. 463, 506 (2009). But Alschuler also notes: "Unlike other instances of Warren Court activism, however (for example, the extension of the exclusionary rule to the states), the Court's whole-cloth invention of qualified immunity for police officers has met with the whole-hearted approval of the Burger, Rehnquist, and Roberts Courts." *Id.*

[33] *Cf.* Yale Kamisar, *The Warren Court (Was It Really So Defense-Minded?), The Burger Court (Is It Really So Prosecution-Oriented?), and Police Investigatory Practices*, *in* THE BURGER COURT: THE COUNTER-REVOLUTION THAT WASN'T 62, 67–68 (Vincent Blasi ed., 1983) (explaining that by the end of its tenure, the Warren Court was issuing pro-police rulings and "had begun a process many associated only with its

a case. In the late 1970s, the Burger Court employed *Wong Sun*'s logic to restrict the scope of the exclusionary rule.

Following *Mapp v. Ohio*, the next important exclusionary rule case decided by the Court was *Wong Sun v. United States*,[34] which was decided in 1963. The case involved a confusing set of facts, with federal drug agents entering the homes of suspected heroin users and dealers in San Francisco's Russian Hill district. The suspects' names and aliases—James Wah Toy, a.k.a. "Blackie Toy," Johnny Yee and Wong Sun, a.k.a. "Sea Dog"—seem to be pulled from a James Bond movie. The arrests produced incriminating statements from the defendants and the discovery of narcotics from one defendant, which the defense claimed should have been excluded from the trial. The two conference discussions in *Wong Sun* focused primarily on whether the agents had probable cause for the various arrests of the defendants.[35] The Court voted five to four that the arrests were unconstitutional, and Brennan was assigned the opinion.[36]

After concluding that the arrests violated the Fourth Amendment, Brennan's opinion turned to whether the statements and physical evidence should have been excluded. Here, Brennan relied upon the attenuation doctrine and the metaphor of "poisonous fruit" that Frankfurter coined in his 1939 opinion in *Nardone II*.[37] (*Nardone II* is discussed in chapter 2.) Frankfurter's discussion was dicta in a case that did not involve the Fourth Amendment. But that did not stop Brennan from adopting Frankfurter's analysis to determine when evidence obtained from a Fourth Amendment violation was subject to exclusion.

Brennan first explained there would be no distinction between physical and verbal evidence. Although the exclusionary rule had traditionally required the suppression of physical items, Brennan found no policy reason justifying suppression of physical evidence but not verbal evidence: "[I]n terms of deterring lawless conduct by federal officers, or closing the doors of the federal courts to any use of evidence unconstitutionally obtained, the danger in relaxing the exclusionary rules in the case of verbal evidence would seem too great to warrant introducing such a distinction."[38] Brennan applied this logic to suppress defendant James Wah Toy's statement obtained immediately after the agents broke into Toy's home and chased him into his bedroom. The government argued the statement was admissible as "an intervening independent act of a free will."[39] But

---

successor—a process of reexamination, correction, consolidation, erosion, or retreat, depending upon your viewpoint").

34 371 U.S. 471 (1963).

35 *See* Bernard Schwartz, Super Chief: Earl Warren and His Supreme Court—A Judicial Biography 453–57 (1983). Schwartz explains that *Wong Sun* was first argued while Frankfurter was still on the Court. After Frankfurter retired from the Court, the case was reargued in 1962, with Arthur Goldberg replacing Frankfurter. *Id.*

36 *Id.* at 455.

37 *Wong Sun*, 371 U.S. at 487–88; *see also* Nardone v. United States (*Nardone II*), 308 U.S. 338, 341 (1939).

38 *Wong Sun*, 371 U.S. at 486 (citations omitted).

39 *Id.*

Brennan rejected this claim. He explained, under such oppressive circumstances, it "is unreasonable to infer that Toy's response was sufficiently an act of free will to purge the primary taint of the unlawful invasion."[40]

Brennan's ruling, however, was no bonanza for criminal defendants. *Wong Sun* made clear that not all evidence obtained from an unconstitutional search or seizure should be suppressed. In other words, *Wong Sun* rejected a "but-for" test for exclusion. In his early years on the Court, Brennan "eschewed absolutes" and preferred "balancing tests that allowed him to weigh competing values."[41] The reasoning of *Wong Sun* fit that mold. Reminiscent of Frankfurter's policy-driven approach to exclusion, Brennan explained that evidence is not subject to exclusion "simply because it would not have come to light but for the illegal actions of the police."[42] Bypassing a clear rule, Brennan framed the inquiry as whether the challenged evidence was obtained "by exploitation" of the illegal intrusion or "instead by means sufficiently distinguishable to be purged of the primary taint."[43]

Brennan found that with respect to Johnny Yee, it was "clear" that his narcotics, which were obtained immediately after the unlawful arrest, were secured by exploitation of the illegal seizure and therefore should have been excluded.[44] On the other hand, Brennan ruled Wong Sun's confession was not tainted fruit of his illegal arrest. The federal agents had entered Wong Sun's home without a warrant and, lacking probable cause, found Wong Sun sleeping in his bedroom and arrested him. Wong Sun was later released from police custody, arraigned by a federal magistrate, and voluntarily returned to the office of the federal agents several days later to give the statement. Without explaining why, Brennan stated that the connection between the illegal arrest and Wong Sun's statement "had 'become so attenuated as to dissipate the taint.'"[45]

It is not obvious why Wong Sun's confession was attenuated from the illegal arrest. As Professor LaFave rightly observes, the statement "quite clearly was caused by the illegal arrest, and thus doesn't admission of the confession permit the government to profit from a Fourth Amendment violation?"[46] Brennan's opinion provides no reason to think that Wong Sun would have confessed without the unlawful arrest. Interestingly, Brennan's articulation and application of the standard for determining whether evidence was sufficiently attenuated as to dissipate the taint of illegal conduct drew no complaints from other members of the Court—either liberal or conservative. Neither Douglas's separate concurring opinion nor Clark's dissent raised any objection. Perhaps,

---

40 *Id.*

41 Seth Stern & Stephen Wermiel, Justice Brennan: Liberal Champion 225 (2010).

42 *Wong Sun*, 371 U.S. at 487–88.

43 *Id.* at 488.

44 *Id.*

45 *Id.* at 491 (quoting Nardone v. United States (*Nardone II*), 308 U.S. 338, 341 (1939)).

46 6 Wayne R. LaFave, Search and Seizure: A Treatise on the Fourth Amendment §11.4(a), at 258 (4th ed. 2004).

no objection was raised because Brennan's test provides little, if any, guidance on when evidence must be excluded.[47]

While Brennan's adoption of the fruit analysis elicited no controversy among the justices, *Wong Sun*, like Frankfurter's opinion in *Nardone II*, never explained why attenuation analysis was consistent with the view that exclusion was a constitutional right of the defendant. When the concept of attenuation was initially acknowledged by the Court, the exclusionary rule rested on the reasoning of *Weeks*, which viewed exclusion as a personal right. In *Nardone II*, Frankfurter "did not explain why or how the admission of attenuated evidence was consistent with the personal entitlement to exclude both direct and indirect products of illegalities."[48] Likewise, Brennan omitted any such explanation in *Wong Sun*. The absence of such an explanation was particularly ironic in light of the recent (and highly controversial) ruling in *Mapp*, which held that "all evidence obtained by searches and seizures in violation of the Constitution is, by that same authority, inadmissible."[49]

In theory, an attenuation exception to the exclusionary rule appears sensible. Perhaps Brennan's embrace of attenuation analysis is another way of saying that an illegal search must be the "proximate cause" of the discovery of evidence. Under tort law, in order to recover damages, a plaintiff must show that a defendant's negligence was not only the "but-for" cause but also the proximate cause of the plaintiff's injury.[50] In tort law, if there is an independent or intervening act that causes the plaintiff's injury, then the defendant's negligence is not the proximate cause of the plaintiff's injury. In Fourth Amendment cases, the concept of attenuation might be viewed as a substitute for "proximate cause." In other words, if an intervening act uncovers the evidence, then exclusion seems unwarranted even though an illegal search was still a "but-for" cause of discovering the evidence. The problem in *Wong Sun*, however, is that Brennan does not explain why Wong Sun's release from custody made his later confession attenuated evidence. An application of tort logic to *Wong Sung* teaches that exclusion would be improper if an

---

47 As Professor Tomkovicz has observed, the "notion of 'taint dissipation' is not particularly helpful in determining *when* evidence is admissible." James J. Tomkovicz, Constitutional Exclusion: The Rules, Rights, and Remedies that Strike the Balance Between Freedom and Order 48 (2011); *see also* 6 LaFave, *supra* note 46, § 11.4(a), at 259 (noting that in neither *Nardone II* nor *Wong Sun* "did the Court elaborate upon the 'attenuated connection' test, thus leaving it rather uncertain exactly what it was that lower courts were expected to look for, to say nothing of what facts would be relevant to an 'attenuation' determination"). Nevertheless, Tomkovicz concedes that Brennan's test does "capture and reflect a belief that exclusion is inappropriate when the connection between a Fourth Amendment wrong and an item of evidence is sufficiently weak—that is, when the acquisition of the evidence is sufficiently remote from the commission of the wrong to diminish the 'poisonous' impact of that wrong." Tomkovicz, *supra*, at 48.

48 Tomkovicz, *supra* note 47, at 102 n.238.

49 Mapp v. Ohio, 367 U.S. 643, 655 (1961).

50 "Proximate cause" is defined as "[a] cause that is legally sufficient to result in liability; an act or omission that is considered in law to result in a consequence, so that liability can be imposed on the actor." Black's Law Dictionary 250 (9th ed. 2009).

independent act truly separate from the police misconduct had produced Wong Sun's confession. But Brennan provides no clear basis for the Court's judgment. It appears as if the Court is conducting a stealth balancing analysis. And, as the Burger Court's later rulings show, attenuation analysis is a convenient and useful tool for justices opposed to exclusion.

The absence of an objection to Brennan's adoption and application of attenuation analysis is telling. Even though *Mapp* had been recently decided, the Court was seemingly retreating from the logical implications of that landmark ruling. Although Wong Sun's confession was not directly derived from his illegal arrest, like the documents copied and later subpoenaed by the government after the illegal search in *Silverthorne Lumber*, Wong Sun's statement was derivative of a Fourth Amendment violation. Excluding the statement not only would have put Wong Sun in the position he occupied prior to his illegal arrest, it would have echoed and reinforced Holmes's admonition that unconstitutionally obtained evidence "shall not be used at all."[51]

Because he failed to clearly identify an independent or intervening act that prompted Wong Sun's confession and thus dissipated the taint of the earlier illegal intrusion, Brennan's attenuation analysis in *Wong Sun* appeared to rest upon an undisclosed balancing analysis. *Wong Sun* thus was a precursor to *Linkletter v. Walker*, decided two years later, which was a major setback for the exclusionary rule.

Twelve years after *Wong Sun* was decided, the Burger Court addressed its first significant case involving attenuation analysis. *Brown v. Illinois*, decided in 1975, concerned whether incriminating statements of the defendant, obtained after a flagrantly illegal arrest and the provision of *Miranda* warnings, were admissible at a murder trial.[52] The Illinois Supreme Court ruled that the statements were admissible because the giving of *Miranda* warnings "served to break the causal connection" between the illegal arrest and the incriminating statements, and that the defendant's making of the statements was—in the language of *Wong Sun*—"'sufficiently an act of free will to purge the primary taint of the unlawful invasion.'"[53] The Illinois Attorney General told the Court that compliance with *Miranda* attenuated the taint of the illegal arrest, and the purpose of the exclusionary rule would not be served by suppressing the statements.

In his pre-argument memo, Blackmun lamented, "this isn't easy."[54] Brown's arrest was patently illegal and his statements—at least, according to Blackmun's law clerk—were made in "a highly coercive atmosphere."[55] On the other hand, Blackmun took note of

---

[51] Silverthorne Lumber Co. v. United States, 251 U.S. 385, 392 (1920).

[52] Brown v. Illinois, 422 U.S. 590 (1975).

[53] People v. Brown, 307 N.E.2d 356, 358 (Ill. 1974) (quoting Wong Sun v. United States, 371 U.S. 471, 486 (1963)).

[54] Harry Blackmun, Memorandum on *Brown v. Illinois* 5 (Mar. 10, 1975), Blackmun Papers, Box 206.

[55] *Id.*

the unanimity of the Illinois Supreme Court, which included Walter Schaefer, a judge known as being sensitive to civil liberties issues. Blackmun speculated that Brown's guilt might have prompted Schaefer to affirm the conviction.[56]

Blackmun commented, "What this really comes down to is a basic test of the validity of the exclusionary rule."[57] He noted that there "have been occasions around the conference table when it looked as though there were enough votes to do away with the exclusionary rule in a proper situation."[58] He suspected, however, that "when the pinch comes," Stewart and White would be "rather reluctant" to eliminate the rule.[59] Blackmun also noted that "it is hard to engage in balancing"[60] competing interests and that "[i]t seems to be that we have to go all one way or all another."[61] At the same time, Blackmun recognized, "[I]f we do away with the exclusionary rule, the defendant is not without his remedies."[62] He ended his memo by observing: "I have always been supercritical of the exclusionary rule," and "I suspect I shall vote to affirm this case although I am not entirely positive."[63]

At the *Brown* conference, Burger opened by stating that the "quality of the misconduct should be a factor in applying the exclusionary rule" but observed that other courts have not accepted his view.[64] He thought the real issue was whether the confession is "voluntary."[65] Burger noted that "if appearing before a magistrate breaks the chain," the provision of *Miranda* warnings could also break the causation chain.[66] Burger stated that the court below had applied a per se rule, "regardless of whether the arrest was pretextual or deliberately brutal."[67] He also felt, despite *Wong Sun*'s holding, that "verbal statements should be treated differently from things."[68] After his remarks, Burger passed on voting.[69]

---

56 *Id.*

57 *Id.*

58 *Id.*

59 *Id.*

60 *Id.* at 6.

61 *Id.*

62 *Id.*

63 *Id.*

64 Lewis Powell, Conference Notes on *Brown v. Illinois* (Mar. 21, 1975), Powell Papers, Box 24.

65 *Id.*

66 *Id.* On this point, Burger probably was referring to *Wong Sun* or *Johnson v. Louisiana*, 406 U.S. 356 (1972). *Johnson* ruled that an illegal arrest did not taint a subsequent lineup identification of the defendant. White's opinion for the Court on this point explained that prior to the lineup, Johnson had been brought before a magistrate and informed of his rights. The lineup was conducted while Johnson was under the authority of the magistrate's commitment and Johnson was represented by counsel. Thus, the lineup was conducted not by exploiting the illegal arrest "but 'by means sufficiently distinguishable to be purged of the primary taint.'" *Johnson*, 406 U.S. at 365 (quoting Wong Sun v. United States, 371 U.S. 471, 488 (1963)).

67 Powell, Conference Notes on *Brown v. Illinois*, *supra* note 64.

68 *Id.*

69 *Id.*

Brennan noted that *Wong Sun* "held that *verbal* statements must be excluded, as well as *physical* evidence."[70] He voted to reverse. Stewart spoke next and emphasized that the case involved the Fourth Amendment, and not the Fifth Amendment. He stated that *Wong Sun* was "decided as a means of enforcing the Fourth and Fourteenth Amendments. It extended *Mapp* to verbal statements."[71] Stewart noted that "unless *Wong Sun* is overruled, we must reverse," though he acknowledged dissenting in *Wong Sun* and said he was not "enthusiastic about *Wong Sun*."[72] Stewart saw "no adequate attenuation" because Brown's interrogation was "continuous" from the time of his arrest.[73] He voted to reverse and said that a remand to the Illinois courts "would serve no purpose."[74]

White then spoke. At best, White acquiesced in applying the exclusionary rule during his early years on the Court. By 1975, however, his colleagues on the Court knew that White was highly critical of the rule. Despite his opposition to the rule, White stated that the arrest of Brown was a "known violation of law," and the "exclusionary rule should therefore apply."[75] He also disagreed with the per se approach adopted by the Illinois Supreme Court. Like Stewart, White acknowledged his dissent in *Wong Sun* but explained that his vote in that case was based on his view that there was probable cause for the arrests. White voted to reverse and not to remand. Marshall also voted to reverse. He agreed with Brennan's position and said that the provision of *Miranda* warnings was "meaningless" under the circumstances of this case.[76]

Blackmun spoke next and reversed the position he had tentatively taken in his pre-argument memo. He explained that he "doesn't admire" the exclusionary rule, because it all too often suppresses the truth.[77] "But it is on the books until we overturn it."[78] Blackmun saw no difference between "verbal and physical fruits."[79] He closed by noting that in the "right case" he "will vote to end the exclusionary rule."[80] Powell followed Blackmun and said he "would not adopt the Illinois per se rule."[81] He continued: "The giving of *Miranda* warnings goes a long ways towards attenuation of taint, but is not necessarily determinative in every case."[82] Repeating the position he had favored since joining the Court, Powell stated a "totality of the circumstances" test should be utilized "in light of the principal purpose of the exclusionary rule. If the arrest is pretextual, the

---

70 *Id.*
71 *Id.*
72 *Id.*
73 *Id.*
74 *Id.*
75 *Id.*
76 *Id.*
77 *Id.*
78 *Id.*
79 *Id.*
80 *Id.*
81 *Id.*
82 *Id.*

attenuation should be *clear*—e.g. the intervention of counsel, etc."[83] On the other hand, if the arrest is "merely technically unlawful, such as an invalid warrant, or otherwise made in good faith," a confession after *Miranda* warnings is "usually admissible."[84] He thought the "nature and extent of the violation was important in determining whether the exclusionary rule's purpose is implicated."[85] Powell voted to reverse and wanted to remand.[86] Rehnquist stated that he did not read the Illinois Supreme Court's opinion as "laying down a per se rule."[87] He thought the "confession attenuates the taint."[88] After the rest of his colleagues had voted, Burger spoke again and noted: "Unless we want to overrule *Wong Sun*, a per se rule as to *Miranda* is not justified."[89] But Burger also stated that he was "willing in a proper case to overrule the exclusionary rule."[90] Ultimately, Burger voted to reverse, which meant that the conference voted seven to one to reverse Brown's conviction.[91]

Blackmun was assigned the *Brown* opinion. At the end of the published opinion, he wrote: "We emphasize that our holding is a limited one."[92] That was an apt way to describe the result. Blackmun's logic followed the views offered at the conference. First, he rejected the per se rule that *Miranda* warnings were always sufficient to remove the taint of an illegal arrest: "If *Miranda* warnings, by themselves, were held to attenuate the taint of an unconstitutional arrest, regardless of how wanton and purposeful the Fourth Amendment violation, the effect of the exclusionary rule would be substantially diluted."[93] Such a rule would encourage illegal arrests because police would know "evidence derived therefrom could well be made admissible at trial by the simple expedient of giving *Miranda* warnings."[94]

Although he rejected Illinois's per se rule, Blackmun's opinion, like Brennan's opinion in *Wong Sun*, did not provide criminal defendants a "get-out-of-jail-free-card." As did Brennan, Blackmun rejected a "but-for" rule concerning exclusion. He stated that *Wong Sun*'s attenuation analysis required a case-by-case determination of whether a confession was tainted evidence.[95] Ultimately, Blackmun ruled that while *Miranda* warnings were an important factor in deciding whether a confession was obtained by exploitation of an illegal arrest, they were not the only factor to consider. Also relevant were the temporal

---

[83] *Id.*
[84] *Id.*
[85] *Id.*
[86] *Id.*
[87] *Id.*
[88] *Id.*
[89] *Id.*
[90] *Id.*
[91] *Id.*
[92] Brown v. Illinois, 422 U.S. 590, 605 (1975).
[93] *Id.* at 602.
[94] *Id.*
[95] *Id.* at 603–04.

proximity of the arrest and confession, the presence of intervening circumstances, and the purpose and flagrancy of the police misconduct.[96] Applying these criteria, Blackmun saw no reason for a remand. Brown's first statement came shortly after his arrest, and there were no intervening events. The facts were "remarkably" similar to the arrest of James Wah Toy in *Wong Sun*.[97] And Brown's second statement was the direct result of the first statement. Moreover, Blackmun took note of the "purposefulness" of the unconstitutional behavior.[98] The arrest was designed for investigatory purposes and executed in a manner "calculated to cause surprise, fright, and confusion."[99]

While no justice offered a dissent in *Brown*, White and Powell did write separate opinions. Unlike Blackmun's consideration of several factors, White and Powell thought the result depended on a single factor: the bad faith of the police. White's opinion was an opaque sentence. Reading between the lines, it was evident that White was again marking grounds for a good-faith exception to the exclusionary rule. His vote in *Brown* turned on the fact that the police "knew or should have known" that the arrest was without probable cause and unconstitutional.[100] The analysis offered by Powell, by contrast, was nearly as extensive as the analysis contained in Blackmun's opinion. Like White, Powell was also laying the foundation for a good-faith exception. But before discussing the basis for that exception, Powell offered a candid view of the concept of attenuation analysis.

Powell did not envision attenuation as a substitute for proximate cause or as a way of determining whether an illegal search actually produced the challenged evidence. Instead, he saw attenuation as a way of taking some of the bite out of the exclusionary rule. According to Powell, implicit in *Wong Sun*'s rejection of a "but-for" test, was the acknowledgment that the Court was unwilling to strictly adhere to the exclusionary rule in every case where the police violated a defendant's Fourth Amendment rights. Fruit analysis, Powell wrote, "attempts to mark the point at which the detrimental consequences of illegal police action become so attenuated that the deterrent effect of the exclusionary rule no longer justifies its cost."[101] Put simply, Powell thought fruit analysis should parallel the deterrent theory justifying exclusion. Although Powell may not have realized it, his comments on fruit analysis echoed Anthony Amsterdam's perceptive observation on the topic. In a 1964 law review article, Amsterdam, the former Frankfurter clerk, had made the same point Powell was now making. As a young law professor, Amsterdam characterized attenuation doctrine as "foggy" and "inarticulately and unsystematically designed."[102] Despite these flaws, he recognized that the purpose of

---

96 *Id.*
97 *Id.* at 604.
98 *Id.* at 605.
99 *Id.*
100 *Id.* at 606 (White, J., concurring in the judgment).
101 *Id.* at 609 (Powell, J., concurring in part).
102 Anthony G. Amsterdam, *Search, Seizure, and Section 2255: A Comment*, 112 U. Pa. L. Rev. 378, 389–90 (1964).

attenuation analysis was to mark "the point of diminishing returns" of the exclusionary rule.[103]

Besides his comment on fruit analysis, Powell's separate opinion in *Brown* mirrored and promoted the ALI proposal for exclusion. His opinion emphasized the difference between the "flagrantly abusive" and "technical" or "good-faith" Fourth Amendment violation.[104] Powell noted that the deterrent purpose of the exclusionary rule assumes that the police have willfully, or at least negligently, violated a defendant's rights. In cases falling outside of this premise, "the deterrence rationale of the exclusionary rule does not obtain, and I can see no legitimate justification for depriving the prosecution of reliable and probative evidence."[105]

Focusing on deterring deliberate police misconduct, Powell proposed a rule narrower than the rule announced by Blackmun, which left considerable discretion to trial judges on whether a confession obtained after an illegal arrest was admissible. In cases of flagrant or deliberate Fourth Amendment violations, Powell would require an obvious break in the causation chain from illegal arrest to incriminating statement, such as consultation with a lawyer or appearance before a magistrate, "before the taint can be deemed removed."[106] He also conceded that a confession secured by the police "in the immediate circumstances" of an illegal arrest was inadmissible under *Wong Sun*'s holding.[107] But in cases involving a "technical" constitutional violation, for example, where police believe their conduct is lawful, Powell was willing to consider "a statement given at the station house after one has been advised of *Miranda* rights to be sufficiently removed from the immediate circumstances of the illegal arrest to justify its admission at trial."[108] In the end, Powell recognized that not every case would fit into the categories outlined in his opinion. For such cases, he stressed that attenuation analysis always should be conducted with the deterrent purpose of the exclusionary rule "sharply in focus."[109] But Powell did not explain why deterrence would not be promoted by excluding evidence discovered as a result of a "technical" violation. Finally, Powell identifies two situations where suppression would not promote deterrence: when officers arrest an individual in good-faith reliance on a warrant subsequently invalidated or pursuant to a statute later deemed unconstitutional.[110] In light of the fact that the Fourth Amendment regulates conduct of all government actors, it is not altogether clear why suppression of evidence under these circumstances would not still advance deterrence goals, and Powell fails to elucidate an explanation.

---

103 *Id.*

104 *Brown*, 422 U.S. at 610–12 (Powell, J., concurring in part).

105 *Id.* at 612.

106 *Id.* at 611.

107 *Id.* at 612.

108 *Id.*

109 *Id.*

110 *Id.* at 611.

Brown v. Illinois avoided per se rules and opted for a multifactor balancing test. Thus, *Brown* followed *Wong Sun*'s approach to deciding when evidence obtained from an illegal search or seizure is admissible. The result in *Brown* was welcomed by liberal commentators because it rejected a rule that permitted police to violate Fourth Amendment rules "with impunity, safe in the knowledge that they could wash their hands" with the provision of *Miranda* warnings.[111] But the balancing model of *Brown* and *Wong Sun* raised other concerns. Neither case provided clear standards to lower courts, and their holdings were subject to misconstruction and manipulation by trial judges unsympathetic to the exclusionary rule.[112]

From a different perspective, however, the balancing model of *Brown* and *Wong Sun* was out of step with the character of the Court's contemporaneous exclusionary rule decisions and, perhaps, obscured how a majority of the justices envisioned the rule in the future. By the late 1970s, the intentions of the Burger Court regarding the exclusionary rule were becoming apparent. The Court had announced significant restrictions on the scope of the rule in *Calandra*, *Janis*, *Peltier*, and *Stone v. Powell*, all of which, as a practical matter, involved unqualified exceptions to the exclusionary rule and prevented judges from applying the rule in specific contexts. From this vantage point, the Court seemed poised to make a similar move regarding attenuation analysis, or so the Solicitor General thought when *United States v. Ceccolini*[113] arrived at the Court.

On December 14, 1974, a North Tarrytown, New York, police officer, Ronald Biro, entered the Sleepy Hollow Flower Shop to talk with a friend, Lois Hennessey, who worked behind the counter. The shop was owned by Ralph Ceccolini and, unbeknownst to Biro, was the subject of FBI surveillance as a drop-off location for Francis Millow's gambling activities during the latter half of 1973. The surveillance ended by December 1973. During his visit with Hennessey, Biro noticed an envelope filled with money lying on the drawer of the cash register behind the counter. He opened the envelope and discovered policy slips associated with gambling operations. Biro returned the envelope to the counter and without informing Hennessey of what he discovered inside, asked her who owned the envelope. Hennessey told Biro that the envelope belonged to Ceccolini, and that he had asked her to give it to someone. Biro subsequently reported his findings to detectives in his police department who then informed an FBI agent. Four months later, the FBI interviewed Hennessey about the events that transpired on the day Biro entered the shop.

In May 1975, Ceccolini testified before a federal grand jury that he had never taken policy bets for Millow. Hennessey told the grand jury a different story, and Ceccolini was later indicted for perjury. A federal district judge granted Ceccolini's motion to suppress

---

111 Gloria J. Studdard, Recent Decision, *Miranda Warnings Do Not Per Se Render Admissible a Confession Following an Arrest Which Violates Fourth Amendment Rights:* Brown v. Illinois, 25 EMORY L.J. 227, 238 (1976).

112 *See id.* at 239-40.

113 435 U.S. 268 (1978).

the policy slips discovered in the envelope and Hennessey's trial testimony because she came to the government's attention as a result of Biro's illegal search, and the government failed to prove that it would have obtained her testimony without the search. The court of appeals affirmed, rejecting the government's argument that Hennessey's testimony was an act of free will sufficient to purge the taint of Biro's illegal search. The court found that the road between Biro's unconstitutional search and Hennessey's testimony was "straight and uninterrupted" and declined to consider the lapse of time between the search and testimony.[114]

Even before the Court decided to review *Ceccolini*, Powell thought the case merited the Court's attention. On the top of a law clerk's preliminary memorandum about *Ceccolini*, Powell wrote: "An interesting and important case involving a drastic extension . . . of *Wong Sun* and *Brown v. Illinois*."[115] He also wrote that the Fourth Amendment violation was "negligible and probably would come within ALI 'good faith rule,'" and that the case provided an "opportunity to make some sense out of use of [the] exclusionary rule in a 'taint' (poisonous tree) case."[116] In the top corner of the memo, Powell underlined "Grant" and wrote, "I'll dissent if not granted."[117] Over a month later, the Court granted the Solicitor General's request to review the case.[118]

The Solicitor General offered the Court several options to restrict the scope of the exclusionary rule in order to admit Hennessey's testimony. One proposal suggested there was sufficient attenuation between the illegal search and Hennessey's testimony at trial. The government offered two ways to achieve that result. First, Hennessey's testimony was admissible under the balancing approach outlined in *Brown v. Illinois* and *Wong Sun*. Alternatively, the Court could rule that live witness testimony was never tainted fruit no matter how direct the nexus between the illegal search and testimony. The government preferred the per se rule, arguing that a balancing model is too uncertain and takes insufficient account of the voluntary nature of live witness testimony.[119]

Burger began the *Ceccolini* conference stating that there was "no basis for suppressing testimony five months after" a constitutional violation.[120] Burger told his colleagues that he "also could hold that *Wong Sun* doesn't apply to live witnesses—although there may be some exceptions."[121] Burger voted to reverse. Brennan also voted to reverse but said *Wong Sun* applies here. Brennan thought "there was attenuation" and stated he "would

114 United States v. Ceccolini, 542 F.2d 136, 142 (2d Cir. 1976).

115 Law Clerk, Preliminary Memorandum to Lewis Powell on *United States v. Ceccolini* (Apr. 18, 1977), Powell Papers, Box 48.

116 *Id.*

117 *Id.*

118 United States v. Ceccolini, 431 U.S. 903 (1977) (mem.).

119 Brief for the United States at 36–38, United States v. Ceccolini, 435 U.S. 268 (1978) (No. 76-1151).

120 Lewis Powell, Conference Notes on *United States v. Ceccolini* (Dec. 7, 1977) [hereinafter Powell, *Ceccolini* Conference Notes], Powell Papers, Box 48.

121 *Id.*

not adopt a 'live witness' exception."[122] Stewart voted to reverse, and like Brennan, thought that the Court "need not accept any per se rule."[123] He agreed that "*Wong Sun* applies" here.[124] "The fact there was 'live witness' testimony is an important attenuation factor."[125] White voted to reverse without comment, while Marshall voted to affirm or dismiss the case as improvidently granted.[126] Powell voted to reverse. He was "not inclined to adopt an inflexible rule" as to live witnesses.[127] The existence of a live witness "is relevant to attenuation," especially in determining whether the testimony is an act of "free will."[128] Powell concluded, "there was abundant attenuation" under the facts.[129] Rehnquist remarked that "attenuation is much more readily found where there is a live witness" and thought the Court should make this point clear.[130] He voted to reverse. Stevens spoke last and voted to reverse but noted that "unless there were a live witness here, the attenuation would be less clear."[131]

In the end, the vote was seven to one in favor of reversing.[132] Brennan, Stewart, and (at least tentatively) Powell opposed a per se exception for live witness testimony and favored deciding the case on traditional attenuation analysis, while Burger and (probably) Rehnquist seemed prepared to adopt a per se rule. White was silent on the issue, and Stevens's vote was keyed to the existence of a live witness. Rehnquist was assigned the opinion.

On January 20, 1978, Rehnquist circulated a draft. The draft began by rejecting, without explanation, the Solicitor General's proposal for a per se exception for live witness testimony. It also reaffirmed *Wong Sun*'s statement that verbal evidence "which derives so immediately from" an unconstitutional search or seizure is considered tainted evidence.[133] But then Rehnquist reversed gears by noting that the cases decided since *Wong Sun* "significantly qualify" its refusal to distinguish between physical and verbal evidence for exclusionary purposes.[134] Rehnquist cited no cases supporting this statement. When dealing with the testimony of a live witness and not a putative defendant, Rehnquist declared the lapse of time between the illegality and testimony to be material, even if there is a direct and uninterrupted nexus between the two.[135]

---

122 *Id.*

123 *Id.*

124 *Id.*

125 *Id.*

126 *Id.*

127 Lewis Powell, Handwritten Notes on *United States v. Ceccolini* (undated), Powell Papers, Box 48.

128 *Id.*

129 Powell, *Ceccolini* Conference Notes, *supra* note 120.

130 *Id.*

131 *Id.*

132 *Id.*

133 Wong Sun v. United States, 371 U.S. 471, 485 (1963).

134 William Rehnquist, First Draft of *United States v. Ceccolini* 6 (Jan. 20, 1978) [hereinafter Rehnquist, *Ceccolini* First Draft], Powell Papers, Box 48.

135 *Id.* at 6–7.

The draft then enumerated the factors courts should consider when determining whether live witness testimony is sufficiently attenuated from a Fourth Amendment violation. Most important was "the degree of free will exercised by the witness."[136] Rehnquist wrote it is "unlikely that the police will regularly conduct illegal searches in the hope of discovering the identity of knowledgeable witnesses who are truly willing and eager to testify."[137] The likelihood of finding such witnesses is "rather speculative," and even when found, there was no certainty that they would help the prosecution.[138] Rehnquist also claimed that witnesses "can, and often do, come forward and offer evidence entirely of their own volition."[139] When evaluated correctly, "the degree of free will necessary to dissipate the taint will very likely be found more often in the case of live-witness testimony than other kinds of evidence." [140] Furthermore, exclusion "would perpetually disable a witness from testifying about relevant and material facts."[141] Here, Hennessey's testimony was "an act of her own free will in no way coerced or even induced" by the illegal search.[142]

In addition to the factor of "free will," Rehnquist offered two other reasons why Hennessey's testimony was attenuated from the unlawful search. First, a substantial period of time elapsed between the constitutional violation and the testimony. And second, there was no evidence that officer Biro's search was motivated by a desire to discover witness testimony. Applying the exclusionary rule here, Rehnquist concluded, would not have "the slightest deterrent effect" on Biro.[143] The draft ended with the general proposition that the exclusionary rule should be employed with "much greater reluctance" in the case of a live witness than when dealing with physical evidence.[144]

After reading Rehnquist's draft, Powell's law clerk, Sam Estreicher, told his boss that the "opinion will be understood by the outside world as recognizing what is, in effect, a *per se* rule for live-witness cases."[145] Estreicher's memo reiterated what he had told Powell in a previous memo. In that earlier memo, Estreicher wrote that when conducting searches, police hope to find useful witnesses as well as discover physical items; "the police are concerned with developing both types of evidence."[146] Consequently, the memo continued, deterrence principles will be promoted in many live-witness cases. Powell

---

136 *Id.* at 7-8.

137 *Id.* at 8.

138 *Id.*

139 *Id.*

140 *Id.*

141 *Id.* at 9.

142 *Id.* at 11.

143 *Id.*

144 *Id.* at 11-12.

145 Sam Estreicher, Memorandum to Lewis Powell on *United States v. Ceccolini* 1 (Jan. 20, 1978) [hereinafter Estreicher, *Ceccolini* Memo], Powell Papers, Box 48.

146 Sam Estreicher, Bench Memorandum to Lewis Powell on *United States v. Ceccolini* 16 (Dec. 2, 1977), Powell Papers, Box 48.

underlined the quoted phrase and wrote "true" in the margin.[147] Powell also underlined a part of the memo where Estreicher wrote: "I do not agree that any principled distinction can be drawn between live witness testimony and non-testimonial evidence."[148] And Estreicher's memo pointed out there was "no basis" for the government's claim that witnesses are more likely to be discovered through normal investigatory procedures and thus less incentive for the police to conduct illegal searches to find such witnesses, two points embraced by Rehnquist's draft.[149]

Furthermore, in the memo prepared after Rehnquist's draft had been circulated, Estreicher told Powell that it was bad police science to assert, as Rehnquist's draft did, that police are unlikely to conduct illegal searches to discover witnesses: "Any policeman worth his salt is interest[ed] in unearthing leads to live witnesses, in addition to non-testimonial evidence."[150] And contrary to what the draft implied, once a witness is discovered, cooperation can be "fairly assumed," and the government has effective tools—subpoenas and grants of immunity "to prod the recalcitrant."[151] Finally, Estreicher noted that Rehnquist's concern that exclusion would "perpetually" disable a witness's testimony did not "distinguish this case from the run-of-the-mill exclusionary rule case."[152] In sum, Estreicher told Powell, "There is simply no need for much of [Rehnquist's] language."[153] Estreicher believed attenuation was clearly present based on the facts, including Hennessey's live testimony, that a substantial period of time had elapsed between the illegal search and the challenged testimony, and that suppression would have little deterrent impact on Biro. Estreicher urged Powell to write a separate opinion distancing himself from Rehnquist's comments on live testimony.[154]

Estreicher's memos had an effect on Powell. The next day, after reading Rehnquist's draft, Powell wrote in the margins: "I am in accord with the essence of much of which Bill says, although a good deal of it is unnecessary to the opinion."[155] He also commented: "I'm not sure I agree with the sharpness of Bill's distinction between 'tangible evidence' and live witness testimony."[156] Two days later, Powell wrote Rehnquist. He agreed that there was "abundant" attenuation in the case, and that "the 'live witness' is in itself an attenuation factor of importance."[157] However, Powell thought the draft "may overemphasize" the distinction between live witness testimony and inanimate evidence for determining

---

147 *Id.*

148 *Id.*

149 *Id.*

150 Estreicher, *Ceccolini* Memo, *supra* note 145, at 1.

151 *Id.*

152 *Id.*

153 *Id.*

154 *Id.* at 2.

155 Rehnquist, *Ceccolini* First Draft, *supra* note 134, at 1.

156 *Id.*

157 Lewis Powell, Letter to William Rehnquist on *United States v. Ceccolini* (Jan. 23, 1978), Powell Papers, Box 48.

attenuation under *Wong Sun*.[158] He also requested that Rehnquist add a footnote "to the effect that the analysis would be different where the search was conducted by the police for the specific purpose of discovering potential witnesses."[159] Powell noted the Solicitor General had conceded the point, and "it would be well to make this explicit."[160]

In the meantime, Brennan wrote Rehnquist pointing out "the conference consensus was that we need not reach the live witness question because even assuming that the live witness was a 'fruit' of the illegality, there was sufficient attenuation under *Wong Sun* to make the evidence admissible."[161] On the same day, Rehnquist replied to Brennan, writing that his conference notes indicated that Burger, Stewart, and Stevens "disagreed to a greater or lesser extent" with Brennan's assessment.[162] Thus, he was unwilling to decide the case narrowly under *Wong Sun*'s attenuation theory.[163] Rehnquist sent a reply to Powell two days later.

Rehnquist's letter to Powell agreed to insert the footnote that Powell requested. But rather than stating that the result "would" be different for a search designed to discover a potential witness, as Powell requested, Rehnquist's new footnote would merely say the analysis "might" be different.[164] Regarding Powell's other concern about the distinction Rehnquist had drawn between live witnesses and physical items, Rehnquist wrote that he was "opposed to resolving this case simply by equating live-witness testimony with inanimate evidence and then applying the normal attenuation principles of *Wong Sun*."[165] That approach, Rehnquist noted, is "unsatisfying to me as a matter of pure logic," and he claimed that based on what was said at the conference, Burger, Stewart, and Stevens "would be loath to join an opinion along those lines."[166]

In the meantime, Burger told his colleagues that he could not join Rehnquist's opinion because he was unwilling to concede any "constitutional or rational basis to exclude the testimony of a human being."[167] Burger's position was no surprise. A year after *Wong Sun* was decided, as a circuit court judge, Burger wrote that the testimony of a live witness should not be mechanically equated with physical evidence.[168] Then, in another opinion, Burger stated: "[L]ive witnesses are not 'suppressed', as inanimate objects may

158 *Id.*

159 *Id.*

160 *Id.*

161 William J. Brennan, Jr., Letter to William Rehnquist on *United States v. Ceccolini* (Jan. 23, 1978), Powell Papers, Box 48.

162 William Rehnquist, Letter to William J. Brennan, Jr. on *United States v. Ceccolini* (Jan. 23, 1978), Powell Papers, Box 48.

163 *Id.*

164 William Rehnquist, Letter to Lewis Powell on *United States v. Ceccolini* 1 (Jan. 25, 1978), Powell Papers, Box 48; *see* United States v. Ceccolini, 435 U.S. 268, 276 n.4 (1978).

165 Rehnquist, Letter to Lewis Powell on *United States v. Ceccolini*, *supra* note 164, at 1.

166 *Id.*

167 Warren Burger, Letter to William Rehnquist on *United States v. Ceccolini* (Jan. 25, 1978), Powell Papers, Box 48.

168 Smith v. United States, 324 F.2d 879, 881–82 (D.C. Cir. 1963), *cert. denied*, 377 U.S. 954 (1964).

be. . . . How he came to be in court is a matter which goes only to the weight, not to the admissibility, of his testimony."[169]

In the end, Powell joined the *Ceccolini* opinion after Rehnquist acceded to making additional minor changes suggested by Powell. Significantly, however, Rehnquist did not alter or withdraw the distinction his opinion made between live witness testimony and non-testimonial evidence. Rehnquist could have written a narrower opinion along the lines suggested by Brennan's letter. Such an opinion probably would have garnered Brennan's vote (but not Burger's), and satisfied Powell's concern over the sharp differences between live testimony and physical evidence. But Rehnquist "opposed" a narrow ruling, because it was "unsatisfying" to him as a matter of logic; he wanted a broader restriction on the exclusionary rule.

Rehnquist lacked the votes to adopt the government's per se rule regarding live witness testimony. He did, however, create a distinction between how verbal and tangible evidence was to be treated for purposes of exclusion, thereby removing an essential element of *Wong Sun*'s reasoning. Without citing any cases, Rehnquist asserted that the Court's decisions had significantly qualified *Wong Sun*'s refusal to distinguish between physical and verbal evidence. *Wong Sun* rejected that distinction because verbal evidence is "no less" the fruit of unconstitutional conduct than tangible evidence. As Stewart told his colleagues in the *Brown v. Illinois* conference, this aspect of *Wong Sun* was "decided as a means of enforcing" the Fourth Amendment and was vital to extending *Mapp*'s protection to verbal statements.[170] Although it is not the only way to read *Ceccolini*, one could interpret Rehnquist's opinion as endorsing a general presumption against the suppression of live testimony. There is no dispute, however, that *Ceccolini* declared that the exclusionary rule "should be invoked with much greater reluctance" where an unconstitutional search discloses the existence of a live witness.[171] As the dissenters in *Ceccolini* remarked, the poisonous tree can now "bear two different kinds of fruit, with one kind less susceptible than the other of exclusion on Fourth Amendment grounds."[172]

* * *

By 1980, most of the justices acknowledged the principle that any physical or verbal evidence immediately derived from an illegal arrest is considered fruit of the poisonous tree and inadmissible against the arrestee in a later prosecution. Thus, if police discover drugs in the pocket of someone illegally arrested, or obtain a confession after arresting a murder suspect without probable cause, the drugs and confession will be excluded from trial. The Court, however, had not directly addressed whether fruit analysis also applies when an illegal arrest provides a direct link to live-witness identification evidence, such as

---

169 Brown v. United States, 375 F.2d 310, 319 (D.C. Cir. 1966) (Burger, J., concurring), *cert. denied*, 388 U.S. 915 (1967).

170 Powell, Conference Notes on *Brown v. Illinois*, *supra* note 64.

171 United States v. Ceccolini, 435 U.S. 268, 280 (1978).

172 *Id.* at 286 (Marshall, J., dissenting).

when a crime victim or witness identifies a suspect in a lineup or identifies the arrestee as the person who robbed him after being shown a photograph by the police. If traditional fruit analysis applied to this scenario, the exclusionary rule would preclude testimony by the victim or witness (or the police, for that matter) that the defendant had been identified in a pretrial procedure as the perpetrator of the crime. And as Professor LaFave has inquired, if fruit analysis does apply to this type of identification evidence, "does it follow that identification of the defendant at the trial itself is also forbidden?"[173]

At the same time, there was no indication the Court was ready to retreat from the *Ker-Frisbie* doctrine that holds that an illegal arrest of an individual would not preclude the government from subsequently prosecuting that individual. *Ker v. Illinois*,[174] decided in 1886, and *Frisbie v. Collins*,[175] decided in 1952, established that an illegal arrest or "forcible abduction" by government officials does not remove the power of a court to prosecute a defendant who has been brought within its jurisdiction.[176] Specifically, in *Frisbie*, a unanimous Court, speaking through Black, held that Due Process concerns are satisfied if a defendant in a state prosecution is given fair notice of the charges against him and a fair trial.[177] Shirley Collins alleged that he had been forcibly and illegally removed from Illinois by Michigan law enforcement officials, and a federal appellate court ruled that he was entitled to a writ of habeas corpus, based in part, on the theory that to allow the conviction to stand "would in practical effect lend encouragement to the commission of criminal acts by those sworn to enforce the law."[178] Black, however, disagreed. He wrote: "There is nothing in the Constitution that requires a court to permit a guilty person rightfully convicted to escape justice because he was brought to trial against his will."[179]

Interestingly, Black's opinion never bothered to reconcile the result in *Frisbie* with a ruling announced two months earlier by the Court. As noted in chapter 2, *Rochin v. California* reversed a state conviction when evidence was obtained by an illegal stomach pump ordered by the police. *Rochin*, like *Frisbie*, was a unanimous ruling that held that evidence obtained by methods that violate Due Process cannot be admitted during a state prosecution. The tension between *Rochin* and *Frisbie* was obvious: "The brutality involved in kidnapping is not far removed in degree from the brutality of the stomach pump."[180]

---

[173] 6 LaFave, *supra* note 46, §11.4(g), at 347.

[174] 119 U.S. 436 (1886).

[175] 342 U.S. 519 (1952).

[176] *Id.* at 522; *see also Ker*, 119 U.S. at 444.

[177] *Frisbie*, 342 U.S. at 522.

[178] Collins v. Frisbie, 189 F.2d 464, 468 (6th Cir. 1951).

[179] *Frisbie*, 342 U.S. at 522.

[180] Austin W. Scott, Jr., *Criminal Jurisdiction of a State Over a Defendant Based Upon Presence Secured by Force or Fraud*, 37 Minn. L. Rev. 91, 98 (1953); *see also* Francis A. Allen, *Due Process and State Criminal Procedures: Another Look*, 48 Nw. U. L. Rev. 16, 25–29, 28 (1953) (explaining that forcible abductions by the police "represent a threat to life and limb which may be at least as serious as the practices pursued by the police in the *Rochin* case"). Moreover, the *Ker-Frisbie* rule, according to one scholar, "represented [a] clear departure[ ] from the constitutional understandings of 1791." Roger Roots, *The Originalist Case for*

Despite its longevity, or maybe because of it, a few scholars and judges questioned the continued validity of the *Ker-Frisbie* doctrine.[181] When *Frisbie* was decided, the exclusionary rule did not apply to the states. More important, neither *Frisbie* nor *Ker* involved the admissibility of evidence from an illegal arrest. Strictly read, the *Ker-Frisbie* doctrine simply meant that an illegal arrest did not prevent the prosecution of the defendant.

While the Court's modern cases established that verbal evidence and physical items, including a suspect's fingerprints, directly obtained from an unconstitutional arrest were "poisonous fruit" when applying the exclusionary rule, the *Ker-Frisbie* doctrine suggested that a defendant's presence in the courtroom could never be challenged. These seemingly distinct rules would intersect in a case, *United States v. Crews*,[182] involving a mugging in the women's restroom of the Washington Monument.

While in a restroom stall at the Washington Monument, Carol Owens was confronted by a young black male who pointed a gun at her. After demanding and receiving money, the assailant made sexual advances at Owens and then left. Owens immediately notified the police and provided a description of her assailant. Owens later testified that she got a close look at the assailant for almost three minutes. Three days later, two other women were assaulted and robbed in the same restroom in a similar manner. All three women described the assailant as a black teenager, approximately 5'5" to 5'8" tall, thin, with a dark complexion and smooth skin. Three days after the second set of robberies, two United States Park Police officers observed Keith Crews, who matched the description of the assailant, in the area where the robberies had occurred. After briefly speaking with him and obtaining his identification, the officers allowed Crews to leave. A few minutes later, the officers spoke with a tour guide, who identified Crews as the person he had seen in the area on the day of the first robbery. The officers then detained Crews and transported him to Park Police headquarters, where he was photographed, questioned, and released.

The next day, Owens was shown a photo of Crews, and she immediately identified him as the person who had robbed her. Crews was then arrested and ordered to appear in a lineup, where Owens and one of the other robbery victims identified him as the robber.

Crews was indicted and charged with three counts of robbery. At a pretrial suppression hearing, the trial judge ruled that Crews's detention at Park Police headquarters constituted an arrest without probable cause. The judge found that the photographic and line-up identifications were fruits of the illegal arrest and thus had to be excluded

the Fourth Amendment Exclusionary Rule, 45 GONZ. L. REV. 1, 32 (2010). According to Professor Roots: "The pretrial discharge of defendants who were improperly arrested represented the *only 'rule' of search and seizure remedies that was generally applied* in criminal cases at the time the Fourth Amendment was proposed and ratified in the late 1700s. Thus, to the extent that there was any 'common law rule' governing search and seizure remedy practices in the Founding period, *it was a rule of exclusion*." *Id.* at 33.

[181] *See* 1 LAFAVE, *supra* note 46, §1.9(a), at 335-36.

[182] 445 U.S. 463 (1980).

from trial. The judge, however, allowed the victims to make in-court identifications of Crews, finding that their observations and memories of Crews during the robberies constituted an independent, and untainted, basis for their in-court identifications.

At trial, Owens and the other victims identified Crews as the robber. Crews was convicted of robbing Owens but acquitted of the two other robberies. An appellate court reversed the conviction. The court ruled that Owens's in-court identification was fruit of the illegal arrest, notwithstanding the fact that Owens's trial testimony was reliable and independent of the tainted pretrial identification. Applying what it considered to be traditional fruit analysis, the appellate court concluded there was a direct link between the illegal arrest and Owens's in-court identification testimony. The Court granted certiorari to decide whether Owens's in-court identification should have been excluded as the fruit of an illegal arrest that produced the initial identification of Crews as the robber.[183]

The conference discussion of *Crews* was straightforward. Eight justices voted to reverse (Marshall did not participate). Brennan thought the ruling below "goes beyond" what *Wong Sun* required under fruit analysis.[184] Stewart believed the *Ker-Frisbie* doctrine controlled the result and stated, "no matter how the defendant got in the courtroom, the victim could testify."[185] Stewart saw this as an "easy case,"[186] noting that under *Calandra*, a grand jury could have indicted a defendant with tainted evidence. White, Blackmun, and Rehnquist agreed with Stewart's assessment. Powell thought it important, even controlling, that the "in-court identification was highly probative."[187] Furthermore, Powell believed it relevant that Owens was "available for cross-examination" and for the "jury to hear."[188] Powell stated, "the taint was dissipated."[189] The consensus among the justices at the conference was that the ruling below should be reversed based on the *Ker-Frisbie* doctrine.

Brennan had not written a majority opinion on the exclusionary rule in the sixteen years since *Wong Sun* was decided in 1963. Throughout the seventies, Brennan's voice was heard only in the vigorous dissents he issued against the Burger Court's steady retrenchment of the rule. Thus, authoring the *Crews* opinion afforded Brennan a rare opportunity to speak on the scope of the exclusionary rule. Brennan circulated a first draft on December 13, 1979. He ruled that Owens's in-court identification was admissible because both the police's knowledge of Crews's identity and Owens's recollections of him antedated the illegal arrest and thus remained untainted by the constitutional violation.[190]

---

183 *Id.* at 465-70.

184 Lewis Powell, Conference Notes on *United States v. Crews* (Nov. 2, 1979), Powell Papers, Box 65.

185 *Id.*

186 *Id.*

187 *Id.*

188 *Id.*

189 *Id.*

190 William J. Brennan, Jr., First Draft of *United States v. Crews* 14 (Dec. 13, 1979) [hereinafter Brennan, *Crews* Draft], Powell Papers, Box 65.

Brennan's draft prompted a flurry of letters among the justices, none of which indicated full support for Brennan's opinion. The problem for the other justices was not Brennan's conclusion—they were unanimous on that point—but several statements he made in the course of reaching his conclusion. As Gregory May, a law clerk for Powell remarked, the opinion "seems to reach the unanimous result rather reluctantly."[191] Although Brennan intended, as he would later admit, to write "a relatively straightforward opinion relying on *Frisbie v. Collins*,"[192] the draft he sent his colleagues raised topics unnecessary to decide the case, and more important, appeared to expand the reach of the exclusionary rule.

For example, in Part II of the draft, Brennan wrote, "the exclusionary sanction applies to any 'fruits' of a constitutional violation . . . even the testimony of witnesses whose existence became known to the police only as a result of the official misconduct."[193] He went on to note that "some courts have suppressed the testimony of the 'tainted' witness, reasoning that the evidence would not have been available had the illegality not occurred."[194] No Supreme Court authority was cited for this statement, and, as May told his boss, it had "little to do with this case" since there were no tainted witnesses in *Crews*.[195] Moreover, Rehnquist told Brennan this statement was inconsistent with *United States v. Ceccolini*, an opinion Rehnquist authored two years earlier.[196] Although *Ceccolini* could be distinguished from *Crews*,[197] Brennan made no effort to do so and did not cite *Ceccolini*. May told Powell that the opinion could prejudice the Court's ability to decide, in an appropriate case, how the fruits doctrine applies to live witness identification evidence.[198] In the margin of May's memo, Powell wrote "yes."[199]

---

[191] Gregory May, Memorandum to Lewis Powell on *United States v. Crews* 1 (Dec. 13, 1979) [hereinafter May, *Crews* Memo], Powell Papers, Box 65.

[192] William J. Brennan, Jr., Memorandum to the Conference on *United States v. Crews* 1 (Jan. 8, 1980) [hereinafter Brennan, *Crews* Memo], Powell Papers, Box 65.

[193] Brennan, *Crews* Draft, *supra* note 190, at 6–7.

[194] *Id.* at 8.

[195] May, *Crews* Memo, *supra* note 191, at 2.

[196] William Rehnquist, Letter to William J. Brennan, Jr. on *United States v. Crews* (Dec. 13, 1979), Powell Papers, Box 65.

[197] As May told Powell in a memo, there was an important factual distinction between *Crews* and *Ceccolini*. In *Ceccolini*, the parties disputed whether the witness's identity was discovered as a result of the illegal search. By contrast, in *Crews*, the police knew the identity of the witness prior to the illegal arrest. Moreover, the witness's willingness to testify in *Crews* was "beside the point in determining the relationship between the evidence [she] would give at trial and the illegal arrest. Rather, it is the *identity of the defendant* that was discovered as a result of the illegal arrest. The ability of the witness[ ] to testify that the man who assaulted [her] was in fact the defendant was a direct result of the illegal arrest." Gregory May, Supplemental Memorandum to Lewis Powell on *United States v. Crews* 2 (undated) (emphasis added), Powell Papers, Box 65.

[198] May, *Crews* Memo, *supra* note 191, at 2–3.

[199] *Id.*

Similarly, in another part of the draft, Brennan explained that a victim's in-court identification has three distinct elements. First, "the victim is present at trial to testify as to what transpired between her and the offender and to identify the defendant as the culprit."[200] Second, based on her memory, the victim can "identify the defendant from her observations of him at the time of the crime."[201] Third, because the defendant is present in the courtroom, "the victim can observe him and compare his appearance to that of the offender."[202] Brennan then wrote: "If any of these three elements 'has been come at by exploitation' of the violation of the defendant's Fourth Amendment rights, the necessary causal link has been established, and in the absence of any attenuating or intervening circumstances, the courtroom identification must be suppressed."[203] Again, Brennan was deciding an issue not before the Court since all agreed Owens's testimony was independent of the constitutional violation. Stewart urged Brennan to delete this last portion about suppressing the identification if any of the three elements were established by exploiting the illegality, which Brennan agreed to do.[204]

Finally, in a section of the draft that would eventually be designated as subparts C and D in the published opinion, Brennan addressed Crews's challenge to his presence in the courtroom. The court below found a direct link between the illegal arrest and Owens's in-court identification of Crews. But in subpart C of his draft opinion, Brennan explained that the *Ker-Frisbie* doctrine defeated Crews's argument on this point: "An illegal arrest, without more, has never been viewed as a bar to subsequent prosecution, nor as a defense to a valid conviction."[205] He explained, Crews "is not himself a suppressible fruit," and the government cannot be denied the opportunity to prove his guilt with lawfully obtained evidence.[206]

Brennan could have stopped here but instead he went on to make comments objectionable to all of his colleagues. Brennan refused to view *Ker-Frisbie* as an absolute rule and explained that the defendant's presence in the courtroom can serve as "evidence."[207] According to Brennan, when a victim testifies, "'That's the man who robbed me,' his physiognomy becomes something of evidentiary value, much like a photograph showing [a defendant] at the scene of the crime." The critical question for exclusionary purposes, Brennan explains, is the same for both the introduction of the photograph and the defendant's physical presence in the courtroom: was the evidence obtained "only as a result

200 Brennan, *Crews* Draft, *supra* note 190, at 7.

201 *Id.*

202 *Id.*

203 *Id.* at 7–8 (citation omitted).

204 Potter Stewart, Letter to William J. Brennan, Jr. on *United States v. Crews* (Dec. 13, 1979), Powell Papers, Box 65; *see also* William J. Brennan, Jr., Letter to Potter Stewart on *United States v. Crews* (Dec. 14, 1979), Powell Papers, Box 65.

205 Brennan, *Crews* Draft, *supra* note 190, at 10.

206 *Id.* at 11.

207 *Id.*

of official misconduct?"[208] In answering that question, Brennan emphasized that prior to Crews's illegal arrest, police knew his identity and had a basis for believing he was involved with the robberies. Further, before the unlawful arrest, police had "obtained access to the 'evidence' that implicated [Crews] in the robberies, i.e., the mnemonic representations of the criminal retained by the victims and related to the police in the form of their agreement upon his description."[209] In other words, the unconstitutional arrest of Crews "yielded nothing of evidentiary value that the police did not already have."[210] Thus, although the facts of Crews's case did not satisfy Brennan's standard, Brennan's opinion unnecessarily created an exception to the *Ker-Frisbie* doctrine and expanded the scope of the exclusionary rule.

Rehnquist wrote Brennan to say that this part of the draft implied that the *Ker-Frisbie* doctrine would be inapplicable if the police had no reason to suspect the defendant of criminal behavior. Rehnquist explained to Brennan that he understood *Frisbie v. Collins* to mean that "regardless of how the defendant came to be in the courtroom, the question was whether the trial accorded the defendant was fair."[211] He questioned then, what impact Brennan's reasoning had on *Frisbie* "[i]f 'taint' analysis might be usable to show that the presence of the defendant in the courtroom is itself an 'exploitation' of an unlawful seizure."[212] While Rehnquist questioned Brennan's analysis of *Ker-Frisbie*, interestingly, Powell wrote Brennan to say "I can agree with your disposition of respondent's claim that his presence itself is 'evidence.'"[213] But Powell did have other concerns with Brennan's draft. Powell's primary objection focused on the discussion of tainted witnesses. He thought that discussion was unnecessary in a case where everyone agreed that Owens's testimony was untainted.[214]

While Brennan was willing to accommodate Powell's concerns, his reply to Rehnquist admitted what his draft had only implied: "I do not . . . believe that *Frisbie* means that the use of the defendant's body as evidence can *never* be 'tainted' in the Fourth Amendment sense."[215] Brennan analogized to *Davis v. Mississippi*, the final Fourth Amendment ruling of the Warren Court. *Davis* suppressed fingerprints obtained from a defendant arrested without probable cause, along with several other persons, as part of a dragnet roundup of suspects in a rape investigation.[216] Brennan told Rehnquist that if Crews's situation

---

[208] *Id.*

[209] *Id.*

[210] *Id.*

[211] William Rehnquist, Letter to William J. Brennan, Jr. on *United States v. Crews* (Dec. 14, 1979), Brennan Papers, Box I: 504.

[212] *Id.*

[213] Lewis Powell, Letter to William J. Brennan, Jr. on *United States v. Crews* 2 (Dec. 14, 1979), Brennan Papers, Box I: 504.

[214] *Id.*

[215] William J. Brennan, Jr., Letter to William Rehnquist on *United States v. Crews* (Dec. 17, 1979) [hereinafter Brennan, *Crews* Letter to Rehnquist], Brennan Papers, Box I: 504.

[216] Davis v. Mississippi, 394 U.S. 721 (1969).

were similar to *Davis*, "and the police had randomly arrested a number of individuals—without any reasonable basis for suspecting them of the robberies—merely to see if the victim could identify one of them," then he would likely exclude the in-court identification. He said he suspected that Rehnquist, by contrast, would nonetheless admit the in-court identification.[217] Brennan ended his letter to Rehnquist by acknowledging that the *Davis* problem was "not presented in this case, and I have endeavored to write the opinion so as to leave the treatment of that situation open."[218]

The next day, Rehnquist circulated a brief concurring opinion joining all of Brennan's opinion "except those [portions] which treat the mere presence of the defendant in the courtroom as 'evidence' for purposes of 'taint' analysis."[219] Rehnquist observed that the question that Brennan was purporting to leave open was resolved by the *Ker-Frisbie* doctrine.[220] Within two weeks, White circulated his own concurrence, agreeing with Rehnquist but offering his opinion in a more emphatic fashion than Rehnquist.[221]

White recognized that there was a direct link between Crews's illegal arrest and his presence in the courtroom. White agreed with Brennan's conclusion that the in-court identification was admissible but read the opinion to reach a different result had there not been some reason to suspect Crews of the robberies at the time of the illegal arrest. He explained: "Such a rule excluding an otherwise untainted, in-court identification is tantamount to holding that an arrest without reasonable suspicion effectively insulates one from conviction for any crime where an in-court identification is essential."[222] Using a hypothetical case, White left no doubt that the *Ker-Frisbie* doctrine permitted no exceptions and that a defendant could never raise an exclusionary rule challenge to his presence in court.

In White's hypothetical, a defendant is arrested for crime *X*, the police interrogate the defendant without *Miranda* warnings, and they obtain answers that implicate the defendant in crime *Y*. The victim of crime *Y* identifies the defendant in court, and her in-court identification is untainted evidence. White explained that he would not suppress the victim's in-court identification even though "the police had no reason to suspect the defendant of crime Y prior to their illegal questioning and that it is only because of that questioning that he is present in the courtroom for trial."[223] White went on to say, "I would reach the same result whether or not his arrest for crime X was without probable cause or reasonable suspicion. The exclusionary rule does not reach so far . . . ."[224]

---

[217] Brennan, *Crews* Letter to Rehnquist, *supra* note 215.

[218] *Id.*

[219] William Rehnquist, Draft of Concurring Opinion in *United States v. Crews* 1 (Dec. 18, 1979), Powell Papers, Box 65.

[220] *Id.*

[221] Byron White, First Draft of Concurring Opinion in *United States v. Crews* (Jan. 2, 1980), Powell Papers, Box 65.

[222] *Id.* at 1.

[223] *Id.*

[224] *Id.* at 1–2.

With this hypothetical, White made clear his view that the *Ker-Frisbie* doctrine had no limits, even in a case where tainted identification evidence was directly obtained from a Fourth Amendment violation.

Powell was considering joining either Rehnquist's or White's concurrence, so his law clerk, Gregory May, summarized the upshot of both for Powell. Both concurring opinions, according to May, gave *Frisbie* "rather broad play without explaining how a jurisdiction case came to take on such meaning."[225] On the other hand, if Powell joined either opinion, May explained, it "could provide a basis for shifting a majority of the Court away from the rather odd view that [Crews's] visage is 'evidence'" subject to the exclusionary rule.[226]

On January 8, Brennan circulated a memo to "clarify" his views.[227] While admitting his original intent was to write a simple opinion based on *Frisbie*, he observed that further thinking convinced him that such analysis "would not adequately resolve the case."[228] He explained that two "characters play crucial roles in the courtroom identification: the victim and the defendant."[229] Brennan acknowledged that the victim's testimony was untainted by the illegal arrest. Whether, however, "the defendant is 'tainted' is a much harder question, and *Frisbie* does not to my mind provide the answer."[230] According to Brennan, *Frisbie* "dealt solely with the power of a court to try a person who had been brought within its jurisdiction" by an illegal arrest.[231] *Frisbie*, which predated *Mapp*, "contains absolutely no discussion about what evidence may be introduced at the defendant's trial; rather, it holds only that an illegal arrest does not bar prosecution of the offender, and that the resulting conviction, if otherwise validly obtained, will withstand collateral attack on that ground."[232] The Court's later cases have never gone beyond this narrow view, and Brennan noted that his various drafts in *Crews* "rather than retreating from that principle, expressly reaffirm[]" that view of *Frisbie*.[233]

Brennan thus believed that *Frisbie* did not answer the question raised in *Crews*. He also could "perceive no basis for concluding that the identification" of a defendant in the courtroom "is anything but 'evidence' in the conventional sense."[234] Brennan noted that in the context of Fifth and Sixth Amendment violations, the Court had ruled that tainted in-court identification evidence was subject to exclusion: "Thus the exclusion of the identification evidence would not be in derogation of *Frisbie*, but would merely prohibit the introduction of specific testimony of the victim concerning a specific property

---

[225] Gregory May, Note to Lewis Powell on *United States v. Crews* (Jan. 2, 1980), Powell Papers, Box 65.

[226] *Id.*

[227] Brennan, *Crews* Memo, *supra* note 192, at 1.

[228] *Id.*

[229] *Id.*

[230] *Id.* at 2.

[231] *Id.*

[232] *Id.*

[233] *Id.*

[234] *Id.* at 2–3.

of the defendant."[235] The fact that illegally obtained identification evidence is crucial, in cases like *Crews*, to prove a defendant's guilt did not call for an exception to the exclusionary rule. Moreover, Brennan told his colleagues that extending *Frisbie* to this case was inconsistent with *Davis*: "I see no reason to distinguish between 'faces' and 'fingerprints' under the Fourth Amendment; both are, in the Court's words, 'something of evidentiary value which the public authorities have caused an arrested person to yield to them during [an] illegal detention.'"[236]

Finally, Brennan stated Crews's courtroom identification resulted from his illegal arrest. Indeed, Brennan thought the logic of *Davis* required the reversal of Crews's conviction. But like the rest of his colleagues, Brennan thought *Davis* was distinguishable.

> I believe the difference is that here, before any illegality had occurred, the police already had access to the information sufficient to produce an identification of the defendant. In other words, unlike the situation in *Davis*, the government here can prove that had the unlawful arrest not taken place, it still could have obtained the defendant's photograph by any number of lawful means and thus secured his presence in the courtroom for identification purposes.[237]

As for White's hypothetical, Brennan seemed to blink momentarily when he confessed that he was "not sure what result I would reach."[238] But he knew of "no rationale for differentiating between the identification testimony and any other evidence gathered as a result of the investigation of the defendant for crime Y."[239] Brennan closed his memo by noting that it was the unique combination of circumstances that justified the admission of Owens's testimony, and "not any untoward extension of the *Ker-Frisbie* doctrine."[240] However, he also recognized that if a majority were not persuaded by his reasoning, then the opinion should be reassigned.[241]

Far from settling the matter, Brennan's January 8 memo occasioned a new round of letters among the justices. The next day, Stevens identified his "problem" with Brennan's rationale:

> In *Davis* the fingerprints sought to be introduced in evidence were excluded because they were the fruit of unlawful police conduct. In this case the prosecutor does not seek to introduce any "faces" into evidence. The presence of defendant's face at trial is merely the inevitable consequence of his being on trial in the first

---

[235] *Id.* at 3.
[236] *Id.*
[237] *Id.* at 4.
[238] *Id.* at 4 n.1.
[239] *Id.*
[240] *Id.* at 5.
[241] *Id.*

> place, which is lawful by virtue of *Ker* and *Frisbie*. The evidence which he offers is the testimony of the victim and, as you have so cogently demonstrated, that testimony is totally untainted.[242]

Two days after receiving Brennan's memo, Powell wrote Brennan to express his agreement with Stevens's view. Powell envisioned a case where a defendant was illegally arrested, and there were ten eyewitnesses to the crime who identified him as the perpetrator, and whose testimony was untainted by the arrest. "The *Frisbie* doctrine," according to Powell, "establishes that the Court has the power to try such a defendant."[243] Yet, Powell read Brennan's analysis to mean that if the "only evidence were the unanimous testimony of the ten eyewitnesses, there could—in effect—be no trial."[244] On the same day, Burger, who had been curiously silent, weighed in on the case. He expressed agreement with Stevens's and Powell's memos. Burger would later join White's separate concurrence, as did Rehnquist.[245]

As he wrote on the top of White's latest draft, Powell too was "inclined to join" White's opinion but would "await developments."[246] After Brennan agreed to make additional changes that Powell proposed to Brennan's third draft, on February 14, Powell agreed to join all of Brennan's opinion except for the discussion of the *Ker-Frisbie* doctrine and *Davis*, now designated as subparts C and D.[247] Powell's correspondence was followed by a letter from Blackmun. Blackmun stated that the case had given him "difficulty as to proper analysis, not as to result."[248] Ultimately, Blackmun agreed with Powell's position and told Brennan that he would join all of the opinion except for subparts C and D.[249] Rehnquist, who had initiated the concern about Brennan's analysis of *Ker-Frisbie*, then sent a letter withdrawing his separate concurring opinion and affirming his joinder of White's opinion.[250]

---

[242] John Paul Stevens, Letter to William J. Brennan, Jr. on *United States v. Crews* (Jan. 9, 1980), Powell Papers, Box 65.

[243] Lewis Powell, Letter to William J. Brennan, Jr. on *United States v. Crews* (Jan. 10, 1980), Brennan Papers, Box I: 504.

[244] *Id.*

[245] Warren Burger, Letter to William J. Brennan, Jr. on *United States v. Crews* (Jan. 10, 1980), Powell Papers, Box 65; *see also* Warren Burger, Letter to Byron White on *United States v. Crews* (Feb. 1, 1980), Powell Papers, Box I: 504.

[246] Byron White, Third Draft of Concurring Opinion in *United States v. Crews* 1 (Feb. 4, 1980), Powell Papers, Box I: 504.

[247] Lewis Powell, Letter to William J. Brennan, Jr. on *United States v. Crews* (Feb. 14, 1980), Brennan Papers, Box I: 504.

[248] Harry Blackmun, Letter to William J. Brennan, Jr. on *United States v. Crews* (Feb. 19, 1980), Brennan Papers, Box I: 504.

[249] *Id.*

[250] William Rehnquist, Letter to William J. Brennan, Jr. on *United States v. Crews* (Feb. 20, 1980), Brennan Papers, Box I: 504.

Finally, Stevens offered a way to salvage Brennan's efforts. In a February 21 letter, Stevens noted that White's separate opinion, which three other justices had now joined, was "predicated on the assumption that the Court would have held the in-court identification inadmissible if there had been no basis for suspecting Crews prior to his arrest."[251] Stevens correctly observed that because no justice had actually joined that portion of Brennan's opinion, White's opinion was only disagreeing with Brennan's view of the matter rather than a majority of the Court's. Second, Stevens proposed that Brennan assume, for purposes of argument, that a defendant's face might be evidence subject to exclusion (a position with which Stevens reaffirmed his disagreement), but to go on and hold that Crews would not prevail in this case for the reasons Brennan had outlined earlier.[252]

Put simply, Stevens suggested that Brennan leave open whether Crews's person could be considered evidence for purposes of the exclusionary rule. If those changes were made, Stevens saw "no reason why the entire Court could not join the opinion."[253] At a minimum, if Brennan accepted these changes, Stevens stated he would join Brennan's opinion even though he would ultimately agree with White on the question whether a defendant's person was tainted evidence. Stewart immediately followed up on Stevens's letter and sent a letter indicating that he too would join the opinion if Brennan made Stevens's proposed changes.[254]

In the end, Brennan agreed to the changes Stevens proposed, but only Stevens and Stewart joined all of Brennan's opinion. Powell, who had told Brennan in December that he agreed with Brennan's disposition that Crews's presence could be evidence, stuck with his position that Crews's face was not subject to suppression. Although Powell never directly stated it, he seemed to draw a distinction between the defendant's "presence" and his "face" as suppressible evidence. In any event, in the published opinion Powell wrote: "I would reject explicitly, rather than appear to leave open, the claim that a defendant's face can be a suppressible fruit of an illegal arrest."[255] Powell agreed with White that the *Ker-Frisbie* doctrine "foreclosed" that claim.[256]

White also stuck to his guns. He made it plain that the issue Brennan left open—whether a defendant's face can ever be considered tainted evidence derived from an illegal arrest—was controlled by *Frisbie*.[257] White, like Brennan, also thought Crews's case was different from *Davis*. The fingerprints in *Davis* were excluded, according to White,

[251] John Paul Stevens, Letter to William J. Brennan, Jr. on *United States v. Crews* 1 (Feb. 1, 1980), Brennan Papers, Box I: 504.

[252] *Id.*

[253] *Id.* at 2.

[254] Potter Stewart, Letter to William J. Brennan, Jr. on *United States v. Crews* (Feb. 21, 1980), Brennan Papers, Box I: 504.

[255] United States v. Crews, 445 U.S. 463, 477 (1980) (Powell, J., concurring in part).

[256] *Id.*

[257] *Id.* at 479 (White, J., concurring in the result).

"because they were the direct product of the unlawful arrest."[258] The eyewitness testimony that Crews sought to exclude "was not the product" of his illegal arrest.[259] The fact that Crews was in the courtroom and capable of being identified by Owens "is merely the inevitable result of the trial being held, which is permissible under *Frisbie*," despite Crews's unlawful arrest.[260]

White went on to note that suppression of the fingerprints in *Davis* would be required regardless of whether the defendant in that case was arrested without any suspicion or "with something just short of probable cause."[261] For good measure, White also explained that he disagreed with the discussion in Brennan's opinion that implied "that a courtroom identification would be inadmissible if the defendant's physical presence had resulted from exploitation" of a Fourth Amendment violation.[262] The hypothetical he posed in his January 2 draft concurrence would also appear in the final opinion—which adopted an absolute view of *Ker-Frisbie*. Finally, to leave no doubt about the line-up of the justices, White pointed out that a majority of the Court agreed that *Frisbie* "forecloses" the claim that a defendant's face can be suppressible as a fruit of the unlawful arrest.[263]

In the end, only two justices—Stewart and Stevens—would join Brennan's discussion of how a defendant's person could be considered tainted evidence for exclusionary purposes and why Crews's situation was different from the issue decided in *Davis*. If there were a "winner" in the case, it would seem to be White. By insisting on an unqualified interpretation of the *Ker-Frisbie* doctrine, White convinced a majority of the justices that he had the better view of the law. And while White never offered a principled distinction between tainted physical or verbal evidence and tainted identification evidence for exclusionary rule purposes, his conclusion reaffirming the *Ker-Frisbie* doctrine and preventing suppression as a remedy for Crews's unconstitutional arrest would prevail.

II. Impeachment (Again)

Professor Tom Davies has stated that the briefs seeking or opposing certiorari "are the ones that are most likely to matter"[264] when trying to discern the motivations of the justices' votes in particular cases, especially in an area "as ideologically charged as criminal

[258] *Id.*

[259] *Id.*

[260] *Id.*

[261] *Id.*

[262] *Id.* at 479 n.*.

[263] *Id.* at 479.

[264] Thomas Y. Davies, *An Account of* Mapp v. Ohio *That Misses the Larger Exclusionary Rule Story*, 4 Ohio St. J. Crim. L. 619, 629 n.34 (2007) (book review).

procedure."[265] Davies's analysis rings true in *United States v. Havens*,[266] which concerned whether evidence obtained from an unconstitutional search can be used to impeach a defendant's false testimony given while undergoing cross-examination when the evidence does not squarely contradict the defendant's direct testimony.

On October 2, 1977, J. Lee Havens and John McLeroth, both attorneys, flew from Lima, Peru, to Miami. In Miami, customs officers found cocaine sewn into improvised pockets in a T-shirt McLeroth was wearing. McLeroth implicated Havens, who had already cleared customs. Havens was arrested, and a search of his luggage revealed a man's T-shirt with missing pieces that matched the pieces that had been sewn to McLeroth's T-shirt. Havens was charged with narcotic offenses. Prior to the trial, the district court found the search of Havens's luggage unconstitutional and suppressed the T-shirt and other evidence derived from the search.

At trial, McLeroth testified for the government and stated that Havens had provided the altered T-shirt and sewn the pockets. Havens took the stand and in his direct testimony denied involvement with cocaine smuggling. When asked on cross-examination whether he was involved with T-shirts or anything involving McLeroth, or this cocaine matter, Havens said, "Absolutely not."[267] And when asked whether his luggage contained a man's T-shirt with missing pieces, he responded, "Not to my knowledge."[268] The prosecutor was then permitted to impeach Havens by introducing the T-shirt found in Havens's luggage and a statement Havens made to federal agents after his arrest that the T-shirt belonged to McLeroth. Havens was convicted, but the court of appeals reversed. The court read *Agnello v. United States* (discussed in chapter 1) and *Walder v. United States* (discussed in chapter 2) to mean that tainted evidence can be used to impeach only if the predicate is found in the defendant's direct testimony and the evidence contradicts a particular statement of the defendant. "An arguable conflict with a simple denial of guilt does not" justify impeachment with tainted evidence.[269]

The Solicitor General's petition for certiorari in *Havens* did not pull any punches. It described the case "as a classic example of the use of the exclusionary rule, not as a shield, but as 'a license to use perjury by way of a defense.'"[270] Acknowledging that *Agnello* rested on the principle that the essence of the exclusionary rule was that illegally obtained evidence shall not be used at all, the Solicitor General told the Court that *Agnello*'s reasoning had been rejected by later decisions. Echoing what Brennan said in his dissent in *Harris v. New York*, the Solicitor General argued that the result in *Harris* went beyond the narrow rule of *Walder* and "flatly repudiated the rationale

265 *Id.* at 629.

266 446 U.S. 620 (1980).

267 *Id.* at 623.

268 *Id.*

269 United States v. Havens, 592 F.2d 848, 851 (5th Cir. 1979).

270 Petition for a Writ of Certiorari at 8–9, *Havens*, 446 U.S. 620 (No. 79-305) (quoting Harris v. New York, 401 U.S. 222, 226 (1971); Oregon v. Hass, 420 U.S. 714, 721-22 (1975)).

relied upon in *Agnello* that illegally obtained evidence must be completely excluded from trial."[271] Rather than attempt to reconcile *Agnello* and *Harris*, "whose underlying rationales are fundamentally inconsistent," the Solicitor General urged the Court to overrule *Agnello*.[272]

The Solicitor General further explained that the Court's cases had already struck the proper balance for resolving the conflict between the need to deter Fourth Amendment violations and the obligation of every witness to testify truthfully. Burger's conclusion in *Harris* that "sufficient deterrence flows when the evidence cannot be used in the prosecution's case in chief" was the Court's resolution to this conflict.[273] In a footnote, the Solicitor General's petition addressed the concern that the government's argument might impinge or have a chilling effect on a defendant's right to testify in his own behalf. The right to testify, the petition explained, "is simply the 'right to testify truthfully,'" and if the potential for impeachment chills false testimony, that effect "'is entirely permissible.'"[274] While the petition did not directly confront Frankfurter's pronouncement in *Walder* that a defendant must be free to deny all elements of the case against him without fear that a prosecutor could introduce tainted evidence, it did acknowledge that impeachment may relate to matters raised on cross-examination. That scenario did not mandate a "no impeachment" rule. Rather, it was "a consequence of the defendant's decision to take the stand, which carries with it the obligation to respond to cross-examination."[275] The Solicitor General's argument convinced Powell. Even before the Court decided to review *Havens*, Powell wrote, "*Agnello* should be overruled" on the top of his law clerk's preliminary memo.[276]

Although the Solicitor General wanted the Court to take *Havens* to overrule *Agnello*, the petition also gave the Court a way to reverse the court of appeals without overruling *Agnello*. Even if *Agnello* was retained for cases in which a prosecutor's cross-examination went beyond the scope of the defendant's direct testimony, impeachment with tainted evidence was still permissible where a cross-examination was proper. While the court of appeals found otherwise, the cross-examination of Havens was proper, according to the government, because it simply required Havens to state more directly the lie he told during his direct testimony.

The government's petition achieved its intended result. Five justices—Stewart, White, Blackmun, Powell, and Rehnquist—voted to grant review in *Havens*. (In light of his authorship of *Harris* and opposition to exclusion in general, Burger's vote to deny review is somewhat surprising.) At the conference vote to grant review, Stewart told

---

271 *Id.* at 10.

272 *Id.* at 15.

273 *Id.* at 12.

274 *Id.* at 13 n.8 (quoting United States v. Grayson, 438 U.S. 41, 54 (1978)).

275 *Id.*

276 Law Clerk, Preliminary Memorandum to Lewis Powell on *United States v. Havens* (Nov. 6, 1979), Powell Papers, Box 70.

his colleagues that "*Agnello* and *Harris* are irreconcilable."[277] After the justices voted to hear the case, Gregory May, one of Powell's law clerks, outlined the problems of overruling *Agnello*. First, prosecutors would be encouraged "to press against the proper limits of the scope of cross-examination in order to introduce evidence that otherwise would be excluded," and in many cases, trial judges would not know "whether the Government has a basis for the question other than knowledge derived from the illegal search itself."[278]

The second problem with overruling *Agnello*, May explained, is the chilling effect on a defendant's willingness to testify on his own behalf. In the normal case, almost anything a defendant says on direct testimony "can open the door to cross-examination that will implicate the illegally seized evidence. It is not a sufficient answer to this problem to say that the defendant has no right to lie. He may well be able to give truthful testimony that avoids matters as to which the evidence would be impeaching."[279] But May conceded that permitting impeachment "obviously contributes to truth-finding—no matter how unpleasant that may be to the guilty defendant."[280]

The third problem, as May saw it, was "the most serious."[281] While acknowledging that the jury is instructed to consider tainted impeachment evidence only to assess the defendant's credibility, May told Powell: "[E]veryone knows that the main reason for introducing it is to prejudice the jury's determination of guilt or innocence. This deplorable practice is so much a part of trial strategy that it seems a pity to encourage it further."[282] A related concern, although not mentioned in May's memo to Powell and denied by the Solicitor General in his brief on the merits, is that overruling *Agnello* would encourage unconstitutional searches. As one commentator noted shortly after *Havens* was announced, permitting impeachment with tainted evidence on cross-examination gives police and prosecutors an incentive to conduct illegal searches that might not otherwise exist if the impeachment exception to exclusion was confined to cases where defendants falsely testified on direct examination. Law enforcement officials "would know that the evidence would be heard by the jury in practically all cases in which the defendant took the stand."[283]

At the *Havens* conference on March 21, 1980, Burger told his colleagues that Havens "opened up the subject by his own testimony. The cross-examination was proper. *Walder* is factually controlling."[284] Because the scope of cross-examination is broad,

---

277 Lewis Powell, Docket Sheet on *United States v. Havens* (Nov. 21, 1979), Powell Papers, Box 70.

278 Gregory May, Bench Memorandum to Lewis Powell on *United States v. Havens* 5 (Mar. 13, 1980), Powell Papers, Box 70.

279 *Id.* at 5–6.

280 *Id.* at 6.

281 *Id.*

282 *Id.*

283 Edward P. Leibensperger, Case Note, *Impeachment by Unconstitutionally Obtained Evidence: The Erosion of the Exclusionary Rule*, 34 OHIO ST. L.J. 706, 717 (1973).

284 Lewis Powell, Conference Notes on *United States v. Havens* (Mar. 21, 1980), Powell Papers, Box 70.

Burger thought that the Court could "decide the case on this basis" without overruling *Agnello*.[285] The case was "different from *Agnello*," where the "defendant did not open the door to cross-examination."[286] Burger voted to reverse. Brennan voted to affirm. He said, "*Agnello* is good law," and that Havens's "direct testimony did not open himself" to impeachment.[287] Stewart also voted to affirm. He stated that the "government can't premise a question on illegally seized evidence. The argument of the Solicitor General would obliterate *Weeks v. United States*."[288] Based on the facts, Stewart thought "the cross-examination was proper. *Walder* controls. But this was not the issue presented. On the issue presented—whether *Agnello* should be reversed"—Stewart rejected the government's argument and voted to affirm the ruling below.[289]

White spoke next and voted to reverse. He stated "*Walder* controls," and the "cross-examination was proper."[290] Marshall voted to affirm and told his colleagues that "*Harris* is wrong."[291] Blackmun voted for reversal and said "*Walder* controls."[292] Powell also wanted to reverse. He was ready to "accept the Solicitor General's position broadly,"[293] which meant reversing *Agnello*. But Powell could also agree to decide the case "narrowly simply on the facts and *Walder*, but would prefer a broader decision."[294] He also stated that *Agnello* and *Walder* require courts to draw lines that "are impossible to draw."[295] Rehnquist voted to reverse and said he agreed with Powell: "When a defendant takes the stand he should be subject to the same rules as any other witness."[296] Finally, Stevens voted to affirm. Stevens "would not overrule *Agnello*."[297] Stevens believed that overruling would do "more than allow a prosecutor to expose lies."[298] And Stevens said that the cross-examination of Havens was improper.[299] After the conference, White was assigned the opinion.

Powell sent his law clerk Gregory May a revealing memo, reflecting on the conference discussion. While acknowledging that five justices (Burger, White, Blackmun, Powell, and Rehnquist) voted to reverse on the narrow ground that Havens's direct testimony justified the cross-examination, Powell told May: "I'd prefer a more fundamental

---

285 *Id.*
286 *Id.*
287 *Id.*
288 *Id.*
289 *Id.*
290 *Id.*
291 *Id.*
292 *Id.*
293 *Id.*
294 *Id.*
295 *Id.*
296 *Id.*
297 *Id.*
298 *Id.*
299 *Id.*

position."[300] Powell stated that the narrow basis for reversal provides no helpful guidance to prosecutors, defense lawyers, or judges. In light of this, Powell explained, the normal rules otherwise applicable to cross-examination should determine the scope of the cross-examination of a defendant. Accordingly, he reasoned: "If normal cross-examination would permit the prosecutor to ask about illegally seized evidence for impeachment purposes (and introduce it, if necessary), this should be permitted."[301]

But Powell was willing to go further. He told May that he supported a result that went beyond the question presented to the Court. In his brief on the merits, the Solicitor General contended that it was "entirely implausible" and "highly speculative" that allowing impeachment in a case like *Havens* would encourage future illegal searches.[302] Again emphasizing the point that sufficient deterrence is achieved when tainted evidence is excluded from the government's case-in-chief, the government claimed that few police officers are "both so sophisticated and so calculating" that they will undertake illegal searches to gather evidence that can be used outside of the prosecution's direct case.[303] Thus, according to the Solicitor General, when the government presents a prima facie case of guilt, and the defendant takes the stand "to adduce testimony that is belied by the illegally seized evidence, such evidence should become admissible on rebuttal for all purposes, not just for impeachment."[304]

Powell agreed with this argument. Powell believed:

> [It] is unrealistic to argue—as some of my Brothers do—that if illegal evidence may be used to impeach or rebut, police officers will be encouraged to violate the Fourth Amendment. No responsible prosecutor or chief of police would so instruct police officers, and few police officers would deliberately violate the Fourth Amendment on the odd chance that it would be needed for this purpose.[305]

He told his clerk to draft an opinion that would permit the use of tainted evidence for "both impeachment and rebuttal" purposes.[306]

Powell also wrote that after he stated his views at conference, Burger, Blackmun, and Rehnquist told Powell they all agreed with his views. Accordingly, Powell wanted "to go on record at least with respect to the full right to cross examine for impeachment purposes."[307] As he had done a decade earlier in *Schneckloth v. Bustamonte* when

---

300 Lewis Powell, Memorandum to Gregory May on *United States v. Havens* 2 (Mar. 21, 1980) [hereinafter Powell, *Havens* Memo], Powell Papers, Box 70.

301 *Id.*

302 Brief for the United States at 32–33, United States v. Havens, 446 U.S. 620 (1980) (No. 79-305).

303 *Id.* at 34–35.

304 *Id.* at 35.

305 Powell, *Havens* Memo, *supra* note 300, at 2–3.

306 *Id.* at 3.

307 *Id.* at 4.

he proposed eliminating the exclusionary rule in habeas corpus proceedings, Powell was again thinking about proposing another categorical restriction on the rule. He closed the memo with the following thought: "When I wrote my concurring opinion in *Bustamonte*, I laid the ground work for *Stone v. Powell*. Possibly we can strike another blow on behalf of the public interest in conducting trials on the assumption that witnesses who take an oath to testify truthfully cannot perjure themselves with impunity."[308]

The draft opinion White circulated on April 30, 1980, was essentially the same as the published opinion. After reviewing the opinion, May wrote to Powell that White's opinion "seems to come quite close to the position" of Powell's recent memo.[309] The bottom line of White's opinion, according to May, was that "all statements made during proper cross-examination can be impeached with illegally seized evidence."[310] The practical result was that "almost nothing of *Agnello* would survive this opinion. *Agnello* would simply stand for the proposition that answers to questions that should not have been asked in the first place cannot be impeached with illegally seized evidence."[311] May closed by observing that White's draft "is about as much as you could ask for."[312] At the end of May's memo, Powell wrote "yes."[313]

White's opinion began by acknowledging that *Agnello*'s per se approach to exclusion, which rested on Holmes's principle that tainted evidence shall not be used at all, had been rejected by *Walder* and *Harris*.[314] The opinion also acknowledged that *Agnello* involved impeachment of testimony initially given on cross-examination, while *Walder* and *Harris* involved testimony by the defendant given during direct examination.[315] This factual difference, however, was inconsequential. White then endorsed the Solicitor General's assertions that the deterrent goal of the exclusionary rule was "sufficiently served" by denying the government the use of tainted evidence in its direct case. White perceived no basis for thinking the admission of impeachment evidence would encourage illegal searches.[316] Additionally, White saw "no difference of constitutional magnitude between the defendant's statements on direct examination and his answers to questions put to him on cross-examination that are plainly within the scope of the defendant's direct examination."[317] This statement was reiterated in the next paragraph and rephrased as *Havens*'s holding.

---

308 *Id.*

309 Gregory May, Memorandum to Lewis Powell on *United States v. Havens* (Apr. 30, 1980) [hereinafter May, *Havens* Memo], Powel Papers, Box 70.

310 *Id.*

311 *Id.*

312 *Id.*

313 *Id.*

314 United States v. Havens, 446 U.S. 620, 624–25 (1980).

315 *Id.* at 625.

316 *Id.* at 626.

317 *Id.* at 627.

Havens was more than a "rewriting" of *Agnello*, as critics of its holding, such as Professor LaFave, have complained.[318] Without explicitly saying so, *Havens* stripped *Agnello* of its constitutional status. While *Agnello* was not expressly overruled, Gregory May accurately captured the impact of White's opinion when he noted that after *Havens*, *Agnello* simply stood for the rule that tainted evidence cannot be used to impeach answers to questions that should have never been asked.[319]

What was less clear was whether White's opinion also embraced the position proposed in Powell's March 21 memo and the Solicitor General's merits brief, namely, whether tainted evidence could be admissible on rebuttal for all purposes, not just impeachment. In any event, the Court had traveled full circle regarding impeachment and the exclusionary rule. In 1925, the Court rejected the government's proposal to create an impeachment exception to the rule. In 1954, *Walder*, authored by Frankfurter, created the first exception to the rule. Then, in 1971, Burger's opinion in *Harris* took a significant step by extending *Walder* when it ruled that tainted evidence could be used to impeach a defendant with evidence directly bearing on his guilt. The result in *Havens* simply followed the path opened by *Walder* and *Harris*. After *Havens*, there was no constitutional basis for distinguishing between a defendant's statement on direct examination and his answers given in response to proper cross-examination. Impeachment with tainted evidence was permissible in either context.

* * *

On April 1, 1969, William Rehnquist sent John Dean a memorandum marked "administratively confidential."[320] At that time, Rehnquist worked in the Office of Legal Counsel, and Dean was the Associate Deputy Attorney General in the Nixon Administration's Department of Justice. The memo discussed changes in constitutional criminal procedure resulting from several Warren Court rulings. Rehnquist characterized the rulings in the 1960s as a "dramatic change" in interpreting the constitutional rights of criminal defendants.[321] Specifically, Rehnquist highlighted rulings that "suppress relevant, competent evidence of guilt" when obtained in violation of the Constitution.[322] Such rulings were formerly only applicable to the federal government, but the Warren Court made these evidentiary prohibitions enforceable against the states. Rehnquist thought

318 *See* 6 LaFave, *supra* note 46, § 11.6(a), at 401-02.

319 *See* May, *Havens* Memo, *supra* note 309; *cf. Havens*, 446 U.S. at 631 (Brennan, J., dissenting) (stating that the Court's current interpretation of *Agnello* and *Walder* "simply trivializes those decisions by transforming their Fourth Amendment holdings into nothing more than a constitutional reflection of the common-law evidentiary rule of relevance"). Professor James Kainen also concluded that *Havens* "delivered [a] death blow" to *Agnello*. James L. Kainen, *The Impeachment Exception to the Exclusionary Rules: Policies, Principles, and Politics*, 44 Stan. L. Rev. 1301, 1309 (1992).

320 William H. Rehnquist, Assistant Attorney General, Memorandum to John W. Dean, III, Associate Deputy Attorney General, on Constitutional Decisions Relating to Criminal Law (Apr. 1, 1969) (on file with author).

321 *Id.* at 1.

322 *Id.*

the Court's decisions had "failed to hold true the balance between the right of society to convict the guilty and the obligation of society to safeguard the accused."[323] Rehnquist touched on the following topics illustrative of this point: "Statements and Confessions Made by the Defendant," "Restrictions Relating to Incrimination of Defendant," and the Fourth Amendment's "Exclusionary Rule." Rehnquist recommended that President Nixon appoint a commission to review the Court's rulings "to determine whether the overriding public interest in law enforcement which is both fair and effective requires a constitutional amendment."[324]

As John Dean subsequently described it, the memo was a "brutal critique" of how the Court had "gone astray" in the field of criminal procedure, and was "a map of Rehnquist's thinking on the Supreme Court's role in criminal justice."[325] Rehnquist's views expressed in the memo seemed to contradict a statement Rehnquist made to a writer for the *New York Times* in 1985. A recommendation to the president to create a commission to consider overturning several landmark Supreme Court rulings by constitutional amendment would not be proposed without serious and careful thought. Yet Rehnquist stated in 1985: "I came to the court sensing, without really having followed it terribly closely, that there were some excesses in terms of constitutional adjudication during the era of the so-called Warren Court."[326] Rehnquist also told the *Times*: "I don't think that the Burger Court has as wide a sense of mission" as did the Warren Court.[327] "Perhaps it doesn't have any sense of mission at all. In the area of constitutional rights of accused criminal defendants, the Court has called a halt to a number of the sweeping rulings that were made in the days of the Warren Court. I don't know if you can describe that as a sense of mission or not."[328]

A decade after writing the memo, Rehnquist, as member of the Court, had more criticism of the Court's seminal decisions on the exclusionary rule. This time, however, Rehnquist's views were available to the public, although few people took note of his opinion in a case involving an ordinary car search by California police.[329] Although the California Attorney General did not ask the Court to do so, Rehnquist urged his colleagues to decide whether, and to what extent, the exclusionary rule announced in *Weeks v. United States* should be retained. A routine case from California seemed an unlikely stimulus for reconsideration of *Weeks*'s exclusionary rule, which even Harlan's dissent in *Mapp* did not question. Rehnquist saw the case as far from ordinary, however, believing it to represent the "culmination of a sport of fox and hound" begun by *Weeks*.[330]

---

[323] *Id.* at ii.

[324] *Id.*

[325] JOHN W. DEAN, THE REHNQUIST CHOICE 268–69 (2001).

[326] John A. Jenkins, *The Partisan: A Talk With Justice Rehnquist*, N.Y. TIMES MAG., Mar. 3, 1985 at 28, 33.

[327] *Id.* at 35.

[328] *Id.*

[329] California v. Minjares, 443 U.S. 916 (1979) (Rehnquist, J., dissenting from denial of stay).

[330] *Id.* at 916.

On the evening of December 19, 1975, a Fremont, California, supermarket was robbed by two individuals armed with handguns. A description of the suspects and their getaway vehicle was broadcast to the police, and shortly thereafter a Fremont officer stopped a vehicle that matched the description. The officer arrested the driver of the vehicle, Paul Minjares. Minjares was the only person in the car. A search of Minjares and the passenger compartment revealed no evidence of the robbery. The police were unable to access the trunk at the scene, so the vehicle was taken to a tow-yard, where the trunk was forcibly opened. Inside the trunk, police found a tote bag in which they discovered evidence of the robbery, including three guns. An officer later testified the police searched the bag without a warrant because it saved "a matter of hours," and the police were still looking for the second suspect.[331]

A trial court denied Minjares's motion to suppress the evidence taken from the bag, and Minjares was convicted. The California Supreme Court, however, reversed the conviction, relying on a recent ruling authored by Burger, *United States v. Chadwick*.[332] *Chadwick* held that absent exigent circumstances, a warrantless search of personal luggage violates the Fourth Amendment. Accordingly, the California Supreme Court ruled that while the police could search the interior of the car without a warrant, the warrantless search of the bag violated *Chadwick*. After this ruling, prosecutors asked the Court to stay the mandate and judgment of the state high court. A majority of the justices denied the motion for a stay, with Blackmun and Rehnquist dissenting. Rehnquist, joined by Burger, filed a dissent from the denial of the stay.

Rehnquist's critique of the exclusionary rule in his dissent began with a curious description of *Weeks* and the evolution of the rule. He said that the *Weeks* Court ruled, "almost casually," that evidence obtained from a Fourth Amendment violation could not be used at trial.[333] Rehnquist did not explain, however, why the holding in *Weeks* was "almost casually" announced. And he seemed to suggest that the deliberate, warrantless search of Weeks's home was "a technical violation" of the Fourth Amendment.[334] Interestingly, when cataloguing the Court's cases subsequent to *Weeks*, Rehnquist omits any reference to Holmes's ruling in *Silverthorne Lumber*, which ruled that evidence derivative of a Fourth Amendment violation "shall not be used at all."

Rehnquist's description of *Mapp* is also telling. He asserted that *Mapp* essentially concluded that "the exclusionary rule represented the only feasible means of enforcing the Fourth Amendment," and victims of Fourth Amendment violations "had no effective redress available."[335] In doing so, Rehnquist seemingly ignored Clark's explicit holding in *Mapp* that "all evidence obtained by searches and seizures in violation of the Constitution is, by that same authority, inadmissible in a state court."[336] Rehnquist also

---

331 *Id.* at 917–18.

332 433 U.S. 1 (1977).

333 *Minjares*, 443 U.S. at 920 (Rehnquist, J., dissenting from denial of stay).

334 *Id.*

335 *Id.* at 922.

336 Mapp v. Ohio, 367 U.S. 643, 655 (1961).

stated that "one of the central themes in the procession of cases from *Weeks* to the present day has been a continuing re-evaluation of past assumptions."[337] Rehnquist conceded that *Weeks* "seemed" to hold that the exclusionary rule was grounded in the Fourth Amendment itself but noted that *Wolf* found the protections of the rule were not sufficiently fundamental to justify imposition on the states.[338] Similarly, he stated that in *Mapp*, a plurality "implied" that the rule was "a necessary corollary" of the amendment, but that the Burger Court's subsequent rulings rejected that conclusion.[339] Thus, according to Rehnquist, defenders of the exclusionary rule "must look beyond the corners of the Fourth Amendment for support."[340]

After noting that the judicial integrity theory for exclusion had failed to persuade the Burger Court, Rehnquist revealed his (and Burger's) willingness to scrap the exclusionary rule even when police deliberately violate the Fourth Amendment—a position that neither White nor Powell were willing to take. He wrote: "Although someone undoubtedly should be disciplined when a deliberate violation of the Fourth Amendment occurs, that proposition does not require the conclusion that the whole criminal prosecution must be aborted to preserve judicial integrity."[341] Rehnquist acknowledged that deterrence was the primary justification for exclusion but stated that since *Mapp*, various changes in the legal landscape have made redress for victims of illegal searches and seizures much easier. Thus, he continued, the arguments supporting exclusion as the "*only* practicable means" for enforcing the Constitution, "whether or not they were true in 1949 or 1961, are no longer correct."[342] He thought it "quite rational" for a prosecution to occur "without any application of the exclusionary rule in either federal or state cases, or at least without any application in state cases," even in cases where the Fourth Amendment has deliberately been violated.[343]

While Rehnquist stated he wanted the parties to brief whether *Weeks* should be "retained,"[344] the tone and direction of his opinion suggested he wanted to overrule *Weeks*, or at least *Mapp*—a prospect that several of the justices had mentioned during conference discussions throughout the 1970s. That was the ultimate goal for both Rehnquist and Burger. Although Rehnquist succeeded Burger as Chief Justice in 1986, he (like Burger) was unable to persuade his colleagues to overrule *Weeks*. Rehnquist did, however, help further curtail the scope of the exclusionary rule in significant ways, building on the anti-exclusion efforts of his predecessor.

* * *

---

337 *Minjares*, 443 U.S. at 922 (Rehnquist, J., dissenting from denial of stay).

338 *Id.* at 923.

339 *Id.* at 923-24.

340 *Id.* at 924.

341 *Id.* at 925.

342 *Id.* at 926.

343 *Id.* at 927.

344 *Id.* at 928.

As far back as 1921, scholars were remarking that the standing limitation allowed the government to profit from unconstitutional searches.[345] By 1941, another commentator observed that the concept of standing contradicted the exclusionary rule.[346] Although he was not the first to say so, in 1964, Professor Anthony Amsterdam pointedly observed that the standing limitation was a response to the judiciary's aversion to the exclusionary rule.[347] At that time, the doctrine of standing restricted invocation of the rule to a defendant who could prove that he was "a victim of a search or seizure, one against whom the search was directed."[348] A defendant could not challenge evidence obtained from a search of someone else. In the waning days of the Warren Court, only Fortas and Douglas dissented when the Court reaffirmed the standing limitation and refused to extend the logic of *Weeks* and *Mapp* to defendants who had not been the victims of Fourth Amendment violations. And by the late 1970s, Rehnquist could comment in *Ceccolini* without igniting controversy that the standing requirement was a means of limiting the exclusionary rule.

The day before *Ceccolini* was decided, the Court granted review in *Rakas v. Illinois*,[349] which presented two standing issues: whether a passenger has standing to challenge the search of a car, and whether a person against whom a search is directed has standing to contest the search. The justices knew the case was about the exclusionary rule.

Police in Kankakee County, Illinois, stopped a car matching the description of a vehicle seen leaving a robbery. Police ordered the four occupants of the car, Frank Rakas, Lonnie King, and two women to exit the car. The officers searched the car and discovered a box of rifle shells in the locked glove compartment and a sawed-off rifle under the front passenger seat. Rakas and King, who were passengers at the time of the stop, were later indicted for the robbery. While neither defendant claimed ownership of either the car or the rifle and shells, they argued the search violated the Fourth Amendment. The prosecutor responded that the defendants lacked standing to challenge the search. The Illinois courts agreed with the prosecutor, the evidence was admitted, and the defendants were convicted. The Illinois courts never did decide whether there was probable cause for the search.[350]

In the Court, the defendants contended Frankfurter's 1960 opinion in *Jones v. United States*[351] established their standing to challenge the search. *Jones* had ruled that anyone "legitimately on premises" where a search occurs may invoke the exclusionary rule.

---

345 Osmond K. Fraenkel, *Concerning Searches and Seizures*, 34 HARV. L. REV. 361, 375 (1921).

346 *See, e.g.*, J.A.C. Grant, *Circumventing the Fourth Amendment*, 14 S. CAL. L. REV. 359, 369 (1941). By 1952, another scholar stated that the standing requirement "is a manifestation of the courts' opposition to the federal exclusionary rule," and by sharply limiting the benefits of exclusion, courts "have in effect adopted much of the Wigmorean antipathy" for the federal exclusionary rule. Richard A. Edwards, *Standing to Suppress Unreasonably Seized Evidence*, 47 NW. U. L. REV. 471, 472 (1952).

347 Amsterdam, *supra* note 102, at 389.

348 Jones v. United States, 362 U.S. 257, 261 (1960).

349 439 U.S. 128 (1978).

350 *Id.* at 130–32.

351 362 U.S. 257 (1960).

Following *Jones*'s reasoning, the defendants argued that because they were "legitimately" occupying the car immediately before the search, they were afforded Fourth Amendment protection. They saw no principled reason not to apply *Jones*'s logic to a car search. Alternatively, the defendants claimed that as the "targets" of the search, they had standing to contest the search.[352] The defendants argued *Jones* also provided support for this theory when it stated that "'one against whom the search was directed'" may challenge a search.[353] While conceding that the Court had not endorsed this theory,[354] the defendants noted that many legal scholars had, and that the "target" theory was consistent with the deterrent purposes of exclusion. Maximum deterrence would be achieved, so argued the defendants, because police would be put on notice that illegally acquired evidence could be excluded by the target of an unlawful search.[355] The state's reply to the defendants' arguments was brief and straightforward: the defendants' claims would expand the exclusionary rule and thus should be rejected. According to the state, the "legitimately on premises" theory should be confined to the situation presented in *Jones*, and the "target" theory conflicted with the standing limitation and the "well established boundaries of the exclusionary rule."[356]

The opening sentence of Blackmun's pre-argument memo in *Rakas* read: "This case focuses on the exclusionary rule and raises an issue as to its expansion."[357] Although Blackmun was not impressed with Illinois's brief—he described it as "short and bare-boned" and noted that "I am not entirely sure that I fully understand some of its thrust"[358]—Blackmun devoted considerable space to restating verbatim the claims made in the amicus brief filed by Americans for Effective Law Enforcement. For example, the amicus brief claimed, and Blackmun restated in his memo: the exclusionary rule was originally imposed in *Weeks* as an exercise of the Court's supervisory power; there is little or no empirical proof that the rule deters; and it exacts a high cost on society.[359]

Regarding his own views after reading the briefs, Blackmun again reaffirmed his antagonism toward the rule for the "obvious reason that it serves to eliminate relevant evidence useful in ascertaining the truth."[360] He distinguished his recent opinion

---

[352] *Rakas*, 439 U.S. at 132–33.

[353] *Id.* at 134–35 (quoting *Jones*, 362 U.S. at 261).

[354] In *Alderman v. United States*, 394 U.S. 165 (1969), Fortas (with Douglas joining him), relying on the language from *Jones*, stated that a defendant has standing when law enforcement officials "conducted their unlawful search and seizure in order to obtain evidence to use against him." *Id.* at 209 (Fortas, J., concurring in part and dissenting in part). Harlan and Stewart specifically rejected this view. *Id.* at 188 n.1 (Harlan, J., concurring in part and dissenting in part). The rest of the *Alderman* Court did not address the point.

[355] Brief for Petitioners at 16–17, *Rakas*, 439 U.S. 128 (No. 77-5781).

[356] Brief for Respondents at 7, *Rakas*, 439 U.S. 128 (No. 77-5781).

[357] Harry Blackmun, Memorandum on *Rakas v. Illinois* 1 (July 3, 1978) [hereinafter Blackmun, *Rakas* Memo], Blackmun Papers, Box 290.

[358] *Id.* at 3.

[359] *Id.* at 4–5.

[360] *Id.* at 6.

in *Franks v. Delaware*,[361] which held that a defendant can challenge a warrant affidavit when he shows that police included a knowingly false statement in the affidavit, and that statement was necessary to the finding of probable cause. Blackmun wrote the result in *Franks* was based on the theory that "the *use* of truth would not have produced the search warrant in the first place. I can defend that position because it, too, rests on truth and utilizes it."[362] He saw no gain in deterrence in *Rakas* because the officers "acted in good faith."[363] He agreed with Illinois's position that if the Court accepted the defendants' arguments "there will be little limit" to applying the exclusionary rule.[364]

Powell also wrote down some tentative views after reading the briefs. In particular, he shared the position taken by the state and amicus brief that adoption of the target theory "would be a major extension of the scope of the exclusionary rule."[365] In light of his views in *Stone v. Powell*, Powell wrote "it will be difficult to persuade me that there is any sound policy reason for such an extension," and there "certainly is no constitutional basis for it."[366] Finally, he thought the standing limitation "also points strongly against [the defendants'] proposed extension of the exclusionary rule."[367]

At the *Rakas* conference, Burger said that a "guest in a car does not have same the expectation of privacy as a guest in a house."[368] The "only issue" for the Court to decide is standing.[369] Burger passed. Brennan said *Jones* was "indistinguishable" and voted to reverse.[370] Stewart said that the target theory "has never been accepted by this Court and should not be."[371] As to the "legitimately on premises" theory, Stewart said he "would not distinguish between automobiles and residences for standing purposes. But *Jones* has been criticized and should be modified."[372] Stewart wanted to redefine *Jones*'s test; the standard "is too gross a test."[373] He also stated that "standing depends on the facts. A guest in a home has standing to object to a search of his bedroom, but not of the wine-cellar, basement or of his host's bedroom. A possessory interest is important."[374] Stewart stated that the defendants in *Rakas* "had no such interest in the car."[375] Stewart voted to affirm.

White spoke after Stewart. He said that the Court "need not decide how far the 'lawfully on premises' test goes, but here it applies."[376] White voted to reverse. Marshall also

---

[361] 438 U.S. 154 (1978).

[362] Blackmun, *Rakas* Memo, *supra* note 357, at 6.

[363] *Id.* at 9.

[364] *Id.*

[365] Lewis Powell, Memorandum on *Rakas v. Illinois* 2 (July 10, 1978), Powell Papers, Box 60.

[366] *Id.*

[367] *Id.* at 2–3.

[368] Lewis Powell, Conference Notes on *Rakas v. Illinois* (Oct. 6, 1978), Powell Papers, Box 60.

[369] *Id.*

[370] *Id.*

[371] *Id.*

[372] *Id.*

[373] *Id.*

[374] *Id.*

[375] *Id.*

[376] *Id.*

voted to reverse. Blackmun's comments focused on the exclusionary rule. There was "no question as to the good faith of the officers."[377] There was "no element of deterrence" to be gained, and he "would not extend the exclusionary rule."[378] He also agreed with Stewart's views on *Jones*. Powell stated that *Jones* was "not applicable to this situation."[379] There is "no comparable expectation of privacy in an automobile search situation."[380] But he also noted, "I can join Potter's analysis. I also certainly agree with Harry as to the exclusionary rule."[381] Powell voted to affirm. Rehnquist also voted to affirm and said he "could go along with Potter's type of analysis."[382] Stevens spoke last and voted to reverse. Stevens "would not entirely reject the 'target theory'—as where police are trying to build-up a case against a particular individual."[383] He also stated that "there is a stronger case for standing of a passenger in a car than a guest in a home."[384] At the end of the discussion, the vote was four to four, with Burger undecided.[385] The next day, Burger voted to affirm.[386] Rehnquist was assigned the opinion.

After working on the opinion, Rehnquist sent a memo to the four members of the majority explaining that his reading of the cases showed that "the term 'standing' means nothing more in an analytical sense than does the statement found in several of our cases that rights secured by the Fourth Amendment are personal, and A will not be heard to assert that evidence was obtained in violation of the constitutional rights of B."[387] He informed his colleagues that he would draft the opinion "so as to subsume 'standing' under the principle that one may only move to suppress when his own Fourth Amendment rights have been violated."[388] This made sense to Rehnquist because in his mind, standing was a concept separate from Fourth Amendment analysis in theory but in practice was "invariably intertwined" in the analysis.[389] The analysis, therefore, would "focus on the extent of the particular defendant's rights under the Fourth Amendment."[390] Concerned that he might lose someone's vote, Rehnquist wrote he would "simply abandon even the trial effort" to write the opinion this way if any one of the four "felt irrevocably committed to the proposition that the notion of

---

377 *Id.*

378 *Id.*

379 *Id.*

380 *Id.*

381 *Id.*

382 *Id.*

383 *Id.*

384 *Id.*

385 *Id.*

386 Warren Burger, Memorandum to the Conference on *Rakas v. Illinois* (Oct. 7, 1978), Powell Papers, Box 60.

387 William Rehnquist, Memorandum to Warren Burger, Potter Stewart, Harry Blackmun, and Lewis Powell on *Rakas v. Illinois* 1 (Oct. 17, 1978), Blackmun Papers, Box 290.

388 *Id.* at 2.

389 *Id.*

390 *Id.*

'standing' in Fourth Amendment cases should be retained exactly as it is."[391] Apparently, none of the four objected because the published opinion in *Rakas* tracked the logic of Rehnquist's memo.

First, *Rakas* rejected the "target theory" as a basis for invoking the exclusionary rule. Relying on *Alderman*, Rehnquist repeated that Fourth Amendment rights are personal and may not be vicariously asserted. A defendant suffers no Fourth Amendment harm by the admission of evidence acquired from a search of a third party.[392] Rehnquist did not dispute the defense claim that maximum deterrence would be achieved by adoption of the target theory; he simply noted, in a footnote, that despite the deterrent purpose of the exclusionary rule, "we never have held that unlawfully seized evidence is inadmissible in all proceedings or against all persons."[393] He also saw practical problems with administering a target theory. Suppression hearings would have to determine the subjective motivations of the police regarding the targets of their searches. More important, Rehnquist stated that the target theory "would necessarily mean a more widespread invocation of the exclusionary rule."[394] All exclusion results in a cost to society, and the Court's "misgivings" about enlarging the number of persons who can invoke the rule are "properly considered when deciding whether to expand standing to assert Fourth Amendment violations."[395]

Next, *Rakas* asked whether Fourth Amendment analysis is advanced by considering the question of a defendant's standing, as distinct from the merits of whether that person's Fourth Amendment rights have been violated. Instead of considering the concepts independently, Rehnquist thought "the better analysis forthrightly focuses on the extent of a particular defendant's rights under the Fourth Amendment, rather than on any theoretically separate, but invariably intertwined concept of standing."[396]

Rakas then addressed the defendants' argument that because they were lawfully in the car at the time of the search, they could contest the legality of the search. Rehnquist explained, undoubtedly relying on Stewart's statement at the conference, that *Jones*'s "legitimately on premises" test "creates too broad a gauge for measurement of Fourth Amendment rights."[397] Although he did not overrule *Jones* expressly, Rehnquist confined *Jones*'s holding to its specific facts. After discarding *Jones*'s formulation for determining standing, Rehnquist finally concluded that Rakas and King, as passengers, held no privacy interests in the glove compartment or area under the front seat: "Like the trunk of an automobile, these are areas in which a passenger *qua* passenger simply would

---

391 *Id.* at 3.

392 Rakas v. Illinois, 439 U.S. 128, 133–34 (1978).

393 *Id.* at 134 n.3.

394 *Id.* at 137.

395 *Id.* at 138.

396 *Id.* at 139.

397 *Id.* at 142.

not normally have a legitimate expectation of privacy."[398] The remarkable aspect of this part of *Rakas* is that the opinion "does not even hint at a stopping point" short of an absolute rule that passengers who do not claim ownership of either the vehicle or items seized by the police will never have standing to challenge a police search.[399]

Powell, joined by Burger, joined Rehnquist's opinion but wrote his own concurrence. He insisted the issue before the Court was narrow: did the search of the car *after* the defendants had been *ordered out* by the police violate their Fourth Amendment rights? For Powell, it was "unrealistic—as the shared experience of us all bears witness" to suggest that Rakas and King reasonably expected that the car would not be searched "after they were lawfully stopped and made to get out."[400] Regarding the exclusionary rule, Powell saw no basis for White's claim, offered in the dissent, that the result in *Rakas* would encourage the police to perform illegal searches every time a car contains more than one occupant. But even if White were correct on that point, Powell thought the result was "justified by society's interest in restricting the scope of the exclusionary rule to those cases where in fact there is a reasonable expectation of privacy."[401]

Besides agreeing that the target theory should be rejected, White's dissent was blunt and highly critical of the result and logic of *Rakas*. The opinion, White asserted, means an "'open season'" on searching cars and the belongings of passengers in cars.[402] He accused the majority of "distorting" substantive Fourth Amendment doctrine in order to diminish the "practical impact of the exclusionary rule."[403] In White's view, the motive and flaw of Rehnquist's opinion was clear: "In the rush to limit the applicability of the exclusionary rule somewhere, anywhere, the Court ignores precedent, logic, and common sense to exclude the rule's operation from situations in which, paradoxically, it is justified and needed."[404]

As *Rakas* showed, when the rules of standing are compressed, fewer defendants are able to invoke the exclusionary rule. It soon became evident that the Court's tightening of standing doctrine would not be limited, as Powell might have thought, to the particular facts presented in *Rakas*. Three cases decided during the final days of the October 1979 Term showed that the logic of *Rakas* would extend not only to cases in which defendants claimed ownership of items acquired through unlawful searches, but also where federal agents deliberately and flagrantly violated the Fourth Amendment.

Rawlings v. Kentucky[405] and *United States v. Salvucci*[406] were decided on the same day, June 25, 1980. David Rawlings was one of several guests inside Lawrence Marquess's

---

398 *Id.* at 148–49.

399 6 LaFave, *supra* note 46, §11.3(e), at 193.

400 *Rakas*, 439 U.S. at 155 (Powell, J., concurring).

401 *Id.* at 152 n.1.

402 *Id.* at 157 (White, J., dissenting).

403 *Id.*

404 *Id.* at 169.

405 448 U.S. 98 (1980).

406 448 U.S. 83 (1980).

home in Bowling Green, Kentucky, when the police arrived with an arrest warrant for Marquess. Marquess was not home, but the police detained some of the guests because they smelled marijuana and saw marijuana seeds in plain view. Forty-five minutes later, other officers arrived with a warrant to search the premises. Under the mistaken impression the search warrant authorized a search of the occupants, police ordered Vanessa Cox to empty her purse, which disclosed illegal narcotics. Cox turned to Rawlings and told him to "take what was his."[407] Rawlings immediately claimed ownership of the drugs. Rawlings was convicted of narcotics violations, and the Kentucky Supreme Court upheld the conviction after concluding that Rawlings lacked standing to challenge the search of Cox's purse because he had no privacy interest in the purse.[408] Writing for the majority, Rehnquist ruled that Rawlings could not challenge the constitutionality of the search.[409] He curtly dismissed Rawlings's contention that his situation was distinguishable from *Rakas* because he had acknowledged ownership of the drugs found in the purse.

John Salvucci and Joseph Zackular were charged in a federal indictment with unlawful possession of stolen mail. The indictment was based on evidence obtained from a search of Zackular's mother's home. The defendants claimed that the warrant authorizing the search was not supported by probable cause. The government argued that the defendants lacked standing to challenge the search, but a federal appellate court disagreed, ruling that the defendants had standing, and the search was unconstitutional. The court explained that under Frankfurter's opinion in *Jones*, the defendants had "automatic standing" because they were charged with a possessory offense and thus were not required to establish a privacy interest in the place searched or property interest in the items seized.[410] But just as he discarded *Jones*'s "legitimately on premises" rule in *Rakas*, Rehnquist dispatched *Jones*'s "automatic standing" rule in *Salvucci*.

As explained in chapter 2, although Frankfurter's opinion in *Jones* ruled that a defendant invoking the exclusionary rule should have to establish his standing by showing "that he himself was the victim of an invasion of privacy,"[411] Frankfurter rejected the then-prevailing view of the federal appellate courts that to establish standing, a defendant could be forced to allege facts in a suppression hearing that could later be used by the prosecutor to convict him. Prior to *Jones*, the federal appellate courts forced defendants

---

[407] *Rawlings*, 448 U.S. at 100-01.

[408] *Id.* at 102–03.

[409] Rehnquist concluded that Rawlings held no privacy interest in the purse because of the following factors: At the time of the search, Rawlings had known Cox "only for a few days"; Rawlings "never sought or received access to [the] purse" prior to the search; Rawlings lacked a "right to exclude" others from the purse; Rawlings did not take "normal precautions to maintain his privacy" in the purse; and finally, upon seeing the arrival of the police at the house, Rawlings admitted that he had no belief that the contents of the purse would be free of police intrusion. *Id.* at 105.

[410] *Salvucci*, 448 U.S. at 84–85.

[411] Jones v. United States, 362 U.S. 257, 261 (1960).

"to choose one horn of the dilemma"[412]—either go forward with a Fourth Amendment challenge and risk being convicted based on what was said at the suppression hearing or refuse to testify, as permitted by the Fifth Amendment, but waive a valid Fourth Amendment claim. Frankfurter found this position "presupposes requirements of 'standing' which we do not find compelling."[413] *Jones* ruled that the same element that caused a dilemma for the defense, "*i.e.*, that possession both convicts and confers standing, eliminates any necessity for a preliminary showing of an interest in the premises searched or the property seized, which ordinarily is required when standing is challenged."[414]

In other words, because the defendant is charged with a crime of possession, he is not required to establish his standing with testimony that could later be used to convict. So began use of the phrase "automatic standing." Frankfurter explained that his ruling was supported by a further consideration: the government should not be free to charge that the defendant possessed items that prove his guilt, while simultaneously arguing that he did not possess them for Fourth Amendment purposes.[415] Automatic standing prevented the government from employing the "vice of prosecutorial self-contradiction"[416] as a basis for conviction.

In *Salvucci*, Rehnquist claimed that subsequent events had eliminated the need for "automatic standing." First, *Simmons v. United States*,[417] decided in 1968, held that "when a defendant testifies in support of a motion to suppress evidence on Fourth Amendment grounds, his testimony may not thereafter be admitted against him at trial on the issue of guilt unless he makes no objection."[418] According to Rehnquist, the result in *Simmons* not only protects defendants charged with possessory crimes but also "grants a form of 'use immunity' to those defendants charged with nonpossessory crimes."[419] Put another way, the rule announced in *Simmons*, according to Rehnquist, was "broader than that of *Jones*."[420]

Second, Rehnquist explained that the additional concern that prompted *Jones*'s "automatic standing" holding—the "vice of prosecutorial self-contradiction"—had ceased to be a constitutional problem. According to Rehnquist, *Rakas* "clearly" established that "a prosecutor may simultaneously maintain that a defendant criminally possessed the seized good, but was not subject to a Fourth Amendment deprivation, without legal contradiction."[421] In the future, defendants could no longer rely on legal possession of an item that was seized during a police search as a basis for invoking the exclusionary rule.

---

412 Connolly v. Medalie, 58 F.2d 629, 630 (2d Cir. 1932).

413 *Jones*, 362 U.S. at 263.

414 *Id.*

415 *Id.* at 263–64.

416 Brown v. United States, 411 U.S. 223, 229 (1973).

417 390 U.S. 377 (1968).

418 *Id.* at 394.

419 United States v. Salvucci, 448 U.S. 83, 90 (1980).

420 *Id.*

421 *Id.*

Referencing the result in *Rawlings*, Rehnquist noted legal possession of an item "is not a proxy" for determining whether the defendant can challenge the search because possession "does not invariably represent the protected Fourth Amendment interest."[422]

Leaving no doubt as to the motivations driving the *Salvucci* holding, Rehnquist closed his opinion by observing that the automatic standing rule was a relic of Fourth Amendment jurisprudence: "The doctrine now serves only to afford a windfall to defendants whose Fourth Amendment rights have *not* been violated."[423] The Court, Rehnquist noted, was "unwilling to tolerate the exclusion of probative evidence under such circumstances," and would continue to limit the "availability of the exclusionary rule to defendants who have been subjected to a violation of their Fourth Amendment rights."[424]

* * *

By the close of the 1970s, there was no doubt that a majority of the justices had decided that the primary, if not sole, purpose of the exclusionary rule was deterrence of unconstitutional searches and seizures. While Burger and Rehnquist signaled their readiness to abolish the rule, the justices who occupied the middle ground in the exclusionary rule debate continued to apply the rule to deliberate or flagrant unconstitutional searches and arrests. White and Powell—despite their strong antipathy to the rule—were willing to apply the rule in cases of bad-faith police conduct. In fact, Powell resisted Burger's intense lobbying to extend the rationale of *Stone v. Powell* (a case Powell wrote) to Sixth Amendment cases, because Powell could not defend the interrogation tactics of the police in *Brewer v. Williams*. And Blackmun, who indicated on more than one occasion his willingness to vote to repeal the exclusionary rule, authored opinions requiring exclusion in the case of a bad-faith arrest, and where police intentionally include false statements in a search warrant affidavit.

Yet, *Rakas* made clear that neither the need nor ability to deter illegal searches would be the touchstone for applying the exclusionary rule. And by rejecting the target theory for exclusion, *Rakas* revealed that the Court was either unconcerned or unconvinced that law enforcement officers would intentionally manipulate the standing limitation to invade the constitutional rights of third parties in order to secure evidence against another person. Perhaps, moderate members of the Court might distinguish *Rakas* and vote to exclude in an egregious case or where there was evidence high-ranking officials had encouraged officers to conduct unconstitutional searches. After all, the facts in *Rakas* were not going to move justices like Blackmun or Powell to support the target theory. The search involved a car (as opposed to a home), an area of reduced privacy in the eyes of Blackmun and Powell, and neither justice saw fault in the police behavior in *Rakas*; nor was there any evidence the police search was conducted in bad faith.

---

422 *Id.* at 91.

423 *Id.* at 95.

424 *Id.*

Therefore, Blackmun and Powell believed that excluding the evidence in *Rakas* would result in little to no gains in terms of deterrence.

On the other hand, before and after *Rakas*, scholars warned that the Court's standing cases encouraged police "to conduct unconstitutional searches against small fish in order to catch big ones."[425] Professor John Burkoff noted that it "takes little exposure to actual police procedures or strategies . . . to realize that law enforcement agents do not treat all criminal suspects as fungible targets for law enforcement efforts."[426] Like other scholars, Burkoff observed that cases like *Rakas* create "no disincentive to the illegal harassment of those individuals who are not the ultimate target of police activity."[427] An Ohio case, decided two days before *Rawlings* and *Salvucci*, proved that the scholars were right about the willingness of police to violate the constitutional rights of third parties to obtain evidence against targeted suspects. But the views of law professors rarely, if ever, matter in Fourth Amendment cases. Despite an egregious Fourth Amendment violation and possibly criminal behavior by federal law enforcement officers, the Court would not require exclusion and remained steadfastly committed to Rehnquist's desire to limit the exclusionary rule whenever possible.

A majority of the justices reaffirmed their allegiance to *Rakas*'s approach to standing, even in cases of deliberate and egregious Fourth Amendment violations, in *United States v. Payner*. In the mid-1960s, the Internal Revenue Service launched "Operation Trade Winds," which investigated the financial dealings of American citizens in the Bahamas. In 1972, IRS Special Agent Richard Jaffe, the lead investigator, enlisted an informant, Norman Casper, to discover information about a Bahamian bank, the Castle Bank and Trust Company, and its depositors. Casper learned that Castle Bank vice president Michael Wolstencroft would be traveling to Miami for a business trip on January 15, 1973, and would have Castle Bank records with him on the trip. Casper introduced Wolstencroft to Sybol Kennedy, a private detective who worked for Casper. When Wolstencroft arrived in Miami, he went to Kennedy's apartment and then went out to dinner with Kennedy.[428]

While Wolstencroft and Kennedy were dining, Casper stole Wolstencroft's briefcase and took it to the home of another IRS employee. There, Casper, Jaffe, and others, with help from a "trusted" locksmith,[429] opened the briefcase and photographed approximately four hundred documents taken from the briefcase. The briefcase was returned before

---

[425] Anthony G. Amsterdam, *Perspectives on The Fourth Amendment*, 58 MINN. L. REV. 349, 433 (1974).

[426] John M. Burkoff, *The Court that Devoured the Fourth Amendment: The Triumph of an Inconsistent Exclusionary Doctrine*, 58 OR. L. REV. 151, 176 (1979).

[427] *Id.* at 176–77 ; *see also* Welsh S. White & Robert S. Greenspan, *Standing to Object to Search and Seizure* 118 U. PA. L. REV. 333, 351 (1970) ("Police are often tempted to make illegal searches during the investigation of a large conspiracy. Once the police have established that several individuals are involved, they may deem it worthwhile to violate the constitutional rights of one member of the conspiracy (particularly a minor member) in order to obtain evidence for use against others." (footnote omitted)).

[428] United States v. Payner, 434 F. Supp. 113, 118–19 (N.D. Ohio 1977).

[429] *Id.* at 119.

Wolstencroft and Kennedy finished dinner. The documents photographed revealed a relationship between Castle Bank and the Bank of Perrine, Florida. Subpoenas to the Florida bank disclosed a loan agreement between Jack Payner and the Florida bank. The loan agreement was the key evidence proving Payner had falsified his 1972 federal income tax return when he denied maintaining a foreign bank account. Payner had pledged the funds in his Castle Bank account as security for a one hundred thousand dollar loan from the Florida bank.[430]

A federal district court found Payner guilty but set aside the conviction after granting Payner's motion to suppress the loan agreement. As an initial matter, the court ruled the government discovered the loan agreement by exploiting the search of Wolstencroft's briefcase, but also that Payner lacked Fourth Amendment standing to challenge the search. Nevertheless, the court suppressed the loan agreement by invoking the supervisory power of the federal courts to exclude evidence obtained by official conduct "which is either purposefully illegal or motivated by an intentional bad faith hostility to a constitutional right."[431]

Among other things, the trial court found government officials knowingly and purposefully obtained the briefcase materials with "bad faith hostility toward the Fourth Amendment rights" of Wolstencroft; Jaffee and others were aware that the standing requirement would permit the admissibility of evidence obtained from searches of third parties against other defendants; the government "affirmatively counsels" its officers that the standing requirements permit them "to purposefully conduct an unconstitutional search and seizure of one individual in order to obtain evidence against third parties, who are the real targets of the governmental intrusion"; and "the IRS agents in this case acted, and will act in the future, according to that counsel."[432] After the court of appeals affirmed, the Solicitor General asked the Court to review the case. The Solicitor General's argument was direct: The district court's use of its supervisory power to exclude evidence was an end run around *Rakas*; the "salutary restriction on the applicability of the exclusionary remedy should not be abandoned under the rubric of supervisory power."[433]

Powell's law clerk, Gregory May, outlined Powell's options in a February 12, 1980, memorandum that Powell described as an "interesting memo."[434] According to May, the government's argument against the use of the supervisory power rested on two claims. First, "the supervisory power should not be used to exclude evidence admissible under the Fourth Amendment."[435] Second, the supervisory power cannot be invoked to regulate the activities of the Executive Branch "in ways not required by rule, statute, or the

430 *Id.* at 119–23.

431 *Id.* at 134–35 (footnotes omitted).

432 *Id.* at 131–33.

433 Petition for a Writ of Certiorari at 16, United States v. Payner, 447 U.S. 727 (1980) (No. 78-1729).

434 Gregory May, Bench Memorandum to Lewis Powell on *United States v. Payner* 1 (Feb. 12, 1980), Powell Papers, Box 62.

435 *Id.* at 5.

Constitution."[436] May told Powell, "Your view of the exclusionary rule as a deterrent to future violations of the Fourth Amendment would allow you to go either way on the first argument."[437] Powell had joined *Rakas*, which established that exclusion was appropriate only when a defendant proved his Fourth Amendment rights were violated. On the other hand, Powell had indicated through his advocacy of the ALI proposal that exclusion was proper when the illegal search is conducted both purposefully and in bad faith. May outlined the consequences of not excluding. "Certainly in a case like this one, the Internal Revenue Service has little incentive to behave itself. Since the Service violates the rights of bank officers solely for the purpose of getting evidence against depositors, there never will be a case where the Fourth Amendment would exclude the fruits of the constitutional violation from a criminal trial."[438]

To accept the government's second argument—i.e., the supervisory power is limited to enforcement of rules that have a textual foundation—May informed Powell that he would have "to take a position somewhat inconsistent with [his] theory of the exclusionary rule."[439] From the time Powell joined the Court, he insisted that exclusion was not a personal right of the defendant, but instead was designed solely to deter future unconstitutional searches. May told Powell it would be difficult to conceive of a deterrence theory that distinguishes between "judicial action to deter searches that will violate the rights of third parties and judicial action to deter 'future violations.' In both cases, the courts act to deter violations that will injure persons other than the defendant. In both cases, the judicial goal is the regulation of police conduct."[440]

In the margin of this part of May's memo, Powell inscribed, "True."[441] After reading May's memo, Powell wrote on the top: "I'm not at rest."[442] He described *Payner* as a "close case, with policy arguments both ways."[443] He acknowledged, however, that under *Rakas*, "the need to deter illegal searches is inapplicable where search doesn't violate right of defendant himself."[444]

At the *Payner* conference, Burger began the discussion stating the question is whether the federal courts "have power to deal with outrageous conduct" by the government.[445] Burger passed and said he "wants to study further."[446] Brennan voted to affirm, stating the "conduct of the government is so shocking, this is a denial of Due Process. Can't

---

436 *Id.* at 5–6.

437 *Id.* at 6.

438 *Id.*

439 *Id.* at 7.

440 *Id.* (citation omitted).

441 *Id.*

442 *Id.* at 1.

443 *Id.*

444 *Id.*

445 Lewis Powell, Conference Notes on *United States v. Payner* (Feb. 22, 1980) [hereinafter Powell, *Payner* Conference Notes], Powell Papers, Box 62.

446 *Id.*

let the government do this."[447] Stewart voted to reverse. He agreed with the Solicitor General's arguments: "Payner's rights were not violated."[448] This was an "erroneous use of the supervisory power."[449] White also voted to reverse: "None of Payner's rights were violated."[450] White also told his colleagues that the Court's "prior precedents would have to be ignored or overruled" to affirm.[451] Payner had "no standing" and the "supervisory power can't be carried this far."[452]

Marshall voted to affirm. He said that this "is not an evidentiary matter, but government conduct deliberately" designed to "get around the standing" requirement.[453] Marshall said the courts must "stop this type of lawless evidence."[454] Blackmun said this was an "uncomfortable case."[455] He noted that the supervisory power had been exercised in *Elkins* and other cases involving improper police interrogation. The "violation was flagrant and with intent to avoid the standing limitation."[456] Blackmun voted to affirm. Powell agreed that the "IRS conduct was outrageous," but the rights violated were those of the banker, not the rights of Payner.[457] He explained, "If we allowed courts to exercise supervisory power in cases like this, the standing principles developed by the Court would be circumvented."[458] He cited *Rakas* as an example. Powell said this was an "erroneous use of supervisory power."[459] He voted to reverse. Rehnquist also voted to reverse. He "would decide the case as Stewart, White and Powell would."[460] Rehnquist said the "standing cases make clear that Payner has no standing."[461] He cited *Alderman* and *Rakas*. This was an "abuse of supervisory power."[462] Stevens voted to reverse. He said that one cannot draw "workable lines as to standing based on the degree of government misconduct."[463] The Court "would have to overrule *Alderman*" to rule in favor of Payner.[464] At the close of the discussion, the vote was five to three in favor of reversing, with Burger undecided.[465] Later, Burger voted to affirm and assigned the opinion to Powell.

---

447 *Id.*
448 *Id.*
449 *Id.*
450 *Id.*
451 *Id.*
452 *Id.*
453 William J. Brennan, Jr., Conference Notes on *United States v. Payner* (undated), Brennan Papers, Box I: 495.
454 Powell, *Payner* Conference Notes, *supra* note 445.
455 *Id.*
456 *Id.*
457 *Id.*
458 *Id.*
459 *Id.*
460 *Id.*
461 *Id.*
462 *Id.*
463 *Id.*
464 *Id.*
465 *Id.*

Except for a footnote responding to a point made in Marshall's dissent, the published opinion in *Payner* largely resembles the eight-page first draft that Powell circulated on April 10, 1980.[466] After some preliminary criticism directed at an "indiscriminate application" and "unbending application" of the exclusionary rule,[467] the core of *Payner* rested on the foundation laid in *Rakas*. Powell ruled that the supervisory power does not permit a federal judge to exclude evidence on the grounds that it was illegally acquired from a third party. Citing *Rakas* and *Alderman*, Powell stated prior rulings had already established "that the interest in deterring illegal searches does not justify the exclusion of tainted evidence at the instance of a party who was not the victim of the challenged practices."[468] The result dictated by *Rakas* does not change because "a court has elected to analyze the question under the supervisory power instead of the Fourth Amendment."[469] The "need to deter" unlawful police behavior and the "detrimental impact" of excluding relevant evidence "remain precisely the same."[470]

As the conference discussion revealed, the *Payner* majority was not going to overrule or even diminish *Rakas*. Of course, the interests at stake in *Payner* were very different from the interests involved in prior cases. Although Powell cited *Alderman* as support, a majority of the *Alderman* Court did not directly address the target theory for exclusion. And while a majority of the justices did reject the target theory in *Rakas*, the facts and constitutional interests in *Rakas* were very different from those in *Payner*.

In *Rakas*, none of the justices questioned the good faith of the officers, and Powell himself saw the issue in that case as narrow. *Payner*, on the other hand, involved a situation where the government intentionally manipulates the standing requirement; purposefully and in bad faith, infringes the Fourth Amendment rights of a third party to discover evidence against contemplated targets; and then prosecutes one of the targets using such evidence.[471] In sum, the justices, or at least Powell, could have easily distinguished *Payner* from *Rakas*. After all, in other Fourth Amendment rulings and constitutional cases generally, Powell was known for his "penchant for hair-splitting distinctions

---

466 Lewis Powell, First Draft of *United States v. Payner* (Apr. 10, 1980), Powell Papers, Box 62.

467 United States v. Payner, 447 U.S. 727, 734 (1980).

468 *Id.* at 735.

469 *Id.* at 736.

470 *Id.*

471 *See* Yale Kamisar, *Does (Did) (Should) The Exclusionary Rule Rest On A "Principled Basis" Rather Than An "Empirical Proposition"?*, 16 Creighton L. Rev. 565, 638 (1983) ("The relevant question in *Payner*, then, was not whether the exclusionary rule should *always* be applied when police illegality is somewhere in the picture, but whether it should *ever* be applied—taking into account the seriousness or flagrancy of the illegality—when the defendant lacks 'standing.' The question was not whether the exclusionary rule should be given 'unbending application,' but whether *the 'standing' requirement* should be. By deciding that even in a case like *Payner* a federal court is *unable* to exercise its supervisory powers to bar the evidence—by holding that 'judicial impotency is *compelled* in the face of such scandalous conduct'—the Court gave us its answer." (footnote omitted)).

and fact-specific decisions."[472] But the justices in the *Payner* majority were committed to confining the exclusionary rule no matter how flagrant the government's conduct.

In the early 1970s, Powell told his law clerk, John Jeffries, that "substantial" violations of Fourth Amendment rights—like the kind described by the ALI—must be deterred. A few years later, Powell resisted Burger's pressure to withhold application of the exclusionary rule in *Brewer v. Williams*. Powell refused to go along with Burger because Powell had "difficulty defending the police conduct."[473] During the conference discussion of *Brown v. Illinois*, Powell told his colleagues that the "nature and extent of the violation was important in determining whether the exclusionary rule's purpose is implicated."[474] And during the deliberations of *Peltier*, Powell told Rehnquist that the exclusionary rule should apply where police knew or should have known their actions violate the Fourth Amendment. The police behavior in *Payner* fit this mold: knowingly illegal actions that were performed in bad faith. But in *Payner*, Powell would not vote to exclude. Instead, he voted to extend *Rakas*'s reasoning to a case quite distinct from *Rakas*. Powell's vote and opinion in *Payner* reveals the impact of *Rakas*—and Powell's deep-seated opposition to exclusion.

---

472 JEFFRIES, *supra* note 2, at 436. Powell's "penchant for hair-splitting distinctions" in Fourth Amendment cases can be seen in his concurring opinions in *Almeida-Sanchez v. United States*, 413 U.S. 266, 275–85 (1973) (Powell, J., concurring), and *Robbins v. California*, 453 U.S. 420, 429–36 (1981) (Powell, J., concurring in the judgment).

473 Powell, Letter to Warren Burger, *supra* note 18, at 2.

474 Powell, Conference Notes on *Brown v. Illinois*, *supra* note 64.

6 The Good-Faith Exception

ALTHOUGH FEDERAL COURT of Appeals Judge Henry Friendly may not have been the first person to suggest limiting the reach of the exclusionary rule to bad faith or brazen Fourth Amendment violations, his criticism of the rule in 1965 attracted considerable attention nonetheless. Friendly saw suppression as an excessive response when police make a technical mistake on the street, or a minor and unintentional blunder. Recognizing that the sole reason for exclusion is to deter Fourth Amendment violations, Friendly thought the benefits of deterrence could be sufficiently achieved if prosecutors were denied the fruit of conduct that was intentionally or flagrantly illegal.[1] Although the comparison was not perfect, Friendly's criticism of the rule aligned him with another influential jurist who opposed exclusion. Almost forty years earlier, Justice Cardozo, while a member of the New York Court of Appeals, summarized similar sentiments: "The criminal is to go free because the constable has blundered."[2] Despite his esteem and influence, the Court did not embrace Cardozo's view on exclusion during the twentieth century.[3] Judge Friendly's criticism of the rule and his proposal to restrict its application to bad-faith searches, unlike Cardozo's, however, would have a substantial and lasting influence on the Court.

---

[1] Henry J. Friendly, *The Bill of Rights as a Code of Criminal Procedure*, 53 CALIF. L. REV. 929, 951–53 (1965).

[2] People v. Defore, 150 N.E. 585, 587 (N.Y. 1926).

[3] *See* Wayne R. LaFave, *The Smell of* Herring*: A Critique of the Supreme Court's Latest Assault on the Exclusionary Rule*, 99 J. CRIM. L. & CRIMINOLOGY 757, 765 (2009) (explaining that Cardozo's "'misleading epigram' has *never* been an ingredient in the pre-[2009] exclusionary rule; it was quoted but then rejected by the Supreme Court in Fourth Amendment cases on more than one occasion" (footnote omitted)).

In 1971, during the deliberations in *Coolidge v. New Hampshire*,[4] White sent Stewart a six-page memo, elaborating his thoughts on the case. One of the issues in *Coolidge* was the legality of the seizure and subsequent search of the defendant's car. The warrant authorizing the search of the car had been issued by the New Hampshire Attorney General, Warren Rudman, who was leading the murder investigation of Coolidge. While a majority of the Court agreed that the warrant was invalid because the Attorney General (like a police officer) could not act as a neutral and detached judge, the Court split on whether a warrantless seizure (and later search) of the car, supported by probable cause, was valid. The closing paragraph of White's memo appeared to contain the seeds for a "good-faith" exception to the exclusionary rule. He wrote:

> Even if the State proceeded on mistaken grounds which they knew were invalid, it is doubtful that the exclusionary rule should be applied if objectively the State's search was sustainable for other reasons. But here the officers proceeded in good faith believing that the warrant issued by the Attorney General, acting as Justice of the Peace, was a good warrant. Excluding the evidence in these circumstances, where there were other grounds to sustain the search, seems to me an extravagant application of the Fourth Amendment.[5]

To be sure, it is unclear whether White opposed exclusion because there were "other reasons" for upholding the search of the car, or because the police acted in good-faith reliance that the warrant was valid. Six months later and four days before *Coolidge* was announced, White told his colleagues that the exclusionary rule "should at least be narrowed," and proposed that the Court consider reargument in *Coolidge* on whether *Mapp v. Ohio* should be overruled.[6] That proposal failed because Harlan thought *Coolidge* was a poor vehicle to overrule *Mapp*. White would spend the 1970s periodically urging his colleagues to adopt a good-faith exception to the rule.

A decade after *Coolidge* was decided, the membership of the Court had changed dramatically. Four members of the Court—Black, Harlan, Douglas, and Stewart—were replaced by Powell, Rehnquist, Stevens, and O'Connor. Although it seemed that the Court was ready to adopt a good-faith exception in the mid-1970s, it never did so. By 1981, however, not only did a majority of the Court share White's objective to bar application of the exclusionary rule when police act in the good-faith belief that their conduct was lawful, this majority was determined to establish such a rule. What remained unresolved was *how* the Court would implement that goal.

* * *

---

[4] 403 U.S. 443 (1971).

[5] Byron White, Memorandum to Potter Stewart on *Coolidge v. New Hampshire* 6 (Jan. 22, 1971), Stewart Papers, Box 66.

[6] Byron White, Memorandum to the Conference on *Coolidge v. New Hampshire* (June 17, 1971), Blackmun Papers, Box 128.

Lance and Susan Gates were drug dealers based in Bloomingdale, Illinois. The Gateses apparently had a profitable racket going until someone familiar with their drug peddling contacted the police. On May 3, 1978, the Bloomingdale Police Department received an anonymous handwritten letter:

> This letter is to inform you that you have a couple in your town who strictly make their living on selling drugs. They are Sue and Lance Gates, they live on Greenway, off Bloomingdale Rd. in the condominiums. Most of their buys are done in Florida. Sue his wife drives their car to Florida, where she leaves it to be loaded up with drugs, then Lance flys down and drives it back. Sue flys back after she drops the car off in Florida. May 3 she is driving down there again and Lance will be flying down in a few days to drive it back. At the time Lance drives the car back he has the trunk loaded with over $100,000.00 in drugs. Presently they have over $100,000.00 worth of drugs in their basement.
>
> They brag about the fact they never have to work, and make their entire living on pushers.
>
> I guarantee if you watch them carefully you will make a big catch. They are friends with some big drugs dealers, who visit their house often.[7]

Law enforcement officers soon corroborated some of the letter's details, including the names and address listed in the letter, and the fact that Lance Gates was scheduled to fly from Chicago to West Palm, Florida on May 5. Surveillance of Gates's trip revealed that he had arrived in West Palm and went to a room in a hotel registered to Susan Gates. Early the next morning, Gates and an unidentified female left in a car with Illinois license plates registered to Gates and drove northbound on an interstate highway used by travelers heading to Chicago. An affidavit explaining these facts was submitted to a judge, along with a copy of the anonymous letter. The judge issued a search warrant, and when the Gateses arrived home, twenty-two hours after they left West Palm, the police searched their car and discovered three hundred and fifty pounds of marijuana. A search of the house revealed marijuana, weapons, and other contraband. The Illinois courts ruled that the affidavit supporting the warrant did not establish probable cause to believe that the Gateses' car or home contained drugs.[8]

The Illinois Attorney General asked the Court to review the case, but the Court initially denied that request. The case was relisted after Burger circulated a dissent from the denial to review the case.[9] The Court then voted to hear the case and decide whether detailed information provided to police by an anonymous informant, coupled with police corroboration of the information, provides probable cause to issue a search warrant. Eight months before the oral argument, Illinois filed a motion asking the Court to

7 Illinois v. Gates, 462 U.S. 213, 225 (1983).

8 *Id.* at 225–27.

9 Warren Burger, First Draft of Dissenting Opinion in *Illinois v. Gates* (Jan. 5, 1982), Powell Papers, Box 92.

also consider whether, assuming the warrant was unconstitutional, evidence obtained pursuant to the warrant should still be admitted "because the police acted in a reasonable good faith belief in the validity of the warrant."[10] Most likely because that question had not been presented to the Illinois courts, the Court unanimously denied Illinois's request to argue the good-faith issue. Thus, *Gates* was argued without either party discussing a good-faith exception.

The *Gates* conference discussion began with Burger and Brennan offering conflicting views on what is required for an informant's tip to establish probable cause. The justices eventually voted six to two to one to reverse the Illinois Supreme Court's ruling. Burger, White, Blackmun, Powell, Rehnquist, and O'Connor thought the warrant was supported by probable cause and voted to reverse. Brennan and Marshall believed there was insufficient information to prove probable cause and voted to affirm. Stevens split his vote. He thought the police had probable cause to search the car but insufficient evidence to search the home.[11]

While six justices favored reversal, that majority could not agree on how to reverse the judgment below. Burger, Blackmun, Rehnquist, and O'Connor seemed to favor overruling two of the Court's precedents that outlined a multipronged test for determining when an informant's tip satisfied the probable cause standard.[12] Under *Spinelli v. United States*[13] and *Aguilar v. Texas*,[14] in order to establish probable cause, a police affidavit had to reveal the "basis of knowledge" for the informant's accusations and the reliability of the informant.

During the conference discussion, White proposed an alternative that would avoid overruling any precedents: "I would prefer to say here that the good faith of the officers means that we ought not to apply the exclusionary rule. This *Aguilar-Spinelli* test is not satisfied—so what? The officers and the magistrate acted in good faith under the authorization of a warrant, so we ought not to apply the exclusionary rule."[15] White saw *Gates* as a "good case to modify the exclusionary rule."[16] Blackmun thought the Court need not decide the good-faith issue but stated his willingness to do so.[17] Powell stated: "I am interested in Byron's good faith exception proposal, and I prefer to do that."[18] Rehnquist also indicated his readiness to approve a good-faith exception, and O'Connor closed the discussion by noting: "I can join in Byron's good faith exception to the exclusionary rule."[19] Thus, five members of the Court openly agreed to join White in creating a good-faith

10 John Paul Stevens, Draft of Dissenting Opinion in *Illinois v. Gates* 1-2 (Nov. 15, 1982), Powell Papers, Box 92.

11 The Supreme Court in Conference (1940–1985): The Private Discussions Behind Nearly 300 Supreme Court Decisions 491–93 (Del Dickson ed., 2001).

12 *Id.*

13 393 U.S. 410 (1969).

14 378 U.S. 108 (1964).

15 Dickson, *supra* note 11, at 492.

16 Lewis Powell, Conference Notes on *Illinois v. Gates* (Oct. 15, 1982), Powell Papers, Box 92.

17 Dickson, *supra* note 11, at 492.

18 *Id.*

19 *Id.* at 492–93.

exception. Although Burger did not express an opinion on the issue during the conference, in light of his longstanding hostility to suppression, there was no reason to think he would oppose White's proposal.

After the conference, Stevens circulated a memo reminding his colleagues that they had already denied Illinois's motion to argue the good-faith issue. In light of that denial, Stevens wrote, "'[I]t seems to me that the Court should not address the question which the parties were not permitted to argue.'"[20] Burger thought Stevens was "'entirely correct'" on this point, and added that the Court "'was quite wrong in deciding *Mapp v. Ohio* on a ground never argued, especially on an important issue.'"[21] While agreeing with the soundness of Stevens's position, White told his colleagues in a memo that he "'would not be averse to rearguing this case with the possible modification of the exclusionary rule in mind.'"[22] White then made a motion for reargument on the exclusionary rule issue. After previously agreeing with Stevens, Burger accepted White's memo as a motion for reargument and voted for it. Eventually, Blackmun, Powell, Rehnquist, and O'Connor also supported White's motion for reargument.[23]

Stevens thought reargument was pointless. He reminded his colleagues that a majority of justices thought the warrant was valid. If the warrant was valid, Stevens saw no need to consider a good-faith exception. He also noted that Illinois had adopted its own exclusionary rule in 1923, almost forty years before *Mapp* imposed the rule on the states. Thus, the Court would still have to decide the probable cause issue before reaching the question of remedy. Stevens wrote: "'I do not understand anyone to suggest that this Court would have the power to require a state court to create a good faith exception to its own exclusionary rule.'"[24] Put simply, Stevens saw no reason to reach the good-faith issue in a case that was "'due for reversal in any event.'"[25] Stevens voted to deny White's motion, as did Brennan and Marshall.[26] White's motion was approved, and he circulated a proposed order for reargument, which asked the parties to address whether the exclusionary rule "should to any extent be modified, so as, for example, not to require the exclusion of evidence obtained in the reasonable belief that the search and seizure at issue was consistent with the Fourth Amendment."[27] A majority again approved White's proposal, while Stevens filed a dissent to the order, which Brennan and Marshall joined.[28]

---

[20] William J. Brennan, Jr., Case Histories, October Term 1982, at XXIX (undated), Brennan Papers, Box II: 7.

[21] *Id.*

[22] *Id.* at XXIX–XXX.

[23] *Id.* at XXX.

[24] *Id.*

[25] *Id.*

[26] *Id.* at XXX–XXXI.

[27] Byron White, Memorandum to the Conference on *Illinois v. Gates* (Nov. 5, 1982), Powell Papers, Box 92.

[28] Illinois v. Gates, 459 U.S. 1028 (1982) (Stevens, J., dissenting from reargument order).

Interestingly, White framed his reargument order broadly. The order did not ask the parties to address whether the exclusionary rule should be modified to allow the admission of evidence obtained by police acting in reasonable reliance on a *search warrant* that was later declared invalid. That was how Illinois framed its earlier request, which tracked the facts in *Gates*. Instead, White was seeking a restriction of the exclusionary rule that went beyond the facts in *Gates*. White's order asked the parties to address whether the rule should be modified when evidence was obtained in the reasonable belief that the search and seizure at issue was valid under the Fourth Amendment. Framed this way, a good-faith exception would be available in every case involving a Fourth Amendment violation and would not be confined to the narrow category of cases where police rely on a warrant that is subsequently ruled illegal. White's decision to frame the question broadly was not surprising.

During the 1970s, White formulated his proposal for a good-faith exception in expansive terms, even in cases where a narrower exception was available. For example, in *Stone v. Powell*,[29] Nevada police relied upon a vagrancy statute to arrest Lloyd Powell. In its companion case, Nebraska law enforcement officers obtained incriminating evidence against David Rice pursuant to a search warrant. The statute and warrant were later declared unconstitutional, and the lower courts suppressed evidence obtained incident to Powell's arrest and the search of Rice's home. In his dissent in *Stone v. Powell*, White eschewed a modification of the exclusionary rule that would permit the admission of evidence where police rely on either a statute or warrant that is later declared invalid. Instead, White proposed a modification of the rule that would apply in every case

> so as to prevent its application in those many circumstances where the evidence at issue was seized by an officer acting in the good-faith belief that his conduct comported with existing law and having reasonable grounds for this belief. . . . . When law enforcement personnel have acted mistakenly, but in good faith and on reasonable grounds, and yet the evidence they have seized is later excluded, the exclusion can have no deterrent effect. The officers, if they do their duty, will act in similar fashion in similar circumstances in the future; and the only consequence of the rule as presently administered is that unimpeachable and probative evidence is kept from the trier of fact and the truth-finding function of proceedings is substantially impaired or a trial totally aborted.[30]

When the parties in *Gates* submitted new briefs on the good-faith issue that the Court had asked them to address, the Solicitor General's amicus brief urged the Court to modify the exclusionary rule along the exact lines proposed by White in *Stone v. Powell*. As a fallback position, the Solicitor General told the Court that no deterrent purpose would

---

29 428 U.S. 465 (1976).

30 *Id.* at 538–40 (White, J., dissenting).

be served by suppressing evidence when police rely in good faith on a warrant issued by a judge.[31]

After the second argument, the conference discussion focused on whether *Gates* was a good vehicle to adopt a good-faith exception. Burger began the discussion with a surprising statement, informing his colleagues that he "never said the exclusionary rule should be abandoned."[32] Burger wanted to "modify" the rule with a "good-faith exception" and commented that he had "said so several times."[33] Burger thought such an exception "clearly applies to a warrant unless it is executed by a policeman who filed the affidavit. Then the question of 'good faith' would be suspect."[34] Burger also would overrule *Spinelli* and *Aguilar*. Burger passed on voting.[35]

At the first conference Brennan had said *Aguilar* and *Spinelli* controlled the probable cause question.[36] On the issue of exclusion, Brennan said there was an adequate and independent state ground for the ruling below.[37] Accordingly, the Court had no jurisdiction to decide the good-faith issue. Brennan voted to affirm. White spoke next and disagreed with Brennan's view on jurisdiction. White said, "there is jurisdiction."[38] The ruling of the Illinois court, according to White, "was decided on federal grounds. The issue is here—it is a Fourth Amendment question and the good-faith defense is within that amendment."[39] White noted that *Mapp* decided a federal issue that was not raised below. And he said that "where a warrant is involved, the exclusionary rule doesn't apply absent bad faith."[40] White voted to reverse.[41]

Marshall voted to affirm. He said there was no jurisdiction to decide the good-faith issue. Blackmun said he regretted that the Court took the case for reargument. He would decide the probable cause issue; the "good-faith issue was not raised below."[42] Powell then spoke and said he "would adopt an exception to the exclusionary rule where the officer acts in the reasonable, good-faith belief that his search and seizure was lawful."[43] But Powell was "concerned that the good-faith issue was not raised below."[44] Ultimately,

---

31 Supplemental Brief for the United States as Amicus Curiae Supporting Reversal at 25, 37, Illinois v. Gates, 462 U.S. 213 (1983) (No. 81-430).

32 Lewis Powell, Conference Notes on *Illinois v. Gates* Reargument (Mar. 4, 1983) [hereinafter Powell, *Gates* Reargument Conference Notes], Powell Papers, Box 92.

33 *Id.*

34 *Id.*

35 *Id.*

36 Lewis Powell, Conference Notes on *Illinois v. Gates*, *supra* note 16.

37 Powell, *Gates* Reargument Conference Notes, *supra* note 32.

38 *Id.*

39 *Id.*

40 *Id.*

41 *Id.*

42 *Id.*

43 *Id.*

44 *Id.*

Powell favored reversing the Court's probable cause precedents, which made him "reluctant to reach the good-faith issue."[45]

Rehnquist agreed with Powell. Rehnquist's "tentative view" was that the Court did not have jurisdiction to decide the good-faith issue.[46] Moreover, "the failure to raise the question below also is a negative against reaching the good-faith issue."[47] Stevens also opposed deciding the good-faith issue. But he noted that if the good-faith issue was addressed, the Court should also "consider deterrence" to judges who issue warrants.[48] For Stevens, the "strongest type case for good faith is where an officer was confronted with exigent circumstances."[49] O'Connor then spoke and said if the Court decided the good-faith issue, she would provide the fifth vote.[50] However, she said the "exception must be carefully framed."[51] But O'Connor preferred not to reach the good-faith issue for the reasons stated by Powell, Blackmun, and Rehnquist. After the discussion ended, Burger voted to reverse.[52] Thus, the Court again voted six to two to one to reverse the Illinois Supreme Court. Rehnquist was assigned the opinion.

In the end, Rehnquist's opinion in *Gates* only decided the probable cause question. His opinion discarded the two-pronged *Aguilar-Spinelli* test and substituted in its place a totality of the circumstances model for determining probable cause. Under the new *Gates* standard:

> The task of the issuing magistrate is simply to make a practical, common-sense decision whether, given all the circumstances set forth in the affidavit before him, including the "veracity" and "basis of knowledge" of persons supplying hearsay information, there is a fair probability that contraband or evidence of a crime will be found in a particular place.[53]

Because the good-faith question had not been presented to the Illinois courts, Rehnquist expressed jurisdictional and prudential concerns about addressing that issue. The fact that Illinois repeatedly opposed the Gateses' Fourth Amendment claims on the merits was not sufficient to reach the good-faith issue. Recognizing the Burger Court's stance in previous cases, Rehnquist explained that the Court had uncoupled the exclusionary rule from the Fourth Amendment: "The question whether the exclusionary rule's remedy is appropriate in a particular context has long been regarded as an issue separate

---

[45] *Id.*

[46] *Id.*

[47] *Id.*

[48] *Id.*

[49] *Id.*

[50] *Id.*

[51] *Id.*

[52] *Id.*

[53] Illinois v. Gates, 462 U.S. 213, 238 (1983).

from the question whether the Fourth Amendment rights of the party seeking to invoke the rule were violated by police conduct."[54] Thus, "modification or abolition" of the rule was not conjoined with the merits of the Fourth Amendment issue.[55] Therefore, the Court would save the question of whether the exclusionary rule should be modified or abolished for another day.

White, however, would not let a jurisdictional barrier prevent him from saying his part on the good-faith issue. He was going to address the "important question" of whether the rule should be modified to contain a good-faith exception, regardless.[56] Moreover, White saw the question of exclusion as inseparable from the Fourth Amendment itself. He explained: "Our decisions concerning the scope of the exclusionary rule cannot be divorced from the Fourth Amendment; they rest on the relationship of Fourth Amendment interests to the objectives of the criminal justice system."[57] White had "no doubt" that the issue was properly before the Court "as an indivisible element of the claim that the Constitution requires exclusion of certain evidence seized in violation of the Fourth Amendment."[58] A year later, White would reverse his position on this point. Whether the exclusionary rule was part of the Fourth Amendment was unimportant to White. What was important was the chance to explain why a good-faith exception should be adopted. White's proposed good-faith exception was expansive, and his reasoning was highly instructive on where the Court was heading in its exclusionary rule jurisprudence.

White began by reaffirming the position he took in *Stone v. Powell*: "[T]he exclusionary rule is an inappropriate remedy where law enforcement officials act in the reasonable belief that a search and seizure was consistent with the Fourth Amendment."[59] White drew support for his exception from the Court's recent cases, as well as from notions of common sense. Accepting "that the rule deters some police misconduct, it is apparent as a matter of logic that there is little if any deterrence when the rule is invoked to suppress evidence obtained by a police officer acting in the reasonable belief that his conduct did not violate the Fourth Amendment."[60]

White did not pull any punches on the scope of the good-faith exception he proposed. He stated, "There are several types of Fourth Amendment violations that may be said to fall under the rubric of 'good faith.'"[61] He recognized that a good-faith exception would be available in cases of warrantless arrests—occasions where judges disagree on the issue of probable cause—"no matter how reasonable the grounds for arrest appeared

54 *Id.* at 223.
55 *Id.*
56 *Id.* at 247 (White, J., concurring in the judgment).
57 *Id.* at 249.
58 *Id.* at 250.
59 *Id.* at 246.
60 *Id.* at 260.
61 *Id.* at 262.

to the officer and though reasonable men could easily differ on the question."[62] White also signaled, in a footnote discussing the concept of judicial integrity, that his good-faith exception was available where police have "reasonably erred in assessing the facts, mistakenly conducted a search authorized under a presumably valid statute, or relied in good faith upon a warrant not supported by probable cause."[63] In such cases, "the question of exclusion must be viewed through a different lens," and the "integrity of the courts is not implicated."[64] White did note, however, that exclusion would remain available for "searches and seizures perpetrated in intentional and flagrant disregard of Fourth Amendment principles."[65]

In another footnote, White acknowledged that his good-faith exception would negatively impact the Court's precedents that seemed to require suppression of illegally acquired evidence.[66] In prior cases, when the Court invalidated a statute authorizing a search without a warrant or probable cause, the evidence obtained pursuant to the unconstitutional statute was excluded as a result of the Court's decision. In *Michigan v. DeFillippo*,[67] Burger's opinion acknowledged that practice but distinguished it from a case in which police have probable cause to suspect a crime as defined by a substantive statute and make a search incident to the arrest for that crime. *DeFillippo* ruled that evidence seized incident to an arrest was admissible, even though the statute authorizing the arrest, a Detroit vagrancy ordinance, was subsequently declared unconstitutional. Although Michigan prosecutors argued in the court below that the evidence seized should have been admissible under a "good-faith" exception, Burger's opinion eschewed that theory to uphold DeFillippo's conviction. Instead, *DeFillippo* explained that the later invalidation of the law did not "undermine the *validity of the arrest* made for violation of that ordinance," and the evidence discovered incident to the arrest of DeFillippo should not have been excluded.[68] Put simply, the arrest and search of DeFillippo, lawful when executed by the police under a presumptively valid statute, did not become unlawful once the statute was declared unconstitutional.

The distinction created in *DeFillippo* became known as the "substantive-procedural dichotomy." On the one hand, as *DeFillippo* illustrated, exclusion is *not* required for the fruits of an arrest or search when police act pursuant to a substantive statute defining criminal conduct that is subsequently declared invalid, provided the police have probable cause to make the arrest and rely on the statute in good faith. On the other hand, evidence obtained pursuant to a procedural statute authorizing a search without a warrant or probable cause that is later declared invalid *is* subject to suppression notwithstanding

---

62 *Id.*

63 *Id.* at 259 n.14.

64 *Id.*

65 *Id.*

66 *Id.* at 256 n.12.

67 443 U.S. 31 (1979).

68 *Id.* at 40 (emphasis added).

good-faith reliance on the statute by the police. In his *Gates* concurrence, White stated that the results in the latter category of cases "may well be different under a 'good-faith' exception to the exclusionary rule."[69]

Despite the fact that five other justices during the two *Gates* conference discussions expressed support for White's position, no other justice joined his *Gates* opinion. But White knew (as did the other justices) that future cases raising the good-faith issue would come to the Court. In the meantime, White's opinion in *Gates* laid the foundation for a broad good-faith exception. A year later, White again would have his say on restricting the exclusionary rule, but this time he would write for a majority of the Court.

* * *

Before *Gates* was decided on June 8, 1983, three other cases presenting a good-faith issue arrived at the Court: *United States v. Leon*, *Massachusetts v. Sheppard*, and *Colorado v. Quintero*.

United States v. Leon[70] concerned the same issue the Court chose not to decide in *Gates*. The defendants were indicted for federal drug offenses after California police officers executed a search warrant that revealed drugs in their homes and cars. After the police had been told by an informant of unproven reliability that two of the defendants sold drugs from their home, police conducted an extensive investigation of the defendants. Several district attorneys reviewed the search warrant application before a magistrate issued the warrant. The federal district court, conceding the question was close, concluded the warrant was not supported by probable cause and granted the defendants' suppression motion. The district court agreed with the government's argument that the police had acted in good faith, but it refused to recognize a good-faith exception. This ruling was affirmed by the Court of Appeals for the Ninth Circuit. The Reagan Administration's Department of Justice was obviously seeking to make "new" law because when *Leon* arrived at the Court, the Solicitor General expressly refused to seek review of the lower courts' probable cause ruling, even though everyone knew that under *Gates*'s new probable cause standard, the Ninth Circuit's ruling would be reversed.

Massachusetts v. Sheppard[71] raised the question of whether the exclusionary rule should be modified to permit the admission of evidence seized in reasonable reliance on a search warrant supported by probable cause, but later held invalid due to a failure to specify the items to be seized. Police in Boston, Massachusetts, had good reason to suspect Osborne Sheppard murdered his girlfriend. After developing substantial evidence of Sheppard's guilt, a detective completed an affidavit for an arrest warrant and a warrant authorizing a search of Sheppard's home. The affidavit listed the evidentiary items the police were seeking in Sheppard's home. The detective showed the affidavit to two district attorneys and a police sergeant. Because it was a Sunday, the detective could only find a warrant

---

69 *Gates*, 462 U.S. at 256 n.12 (White, J., concurring in the judgment).

70 468 U.S. 897 (1984).

71 468 U.S. 981 (1984).

application form for "controlled substances." Although the detective made certain corrections and changes to the form, the warrant that the judge actually signed retained reference to "controlled substances."[72]

The detective took the affidavit and warrant form to a local judge's home. After examining the affidavit, the judge said he would authorize the search. The detective informed the judge about the changes he made to the form. The judge made other changes to the form and told the detective that everything was in order. But the judge did not change the substantive portion of the warrant, which authorized a search for "controlled substances." And the judge did not alter the warrant to incorporate the affidavit. The detective took the warrant to Sheppard's home and conducted a search limited to the items listed in the affidavit. He discovered evidence linking Sheppard to the crime, and Sheppard was later charged with first degree murder.[73]

The trial court concluded that the warrant was illegal because it did not, as the text of the Fourth Amendment requires, particularly describe the items to be seized from Sheppard's home. Nonetheless, the court admitted the evidence because the police acted in good faith when procuring and executing the warrant. Sheppard was convicted. The Supreme Judicial Court of Massachusetts, however, reversed the conviction. The court held that the evidence discovered from the search had to be suppressed because the United States Supreme Court had not recognized a good-faith exception to the exclusionary rule.[74]

The third case, *Colorado v. Quintero*,[75] presented the most serious threat to the exclusionary rule besides outright elimination of the suppression remedy: whether the rule should be modified to allow the admission of evidence seized in the mistaken, but reasonable, belief that a warrantless arrest did not violate the Fourth Amendment. Darlene Bergan was sweeping her porch in a Denver neighborhood when she observed a man peering into two of her neighbors' residences around 12:45 p.m. The man disappeared, but approximately one hour later, Bergan saw the man at a bus stop next to her home. He had taken off his shirt and was using it to cover a television. He paced nervously and appeared to be trying to thumb a ride while waiting for the bus. Bergan called the police.[76]

Five minutes later, an officer arrived and asked the man, Fidel Quintero, for identification. Quintero told the officer he had no identification and that he had purchased the television for one hundred dollars and was trying to get home. After the officer requested assistance, Quintero was frisked. Police found two wool gloves in his pocket on a day when the temperature was above eighty degrees. While the police were questioning

[72] *Id.* at 984–86.

[73] *Id.* at 986–87.

[74] *Id.* at 987; *see also* Commonwealth v. Sheppard, 441 N.E.2d 725, 733–36 (Mass. 1982).

[75] 657 P.2d 948 (Colo. 1983), *cert. granted*, 463 U.S. 1206 (1983), *and cert. dismissed*, 464 U.S. 1014 (1983).

[76] *Quintero*, 657 P.2d at 949.

Quintero, Bergan arrived and told the officers she was the person who had called the police, but she did not repeat the information about Quintero peering into homes in the neighborhood. Police arrested Quintero and searched him. They found one hundred and forty dollars in cash, five rings (including two class rings bearing different initials and class years), and ladies' jewelry. Five hours after the arrest, the police learned that a home in the neighborhood had been burglarized, and the items found on Quintero had been taken from it. Quintero was later convicted of burglary.[77]

The Colorado Supreme Court overturned Quintero's conviction; it ruled there was no probable cause to arrest Quintero. The court conceded the police had grounds to stop and question Quintero, but his explanation about purchasing the television merely provided a suspicion of theft. Because the police did not know that a crime had been committed until five hours later, they lacked probable cause. The Colorado court refused to recognize a good-faith exception to the suppression doctrine.[78] In their petition requesting the Court to review *Quintero*, Colorado prosecutors did not argue police had probable cause to arrest Quintero. Instead, they argued the police had a good-faith belief that the facts they confronted were sufficient to establish probable cause.[79] Put another way, the prosecutors wanted the Court to conclude that the good-faith mistake by the police did not require suppression of evidence found as a result of Quintero's illegal arrest.

The conference discussions in *Gates* revealed that six members of the Court wanted to create a good-faith exception. There was, however, no consensus among the six on the substance or scope of a good-faith exception. While individual justices had occasionally written or spoken on the need for a good-faith exception, only White had provided a framework for a good-faith standard. White envisioned a broad exception that confined exclusion to instances of deliberate or flagrant police misconduct, or cases where no well-trained officer could reasonably have thought his or her behavior was constitutional. By contrast, O'Connor stated in the second *Gates* conference discussion that the "exception must be carefully framed."[80] Although its content and scale were undetermined, a good-faith exception was emerging.

Indeed, some members of the Court wanted it sooner than others. While Rehnquist chose not to decide the good-faith issue in *Gates*, he continued to look for cases that would make new law. In a memo describing *Quintero*, Rehnquist told his colleagues that the Colorado case made a better vehicle for a good-faith exception because it did not raise the difficulties present in *Gates* "of inquiring into the reasonableness of a magistrate's conduct."[81] According to Rehnquist, *Quintero* "involves on-the-street conduct of

[77] *Id.* at 949–50.

[78] *Id.* at 950–51.

[79] *See* Petition for Writ of Certiorari at 10-13, Colorado v. Quintero, 464 U.S. 1014 (1983) (No. 82-1711). *See generally* Brief for the United States, United States v. Leon, 468 U.S. 897 (1984) (No. 82-1771), *Sheppard*, 468 U.S. 981 (No. 82-963), *Quintero*, 464 U.S. 1014 (No. 82-1711).

[80] Powell, *Gates* Reargument Conference Notes, *supra* note 32.

[81] William Rehnquist, Memorandum to the Conference on *Colorado v. Quintero* 3 (June 15, 1983), Powell Papers, Box 109.

police officers of the sort that the reasonable, good faith exception generally is associated with."[82] Rehnquist thought the case provided "a potentially good vehicle for considering the good-faith issue" and would vote to review it.[83]

Rehnquist then sent a memo to his colleagues on *Leon*. This memo noted that a "fairly persuasive argument can be made that" the Ninth Circuit's ruling in *Leon* was inconsistent with the result in *Gates*, and the case should be sent back to the appellate court.[84] But Rehnquist also thought that *Leon* was a "useful vehicle" for consideration of a good-faith exception.[85] "On balance," Rehnquist thought the briefs in *Leon* would "provide useful guidance if we should decide to formulate a good faith exception."[86] As in *Quintero*, Rehnquist told his colleagues he would vote to review *Leon*.[87]

Powell's law clerk, Rives Kistler, summarized the three cases for his boss in a short memo. The memo explained that *Sheppard* was "clearly the narrowest" of the cases, presenting the issue of whether a good-faith exception applies to a technical mistake or a mistake of fact.[88] *Leon* raised "the broader issue" of whether a decision by a "neutral body" will trigger the good-faith exception.[89] Finally, *Quintero* presented "the broadest holding of all": whether exclusion is required "whenever the police themselves have a good faith belief that probable cause exists."[90] Kistler recommended granting review in *Sheppard*. He cautioned: "Recognizing a good-faith exception is a significant step and it would seem best to allow the idea to develop in the lower courts on a case-by-case basis."[91] Moreover, *Sheppard* was the type of case where everyone seemed to agree there was good faith. It "might provide a solid first step."[92]

For his part, Powell was "inclined" to review *Leon* and *Sheppard*.[93] Powell viewed *Sheppard* as the "least complicated" of the three cases.[94] On *Leon*, he acknowledged that the case could be remanded in light of *Gates* but also recognized that the Solicitor General wanted the Court to decide the good-faith issue.[95] Initially, Powell opposed taking *Quintero*. Before receiving Kistler's memo, Powell wrote that the Colorado case was

---

82 *Id.*

83 *Id.*

84 William Rehnquist, Memorandum to the Conference on *United States v. Leon* (June 22, 1982), Powell Papers, Box 109.

85 *Id.*

86 *Id.*

87 *Id.*

88 Rives Kistler, Memorandum to Lewis Powell on *United States v. Leon* 3 (June 11, 1983), Powell Papers, Box 109.

89 *Id.*

90 *Id.*

91 *Id.*

92 *Id.*

93 Lewis Powell, Notes on *United States v. Leon*, *Massachusetts v. Sheppard*, and *Colorado v. Quintero* (undated), Powell Papers, Box 109.

94 *Id.*

95 *Id.*

not a good case to consider a good-faith exception, because "there may have well been probable cause to arrest" Quintero, but that highly factual issue was not presented to the Court.[96]

After the Court agreed to review all three cases, the Solicitor General filed a consolidated brief, the bulk of which urged the Court to adopt a broad "reasonable mistake" exception to the exclusionary rule.[97] Specifically, the brief argued the exclusionary rule was inapplicable where "a reasonably well-trained police officer should not have known that the search and seizure in question violated the Fourth Amendment" or where the violation "did not substantially affect the rights of the subject of the search."[98] The government's "reasonable mistake" exception mirrored the good-faith exception outlined in White's *Gates* opinion. It would not only allow admission of evidence obtained when police rely on the unconstitutional determinations of neutral judges or legislators unconnected with law enforcement personnel, but also when police themselves are responsible for the legal errors. According to the Solicitor General, neither the fundamental values of the Fourth Amendment nor the deterrent purposes behind the exclusionary rule are promoted when "law enforcement officers, even though acting without a warrant, reasonably attempt to navigate the intricate channels of Fourth Amendment law."[99] The "honest mistakes" of police officers should not trigger "the severe sanction of suppression."[100]

While the Solicitor General's "reasonable mistake" exception was broad enough to encompass cases like *Quintero*, should the Court prefer a more cautious approach, the government offered the Court a narrower rule for cases like *Leon* and *Sheppard*. The government claimed "*no* credible justification" had ever been offered for invoking the exclusionary rule in cases like *Leon* and *Sheppard* when police have not engaged in any misconduct, "but a judicial officer has issued a search warrant that is subsequently held to be defective."[101] Suppression, according to the brief, is "inherently inappropriate" for deterring judicial mistakes.[102] Therefore, exclusion of evidence obtained through an invalid warrant is only proper if it promotes the basic purpose of deterring police misconduct. But exclusion made no sense in cases like *Leon* and *Sheppard* "because law enforcement officers will never be deterred from executing a search warrant that a judge has told them is valid."[103]

Before the Court heard oral arguments in the three cases, the justices learned that Fidel Quintero had died of a gunshot wound, which removed *Quintero* from the Court's

---

[96] Lewis Powell, Preliminary Memorandum on *Colorado v. Quintero* 1 (June 6, 1983), Powell Papers, Box 109.

[97] Brief for the United States, *supra* note 79, at 19.

[98] *Id.*

[99] *Id.* at 56–57.

[100] *Id.* at 57.

[101] *Id.*

[102] *Id.* at 58.

[103] *Id.* at 61.

argument list.[104] Although he had earlier opposed taking *Quintero*, Powell told his law clerk, Rob Couch, that it was "regrettable" *Quintero* was gone because it presented "the pure 'good faith' issue as distinguished from the 'defective warrant' issue" raised in *Leon* and *Sheppard*.[105] Powell admitted that the issue presented in *Quintero* was "a considerably more difficult question," and he would not want to address it in *Leon* and *Sheppard*.[106]

As for *Leon* and *Sheppard*, Powell wrote, "[T]hese are easy cases for me. I would reverse both of them."[107] Essentially, Powell had already decided the questions presented in *Leon* and *Sheppard* nine years earlier when he wrote his concurring opinion in *Brown v. Illinois*. Although *Brown* involved a flagrant and bad-faith arrest, and the issue addressed was quite different than the questions raised in *Leon* and *Sheppard*, Powell's concurrence stated exclusion should not be available where police "in good faith arrest an individual in reliance on a warrant later invalidated or pursuant to a statute that subsequently is declared unconstitutional."[108] As for the many amicus briefs filed in *Leon* and *Sheppard*, Powell told his clerk: "[A]ll one need do is identify the source of the brief to predict with reasonable certainty its position. I doubt the reading of any of them will shed any light on this case which otherwise is fully briefed."[109]

The conference notes of Brennan and Powell reveal that the good-faith exception approved in *Leon* and *Sheppard* could easily have been avoided. Powell's notes state that the justices discussed and voted on the cases together and explained, "I would not have done this."[110] Burger began the discussion on *Leon* with a rather surprising statement: "I would adopt the good-faith exception. It would be a disaster to write anything that might be read as wiping out the exclusionary rule. We must write tightly to avoid that."[111] Regarding *Sheppard*, Burger observed that "if the affidavit were clipped to the warrant that referenced to it, no Fourth Amendment violation" would exist.[112]

Brennan thought *Leon* should be returned to the lower court in light of *Gates*: "It seems to me quite reasonable to assume that the search warrant found to be defective

104 Alex L. Stevas, Memorandum to the Conference on *Colorado v. Quintero* (Nov. 30, 1983), Powell Papers, Box 109.

105 Lewis Powell, Memorandum to Rob Couch on *United States v. Leon* and *Massachusetts v. Sheppard* 7 (Jan. 3, 1984) [hereinafter Powell, *Leon* and *Sheppard* Memo], Powell Papers, Box 109.

106 *Id.*

107 *Id.* at 5.

108 Brown v. Illinois, 422 U.S. 590, 611 (1975) (Powell, J., concurring in part) (footnote omitted).

109 Powell, *Leon* and *Sheppard* Memo, *supra* note 105, at 7.

110 Lewis Powell, Conference Notes on *Massachusetts v. Sheppard* (Jan. 20, 1984) [hereinafter Powell, *Leon* and *Sheppard* Conference Notes], Powell Papers, Box 106. While Powell's conference notes state that *Leon* and *Sheppard* were discussed simultaneously, Brennan had separate documents for the *Leon* and *Sheppard* discussions. *See* William J. Brennan, Jr., Conference Notes on *United States v. Leon* (undated) [hereinafter Brennan, *Leon* Conference Notes], Brennan Papers, Box I: 627; William J. Brennan, Jr., Conference Notes on *Massachusetts v. Sheppard* (undated) [hereinafter Brennan, *Sheppard* Conference Notes], Brennan Papers, Box I: 626.

111 Brennan, *Leon* Conference Notes, *supra* note 110.

112 Brennan, *Sheppard* Conference Notes, *supra* note 110.

in this case . . . would, under the new 'totality of the circumstances' test announced in *Gates*, be found valid."[113] Brennan noted because the police in *Leon* conducted an extensive investigation, "the lower court, if given the opportunity to consider the warrant application in light of *Gates*, might well find [the application] provides a sufficient showing of probable cause to support the issuance of the warrant."[114] As for *Sheppard*, Brennan stated the "error was trivial. In all other respects, the warrant was okay."[115] Brennan stated he "could reverse on this ground."[116]

White's views were well known: "I would adopt a good-faith exception."[117] Marshall agreed with Brennan and voted to reverse. Blackmun seemed uncertain on what to do. He asked: "Can we confine good faith to the warrant context?"[118] He then stated that "both cases could be decided without reaching the 'good faith'" issue.[119] He commented that *Sheppard* could be decided under *Gates*'s totality of the circumstances test. He also noted that a "good-faith rule has some negatives."[120] He thought it "would encourage Fourth Amendment violations and let up on police training."[121] He wanted to keep any exception "narrow."[122] He said he would "accept good faith for this type of case" and "limit these cases to magistrates."[123] However, he also indicated a preference "to vacate on *Gates*."[124]

Powell agreed "with much of what" Blackmun said.[125] Powell stated the Court "can reverse both without going to good faith, but an objective exception appeals to me."[126] Possibly thinking of *Quintero*, Powell opposed "a simple 'good-faith' exception."[127] Again, Powell spoke of the ALI model as identifying some of the objective factors to consider: "I could perhaps go with an objective reasonable good-faith test."[128] But Powell emphasized that he "wouldn't abandon the exclusionary rule as such under any circumstances."[129]

Rehnquist agreed that "under *Gates* there would be a different result" in *Leon*, but the probable cause issue had not been presented to the Court.[130] He concluded, "we must

---

113 Dickson, *supra* note 11, at 495.
114 *Id.*
115 Powell, *Leon* and *Sheppard* Conference Notes, *supra* note 110.
116 *Id.*
117 Brennan, *Leon* Conference Notes, *supra* note 110.
118 Brennan, *Sheppard* Conference Notes, *supra* note 110.
119 Powell, *Leon* and *Sheppard* Conference Notes, *supra* note 110.
120 *Id.*
121 Brennan, *Sheppard* Conference Notes, *supra* note 110.
122 Powell, *Leon* and *Sheppard* Conference Notes, *supra* note 110.
123 *Id.*
124 Brennan, *Leon* Conference Notes, *supra* note 110.
125 Powell, *Leon* and *Sheppard* Conference Notes, *supra* note 110.
126 Brennan, *Sheppard* Conference Notes, *supra* note 110.
127 Powell, *Leon* and *Sheppard* Conference Notes, *supra* note 110.
128 Brennan, *Sheppard* Conference Notes, *supra* note 110.
129 *Id.*
130 Brennan, *Leon* Conference Notes, *supra* note 110.

therefore reach the good-faith issue."[131] On *Sheppard*, Rehnquist said he "would adopt a good-faith exception limited to the warrant situation—and not allow subjective good faith."[132] Stevens stated there were "no Fourth Amendment violations in these cases," and the Court "should not adopt a good-faith exception."[133] Referring to a speech retired Justice Potter Stewart had given at Columbia Law School on the exclusionary rule, Stevens said he agreed with Stewart's conclusion that a good-faith exception should not be adopted. He also noted that there is "greater reason to be concerned with the warrant and the power of a magistrate."[134] Finally, Stevens said the "need for good faith is perhaps greater in warrantless searches."[135] O'Connor ended the discussion. Regarding *Sheppard*, she stated the Court "could reverse without addressing the good-faith exception. If a 'good-faith' test were applied to *Sheppard*, I can't say that the police acted in objective good faith."[136] But O'Connor said she would "go along with a good-faith exception on an objective standard."[137] She noted her agreement "with what Harry Blackmun and Lewis Powell said generally."[138] On *Leon*, O'Connor noted: "It is time to restrict the scope of the exclusionary rule. The Founders relied on tort law to remedy search and seizure violations, as did the English. A good-faith exception will require an adjustment of tort remedies to replace the exclusionary rule."[139] Finally, she noted that *Gates* and *Franks v. Delaware* have "alleviated some of the abuses of the exclusionary rule."[140]

When all was said and done, the justices were unanimous in voting to reverse both *Leon* and *Sheppard*. Powell's conference notes show that the vote was nine to zero for reversal in *Sheppard*.[141] The Court could easily have avoided the good-faith issue in *Sheppard*. As Professors LaFave and Alschuler would note a few months later in separate articles, the lower courts had already established that when an affidavit is attached to a warrant that improperly described the items to be seized, reference to the affidavit's specificity can cure the constitutional defect in the warrant.[142] Even Sheppard's lawyer, John Reinstein, an experienced civil liberties litigator, admitted during the oral argument that if the judge had indicated somewhere in the warrant that he intended to adopt the affidavit as a substitute for describing the items to be seized, that action would make

---

131 *Id.*
132 Brennan, *Sheppard* Conference Notes, *supra* note 110.
133 Powell, *Leon* and *Sheppard* Conference Notes, *supra* note 110.
134 *Id.*
135 Brennan, *Leon* Conference Notes, *supra* note 110.
136 Powell, *Leon* and *Sheppard* Conference Notes, *supra* note 110.
137 *Id.*
138 *Id.*
139 Brennan, *Leon* Conference Notes, *supra* note 110.
140 Powell, *Leon* and *Sheppard* Conference Notes, *supra* note 110.
141 *Id.*
142 Albert W. Alschuler, *"Close Enough For Government Work": The Exclusionary Rule After* Leon, 1984 SUP. CT. REV. 309, 343–44; Wayne R. LaFave, *"The Seductive Call of Expediency":* United States v. Leon, *Its Rationale and Ramifications*, 1984 U. ILL. L. REV. 895, 911.

the warrant valid.[143] Thus, under the facts in *Sheppard*, the Court could have ruled "that the lack of a specific reference or a staple should not be determinative" when the officer who conducted the search was also the affiant, "and he acted on the basis of his words in the affidavit rather than the improper words printed on the warrant."[144]

Similarly, in *Leon*, none of the justices expressly voted to affirm the Ninth Circuit's ruling. *Leon* could have been sent back to the Ninth Circuit to allow that court the opportunity to reconsider the validity of the warrant under *Gates*'s new totality of the circumstances test; three justices favored this result: Brennan, Marshall, and Stevens.[145] Alternatively, the Court itself could have decided the warrant was valid under the *Gates* test; three justices, Blackmun, Powell, and O'Connor, expressly stated the Court could reverse without deciding the good-faith issue.

Under any of these alternatives, the Court could have refrained from deciding whether the exclusionary rule should be modified, which would have been consistent with the Court's tradition of avoiding ruling on constitutional questions unless necessary to decide a case. Moreover, any of these alternatives would have allowed the Court to avoid the awkward position of imposing a good-faith exception in two cases where most, if not all, of the justices agreed there was no Fourth Amendment violation. But as Stevens commented in his separate opinion, six justices were "determined" to decide *Leon* and *Sheppard* on the "broadest possible grounds."[146] That approach, Stevens observed, was "utterly at odds with the Court's traditional practice as well as any principled notion of judicial restraint."[147]

White wrote the opinion for the Court in both *Leon* and *Sheppard*. *Leon* was the lead case, and its holding was applied to the facts of *Sheppard*. *Leon* held that exclusionary rule does not forbid the use in the prosecution's case-in-chief of evidence obtained by police acting in reasonable reliance on a search warrant issued by a judge, but later determined to be unsupported by probable cause. Several of the themes of White's opinions in *Gates* and *Stone v. Powell* were repeated in *Leon*. As Powell's law clerk, Rob Couch, told his boss, in *Leon*, White often "cites his own concurring and dissenting opinions in prior

---

143 Transcript of Oral Argument at 28-29, Massachusetts v. Sheppard, 468 U.S. 981 (1984) (No. 82-963); *see also Sheppard*, 468 U.S. at 990 n.7.

144 LaFave, *supra* note 142, at 911. Indeed, a Court less eager to decide the good faith question could have found the search in *Sheppard* constitutional, despite the technical defect in the warrant. *See* Silas Wasserstrom & William J. Mertens, *The Exclusionary Rule on the Scaffold: But Was It a Fair Trial?*, 22 AM. CRIM. L. REV. 85, 99-101 (1984) (explaining that in *Sheppard*, the police obtained a warrant before searching, and the warrant was supported by probable cause established in the affidavit; the magistrate reviewed the affidavit before authorizing the search; the search and seizure were confined to those areas and items specified in the affidavit; the technical error in the warrant did not make the search unreasonable; and the magistrate's error, unlike a lack of probable cause, did not cause an unconstitutional search).

145 *See* United States v. Leon, 468 U.S. 897, 961-62 (1984) (Stevens, J., dissenting); *id.* at 959 (Brennan, J., dissenting).

146 *Id.* at 962 (Stevens, J., dissenting).

147 *Id.*

cases. Many times, those opinions are the only authority available for the proposition he is trying to support."[148] White's writing style prompted Couch to comment: "While reading the opinion, I sometimes got the feeling that Justice White was saying 'I told you so.'"[149]

But it was not White's blunt writing style that made *Leon* an extremely important and pivotal ruling in the Court's exclusionary jurisprudence. Like *Wolf*'s view of the exclusionary rule, *Leon*'s analysis of the rule was unprecedented. It fundamentally altered how the Court would approach future cases involving Fourth Amendment violations. The good-faith exception embraced in *Leon*, although announced in a case involving a defective judicial warrant, was capable of expansive growth beyond contexts involving unlawful warrants. The logic of *Leon*'s good-faith exception, as White explained in his opinions in *Gates* and *Stone v. Powell*, was broad enough to encompass other "reasonable mistakes" by the police. *Leon*'s good-faith exception, for instance, could encompass situations where police search a car, execute a warrantless arrest, or perform an investigative detention and frisk, all of which are permissible without a judicial warrant. Indeed, the natural and logical endpoint of the good-faith exception outlined in *Leon* would ultimately embrace most, if not all, reasonable mistakes by police that violate the Fourth Amendment and would limit the exclusionary rule to cases of deliberate and egregious police misconduct, which was the argument urged by the Solicitor General in *Leon*.[150] This, of course, was the same position White proposed in his *Stone v. Powell* dissent.

Leon and *Sheppard* Opinions

Leon ruled that when police reasonably rely on a facially valid search warrant, the evidence obtained is admissible in the prosecution's case-in-chief, even when the warrant is later shown to be constitutionally invalid. While sometimes referring to the "good faith" of police officers, White's opinion made plain that the subjective good faith of officers was irrelevant to the standard announced by the Court. He stated, "We emphasize that the standard of reasonableness we adopt is an objective one,"[151] meaning *Leon*'s "good faith" standard focused on the "reasonably well-trained officer"[152] and "requires officers to have a reasonable knowledge of what the law prohibits."[153]

White's opinion did not abolish the exclusionary rule—even in cases where police obtain judicial warrants. He explained that exclusion remained an "appropriate remedy"

148 Rob Couch, Memorandum to Lewis Powell on *United States v. Leon* (Feb. 24, 1984), Powell Papers, Box 109.

149 *Id.*

150 Brief for the United States, *supra* note 79, at 57.

151 *Leon*, 468 U.S. at 919 n.20.

152 *Id.* at 922 n.23.

153 *Id.* at 920 n.20.

in four scenarios.[154] First, if a judge issues a warrant based on false statements deliberately or recklessly made in a police affidavit, the good-faith exception will not apply. Second, the exception does not apply where the judge "wholly abandoned his judicial role" and, in effect, becomes part of the law enforcement team. Under such circumstances, a reasonably well-trained officer cannot rely on that warrant.[155] Third, police cannot rely on a warrant "'so lacking in indicia of probable cause as to render official belief in its existence entirely unreasonable.'"[156] Finally, if the warrant is "so facially deficient" as to be invalid—for example, it fails to particularize the place to be searched or things to be seized, the good-faith exception is unavailable.[157] But beyond these four "unusual cases," White signaled that motions to suppress should rarely be granted when police obtain warrants.[158]

Leon also planted the seeds for future expansion of the good-faith exception. Although the holdings in *Leon* and *Sheppard* were limited to cases where police obtained warrants, White sprinkled dicta throughout his opinion suggesting the good-faith exception would embrace various types of reasonable police mistakes.[159] This language was consistent with the expansive good-faith exception White had proposed in his separate opinions in *Gates* and *Stone v. Powell.* And should there be any doubt as to White's view on this matter, his characterization of *Leon*'s holding in a dissent he filed on the same day that *Leon* was decided makes his expansive viewpoint patently clear. *INS v. Lopez-Mendoza*[160] concerned whether evidence obtained pursuant to illegal warrantless arrests by federal border agents was admissible in deportation hearings. The Court held the exclusionary rule does not apply in such proceedings. White dissented because he thought the rule should apply in deportation hearings. White noted, however, that "if the agents neither knew nor should have known that they were acting contrary to the dictates of the Fourth Amendment, evidence will not be suppressed even if it is held that their conduct was illegal."[161] White cited *Leon* as the basis for this assertion. He wrote that *Leon* "held that the exclusionary rule is not applicable when officers are acting in objective good faith."[162]

---

154 *Id.* at 923.

155 *Id.*

156 *Id.* (quoting Brown v. Illinois, 422 U.S. 590, 610-11 (1975) (Powell, J., concurring in part)).

157 *Id.*

158 *Id.* at 918 (concluding that "suppression of evidence obtained pursuant to a warrant should be ordered only on a case-by-case basis and only in those unusual cases in which exclusion will further the purposes of the exclusionary rule"); *id.* at 922 ("'[S]earches pursuant to a warrant will rarely require any deep inquiry into reasonableness . . . .'" (quoting Illinois v. Gates, 462 U.S. 213, 267 (1983) (White, J., concurring in the judgment)) (alteration in original)). Whether *Leon* intended this list of four cases to be exhaustive, or merely illustrative, of exceptions to the good-faith standard is not clear from its opinion. Wasserstrom & Mertens, *supra* note 144, at 115-17.

159 *Leon*, 468 U.S. at 907–08, 918–19.

160 468 U.S. 1032 (1984).

161 *Id.* at 1056 (White, J., dissenting).

162 *Id.*

Thus, at least in White's view, the "holding" in *Leon* covered every type of good-faith or reasonable mistake by law enforcement officers.

Finally, applying the principles outlined in *Leon*, the Court concluded that the unconstitutional police conduct in *Leon* and *Sheppard* easily satisfied the newly minted good-faith exception. The affidavit in *Leon* revealed the results of an extensive investigation and produced enough evidence that reasonably minded judges could differ over the existence of probable cause. Thus, the officers' reliance on the warrant subsequently issued was "objectively reasonable," and exclusion was unwarranted.[163] Likewise, in *Sheppard*, the police took "every step that could reasonably be expected of them."[164] The detective informed the judge about the problems on the warrant form. The judge assured the officer that the necessary changes would be made. Consequently, the Court concluded, suppression under these facts would not serve the deterrent purpose the exclusionary rule was designed to achieve.[165]

Much has been written about *Leon* and the good-faith exception to the exclusionary rule it created.[166] Here, three points about *Leon* are highlighted. First, the result in *Leon* was unprecedented, and its mode of analysis would prove to be crucial for future cases. The substance and tone of White's opinion was established quickly. Assertions were substituted for principled arguments. Evidence undermining the desired result was ignored or dismissed. And no effort was undertaken to explain why the Court's reasoning was consistent with the historical purposes of the Fourth Amendment. In short, White seemed interested only in the result.

Early in his opinion, White explains: "Whether the exclusionary sanction is appropriately imposed in a particular case, our decisions make clear, is 'an issue separate from the question whether the Fourth Amendment rights of the party seeking to invoke the rule were violated by police conduct.'"[167] Of course, a year earlier in his *Gates* opinion, White stated: "Our decisions concerning the scope of the exclusionary rule cannot be divorced from the Fourth Amendment . . . ."[168] White never paused to explain this inconsistency. Returning to the merits of *Leon*, White then explains that the balancing approach utilized in previous cases where the Court weighs the costs and benefits of exclusion in a particular context justifies modifying the exclusionary rule to allow the admission, in the prosecution's case-in-chief, of evidence "obtained in the reasonable good-faith belief that a search or seizure was in accord with the Fourth Amendment."[169]

---

163 *Leon*, 468 U.S. at 926.

164 Massachusetts v. Sheppard, 468 U.S. 981, 989 (1984).

165 *Id.* at 990–91.

166 For other informative articles on *Leon*, in addition to those already cited in this chapter, *see* Craig M. Bradley, *The "Good Faith Exception" Cases: Reasonable Exercises in Futility*, 60 Ind. L.J. 287 (1985); William C. Heffernan, *On Justifying Fourth Amendment Exclusion*, 1989 Wis. L. Rev. 1193; George C. Thomas, III & Barry S. Pollack, *Balancing the Fourth Amendment Scales: The Bad-Faith "Exception" to Exclusionary Rule Limitations*, 45 Hastings L.J. 21 (1993).

167 *Leon*, 468 U.S. at 906 (quoting Illinois v. Gates, 462 U.S. 213, 223 (1983)).

168 *Gates*, 462 U.S. at 249 (White, J., concurring in the judgment).

169 *Leon*, 468 U.S. at 909 (internal quotation marks and citation omitted).

Although White asserted that prior cases provide "strong support" for *Leon*'s modification of the exclusionary rule,[170] the Court's holding was not supported by earlier rulings. Prior to *Leon*, the Court had never permitted the introduction of illegally acquired evidence (taken from the defendant) during the direct phase of a criminal trial where the prosecution is seeking to establish the defendant's guilt. Prior cases like *Stone v. Powell*, *Janis*, and *Calandra*, which White cited in support, barred invocation of the exclusionary rule only in collateral contexts, such as habeas corpus proceedings, civil trials, and grand jury hearings. But as White recognized in another exclusionary rule case decided on the same day as *Leon*: "In all of these cases it was unquestioned that the illegally seized evidence would not be admissible in the case in chief of the proceeding for which the evidence was gathered; only its collateral use was permitted."[171] The rulings in *Stone v. Powell*, *Janis*, and *Calandra* were based on the conclusion that because unlawfully obtained evidence was already barred from the criminal trial, further exclusion in collateral proceedings would not provide sufficient additional deterrence. Put simply, although court watchers were not surprised by the result, as a matter of Fourth Amendment jurisprudence, *Leon* was a novel and pivotal case.

A second aspect of *Leon* that deserves attention is the Court's immunization of judicial errors from the exclusionary sanction. White wrote that the exclusionary rule is designed to deter law enforcement officers rather than judges' errors. He dismissed studies suggesting that judges sometimes act as rubber stamps for the police. And he found no basis for believing that suppression of evidence will have a deterrent impact on magistrates. Judicial officers, White insisted, "are not adjuncts to the law enforcement team; as neutral judicial officers, they have no stake in the outcome of particular criminal prosecutions."[172] The consequence of *Leon*'s logic regarding the errors of judges is that exclusion is forbidden when judges make constitutional mistakes.

The Court's decision to exempt judicial conduct as a target of the exclusionary rule, like its determination to allow the admission of illegally acquired evidence in the prosecution's case-in-chief, was new lawmaking.[173] Moreover, *Leon*'s reasoning concerning judges is odd on at least two fronts. First, the history of the Fourth Amendment and its text indisputably demonstrates the Framers' intent to ban warrants not supported by

---

170 *Id.* at 913.

171 INS v. Lopez-Mendoza, 468 U.S. 1032, 1053 (1984) (White, J., dissenting).

172 *Leon*, 468 U.S. at 917.

173 *See* James J. Tomkovicz, Constitutional Exclusion: The Rules, Rights, and Remedies That Strike the Balance Between Freedom and Order 53 n.248 (2011) (noting that while the deterrent goals of the exclusionary rule had always been framed in terms of police conduct, the Court had not ruled out deterring judicial errors as a proper goal of exclusion; "*Leon* marked the first announcement that deterring future judicial errors is not an aim of the exclusionary rule"). Furthermore, White's description of the "design" of the exclusionary rule – to deter police misconduct, rather than to deter judicial mistakes – shows how far the Court had distanced itself from the reasoning of *Boyd v. United States*, 116 U.S. 616 (1886) and *Weeks v. United States*, 232 U.S. 383 (1914). "When it was initially 'designed,' [the exclusionary rule] was seen as a constitutional requirement which vindicated the personal rights of the accused and preserved the integrity of the federal courts." Wasserstrom & Mertens, *supra* note 144, at 106.

probable cause. Scholars, who sharply differ over other aspects of search and seizure history, agree that the Framers intended to outlaw general warrants.[174] The clear language of the Fourth Amendment that "no Warrants shall issue, but upon probable cause" unmistakably memorializes this objective. Under *Leon*, however, evidence secured pursuant to an unconstitutional warrant is nevertheless admissible against a person whose Fourth Amendment rights were violated.

On a more practical level, *Leon* removes an effective device for reviewing the Fourth Amendment decisions of magistrates and providing constitutional guidance to judges and law enforcement officials generally. As Professor Alschuler has explained, before *Leon* the exclusionary rule supplied the mechanism for reviewing the issuance of arrest and search warrants:

> Through the review mechanism established by the exclusionary rule, courts had developed a variety of familiar rules to guide the determination of probable cause—rules, for example, concerning the significance of an informant's admission against penal interest, the presumed reliability of a "citizen informant," the need to confirm the statements of an anonymous informant through independent investigation before issuing a warrant or conducting a search, the propriety of considering hearsay evidence in deciding whether to issue a search or arrest warrant, and the inadequacy of an affidavit that fails to specify the underlying circumstances in sufficient detail to enable a magistrate to make an independent determination of probable cause.[175]

After *Leon*, the review process boils down to asking whether the police reasonably relied upon a warrant, which White acknowledges, will not require a lot of work from judges or prosecutors.[176] But White pays no attention to the irony his holding creates. "The issuance of warrants without probable cause was one of the grievances of the American Revolution, and it was an evil that the framers of the Constitution

---

[174] *Compare* William J. Cuddihy, The Fourth Amendment: Origins and Original Meaning 602-1791, at 739–72 (2009) (finding that the protection intended by the Fourth Amendment is much broader than the protection granted by the Warrant Clause and that this broader protection captures many kinds of searches and seizures that the Framers found to be unreasonable), *with* Thomas Y. Davies, *Recovering the Original Fourth Amendment*, 98 Mich. L. Rev. 547, 551 (1999) (explaining that the primary concern of the Framers was the need to ban house searches under general warrants; "the Framers clearly understood the warrant standards to be the operative content of the Fourth Amendment").

[175] Alschuler, *supra* note 142, at 312–13 (footnotes omitted). *See also* Carol S. Steiker, *Second Thoughts About First Principles*, 107 Harv. L. Rev. 820, 851 (1994) (explaining how the exclusionary rule "involves the courts in the ongoing project of developing a detailed body of Fourth Amendment law"); William J. Stuntz, *The Virtues and Vices of the Exclusionary Rule*, 20 Harv. J.L. & Pub. Pol'y 443, 446 (1997) (noting that the virtues of exclusion – deterring police misconduct without the overdeterrence caused by officer or governmental damages liability, "coupled with the ability to define the law—are very substantial indeed").

[176] *Leon*, 468 U.S. at 924 ("[T]he good-faith exception ... should not be difficult to apply in practice. When officers have acted pursuant to a warrant, the prosecution should ordinarily be able to establish objective good faith without a substantial expenditure of judicial time.").

condemned unmistakably."[177] After *Leon*, "virtually the only check on the issuance of a warrant without probable cause is the conscience of a single magistrate."[178]

Last, on a related note, *Leon* leaves victims of Fourth Amendment violations without any remedy whatsoever. Opponents of the exclusionary rule contend that rather than provide guilty defendants the windfall of suppressing probative evidence in criminal trials, the victims of illegal searches should do what the Framers would have done when their Fourth Amendment rights were violated: bring a civil rights lawsuit seeking monetary damages. For example, O'Connor made this point in the *Leon* conference.[179] The problem with this proposed solution is that if Alberto Leon and his codefendants had consulted a competent lawyer about the prospects for a successful federal civil rights lawsuit against the police who illegally searched their homes and possessions, he would have been told the following: *Leon*'s objective reasonableness test is also the test used to determine whether police officers are liable in civil lawsuits for violating the rights of citizens. Thus, in order for Leon to win his lawsuit, a judge would have to find that the officer who searched Leon's home would have known that his affidavit failed to establish probable cause and that he should not have applied for the warrant.[180] Because the Court had already found the police acted reasonably in relying on the warrant in the criminal context, there was no way for Leon to succeed in the civil context. Put simply, even though Leon's constitutional rights had been violated, no court *anywhere* could provide a remedy. Professor Donald Dripps, who defends the result in *Leon* on other grounds, characterizes this reality as probably the most troubling aspect of *Leon*: "In effect, the Court maintains that searches pursuant to defective warrants violate the Fourth Amendment, but that nothing happens when such violations take place."[181]

* * *

On the same day *Leon* and *Sheppard* were decided, the Court also decided *INS v. Lopez-Mendoza*.[182] At issue was whether the exclusionary rule applied in deportation hearings. Two Mexican residents, Adan Lopez-Mendoza and Elias Sandoval-Sanchez, were arrested by Immigration and Naturalization Service (INS) officers in separate cases while working in the United States. After their arrests, both men were subject to deportation charges. Lopez-Mendoza made a motion to terminate the deportation proceeding claiming that he had been illegally arrested. Sandoval-Sanchez also contested the legality of his arrest, and moved to suppress a statement he had given to the officers after his arrest. The Court of Appeals for the Ninth Circuit ruled in favor of both men and held that the exclusionary rule applies in deportation hearings.[183] After the Court took the

[177] Alschuler, *supra* note 142, at 322.

[178] *Id.*

[179] *See* Brennan, *Leon* Conference Notes, *supra* note 110.

[180] *See* Malley v. Briggs, 475 U.S. 335 (1986).

[181] Donald Dripps, *Living with* Leon, 95 YALE L.J. 906, 934 (1986).

[182] 468 U.S. 1032 (1984).

[183] *Id.* at 1034–38.

case, the Solicitor General's office insisted reversal was required because the Court had never applied the rule to civil proceedings.[184] Moreover, the government argued that permitting invocation of the rule in deportation hearings would unduly burden the INS.[185]

Burger began the *Lopez-Mendoza* conference discussion by stating that deportation cases are not like criminal cases, despite the hardship imposed on illegal aliens. Burger said there is "no basis for extending the exclusionary rule to non-criminal cases."[186] Burger asserted the burden on the immigration service imposed by the exclusionary rule would be "enormous."[187] He stated: "I wouldn't extend the exclusionary rule to any civil proceedings."[188] Burger voted to reverse.[189]

Brennan said that the reasoning of *Janis*, which held that the exclusionary rule could not be invoked in a federal tax proceeding to forbid the use of evidence unlawfully seized by a state police officer, supported application of the rule in this case. Brennan emphasized three points: First, "unlike *Janis*, there is a direct connection between the conduct of INS agents and the application of the exclusionary rule in deportation proceedings."[190] The mission of the INS "is to see to it that undocumented aliens are deported; criminal prosecutions against deportable aliens are very rare, and the deportation hearing is therefore the only forum in which the agency's efforts are tested."[191] Second, "the fact that the INS is a single, integrated federal agency actually weighs in favor of applying the rule here.... We can be especially confident that applying the exclusionary rule will yield substantial benefits in terms of deterring unconstitutional law-enforcement activity."[192] Finally, Brennan noted that the rule had applied in deportation proceedings until 1979. In that year, the Board of Immigration Appeals ruled that the rule was inappropriate in deportation hearings. Brennan voted to affirm.[193]

White spoke next. In 1976, White openly stated his uncertainty over whether he would have joined the Court's opinion in *Mapp*. He also expressed his unwillingness to overrule *Weeks* or *Mapp* but did believe the exclusionary rule should be modified by a good-faith exception. Now, White told his colleagues that he "would not have voted for *Mapp* or *Weeks*."[194] White continued: "I am no fan of the exclusionary rule, but as long as we have it and we regard deterrence as the only factor to be considered, I don't see how

184 Brief for the Petitioner at 21-22, *Lopez-Mendoza*, 468 U.S. 1032 (No. 83-491).

185 *Id.* at 31-33.

186 Lewis Powell, Conference Notes on *INS v. Lopez-Mendoza* (Apr. 20, 1984) [hereinafter Powell, *Lopez-Mendoza* Conference Notes], Powell Papers, Box 112.

187 *Id.*

188 *Id.*

189 *Id.*

190 Dickson, *supra* note 11, at 497.

191 *Id.*

192 *Id.*

193 *Id.*

194 Harry Blackmun, Conference Notes on *INS v. Lopez-Mendoza* (Apr. 20, 1984) [hereinafter Blackmun, *Lopez-Mendoza* Conference Notes], Blackmun Papers, Box 407.

we can fail to apply it here."[195] White considered immigration agents "law enforcement officers" who could be deterred, and concluded "until we overrule it, it applies here."[196] According to White, "there is no principled way to distinguish" INS officers and police officers for purposes of the exclusionary rule.[197] White added that the "consequences to aliens are severe."[198] He voted to affirm, as did Marshall.[199]

Blackmun considered deportation hearings "a civil proceeding" and said he would not vote to "extend a judge-made rule to cover it."[200] He thought it "a serious step" to extend the exclusionary rule in deportation hearings and said it would "create a special class of privileged illegal aliens."[201] He felt the "societal costs would be great."[202] Blackmun voted to reverse, as did Powell who spoke next. In a preconference memo he dictated, Powell wrote that the question confronting the Court was "straightforward, important, and—at least for me at this time—not difficult to answer."[203] After outlining the arguments for both sides, Powell ended his memo with the observation that the lower court's ruling was theoretically sound: "If the Fourth Amendment applies to aliens, the exclusionary rule certainly would protect them in a criminal proceedings [sic]. The question therefore, is whether the rationale of the rule applies with equal force in a civil proceedings [sic]. I am inclined to think not."[204]

By the time of the *Lopez-Mendoza* conference discussion, Powell still opposed exclusion. His comments focused less on the exclusionary rule and more on the politics of illegal immigration. It was important to Powell that the typical illegal alien arrested by border agents "is *not* faced with imprisonment. He has the option of returning to his country. The government interest is *not* in punishing—only in sending illegals home."[205] There is "no criminal penalty—not even a 'record' of being charged with crime."[206] Powell thought the federal government "is generous in *not* punishing for illegal entry."[207] Powell observed that "the exclusionary rule never extended to civil proceedings," and that its "deterrence rationale is weak here."[208] Finally, Powell considered the public interest in

---

195 Dickson, *supra* note 11, at 497.

196 Blackmun, *Lopez-Mendoza* Conference Notes, *supra* note 194.

197 Powell, *Lopez-Mendoza* Conference Notes, *supra* note 186.

198 *Id.*

199 *Id.*

200 William J. Brennan, Jr., Conference Notes on *INS v. Lopez-Mendoza* (undated) [hereinafter Brennan, *Lopez-Mendoza* Conference Notes], Brennan Papers, Box I: 628.

201 Powell, *Lopez-Mendoza* Conference Notes, *supra* note 186.

202 *Id.*

203 Lewis Powell, Memorandum on *INS v. Mendoza* and *Sandoval Sanchez* 1 (Apr. 13, 1984), Powell Papers, Box 112.

204 *Id.* at 5.

205 Lewis Powell, Handwritten Notes on *INS v. Lopez-Mendoza* (undated) [hereinafter Powell, *Lopez-Mendoza* Handwritten Notes], Powell Papers, Box 112.

206 Powell, *Lopez-Mendoza* Conference Notes, *supra* note 186.

207 *Id.*

208 *Id.*

stemming illegal immigration important. He noted, "illegals hold millions of jobs—with unemployment high."[209]

Rehnquist's views were upfront: "Don't let the exclusionary rule spread is my base belief."[210] Application of the rule "would make another layer of issues" at deportation proceedings.[211] Rehnquist concluded, "a *Janis* cost-benefit analysis comes out in favor of INS."[212] He voted to reverse. Stevens voted to affirm. He was persuaded that the rule had been applied in deportation hearings prior to 1979. He stated: "[T]he government's argument that this is now a flood is purely phony. A cost-benefit analysis tips in favor of applying the exclusionary rule."[213] O'Connor spoke last and provided the fifth vote to reverse: "Even if the exclusionary rule has been applied, we should not compel it. There could be a violation so severe as to amount to a due process violation."[214] That would present a "different situation."[215] Ultimately, the Court voted five to four to reverse.

O'Connor was assigned the opinion, and she sent Blackmun a draft to "preview" because she relied primarily on *Janis*, which Blackmun authored.[216] But there were good reasons to distinguish *Janis* from *Lopez-Mendoza*. *Janis* ultimately rested on Blackmun's "common sense" conclusion that exclusion would have no deterrent impact when the illegally acquired evidence is used in a forum that "falls outside the offending officer's zone of primary interest."[217] *Janis* reasoned that the deterrent impact of excluding evidence in a civil tax proceeding would be minimal because the state police officer would already be deterred by the fact that any evidence he illegally acquired would be suppressed in both state and federal criminal prosecutions.

In contrast, the job of INS agents is to discover illegal aliens in order to deport them. Also, INS agents are employed by the same sovereign that seeks to use the fruit of the illegal conduct. Put simply, unlike in *Janis*, in *Lopez-Mendoza* there was a direct connection between the constitutional violation and the government agency that seeks to use the fruits of the constitutional violation. *Janis* specifically left open whether the exclusionary rule would apply to intra-sovereign violations.[218]

Moreover, *Janis* involved a case where the officer who violated the Fourth Amendment acted in good-faith reliance on a warrant issued by a judge that was later found unlawful. Although no reference was made of that fact in *Janis*'s holding, the good faith of the officer's conduct seemed an important factor to several justices. Blackmun mentioned it

---

209 Powell, *Lopez-Mendoza* Handwritten Notes, *supra* note 205.

210 Brennan, *Lopez-Mendoza* Conference Notes, *supra* note 200.

211 Blackmun, *Lopez-Mendoza* Conference Notes, *supra* note 194.

212 Brennan, *Lopez-Mendoza* Conference Notes, *supra* note 200.

213 *Id.*

214 Powell, *Lopez-Mendoza* Conference Notes, *supra* note 186.

215 *Id.*

216 Sandra Day O'Connor, Letter to Harry Blackmun on *INS v. Lopez-Mendoza* (May 22, 1984), Blackmun Papers, Box 407.

217 United States v. Janis, 428 U.S. 433, 457–58 (1976).

218 *Id.* at 455 n.31.

in his preconference notes.[219] So did both Powell and Rehnquist during the *Janis* conference. Indeed, Powell stated he wanted the Court to "write narrowly," noting that the IRS was not responsible for the illegal seizure, and there was no proof of collaboration between the offending officer and the IRS.[220] Thus, *Janis* was a very different case from *Lopez-Mendoza,* or so the Court could have determined if it had wanted to distinguish the two.

Principled legal analysis, however, was not the focus of the Court; forbidding use of the exclusionary rule in civil proceedings was the objective. Despite the factual and legal differences between *Janis* and *Lopez-Mendoza*, O'Connor's opinion concluded that *Janis*'s cost-benefit analysis demanded that the rule not apply in deportation hearings. After reviewing O'Connor's draft opinion, Blackmun's law clerk, knowing that Blackmun opposed exclusion, encouraged Blackmun to await the dissent before casting his final vote to join O'Connor's opinion. The law clerk thought O'Connor had circulated the draft to Blackmun because she viewed him as the crucial fifth vote for a majority. Among other things, the law clerk took issue with O'Connor's argument that exclusion would have a minimal deterrent impact because the chances of a particular arrestee invoking it were small. This assertion, Blackmun's clerk believed, conflicted with O'Connor's argument that application of the rule in deportation hearings would bog down the process.[221] This conflict apparently did not bother Blackmun because he joined O'Connor's opinion without objection, and before reading the dissent.[222]

O'Connor's published opinion in *Lopez-Mendoza* certainly achieves the result desired by the majority: forbidding extension of the exclusionary rule to any civil proceeding. But besides reaching that outcome, the opinion is unconnected to the legal reasoning of past cases and does not reflect any legal principles, other than opposition to the exclusionary rule. The exceptions to the exclusionary rule that the Burger Court had constructed in prior cases were obviously unavailable in *Lopez-Mendoza*. There was no proof the INS officers had acted in a mistaken but good-faith manner when arresting the illegal aliens. Nor did the case remotely resemble the exception the Court created when it ruled in several cases that the exclusionary rule was inapplicable in collateral proceedings like grand juries, habeas corpus hearings, and federal tax proceedings. There was nothing "collateral" about deportation proceedings. Indeed, O'Connor's opinion acknowledges that the primary objective of INS officers is to gather evidence for use in deportation hearings. And unlike the situation in *Janis* where a state police officer unlawfully acquired evidence that was originally sought for a criminal prosecution, but was later used in a federal civil tax proceeding, here O'Connor concedes that the INS

---

219 Harry Blackmun, Memorandum on *United States v. Janis* 9 (Dec. 5, 1975), Blackmun Papers, Box 219.

220 Lewis Powell, Conference Notes on *United States v. Janis* (Dec. 10, 1975), Powell Papers, Box 30.

221 Law Clerk, Memorandum to Harry Blackmun on *INS v. Lopez-Mendoza* 1-2 (May 23, 1984), Blackmun Papers, Box 407.

222 Harry Blackmun, Letter to Sandra Day O'Connor on *INS v. Lopez-Mendoza* (May 29, 1984), Blackmun Papers, Box 407.

officers "who effect the unlawful arrest are the same officials who subsequently bring the deportation action."[223]

O'Connor acknowledges that *Janis* recognized that in such circumstances exclusion is likely to have a deterrent impact.[224] Nevertheless, she finds that other factors reduce the deterrent effect of exclusion. First, she notes illegal aliens will still be deported when other lawfully obtained evidence is sufficient to support deportation.[225] Second, she states that because over 97.5 percent of the persons arrested for being in the country illegally agree to voluntary deportation, illegal aliens are unlikely to invoke the exclusionary rule. Accordingly, she explains: "In these circumstances, the arresting officer is most unlikely to shape his conduct in anticipation of the exclusion of evidence at a formal deportation hearing."[226] Third, O'Connor notes the INS has a "comprehensive scheme" for deterring Fourth Amendment offenses.[227] Finally, she concludes that exclusion will have a reduced deterrent impact due to the availability of alternative remedies for institutional practices of the INS that violate the Fourth Amendment.[228]

It is hard to take this reasoning seriously. O'Connor's first reason for barring suppression—the fact that illegal aliens will still be deported when there is sufficient lawful evidence to support deportation—is true but irrelevant. Most criminal defendants who raise successful Fourth Amendment claims are eventually convicted, but the Court has never relied on that fact as a reason for prohibiting invocation of the exclusionary rule in criminal trials. Likewise, the fact that the overwhelming majority of aliens arrested by INS agents choose voluntary deportation does not prove that deterrence is reduced. As White's dissent countered, "that fact no more diminishes the importance of the exclusionary sanction than the fact that many criminal defendants plead guilty dilutes the rule's deterrent effect in criminal cases."[229] O'Connor's other reasons for finding little deterrent value from exclusion—the "comprehensive scheme" the INS had put in place and the availability of "alternative remedies"—were cosmetic rather than substantive. No officer had ever been disciplined by the INS for Fourth Amendment violations. And the notion that someone like Lopez-Mendoza, after being deported back to Mexico, is going to bring a lawsuit against the INS for its institutional practices is laughable. The prospect of such legal action, White correctly commented, is unlikely to "strike fear into the hearts of those who enforce the Nation's immigration laws."[230]

---

[223] INS v. Lopez-Mendoza, 468 U.S. 1032, 1043 (1984). In other words, "the deportation hearing is to the INS agent what the criminal trial is to the police." Wasserstrom & Mertens, *supra* note 144, at 91 (footnote omitted).

[224] *Lopez-Mendoza*, 468 U.S. at 1043.

[225] *Id.*

[226] *Id.* at 1044.

[227] *Id.*

[228] *Id.* at 1045.

[229] *Id.* at 1054 (White, J., dissenting).

[230] *Id.* at 1055. Research reveals no reported cases in the years prior to and following *Lopez-Mendoza* in which an alien unlawfully in the country suffered a Fourth Amendment violation at the hands of the INS, was

On the "costs" side of her balancing analysis, O'Connor made three points. Allowing use of the exclusionary rule in deportation proceedings would produce "unusual and significant" costs.[231] First, successful invocation of the rule would "require the courts to close their eyes to ongoing violations of the law."[232] Second, the possibility of even occasional Fourth Amendment challenges "might significantly change and complicate the character" of deportation hearings.[233] Finally, because of the chaotic circumstances surrounding arrests of many illegal aliens, INS officers "cannot be expected to compile elaborate, contemporaneous, written reports detailing the circumstance of every arrest."[234] Under these conditions, O'Connor worried that application of the rule "might" result in the exclusion of large amounts of evidence lawfully obtained.[235]

O'Connor's concern about courts ignoring continuing violations of the immigration laws, which would thereby create a "special class" of illegal aliens who continue to roam throughout the nation is a colorful description but not relevant to the question addressed by the Court. First, the Court had not decided whether an illegal alien's remaining in the country after an unlawful entry is a continuing or a completed crime. And even if an illegal alien's presence inside the country was a continuing crime, that fact was irrelevant to the issue of whether exclusion at deportation hearings would deter INS agents from violating the Fourth Amendment. Further, the concern about complicating deportation proceedings due to the even occasional invocation of the exclusionary rule was inconsistent with O'Connor's earlier assertions that illegal aliens are unlikely to raise Fourth Amendment challenges, and that the INS already provides sufficient training to deter illegal searches and seizures. If very few aliens will invoke the rule, only a few proceedings would be disrupted by Fourth Amendment claims. And if INS officers are properly trained and disciplined for their offenses, the judiciary should expect few hearings on the issue of exclusion.

---

deported, and subsequently brought a *Bivens* action against the responsible federal officers. The court of appeals had found the possibility of such a suit so unlikely as to be an "unrealistic and unacceptable" alternative to the exclusionary rule. Lopez-Mendoza v. INS, 705 F.2d 1059, 1073 (9th Cir. 1983). O'Connor's opinion offered no reason to dispute the appellate court's conclusion.

Moreover, as other scholars have explained, the comprehensive scheme instituted by the INS was a "reason for retaining the exclusionary rule, not for abandoning it" in deportation hearings:

> This scheme was instituted at a time when it was generally assumed that the exclusionary rule did apply in deportation proceedings; . . . the rule created the incentives for the agency to ensure that its officers comply with the law. Eliminating the exclusionary rule because law enforcement agencies have instituted administrative mechanisms for punishing fourth amendment violations is like cutting off a diabetic's insulin supply because his illness seems to be under control.

Wasserstrom & Mertens, *supra* note 144, at 129.

[231] *Lopez-Mendoza*, 468 U.S. at 1046.

[232] *Id.*

[233] *Id.* at 1048–49.

[234] *Id.* at 1049.

[235] *Id.*

Moreover, O'Connor's concern that border agents cannot be expected to keep up with the paperwork related to arrests occurring under "crowded and confused circumstances,"[236] which might mean the loss of large amounts of lawfully obtained evidence if exclusion were available, exposes the justices' real motivations in these cases. Imagine a small, local police department, saddled with budget cuts, the loss of officers from layoffs, and soaring crime rates in its jurisdiction. Would the Court take seriously the argument that officers from this department "cannot be expected to compile elaborate, contemporaneous, written reports detailing the circumstances of every arrest," and thus evidence acquired from illegal searches and seizures effectuated by this department should not be subject to exclusion? Probably not. As White's dissent noted, O'Connor's concerns amount to "a rejection of the application of the Fourth Amendment to the activities of INS agents."[237] One might surmise that, at bottom, the result in *Lopez-Mendoza* rests on the unspoken belief that illegal aliens are undeserving of Fourth Amendment protection.

In the mid-1970s, the Burger Court loosened constitutional rules on INS officers due to the legitimate needs of the government in enforcing the immigration laws and the difficulty of policing a two-thousand-mile border with Mexico. The Court made it easier for officers to stop vehicles traveling near the border and permitted officers to interrogate the occupants of vehicles based on the ancestry of persons inside the vehicles.[238] In the same Term that *Lopez-Mendoza* was announced, the Court also ruled that INS officers do not trigger Fourth Amendment protections when they enter factories and other workplaces to interrogate workers about their immigration status.[239] Thus, the worries voiced in *Lopez-Mendoza* about further burdening INS officers seemed strained. As a law clerk told Blackmun: "Because the standards are so low, it is hardly placing an onerous burden on the INS to force it to abide by those standards or forgo use of evidence obtained in an illegal manner."[240]

To be sure, *Lopez-Mendoza* assumed that illegal aliens are protected by the Fourth Amendment while in this country. But six years later, the Court was more candid about its views on whether illegal aliens are actually protected by the Fourth Amendment when it noted that statements from *Lopez-Mendoza* were "not dispositive of how the Court would rule on a Fourth Amendment claim by illegal aliens in the United States if such a claim were squarely before us."[241] One scholar, doubtful of the benefits of exclusion, reacted to this statement by observing that the "practical consequence, if not the

---

236 *Id.*

237 *Id.* at 1059 (White, J., dissenting).

238 *See* United States v. Martinez-Fuerte, 428 U.S. 543 (1976); United States v. Brignoni-Ponce, 422 U.S. 873 (1975).

239 INS v. Delgado, 466 U.S. 210 (1984).

240 Law Clerk, Memorandum to Harry Blackmun on *INS v. Lopez-Mendoza* 18 (Apr. 16, 1984), Blackmun Papers, Box 407.

241 United States v. Verdugo-Urquidez, 494 U.S. 259, 272 (1990).

intent," of *Lopez-Mendoza* and the Court's subsequent cases is "the creation of an illegal alien exception to the Fourth Amendment."[242]

Finally, after spending over fifteen pages slamming the door on the ability of illegal aliens to invoke the exclusionary rule in deportation hearings, O'Connor nonetheless appears to leave the door slightly ajar. In Part V of her opinion, which Burger refused to join without explanation, O'Connor stated that the Court's "conclusions concerning the exclusionary rule's value might change, if there developed good reason to believe that Fourth Amendment violations by INS officers were widespread."[243] She also left open whether exclusion was appropriate in cases of "egregious violations of Fourth Amendment or other liberties that might transgress notions of fundamental fairness and undermine the probative value of the evidence obtained."[244]

The point of this section of O'Connor's opinion is unclear. It was classic obiter dicta. Perhaps it was an early example of O'Connor's style of judging: she liked to split the difference.[245] After making clear that evidence from garden-variety Fourth Amendment violations was always admissible in deportation hearings, O'Connor dangled the remote chance that evidence from an outlandish intrusion might warrant a different result.

Although the public was unaware of Burger's reason for not joining Part V, he told O'Connor that he saw "no point in intimating that constitutional adjudication will weave and bob with some sort of Gallup Poll reflection of how many [Fourth] [A]mendment violations occur."[246] Burger's complaint was consistent with his antipathy toward suppression in general, but he had a valid point. O'Connor did not explain how the justices (or anyone else) would know whether INS officers were engaged in "widespread" Fourth Amendment violations particularly since illegal aliens had no incentive to raise such claims now that the exclusionary rule was inoperable in deportation proceedings.

Her second point—the possibility of exclusion for "egregious" violations of "Fourth Amendment or other liberties"—raised more questions than it provided answers. The reference to "fundamental fairness" suggests that exclusion might be warranted for INS searches and seizures that violate Due Process protections. But O'Connor's use of the conjunction "and" might mean that exclusion is proper only when the constitutional offense both violates Due Process rights *and* produces evidence of dubious reliability: for example, a coerced statement. The problem here is that pure Fourth Amendment violations rarely, if ever, result in the discovery of non-probative evidence. O'Connor's cite to *Rochin v. California* did not clarify her intentions or thoughts. The Court suppressed the evidence in *Rochin* after ruling that an illegal stomach pump violated Due Process. But the evidence produced by the offense—capsules containing morphine—was highly

---

242 Christopher Slobogin, *The Poverty Exception to the Fourth Amendment*, 55 FLA. L. REV. 391, 396 (2003).

243 INS v. Lopez-Mendoza, 468 U.S. 1032, 1050 (1984).

244 *Id.* at 1050–51.

245 *See* JEFFREY TOOBIN, THE NINE: INSIDE THE SECRET WORLD OF THE SUPREME COURT 204 (2007).

246 Warren Burger, Letter to Sandra Day O'Connor on *INS v. Lopez-Mendoza* (June 25, 1984), Blackmun Papers, Box 407.

probative of the crime that Rochin was alleged to have committed. Moreover, the Court had long ago confined the rule announced in *Rochin* to physical violence exerted by governmental officials.

Thus, a lower court judge reading Part V might understand that if INS officers physically assault an alien, which causes the alien to make an incriminating statement, that statement might be subject to exclusion under O'Connor's dicta. But would an arbitrary stop of a Hispanic male on the streets of Los Angeles or Phoenix, Arizona, who turns out to be an illegal alien, be enough to justify exclusion or dismissal of deportation charges? If the illegal arrest produces no physical evidence besides identification, the alien has no remedy notwithstanding what was said in Part V. Earlier in her opinion, O'Connor wrote: "The 'body' or identity of a defendant or respondent in a criminal or civil proceeding is never itself suppressible as a fruit of an unlawful arrest, even if it is conceded that an unlawful arrest, search, or interrogation occurred."[247] And despite her contrary suggestion in Part V, even a warrantless nighttime entry into an illegal alien's home that produces tangible evidence, such as a Mexican identification card or other evidence indicating the alien's illegal presence in the nation, would not seem to merit exclusion. Even assuming that the Court would find a warrantless nighttime entry to be an "egregious" Fourth Amendment offense and fundamentally unfair, the violation in no way undermined "the probative value of the evidence obtained." Thus, exactly what O'Connor had in mind concerning Part V of her opinion is a mystery.[248]

* * *

A weak link in the chain holding together the Burger Court's exclusionary rule jurisprudence was the cost-benefit balancing analysis used to decide whether exclusion would promote sufficient deterrence of illegal searches and seizures. White's opinion in *Alderman* introduced this methodology, and it has been a mainstay of the Court's analysis in suppression cases ever since. To the neophyte, the Court's conclusions on the exclusionary rule's behavioral effects might seem based on empirical data or some other neutral grounds. But the Court's judgments were based neither on empirical facts nor legal principle. As Brennan put it in his dissent in *Leon*, "the reality is that the Court's opinions represent inherently unstable compounds of intuition, hunches, and occasional pieces of partial and often inconclusive data."[249] On a rare occasion, even justices opposed to exclusion acknowledged the point. Blackmun, an ardent opponent of suppression and

---

247 *Lopez-Mendoza*, 468 U.S. at 1039.

248 *See* Elizabeth Rossi, Revisiting *INS v. Lopez-Mendoza*: Why the Fourth Amendment Exclusionary Rule Should Apply in Deportation Proceedings 37–46 (May 13, 2011) (unpublished manuscript) (on file with author) (describing the split among federal courts of appeals on *Lopez-Mendoza*'s definition of "egregious violation"). *See generally* Irene Scharf, *The Exclusionary Rule in Immigration Proceedings: Where It Was, Where It Is, Where It May Be Going*, 12 San Diego Int'l L.J. 53 (2010); Matthew S. Mulqueen, Note, *Rethinking the Role of the Exclusionary Rule in Removal Proceedings*, 82 St. John's L. Rev. 1157 (2008).

249 United States v. Leon, 468 U.S. 897, 942 (1984) (Brennan, J., dissenting).

a member of the *Leon* majority, ultimately recognized, after twice characterizing the conclusion reached in *Leon* as an "empirical judgment,"[250] that *Leon*'s conclusion regarding deterrence rested on "assumptions."[251] Despite this acknowledgment, White continued to employ this analysis to limit application of the rule. In one case, however, White pushed too far, exposing the weak link of his methodology and prompting a reaction even from justices who were confirmed enemies of the exclusionary rule.

During the same Term that *Leon* and *Lopez-Mendoza* were under review, the Court first considered Terry Lee Owens's case. The issue in *New Jersey v. T.L.O.*[252] was straightforward: did the exclusionary rule apply in a criminal proceeding to challenge an illegal search made by a public school official? On March 7, 1980, a teacher discovered fourteen-year-old Owens and another student smoking cigarettes in the girls' restroom in Piscataway High School, in Piscataway, New Jersey. Although possession of cigarettes was not a violation of school rules, smoking in the restroom was. Owens and the other girl were taken to Assistant Vice Principal Theodore Choplick's office. After being questioned by Choplick, the other student admitted the infraction and was given a "punishment" to attend a three-day smoking clinic. Owens, however, denied smoking in the lavatory and told Choplick she "did not smoke at all."[253]

Choplick then took Owens into his private office and requested Owens's purse. He opened the purse and saw a package of Marlboro cigarettes. Next to the cigarettes in plain view was a package of rolling papers. After discovering the rolling papers, Choplick continued to search the purse and eventually found marijuana, drug paraphernalia, several one-dollar bills, and documentation of Owens's sale of marijuana to other students. Choplick then called Owens's mother and notified the police.[254]

Owens was later charged with delinquency based on possession of marijuana with the intent to distribute. She filed a motion to suppress the evidence obtained from the search of her purse, but the trial court denied the motion, and she was adjudicated a delinquent.[255] The New Jersey Supreme Court later ruled that Choplick's search was unconstitutional, and the evidence seized should have been excluded from the juvenile delinquency hearing. That court concluded that "if an official search violates constitutional rights, the evidence is not admissible in criminal proceedings."[256] When the Attorney General of New Jersey petitioned the Court to review the case, he did not contest the state court's ruling that Choplick's search was illegal. Further, the Attorney General did not challenge the

---

250 *Id.* at 927 (Blackmun, J., concurring).

251 *Id.* at 928.

252 469 U.S. 325 (1985). Justice Brennan's private notes provide interesting insight into the behind-the-scenes development of the case. *See* William J. Brennan, Jr., Case Histories, October Term, 1983, at XCVI-CII (undated) [hereinafter Brennan, Case Histories O.T. 1983], Brennan Papers, Box II: 7.

253 *T.L.O.*, 469 U.S. at 328.

254 State *ex rel.* T.L.O. v. Engerud, 463 A.2d 934, 936 (N.J. 1983).

255 *T.L.O.*, 469 U.S. at 329.

256 *T.L.O.*, 463 A.2d at 939.

judgment that the Fourth Amendment applies to in-school searches by school officials and teachers; nor did he challenge the standard of reasonableness employed by the state court. Thus, the only issue confronting the justices was whether the exclusionary rule applied in a juvenile delinquency proceeding to bar evidence unlawfully acquired by a school official without participation of law enforcement officers. All of the justices who would eventually comprise the *Leon* majority (Burger, White, Blackmun, Powell, Rehnquist, and O'Connor) voted to review the case.[257]

At the oral argument, many of the justices attempted to get New Jersey's lawyer to discuss whether the search was lawful. Counsel, however, remained steadfast that the exclusionary rule issue was the only question before the Court, and he told the justices that "we don't feel that exclusion of evidence from a later criminal proceeding should ever occur when the search was instituted by school teachers and school officials."[258] The conference discussion of *T.L.O.* was held two months after *Leon* was argued and four months before the results in *Leon* and *Lopez-Mendoza* were announced.

Burger began the discussion by stating he "wants the exclusionary rule held inapplicable."[259] Burger wondered whether the Court could reach that decision "without addressing whether there was a Fourth Amendment violation."[260] He also asked whether a teacher is more like an officer of the state or a parent. Burger voted to reverse or dismiss the case.[261] Brennan wanted to affirm the judgment of the New Jersey court. "We have never even intimated that the exclusionary rule should not apply in the prosecution's case-in-chief in a criminal proceeding."[262] Brennan acknowledged that some on the Court decided to review the case "with an eye toward reaching the question whether the Fourth Amendment should apply at all in the school context."[263] But that issue was not presented. Brennan told his colleagues that he would not oppose dismissing the case without reaching the merits.[264]

White said the "exclusionary rule doesn't apply to school officials."[265] He saw no deterrent impact, and said exclusion would not "stop teachers from doing this."[266] White voted to reverse. Marshall saw no difference between teachers and police officers regarding the

---

[257] New Jersey v. T.L.O., 464 U.S. 991 (1983) (mem.).

[258] Transcript of Oral Argument at *7, *T.L.O.*, 469 U.S. 325 (No. 83-712), 1984 U.S. Trans. LEXIS 140.

[259] William J. Brennan, Jr., Conference Notes on *New Jersey v. T.L.O.* (undated) [hereinafter Brennan, *T.L.O.* Conference Notes], Brennan Papers, Box I: 661.

[260] *Id.*

[261] *Id.*

[262] William J. Brennan, Jr., Memorandum to the Conference on *New Jersey v. T.L.O.* (undated), Brennan Papers, Box I: 669.

[263] *Id.*

[264] *Id.*

[265] Lewis Powell, Conference Notes on *New Jersey v. T.L.O.* (Mar. 30, 1984) [hereinafter Powell, *T.L.O.* Conference Notes], Powell Papers, Box 117.

[266] Brennan, *T.L.O.* Conference Notes, *supra* note 259.

use of evidence in criminal cases. Marshall voted to affirm but indicated he would be willing to dismiss the case. Blackmun and Powell agreed with White's position that the exclusionary rule did not apply to school searches. They both voted to reverse.[267]

Rehnquist noted the "odd posture" of the case.[268] He thought only "school discipline was involved."[269] Surprisingly, he told his colleagues that he was "not at rest whether the exclusionary rule should apply to evidence obtained by persons other than police."[270] This statement seemed to conflict with Rehnquist's remarks in the *Lopez-Mendoza* conference where he stated that not letting the exclusionary rule spread was his "base" belief. He also expressed uncertainty on whether the good-faith exception "should apply only to law enforcement officers."[271] Rehnquist voted "pass."[272]

Stevens wanted to dismiss the case. At the same time, he thought that it was "appalling" that a state actor could perform this search, and the Court would find that the search does not violate the Fourth Amendment in these circumstances.[273] He voted to dismiss the case or to affirm the judgment of the New Jersey Supreme Court. Finally, O'Connor said that the Court should not have reviewed the case. She felt the search was lawful, but that issue was not presented. She stated, however, that she "would apply the exclusionary rule in a criminal case."[274] O'Connor voted to dismiss the case or affirm.[275]

The conference vote was inconclusive. There were four votes for reversal (Burger, White, Blackmun, and Powell) and four votes for affirming or dismissing the case (Brennan, Marshall, Stevens, and O'Connor). And there was one undecided vote (Rehnquist). After the conference, Rehnquist provided the fifth vote for reversal and sent his colleagues a memo that Brennan privately described as the "most forthright memo of the Term."[276] In its entirety, Rehnquist's memo stated: "I now vote to reverse this case. Whatever may be the arguments for and against this particular limitation on the Exclusionary Rule, my disagreement with *Mapp v. Ohio* remains so fundamental that I will seize any opportunity to limit the damage done by that case."[277]

White was assigned the opinion, and he sent a draft to Powell to review prior to circulating it to the other justices.[278] White's opinion explained that the issue before the

---

267 *Id.*

268 Powell, *T.L.O.* Conference Notes, *supra* note 265.

269 *Id.*

270 *Id.*

271 Brennan, *T.L.O.* Conference Notes, *supra* note 259.

272 Powell, *T.L.O.* Conference Notes, *supra* note 265.

273 Brennan, *T.L.O.* Conference Notes, *supra* note 259.

274 Powell, *T.L.O.* Conference Notes, *supra* note 265.

275 *Id.*

276 Brennan, Case Histories O.T. 1983, *supra* note 252, at XCVIII.

277 William Rehnquist, Letter to the Conference on *New Jersey v. T.L.O.* (Mar. 30, 1984), Blackmun Papers, Box 414.

278 Byron White, First Draft of *New Jersey v. T.L.O.* (undated) [hereinafter White, *T.L.O.* first draft], Powell Papers, Box 117.

Court would be resolved "by weighing the costs and benefits of excluding from juvenile delinquency proceedings evidence illegally obtained by a school official who sought to enforce school disciplinary rules and who acted without the participation of law-enforcement authorities."[279] The opinion noted that before exclusion is required, the Court "must be convinced that an appreciable deterrent effect has been shown. Speculative benefits do not warrant the 'strong medicine' of the exclusionary rule."[280]

White concluded that exclusion was unwarranted. He explained that school officials are not similar to police officers. Searches by school officials and teachers serve interests "distinct from those served by the criminal-justice system."[281] Suppressing evidence obtained from school searches "may well have none of the behavioral effects on either school officials or school boards that exclusion of illegally obtained evidence in criminal prosecutions generally is thought to have on the typical law-enforcement official."[282] Quoting an Alaska appellate court decision, White wrote that enforcing school regulations, protecting the safety of students, and maintaining a drug-free environment provide substantial incentives to school officials to search students "that would not be lessened by suppression of evidence at a subsequent delinquency proceeding."[283] He also asserted that the admissibility of evidence in a criminal proceeding "is not a substantial concern" to teachers and will not "appreciably control their conduct."[284]

Finally, to the extent school officials may be deterred by exclusion, White asserted that result would be achieved by barring the fruits of illegal searches in school disciplinary proceedings. (In a separate lawsuit, a New Jersey trial court ruled in favor of Owens when she claimed that the fruits of Choplick's search should not have been used in the school disciplinary hearings against Owens. That ruling was not before the justices.) White insisted that school officials are more interested in the outcome of those proceedings.[285] And he was "quite convinced" that excluding evidence in juvenile delinquency hearings, which fall outside of school teachers' "'zone of primary interest,'" would produce only marginal deterrence that was insufficient to justify the costs to effective law enforcement.[286] Correspondingly, since barring unlawfully obtained evidence from school disciplinary hearings would sufficiently deter violations by school officials and teachers, White thought it "unlikely" that further suppression in criminal cases would produce appreciable deterrence to outweigh the state's interest in punishing guilty students.[287]

[279] *Id.* at 7.

[280] *Id.* at 8.

[281] *Id.* at 10.

[282] *Id.*

[283] *Id.* (quoting D.R.C. v. State, 646 P.2d 252, 258 (Alaska Ct. App. 1982)).

[284] *Id.*

[285] *Id.* at 10–11.

[286] *Id.* at 11 (quoting United States v. Janis, 428 U.S. 433, 458 (1976)).

[287] *Id.*

After reviewing White's draft opinion, Powell sent White a letter indicating his willingness to join the opinion. Powell specifically agreed with White's conclusion that exclusion would produce little deterrent impact because school authorities "have no responsibility for enforcing the criminal law."[288] But Powell thought White's discussion of the deterrent effects achieved by exclusion in school disciplinary proceedings was unnecessary and should be omitted from the case.[289] Even when school officials violate the rights of students, Powell believed those officials were entitled to more deference from judges. Powell wrote: "On any cost/benefit analysis, as I view it, deterring Fourth Amendment violations weighs far less in the scales than leaving the school authorities with broad discretion to enforce disciplinary rules that are essential to the proper operation of the schools."[290]

White's response to Powell's letter was telling. Although he cited no empirical evidence or any other type of evidence for the conclusions in his draft, White thought his discussion on the deterrence created when evidence is excluded in school disciplinary hearings "relevant and persuasive in negating a deterrence justification" for applying the exclusionary rule in criminal proceedings.[291] White acknowledged that his draft was written against a background in which the Court had not addressed the application of the exclusionary rule in civil proceedings. He noted if *Lopez-Mendoza* was decided before *T.L.O.* and held that the rule never applies in civil cases, his discussion on school disciplinary proceedings would have to be changed. But for now, White did not want to delete the section on exclusion in school disciplinary hearings.[292]

Two weeks later, Powell circulated a concurrence. In it, he agreed with White's conclusion that exclusion was unwarranted because Choplick was acting pursuant to his duty to enforce school regulations and ensure a drug-free learning environment. Choplick, Powell wrote, had "no responsibility for enforcing the criminal laws."[293] Like White, Powell thought suppression "would be unlikely to result in appreciable deterrence."[294] But Powell's concurrence objected to White's analysis that illegal searches and seizures will be adequately deterred by the exclusion of evidence from school disciplinary proceedings. Ironically, Powell objected that White's analysis was "unsupported" by the record and suggested an answer to a question not before the Court.[295] Revealing his view of the scope of *Lopez-Mendoza*'s holding, which had not been decided at this point, Powell

---

[288] Lewis Powell, Letter to Byron White on *New Jersey v. T.L.O.* 1 (Apr. 24, 1984), Blackmun Papers, Box 414.

[289] *Id.*

[290] Lewis Powell, Letter to Byron White on *New Jersey v. T.L.O.* 3 (April 21, 1984), Powell Papers, Box 117.

[291] Byron White, Letter to Lewis Powell on *New Jersey v. T.L.O.* (Apr. 30, 1984), Blackmun Papers, Box 414.

[292] *Id.*

[293] Lewis Powell, First Draft of Concurring Opinion in *New Jersey v. T.L.O.* 1 (May 15, 1984), Blackmun Papers, Box 414.

[294] *Id.*

[295] *Id.* at 2.

also stated that White's analysis was contrary to the Court's consistent refusal "to extend the rule to civil proceedings."[296]

In the meantime, Burger and Rehnquist joined White's opinion. Then, a month later, Stevens and O'Connor circulated separate dissenting opinions. Stevens's dissent was caustic and directly challenged White's cost-benefit analysis. The opening lines of Stevens's dissent read:

> ". . . One nation, under God, indivisible, with liberty and justice for all."
> "But, my child, you must remember that there are certain exceptions . . . ."[297]

Stevens attacked White's conclusion that exclusion would not deter illegal searches by school officials: "The Court cites no empirical evidence in support of its conclusion; there is none in the record. The Court's assumptions about the sociology of schools may be correct, but they are based not on any principle of law, nor on anything in the record. Instead, they are premised on five Justices' personal experiences and beliefs."[298] Stevens thought it "unwise to make law based on little more than our best guesses."[299]

Although it did not employ the purple prose Stevens used, O'Connor's dissent was more significant because of its author. O'Connor was a solid Republican. Although she would become known as a "moderate" or centrist jurist by the end of her time on the Court, throughout her tenure as a justice, O'Connor was "a hard-liner" when it came to issues of criminal law.[300] By the time she retired from the Court, O'Connor would vote for the defendant in only two Fourth Amendment exclusionary rule cases.[301] Thus, her vote to dissent at the *T.L.O.* conference, as Brennan privately noted, surprised almost everyone.[302] And the dissent O'Connor circulated in *T.L.O.* pulled no punches.

She began by noting that White's "empirical speculation" in *T.L.O.* cannot be reconciled with the presumption, consistently applied by the Court's precedents, "that exclusion of evidence from the prosecution's case-in-chief at criminal trials will tend to deter unlawful searches and seizures by any and all officials of the State."[303] (Of course, O'Connor found this presumption not dispositive in *Leon*.) O'Connor thought White's

---

296 *Id.*

297 John Paul Stevens, First Draft of Dissenting Opinion in *New Jersey v. T.L.O.* 1 (June 11, 1984), Blackmun Papers, Box 414.

298 *Id.* at 3–4 (footnote omitted).

299 *Id.* at 4.

300 Toobin, *supra* note 245, at 208. For an informative biography of O'Connor, see Joan Biskupic, Sandra Day O'Connor: How the First Woman on the Supreme Court Became Its Most Influential Justice (2005).

301 *See* Murray v. United States, 487 U.S. 533, 544-51 (1988) (Marshall, J., dissenting); Illinois v. Krull, 480 U.S. 340, 361-69 (1987) (O'Connor, J., dissenting).

302 Brennan, Case Histories O.T. 1983, *supra* note 252, at XCVIII.

303 Sandra Day O'Connor, First Draft of Dissenting Opinion in *New Jersey v. T.L.O.* 1 (June 12, 1984), Blackmun Papers, Box 414.

analysis was unprecedented for a second reason. She stated that the Court had "never before" considered whether a "particular class" of government officials actually will be deterred by exclusion.[304] None of the Court's prior cases rejecting use of the exclusionary rule were based on "judicial intuition" that the offending state officials would not be deterred by application of the rule in criminal proceedings.[305]

O'Connor also distinguished the soon-to-be-announced *Leon* ruling. According to O'Connor, *Leon* found that certain constitutional violations would not be deterred by exclusion. "By striking contrast," in *T.L.O.*, White had "categorically determined that deterrence of certain *persons*, as opposed to the commission of certain *errors*, will not result by excluding the evidence illegally seized."[306] White's conclusion, in O'Connor's view, was "irreconcilable with the Court's consistently applied assumption that all government officials can and should be encouraged to incorporate Fourth Amendment ideals into their value systems."[307]

Finally, O'Connor asserted that White's opinion would lead to unprincipled judicial rulings. She wrote: "It makes little sense, in the absence of determinate empirical evidence, to expect judges in state and federal courts to be able to draw reliable and consistent conclusions about the exclusionary rule's deterrent effect on various government officials."[308] She thought White had made an "arbitrary distinction" when he singled out school officials as not subject to deterrence[309]:

> Like firefighters, building inspectors, and alcohol tax collectors, public school officials are charged with enforcing government regulations and with administering a government program . . . . School officials, like these other regulatory agents, are often obliged to seek out and report to the police evidence of criminal conduct. If the presumption of deterrence properly applies to these other public officials, then it should apply to public school officials as well.[310]

White's second draft responded to Stevens's and O'Connor's criticism. White conceded that the Court's previous exclusionary rule cases were not grounded on empirical data, which the Court had previously described as "flawed and inconclusive."[311] Rather, those decisions, White claimed, were based on "an informed judgment concerning the rule's behavioral effects."[312] White acknowledged that when rejecting application of the

304 *Id.* at 3.
305 *Id.*
306 *Id.* at 4.
307 *Id.*
308 *Id.*
309 *Id.* at 5.
310 *Id.* (citation omitted).
311 Byron White, Second Draft of *New Jersey v. T.L.O.* 10 n.6 (June 12, 1984), Blackmun Papers, Box 414.
312 *Id.*

rule in prior cases, "the Court acted in the absence of convincing empirical evidence and relied, instead, on its own assumptions of human nature and the interrelationship of the various components of the law enforcement system."[313] White saw no persuasive reason why the Court's judgment "should not vary depending on the identity, duties, and responsibilities of the governmental official who conducted the search in question."[314] Put differently, White thought "common sense" and "reasoned analysis" should also guide the Court's thinking when deciding whether exclusion would deter school authorities.[315]

After the circulation of White's second draft, the only member of the Court who had not been heard from was Blackmun. The next day, Blackmun sent a memo to his colleagues acknowledging his vote was the "last one out in this difficult case."[316] Although Blackmun voted to reverse at the conference, "after some soul-searching," he now thought the proper resolution was to dismiss the case.[317] Any other resolution "will tend only to confuse and not to assist."[318] White immediately replied to Blackmun's letter with the suggestion that the good-faith exception be extended to school searches. Never mind that in his first draft White stated that because the New Jersey Supreme Court found Choplick had "'no reasonable grounds'" to believe Owens's purse contained cigarettes, there was no reason to remand the case for reconsideration under *Leon*'s good-faith exception.[319] Now, White wanted to remand the case. He proposed that *T.L.O.* be held until *Leon* was announced and then sent back to the New Jersey Supreme Court for consideration in light of *Leon*. White's letter to Blackmun stated: "I have substantial doubt that the school official should have known that his conduct was in violation of the Fourth Amendment."[320] He also asserted: "*Leon* has a direct bearing" on the admissibility of the evidence seized by Choplick.[321]

White's proposals attracted no support from the other justices, and it seemed as if Blackmun would provide the fifth vote to dismiss the case. At the next conference discussion, however, O'Connor, after conferring with White, proposed that *T.L.O.* be reargued on the question whether Choplick's search violated the Fourth Amendment.[322] Four other justices agreed, so *T.L.O.* was set for reargument in the fall. The order for reargument prompted Stevens to file a strong dissent. Stevens accused his colleagues of

---

313 *Id.* (quoting United States v. Janis, 428 U.S. 433, 459 (1976)).

314 *Id.*

315 *Id.*

316 Harry Blackmun, Memorandum to the Conference on *New Jersey v. T.L.O.* (June 13, 1984), Blackmun Papers, Box 414.

317 *Id.*

318 *Id.*

319 White, *T.L.O.* First Draft, *supra* note 278, at 6 n.3.

320 Byron White, Letter to Harry Blackmun on *New Jersey v. T.L.O.* (June 14, 1984), Powell Papers, Box 117.

321 *Id.*

322 Sandra Day O'Connor, Memorandum to the Conference on *New Jersey v. T.L.O.* (June 26, 1984), Powell Papers, Box 117.

acquiring "a voracious appetite for judicial activism in its Fourth Amendment jurisprudence, at least when it comes to restricting the constitutional rights of the citizen."[323] After reargument, six justices, including O'Connor and Blackmun, concluded that the search of Owens's purse was valid. Thus, the evidence was admissible in the juvenile delinquency hearing.[324] The Court would not have to decide the exclusionary rule issue after all. The episode revealed that even fervent opponents of exclusion like Blackmun and O'Connor could only be pushed so far. But it also showed that the foundation of the Burger Court's exclusionary rule jurisprudence was built on assumptions rather than empirical data or neutral legal principles.

323 New Jersey v. T.L.O., 468 U.S. 1214, 1215 (1984) (Stevens, J., dissenting from reargument order).

324 New Jersey v. T.L.O., 469 U.S. 325 (1985).

7 Warren Burger's Triumph

NEARLY A DECADE before they would take their seats as justices on the Supreme Court, federal appellate judges Warren Burger and Harry Blackmun were condemning the exclusionary rule and strategizing to create a significant exception to the rule. Late in 1961, *Killough v. United States*[1] was pending before an *en banc* panel of the Court of Appeals for the District Columbia, where Burger sat as a judge. James Killough was convicted of murdering his wife, Goldie Killough. Police illegally detained Killough and obtained a confession from him, in which he admitted the killing, and he later led police to the location of the body. In his appeal, Killough argued that the coroner's testimony about the condition of the body should have been suppressed as fruit of the illegal detention and confession.[2]

In an October 21, 1961, letter to Blackmun, who was then a member of the Court of Appeals for the Eighth Circuit, Burger complained that the Supreme Court's exclusionary rule decisions required suppression of a murder victim's body: "If those cases make any sense the body must be ignored as if non-existent—except that it must be buried out of a decent respect for the dead and local sanitary regulations."[3] Burger asked Blackmun for advice on how to distinguish the Court's precedents and told him, "I am going to try to write the opinion so as to force" the Court to review it.[4] A few months later, Burger sent Blackmun another letter and a draft of his *Killough* opinion. The letter noted: "For

[1] (*Killough I*), 315 F.2d 241 (D.C. Cir. 1962).

[2] *Id.* at 241–45.

[3] Warren Burger, Letter to Harry Blackmun 2 (Oct. 21, 1961), Blackmun Papers, Box 50.

[4] *Id.*

5 plus years I have had a growing feeling that the universal application of the Suppression Doctrine made no sense."[5] Nonetheless, in acknowledgment of several of the justices' adherence to *Weeks v. United States*, which launched the Fourth Amendment exclusionary rule in 1914, Burger told Blackmun that he tried to eliminate his "grating comments" about exclusion from his draft opinion. He wrote, "for after all I must persuade the Oracles. To most of them, I fear, an attack on *Weeks* is like an attack in Texas on home, mother and the 27 ½ [percent] depletion rate."[6]

Two weeks later, Blackmun sent his comments on the draft. Blackmun was complimentary of Burger's opinion and its attempt to limit the scope of the exclusionary rule. Blackmun agreed that it did not "make good common or judicial sense" to exclude in *Killough*.[7] He remarked, "It makes one naturally question the validity of the Rule itself. I suspect that in due time the Rule will be changed or largely modified but this may take many years."[8] Regarding suppression of a murder victim's body, Blackmun commented: "The Rule cannot apply to the corpus delicti (whatever that may be in the particular case) to defeat utterly the process of criminal justice. The Rule as it is today is enough of a hamper."[9] Blackmun thought the draft seemed "defensive" in its criticism of exclusion.[10] Blackmun added: "It seems to me that there must be a general rule that the corpus delicti stands by itself, that it is, so to speak, sui generis, and that it is not subject to the exclusionary rules of evidence."[11]

Burger immediately replied in another letter and explained that the draft he sent Blackmun was "concentrating on the basic idea of (1) an attack or challenge to the validity of the rule itself and (2) possible alternatives, or additions. With *Elkins* and *Mapp* hardly dry on the books this is a helluva time, at best, to be doubting the Sacred Cow of Suppression."[12] Burger wrote that a new draft removed "some of the gravelly remarks which would be bound to raise the hackles of almost all 9 if not all 9 of the oracles."[13] Burger conceded, however, his opinion was not supported by Supreme Court rulings: "If you have not recently read *Elkins* and *Mapp* they will explain the 'defensive' attitude you refer to. In fact there is really not the slightest support in any opinion of the last 50 years for making an exception for a body."[14] Burger told Blackmun that he wanted to "carve out a rule that excludes corpus delicti evidence from the exclusion rule" but recognized that the Court's precedents stood in the way.[15]

---

5 Warren Burger, Letter to Harry Blackmun (Jan. 10, 1962), Blackmun Papers, Box 50.

6 *Id.*

7 Harry Blackmun, Letter to Warren Burger on *Killough v. United States* 1 (Jan. 24, 1962), Blackmun Papers, Box 50.

8 *Id.*

9 *Id.*

10 *Id.*

11 *Id.*

12 Warren Burger, Letter to Harry Blackmun 1 (Jan. 28, 1962), Blackmun Papers, Box 50.

13 *Id.*

14 *Id.*

15 *Id.*

Blackmun wrote back and explained that his comment about the corpus delicti was "largely an agonizing groan to the general effect that a homicide victim's body just cannot possibly be excluded."[16] Blackmun then elaborated on his views toward exclusion:

> That it is excludable by the extended logic of the suppression doctrine shows conclusively, it seems to me, that the doctrine itself is unsound. But if we are to live with it a human victim's body ought to be an exception. If so, perhaps it is a good first or starting exception. If it could be established as an exception, more exceptions ought to follow. I realize I am crying in the wilderness but I am oldfashioned enough to feel that the criminal law ought to consist, even in these days, of some measure of a search for truth and that the so-called protections were not intended to be utilized to defeat truth, at least to this extent. If it is otherwise, then, as I have somewhat suspected, the application of the criminal law is something of a game; I wonder if it should be.[17]

As things turned out, Burger's dissent in *Killough* did not directly attack the exclusionary rule, although he commented in a footnote that "the Suppression Doctrine has totally failed to achieve its stated objective" of compelling police compliance with the Fourth Amendment, and that exclusion "is a manifestation of sterile indignation, and is essentially negative."[18] Burger also asserted, without providing any legal analysis, that evidence related to the discovery of Goldie Killough's body was not subject to exclusion. While the full court did not address that issue, it did reverse Killough's conviction and order a new trial. Burger worried that if exclusion of the body was eventually ordered, the judiciary would have fulfilled Justice Cardozo's prophetic warning that the exclusionary rule would be carried to "ridiculous lengths" by the suppression of a murder victim's body.[19] Burger remarked: "Cardozo did not really believe this could happen; he was indulging in a form of judicial hyperbole to make a point. It is inconceivable that judges would go to such lengths ignoring a reasonable balance between individual rights and protection of the public."[20]

After a second trial, James Killough was again convicted of murdering his wife. He filed another appeal in the court of appeals. That court (without Burger sitting) again reversed Killough's conviction and ordered a new trial, although this time the court rejected his argument that testimony related to the discovery of the body was inadmissible. That Killough's illegal confession was the "but-for" cause of the discovery of the body was not decisive. The evidence concerning the body was admissible because "[i]n

16 Harry Blackmun, Letter to Warren Burger on *Killough v. United States* 1 (Jan. 30, 1962), Blackmun Papers, Box 50.

17 *Id.*

18 *Killough I*, 315 F.2d 241, 257 n.5 (D.C. Cir. 1962) (Burger, J., dissenting).

19 *Id.* at 259.

20 *Id.*

time the body (or its bones) would have been discovered and would have been identified as that of Mrs. Killough."[21] Notably, the court did not explain why this conclusion was consistent with the Supreme Court's exclusionary rule precedents.

Thirteen years later, and somewhat surprisingly in light of its absence of legal analysis, Stewart cited *Killough II* in a footnote in *Brewer v. Williams*,[22] which held that police violated Robert Williams's Sixth Amendment right to counsel when they deliberately sought to elicit information from Williams at a time when he was entitled to counsel's assistance. In the footnote, Stewart explained that although neither direct evidence obtained from the illegal interrogation of Williams nor any evidence describing Williams having led police to the victim's body was admissible at a retrial, evidence of where the body was found and of its condition might be admissible on the theory that the body would have been found in any event.[23] *Killough II* was the only case Stewart cited as support. This theory was known as the "inevitable discovery" exception to the exclusionary rule. Burger, now sitting as Chief Justice, ridiculed the footnote as proposing an "unlikely theory" to obtain a conviction of Williams at a second trial.[24]

Burger's dismissive remark in 1977 ignored the fact that the lower courts had already embraced the inevitable discovery theory as a way of bypassing the exclusionary rule. In 1968, Professor Robert Pitler published an informative law review article explaining how lower courts in the 1960s used the inevitable discovery exception to avoid suppressing evidence obtained from illegal searches and seizures.[25] To satisfy the exception, it was not enough to show that the police "could" or "should" have pursued lawful, alternative ways to get the evidence. Rather, a prosecutor would have to convince a judge that the proffered evidence *would* have been obtained through lawful means, even if the unconstitutional conduct had not occurred. In other words, if the prosecution establishes that an illegal search or seizure "was not an *indispensable* cause of the discovery" of the evidence, the exclusionary rule is inapplicable.[26] According to its supporters, the inevitable discovery exception promotes the purpose behind suppression by withholding from the prosecution evidence obtained by illegal conduct and at the same time minimizes the chances of a guilty defendant receiving "an undeserved and socially undesirable bonanza."[27]

While acknowledging that several courts and academic scholars had endorsed inevitable discovery as a valid exception to the Fourth Amendment's exclusionary rule, Professor Pitler remained dubious. He thought the rule would be rendered "useless if

---

[21] Killough v. United States (*Killough II*), 336 F.2d 929, 934 (D.C. Cir. 1964).

[22] *See* Brewer v. Williams (*Williams I*), 430 U.S. 387, 406 n.12 (1977).

[23] *Id.*

[24] *Id.* at 416 n.1 (Burger, C.J., dissenting).

[25] Robert M. Pitler, *"The Fruit of the Poisonous Tree" Revisited and Shepardized*, 56 CALIF. L. REV. 579 (1968).

[26] Robert F. Maguire, *How to Unpoison the Fruit, The Fourth Amendment and the Exclusionary Rule*, 55 J. CRIM. L. CRIMINOLOGY & POLICE SCI. 307, 313 (1964) (emphasis added).

[27] *Id.* at 317.

the police may unlawfully invade a man's home, illegally seize evidence and then claim 'we would have obtained it anyway.'"[28] Acknowledging that the logic of an inevitable discovery exception has "a certain appeal,"[29] Pitler argued that the theory conflicted with the fundamental purpose of suppression: "The preservation of the exclusionary rule as a viable deterrent to illicit police activity requires the spotlight to focus 'on actualities not probabilities.'"[30]

The problem with the inevitable discovery exception that Pitler identified was highlighted in a federal appellate case in 1974.[31] In that case, federal narcotics officers had probable cause to search a home. While an officer was sent to obtain a search warrant, other officers secured the apartment. Instead of waiting for the officer to obtain the warrant, the officers assigned to guard the apartment illegally entered and seized the drugs. Four hours later, the other officer arrived with the search warrant. The government argued the drugs were admissible under the inevitable discovery exception. The government's position was certainly plausible. If the feds had been patient and complied with the Constitution, they would have inevitably obtained the evidence. Thus, the illegal entry was not an indispensable cause of the discovery of the drugs.[32]

On the other hand, it is hard to fathom how admitting the evidence from this illegal search would promote the theory behind exclusion: encouraging police to comply with the Fourth Amendment. The Court of Appeals for the Sixth Circuit understood the implications of embracing an inevitable discovery exception in this context: "The assertion by police (after an illegal entry and after finding evidence of crime) that the discovery was 'inevitable' because they planned to get a search warrant and had sent an officer on such a mission, would as a practical matter be beyond judicial review."[33] The government's argument, the court noted, would "emasculate the search warrant requirement of the Fourth Amendment."[34] Although the Sixth Circuit did not put it in such terms, the government's reliance on the inevitable discovery exception amounted to the claim "If we hadn't done it wrong, we would have done it right."[35]

Against this legal backdrop, Robert Williams's case returned to the Court—this time under the caption *Nix v. Williams*[36]—in the same Term that the Court was considering *Leon*, *Lopez-Mendoza*, and *T.L.O.* As explained in chapter 5, in 1977, the Court reversed Williams's conviction in *Brewer v. Williams* despite the "bloodcurdling" dissents of four

---

[28] Pitler, *supra* note 25, at 630.

[29] *Id.*

[30] *Id.* (quoting United States v. Paroutian, 299 F.2d 486, 489 (2d Cir. 1962)).

[31] United States v. Griffin, 502 F.2d 959 (6th Cir. 1974) (per curiam), *cert. denied*, 419 U.S. 1050 (1974).

[32] *Griffin*, 502 F.2d at 960.

[33] *Id.* at 961.

[34] *Id.*

[35] Professor Alschuler states that this phrase was offered in 1992 by Chief Judge Sam Ervin III in *United States v. Thomas*, 955 F.2d 207, 210 (4th Cir. 1992). *See* Albert W. Alschuler, Herring v. United States*: A Minnow or a Shark?*, 7 OHIO ST. J. CRIM. L. 463, 482 & n.95 (2009).

[36] (*Williams II*), 467 U.S. 431 (1984).

justices.[37] During the same Term in which the Court would finally adopt a good-faith exception to the exclusionary rule and hold the exclusionary rule inapplicable in deportation hearings, the justices would again have to decide whether evidence should have been suppressed in Williams's prosecution for murdering ten-year-old Pamela Powers. This time, the exclusionary rule would not help Williams gain a new trial. His conviction would be affirmed, and Williams would be sent to prison. More important, unlike the outcome in *Williams I*, when the Chief Justice failed to persuade his colleagues to retreat from the exclusionary rule, in *Williams II*, Burger would create an exception to exclusion that functions in most cases the same way a corpus delicti exception would function.

At a second trial, Iowa prosecutors were precluded from offering as evidence Williams's statements to the police and the fact that he led police to Pamela Powers's body. Relying on a theory of inevitable discovery, the same theory suggested by Stewart's footnote in *Brewer v. Williams* and ridiculed by Burger, the prosecution was permitted to admit as evidence the condition of the body, articles and photographs of Powers's clothing, and the results of autopsy tests on the body.[38] The prosecution argued that after Powers was discovered missing, the Iowa Bureau of Criminal Investigation began a wide-scale search for the girl with two hundred volunteers.[39] Starting at the location where some of Powers's clothing had been found, searchers were instructed to check all locations: roads, abandoned farm property, buildings, ditches, culverts, and any other location where the body of a small child might be found. When officials learned that Williams had agreed to show police where Powers's body was located, they suspended the search. At that point, searchers were two and one-half miles from where the body was located, next to a culvert in a ditch beside a road.[40]

Because he led police to Powers's body after being illegally questioned, Williams argued that the evidence relating to the condition of the body as well as the autopsy evidence was the fruit of his illegal interrogation and should have been excluded. The trial court, however, concluded the state had proven the evidence would inevitably have been discovered. The trial court ruled the body would have been found irrespective of Williams leading the police to the body after unlawful interrogation and the search having been suspended. Williams was again convicted of murder.[41] After the Iowa courts

---

[37] That is how Justice Marshall described the dissenting opinions in *Brewer v. Williams*. *See Williams I*, 430 U.S. 387, 408-09 (1977) (Marshall, J., concurring). In *Williams I*, all of the justices assumed that Williams was guilty of murder. When Williams's case returned to the federal Court of Appeals for the Eighth Circuit, the appellate court stated that the defense claim of Williams's innocence "is not so far-fetched as it sounds." Williams v. Nix, 700 F.2d 1164, 1168 (8th Cir. 1983). *See* Phillip E. Johnson, *The Return of the "Christian Burial Speech" Case*, 32 Emory L.J. 349, 357-60 (1983) (explaining defense theory that Williams was innocent of the murder of Pamela Powers).

[38] *Williams II*, 467 U.S. at 437–38.

[39] Brief for the United States as Amicus Curiae Supporting Reversal at 17–18, *Williams II*, 467 U.S. 431 (No. 82-1651).

[40] *Williams II*, 467 U.S. at 435–36.

[41] *Id.* at 437–38.

affirmed his conviction, Williams filed a federal habeas corpus petition. His petition argued that the testimony concerning the condition of the victim's body was derivative fruit of the same Sixth Amendment violation the Court had found in *Brewer v. Williams*, and thus should have been suppressed. The district court denied relief, concluding that the body inevitably would have been found.[42] The Court of Appeals for the Eighth Circuit, however, granted the petition. It ruled that even assuming the validity of the inevitable discovery exception, the exception was available only upon a showing that police did not act in bad faith.[43] The Court then agreed to review the case.

Although the question presented in *Williams II*—whether there should be an inevitable discovery exception to the exclusionary rule—had never been addressed by the Court, it was a foregone conclusion the Court would endorse the exception. Every federal appellate court had adopted the exception. Moreover, the results in *Leon* and *Lopez-Mendoza* revealed a desire by a majority of the justices to develop new ways to curtail the exclusionary rule. The only issue that Williams had a remote chance of winning was whether the Court would deny use of an inevitable discovery exception when police acted in bad faith. As *Leon* would subsequently note, "an assessment of the flagrancy of the police misconduct constitutes an important step in the calculus" when deciding whether to recognize an exception to the suppression doctrine.[44] The Solicitor General's amicus brief argued, however, that the bad faith of the police was irrelevant to the theory of inevitable discovery:

> The absence of bad faith is neither a logical nor an appropriate component of the inevitable discovery doctrine. The premise of that doctrine is the lack of a necessary causal connection between the police misconduct and the discovery of the evidence, and the *mens rea* of the offending officer is irrelevant to the question of the presence or absence of that causal connection. The important point is to ensure that the police do not profit by their misconduct . . . .[45]

This argument reflected an opportune position since five justices had previously described the police misconduct in Williams's case as "deliberately" and "purposely" undertaken in violation of the Sixth Amendment right to counsel.[46]

The conference discussion in *Williams II* revealed that a majority of the justices agreed with the Solicitor General. Burger stated that the "inevitable discovery rule acknowledges a prior violation."[47] Thus, in Burger's view, the "good or bad faith of the

---

[42] Williams v. Nix, 528 F. Supp. 664 (S.D. Iowa 1981).

[43] Williams v. Nix, 700 F.2d 1164, 1169–70 (8th Cir. 1983).

[44] United States v. Leon, 468 U.S. 897, 911 (1984).

[45] Brief for the United States as Amicus Curiae Supporting Reversal, *supra* note 39, at 9.

[46] *Williams I*, 430 U.S. 387, 399 (1977).

[47] Lewis Powell, Conference Notes on *Nix v. Williams* (Jan. 20, 1984) [hereinafter Powell, *Williams II* Conference Notes], Powell Papers, Box 109.

police at the time of that violation is irrelevant."[48] Burger voted to reverse.[49] Brennan focused on the meaning of the Sixth Amendment. According to Brennan, if an accused is questioned by police at a time when he is entitled to counsel's assistance, but evidence from that interrogation is never used at trial, there has been no Sixth Amendment violation. A violation only occurs when the fruits of unlawful questioning are admitted at trial to facilitate the prosecution. Applied to this case, Brennan explained, "that would occur when the result of that questioning—the girl's body—is introduced at trial. At the [sic] point, the accused can no longer be said to have 'enjoy[ed] the right . . . to have the Assistance of Counsel for his defense' in a 'criminal prosecution.'"[50] Thus, in Brennan's view, exclusion was required to prevent a constitutional violation, not as a "remedy for a violation that has already occurred."[51] Therefore, the inevitable discovery exception was available only if the unlawful questioning "did not really *cause* the discovery of evidence at issue."[52] Brennan voted to affirm.[53]

White voted to reverse. He stated the inevitable discovery exception is "sound and applies" here.[54] The bad faith of the police "is irrelevant."[55] Marshall agreed with Brennan's views and voted to affirm. Blackmun spoke next. Perhaps forgetting the view he expressed to Burger in 1962 that exclusion should never apply to corpus delicti evidence, now Blackmun was willing to accept an inevitable discovery rule, but with a good-faith requirement. He voted to reverse.[56]

Powell stated that three courts had found that the body would have been inevitably discovered, and "whether there was bad faith is irrelevant."[57] He added that the "inevitable discovery doctrine is reached only if there is a constitutional violation."[58] Powell voted to reverse. Rehnquist agreed with Powell's views and voted to reverse. Stevens thought the "inevitable discovery rule is sound" and stated that "logically the good or bad faith of the police is irrelevant."[59] But Stevens "wouldn't find bad faith in this case."[60] Stevens voted to reverse and remand. Finally, O'Connor agreed to support an inevitable discovery exception and thought the good faith of the police is irrelevant.[61]

---

48 *Id.*

49 *Id.*

50 William J. Brennan, Jr., Memorandum to the Conference on *Nix v. Williams* 1 (undated), Brennan Papers, Box I: 648 (alterations in original).

51 *Id.*

52 *Id.* at 1–2.

53 Powell, *Williams II* Conference Notes, *supra* note 47.

54 *Id.*

55 *Id.*

56 *Id.*

57 *Id.*

58 *Id.*

59 *Id.*

60 *Id.*

61 *Id.*

Burger assigned *Williams II* to himself, and his opinion shows just how determined Burger was to create a substantial exception to the exclusionary rule. Rather than write an opinion that closely tracks the facts of the case and the Sixth Amendment issue before the Court, Burger's opinion embraces a broad inevitable discovery exception applicable to Fourth Amendment, as well as Sixth Amendment violations.

Burger begins his opinion by equating an inevitable discovery exception with the independent source rule.[62] The independent source rule, which was first acknowledged by Holmes in 1920, permits the admission of evidence gained from a source or means independent and distinct from an illegal search or seizure that uncovered the exact same evidence. The independent source rule is sometimes mislabeled as an exception to the exclusionary rule, a mistake that Burger and Brennan both made in *Williams II*. In order to invoke the exclusionary rule, the challenged evidence must have a "but-for" causal connection to an illegal search. Evidence or knowledge of evidence that lacks any connection to an unlawful search, that is, evidence that comes from an independent source, is not subject to exclusion even though the evidence is identical to evidence unlawfully acquired by the police. When properly applied, the independent source rule permits the admission of evidence only if it was obtained by truly independent, lawful means.

In *Williams II*, Burger correctly notes that notwithstanding a prior or simultaneous constitutional offense, the independent source rule permits the admission of evidence that comes from independent means to avoid putting the prosecution in a *worse* position than it would have been if no police misconduct had occurred. He also correctly concedes that the independent source rule did not apply in *Williams II* because Williams's unlawfully obtained statements led police to the body. However, Burger goes on to state that there is a "functional similarity" between the independent source rule and the inevitable discovery exception "in that exclusion of evidence that would inevitably have been discovered would also put the government in a worse position, because the police would have obtained that evidence if no misconduct had taken place."[63]

In theory, the independent source rule and inevitable discovery exception are similar. The premise of both doctrines is that because there is no causal connection between the unconstitutional police conduct and the discovery of the challenged evidence, that evidence is admissible notwithstanding the police misconduct. While Burger saw a "functional similarity" between the independent source rule and the inevitable discovery exception, he overlooks critical differences between the two legal doctrines. First, Burger suggests that exclusion is unwarranted under the independent source rule because when "properly balanced," the interest in deterring unlawful police conduct and the interest of society in having juries receive all probative evidence requires that the prosecution be put "in the same, not a *worse*" position than it would have been in if no police misconduct had occurred.[64]

---

62 *Williams II*, 467 U.S. 431, 440–41 (1984).

63 *Id.* at 444.

64 *Id.* at 443.

But, as it was envisioned by Holmes, evidence is admissible under the independent source not because of a balancing of interests, but because evidence that comes from an independent source is acquired without violating the defendant's constitutional rights. There is no need for balancing under the independent source rule because evidence obtained from a truly independent source "does not fall within the presumptive scope of the suppression doctrine."[65]

By contrast, the inevitable discovery doctrine is an *exception* to the exclusionary rule. And as the facts in *Williams II* clearly demonstrate, it permits the admission of evidence that was in fact obtained by conduct that violated the defendant's constitutional rights. Although the Solicitor General twice stated in his brief that the independent source rule and the inevitable discovery exception both rest on the premise that suppression is unwarranted "in the absence of a sufficiently close causal connection" between police misconduct and the discovery of the disputed evidence,[66] the misconduct and discovery of the body in *Williams II* were causally connected. In fact, as Powell's law clerk told her boss, "the constitutional violation was the direct and immediate source of the discovery of evidence."[67] Thus, to equate the independent source rule with the inevitable discovery exception ignores a fundamental difference between the two doctrines. Equally important, the inevitable discovery exception encompasses primary as well as derivative fruits of unconstitutional police behavior. Although the contested evidence in *Williams II*—testimony regarding the condition of Pamela Powers's body and autopsy evidence—was the derivative fruit of an unlawful police interrogation, the logic of an inevitable discovery exception also extends to evidence that is the direct and immediate fruit of unconstitutional behavior.[68]

Another significant difference between the independent source rule and the inevitable discovery exception that Burger glosses over is the burden of proof required to

---

65 James J. Tomkovicz, Constitutional Exclusion: The Rules, Rights, and Remedies that Strike the Balance Between Freedom and Order 42 (2011); Silas Wasserstrom & William J. Mertens, *The Exclusionary Rule on the Scaffold: But Was It a Fair Trial?*, 22 Am. Crim. L. Rev. 85, 157 (1984) (explaining that as originally formulated, Holmes's independent source rule did not propose balancing competing interests to determine the admissibility of tainted evidence); *id.* at 159 (noting that Holmes's obvious concern was that tainted evidence not be available to the prosecution: "The reason for permitting use of evidence where an independent source could be demonstrated was not based on the concern that the police not suffer a net disadvantage because of their conduct. Rather, the reasoning was that when an independent source could be demonstrated, the prohibited exploitation of the prior wrong had not occurred.").

66 Brief for the United States as Amicus Curiae Supporting Reversal, *supra* note 39, at 8, 12.

67 Cammie Hauptfuhrer, Memorandum to Lewis Powell on *Nix v. Williams* 1 (Mar. 18, 1984), Powell Papers, Box 109.

68 As Professor Robert M. Bloom has shown, less than a decade after *Williams II* endorsed the inevitable discovery exception, most federal courts of appeals, without any discussion of the difference between primary and derivative evidence, applied the exception to direct evidence acquired from an illegal search. Some state courts did the same. *See* Robert M. Bloom, *Inevitable Discovery: An Exception Beyond the Fruits*, 20 Am. J. Crim. L. 79, 87 (1992).

establish each doctrine's applicability in a given case. When *Williams II* was decided, the Court had never used the independent source doctrine to authorize the admission of evidence. Thus, how the doctrine would actually function in a real case and its precise meaning and scope had not been addressed by the Court. In theory, the rule allows the introduction of disputed evidence only if the evidence was, *in fact*, obtained by lawful means distinct from unconstitutional police behavior. Proving that the government had an independent source for the same evidence that was also discovered by an illegal search is not difficult. The government simply has to identify the source and prove that evidence came from a source independent of an illegal search or seizure.

By contrast, and despite its name, the inevitable discovery exception does not require the prosecution to prove that the discovery of the evidence was "inevitable." Instead, all the prosecution has to do is show "by a preponderance of the evidence"—which is the lowest legal standard of proof in American law—that the evidence likely would have been discovered by lawful efforts. In other words, under the test Burger announced in *Williams II*, the discovery of the evidence "need not be certain or inevitable at all; it need only be probable."[69]

Finally, Burger neglects to discuss the greatest tension between an inevitable discovery exception and the exclusionary rule. As Professor Pitler first recognized, an inevitable discovery exception renders the exclusionary rule worthless. It allows the police to conduct an illegal search or seizure and obtain evidence from that violation, and then authorizes the admission of that evidence under the theory that the police probably would have obtained the same evidence by lawful means. In other words, if the police hadn't done wrong, they (or someone else) would have done right. One way to avoid this dilemma is to make the inevitable discovery exception unavailable for Fourth Amendment violations, which was what the Court of Appeals for the Sixth Circuit did in 1974. But this is not the result Burger had in mind when he wrote *Williams II*.

Although *Williams II* never explicitly states that its reasoning is also applicable to Fourth Amendment violations, there is no doubt Burger intended the inevitable discovery rule to apply to illegal searches and seizures as well as to Sixth Amendment violations. For one thing, Burger frequently cites Fourth Amendment cases when making the case for an inevitable discovery exception.[70] Moreover, Burger employed the same cost-benefit balancing analysis used in Fourth Amendment cases to decide whether evidence acquired from a Sixth Amendment violation was admissible at trial. Thus, Burger rejected Williams's argument that because his case involved the right to counsel protected by the Sixth Amendment, the Court was not free to balance competing values in deciding whether the illegally obtained evidence was properly admitted. Addressing Williams's claim that the Sixth Amendment right to counsel guaranteed him a fair trial process, Burger asserted that suppressing evidence that would inevitably have been discovered

[69] Albert W. Alschuler, *The Exclusionary Rule and Causation:* Hudson v. Michigan *and Its Ancestors*, 93 Iowa L. Rev. 1741, 1805 (2008) [hereinafter Alschuler, *The Exclusionary Rule and Causation*].

[70] *See Williams II*, 467 U.S. 431, 441–48 (1984).

"adds nothing to either the integrity or fairness of a criminal trial."[71] Rather, Burger reasoned, exclusion would "inflict a wholly unacceptable burden on the administration of criminal justice."[72] Nor would suppression promote "fairness."[73] According to Burger: "Fairness can be assured by placing the State and the accused in the same positions they would have been in had the impermissible conduct not taken place."[74] He explained exclusion would undermine the adversary system by "putting the State in a *worse* position than it would have occupied without any police misconduct."[75] Of course, each of these assertions equally applies to evidence directly obtained from an unreasonable search or seizure, but, in theory, would inevitably have been discovered by lawful means.

Another way Burger could have avoided the problem Professor Pitler identified was to withhold the exception in cases of bad-faith police conduct. Requiring good-faith police conduct was consistent with the theoretical basis of exclusion, namely, encouraging lawful police conduct. But again, Burger rejected that option with seemingly empirical assertions that were neither empirical nor self-evident. Rephrasing claims made in the Solicitor General's brief, Burger asserted: "A police officer who is faced with the opportunity to obtain evidence illegally will rarely, if ever, be in a position to calculate whether the evidence sought would inevitably be discovered."[76] He also stated that "when an officer is aware that the evidence will inevitably be discovered, he will try to avoid engaging in any questionable practice."[77] In those circumstances, according to Burger, the officer has "little to gain from taking any dubious 'shortcuts' to obtain the evidence."[78] No empirical data was provided for these assertions; indeed, the facts of a few lower court cases directly undermined Burger's second assertion. In these cases, lower courts were asked to apply the inevitable discovery exception to Fourth Amendment violations, like the case in which the Court of Appeals for the Sixth Circuit rejected the government's request to apply an inevitable discovery exception to permit the admission of drugs seized during an illegal search of a home.[79] Ultimately, however, Burger concluded that

---

71 *Id.* at 446.

72 *Id.* at 447.

73 *Id.*

74 *Id.*

75 *Id.*

76 *Id.* at 445; *see* Brief for the United States as Amicus Curiae Supporting Reversal, *supra* note 39, at 21 ("It seems quite improbable that a police officer would engage in conduct he knew to be illegal in the hope that the government could later prove that it would have found the same evidence through lawful means.").

77 *Williams II*, 467 U.S. at 445–46.

78 *Id.* at 446; *see* Brief for the United States as Amicus Curiae Supporting Reversal, *supra* note 39, at 22 ("[T]he possibility that the evidence [the officer] seeks would be discovered absent any illegality seems far too speculative to encourage unlawful 'shortcuts.' . . . [An] officer at the point of his misconduct may occasionally be able to anticipate that evidence obtained thereby will be admissible at trial under the inevitable discovery doctrine. But the more confident he is in that assessment, the less motivated he will be to seek the evidence by illegal means.").

79 4 Wayne R. LaFave, Search and Seizure: A Treatise on the Fourth Amendment § 11.4(a), at 380 & n.56 (2d ed. 1987) (citing cases).

the societal costs of suppression "far outweigh any possible benefits to deterrence that a good-faith requirement might produce."[80]

In 1961, as a federal appellate judge, Burger wanted to create an exception to the exclusionary rule that would allow the admission of corpus delicti evidence that was the direct fruit of an unlawful detention and subsequent confession of the defendant. Burger knew that the Supreme Court's exclusionary rule precedents barred such a result and lamented that someday Cardozo's prophecy that the judiciary will suppress a murder victim's body will ring true. Twenty-three years later, in *Williams II*, Burger would again invoke Cardozo's warning about the exclusionary rule, but this time Burger was writing as Chief Justice of the United States, and more important, writing for a majority of the Court. In *Williams II*, Burger engineered the Court's approval of the same result that he and Harry Blackmun plotted in 1961—an exception to the exclusionary rule broad enough to admit corpus delicti evidence—the inevitable discovery exception.

Two months before *Williams II* was announced, Powell sent Burger a letter noting that the results in *Leon*, *Sheppard*, and *Williams II* (Powell did not mention *Lopez-Mendoza*) would be viewed by the news media and others "as foreshadowing the abandonment of the exclusionary rule."[81] Powell's letter continued: "I know that you would favor that, but it is now too deeply rooted in the jurisprudence of this Court for abandonment to be a realistic possibility. This Term's decisions will have put the rule in a proper balance."[82] Burger immediately replied to Powell's letter with the following comment: "You are quite wrong that I would 'overrule' the Exclusionary Rule; I would just 'trim' it, as I set out in a 1960 lecture and in my *Bivens* dissent."[83]

Burger's opinion in *Williams II* did a lot more than "trim" the exclusionary rule. Although it was not obvious at the time, *Williams II* unleashed "a virus capable of killing" the Fourth Amendment exclusionary rule.[84] After *Williams II*, when police obtain evidence through a Fourth Amendment violation, prosecutors routinely argue, "if the police hadn't done it wrong, they would have done it right," and courts often admit the illegally acquired evidence under the inevitable discovery exception. For example, in 1999, the Michigan Supreme Court relied upon the exception to permit the admission of evidence police seized after entering the defendant's home at 12:32 a.m. without complying with the constitutional knock-and-announce requirement.[85] The Michigan court explained that exclusion was unwarranted because the police had a lawful warrant and "the evidence would have been discovered despite any police misconduct."[86]

---

80 *Williams II*, 467 U.S. at 446; *cf.* Brief for the United States as Amicus Curiae Supporting Reversal, *supra* note 39, at 25 ("[T]he costs of the exclusionary rule are simply too great to pay where the government would have discovered the challenged evidence regardless of the police misconduct.").

81 Lewis Powell, Letter to Warren Burger on *Nix v. Williams* (Apr. 12, 1984), Powell Papers, Box 109.

82 *Id.*

83 Warren Burger, Letter to Lewis Powell on *Nix v. Williams* (Apr. 12, 1984), Powell Papers, Box 109.

84 Alschuler, *The Exclusionary Rule and Causation*, *supra* note 69, at 1808 n.331.

85 People v. Stevens, 597 N.W.2d 53 (Mich. 1999).

86 *Id.* at 62.

Currently, there is a growing multitude of cases where lower courts rely on the inevitable discovery exception to admit evidence obtained from illegal car searches, illegal frisks, and other Fourth Amendment violations where the government can argue with a straight face that the disputed evidence would have been found by other lawful means.[87] In *Williams II*, even dissenting justices Brennan and Marshall were willing to embrace an inevitable discovery exception that admitted tainted evidence if such evidence inevitably would have been discovered "by an independent line of investigation that was already being pursued when the constitutional violation occurred."[88] The dissenters did not anticipate the reality that an inevitable discovery exception would become a virtual cure-all device for admitting evidence obtained in violation of the Fourth Amendment. In other words, Brennan and Marshall did not foresee what Burger and Blackmun had already envisioned in 1961 when they agreed that the exclusionary rule "cannot apply to the corpus delicti (whatever that may be in the particular case) to defeat utterly the process of criminal justice."[89]

* * *

Although Burger's comment about simply wanting to "trim" the exclusionary rule conflicted with his words and actions in *Stone v. Powell* when he proposed to his colleagues the option of modifying or eliminating the rule, the result in *Nix v. Williams* did more than prune the rule. The inevitable discovery doctrine was a significant restriction on exclusion. Yet, Burger's "trimming" of the rule was not complete with the announcement in *Williams II*. In another case decided in the same Term, *Segura v. United States*,[90] Burger solidified another important limitation on exclusion that would pay dividends for opponents of exclusion years after Burger left the Court.

In January 1981, federal law enforcements officers obtained information that Andres Segura and Luz Marina Colon were trafficking cocaine from their New York City apartment. Surveillance of the suspects established probable cause to arrest Segura and search the apartment. On the evening of February 12, after learning that the suspects had made another delivery of cocaine, officers stationed outside of Segura's residence received permission to arrest Segura from a federal prosecutor. But the prosecutor told the officers that a search warrant was unobtainable because of the lateness of the hour and that the officers should merely secure Segura's residence without searching it.[91]

When Segura arrived home alone around 11:15 p.m., he was arrested in the lobby of his building and taken to his apartment on the third floor. After the officers knocked on the door of the apartment, Luz Colon opened the door. The officers entered without permission and arrested Colon and three other persons found inside. The officers

---

[87] *See* 6 WAYNE R. LAFAVE, SEARCH AND SEIZURE: A TREATISE ON THE FOURTH AMENDMENT § 11.4(a), at 278 n.99, 279 n.101 (4th ed. 2004).

[88] *Williams II*, 467 U.S. at 459 (Brennan, J., dissenting).

[89] Harry Blackmun, Letter to Warren Burger on *Killough v. United States*, *supra* note 7.

[90] 468 U.S. 796 (1984).

[91] *Id.* at 799–800.

conducted a security check to ensure that no one was present who might threaten the officers or destroy evidence. During the sweep of the premises, officers saw in plain view evidence of drug trafficking; those items were not seized. The suspects were taken from the apartment, and two officers remained inside the premises to await the issuance of a search warrant.[92]

Nineteen hours later, a federal magistrate issued a warrant to search the apartment. In the search pursuant to the warrant, officers found cocaine, ammunition for a .38 caliber revolver, and more than fifty thousand dollars cash. The officers seized these items, along with the evidence observed in plain view during the earlier entry. After Segura and Colon were indicted, they made a motion to suppress all the evidence seized from their apartment. A federal district court found there were no exigent circumstances justifying the initial entry to the premises. Thus, the arrest of Colon and the discovery of the evidence in plain view were illegal. The court also concluded that although the search warrant was supported by untainted information providing probable cause, the evidence discovered after the execution of the warrant was "fruit of the poisonous tree." The court reasoned that this evidence was tainted because absent the unlawful entry and occupation of the apartment, the defendants might have arranged to have the evidence removed or destroyed.[93]

The court of appeals affirmed in part and reversed in part. It agreed that the entry of the premises was illegal and that the evidence discovered in plain view was inadmissible. On this issue, the appellate court rejected the government's claim that the evidence in plain view was not actually seized until *after* the search warrant was obtained. It also rejected the government's argument that all of the evidence found in the apartment was admissible under either the inevitable discovery exception or independent source doctrine. But the appellate court reversed the ruling that the evidence seized under the valid warrant also had to be suppressed. As for the defendants' claim that they had a right to exclude this evidence because it might have been removed or destroyed absent the illegal entry, the appellate court characterized that argument as "prudentially unsound."[94]

When *Segura* arrived at the Court, Powell agreed with his law clerk's description that this was "a very troubling case."[95] The government did not challenge the ruling below that the evidence discovered in plain view during the security check had to be suppressed.[96] Tellingly, the Solicitor General noted that this evidence could have been

---

[92] *Id.* at 800–01.

[93] *Id.* at 801–02.

[94] United States v. Segura, 663 F.2d 411, 416-17 (2d Cir. 1981). *But cf.* Joshua Dressler, *A Lesson in Incaution, Overwork, and Fatigue: The Judicial Miscraftsmanship of* Segura v. United States, 26 WM. & MARY L. REV. 375, 408 n.175 (1985) ("The claim that there is no 'constitutional right' to destroy evidence is a strawman. Nobody made such a claim. Colon and the others in the apartment did have a constitutional right not to be arrested, and Colon had the right not to have the home entered. The real issue is what should be the evidentiary implication of these violations.").

[95] Robert M. Couch, Bench Memorandum on *Segura v. United States* 7 (Nov. 2, 1983) [hereinafter Couch, *Segura* Bench Memorandum], Powell Papers, Box 110.

[96] *Segura*, 468 U.S. at 802 n.4.

admitted under the independent source[97] or inevitable discovery doctrines.[98] Thus, the only question before the Court was whether the evidence seized during the execution of the valid warrant had to be suppressed.[99] The defendants argued that this evidence was tainted by the initial unlawful entry and later seizure of the apartment.[100] The subsequent issuance of a valid warrant could not cure the unconstitutional entry and seizure. Otherwise, the defendants argued, police will have every incentive to search first before getting a warrant.[101]

The Solicitor General, on the other hand, pointed out that exclusion is appropriate only where there is a causal connection between a Fourth Amendment violation and the discovery of evidence.[102] Here, there was no nexus between the illegal entry and the discovery of the evidence concealed in the apartment.[103] The probable cause supporting the warrant was obtained *before* the illegal entry.[104] Further, the officers were entitled to secure the premises until the warrant issued. The fact that the premises were secured via an internal stakeout rather than an external stakeout was inconsequential.[105] Because the illegal entry and occupation did not lead to the discovery of the evidence, there was no basis for exclusion. Put differently, the search warrant was an independent source for the concealed evidence and, thus, the evidence was not fruit of the poisonous tree.

The government's causation argument was appealing. Indeed, it was similar to the argument urged by prosecutors in *Nix v. Williams*: "if we have hadn't done it wrong, we would have done it right." But if the Court agreed with the Solicitor General's argument that the warrant was an independent source and that there was no exploitation of the illegal entry, what would that mean for the warrant requirement, and what would stop police from performing similar illegal entries and occupations in the future? After all, even opponents of exclusion like Powell acknowledged that the home was afforded the most scrupulous protection under the Fourth Amendment.[106] Powell's law clerk, Rob Couch, observed that although police "are entitled to sit on the front lawn of a dwelling suspected of containing contraband while awaiting a search warrant, they should not be entitled to perform the same tasks from the living room."[107]

And once the Court announced that the illegal conduct in *Segura* had no adverse consequences for suppression purposes, police would have no meaningful incentives to obey Fourth Amendment rules whenever they had probable cause to search a home.

---

[97] *See generally* Brief for the United States, *Segura*, 468 U.S. 796 (No. 82-5298).

[98] *Id.* at 36 n.21.

[99] *Segura*, 468 U.S. at 802 n.4.

[100] *Id.* at 805–06, 813; *see also* Brief of Petitioners at 7, *Segura*, 468 U.S. 796 (No. 82-5298).

[101] *Segura*, 468 U.S. at 811 (Burger, C.J.).

[102] Brief for the United States, *supra* note 97, at 24–27.

[103] *Id.* at 25.

[104] *Id.* at 8, 14.

[105] *Id.* at 21–22.

[106] Couch, *Segura* Bench Memorandum, *supra* note 95, at 8.

[107] *Id.*

Rob Couch told Powell that alternatives to exclusion, such as a civil damages lawsuit, were unlikely to be effective in a case like *Segura* because of the difficulty of proving the requisite mental state of officers, and the damages incurred by the defendants were nominal or nonexistent.[108] And while the Solicitor General argued that police would be deterred from similar conduct in the future by the prospect that a court would exclude any evidence found in plain view upon an illegal entry, this argument contradicted the government's reserved claim that either the inevitable discovery or independent source rule justified admission of *all* of the evidence in the apartment. Put another way, if the government's causation theory was correct, the valid warrant also provided an independent source for the evidence found in plain view, as well as the concealed evidence.

Prior to *Segura*, the Court had not directly addressed the independent source doctrine, although the validity of the doctrine seemed beyond challenge. The venerable status of the doctrine stemmed from Holmes's language in his *Silverthorne Lumber* opinion. Holmes wrote:

> The essence of a provision forbidding the acquisition of evidence in a certain way is that not merely evidence so acquired shall not be used before the Court but that it shall not be used at all. Of course this does not mean that the facts thus obtained become sacred and inaccessible. *If knowledge of them is gained from an independent source they may be proved like any others. . . .*[109]

The last sentence was obiter dictum, and Holmes did not elaborate on its meaning. Holmes never explained that knowledge or evidence gained from an independent source is admissible because the government obtained such evidence without violating the defendant's rights. Since Holmes considered exclusion a personal right of the defendant, however, this is likely what he had in mind. Nor did Holmes say that evidence from an independent source is admissible because suppression would not promote the policy behind the exclusionary rule. Holmes did not identify deterrence or any other policy as

---

108 *Id.* at 11. Modern scholars recognize that damages lawsuits against police continue to be an inadequate remedy for Fourth Amendment violations. For example, Professor Chris Slobogin writes, "The best argument for retaining the [exclusionary] rule despite its flaws is that current alternatives to it are worse." Christopher Slobogin, Privacy at Risk: The New Government Surveillance and the Fourth Amendment 215 (2007) (describing numerous problems with current damages remedies and outlining an alternative damages regime); *cf.* Alison L. Patton, *The Endless Cycle of Abuse: Why 42 U.S.C. § 1983 Is Ineffective in Deterring Police Brutality*, 44 Hastings L.J. 753, 767 (1993) ("Section 1983 suits generally do not deter abusive police behavior, except in rare instances when there is either a large award, media attention, or both. This lack of deterrence comes about because '[m]any officers lose nothing as a result of being sued. It costs them nothing financially, it never results in discipline, it has no effect on promotion, and it does not affect the way officers are regarded by their peers and superiors.' Moreover, the threat of a lawsuit is minimal; 'only a small minority of abuses will ever end up in a lawsuit and the police know that.'" (alteration in original) (footnotes omitted)).

109 Silverthorne Lumber Co. v. United States, 251 U.S. 385, 392 (1920) (emphasis added).

the purpose for exclusion. In any event, this solitary sentence gave rise to the independent source rule, which has been a fixture of Fourth Amendment law ever since.

When *Segura* was before the Court, exclusion was justified as the most effective way to deter police misconduct. As Powell's law clerk, Rob Couch, put it: "Despite the absence of a nexus between the unlawful police conduct and the obtainment of the challenged evidence, the Court may wish to apply the exclusionary rule to deter the police from future misconduct."[110] Couch told Powell that *Segura* "boils down to whether you feel that the occupation of dwellings while waiting for search warrants is sufficiently egregious to warrant application of the exclusionary rule."[111]

After reviewing Couch's memo, which Powell described as "excellent,"[112] Powell dictated a memo to himself. Powell seemed conflicted by the case. He disagreed with the Solicitor General's claim that a warrantless entry and occupation of a private residence is the equivalent of an external stakeout.[113] But he also thought the search warrant was an "intervening" or "independent event," which meant that the evidence was not, "strictly speaking" poisonous fruit.[114] Regarding exclusion, Powell conceded that the nineteen-hour occupation was "outrageous," but he also believed that "the public pays a high price" for exclusion, and here the evidence was seized pursuant to a lawful warrant.[115]

The conference discussion of *Segura* began with Burger stating there was "no difference whether the warrant came back in one hour or nineteen hours."[116] The police "could have secured the apartment from the outside, but this is irrelevant."[117] Burger also thought the fruit of the poisonous tree doctrine was "inapplicable" because there was "no taint" from the entry.[118] Burger rejected the defense claim that the illegal entry amounted to a "constructive seizure" of the premises.[119] According to Burger, the "guts of the case is whether the police had an independent source" for the evidence. Burger voted to affirm.[120]

Brennan voted to reverse. While conceding that prior precedent supported a perimeter stakeout, the police here did not pursue that option. "The illegal entry constituted a 'seizure' of the apartment and *all* of its contents."[121] According to Brennan, "all of the evidence—whether or not in plain view—was seized."[122] If no seizure had occurred, the "evidence would have been removed."[123] White agreed with Burger and voted to affirm.

---

110 Couch, *Segura* Bench Memorandum, *supra* note 95, at 10.

111 *Id.* at 11–12.

112 *Id.* at 1.

113 Lewis Powell, Memorandum on *Segura v. United States* 2 (Nov. 7, 1983), Powell Papers, Box 110.

114 *Id.* at 2–3.

115 *Id.* at 3.

116 Lewis Powell, Conference Notes on *Segura v. United States* (Nov. 11, 1983), Powell Papers, Box 110.

117 *Id.*

118 *Id.*

119 *Id.*

120 *Id.*

121 *Id.*

122 *Id.*

123 *Id.*

Marshall also agreed with Burger, which prompted Powell to write on his conference notes that this "may be the first time Thurgood Marshall agreed with the Chief Justice on a Fourth Amendment issue—cheers!"[124]

Blackmun voted to affirm, as did Powell. Powell noted that "probable cause existed *before* the illegal entry."[125] It would be a "different case if this were not so."[126] And the "pre-existing probable cause was an independent source" for the discovery of the evidence.[127] Rehnquist voted to affirm. Stevens stated that *Segura* was a "difficult case."[128] He asked: "Would the evidence have been there if police had not seized the apartment?"[129] Ultimately, Stevens voted to affirm. O'Connor spoke last and said that "a per se rule was okay when the evidence is the product of a warrant and not the apartment seizure."[130] O'Connor also voted to affirm.[131] Thus, the conference vote was eight to one to affirm the convictions. Burger assigned *Segura* to himself.

Burger's first draft, which was circulated in December, 1983, addressed only whether the concealed evidence that was discovered when officers executed the warrant should have been suppressed. Although not necessary to resolve the exclusionary rule issue, he rejected the defense claim that this evidence was constructively seized as soon as the officers entered the premises. Burger explained that the entry was not conducted to *discover* evidence but to prevent the destruction or removal of it. He stated that "a mere securing of premises does not constitute a seizure of all items therein."[132] As for the defendants' exclusion argument, Burger concluded that the warrant was an independent source for the discovery of the concealed evidence. He explained that "what was discovered and seized under the warrant had no nexus with the initial entry or the 19 hour occupation."[133] While the occupation violated the defendants' privacy, it had no "impact on what evidence was found later under the warrant search."[134]

Four days after its circulation, White, Powell, and Rehnquist joined the opinion. Stevens, however, who voted in conference to affirm the convictions, sent Burger a letter indicating that he would be "writing separately" because he found the case "more difficult than your opinion indicates."[135] Later, Stevens circulated a dissent that Brennan and Marshall joined. By the middle of May, 1984, Burger still did not have five votes for his

[124] *Id.*
[125] *Id.*
[126] *Id.*
[127] *Id.*
[128] *Id.*
[129] *Id.*
[130] *Id.*
[131] *Id.*
[132] Warren Burger, First Draft of *Segura v. United States* 8 (Dec. 30, 1983), Powell Papers, Box 110.
[133] *Id.* at 9.
[134] *Id.* at 10.
[135] John Paul Stevens, Letter to Warren Burger on *Segura v. United States* (Jan. 3, 1984), Powell Papers, Box 110.

opinion. He then took "the unusual step" of circulating two additional drafts to White, Powell, Rehnquist, and O'Connor.[136] As he explained in his cover letter, Draft A was close to his original draft. It would "hold that we need not decide whether there was a *seizure* of the evidence when agents entered and later secured the apartment, since there was a wholly independent source for its discovery."[137]

Draft B was the theory proposed by the Solicitor General and the one preferred by O'Connor, with whom Burger had consulted. Draft B "assumes that there was a seizure of the evidence when the agents entered the apartment, and goes on to hold that the seizure was not unreasonable, primarily because the occupants of the apartment were in the custody of the officers throughout the duration of the seizure."[138] This draft would also hold that the concealed evidence should not have been suppressed as derivative evidence on the basis that the warrant provided an independent source for discovering the evidence. Burger told his colleagues that he preferred Draft A because "the inquiry into the independent source is all that is necessary" to decide the case.[139] But he acknowledged the "merit" of Draft B, which, *inter alia*, "has the benefit of giving us maximum flexibility in this sensitive area in future cases."[140]

After receiving Burger's new drafts, Powell's law clerk, Rob Couch, summarized the significance of the different drafts. Couch recommended that Powell support the original draft because it was "the most straightforward" and consistent with the majority of the federal appellate court holdings.[141] Couch remarked, however, that Burger seemed unable to convince O'Connor to join the original draft.[142] Given the choice between drafts A and B, Couch recommended that Powell support Draft B. According to the lower courts, the independent source rule applied only to derivative evidence. The problem with Draft A was that Burger "applies the 'independent source rule' without deciding whether the evidence is primary or derivative."[143] If Draft A became the law, Couch told Powell that police could "seize evidence without a warrant and hold it as long as necessary to get probable cause from an independent source."[144] This would constitute "a significant change in the law," and the "egregiousness of the police conduct in seizing the evidence is irrelevant" under Draft A.[145]

---

[136] Warren Burger, Letter to Byron White, Lewis Powell, William Rehnquist, and Sandra Day O'Connor on *Segura v. United States* 1 (May 16, 1984), Powell Papers, Box 110.

[137] *Id.*

[138] *Id.*

[139] *Id.* at 1–2.

[140] *Id.* at 2.

[141] Rob Couch, Memorandum to Lewis Powell on *Segura v. United States* 2 (May 17, 1984), Powell Papers, Box 110.

[142] *Id.*

[143] *Id.*

[144] *Id.*

[145] *Id.*

Under Draft B, Couch explained that Burger addresses the seizure issue without actually deciding that a seizure has taken place. According to Couch, the concealed evidence would also be admissible under the independent source doctrine. Draft B also leaves open the possibility that future police occupations might be deemed unreasonable, "[which] seems analytically preferable to the reasoning in Draft A."[146] Powell followed Couch's recommendation and sent Burger a letter indicating his preference for the original draft but also noting that he was inclined toward Draft B over Draft A.[147]

Rehnquist told Burger that he preferred Draft A because it was "closer to the position taken by the conference majority" and applies the independent source rule in "a useful way."[148] White also preferred Draft A "but could join" Draft B.[149] O'Connor, on the other hand, preferred Draft B.[150] In the end, Burger went with Draft B, which was O'Connor's choice all along. The first section of Part IV of Draft B contained a controversial section in which Burger concluded that even assuming that the initial illegal entry and nineteen-hour occupation constituted a seizure of *all* the evidence, that seizure was not unreasonable under the totality of the circumstances.[151]

This conclusion—that the illegal entry and occupation was a legal seizure—was too much, even for White and Rehnquist. White wrote Burger explaining that he would not join this section of the opinion and that he was planning to file a separate concurrence. White's position was that, irrespective of whether the entry and occupation was an unreasonable seizure, the challenged evidence came from an independent source, and thus admissible for that reason alone.[152] After "ruminating" about *Segura*, Rehnquist also refused to join Part IV and told Burger he would join White's separate opinion.[153] Soon, Powell would also abandon Burger on this issue. Powell was concerned that upholding the nineteen-hour occupation would encourage deliberate or negligent occupations of private premises for unreasonable periods of time. Powell believed the occupation in *Segura* violated the defendants' privacy. Powell, who had privately sent Burger a separate concurring opinion, would also join White's concurrence,[154] leaving O'Connor as the only member of the Court to join Burger's full opinion.[155]

---

146 *Id.* at 2.

147 Lewis Powell, Letter to Warren Burger on *Segura v. United States* (May 18, 1984), Powell Papers, Box 110.

148 William Rehnquist, Letter to Warren Burger on *Segura v. United States* (May 18, 1984), Powell Papers, Box 110.

149 Byron White, Letter to Warren Burger on *Segura v. United States* (May 21, 1984), Powell Papers, Box 110.

150 Sandra Day O'Connor, Letter to Warren Burger on *Segura v. United States* (May 21, 1984), Powell Papers, Box 110.

151 Warren Burger, Second Draft of *Segura v. United States* 9 (May 29, 1984), Powell Papers, Box 110.

152 Byron White, Letter to Warren Burger on *Segura v. United States* (June 11, 1984), Powell Papers, Box 110.

153 William Rehnquist, Letter to Warren Burger on *Segura v. United States* (June 12, 1984), Powell Papers, Box 110.

154 Lewis Powell, Letter to Warren Burger on Segura v. United States (June 15, 1984), Powell Papers, Box 110.

155 Sandra Day O'Connor, Letter to Warren Burger on *Segura v. United States* (June 12, 1984), Powell Papers, Box 110.

In response to Powell's move to join White's opinion, Burger sent Powell a "personal" letter.[156] Burger complained that the White-Rehnquist position meant that "evidence obtained as a *direct* result of unconstitutional conduct need not be suppressed."[157] Even though his own opinion upheld a nineteen-hour occupation of a private home that the Solicitor General did not attempt to defend, ironically, Burger criticized the White-Rehnquist position because it "provides no discernible check on police misconduct," and because the Court need not go that far in *Segura*.[158]

Burger also believed that the White-Rehnquist position was logically flawed. He explained that if the first entry into the premises constituted a seizure, "there could be no 'independent source' for *that* seizure."[159] Since the valid warrant, which was the only real independent source, was not obtained until the following day, "it could not serve as an 'independent source' *for the earlier seizure*."[160]

In sum, Burger thought that White's concurrence "either accepts that there can be multiple unconstitutional seizures—and presumably searches—so long as the last in the series is pursuant to a warrant, or it simply misunderstands the difference between the doctrines of independent source and inevitable discovery."[161] For similar reasons, Burger believed it necessary to decide whether the entry and occupation was constitutional. Indirectly referring to O'Connor, Burger admitted to Powell that it was "too bad I have been 'coerced' into dealing with the initial entry, but one colleague can do that!"[162]

Draft B, with some changes, eventually became the final opinion in *Segura*. Part IV of the final version of *Segura* rejected the defense argument that the concealed evidence found by the officers was direct evidence of an unreasonable seizure. This part ruled that the entry and occupation was a reasonable seizure. Only O'Connor joined this section of the opinion. Responding to the defense claim that his conclusion on this point would encourage future illegal entries, Burger offered a few throwaway reasons why such future misconduct was unlikely to occur.[163] Burger's only substantive response to the concern about deterrence was carefully phrased. He stated that future illegal entries and occupations were improbable because "officers who enter illegally will recognize that whatever

[156] Warren Burger, Letter to Lewis Powell on *Segura v. United States* (June 15, 1984), Powell Papers, Box 110.

[157] *Id.*

[158] *Id.*

[159] *Id.*

[160] *Id.*

[161] *Id.*

[162] *Id.*

[163] Burger dismissed the need for deterrence because he was "unwilling to believe that officers will routinely and purposely violate the law as a matter of course." Segura v. United States, 468 U.S. 796, 812 (1984) (Burger, C.J.). Also, "as a practical matter, officers who have probable cause and who are in the process of obtaining a warrant have no reason to enter the premises before the warrant issues." *Id.* And finally, if officers enter without exigent circumstances to justify the entry, they expose themselves to potential civil liability. *Id.*

evidence they discover as a direct result of the entry *may* be suppressed," as the appellate court did in *Segura*.[164]

Part V of *Segura*, which a majority of the Court joined, rejected the defendants' alternative claim that the concealed evidence should have been suppressed as derivative fruit of the entry and occupation. Exclusion was not warranted, according to Burger, because the valid warrant served as an independent source for the evidence. The unlawful entry and occupation "did not contribute in any way to discovery of the evidence seized under the warrant."[165] Thus, as Wayne LaFave observes, the upshot of *Segura* is clear: police know that if they illegally enter and occupy a home to facilitate the execution of a search warrant, "that illegality will have no effect upon the evidence first discovered during the warrant execution."[166] While *Segura* claimed to be following Holmes's vision of exclusion, Holmes never said that the independent source doctrine applied in situations where the government intentionally violated a defendant's Fourth Amendment rights.

Stevens wrote a scathing dissent in *Segura*, which Brennan, Marshall, and Blackmun joined, even though the latter two had voted at conference to affirm the convictions. Among other things, Stevens's dissent pointed out that the majority's independent source analysis was analytically flawed. While the *Segura* majority distinguished between the pre-warrant evidence and the post-warrant evidence for purposes of exclusion, Stevens thought that distinction made no sense. He noted that the warrant embraced both categories of evidence equally: "The warrant provided an 'independent' justification for seizing all the evidence in the apartment—that in plain view just as much as the items that were concealed."[167] It follows then, he explained, that "[i]f the execution of a valid warrant takes the poison out of the hidden fruit, I should think that it would also remove the taint from the fruit in plain view."[168] Tellingly, Burger did not respond to Stevens's point, implying that it was only a matter of time before the independent source doctrine would expand to allow the admission of evidence first seen during an illegal entry and search.

Fours year later, the other shoe fell in *Murray v. United States*.[169] At issue was whether evidence observed during a warrantless search that violated the Fourth Amendment may nevertheless be admitted under the independent source rule. Relying on the foundation built in *Segura*, and to no one's surprise, *Murray* expanded the independent source doctrine to allow the admission of such evidence.

Federal law enforcement officers had probable cause to suspect Michael F. Murray and James D. Carter were trafficking marijuana in a warehouse in South Boston. On April

---

164 *Id.* (emphasis added).

165 *Id.* at 815 (majority opinion).

166 6 LaFave, *supra* note 87, § 11.4(d), at 319. Professor Dressler describes the reasoning of *Segura* in harsher terms. Dressler, *supra* note 94, at 422 ("*Segura* is a disaster as a written opinion.").

167 *Segura*, 468 U.S. at 831 (Stevens, J., dissenting) (footnote omitted).

168 *Id.*

169 487 U.S. 533 (1988).

6, 1983, federal officers were notified that two vehicles, which were driven by Murray and Carter, had recently left the warehouse and contained marijuana. The officers forcibly entered the warehouse without a warrant and discovered in plain view several burlap-wrapped bales that were later confirmed to contain marijuana. The officers left the warehouse without seizing the bales and did not reenter the warehouse until they obtained a search warrant. In the warrant application, the officers made no mention of the forcible entry and search and did not use any information from the search to obtain the warrant. Several hours later, a warrant was issued, a new search was performed, and the officers seized two hundred and seventy bales of marijuana and other incriminating evidence.[170]

Before trial, the defendants unsuccessfully moved to suppress the evidence found in the warehouse. The Court of Appeals for the First Circuit ruled that the defense motion was properly denied because there was no causal connection between the illegal entry and search and the subsequent issuance of the search warrant. The Court then granted the defendants' request to decide whether the bales of marijuana first discovered during the illegal entry and search should have been excluded as tainted fruit.[171]

In the Court, the defendants argued that because the officers' knowledge about the bales of marijuana was primary evidence, exclusion was mandatory.[172] Even in *Segura*, the Court stated that evidence "obtained as a direct result of an unconstitutional search or seizure is plainly subject to exclusion."[173] The defendants also correctly pointed out that the inevitable discovery exception announced in *Williams II* was inapplicable because the warrant here was obtained long after the illegal search of the warehouse had disclosed the marijuana. By contrast, in *Williams II*, the search team looking for Pamela Powers had started their search shortly after her disappearance and probably would have discovered her body, even if Williams had never agreed to direct police to its location.[174] Further, *Williams II* concerned the admissibility of derivative evidence under the inevitable discovery rule, whereas *Murray* concerned primary evidence.[175]

Finally, and most important, the defendants' argument for exclusion relied on *Segura*'s premise that any evidence immediately observed by police during an illegal entry would be excluded at a subsequent prosecution.[176] *Segura*'s holding on the independent source doctrine rested on a distinction between primary evidence, which was inadmissible, and derivative evidence, which was admissible.[177] As Blackmun's law clerk told his boss in a memorandum, neither *Segura* nor *Williams II* permitted the admission of primary

---

170 *Id.* at 535–36.

171 *Id.* at 536.

172 Brief for the Petitioners at 16-18, *Murray*, 487 U.S. 533 (No. 86-995).

173 Segura v. United States, 468 U.S. 796, 804 (1984).

174 For an informative and perceptive analysis of this aspect of the inevitable discovery exception, see Stephen E. Hessler, *Establishing Inevitability Without Active Pursuit: Defining the Inevitable Discovery Exception to the Fourth Amendment Exclusionary Rule*, 99 Mich. L. Rev. 238 (2000).

175 Brief for the Petitioners, *supra* note 172, at 27.

176 *Id.* at 36-37.

177 *Segura*, 468 U.S. at 813–16.

evidence. He wrote, "Indeed, both take as a given that [primary] evidence should not be admitted."[178]

The government's argument in *Murray* was straightforward: the independent source doctrine applies to any evidence initially discovered during, or as a result of, an illegal search but later obtained from a lawful source untainted by the illegal search. The Solicitor General, moreover, contended that the defendants were misinterpreting *Segura*. During the oral argument, the lawyer representing the Solicitor General's Office, Roy Englert, reminded the Court that the government's brief in *Segura* was careful to state that none of the evidence detected in the illegal entry and nineteen-hour occupation—the plain view evidence, as well as the concealed evidence—should have been suppressed. Englert also pointed out that *Segura* only addressed whether the concealed evidence that was later discovered after the warrant had been executed should have been suppressed.[179] Then the following exchange occurred:

> QUESTION: But is it not correct that the Chief Justice in his opinion said that one reason that there will be a deterrent against this kind of activity is that the—whatever evidence they discover as a direct result of the entry will be suppressed?
>
> MR. ENGLERT: No, Your Honor. He said it may. May be suppressed.
>
> QUESTION: Yes. May be.
>
> MR. ENGLERT: I think that's an important distinction.
>
> QUESTION: You don't think he meant that it would automatically be suppressed?
>
> MR. ENGLERT: We do not . . . .
>
> QUESTION: What is the deterrent then if it won't be suppressed? If you say it may. Of course, anything might be suppressed. I don't understand his reasoning there if he isn't assuming that it would be suppressed on the facts of that case.
>
> MR. ENGLERT: Your Honor, he was, of course, assuming that, but that was one of several deterrents that the Chief Justice discussed.
>
> QUESTION: And the other is that he might sue the police officers.
>
> MR. ENGLERT: Civil liability was one of the deterrents. Administrative sanctions were another deterrent that he discussed.[180]

Englert then explained to the justices that what Chief Justice Burger had said in *Williams II* was equally applicable here. In *Williams II*, Burger wrote that the exclusionary rule was intended to put the government "in the same, not a *worse*," position than it would have been in if no police misconduct had occurred. Englert noted that exclusion

[178] Law Clerk, Memorandum to Harry Blackmun on *Murray v. United States* 8 (Dec. 7, 1987), Blackmun Papers, Box 496.

[179] Transcript of Oral Argument at 18, Murray v. United States, 487 U.S. 533 (1988) (No. 86-995).

[180] *Id.* at 19-20.

is warranted only if there is a causal relationship between the police illegality and the discovery of evidence.[181]

The conference discussion of *Murray* began with Chief Justice Rehnquist pointing out that *Segura* and *Williams II* stand for the proposition that even if the government violates the Constitution, exclusion is unwarranted if there is no causal connection between the illegality and the discovery of evidence. Rehnquist voted to affirm. White agreed with Rehnquist and said the exclusionary rule was not applicable here. Marshall wanted to remand the case "to find out the connection of the first search with the second search."[182] Blackmun voted to affirm,[183] but he also proposed, following the suggestion of his law clerk, a remand to determine whether the evidence was, in fact, obtained by an independent source.[184] Stevens voted to reverse, saying that there is "nothing left of the exclusionary rule unless you do so."[185] O'Connor also voted to reverse. She recalled: "I joined Part IV of *Segura*; the stuff observed should be suppressed—this is what *Segura* said."[186] O'Connor also noted, "If there's any deterrent effort left to the exclusionary rule, this case covers it."[187] Finally, Scalia voted to affirm.[188] Thus, the vote was four to two to affirm, with Marshall voting to remand. (Brennan and Kennedy did not participate in *Murray*.)

Scalia's majority's opinion in *Murray* did just want Stevens's dissent in *Segura* predicted: enlarge the independent source doctrine to permit the admissibility of evidence first seen during an illegal search with one condition—the government prove that the unlawful intrusion neither influenced the decision to seek a warrant or the magistrate's decision to grant it.[189] Scalia explained that the officers surely learned about the marijuana during the unlawful search. But they also learned about it during the lawful search pursuant to the warrant, "and if that later acquisition was not the result of the earlier entry there is no reason why the independent source doctrine should not apply."[190]

Relying on Burger's logic in *Williams II*, Scalia found ordering exclusion in *Murray* would not put the government "in the *same* position they would have occupied if no violation occurred, but in a *worse* one."[191] This analysis also applied to the tangible evidence observed during the illegal entry and search—the burlap-wrapped bales. Application

---

181 *Id.* at 24-25.

182 William J. Brennan, Jr., Conference Notes on *Murray v. United States* (undated), Brennan Papers, Box I: 773.

183 *Id.*

184 Antonin Scalia, Memorandum to the Conference on *Murray v. United States* (Mar. 22, 1988), Blackmun Papers, Box 496.

185 Brennan, Conference Notes on *Murray v. United States*, *supra* note 182.

186 Harry Blackmun, Conference Notes on *Murray v. United States* (undated), Blackmun Papers, Box 496.

187 Brennan, Conference Notes on *Murray v. United States*, *supra* note 182.

188 *Id.*

189 Murray v. United States, 487 U.S. 533, 540 (1982).

190 *Id.* at 541.

191 *Id.*

of the independent source doctrine did not turn on whether the officers had actually seized the bales of marijuana during the illegal search. Even assuming that a seizure had occurred, Scalia explained that the evidence was still admissible provided "a later, lawful seizure is genuinely independent of an earlier, tainted one."[192]

The "ultimate" question under the independent source doctrine is whether the lawful acquisition of the challenged evidence came by a genuinely independent source. Scalia instructs that the doctrine is not available if the police decision to seek a warrant was prompted by what was seen during an illegal search, or if information obtained during such a search was presented to a magistrate and affected the decision to grant the warrant.[193] Of course, those are not major obstacles for law enforcement officers, especially when, as was true in *Murray*, the officers performing the unlawful search control the flow of information regarding both why a warrant was sought and what data is put in the application. While *Murray* addressed the scope of the independent source rule, Scalia's opinion and logic supports admitting the bales of marijuana, primary evidence of the illegal search, under the inevitable discovery exception as well.[194] Thus, the result in *Murray* expanded a prosecutor's authority to admit evidence acquired from an illegal search under either the independent source doctrine or inevitable discovery exception.

* * *

In some circles, especially among political conservatives, Warren Burger's tenure as Chief Justice was a "failure."[195] Some academics have taken a similar view. Bernard Schwartz, a prodigious and well-known scholar of the Court, has written that Burger's tenure as Chief Justice "was not marked by strong leadership in molding Supreme Court jurisprudence."[196] While many saw Burger's appointment as Chief Justice as the first step in dismantling the landmark rulings of the Warren Court, Schwartz observes that on the two most controversial criminal procedure rulings announced by the Warren Court, *Mapp v. Ohio* and *Miranda v. Arizona*, Burger was "never able to persuade a majority to cast those cases into constitutional limbo."[197]

To be sure, the exclusionary rule remained intact when Warren Burger left the Court in 1986. But it was certainly not the same rule that existed when Burger was appointed in 1969. Whatever impact Burger had on other areas of constitutional law, his impact on the Court's exclusionary rule jurisprudence cannot be measured simply by asking whether the exclusionary rule was abandoned during his tenure. After all, while Rehnquist was

---

[192] *Id.* at 542.

[193] *Id.*

[194] *Id.* at 540–41; *see also* Bloom, *supra* note 68, at 92–93.

[195] David G. Savage, Turning Right: The Making of the Rehnquist Supreme Court 4 (1992).

[196] Bernard Schwartz, The Ascent of Pragmatism: The Burger Court in Action 2 (1990).

[197] *Id.* at 8; *cf.* Earl M. Maltz, The Chief Justiceship of Warren Burger 1969–1986, at 163 (2000) (acknowledging that although the Burger Court did not overrule core principles established by the Warren Court's criminal procedure rulings, such as *Mapp* and *Miranda*, the Burger Court conservatives "could at least claim to have slowed (if not reversed) the trend toward nationalization of criminal procedure").

willing to join Burger in repealing the rule, neither Burger nor Rehnquist constituted "the Burger Court."[198] As previous chapters have shown, despite their fierce opposition to exclusion, neither White nor Powell was willing to completely discard the exclusionary rule. Similarly, though Blackmun was personally disposed to abolishing the exclusionary rule, he made no effort to convince his colleagues to repeal it. As John Jeffries would later observe, as far as White, Blackmun, and Powell were concerned, there was "a lot of anti-*Mapp v. Ohio* sentiment, but little anti-*Mapp v. Ohio* courage."[199]

Moreover, focusing on whether the rule was abolished overlooks the significant restrictions the Burger Court imposed on suppression as a remedy for Fourth Amendment violations. In *Lopez-Mendoza*, the Court did effectively "repeal" the rule in civil proceedings. The Court also created major exceptions to exclusion in cases like *Calandra* and *Janis*, which allowed the admission of illegally acquired evidence in grand jury proceedings and federal tax hearings; and in *Nix v. Williams* and *Segura*, which approved and solidified the inevitable discovery exception and independent source doctrine. Equally important, the Court substantially reduced the federal judiciary's oversight of searches and seizures when it decided in *Stone v. Powell* that state prisoners cannot invoke the rule in federal habeas corpus proceedings to challenge state convictions. The combined result of these rulings has left state judges as the primary decision makers on whether unlawfully obtained evidence is admissible in legal proceedings.[200] Thus, while each of these decisions chipped away at the force of the exclusionary rule in a piecemeal fashion, their cumulative effect seemingly amounts to a partial overruling of *Mapp*.

Finally, the creation of the good-faith exception in *Leon* was a monumental achievement that continues to expand today. When viewed from this perspective, the Burger Court's impact on the jurisprudence of the exclusionary rule was not only meaningful, but also permanent. Thus, while Burger's leadership skills as Chief Justice may have been lacking, the law of exclusion underwent significant and permanent change during his tenure. By the end of Burger's tenure as Chief Justice, the Court had given prosecutors numerous tools to oppose criminal defendants' efforts to suppress illegally acquired evidence. Unless a case involved a flagrant Fourth Amendment violation, exclusion was a rare remedy. The Burger Court had effectively transformed the exclusionary rule from an important constitutional right into "chicken broth."[201]

---

198 Yale Kamisar, *The Warren Court (Was It Really So Defense-Minded?), The Burger Court (Is It Really So Prosecution-Oriented?), and Police Investigatory Practices, in* THE BURGER COURT: THE COUNTER-REVOLUTION THAT WASN'T 62, 81 (Vincent Blasi ed., 1983).

199 Email from John C. Jeffries, Jr., Professor of Law, University of Virginia School of Law to author (Apr. 12, 2011) (on file with author).

200 John C. Jeffries, Jr. & George A. Rutherglen, *Structural Reform Revisited*, 95 CALIF. L. REV. 1387, 1407 (2007) (noting that the "combined effect of exceptions to the rule and restrictions on collateral review has been to leave exclusion of illegally seized evidence primarily in the hands of state courts").

201 Steven Duke, *Making* Leon *Worse*, 95 YALE L.J. 1405, 1414 (1986).

8 The Rehnquist and Roberts Courts: Making the Exclusionary Rule Largely Irrelevant

ON SEPTEMBER 17, 1986, the Senate confirmed William H. Rehnquist to succeed Warren Burger as Chief Justice of the United States. By that point, Rehnquist's opposition to the Fourth Amendment exclusionary rule was well known. As an associate justice, Rehnquist tried, but had been unable to persuade a majority of his colleagues to overrule *Weeks* and *Mapp*; he did, however, in his own words, "seize any opportunity to limit the damage done" by those cases.[1]

On the same day that the Senate confirmed Rehnquist to be the nation's new Chief Justice, it also unanimously confirmed Antonin Scalia to fill the seat vacated by Rehnquist's elevation to the post of Chief Justice. During the brief time he sat on the federal Court of Appeals for the District of Columbia, Scalia was known as a "law and order" judge.[2] Tellingly, in a dissenting opinion, Scalia took a gratuitous shot at the exclusionary rule in a double jeopardy case when he noted the "public disrepute" the rule brings to the criminal justice process.[3] If that remark did not provide convincing evidence of Scalia's opposition toward exclusion, his hostility to the rule would eventually become evident to the other justices and the public. And unlike some of his conservative colleagues on the Court, if given the opportunity, Scalia was prepared to repeal the rule

[1] William Rehnquist, Letter to the Conference on *New Jersey v. T.L.O.* (Mar. 30, 1984), Blackmun Papers, Box 414.

[2] George Kannar, *The Constitutional Catechism of Antonin Scalia*, 99 YALE L.J. 1297, 1321 (1990).

[3] United States v. Richardson, 702 F.2d 1079, 1086 (D.C. Cir. 1983) (Scalia, J., dissenting).

forthwith. But before the newly formed Rehnquist Court would continue the retrenchment of the exclusionary rule begun by the Burger Court, Brennan would manage one last victory for the rule in *James v. Illinois*.[4]

In late August 1982, Chicago police detectives suspected that fifteen-year-old Darryl James was involved in the shooting and murder of two teenagers. Witnesses to the shooting told police that the shooter had "reddish" straight hair. These same witnesses also said they had seen James several weeks earlier at a parade, and that James's hair was "reddish" and straight.[5] The day after the shooting, detectives found James at his mother's beauty parlor sitting under a hair dryer. When he emerged, his hair was black and curly. After arresting James, the detectives questioned him about his prior hair color. James told the detectives that the previous day his hair had been reddish brown, long, and combed straight back. He also told the police that he had changed his hair color and style on the day of his arrest in order "'to change his appearance.'"[6]

After James was indicted for murder and attempted murder, the trial court ruled that James's statements to the detectives were inadmissible because they were the fruit of an arrest without probable cause. Although James did not testify at the trial, the defense called a family friend, Jewell Henderson, who testified that on the day of the shooting, she had taken James to register for high school, and on that day, his hair was black and curly. The prosecutor was allowed to impeach Henderson's testimony by introducing James's statements to the police.[7] During closing arguments, the prosecutor told the jury that the state's evidence contained an admission by the defendant that he changed the color of his hair.[8] James was convicted of murder and attempted murder.[9]

The Illinois Supreme Court upheld the convictions. A majority of the Illinois court acknowledged that the Supreme Court's impeachment exception cases from *Walder v. United States* to *United States v. Havens* all involved scenarios where the defendant himself had testified, and it was the defendant's own testimony that was impeached by tainted evidence. Nonetheless, the court ruled the balancing analysis of those cases was equally applicable to the impeachment of defense witnesses. Thus, it ruled that to prevent perjury "by proxy," the prosecution was authorized to use James's statements to impeach Henderson.[10]

During the deliberations in *James*, some of the justices were troubled by the Illinois Supreme Court ruling. Blackmun, for example, thought the prosecution had used

4 493 U.S. 307 (1990).

5 *Id.* at 310.

6 *Id.*

7 *Id.* at 309–10.

8 People v. James, 528 N.E.2d 723, 725 (Ill. 1988).

9 *James*, 493 U.S. at 310.

10 *James*, 528 N.E.2d at 728–30 (holding that "when a defense witness testifies on direct examination in a manner squarely at odds with the evidence which has been suppressed, that evidence may be introduced to challenge the veracity of the testimony").

James's statements not as impeachment evidence, but instead as rebuttal evidence. In a preliminary memo, Blackmun's law clerk told his boss that the Illinois Supreme Court ruling "expanded the scope of the impeachment exception to the exclusionary rule beyond any of this Court's precedents,"[11] and the use of James's statements "to contradict the testimony of another witness is not 'impeachment' as traditionally understood, but rather is substantive *rebuttal* evidence."[12] The latter observation repeated a point raised by a dissenting justice on the Illinois Supreme Court, Justice William G. Clark, who argued that James's statements were used as substantive evidence to prove his guilt.[13] Using tainted evidence in this manner was impermissible. *Havens*, for example, had clearly stated that tainted evidence "is inadmissible on the government's direct case, or otherwise, as substantive evidence of guilt."[14] Indeed, Blackmun made a similar point in a *Miranda* impeachment case he authored, *Oregon v. Hass*,[15] when he emphasized that the trial court had instructed the jury that the defendant's illegally acquired confession "could be used only in passing on his credibility and not as evidence of guilt."[16]

The Solicitor General's amicus brief in *James* exacerbated Blackmun's unease about the ruling below. The brief contended that there is no significant difference between impeachment and rebuttal evidence.[17] After the oral argument in *James*, Blackmun's personal notes outlined his concerns. He wrote, "this seems as rebuttal testimony, not merely as impeachment evidence." He observed that the "Solicitor General abandons any effort to deny this." He worried a ruling for the state "would probably lead to additional exceptions." His notes ended with the remark, "this is close for me, but I suspect it goes too far."[18]

Brennan had different concerns. While he shared Blackmun's view that Illinois was seeking a broad "rebuttal" exception to the exclusionary rule, Brennan was also concerned that such an exception would impair a defendant's willingness to present a defense. In a preconference memo explaining the basis for his vote at the *James* conference, Brennan wrote: "Out of a legitimate fear that illegally obtained evidence will come in the back door through this exception, many defendants might be deterred from putting on *any* defense at all. This distorts the truth-seeking function in that it excludes from the jury's consideration probative exculpatory evidence."[19]

---

11 Law Clerk, Preliminary Memorandum to Harry Blackmun on *James v. Illinois* 8 (Jan. 27, 1989), Blackmun Papers, Box 553.

12 *Id.* at 11.

13 *James*, 528 N.E.2d at 733–34 (Clark, J., dissenting).

14 United States v. Havens, 446 U.S. 620, 628 (1980).

15 420 U.S. 714 (1975).

16 *Id.* at 721.

17 Brief for the United States as Amicus Curiae Supporting Respondent at 16–18, James v. Illinois, 493 U.S. 307 (1990) (No. 88-6075).

18 Harry Blackmun, Handwritten Notes on *James v. Illinois* (Sept. 23, 1989), Blackmun Papers, Box 553.

19 William J. Brennan, Jr., Memorandum on *James v. Illinois* 1 (undated), Brennan Papers, Box I: 859.

Brennan had another concern related to deterrence. Relying on the state's argument that illegally acquired evidence will almost always be admissible in rebuttal, Brennan believed that the threat of losing evidence for the prosecution's case-in-chief was an insufficient deterrent to police misconduct. Forbidding the use of evidence in the prosecution's direct case "is hardly a realistic deterrent; the burden of presenting a prima facie case sufficient to withstand a defendant's motion for a directed verdict is quite low. Indeed, I wonder whether trial courts *ever* grant directed verdicts for defendants based on the state's failure to make out a prima facie case."[20] Although *James* was a search and seizure case, Brennan was especially troubled by the impact a rebuttal exception would have for *Miranda* violations. Ironically, Scalia's exchange with the assistant Attorney General of Illinois, Terence Madsen, during oral argument highlighted Brennan's concerns. Scalia asked Madsen the following:

> QUESTION: I must say, what—what you say about the negligible effect on deterrence is a—is a lot truer with respect to Fourth Amendment violations than with respect to—confessions unlawfully obtained. It seems to me the police officer knows very well that if he—if he asks the person under arrest, does he-does he want a lawyer, and tells him you don't have to answer any questions if you have a lawyer, he knows doggone well that as soon as he gets a lawyer the lawyer's going to tell him, don't answer any questions. So he has nothing to lose. Trick—trick him out of a confession right away. You wouldn't get a confession if you did it right so why not do it—do it this way? What—what's to lose? Isn't that the reality of the thing? I mean, the Fourth Amendment is—something different, but as far as—as far as confessions go—
>
> MR. MADSEN: It is harder to—to extend into a *Miranda* situation. I agree with that.[21]

In his preconference memo, Brennan emphasized Scalia's point that "police officers have no reason *not* to try to elicit defendants' testimony illegally."[22] Brennan felt that because the evidence in *James* involved a defendant's incriminating statements, "the special need for a broad exclusionary rule to deter fifth amendment violations applies here."[23]

At the *James* conference vote, only Chief Justice Rehnquist was clearly committed to affirming James's conviction.[24] All the remaining justices, including O'Connor and Scalia, voted to reverse the conviction. Rehnquist seemed to concede that the ruling below had expanded the impeachment exception beyond any of the Court's prior rulings.

---

20 *Id.* at 1–2.

21 Transcript of Oral Argument at 23–24, *James*, 493 U.S. 307 (No. 88-6075).

22 Brennan, Memorandum on *James v. Illinois*, *supra* note 19, at 2.

23 *Id.*

24 William J. Brennan, Jr., Case Histories, October Term, 1989, at 69 (undated) [hereinafter Brennan, Case Histories O.T. 1989], Brennan Papers, Box II: 8.

He said, "*Walder v. United States*, *Harris v. New York*, and others were expanded" by the ruling below.[25] Rehnquist also acknowledged that the challenged evidence "is not impeachment but rebuttal."[26] Nonetheless, Rehnquist voted to affirm on the "ground that the exclusionary rule must give way to truth seeking."[27] Brennan voted to reverse. He told his colleagues that the state concedes this is "okay as rebuttal" evidence.[28]

White voted to reverse; he was troubled about how far the ruling below would extend. White stated that he did not "see how limits can be put on this kind of evidence."[29] Marshall also voted to reverse. He stated: "If evidence is inadmissible in the prosecution's case-in-chief, I can't see it being admissible on cross-examination."[30] Blackmun said this was "rebuttal evidence," and he voted to reverse.[31] Stevens noted his agreement with the dissenting justices on the Illinois Supreme Court and voted to reverse. O'Connor told her colleagues that an affirmance "would encourage improper police conduct."[32] She too voted to reverse. Scalia said that unless the Court was "going to discard the exclusionary rule," he would vote to reverse.[33] Kennedy signaled "he was on the fence"[34] but ultimately voted to reverse.[35] Thus, the vote was eight to one for reversal.

As the senior justice in the majority, Brennan assigned *James* to himself and circulated a first draft that closely resembled the published opinion. He repeated his concern that expanding the impeachment exception to the exclusionary rule to encompass the testimony of all defense witnesses "likely would chill some defendants from presenting their best defense—and sometimes any defense at all—through the testimony of others."[36] Accordingly, Brennan explained that this potential "chilling" effect changed the balance of values that had informed the Court's earlier impeachment rulings. While the Court's prior impeachment cases recognized that defendants were not permitted to exploit tainted evidence as a shield for perjury, Brennan explained: "[I]t seems no more appropriate for the State to brandish such evidence as a sword with which to dissuade defendants from presenting a meaningful defense through other witnesses."[37]

Brennan also wrote that an expanded impeachment exception would undermine the deterrent effects of exclusion. He explained that authorizing the impeachment of

---

25 William J. Brennan, Jr., Conference Notes on *James v. Illinois* (undated) [hereinafter Brennan, *James* Conference Notes], Brennan Papers, Box I: 859.

26 *Id.*

27 *Id.*

28 Harry Blackmun, Conference Notes on *James v. Illinois* (Oct. 6, 1989), Blackmun Papers, Box 553.

29 Brennan, *James* Conference Notes, *supra* note 25.

30 *Id.*

31 *Id.*

32 *Id.*

33 *Id.*

34 Brennan, Case Histories O.T. 1989, *supra* note 24, at 69.

35 Brennan, *James* Conference Notes, *supra* note 25.

36 William J. Brennan, Jr., First Draft of *James v. Illinois* 6 (Nov. 2, 1989), Blackmun Papers, Box 553.

37 *Id.* at 8.

defense witnesses was appreciably different from the impeachment of defendants for at least two reasons. First, enlarging the impeachment exception would multiply the occasions in which tainted evidence could be used because defense witnesses testify more often than does the defendant himself. Second, the threat of admitting tainted evidence gives the prosecution leverage not only to deter perjury, but "also [to] deter defendants from calling witnesses in the first place, thereby keeping from the jury much probative exculpatory evidence."[38] Interestingly, neither Brennan's draft opinion nor the published opinion mentioned his earlier concern that an expanded impeachment exception would encourage police to violate *Miranda*.

Soon after Brennan circulated his first draft, White, Marshall, Blackmun, and Stevens all joined the opinion. Brennan's private papers also noted: "For a while, it even appeared that the Chief might switch his vote and join as well."[39] Rehnquist had told his law clerk "to tinker with a draft dissent but said that he wasn't sure he would circulate anything."[40]

In the meantime, Kennedy wrote Brennan a letter stating, "[I]t seems to me that reversal here requires a rule far more sweeping than I had thought at Conference."[41] Kennedy also thought that the state's position would not undermine the purpose of exclusion, because permitting "rebuttal of the false testimony here need not lower the level of deterrence."[42] Kennedy, whose vote to affirm at the conference was shaky, informed Brennan that he would dissent.[43] Kennedy, according to Brennan's records, "was convinced after a strong lobbying from one of his clerks to write a dissent himself."[44]

The first draft that Kennedy circulated dismissed Brennan's fears that permitting the use of tainted evidence would encourage future lawless behavior by the police. Kennedy pointed out that similar fears had been raised and rejected in prior cases.[45] This concern—encouraging police misconduct—was the basis for O'Connor's vote at conference. In addition, Kennedy argued that any gain in deterrence achieved by excluding the evidence was "marginal."[46]

Within three hours of receiving Kennedy's draft, Rehnquist and O'Connor joined his dissent.[47] The next day, O'Connor wrote Brennan to explain that she found Kennedy's

---

38 *Id.* at 9.

39 Brennan, Case Histories O.T. 1989, *supra* note 24, at 69.

40 *Id.*

41 Anthony Kennedy, Letter to William J. Brennan, Jr. on *James v. Illinois* (Nov. 21, 1989), Blackmun Papers, Box 553.

42 *Id.*

43 *Id.*

44 Brennan, Case Histories O.T. 1989, *supra* note 24, at 69.

45 Anthony Kennedy, First Draft of Dissenting Opinion in *James v. Illinois* 6 (Nov. 21, 1989), Brennan Papers, Box I: 859.

46 *Id.* at 7.

47 Brennan, Case Histories O.T. 1989, *supra* note 24, at 69.

dissent "persuasive" and decided to switch her conference vote.[48] After *James* was announced, Brennan's private papers recalled that O'Connor found Kennedy's dissent "'persuasive' (though it merely relied on the same arguments she had herself rejected at Conference)."[49] Two weeks after Kennedy circulated his dissent, Scalia also joined it and changed his conference vote as well.[50] Even with O'Connor and Scalia's defections, Brennan still retained five votes to reject expanding the impeachment exception to the exclusionary rule.

In the mid-1970s and then again in *Leon*, Brennan frequently complained that the Court was poised to abolish the exclusionary rule.[51] His sentiments shifted after *James* was announced. He believed the result in *James* "casts into some doubt the frequent suggestion that the Court is on the verge of overruling *Mapp v. Ohio* and jettisoning the exclusionary rule altogether."[52] For Brennan, *James* revealed that White, "the most ardent foe of the rule through his proposed 'good faith' exception, is still the key to preserving the rule against being gutted by attacks along other fronts."[53]

Certainly, White's support was essential for preventing an enlargement of the impeachment exception to the exclusionary rule. But another critical fact *James* exposed was that Kennedy was an opponent of exclusion. To be sure, Kennedy's dissent in *James* did not call for repealing the rule, so the depth of his hostility to exclusion could not be judged by this single opinion. *James* did reveal, however, that Kennedy wanted to restrict the rule even knowing that an expansion of the impeachment exception would impact future prosecutions involving defense witnesses, and provide additional incentives for police to violate the constitutional rights of criminal suspects in order to obtain incriminating statements.[54] In *James*, Kennedy stood ready to limit exclusion even when

---

[48] Sandra Day O'Connor, Letter to William J. Brennan, Jr. on *James v. Illinois* (Nov. 22, 1989), Brennan Papers, Box I: 859.

[49] Brennan, Case Histories O.T. 1989, *supra* note 24, at 69.

[50] Antonin Scalia, Letter to William J. Brennan, Jr. on *James v. Illinois* (Dec. 7, 1989), Brennan Papers, Box I: 859.

[51] For example, in 1974, Brennan's dissent in *Calandra* stated the Court's holding "may signal that a majority of my colleagues have positioned themselves to . . . abandon altogether the exclusionary rule in search-and-seizure cases." United States v. Calandra, 414 U.S. 338, 365 (1974) (Brennan, J., dissenting). Again, in 1984 in his *Leon* dissent, Brennan expressed the view that the good-faith exception announced in *Leon* would expand to the point where the Court determines "that we simply cannot afford to protect Fourth Amendment rights" through the exclusionary rule. United States v. Leon, 468 U.S. 897, 959 (1984) (Brennan, J., dissenting).

[52] Brennan, Case Histories O.T. 1989, *supra* note 24, at 68.

[53] *Id.* at 68–69.

[54] During this era, police departments across the country were training their officers to violate *Miranda* in order to obtain statements and evidence that could be used in contexts outside of the prosecution's case-in-chief, such as for impeachment purposes. This practice became known as questioning suspects "outside of *Miranda*." *See* Charles D. Weisselberg, *Saving* Miranda, 84 CORNELL L. REV. 109 (1998); *see also* RICHARD A. LEO, POLICE INTERROGATION AND AMERICAN JUSTICE 131 (2008) ("The purpose of questioning suspects outside *Miranda* is to capitalize on the Supreme Court's ruling in *Harris v. New York*, which established the impeachment exception to *Miranda*."); *cf.* David A. Wollin, *Policing the Police: Should* Miranda

like-minded, conservative justices were initially unwilling to approve such a broad new exception to the rule.

While Brennan was undoubtedly pleased to have White's vote in *James*, the result in *James* did not mean that White had become a supporter of the exclusionary rule. Indeed, four months later, White returned to his anti-exclusion position and abandoned Brennan and the other liberal justices in *New York v. Harris*, a case involving police misconduct even more egregious than the misconduct in *James*. In January 1984, New York City police officers had probable cause to suspect Bernard Harris killed his girlfriend, Thelma Stanton. Five days after finding Stanton's body, police went to Harris's apartment without an arrest warrant. After hearing the police knocking on his door, Harris opened the door; police entered and Harris was read his *Miranda* rights. Harris then admitted to killing Stanton. Police took Harris to the police station and an hour later read him his *Miranda* rights again. Harris then signed a written confession. Finally, Harris was given *Miranda* warnings a third time prior to a videotaped interrogation with a prosecutor in which Harris again confessed to the murder. The interrogation with the prosecutor proceeded even though Harris stated he no longer wanted to talk.

The trial court suppressed Harris's first and third confessions. The first confession was the direct fruit of Harris's illegal arrest. The court found that arresting Harris in his home was a clear violation of *Payton v. New York*,[55] which held that the Fourth Amendment bars the police from forcibly entering a person's home without a warrant to make a routine felony arrest. The court suppressed the third confession because it was obtained after Harris said he wanted to end the interrogation. But the trial court admitted the second confession obtained at the police station, concluding that it had been voluntarily given after a new set of *Miranda* warnings. Harris was then convicted of murder in a bench trial.[56]

The New York Court of Appeals reversed the conviction finding the second confession to be fruit of the illegal arrest, which should have been excluded under *Brown v. Illinois*. Because the police had purposefully violated *Payton*, the New York court, following the dictates of *Brown v. Illinois* and its progeny, stated the admission of Harris's statement turned on whether the taint of the illegal arrest had dissipated when the confession was obtained.[57] *Brown*'s attenuation analysis required the consideration of three factors: the temporal proximity of the arrest and confession, the presence of intervening events, and the purpose and flagrancy of the police misconduct.

Violations Bear Fruit?, 53 OHIO ST. L.J. 805, 845–46 (1992) (explaining that reported cases show that police violate *Miranda* in order to discover the existence and location of physical evidence: "Police officers seeking physical evidence are not likely to view the loss of an unwarned confession as particularly great when weighed against the opportunity to recover highly probative nontestimonial evidence, such as a murder weapon or narcotics. Recovery of such evidence might well convince a suspect to forego [sic] a trial and plead guilty, thereby preventing the *Miranda* issue from ever being raised." (footnote omitted)).

55 445 U.S. 573 (1980).

56 People v. Harris, 532 N.E.2d 1229, 1231 (N.Y. 1988).

57 *Id.* at 1232–33.

Under that test, the court concluded the statement was inadmissible. First, the confession was obtained shortly after the illegal arrest. There were no intervening circumstances between the arrest and confession. And the flagrancy of the police misconduct was patent. Although the police were aware of the warrant requirement for making in-home arrests, an officer testified that it was departmental policy not to get arrest warrants. The court inferred that the policy of not obtaining arrest warrants was designed to avoid restrictions on interrogating suspects.[58] Under prevailing New York law, an arrest warrant may not be issued until an "accusatory instrument" has been filed against the suspect, and police may not question a suspect without a lawyer being present once an accusatory instrument has been filed.[59] Last, the New York Court of Appeals rejected the prosecution's argument that *Brown*'s "fruit" analysis was inapplicable because the police had probable cause to detain Harris, and there was no causal nexus between the *Payton* violation and securing the confession.[60] The court found that claim was grounded on a "'gross misapplication' of the inevitable discovery rule."[61]

The conference discussion in *Harris* was brief. Rehnquist voted to reverse. He stated that "unlike in *Brown v. Illinois*, the police had probable cause."[62] He wanted the Court to "be careful in extending the fruits doctrine."[63] He stated, the "illegality ceases, with probable cause, once the defendant leaves the home."[64] Rehnquist thought it "sufficient to suppress" the evidence inside the home, but not anything obtained outside.[65] Brennan voted to affirm. This was a "clear violation of *Payton*."[66] White voted to reverse. He noted that Harris was "arrested on the doorsteps," and because the police had probable cause, Harris could have been arrested "as he walked out of the door."[67] White told his colleagues, "I am not a fan of *Payton*."[68]

Marshall voted to affirm, as did Blackmun. Normally an opponent of exclusion, Blackmun spelled out the basis for his vote in a handwritten preconference memorandum. He thought this was "a clear violation of *Payton*."[69] He added that "surely there was a causal connection between the arrest and the confession."[70] He also believed that "a deterrence approach leads to the same result."[71] The "police misconduct was flagrant."[72]

---

58 *Id.* at 1233.

59 *See* N.Y. CRIM. PROC. LAW §§ 120.10-.20 (McKinney 1981); People v. Samuels, 400 N.E.2d 1344 (N.Y. 1980).

60 *Harris*, 532 N.E.2d at 1232–34.

61 *Id.* at 1234 n.2.

62 Harry Blackmun, Conference Notes on *New York v. Harris* (Jan. 12, 1990) [hereinafter Blackmun, *Harris* Conference Notes], Blackmun Papers, Box 545.

63 *Id.*

64 *Id.*

65 *Id.*

66 *Id.*

67 *Id.*

68 *Id.*

69 Harry Blackmun, Handwritten Notes on *New York v. Harris* (Jan. 9, 1990), Blackmun Papers, Box 545.

70 *Id.*

71 *Id.*

72 *Id.*

Stevens voted to affirm. He noted that the police were trying to get around New York's restrictions on interrogating suspects. Stevens wanted to defer to the New York Court of Appeals' conclusion. O'Connor voted to reverse. She noted that there was "no coercion" of Harris, and she did not want to extend *Brown v. Illinois*.[73] Scalia also voted to reverse. He stated that the "but-for" connection between the illegal arrest and confession is "reduced" when the police have probable cause.[74] Kennedy also voted to reverse.[75] Thus, the vote was five to four for reversal.

White was assigned *Harris*. He circulated his first draft on February 20, 1990, which Brennan privately described as "virtually incomprehensible."[76] Blackmun's law clerk told his boss the draft was "pretty awful; it seems clear that Justice White did not take a great deal of time in crafting this one."[77] Two months later, *Harris* was announced on April 18. White's opinion overruling the decision below emphasized two points. First, when officers obtained Harris's police station confession, he was lawfully in police custody, and the prior *Payton* violation did not affect his custodial status. White explained, *Payton* was "designed to protect the physical integrity of the home."[78] It was not intended to protect a suspect from making a statement outside of his home where police have probable cause to arrest him. According to White, nothing in *Payton* suggests "that an arrest in a home without a warrant but with probable cause somehow renders unlawful continued custody of the suspect once he is removed from the house."[79]

Second, White believed the fruit analysis of *Brown v. Illinois* and its progeny was inapplicable because there was probable cause to arrest Harris. He explained that *Brown* was a case where the police lacked probable cause to arrest; it announced the familiar rule "that the indirect fruits of an illegal search or arrest should be suppressed when they bear a sufficiently close relationship to the underlying illegality."[80] In *Brown,* the disputed evidence, the defendant's voluntary confession, was undoubtedly the fruit of police misconduct, which was the wrongful detention of Brown.[81]

By contrast, because the police had probable cause to arrest Harris, his police station confession was not the product of an illegal detention. And the confession was not the "fruit of having been arrested in the home rather than someplace else."[82] According to White, *Harris* was analogous to another exclusionary rule decision, *United States v. Crews*,[83] where the Court refused to exclude a victim's in-court identification despite Crews's illegal arrest at the Washington Monument. Because the police knew of the

---

73 Blackmun, *Harris* Conference Notes, *supra* note 62.

74 *Id.*

75 *Id.*

76 Brennan, Case Histories O.T. 1989, *supra* note 24, at 85.

77 Law Clerk, Letter to Harry Blackmun on *New York v. Harris* (Feb. 22, 1990), Blackmun Papers, Box 545.

78 New York v. Harris, 495 U.S. 14, 17 (1990).

79 *Id.* at 18.

80 *Id.* at 19.

81 *Id.*

82 *Id.*

83 445 U.S. 463 (1980).

victim and her ability to identify Crews before his illegal arrest, the *Crews* Court ruled the victim's in-court identification was not the fruit of a Fourth Amendment violation. Therefore, the Court explained, it was unnecessary to employ the three-part test of *Brown v. Illinois* to determine whether the in-court identification was tainted by Crews's illegal arrest. Similarly, in *Harris*, the police had good cause to question Harris prior to his arrest. Therefore, White asserted, Harris's police station confession was not an exploitation of the *Payton* violation.[84]

As for the need to deter future *Payton* violations, White explained that excluding any evidence obtained in the home provides the key incentive to comply with *Payton*. Any additional deterrence gained by suppressing the police station confession would be "minimal," since police do not need to violate *Payton* to question a suspect they have probable cause to arrest. They can arrest that suspect outside his home and then interrogate him. Thus, in what amounted to a per se rule, White held that "where the police have probable cause to arrest a suspect, the exclusionary rule does not bar the State's use of a statement made by the defendant outside of his home, even though the statement is taken after an arrest made in the home in violation of *Payton*."[85]

White's opinion in *Harris* was not surprising as it represented White's standard anti-exclusion views. In *Harris*, White rewrote the legal reasoning of *Brown v. Illinois* to fit his opposition to suppression. *Brown* rejected the request of prosecutors to adopt a per se rule that *Miranda* warnings necessarily purge the taint of an illegal arrest to permit use of voluntary confessions obtained after unlawful arrests. Writing for the majority, Blackmun ruled that whether the taint of an illegal arrest had dissipated to allow the admission of a later voluntary confession turned on a case-by-case analysis with the consideration of several factors. After White's opinion in *Harris*, however, *Brown*'s holding rested not on a concern with the lingering taint of an illegal arrest, but instead only on whether a later confession was obtained during an illegal detention. White's refusal to apply the multifactor *Brown* test is not surprising since he never signed on to Blackmun's analysis in that case. White merely concurred in the judgment in *Brown*, resting his vote solely on his conclusion that the police had acted in bad faith. As he told his colleagues during the *Brown* conference, Brown's arrest was a "known violation of the law."[86]

Interestingly, White was willing to overlook the purposeful and bad-faith actions of the police in *Harris*. His willingness to do so likely reflected his continued disagreement with *Payton*. White wrote a long dissent in *Payton*. His main complaint was that the majority's holding was "founded on erroneous assumptions concerning the intrusiveness of home arrest entries."[87] White believed that a front-door arrest—which is how he characterized the arrest of Harris in the conference—was no more intrusive of

[84] *Harris*, 495 U.S. at 19.

[85] *Id.* at 21.

[86] Lewis Powell, Conference Notes on *Brown v. Illinois* (Mar. 21, 1975), Powell Papers, Box 24.

[87] Payton v. New York, 445 U.S. 573, 603 (1980) (White, J., dissenting).

personal privacy than the public warrantless arrests the Court had approved in *United States v. Watson*,[88] another ruling authored by White.[89] While White did not have the votes to overrule *Payton*, he certainly had the votes to restrict the consequences of violating *Payton*. As Marshall's dissent noted, under *Harris*, police officers know that after a *Payton* violation, exiting the home automatically breaks the causal chain between the illegality and any subsequent statement or evidence taken from the suspect outside of the home.[90]

There is, however, another aspect to White's opinion that may have even greater significance in the future. The state did not challenge the ruling below excluding Harris's first confession. Thus, White explained that the "sole" issue in *Harris* was whether the second confession should have been excluded.[91] Later in the opinion, however, White plainly indicates that Harris's first confession was properly excluded,[92] yet he never explains the reasoning for the disparate treatment. As Professor Alschuler has noted, rather than directly explain why the two confessions are accorded separate results under a causation analysis, White provided a "split-the-difference resolution of the case—admitting one piece of evidence and excluding the other in the belief that a fifty-percent solution would provide 'sufficient' deterrence."[93] But the failure to explain why Harris's first confession was tainted fruit under the logic of *Harris* provides an opening for a future justice (or Court) to explain why it is not.

After all, if the basis for discarding the traditional attenuation analysis was the fact that police had probable cause to arrest Harris prior to their unlawful entry of his home, and if the point of *Payton* is to protect the physical integrity or privacy of the home, why was exclusion required for Harris's first confession? The *Payton* violation did not negate the probable cause to arrest Harris or eliminate the justification to question him. Nor is it obvious why obtaining Harris's first confession jeopardized the sanctity of his home or its privacy. Logically, under White's reasoning in *Harris*, there appeared to be no reason to suppress Harris's first confession—other than the fact that *Brown* and its progeny had earlier required exclusion. Unlike White's concerted efforts in the 1970s and early 1980s to convince the Court to adopt a good-faith exception, there is no proof that White intended his opinion in *Harris* to be the basis for overturning *Brown v. Illinois* and its progeny. Nonetheless, the logic of *Harris* provides an opening for undermining *Brown* and further limiting the application of the exclusionary rule.

Finally, and perhaps more important, the logic of *Harris* offers the Court another way to severely restrict the exclusionary rule without overruling it outright. In *Harris*,

---

88 423 U.S. 411 (1976).

89 *See Payton*, 445 U.S. at 617 (White, J., dissenting).

90 *Harris*, 495 U.S. at 26 (Marshall, J., dissenting).

91 *Id.* at 16 (majority opinion).

92 *Id.* at 20.

93 Albert W. Alschuler, *The Exclusionary Rule and Causation:* Hudson v. Michigan *and Its Ancestors*, 93 Iowa L. Rev. 1741, 1790 (2008).

White's opinion did not reject the defendant's argument for exclusion because of a lack of "but-for" causality between the Fourth Amendment violation and obtaining the confession, or because Harris's confession was not sufficiently close, either physically or temporally, to the *Payton* violation. Rather, White rejected the defendant's argument because the "causal connection was not of the right kind: the confession did not flow from a violation of the interest that the *Payton* rule was designed to protect, namely, the occupant's interest in preventing exposure of the home's contents."[94] Of course, this logic is applicable to other Fourth Amendment violations besides violations of *Payton*. As this chapter will explain, sixteen years later, Scalia employed similar reasoning to create another significant exception to the exclusionary rule.

* * *

More "Good Faith"

Before *Leon* established the first good-faith exception to the exclusionary rule in 1984, justices who favored a good-faith exception rarely spoke in terms of a restricted or limited exception. As chapter 6 detailed, White pushed his colleagues to adopt a good-faith exception that would apply anytime the police act mistakenly, but with a good faith and reasonable belief that their conduct was lawful. Powell, on the other hand, did not push for the type of general good-faith exception urged by White; but he too envisioned a good-faith exception that would apply to different categories of cases. For example, in his concurrence in *Brown v. Illinois*, Powell signaled his support for a good-faith exception in cases where police arrest a suspect "in reliance on a warrant later invalidated or pursuant to a statute that subsequently is declared unconstitutional."[95]

Although he ended up not participating in the case, Powell also believed that a good-faith exception was applicable to the facts in *Dunaway v. New York*.[96] At issue in *Dunaway* was the legality of custodial interrogation where the police lacked probable cause to arrest a suspect. A detective in Rochester, New York, told officers to "pick up" Irving Dunaway and bring him in for questioning,[97] though the detective knew he did not have probable cause to arrest Dunaway for the killing of an owner of a pizza parlor during an attempted robbery. After finding Dunaway at a neighbor's home, but without formally arresting him, officers took Dunaway to the police station where he was given *Miranda* warnings. Dunaway waived his rights and made statements and drew sketches that implicated him in the crime. In seizing Dunaway, the police relied on a questionable and controversial ruling of New York's highest court that permitted this form of investigation so long as the police have reasonable suspicion for questioning a suspect about

94 Eric A. Johnson, *Causal Relevance in the Law of Search and Seizure*, 88 B.U. L. Rev. 113, 114 (2008).

95 Brown v. Illinois, 422 U.S. 590, 611 (1975) (Powell, J., concurring in part) (footnote omitted).

96 442 U.S. 200 (1979).

97 *Id.* at 203.

a crime, and the manner of the questioning protects the Fifth and Sixth Amendment rights of the suspect.[98]

Before he removed himself from the case, Powell was uncertain where he stood on the merits of Dunaway's claim that seizing a suspect for custodial interrogation on less than probable cause violated the Fourth Amendment. But Powell was certain exclusion was inappropriate. On the top of his law clerk's memo about the case, he wrote: "No case for exclusionary rule. Police acted reasonably."[99] Six months later, after the Court decided to review Dunaway's appeal, Powell wrote his law clerk a memo outlining his views on the case. By this time, Powell was more inclined to uphold the constitutional validity of custodial interrogation without probable cause. But he also wrote that he "could decide this case on the view I expressed in my concurring opinion in *Brown v. Illinois*, as the police certainly acted in good faith."[100] Ultimately, the Court ruled that the Fourth Amendment does not permit the police to seize a person for custodial interrogation without probable cause. Rehnquist wrote a dissent, which Burger joined. Brennan's majority opinion in *Dunaway* did not mention the good-faith issue.

While the Court was deliberating in *Dunaway*, it was also considering *Payton v. New York*.[101] As he did in *Dunaway*, Powell again voiced support for a good-faith exception in *Payton*, which addressed whether police may forcibly, and without a judicial warrant, enter a private residence to effectuate a routine felony arrest. *Payton* involved two companion cases in which Theodore Payton and Obie Riddick challenged entries and searches of their homes where police sought to arrest each defendant without a warrant. On January 15, 1970, New York City police had probable cause to believe that Payton murdered the manager of a gas station. Without a warrant, they broke into his residence. Although Payton was not home, police saw in plain view a rifle shell casing that tied Payton to the murder. Payton was subsequently convicted of murder. On March 14, 1974, police offers went to Riddick's apartment in Queens, New York, to arrest him for two armed robberies. Without a warrant, the officers knocked on the door. When Riddick's three-year-old son opened the door, officers could see Riddick lying in bed. Officers arrested Riddick and searched a cabinet near the bed where they found narcotics. Riddick was later convicted of narcotics violations.[102]

---

98 *See* People v. Dunaway, 402 N.Y.S.2d 490, 492 (N.Y. App. Div. 1978) (finding the brief detention of Dunaway for interrogation based on reasonable suspicion to be proper under the recent Court of Appeals decision in *Morales*). In *People v. Morales*, the New York Court of Appeals held that the Fourth Amendment permits police to "detain an individual upon reasonable suspicion for questioning for a reasonable and brief period of time under carefully controlled conditions which are ample to protect the individual's Fifth and Sixth Amendment rights." People v. Morales, 366 N.E.2d 248, 251 (N.Y. 1977), *cert. denied*, 434 U.S. 1018 (1978).

99 Law Clerk, Preliminary Memorandum to Lewis Powell on *Dunaway v. New York* 1 (Aug. 29, 1978), Powell Papers, Box 63.

100 Lewis Powell, Memorandum to Eric Andersen on *Dunaway v. New York* 4 (Mar. 6, 1979), Powell Papers, Box 63.

101 445 U.S. 573 (1980).

102 *Id.* at 576–78.

The New York courts upheld the convictions of Payton and Riddick and rejected their claims that the warrantless entries into their homes violated the Fourth Amendment. The New York Court of Appeals relied on two separate provisions of the New York Code of Criminal Procedure that permitted police to forcibly enter a home without a warrant after providing notice and after being refused entry.[103]

After the Court decided to review *Payton*, Powell sent a memo to his law clerk. He noted his "serious doubt" about the validity of warrantless forcible entries to effect routine felony arrests.[104] But on the issue of exclusion, Powell wrote that if the only question presented was whether to suppress the evidence, he would not exclude, reasoning that "the officers acted in good faith pursuant to a New York statute that has been on the books for many years, and indeed in accord with the law of this country since colonial days."[105] Finally, Powell told his clerk that he wanted "advice as to whether I can reach the constitutional issue in view of my long-held opinion that the exclusionary rule does not apply where an officer acts pursuant to a presumptively valid statute."[106] Eventually, Powell joined Stevens's majority opinion in *Payton* that held that the Fourth Amendment bars police from conducting a warrantless and nonconsensual entry into a suspect's home to effectuate a routine felony arrest. Even though New York's brief argued that the evidence seized was not subject to suppression under a good-faith exception, Stevens's opinion did not reach that issue.

Powell's views on the breadth of a good-faith exception were an important indicator of how the Court would resolve future cases after *Leon* announced a good-faith exception. During his final years on the Court, Powell was the key swing vote on the Court. As Linda Greenhouse of the *New York Times* put it after his death, Powell was a "crucial centrist" on an "increasingly polarized Court."[107] In Fourth Amendment exclusionary rule cases, a defendant had almost no chance of succeeding without Powell's vote. In fact, from the time of his appointment to his retirement, only one defendant prevailed on a suppression claim without it.[108] Therefore, Powell's willingness to extend *Leon*'s good-faith exception mattered. On its face, *Leon*'s holding was narrow; the good-faith exception was limited to cases where police obtained warrants. But Burger, White, and Rehnquist wanted to enlarge the good-faith exception, and few criminal procedure scholars believed the Court would cabin the good-faith exception to scenarios of defective warrants.

---

103 *Id.* at 577 nn.6-7, 577–78.

104 Lewis Powell, Memorandum to Eric Andersen on *Payton v. New York* and *Riddick v. New York* 3 (Mar. 6, 1979), Powell Papers, Box 69.

105 *Id.*

106 *Id.* at 4.

107 Linda Greenhouse, *Lewis Powell, Crucial Centrist Justice, Dies at 90*, N.Y. Times, Aug. 26, 1998, at A1.

108 *See* Taylor v. Alabama, 457 U.S. 687 (1982). In *Taylor* the Court ruled five to four that the defendant's confession was the tainted fruit of an illegal arrest. Powell joined O'Connor's dissent.

Thus, when the Court finally addressed whether the good-faith exception would extend beyond the line drawn by *Leon* to allow the admission of evidence gathered by police in reliance upon a statute that was later declared unconstitutional, the prospects for a defense victory seemed remote. *Illinois v. Krull*[109] presented that issue in the context of a law that authorized warrantless administrative searches of automobile junkyards. To no one's surprise, the Court extended the good-faith exception announced in *Leon*.

An Illinois law permitted warrantless inspections of the records of businesses licensed to sell motor vehicles and vehicle parts. Relying on the law, a Chicago police detective searched the records of Action Iron & Metal, Inc., an automobile wrecking business owned by Albert Krull and others. The search revealed several stolen vehicles. After a state trial court found the statute unconstitutional and granted the defendants' motion to suppress the evidence seized pursuant to the search, the Illinois Supreme Court affirmed the trial court's decision.[110] The Illinois Supreme Court also rejected the state's claim that the evidence seized from the defendants' wrecking yard should be admissible, because the detective had acted in good faith pursuant to a presumptively valid statute authorizing the search. As grounds for denying the good-faith claim, the Illinois court relied upon the "substantive-procedural dichotomy" Burger created in *Michigan v. DeFillippo*.[111]

Under *DeFillippo*'s analysis, exclusion was *not* required for the fruits of an arrest or search when police act pursuant to a substantive statute defining criminal conduct that is subsequently declared invalid, provided the police have probable cause to make the arrest, and they rely on the statute in good faith. On the other hand, evidence obtained pursuant to a procedural statute authorizing a search without a warrant or probable cause that is later declared invalid *was* subject to suppression, notwithstanding good-faith reliance on the statute by the police.[112]

Significantly, in a footnote, White's opinion in *Leon* endorsed the distinction recognized in *DeFillippo* when it noted that suppression is still required for evidence obtained "pursuant to statutes, not yet declared unconstitutional, purporting to authorize searches and seizures without probable cause or search warrants."[113] In other words, an officer's good-faith reliance on a procedural statute authorizing a warrantless search is irrelevant when deciding whether to exclude tainted evidence. The Illinois law authorizing junkyard searches was a procedural statute, and thus, according to the Illinois Supreme Court, the good-faith exception to exclusion was unavailable.

When the Attorney General of Illinois asked the Court to review *Krull*, the state's petition told the Court that suppression of evidence seized in good-faith reliance on

---

109 480 U.S. 340 (1987).

110 Illinois v. Krull, 481 N.E.2d 703 (Ill. 1985).

111 *Id.* at 708.

112 Michigan v. DeFillippo, 443 U.S. 31, 39–40 (1979).

113 United States v. Leon, 468 U.S. 897, 912 n.8 (1984).

a facially valid procedural law was inconsistent with the deterrent purpose behind the exclusionary rule.[114] While *Leon* and *DeFillippo* recognized a "substantive-procedural" distinction between statutes for exclusion purposes, the state informed the Court that Rehnquist's opinion in *United States v. Peltier* established that exclusion was improper where law enforcement officers conduct a search in good-faith reliance on a statute authorizing a search that is later invalidated.[115] As discussed in chapter 4, Rehnquist purposefully left vague the precise holding of *Peltier*. Nevertheless, the language from *Peltier* certainly bolstered Illinois's argument in *Krull*:

> If the purpose of the exclusionary rule is to deter unlawful police conduct then evidence obtained from a search should be suppressed only if it can be said that the law enforcement officer had knowledge, or may properly be charged with knowledge, that the search was unconstitutional under the Fourth Amendment.[116]

As chapter 4 revealed, this was the same sentence that Powell had objected to and asked Rehnquist to change, but Rehnquist refused to do so because it would make *Peltier* just an ordinary retroactivity case and diminish its precedential weight in restricting the exclusionary rule. In any event, Illinois told the Court that the logic of this passage from *Peltier* meant that exclusion was unwarranted in *Krull*.

While the Court was deciding whether to review *Krull*, Blackmun received two memos from his law clerk. The first memo noted that Illinois makes "a persuasive point in arguing that *Peltier* implies that a good-faith rule"[117] should apply in cases where police rely upon facially valid statutes. At the same time, the Illinois Supreme Court "also ha[d] a persuasive point" when it followed the "substantive-procedural" distinction endorsed in *Leon* and *DeFillippo*.[118] The second memo provided Blackmun with a way to resolve the conflict. Conceding that the passage from *Peltier* means that exclusion is warranted only when police knowingly violate the Fourth Amendment, the memo observed that "the holding in *Peltier* can be seen simply as a refusal to retroactively apply a 'new' Fourth Amendment rule."[119] Put differently, Blackmun could reconcile the conflict between *Peltier* and the "substantive-procedural" distinction by concluding that "[an] officer's good faith reliance on a procedural statute is only relevant if the invalidation of the statute involves application

[114] *See* Chai Feldblum, Memorandum to Harry Blackmun on *Illinois v. Krull* 8 (Oct. 19, 1986), Blackmun Papers, Box 464.

[115] *See id.* at 10.

[116] United States v. Peltier, 422 U.S. 531, 542 (1975).

[117] Law Clerk, Preliminary Memorandum to Harry Blackmun on *Illinois v. Krull* 7 (Nov. 20, 1985), Blackmun Papers, Box 464.

[118] *Id.*

[119] Law Clerk, Supplemental Preliminary Memorandum to Harry Blackmun on *Illinois v. Krull* 3 (Jan. 6, 1986), Blackmun Papers, Box 464.

of a new Fourth Amendment rule announced by this Court after the date of the search in question."[120]

While that explanation apparently satisfied Blackmun, who voted against reviewing *Krull*, it did not satisfy Burger. After the Court voted to deny Illinois's request to review *Krull*, Burger filed a dissent.[121] Burger wanted the Court to review *Krull*, and he characterized the passage from *Peltier* quoted above as *Peltier*'s "holding."[122] Burger wrote that *Peltier* directly supported Illinois's argument that exclusion would serve no valid purpose because the search of Krull's business was based on a statute that had not yet been declared invalid. Although Burger's opinion in *DeFillippo* crafted the "substantive-procedural dichotomy," Burger now stated that distinction was "dicta" and thought it conflicted with *Peltier*'s "holding."[123] After reading Burger's dissent, Powell joined it, although his original vote at the *Krull* conference was for summary reversal.[124] Eventually, the Court reconsidered whether to review *Krull*, and four justices (Burger, White, Powell, and Rehnquist) voted to hear the case. Convincing three other justices to hear *Krull* was Burger's final victory in his efforts to reduce the scope of the exclusionary rule. A few months later, Burger informed President Reagan of his desire to retire from the Court in order to head the campaign celebrating the 1987 bicentennial of the United States Constitution.[125]

When *Krull* was argued in the fall of 1986, William Rehnquist was Chief Justice, and Antonin Scalia was the newest member of the Court. Blackmun's new law clerk wrote an extensive memo for the case. In that memo, the clerk told Blackmun that the "substantive-procedural dichotomy" created in *DeFillippo* and endorsed in a footnote in *Leon* did not foreclose application of the good-faith exception in *Krull*.[126] None of the Court's previous rulings invalidating statutes that authorized warrantless searches discussed application of the good-faith exception. In other words, the clerk explained, Burger's analysis in *DeFillippo*'s was obiter dicta.

Moreover, the law clerk noted that White's concurrence in *Illinois v. Gates*, which was the forerunner of the good-faith exception, specifically recognized that exclusion would be unwarranted for evidence obtained pursuant to procedural statutes authorizing warrantless searches that were later declared invalid. What was puzzling, according to the law clerk, was that White "repeated the *DeFillippo* language in toto in *Leon*" in a footnote.[127] Besides the fact that the footnote's purpose in *Leon* was unclear, the law

---

120 *Id.* at 4.

121 Warren Burger, First Draft of Dissenting Opinion in *Illinois v. Krull* (Mar. 20, 1986), Powell Papers, Box 132.

122 *Id.* at 4.

123 *Id.* at 5.

124 Lewis Powell, Letter to Warren Burger on *Illinois v. Krull* (Mar. 19, 1986), Powell Papers, Box 132.

125 David G. Savage, Turning Right: The Making of the Rehnquist Supreme Court 4–5 (1992).

126 Chai Feldblum, Memorandum to Harry Blackmun on *Illinois v. Krull*, *supra* note 114, at 22–23.

127 *Id.* at 22.

clerk told Blackmun that "the Court is not bound by the language in the *Leon* footnote, particularly because the cases cited there never dealt directly with the good faith exception."[128]

Chief Justice Rehnquist began the conference discussion of *Krull* by noting that the substantive-procedural distinction adopted by the Illinois Supreme Court "doesn't make sense and should be abandoned."[129] Rehnquist said the Illinois statute was "procedural, and so we do not need to reconcile the distinction."[130] Rehnquist "would allow the good-faith exception here."[131] Because the Illinois courts did not address this question, a "remand was required on this question."[132] Rehnquist voted to reverse and remand. Brennan voted to affirm but also to remand. He distinguished *Leon*, which involved a "neutral and detached magistrate" issuing a warrant.[133] Here, by contrast, "a legislative body enacted the statute."[134] Brennan also noted that there had been, unlike in *Leon*, no finding of good faith by the lower court. White voted to reverse and said he agreed with Rehnquist's comments.[135]

Marshall voted to affirm and said that he "would not apply a good-faith analysis."[136] Blackmun voted to reverse and remand. He said: "With *Leon* on the books, I can't distinguish a warrant from legislation."[137] Blackmun also noted that the "statute was presumptively valid."[138] Finally, he commented that White's "footnote 8 in *Leon* is troublesome but not controlling."[139] Powell voted to reverse and remand. Powell said he "agrees with the Chief Justice."[140] Powell saw "no difference between a presumptively valid warrant and a presumptively valid statute."[141] Powell wanted a remand on the question of whether there was good faith by the detective.[142]

Stevens said that the "statute is probably constitutional, but reversal is inconsistent with the Court's retroactivity cases."[143] He noted that in a case like *Krull*, the "litigant succeeds on his constitutional attack, but loses on good faith grounds. That's wrong."[144]

---

128 *Id.* at 23.

129 Lewis Powell, Conference Notes on *Illinois v. Krull* (Nov. 7, 1986) [hereinafter Powell, *Krull* Conference Notes], Powell Papers, Box 132.

130 *Id.*

131 *Id.*

132 *Id.*

133 *Id.*

134 *Id.*

135 *Id.*

136 *Id.*

137 William J. Brennan, Jr., Conference Notes on *Illinois v. Krull* (undated) [hereinafter Brennan, *Krull* Conference Notes], Brennan Papers, Box I: 728.

138 Powell, *Krull* Conference Notes, *supra* note 129.

139 *Id.*

140 *Id.*

141 Harry Blackmun, Conference Notes on *Illinois v. Krull* (Nov. 7, 1986), Blackmun Papers, Box 464.

142 Lewis Powell, Handwritten Notes on *Illinois v. Krull* (Nov. 6, 1986), Blackmun Papers, Box 464.

143 Brennan, *Krull* Conference Notes, *supra* note 137.

144 *Id.*

O'Connor agreed with Stevens's comments and "thought footnote 8 in *Leon* rightly made a distinction" between substantive and procedural laws.[145] Finally, Scalia said he agreed with Rehnquist's views. Ultimately, the Court voted five to four for reversal. The only remarkable feature of the conference was O'Connor's vote in favor of exclusion, given that she had joined the *Leon* opinion. Her dissenting opinion in *Krull*, although not disavowing the good-faith exception, would contend that *Leon*'s logic should not extend to legislatures who are more subject to political pressures than are independent judges.[146]

Although he originally voted not to hear *Krull*, Blackmun was assigned to write the opinion. Blackmun's opinion followed the template created in *Leon* and held that "a good-faith exception to the Fourth Amendment exclusionary rule applies when an officer's reliance on the constitutionality of a statute is objectively reasonable, but the statute is subsequently declared unconstitutional."[147] In justifying this result, Blackmun repeated the themes announced in *Leon*. First, exclusion here would serve no deterrent purpose because the detective was simply doing his job when he searched Krull's business pursuant to the statute. The deterrent impact of exclusion was no different than if the officer had relied on a warrant. Second, the exclusionary rule is aimed at deterring police misconduct, and "legislators, like judicial officers, are not the focus of the rule."[148] Last, Blackmun concluded there is no reason to believe that exclusion will have a significant deterrent effect on the actions of legislators, because "[l]egislators enact statutes for broad, programmatic purposes, not for the purpose of procuring evidence in particular criminal investigations."[149] Blackmun observed that Krull offered no evidence to persuade the Court that suppression of fruits obtained from a search made prior to the statute being declared invalid would provide "a significant, additional deterrent."[150] And whatever incremental deterrence that might be gained "must be weighed against the 'substantial social costs exacted by the exclusionary rule.'"[151]

As White did in *Leon*, Blackmun's opinion in *Krull* offered two limitations on the scope of the newly expanded good-faith exception. Police cannot rely on a statute where "the legislature wholly abandoned its responsibility to enact constitutional laws."[152] Additionally, the exception is unavailable if "a reasonable officer should have known that the statute was unconstitutional."[153] Blackmun did not, however, explain how a defendant could prove that a legislature "wholly abandoned" its constitutional obligations to

---

145 *Id.*

146 Illinois v. Krull, 480 U.S. 340, 365–66 (1987) (O'Connor, J., dissenting).

147 *Id.* at 346 (majority opinion).

148 *Id.* at 350.

149 *Id.* at 352.

150 *Id.*

151 *Id.* at 352–53 (quoting United States v. Leon, 468 U.S. 897, 907 (1984)).

152 *Id.* at 355.

153 *Id.*

pass valid laws, or show that an officer should have known that a law was constitutionally defective.

Finally, in a long footnote, Blackmun resolved the conflict between the "substantive-procedural dichotomy" created in *DeFillippo* and endorsed by *Leon*, and the passage from *Peltier* confining exclusion to cases where police knowingly violate the Fourth Amendment.[154] Following the suggestion of his law clerk, Blackmun explained that the Court's prior cases invalidating procedural statutes that authorize warrantless searches did not address whether a good-faith exception should be adopted when police search pursuant to a presumptively valid law.[155] Thus, the distinction crafted in *DeFillippo*, Blackmun concluded, was dicta and not controlling in *Krull*.

Blackmun added there was "no valid reason to distinguish between statutes that define substantive criminal offenses and statutes that authorize warrantless administrative searches."[156] In either situation, suppression will not deter police misconduct, and "there is no basis for assuming" that suppression is needed to deter legislators from enacting unconstitutional laws.[157] In effect, *Krull* established that exclusion was unwarranted whenever police act reasonably and objectively upon a statute authorizing a search, "regardless of whether the statute may be characterized as 'substantive' or 'procedural.'"[158]

Although this footnote specifically addressed statutes that permit warrantless *administrative* searches, there was no doubt that its logic extended to statutes that authorize searches and seizures for *criminal* investigations, like the New York statutes at issue in *Payton v. New York*. Accordingly, a good-faith exception would apply beyond the administrative inspections at issue in *Krull* to all types of statutes, just as Powell envisioned during the *Payton* deliberations. Finally, the footnote showed the continued influence of White's *Gates* concurrence. In *Gates*, White predicted his proposal for a good-faith exception would reverse the results of prior cases where the Court had suppressed evidence obtained in warrantless searches authorized by statute. While none of his colleagues joined the *Gates* concurrence, over time, a majority of the justices began to see exclusion the same way White had envisioned it in *Gates*.

The next opportunity for extending the good-faith exception came in *Arizona v. Evans*.[159] After a Phoenix, Arizona, police officer stopped Issac Evans for a traffic violation, the officer's patrol car computer indicated Evans had an outstanding arrest warrant. The officer arrested Evans and discovered marijuana incident to the arrest. It was later learned that the outstanding warrant had been quashed by a judge, but because of an error by either a court employee or employee in the sheriff's office, the warrant was

---

[154] *Id.* at 355 n.12.

[155] *Id.*

[156] *Id.*

[157] *Id.*

[158] *Id.*

[159] 514 U.S. 1 (1995).

not removed from the police computer records. Without resolving who was responsible for the error, the Arizona Supreme Court ruled that the arrest of Evans, "based entirely as it was on an erroneous computer entry, was plainly illegal."[160] Assuming that the error rested with a court employee, the Arizona court distinguished *Leon* because "no warrant at all was in existence at the time of the arrest."[161] Therefore, it upheld the trial court's order suppressing the narcotics obtained from Evans's arrest.

Rehnquist's opinion for a six-to-two majority reversed, concluding the Arizona court's ruling was contrary to the reasoning of *Leon* and *Krull*. Assuming both that Evans's arrest was illegal and that a court employee was responsible for the computer error, Rehnquist explained that any gains in terms of future deterrence that exclusion would achieve were insufficient to justify "such a severe sanction."[162] Rehnquist's opinion followed the script written in *Leon*. First, exclusion was designed to deter the mistakes of police officers, not court employees. Second, there was no evidence that court employees were inclined to ignore or violate the Fourth Amendment.[163] Third, "and most important," there was no reason to think that suppression of tainted evidence would have a significant impact on court employees responsible for informing police agencies that a warrant has been quashed.[164] Last, exclusion "could not be expected to alter the behavior of the arresting officer."[165] The officer who arrested Evans was required to make an arrest after discovering the arrest warrant, and failure to do so would have been dereliction of his duty.[166]

O'Connor, joined by Justices Souter and Breyer, wrote a brief concurring opinion that appeared to be an effort to narrow the scope of Rehnquist's opinion. O'Connor wrote that the majority's ruling was limited to cases involving errors by court employees. She then opined that other types of computer errors *might* justify exclusion. She observed "it would *not* be reasonable for the police to rely, say, on a recordkeeping system, their own or some other agency's, that has no mechanism to ensure its accuracy over time and that routinely leads to false arrests, even years after the probable cause for any such arrest has ceased to exist (if it ever existed)."[167] O'Connor closed her opinion by commenting that while police are entitled to rely on the advantages afforded by computer technology, they may not "rely on [them] blindly."[168] Stevens's dissent urged an even further limitation on the good-faith exception. He insisted that *Leon*'s logic assumed the existence of a facially valid warrant, and was therefore "wholly inapplicable" to warrantless searches and seizures.[169] Moreover, Stevens thought the reasoning of *Leon* did not extend to the

---

160 State v. Evans, 866 P.2d 869, 871 (Ariz. 1994).

161 *Id.*

162 *Evans*, 514 U.S. at 14.

163 *Id.* at 14–15.

164 *Id.* at 15.

165 *Id.*

166 *Id.*

167 *Id.* at 17 (O'Connor, J., concurring).

168 *Id.*

169 *Id.* at 20 (Stevens, J., dissenting).

time after the warrant had issued, let alone to the errors of court clerks or employees who have regular contact with police officers.[170]

Despite these efforts to contain the good-faith exception, *Evans* marked an important expansion of *Leon* and signaled that an even more substantial one was soon to come. The Solicitor General's amicus curiae brief argued that a good-faith exception should apply to *police* error, depending on the type of error and the circumstances in which it arises.[171] Since the state of Arizona did not make that argument, Rehnquist conceded the issue was not adequately presented in *Evans*. Nevertheless, Rehnquist included a not-so-subtle footnote, indicating that his reasoning would apply even if police personnel were responsible for the computer error.[172] Evidently, this was just the other shoe waiting to drop.

While O'Connor wrote that Rehnquist's analysis in *Evans* was confined to cases involving errors by court employees, her proposed limitation on *Evans*'s reach ignored Rehnquist's tacit overruling of a prior precedent, *Whiteley v. Warden*,[173] and his dismissal of her own reasoning in *United States v. Hensley*.[174] In its brief, Arizona emphasized that the officer who arrested Evans had no knowledge that the warrant had been quashed and had acted in good faith.[175] This argument conflicted with the results in *Whiteley* and *Hensley*. In *Whiteley* (discussed in chapter 4), an officer, relying in good faith on a radio bulletin issued by another department, arrested Whiteley and a companion and discovered incriminating evidence incident to the arrest. Notwithstanding the good faith of the arresting officer, Harlan's opinion in *Whiteley* ruled that "an otherwise illegal arrest cannot be insulated from challenge by the decision of the instigating officer to rely on fellow officers to make the arrest," and the evidence obtained from that arrest "should have been excluded from his trial."[176] Significantly, the result in *Whiteley* was cited with approval in *Leon*.[177]

In *United States v. Hensley*, authored by O'Connor and decided subsequent to *Leon*, the Court reaffirmed *Whiteley* and invoked its reasoning to explain that

> when evidence is uncovered during a search incident to an arrest in reliance merely on a flyer or bulletin, its admissibility turns on whether the officers who *issued* the flyer possessed probable cause to make the arrest. It does not turn on whether those relying on the flyer were themselves aware of the specific facts which led their colleagues to seek their assistance.[178]

---

170 *Id.*

171 Brief for the United States as Amicus Curiae Supporting Petitioner at 12–13, *Evans*, 514 U.S. 1 (No. 93-1660).

172 *Evans*, 514 U.S. at 6 & n.1.

173 401 U.S. 560 (1971).

174 469 U.S. 221 (1985).

175 Brief of Petitioner at 9, 12, *Evans*, 514 U.S. 1 (No. 93-1660).

176 *Whiteley*, 401 U.S. at 568–69.

177 United States v. Leon, 468 U.S. 897, 923 n.24 (1984).

178 *Hensley*, 469 U.S. at 231.

Rehnquist's response to *Hensley* was curt. Because there was no constitutional violation in that case, O'Connor's discussion on exclusion was dicta. As for *Whiteley*, he described its precedential value as "dubious" because it was decided at a time when the "Court treated identification of a Fourth Amendment violation as synonymous with application of the exclusionary rule to evidence secured incident to that violation."[179] While Rehnquist did not explicitly overrule *Whiteley*, his message was clear. *Whiteley* was dispatched. And without *Whiteley* as controlling law, the Court was free to deny exclusion where an officer relied in good faith on a police department employee's negligent handling of computer data, or even to deny exclusion where, as in *Whiteley*, an officer relied on another officer's judgment regarding the existence of probable cause for an arrest. Needless to say, Rehnquist's opinion in *Evans* took the Court another step closer to a general good-faith exception.

* * *

Many scholars and lawyers viewed the result in *Evans* as just another incremental step in limiting the scope of the exclusionary rule, rather than a frontal assault on the rule. Certainly, that is how O'Connor wanted *Evans* to be read. But the same could not be said about *Hudson v. Michigan*,[180] a case in which O'Connor participated, but on which she ultimately did not vote because she retired from the Court before the decision was announced.[181]

Police in Detroit, Michigan, possessed a lawful warrant to search for drugs and guns in Booker Hudson's home. After announcing their presence, police waited only three to five seconds before entering. Inside they found Hudson, drugs, and a gun.[182] After Hudson was convicted of narcotics and gun possession, Michigan prosecutors conceded the manner of entry violated the Fourth Amendment's knock-and-announce rule.[183] Thus, the only issue confronting the justices in *Hudson* was whether suppression is appropriate when police violate the knock-and-announce rule.[184]

Scalia's opinion for the Court in *Hudson* held that suppression is never a remedy for knock-and-announce violations. At first glance, this is a rather remarkable holding because a decade earlier, a unanimous Court had declared that the knock-and-announce

---

[179] *Evans*, 514 U.S. at 13.

[180] 547 U.S. 586 (2006).

[181] O'Connor participated when *Hudson* was originally argued on January 9, 2006. Her resignation was effective upon the nomination and confirmation of her successor, Samuel Alito, who took his seat on January 31, 2006. On April 19, 2006, the Court ordered reargument in *Hudson*, which suggested that the Court was evenly split after O'Connor's resignation. *Hudson* was reargued on May 18, 2006, and decided nearly a month later, this time with Alito providing the fifth vote to affirm Hudson's conviction.

[182] *Hudson*, 547 U.S. at 588.

[183] *Id.* at 590.

[184] While Scalia's opinion does not precisely frame the issue this way, surely this *was* the issue addressed and decided by the Court. *See* James J. Tomkovicz, Hudson v. Michigan *and the Future of Fourth Amendment Exclusion*, 93 IOWA L. REV. 1819, 1822 n.13, 1823 n.19 (2008) [hereinafter Tomkovicz, *The Future of Fourth Amendment Exclusion*].

rule was constitutionally required.[185] Scalia's ruling rested on three distinct and independent bases. First, he explained that the unlawful entry "was *not* a but-for cause of obtaining the evidence."[186] The failure to comply with the announcement rule had no causal nexus to obtaining the evidence, because regardless of whether the police complied with the Constitution, they would have executed the warrant and discovered the evidence. This reasoning alone was sufficient to affirm Hudson's conviction and end the case, but Scalia had more on his mind.[187]

Second, Scalia explained that even if the constitutional violation was the but-for cause of obtaining the evidence, admission of the evidence is nevertheless proper when the connection between the police illegality and the discovery of the evidence is "too attenuated to justify exclusion."[188] Here, Scalia invoked the attenuation exception to the exclusionary rule. He accurately noted that in prior cases, suppression was denied where the nexus between the Fourth Amendment violation and the seizure of evidence was "remote."[189] Although Scalia did not acknowledge it, this traditional attenuation exception was unavailable in *Hudson* since the discovery of the evidence immediately followed on the heels of the illegal entry, and there were no intervening circumstances that severed the connection between the violation and discovery.

Alternatively, Scalia created a new form of attenuation, noticeably lacking in precedential support. He explained: "Attenuation also occurs when, even given a direct causal connection, the interest protected by the constitutional guarantee that has been violated would not be served by suppression of the evidence obtained."[190] Scalia then noted that the interests protected by the announcement rule included protecting human life and limb, preventing the destruction of property, and protecting aspects of privacy and dignity that can be disturbed by a sudden entry. Scalia then distinguished these interests from the interest protected by the warrant requirement.[191] When police violate the warrant requirement, he explained, the government infringes a person's right to "shield 'their persons, houses, papers, and effects' from the government's scrutiny."[192]

---

185 *See* Wilson v. Arkansas, 514 U.S. 927 (1995). *Wilson* was reaffirmed in a series of subsequent rulings, and its validity had not been questioned by the Court.

186 *Hudson*, 547 U.S. at 592.

187 *See* Tomkovicz, *The Future of Fourth Amendment Exclusion*, *supra* note 184, at 1825 ("Justice Scalia could have ended his opinion at this point. His conclusion about the absence of a causal connection between the knock-and-announce violation and the discoveries in the home foreclosed application of the *Mapp* rule to this case. Justice Scalia continued, however, turning to additional, broader grounds for declaring the [exclusionary] rule inapplicable to Hudson's gun and drugs." (footnote omitted)); *id.* at 1825 n.31 ("The fact that [Scalia] did not pen a short, simple opinion that rested solely on the absence of causation is just one of many indications that the *Hudson* majority was bent upon accomplishing more than simply eliminating the exclusionary remedy for knock-and-announce violations.").

188 *Hudson*, 547 U.S. at 592.

189 *Id.* at 593.

190 *Id.*

191 *Id.* at 594.

192 *Id.* at 593 (quoting U.S. Const. amend. IV).

Exclusion of evidence obtained in violation of the warrant requirement "vindicates that entitlement."[193] The knock-and-announce rule, however, does not protect a person's interest in precluding police from seizing evidence described in a valid warrant. That being the case, Scalia concluded: "Since the interests that *were* violated in this case have nothing to do with the seizure of the evidence, the exclusionary rule is inapplicable."[194]

The third basis for *Hudson*'s holding was that "the exclusionary rule has never been applied except 'where its deterrence benefits outweigh its "substantial social costs."'"[195] The origins of this amorphous balancing test dates back to *Alderman v. United States*,[196] and the test has been a central element of the Court's exclusionary rule cases ever since. The content of Scalia's balancing analysis in *Hudson*, however, is novel.

Scalia's contempt and hostility toward the exclusionary rule is palpable in *Hudson*.[197] Amazingly, Scalia characterizes the holding in *Mapp v. Ohio* as "[e]xpansive dicta."[198] Professor LaFave says "one would be hard-pressed to find another case with so many bogus arguments piled atop one another."[199] In any event, four members of the Court (Roberts, Scalia, Thomas, and Alito) were seemingly prepared to abolish the exclusionary rule entirely in *Hudson*. Kennedy, however, stood in the way. Kennedy, who provided the fifth vote and concurred in the three key sections of Scalia's opinion, said the following about suppression: "[T]he continued operation of the exclusionary rule, as settled and defined by our precedents, is not in doubt."[200] Deciphering the meaning of Kennedy's statement is no easy task. Indeed, the statement itself raises the suspicion that the Court is ready to bury the rule. Those distrustful of the Court's motives might wonder why, "if the current operation of the exclusionary rule were *not* in doubt, such a declaration would be required."[201]

---

[193] *Id.* at 593.

[194] *Id.* at 594.

[195] *Id.* (citations omitted).

[196] 394 U.S. 165 (1969).

[197] *See* Thomas K. Clancy, *The Irrelevancy of the Fourth Amendment in the Roberts Court*, 85 CHI.-KENT L. REV. 191, 202 (2010) (stating that at its "most fundamental level," the result in *Hudson* "called into question the future of the exclusionary rule," and that abolition of the rule "is Scalia's clear aim; he has planted the seeds in *Hudson* and needs one more vote to reap the harvest"). Professor Tomkovicz agrees that *Hudson* can be read as a sign that the Court is ready to abolish the rule. *See* Tomkovicz, *The Future of Fourth Amendment Exclusion, supra* note 184, at 1841–47. Professor Tomkovicz explains that when *Hudson* is broadly read, it "foreshadows and anticipates outright abolition" of the exclusionary rule, *id.* at 1841, but he believes that is not the best way to interpret *Hudson*, "at least for the present," *id.* at 1847–49.

[198] *Hudson*, 547 U.S. at 591.

[199] 6 WAYNE R. LAFAVE, SEARCH AND SEIZURE: A TREATISE ON THE FOURTH AMENDMENT § 11.4, at 52 (4th ed. Supp. 2011–2012).

[200] *Hudson*, 547 U.S. at 603 (Kennedy, J., concurring in part and concurring in the judgment). For a discerning analysis of Kennedy's concurrence in *Hudson*, see Tomkovicz, *The Future of Fourth Amendment Exclusion, supra* note 184, at 1832–33, 1848–49, 1880–81.

[201] Donald Dripps, *The Fourth Amendment, the Exclusionary Rule, and the Roberts Court: Normative and Empirical Dimensions of the Over-Deterrence Hypothesis*, 85 CHI.-KENT L. REV. 209, 235 (2010).

Perhaps Kennedy's comments reflect the fact that Scalia had initially lined up the votes to repeal the rule, but Kennedy decided against that move and was signaling his support for the rule, at least for now. On the other hand, why would Kennedy join an opinion designed to bury the rule?[202] Or maybe Kennedy got "cold feet" after reading Scalia's draft in *Hudson* and was unwilling to go along. Alternatively, perhaps Kennedy had not decided what to do about the rule. A concurring opinion would permit Kennedy to join the result and reasoning in *Hudson*, which moved the Court closer to abolishing the rule than it had ever been. But it would also allow him more time to think about repealing the rule outright. Whatever Kennedy meant in *Hudson*, his influence on the future existence of the exclusionary rule is enormous.

While Kennedy's comment in *Hudson* has triggered a wide-ranging debate over whether the Court is poised to repeal the exclusionary rule, academics generally agree that Scalia's opinion is a direct attack on the rule on several levels. Unsurprisingly, both of these reasons have made *Hudson* the subject of intense scholarly criticism.[203] Those views will not be repeated here. Instead, the point emphasized is the expansive nature of Scalia's logic. As written, *Hudson* lays the foundation for abolishing exclusion *as a categorical matter* in contexts beyond knock-and-announce cases; its logic can be extended to other Fourth Amendment violations.

For example, the first basis for withholding exclusion in knock-and-announce cases is that the unlawful police entry "was *not* a but-for cause of obtaining the evidence." In Scalia's words, whether a lawful announcement "had occurred *or not*, the police would have executed the warrant" and discovered the gun and drugs inside of Hudson's home.[204] This is another way of saying that the discovery of the evidence was inevitable regardless of whether or not the police complied with the knock-and-announce rule. In other words, suppression is unwarranted here because "if the police hadn't done it wrong, they would have done it right." More important, the logic of this reasoning would require a different result in many cases now mandating suppression.

---

[202] *See* David A. Moran, *The End of the Exclusionary Rule, Among Other Things: The Roberts Court Takes on the Fourth Amendment*, 2006 CATO SUP. CT. REV. 283, 308 ("If [Kennedy] really believes in the continuing vitality of the exclusionary rule, it is an absolute mystery to me why he would cast the crucial fifth vote for an opinion that openly declared war on the exclusionary rule."); *see also* Sharon L. Davies & Anna B. Scanlon, *Katz in the Age of* Hudson v. Michigan*: Some Thoughts on "Suppression as a Last Resort,"* 41 U.C. DAVIS L. REV. 1035, 1068 (2008) (explaining that Kennedy's "cautionary language [in *Hudson*] may mean that [he] will be unwilling to provide that last-needed vote" to repeal the exclusionary rule, yet "Kennedy's willingness to align himself with the most wide-reaching points" in Scalia's opinion "leaves this unclear").

[203] *See* Alschuler, *supra* note 93; Davies & Scanlon, *supra* note 202; Johnson, *supra* note 94; *see also* 1 LAFAVE, *supra* note 199, § 1.6, at 43–49 (Supp. 2011–2012); 6 *id.* § 11.4, at 44–48, 52–60; Tomkovicz, *The Future of Fourth Amendment Exclusion*, *supra* note 184. For a thorough survey of the lower courts' use of *Hudson*'s logic, see Christopher D. Totten, *The Exclusionary Rule After* Hudson v. Michigan*: Mourning the Death of the Knock and Announce Rule*, 46 No. 5 CRIM. L. BULL. 843 (2010).

[204] *Hudson*, 547 U.S. at 592.

As noted in chapter 1, in cases like *Weeks* and *Agnello*, the Court mandated exclusion because law enforcement officers failed to obtain a warrant before searching a home, even though they had probable cause for the search. In both cases, the Court dismissed government claims similar to the argument embraced in *Hudson*. For example, in *Agnello*, the Court stated: "Belief, however, well founded, that an article sought is concealed in a dwelling house furnishes no justification for a search of that place without a warrant. And such searches are held unlawful notwithstanding facts unquestionably showing probable cause."[205]

An application of *Hudson*'s causation analysis, however, would produce a contrary result in a case like *Weeks* or *Agnello*. Using Scalia's logic, these cases can be rewritten to forbid exclusion: failure to obtain a warrant before searching a home or a footlocker does not justify excluding evidence found within. Because there was probable cause to search, the failure to obtain the warrant was not a but-for cause of obtaining the evidence. Although police could have complied with the Constitution, the fact that they did not does not justify suppression because a judge would have issued a warrant if the police had bothered to ask for one, and the evidence would have been lawfully discovered.[206] To be sure, in *Hudson*, Scalia distinguishes a violation of the warrant requirement and suggests that exclusion is proper where police fail to obtain a warrant because such action infringes a person's right to "shield 'their persons, houses, papers, and effects' from the government's scrutiny."[207] But it will not be surprising if this passage from *Hudson* is treated as dicta in a future case. All the Court need say is that a criminal has no constitutional right to bar a search when police have probable cause he is concealing evidence of a crime. The warrant requirement is not intended to prevent searches, but to ensure that an officer's probable cause determination is scrutinized by a neutral and detached magistrate.[208]

Thus, *Hudson*'s "but-for" analysis raises the same concerns that Professor Pitler identified when he wrote about the implications for the warrant requirement if the Court adopted an inevitable discovery exception to the exclusionary rule.[209] Further, both

---

[205] Agnello v. United States, 269 U.S. 20, 33 (1925).

[206] Professor Amar has not only made this argument as a basis for denying exclusion when the police fail to obtain warrants, *see* AKHIL REED AMAR, THE CONSTITUTION AND CRIMINAL PROCEDURE: FIRST PRINCIPLES 26 (1997) (contending that when police could have obtained a warrant prior to a search, "the illegality is not a but-for cause of the introduction of the [tainted] evidence"), more recently, he has argued that *Hudson*'s logic supports barring exclusion where police fail to obtain warrants, *see* Akhil Reed Amar, *The Battle of Hudson Heights*, SLATE MAG. (June 19, 2006, 3:01 PM), http://www.slate.com/articles/news_and_politics/jurisprudence/2006/06/the_battle_of_hudson_heights.html.

[207] *Hudson*, 547 U.S. at 593 (quoting U.S. CONST. amend. IV).

[208] *Cf.* Johnson, *supra* note 94, at 149 (stating that police are required to obtain search warrants "not because warrantless searches are harmful in themselves, but because the interposition of the magistrate between the police and the citizen will generally tend to prevent searches from being conducted on the basis of something less than probable cause").

[209] Robert M. Pitler, *"The Fruit of the Poisonous Tree" Revisited and Shepardized*, 56 CALIF. L. REV. 579, 630 (1968) ("[T]he exclusionary rule, designed to discourage illegal police activity, is useless if the police

Hudson and the inevitable discovery exception provide law enforcement officials with an incentive to ignore the warrant requirement. "The police might seek the most expeditious method of obtaining the evidence without regard to its illegality, knowing that, as long as they could have obtained the evidence legally, their efforts will not result in its suppression."[210] Although the Court has not yet interpreted the inevitable discovery exception this way, there is nothing to prevent a future Court from reading it this way. That is why Professor Alschuler has described *Hudson*'s but-for causation analysis and the inevitable discovery exception as "clones."[211] As Professor Alschuler explains: "To say that the police would have obtained the challenged evidence even if they had not violated the Constitution is to say both that this evidence inevitably would have been discovered lawfully and that the constitutional violation was not a but-for cause of its discovery."[212]

Scalia's second independent basis for denying suppression in *Hudson*, the attenuation exception to the exclusionary rule, is similarly capable of removing situations from the exclusionary rule's reach that have long been subject to exclusion. According to Scalia, attenuation can occur when, even recognizing a direct or but-for nexus between police illegality and the discovery of evidence, "the interest protected by the constitutional guarantee that has been violated would not be served by suppression of the evidence obtained."[213] Although Scalia did not admit it, the attenuation analysis launched in *Hudson* is not only novel and expansive, it is quite different from traditional attenuation analysis. As Professor Tomkovicz explains in his recent book on constitutional exclusion:

> "Attenuation" seems like a misnomer for this alternative version of the exception. The connection between the violation and the evidence at issue can be very close and very strong. Indeed, this offshoot of the attenuation doctrine encompasses even *primary* evidence acquired as an immediate result of a Fourth Amendment violation and is unconcerned with the culpability of the officers or the egregiousness of their transgression. Considering its very different character, it is at least odd to pair it with the traditional form of the attenuation.[214]

---

may unlawfully invade a man's home, illegally seize evidence and then claim 'we would have obtained it anyway.'").

210 Robert M. Bloom, *Inevitable Discovery: An Exception Beyond the Fruits*, 20 AM. J. CRIM. L. 79, 95 (1992).

211 Alschuler, *supra* note 93, at 1809.

212 *Id.* Others, however, disagree with Alschuler's assessment. Professor LaFave, for example, insists that the inevitable discovery exception is *not* applicable merely because police *could* or *might* have obtained the challenged evidence lawfully. *See* WAYNE R. LAFAVE ET AL., CRIMINAL PROCEDURE § 9.3, at 532 (5th ed. 2009). In his treatise on the Fourth Amendment, LaFave acknowledges that the concerns expressed about the inevitable discovery exception are legitimate, but he contends that the arguments of those who criticize the inevitable discovery exception "are directed not so much to the rule itself as to its application in a loose and unthinking fashion." 6 LAFAVE, *supra* note 199, § 11.4(a), at 269.

213 Hudson v. Michigan, 547 U.S. 586, 593 (2006).

214 JAMES J. TOMKOVICZ, CONSTITUTIONAL EXCLUSION: THE RULES, RIGHTS, AND REMEDIES THAT STRIKE THE BALANCE BETWEEN FREEDOM AND ORDER 51 (2011).

It is also imperative to appreciate how easily *Hudson*'s attenuation analysis can be applied to other search and seizure violations. Similar to the fruit analysis of *New York v. Harris*, under *Hudson*, the exclusionary rule applies only when suppression serves the constitutional interest promoted by the Fourth Amendment rule that the police have failed to follow. The Court could extend *Hudson*'s logic to bar exclusion in a number of contexts.

For example, *Hudson*'s attenuation rule bars exclusion when the *manner* of a police entry into a home violates the Constitution because rarely do the constitutional rules governing the manner in which police execute a warrant protect interests that would be vindicated by suppression. Thus, exclusion is never appropriate when the police allow journalists or other third parties to accompany them when they enter a home to make an arrest or conduct a search. A decade ago, *Wilson v. Layne*[215] found this practice unconstitutional because the Fourth Amendment requires that police actions in execution of a warrant be "related to the objectives of the authorized intrusion," and, as a general matter, the presence of reporters in a home does not aid the police in executing a warrant.[216] While *Wilson* did mention the "privacy" afforded the home,[217] the Court was also careful to observe that the Fourth Amendment violation "is the presence of the media and not the presence of the police in the home," and thus it was reserving the question "whether the exclusionary rule would apply to any evidence discovered or developed by the media representatives."[218] Despite the ruling in *Wilson*, television news programs continue to show videos of police raiding private homes and businesses, indicating that police continue to violate *Wilson* in some locales. But after *Hudson*, there is no reason to think the Court will countenance exclusion for this offense. The Court could easily use *Hudson*'s attenuation logic to conclude that because suppression does not vindicate the interests protected by prohibiting the presence of the media, the exclusionary rule is inapplicable.

Similarly, the logic from *Hudson*'s attenuation analysis may also prevent exclusion when police fail to present their search warrant to a homeowner before entering the home to effectuate a search or arrest. Although the Court has not definitively decided whether a homeowner has a right, circumstances permitting, to inspect the warrant before police entry, language from some of the Court's rulings implicitly recognizes a such a right. Over forty years ago, in *Camara v. Municipal Court*,[219] Justice White acknowledged the dilemma facing a homeowner when confronted with a municipal inspector's demand to perform a warrantless search of his home: the homeowner "has no way of knowing whether enforcement of the municipal code involved requires inspection of his premises,

---

[215] 526 U.S. 603 (1999).

[216] *Id.* at 611.

[217] *Id.* at 610.

[218] *Id.* at 614 n.2.

[219] 387 U.S. 523 (1967).

no way of knowing the lawful limits of the inspector's power to search, and no way of knowing whether the inspector himself is acting under proper authorization."[220]

Likewise, the logic behind the common-law knock-and-announce requirement supports a constitutional right to inspection. One of the interests served by the common-law announcement rule was to allow a homeowner the opportunity to demand identification from officers seeking entry and to allow the resident to explain to the officers that the person or premises are mistakenly described in the warrant.[221] Of course, these purposes could not be served if the homeowner had no right to see the warrant before police entry.

Finally, when *Groh v. Ramirez*[222] explained why the presence of a search warrant serves a high function (that could not necessarily be vindicated by some other document not made available to the homeowner), the Court suggested that a homeowner could see the warrant "for her inspection" before police entry.[223] These statements provide the basis for concluding that a homeowner has a constitutional right to see a warrant prior to entry. That right would, *inter alia*, advance an occupant's interest in assuring that the law requires entry, inform the occupant of the scope of the power of the police to search or seize, and establish that the police are acting under proper authority.

To be sure, more recently in *United States v. Grubbs*,[224] Scalia's majority opinion observed in dicta that the Fourth Amendment imposed no requirement to present a homeowner with a warrant.[225] Souter's concurrence, however, pointed out that the Court had previously reserved that question in *Groh v. Ramirez*, and that it remained unsettled after *Grubbs*.[226] Souter observed that displaying a warrant to a homeowner "'assures the individual whose property is searched or seized of the lawful authority of the executing officer, his need to search, and the limits of his power to search.'"[227]

Even assuming the Court will find that the Fourth Amendment grants a homeowner a right to see a warrant before a police entry, *Hudson*'s attenuation logic ensures that exclusion will never be an appropriate remedy in cases where it is violated. As in *Hudson*, the Fourth Amendment interests protected by a "right to see a warrant" do not "include the shielding of potential evidence from the government's eyes."[228] In fact, some lower federal courts have already applied *Hudson*'s attenuation logic to conclude that the exclusionary rule does not apply when the police fail to present the defendant with a search warrant.[229]

---

220 *Id.* at 532.

221 *See* Charles Patrick Garcia, Note, *The Knock and Announce Rule: A New Approach to the Destruction-of-Evidence Exception*, 93 Colum. L. Rev. 685, 687–88 (1993).

222 540 U.S. 551 (2004).

223 *Id.* at 557.

224 547 U.S. 90 (2006).

225 *Id.* at 98–99.

226 *Id.* at 101 (Souter, J., concurring in part and concurring in the judgment).

227 *Id.* (internal quotation marks and citation omitted).

228 Hudson v. Michigan, 547 U.S. 586, 593 (2006).

229 *See* United States v. Hector, 474 F.3d 1150, 1155 (9th Cir. 2007), *cert. denied*, 552 U.S. 1104 (2008); United States v. Makki, No. 06-20324, 2007 WL 1100453, at *4 (E.D. Mich. Apr. 12, 2007).

Hudson's attenuation analysis would also seem to bar exclusion where police arbitrarily destroy property while executing a warrant. In *United States v. Ramirez*,[230] the Court stated in dicta: "Excessive or unnecessary destruction of property in the course of a search may violate the Fourth Amendment, even though the entry itself is lawful and the fruits of the search are not subject to suppression."[231] And *Ramirez* reserved whether, if breaking a window to enter a garage violated the Fourth Amendment, there was a "sufficient causal relationship" between the breaking and the discovery of evidence to justify suppression.[232] However, even assuming a direct connection between the breaking and the discovery of evidence, *Hudson*'s attenuation analysis would bar suppression because the constitutional interest protected here is the preservation of property, not "the shielding of potential evidence from the government's eyes."[233]

Professor Tomkovicz has written that "[i]t *would seem*" that *Hudson*'s attenuation analysis is applicable "to violations of other rules that prescribe the constitutional *manner* of home entries or other searches."[234] Tomkovicz's cautious qualification is unnecessary. There is no principled difference in the conclusion that the announcement rule does not promote the "shield" function identified by Scalia's new attenuation theory, and the conclusion that the "no-press" rule, the "right-to-see-a-warrant" rule, and the "no-arbitrary-destruction-of-property" rule, also do not promote the "shield" function.

Professor Tomkovicz also believes that *Hudson*'s attenuation theory is potentially applicable "to any case involving evidence found as a result of an unconstitutional *seizure* of a person or property."[235] According to Tomkovicz:

> The Fourth Amendment's prohibitions of unreasonable seizures of individuals and effects are arguably designed to serve liberty and possessory interests, respectively, not to shield potential evidence from government eyes. According to the logic of *Hudson*, because suppression does not serve the interests beneath those rules, the exclusionary rule is inapplicable.[236]

Just as reasonable persons could conclude that suppression does not serve the purposes behind the constitutional bar on unreasonable seizures, reasonable persons could also decide that exclusion does not promote the purposes the Court has identified in its rulings on inventory searches by police. In several cases, the Court has upheld the

---

230 523 U.S. 65 (1998).

231 *Id.* at 66.

232 *Id.* at 72 n.3. In *Hudson*, Scalia, speaking for four justices, viewed *Ramirez*'s reservation of this issue as a clear expression of the "proposition that an impermissible manner of entry does not necessarily trigger the exclusionary rule." *Hudson*, 547 U.S. at 602.

233 *Hudson*, 547 U.S. at 593.

234 Tomkovicz, *The Future of Fourth Amendment Exclusion*, *supra* note 184, at 1864–65 (emphasis added).

235 *Id.* at 1865.

236 *Id.*

government's power to conduct inventory searches of impounded cars and an arrestee's effects. The searches involved can be quite extensive, like the search in *Colorado v. Bertine*,[237] which included the detailed inspection of a backpack located inside a vehicle after the driver had been arrested for drunk driving.[238] The *Bertine* Court, relying on earlier inventory search cases, *South Dakota v. Opperman*[239] and *Illinois v. Lafayette*,[240] held that the police do not violate the Fourth Amendment when they discover evidence pursuant to police department standardized guidelines for inventory searches.

These cases explain that neither the warrant nor probable cause requirements govern inventory searches.[241] Because inventory searches are not designed to advance criminal investigations, traditional Fourth Amendment safeguards, like a magistrate's independent determination that a search is proper or individualized suspicion of wrongdoing exists, are inapplicable.[242] The Court has also explained that the purposes served by inventory searches include protecting a person's property while in police custody; guarding the government against frivolous lawsuits over lost, stolen, or vandalized property; and ensuring police safety.[243] Thus, the Court has authorized inventory searches if law enforcement agencies provide standardized guidelines to control police discretion when conducting such searches.

Keeping in mind the constitutional interests served by inventory searches, under *Hudson*'s attenuation logic, suppression would yet again be unwarranted when police conduct an illegal inventory search. While reasonable persons might differ, an opponent of the exclusionary rule could argue that the interests protected by the Court's inventory cases "are quite different—and do not include the shielding of potential evidence from the government's eyes."[244] Thus, even if an officer conducts an unreasonable inventory search by ignoring standardized procedure, the Court could find suppression inappropriate. Because the interests served by inventory searches—safeguarding an owner's property; shielding the government from lawsuits over lost, stolen, or vandalized property;

---

[237] 479 U.S. 367 (1987).

[238] *Id.* at 368-69. In the backpack, the officer came across a nylon bag containing metal canisters. After opening the canisters, the officer found drugs, drug paraphernalia, and cash. He also discovered cash in a *sealed* envelope located in a zippered outside pocket of the backpack. The officer took the backpack and its contents to the police station, and Bertine was charged with possession and intent to sell the drugs.

[239] 428 U.S. 364 (1976) (holding that the search of a closed glove compartment pursuant to a routine inventory search of a lawfully impounded car did not violate the Fourth Amendment).

[240] 462 U.S. 640 (1983) (holding that the inventory search of an arrestee's personal effects at the police station did not violate Fourth Amendment's warrant requirement).

[241] *See, e.g., Bertine*, 479 U.S. at 371 (explaining that inventory searches are not subject to the warrant requirement); *Lafayette*, 462 U.S. at 643-44 (same); *Opperman*, 428 U.S. at 367 (noting that although vehicles are "effects" within the reach of the Fourth Amendment, the inherent mobility of cars and the reduced expectation of privacy within a vehicle makes "rigorous enforcement of the warrant requirement impossible").

[242] *Bertine*, 479 U.S. at 371.

[243] *Id.* at 372.

[244] Hudson v. Michigan, 547 U.S. 586, 593 (2006).

and promoting police safety—"have nothing to do with the seizure of [ ] evidence,"[245] the Court could easily rule that exclusion is unwarranted in this context.

In sum, *Hudson*'s attenuation theory can plausibly expand beyond the confines of knock-and-announce violations. By insisting that suppression is only appropriate when exclusion will vindicate the underlying Fourth Amendment value the police have violated, *Hudson* not only brazenly contradicted the notion that exclusion was not intended to vindicate a defendant's constitutional rights,[246] it also moved the Court a long way toward confining the exclusionary rule to a small and discrete category of cases, if not outright repeal of the rule.

The third and final basis for the result in *Hudson* was Scalia's assertion that "the exclusionary rule has never been applied except 'where its deterrence benefits outweigh its "substantial social costs."'"[247] As part of his balancing analysis, Scalia dismisses out of hand the concern that without exclusion, police will have no reason to comply with the announcement rule. But then he makes an astonishing statement: "Of course even if this assertion were accurate, it would not necessarily justify suppression."[248] This statement is jarring because for over forty years, the Court has repeatedly stated that exclusion is necessary to deter police illegality. Scalia now seems to be taking the position (along with the four justices who joined this section of his opinion) that even if exclusion is the only way to deter police misconduct, suppression still may not be required.

Scalia then offers the following reasons for not excluding in *Hudson*, all of which have become a staple of the Rehnquist and Roberts Courts' exclusionary rule opinions. Scalia writes suppression of tainted evidence exacts substantial social costs; he *assumes* that civil damage lawsuits are an effective deterrent against police violation of the announcement rule, and that police professionalism, internal police discipline, and citizen review

---

[245] *Id. at* 594.

[246] Professor Alschuler cogently explains why *Hudson*'s analysis contradicts a central tenant of the Burger and Rehnquist Courts' exclusionary rule jurisprudence:

> For more than forty years, the Court has denigrated "rights" theories of the [exclusionary] rule and contended that exclusion never vindicates the interest of the defendant before the court. The Court has insisted that exclusion is always what the *Hudson* Court said it never can be—a windfall awarded to a defendant for the sake of protecting the rights of others. If, as the Court has said repeatedly, exclusion cannot restore the defendant's violated interests and is not designed to do so, *Hudson*'s declaration that exclusion is inappropriate *unless* it restores the defendant's violated interests is simply a formula for abolishing the rule.

Alschuler, *supra* note 93, at 1764 (footnote omitted). It is incredible that Scalia was unaware of the inconsistency between the conclusion that exclusion is not a personal right and his newly announced theory in *Hudson*. Scalia is simply too smart and savvy not to have noticed the conflict. This is another example of Scalia's and the conservative majority's willingness to find or create theories to promote their anti-exclusionary rule agenda. *See id.* at 1756 ("The Court shifts to whichever reason for exclusion gives it a reason not to exclude.").

[247] *Hudson*, 547 U.S. at 594.

[248] *Id.* at 596.

have reduced police misconduct.[249] As Professor Donald Dripps has commented, if this part of Scalia's opinion "isn't a brief for abolition" of the exclusionary rule, "it sure looks like one."[250] In the final analysis, *Hudson* essentially eliminates the knock-and-announce rule from Fourth Amendment protection, and one need not be a constitutional scholar or even trained in the law to understand why this is so.[251]

* * *

In *Hudson*, four justices tipped their hand regarding their intentions for the exclusionary rule. The Roberts Court next addressed the issue of suppression in *Herring v. United States*.[252] While *Herring*'s tone was not as hostile as *Hudson*'s toward exclusion, the Court's reasoning in *Herring* similarly signaled the future demise of exclusion. Beyond *Herring*'s rationale, what was most significant was Kennedy's willingness to join the majority opinion without qualification. Nominally, *Herring* addressed the question left open in *Arizona v. Evans*: whether exclusion is warranted for evidence obtained after police arrest someone relying on a warrant that other police personnel erroneously left in a computer database. But the substance of *Herring* was different from *Evans*. While Rehnquist's opinion in *Evans* certainly followed *Leon*'s anti-suppression script, *Herring* made clear that the Roberts Court was not content to merely chip away at the exclusionary rule, as *Krull* and *Evans* did. As the remainder of this chapter demonstrates, the point of *Herring* is to confine the exclusionary rule to cases of deliberate or recurring police misconduct. Put differently, *Herring* effectively adopts a general good-faith exception to suppression. When combined with the ruling in *Hudson v. Michigan*, the result and reasoning of *Herring* is another sign that the Roberts Court intends to either abolish the rule or confine it to cases of egregious Fourth Amendment violations.

---

249 *Id.* at 596–99. Interestingly, Scalia implies that police professionalism is responsible for the fact that police departments "take the constitutional rights of citizens seriously," *id.* at 599, and cites Samuel Walker's book, TAMING THE SYSTEM: THE CONTROL OF DISCRETION IN CRIMINAL JUSTICE 1950–1990 (1993), as support for his claim. After *Hudson* was announced, Dr. Walker wrote an op-ed article stating that Scalia had cited his work "to support a terrible decision" and had "twisted" his thesis to reach a conclusion that was the "exact opposite" of what Walker had found. Samuel Walker, Editorial, *Thanks for Nothing, Nino*, L.A. TIMES, June 25, 2006, at M5. According to Walker,

> Scalia's opinion suggests that the results I highlighted have sufficiently removed the need for an exclusionary rule to act as a judicial-branch watchdog over the police. I have never said or even suggested such a thing. To the contrary, I have argued that the results reinforce the Supreme Court's continuing importance in defining constitutional protections for individual rights and requiring the appropriate remedies for violations, including the exclusion of evidence.

Id.

250 Dripps, *supra* note 201, at 212.

251 *See* Craig M. Bradley, *Mixed Messages on the Exclusionary Rule*, TRIAL, Dec. 2006, at 56, 57 (stating that non-lawyers understand that the impact of *Hudson* means police no longer have a reason to comply with the announcement rule and "[o]nly a (naïve) lawyer could think otherwise").

252 555 U.S. 135 (2009).

While Bennie Dean Herring was checking on his impounded vehicle at the Coffee County, Alabama, sheriff's office, sheriff's deputy Mark Anderson, who was aware of Herring's less-than-perfect background, requested that the Coffee County warrant clerk run a warrant check on Herring. When the search came back negative, Anderson had the clerk call neighboring Dale County to see if there were any outstanding warrants for Herring. This time, the clerk reported an outstanding arrest warrant for Herring. With this information, Anderson arrested Herring as he was driving away from the impoundment lot. A search of Herring's person and vehicle incident to the arrest revealed narcotics and a weapon. Ten to fifteen minutes later, it was learned that the warrant listed in the Dale County database was erroneous. It had been recalled five months earlier, and a negligent employee of the sheriff's office failed to remove it.[253] That being the case, Herring's arrest was illegal.

Although Herring's arrest violated the Fourth Amendment, the evidence discovered was admitted at his federal narcotics prosecution under the good-faith exception. The lower federal courts ruled that suppression of the evidence would serve no deterrent purpose. The officers who arrested Herring were innocent of any wrongdoing or carelessness; the failure to update the computer records was negligent, not a deliberate or tactical decision.[254]

After losing his argument for exclusion in the lower courts, Herring appealed to the Court. Chief Justice Roberts's opinion for a five-to-four majority ruled that exclusion is unjustified when police error is the result of isolated negligence attenuated from an illegal arrest. Roberts's ruling has been subject to extensive scrutiny and debate. Wayne LaFave characterizes *Herring* as "not simply wrong; it is wrong over and over again!"[255] Likewise, Al Alschuler has described the scope of *Herring* as "breathtaking."[256] Others, however, reject the notion that the result in *Herring* is cause for alarm. These scholars interpret *Herring* narrowly.[257] In light of the current Court's proclivities in suppression

---

253 *Id.* at 137–38.

254 United States v. Herring, 492 F.3d 1212, 1218 (11th Cir. 2007).

255 Wayne R. LaFave, *The Smell of* Herring*: A Critique of the Supreme Court's Latest Assault on the Exclusionary Rule*, 99 J. Crim. L. & Criminology 757, 758 (2009) [hereinafter LaFave, *The Smell of* Herring].

256 Albert W. Alschuler, Herring v. United States*: A Minnow or a Shark?*, 7 Ohio St. J. Crim. L. 463, 463 (2009) [hereinafter Alschuler, *A Minnow or a Shark?*]; *see also* Jennifer E. Laurin, *Trawling for* Herring*: Lessons in Doctrinal Borrowing and Convergence*, 111 Colum. L. Rev. 670, 679–88 (2011) (arguing that the reasoning of *Herring* is a significant departure from the Court's prior good-faith precedents).

257 Professor Craig Bradley originally read *Herring* as an insignificant ruling. *See* Craig M. Bradley, *Red* Herring *or the Death of the Exclusionary Rule?*, Trial, Apr. 2009, at 52, 53–54 [hereinafter Bradley, *Red* Herring] (observing that *Herring* "is only a slight change from *Arizona v. Evans*," and that *Herring* "represents another chip out of the exclusionary rule, albeit a minor one since most illegal searches will not be attenuated from the error that caused them"). But Bradley did caution that if four of the justices "get their way, the major pillar upholding Fourth and Fifth Amendment rights, will soon collapse." *Id.* at 54. Professor Orin Kerr wrote, "*Herring* is a minor case. . . . I think it's a narrow and interstitial decision, not one that is rocking the boat. In particular, I don't see it as suggesting a general good faith exception for police conduct. Such a position would be an extraordinary shift in Fourth Amendment law that would effectively

cases and Roberts's language in *Herring*, it is unlikely that Roberts intended *Herring* to be read narrowly.

At first glance, the issue addressed in *Herring* seems narrow: whether the exclusionary rule applies to suppress evidence obtained from an illegal arrest that was the result of another law enforcement department's erroneous recordkeeping. But Roberts's opening paragraph suggests that his logic and holding apply beyond the specific facts of the case. Roberts asks: "What if an officer reasonably believes there is an outstanding arrest warrant, but that belief turns out to be wrong because of a negligent bookkeeping error by another police employee?"[258] The Chief Justice provides the following answer: exclusion of evidence obtained from an illegal arrest is not a mechanical reaction to a Fourth Amendment violation. Rather, "the question turns on the culpability of the police and the potential of exclusion to deter wrongful police conduct. Here the error was the result of isolated negligence attenuated from the arrest. We hold that in these circumstances" exclusion is not appropriate.[259] Of course, the error in *Herring* involved negligence by a police employee in *another county*, but Roberts's framing of the issue suggested that error by an officer in the same police department should not result in exclusion either.[260]

In finding that the tainted evidence was properly admitted at trial, Roberts follows the anti-exclusion guideposts marked in *Leon* and *Hudson*. Quoting Scalia's opinion in *Hudson*, Roberts observes that suppression is a "'last resort, not our first impulse.'"[261] And relying on *Leon* and its progeny, Roberts explains that the flagrancy and culpability of police conduct is an important factor in determining whether exclusion is proper. These statements were neither noteworthy nor critical in a suppression ruling from the Court. However, Roberts's statements regarding the type of police conduct that justifies exclusion as a remedy were striking. In prior cases, the culpability *vel non* of the police was certainly an important *factor* in whether the Court would authorize exclusion. By contrast, in *Herring*, culpability is now the *dispositive* factor.

Specifically, *Herring* stated: "To trigger the exclusionary rule, police conduct must be sufficiently deliberate that exclusion can meaningfully deter it, and sufficiently culpable

---

overrule a ton of cases. . . . The decision was quite narrow." Orin Kerr, *Responding to Tom Goldstein on* Herring, Volokh Conspiracy (Jan. 14, 2009, 2:38 PM), http:volokh.com/posts/1231961926.shtml; *see also* Matthew J. Franck, *Hyperventilating About the Exclusionary Rule*, Nat'l Rev. Online (Feb. 16, 2009, 11:21 AM), http://www.nationalreview.com/bench-memos/50452/hyperventilating-about-exclusionary-rule/matthew-j-franck# (describing *Herring* as "really pretty ordinary, and simply appl[ying] a principle established" in *United States v. Leon*, and stating that "there's no sign that the Roberts Court has lost its interest in maintaining" the exclusionary rule).

258 *Herring*, 555 U.S. at 136–37.

259 *Id.* at 137.

260 Alschuler, *A Minnow or a Shark?*, *supra* note 256, at 471 ("[Roberts] asked about the significance of a negligent error by *any* officer other than the one who conducted the search. His opinion implied that even negligence by another officer in the same police agency might be regarded as 'attenuated.'").

261 *Herring*, 555 U.S. at 140 (quoting Hudson v. Michigan, 547 U.S. 586, 591 (2006)).

that such deterrence is worth the price paid by the justice system."[262] Purporting to rely on prior cases, *Herring* asserted: "[T]he exclusionary rule serves to deter deliberate, reckless, or grossly negligent conduct, or in some circumstances recurring or systemic negligence."[263] Roberts then stated that Deputy Anderson's illegal arrest of Herring did "not rise to that level."[264]

A few points about this language should be highlighted. First, these assertions in *Herring*—what Professor Alschuler calls the "big blast" statements[265]—were unprecedented and controversial. No decision prior to *Herring* had asserted or even implied that suppression turns on deliberate or grossly negligent police conduct.[266] Although these statements may appear as obiter dicta, it is a mistake to interpret them as such. This part of *Herring*, like Rehnquist's language in *Peltier* that exclusion only applies when police knowingly violate the Fourth Amendment, is the core of Roberts's reasoning. His description of the level of police culpability necessary to trigger exclusion was stated without qualification. Equally important, this language does not mention "attenuation." Unlike the unexplained references to "attenuation" in other parts of his opinion, the discussion on the need for culpable police conduct to trigger the exclusionary rule appears as part of a "sustained argument."[267]

Second, it is also a mistake to think that this language from *Herring* will not be cited by the Court when future defendants invoke the exclusionary rule in the context of

---

262 *Id.* at 144.

263 *Id.*

264 *Id.*

265 Alschuler, *A Minnow or a Shark?*, *supra* note 256, at 472.

266 *See* LaFave, *The Smell of* Herring, *supra* note 255, at 760–70; *see also* Alschuler, *A Minnow or a Shark?*, *supra* note 256, at 488–89 ("No decision prior to *Herring*... had suggested or implied that the exclusionary rule should be limited [to culpable police misconduct].... *Herring*'s 'big blast' statements would preclude exclusion even when an officer was not 'objectively reasonable' as long as he was not grossly negligent. Declaring that this standard had been 'laid out in our cases' took chutzpa.").

267 Alschuler, *A Minnow or a Shark?*, *supra* note 256, at 474 (explaining that *Herring*'s "'big blast' statements look more like *ratio decidendi* (or the Court's 'reason for deciding' as it did) than like obiter dicta (or things 'said by the way.')" and that *Herring*'s "big blast" statements "appeared as part of a sustained argument"). Professor David Moran takes a different view of Roberts's language. He states the distinction drawn by the *Herring* majority

> between various culpable mental states that police officers might have while violating the Fourth Amendment is entirely unnecessary to the result. Since, according to the majority, the police acted reasonably in relying on a database of warrants that was well-maintained and relatively error-free, the case seemed to provide no occasion for the Court to distinguish between officers who are merely negligent and officers acting with more culpable mental states. On the contrary, the majority concluded that the police in *Herring* were not negligent at all.
>
> To put it simply, the language in *Herring* limiting the exclusionary rule to violations committed by grossly negligent (or worse) police officers looks like dicta. The four justices in dissent in *Herring* were careful not to refer to the culpability language in the majority opinion as a holding.

David A. Moran, *Hanging on by a Thread: The Exclusionary Rule (Or What's Left of It) Lives for Another Day*, 9 OHIO ST. J. CRIM. L. 363, 364-65 (2011) (footnote omitted).

ordinary Fourth Amendment violations. To be sure, the "holding" of *Herring* appeared to be bound by the facts. But the opening paragraph of *Herring*, which frames the issue before the Court, suggests that the Chief Justice sees the case as involving a broader concern beyond the specific facts of the case. If Roberts truly intended a narrow reading of *Herring*, he certainly knew how to write an opinion that would convey to the lower courts that *Herring*'s holding and reasoning were confined to negligent recordkeeping cases. If *Herring* were meant to be narrowly read, if *Herring* was simply deciding the issue left open in *Evans*, the "big blast" statements were unnecessary to decide the case. It borders on the naïve to think these statements were heedlessly included without an eye toward their future application. Inclusion of those statements served an intentional purpose: the Roberts Court intends to restrict the exclusionary rule to instances of culpable police behavior.

In fact, the Court's recent ruling in *Davis v. United States*[268] embraced and expanded *Herring*'s edict that only sufficiently deliberate police conduct would trigger exclusion. Also, *Davis* reaffirmed *Herring*'s statement that police misconduct must be sufficiently deliberate such that suppression can meaningfully deter it, and sufficiently culpable that such deterrence is "'worth the price paid by the justice system.'"[269] *Davis*, written by Alito, decided whether the good-faith exception should extend to a case where police conduct a search relying on binding judicial precedent that is subsequently overruled. By a seven-to-two vote, the Court ruled that the exclusionary rule does not apply in this context.[270] *Davis* indicates that six (and maybe seven) of the current justices read *Herring* broadly.

Davis involved a police search of a car that was lawful under the Court's precedents at the time of the search but which the Court later overruled while Davis's appeal was pending. When *Davis* arrived at the Court, few thought that the defendant had any chance of winning because police reasonably relied on existing law to perform the search. Although all agreed that the search was unconstitutional, excluding the evidence found from the now-illegal search would serve no deterrent purpose because the officer was neither culpable nor did anything wrong when performing the search. As far as the good-faith exception went, the facts in *Davis* appeared to be on all fours with *Herring* and the Court's previous good-faith cases.[271]

---

[268] 131 S. Ct. 2419 (2011).

[269] *Id.* at 2428 (quoting *Herring*, 555 U.S. at 144).

[270] *Id.* at 2434.

[271] At first glance, *Davis* might qualify "as a 'no-brainer.'" *See* 1 LaFave, *supra* note 199, § 1.3, at 21 (Supp. 2011–2012). But as Fourth Amendment scholars know, the Court's rulings in this area often require close scrutiny. According to Professor LaFave, "some questions exist with respect to either the result or the majority's reasoning [in *Davis*] that might give one pause." *Id.* Moreover, the result in *Davis* raises significant disincentives for future defendants to challenge search and seizure practices that might result in the creation of new Fourth Amendment law. *See* Orin S. Kerr, *Good Faith, New Law, and the Scope of the Exclusionary Rule*, 99 Geo. L.J. 1077, 1082 (2011).

Indeed, Alito held that because suppression "would do nothing to deter police misconduct" and would impose a high cost to "both the truth and the public safety,"[272] the exclusionary rule does not apply in this context.[273] His opinion explains, relying on *Herring*, the deterrent value of suppression varies with the culpability of the challenged police misconduct: "When the police exhibit 'deliberate,' 'reckless,' or 'grossly negligent' disregard for Fourth Amendment rights, the deterrent value of exclusion is *strong* and *tends* to outweigh the resulting costs."[274] On the other hand, Alito also elaborates, in line with *Herring*'s focus on culpable police conduct, that when police search or seize "with an objectively 'reasonable good-faith belief' that their conduct is lawful,"[275] or when their unconstitutional behavior "involves only simple, 'isolated' negligence,"[276] deterrence "'loses much of its force,'" and exclusion is not required.[277]

Significantly, as Breyer's dissent recognizes, *Davis* expands *Herring*.[278] Recall that *Herring*'s "holding" suggested that exclusion is not required in circumstances where the constitutional offense "was the result of isolated negligence *attenuated* from the arrest."[279] Commentators and lower courts who read *Herring* narrowly believed that the attenuation element would contain *Herring*'s impact and prevent its logic from applying to garden-variety Fourth Amendment violations.[280] Interestingly, Tom Goldstein, a Supreme Court litigator who represented Herring, discounted this view of *Herring*'s

---

272 *Davis*, 131 S. Ct. at 2423.

273 *Id.* at 2423–24.

274 *Id.* at 2427 (emphasis added). Notice that *Davis* is unwilling to categorically state that when police are culpable, exclusion *is* required. Alito will only say that such conduct provides a "strong" reason to exclude and that exclusion "tends" to outweigh the costs to society.

275 *Id.* (quoting United States v. Leon, 468 U.S. 897, 909 (1984)).

276 *Id.* at 2427–28 (quoting Herring v. United States, 555 U.S. 135, 137 (2009)).

277 *Id.* at 2428 (quoting *Leon*, 468 U.S. at 919); *cf.* Moran, *supra* note 267, at 365 (stating that "Justice Alito tried his best to elevate the *Herring* dicta to established precedent even though that dicta has no arguable application at all to the facts in *Davis*").

278 *Davis*, 131 S. Ct. at 2439–40 (Breyer, J., dissenting).

279 *Herring*, 555 U.S. at 137 (emphasis added).

280 *See, e.g.*, Bradley, *Red* Herring, *supra* note 257, at 53 ("[*Herring*'s holding] won't apply to most cases, despite the majority's apparent attempt to establish a new approach to the exclusionary rule that would apply to *all* cases. In most cases, the police error will not be 'attenuated' from the search, but will be committed by the same officers who did the searching."); United States v. Green, No. 1:08–CR–0041, 2009 WL 230890, at *10 (M.D. Pa. Jan. 30, 2009) (granting a suppression motion following an officer's illegal search and explaining that "the Supreme Court clearly restricted the reach of *Herring's* limitation on the exclusion rule to police misconduct that is 'attenuated' from the arrest" and that "[u]nlike the case at bar, *Herring* involved a computer error by police that was remote in both time and location from the unlawful arrest"); State v. Handy, 18 A.3d 179 (N.J. 2011) (affirming the suppression motion and concluding that although the police officer reasonably relied on a mistake by a dispatcher, the conduct of the dispatcher was not sufficiently attenuated from the arrest to trigger the good-faith exception in *Herring*); State v. Hess, 785 N.W.2d 568, 579 (Wis. 2010) (explaining that the Supreme Court "held that the police conduct in *Herring* did not warrant exclusion because it 'was the result of isolated negligence attenuated from the arrest'" and holding that the good-faith exception to the exclusionary rule did not apply to a civil bench warrant that was invalid when issued (quoting *Herring*, 555 U.S. at 137)).

scope. Goldstein conceded that the attenuation element temporarily contained the reach of *Herring*'s holding, but he observed that "the logic of [*Herring*] spans far more broadly, and the next logical step—which I predict is 2 years away—is abandoning the 'attenuation' reference altogether."[281] Goldstein's prediction was dead on. When describing the type of police conduct that justifies suppression, *Davis*, decided two years after *Herring*, never mentions "attenuation."[282]

Will the Roberts Court abolish the exclusionary rule? Roberts, Scalia, Thomas, and Alito are ready to do so. Determining where Kennedy stands on this issue "turns out to be a challenge."[283] But even if that prediction is wrong, the logic and results in *Herring* and *Davis* move the Court nine-tenths of the way toward repealing the exclusionary rule. Even before the recent holding in *Davis*, *Herring*'s "big blast" statements significantly undermined and confined application of the exclusionary rule to a small number of cases. Put succinctly, Roberts's opinion in *Herring* laid the foundation for a general good-faith exception for routine search-and-seizure cases.

After *Herring*, will the Court countenance the suppression of evidence obtained after an officer negligently, but in good faith, decides he has probable cause to search a car or make an arrest, or sufficient suspicion to conduct a *Terry* frisk? If the officer's judgment is wrong, but not culpable, and there is no proof that he has engaged in recurring violations of this kind, the logic of *Herring* dictates that exclusion is not justified. Why *would* the exclusionary rule apply in such circumstances? An "officer who conducts a search that he believes complies with the Constitution but which, it ultimately turns out, falls just outside the Fourth Amendment's bounds is no more culpable than an officer who follows erroneous 'binding precedent,'"[284] or one who relies upon an arrest warrant that had been recalled five months earlier or a statute that is later declared unconstitutional.

Professor Richard McAdams has grasped the Roberts Court's thinking about the good-faith exception. Consider what McAdams had to say about the logic of *Herring* even when viewed as a case that merely decides the issue left open in *Arizona v. Evans*. Shortly after the oral argument in *Herring*, McAdams noted that if the Court was unwilling to distinguish between the errors of judicial employees and police employees who operate databases, it was unlikely to "draw a line between a sworn field officer and a police clerk."[285] As McAdams saw it, if an officer can act in good faith on the error of a police clerk, as *Herring* now permits, she can likely act in good faith on the error of a fellow

---

[281] Tom Goldstein, *The Surpassing Significance of* Herring, SCOTUSBLOG (Jan. 14, 2009, 11:32 AM), http://www.scotusblog.com/2009/01/the-surpassing-significance-of-herring/.

[282] *See* 1 LAFAVE, *supra* note 199, § 1.3, at 28 n.181.30 (Supp. 2011–2012) ("The *Davis* majority's 'restatement' of the *Herring* rule omits its most significant limitation, namely, that 'negligent' conduct by police supports a good-faith claim only if the negligence was 'attenuated.'").

[283] Davies & Scanlon, *supra* note 202, at 1066.

[284] Davis v. United States, 131 S. Ct. 2419, 2439 (2011) (Breyer, J., dissenting).

[285] Richard McAdams, *Wither the Exclusionary Rule?*, U. CHI. L. SCH. FAC. BLOG, (Oct. 29, 2008, 5:23 PM), http://uchicagolaw.typepad.com/faculty/2008/10/wither-the-excl.html.

detective. Furthermore, if a court will not exclude when detective *A* relies on a negligent error by detective *B*, then why would it exclude when detective *A* relies on *her own* negligent, but isolated error?[286]

If under *Herring*, only culpable or deliberate violations of the Fourth Amendment merit suppression, then a great number, perhaps the overwhelming majority, of unconstitutional searches and seizures will be immunized from the exclusionary rule. After all, most search and seizure violations that are the subject of suppression hearings across the nation involve good-faith or negligent, *not* deliberately culpable, mistakes by police officers. Before and after *Herring*, Fourth Amendment scholars have made this point, and the justices know this as well.[287] Justice Breyer's dissent in *Davis*, however, seemed surprised, if not alarmed, by the prospect of the *Herring-Davis* logic applying to routine violations of the Fourth Amendment. He noted:

> [*I*]*f* the Court means what it now says, *if* it would place determinative weight upon the culpability of an individual officer's conduct, and *if* it would apply the exclusionary rule only where a Fourth Amendment violation was "deliberate, reckless, or grossly negligent," then the "good faith" exception *will* swallow the exclusionary rule.[288]

Surely Breyer knows his colleagues better than that. Of course, the Court meant what it said in *Herring* and *Davis*. That was the point of *Herring*: to confine application of the exclusionary rule to the type of purposeful, bad-faith police misconduct seen in *Mapp v. Ohio*.[289] The *Herring* majority knows that egregious Fourth Amendment violations are rarely seen in suppression hearings. Breyer could not seriously believe that his colleagues have not made up their minds to extend the *Herring-Davis* logic to routine violations of the Fourth Amendment. Yet he insists on repeatedly beginning the assertions in his dissent with "if." The more accurate question is *when*, not *if*, as the Court has already resolved to do precisely what the language and logic of *Herring* and *Davis* suggest. And as

---

[286] *Id.*

[287] *See, e.g.*, *Davis*, 131 S. Ct. at 2439 (Breyer, J., dissenting) (explaining that most suppression motions challenge conduct where, "police, uncertain of how the Fourth Amendment applied to the particular factual circumstances they faced, will have acted in objective good faith" and "[y]et, in a significant percentage of these instances, courts will find that the police are wrong"); Potter Stewart, *The Road to* Mapp v. Ohio *and Beyond: The Origins, Development and Future of the Exclusionary Rule in Search-and-Seizure Cases*, 83 COLUM. L. REV. 1365, 1388–89 (1983) ("[Civil damages lawsuits and criminal prosecutions] punish and perhaps deter the grossest of violations, as well as governmental policies that legitimate these violations. They compensate some of the victims of the most egregious violations. But they do little, if anything, to reduce the likelihood of the vast majority of fourth amendment violations—the frequent infringements motivated by commendable zeal, not condemnable malice.").

[288] *Davis*, 131 S. Ct. at 2439 (Breyer, J., dissenting) (emphasis added).

[289] 367 U.S. 643 (1961).

Breyer recognized, some lower courts are already heading in that direction after reading *Herring*.[290]

* * *

After John Roberts finished his clerkship with then-Justice Rehnquist in the early 1980s, he began a four-year stretch in the office of President Ronald Reagan's White House counsel. This was a significant time in the evolution of the exclusionary rule. White was pressing his colleagues to adopt a broad good-faith or "reasonable mistake" exception to the rule. The Reagan Justice Department filed briefs in *Leon*, *Sheppard*, and *Quintero* urging the Court to follow White's proposal. In fact, while employed in the White House counsel office in 1983, Roberts "was hard at work on what he called in a memorandum 'the campaign to amend or abolish the exclusionary rule.'"[291] Roberts, of course, would later become Chief Justice of the United States and the author of *Herring*.

The reasoning of *Herring* suggests that, as Chief Justice, Roberts is following White's roadmap for limiting the exclusionary rule to bad-faith or egregious Fourth Amendment violations. *Davis* effectively eliminates the possibility of a narrow reading of *Herring*. Moreover, as the expansive reasoning and result in *Hudson* show, when it comes to the exclusionary rule, the Roberts Court does not have a narrow agenda. Certain members of the Burger and Rehnquist Courts once considered *Leon*'s good-faith exception to be confined to defective warrants. The results in *Krull* and *Evans* proved that interpretation

---

290 *See, e.g.*, United States v. Master, 614 F.3d 236, 243 (6th Cir. 2010) (finding that the "*Herring* Court's emphasis" weighed in favor of not suppressing illegally seized evidence unless the officers engage in "'deliberate, reckless, or grossly negligent conduct'" (quoting Herring v. United States, 555 U.S. 135, 144 (2009))). United States v. Julius, 610 F.3d 60, 66–67 (2d Cir. 2010) (remanding to the district court for a determination of "whether the degree of police culpability in this case rose beyond mere administrative negligence such that application of the rule is necessary" to deter Fourth Amendment violations under the "cost/benefit analysis required by *Herring*"); United States v. Tracey, 597 F.3d 140, 151 (3d Cir. 2010) (stating that "the Supreme Court has instructed that the exclusionary rule should only be applied when 'police conduct [is] . . . sufficiently deliberate that exclusion can meaningfully deter it, and sufficiently culpable that such deterrence is worth the price paid'" and holding that the exclusionary rule does not apply because the officer's actions did "not amount to 'deliberate, reckless, or grossly negligent conduct'" or indicate "'recurring or systemic negligence'" (quoting *Herring*, 555 U.S. at 144)); People v. McDonough, 917 N.E.2d 590, 594 (Ill. App. Ct. 2009) (claiming that "absent police misconduct, the exclusionary rule does not apply . . . if the justification for the exclusionary rule is solely to deter police misconduct (as the Supreme Court reaffirmed in *Herring*), then the necessary condition precedent for the exclusionary rule's application is police misconduct").

291 Adam Liptak, *Justices Step Closer to Repeal of Evidence Ruling*, N.Y. TIMES, Jan. 30, 2009, at A1. According to one close observer of the Court, John Roberts was a strong believer in President Ronald Reagan's legal agenda. *See* JOAN BISKUPIC, AMERICAN ORIGINAL: THE LIFE AND CONSTITUTION OF SUPREME COURT JUSTICE ANTONIN SCALIA 295 (2009) (describing how, as a young lawyer in the Reagan Administration, Roberts had "hitched [his] hopes to Reagan's promise of a different legal world," and how Roberts "considered [Reagan] an inspiration in the 1980s"). During the second term of the Reagan Administration, the Department of Justice recommended "complete abolition" of the exclusionary rule. *See* OFFICE OF LEGAL POLICY, U.S. DEP'T OF JUSTICE, 'TRUTH IN CRIMINAL JUSTICE' SERIES, REPORT NO. 2: THE SEARCH AND SEIZURE EXCLUSIONARY RULE 66 (1986), *reprinted in* 22 U. MICH. J.L. REF. 573 (1989).

wrong. *Davis* demonstrates that interpreting *Herring* as a ruling confined to negligent police recordkeeping is merely wishful thinking.

To ensure that the rest of the lower courts receive the message that suppression is justified only upon a showing of culpable police conduct, the Court will probably have to take a case involving a routine search and seizure violation: for example, a car search or *Terry* frisk case. If the Court decides to hear such a case, the intentions of the Roberts Court that have underlain their recent exclusionary rule decisions will fully surface. The Court will rule that the exclusionary rule does not apply unless there is proof of culpable police conduct. If this occurs, the exclusionary rule will no longer matter. As Breyer put it in *Davis*, if exclusion is warranted only when the police deliberately or recklessly violate the Fourth Amendment, "then the 'good faith' exception will swallow the exclusionary rule."[292]

Despite the rulings in *Hudson*, *Herring*, and *Davis*, some judges and legal commentators insist that the exclusionary rule is alive and well, although somewhat staggered. This view is fueled by Justice Kennedy's statement in *Hudson* that "the continued operation of the exclusionary rule, as settled and defined by our precedents, is not in doubt."[293] Kennedy's vote obviously matters in suppression cases, as it does in most cases decided by the Court.[294] In *Hudson*, Kennedy provided the crucial fifth vote for the result, joining Scalia's "but-for" causation, attenuation, and balancing analysis, but refusing to join another part of Scalia's opinion. In *Herring*, Kennedy joined the majority, probably again providing the crucial fifth vote. More important, Kennedy joined Roberts's entire opinion in *Herring* without qualification, joining Roberts even in his crucial declarations limiting the applicability of the exclusionary rule to deliberate, reckless, or grossly negligent police violations. One might have thought in light of his comment in *Hudson* about preserving the exclusionary rule, that Kennedy would have distanced himself from this reasoning.[295]

---

292 Davis v. United States, 131 S. Ct. 2419, 2439 (2011) (Breyer, J., dissenting).

293 Hudson v. Michigan, 547 U.S. 586, 603 (2006) (Kennedy, J., concurring in part and concurring in the judgment).

294 *See* Adam Liptak, *A Significant Term, With Bigger Cases Ahead*, N.Y. Times, June 29, 2011, at A12 (reporting that during the 2011 Supreme Court Term, 12 of the 14 closely divided 5–4 cases were split between the four liberal justices and four conservative justices, with "[Justice Kennedy] casting the decisive vote"); Adam Liptak, *Roberts Court Shifts Right, Tipped by Kennedy*, N.Y. Times, July 1, 2009, at A1 (observing that during the 2009 Term, Justice Kennedy was in the majority for 18 of the 23 cases where the justices split 5–4; "in 16 [of these decisions], all four members of the court's liberal wing were on one side and all four of its conservatives were on the other. And in between them was Justice Kennedy, the most powerful jurist in America").

295 Alschuler, *A Minnow or a Shark?*, *supra* note 256, at 476 ("As the indispensible [sic] fifth vote, Kennedy probably had the bargaining power to excise the 'big blast' statements from Chief Justice Roberts's opinion if he wished to do so. He certainly could have disassociated himself from these statements in a concurring opinion."); *see also* Bradley, *Red* Herring, *supra* note 257, at 53 (observing that it "was a mistake for Kennedy, if he wishes to preserve the exclusionary rule in its present form—as he declared in *Hudson*—to go along with the four conservatives in [*Herring*]").

Kennedy is often characterized as a "moderate" member of the Court's conservative majority.[296] His votes in a 1992 Pennsylvania abortion case[297] and a 2003 case invalidating Texas's criminal sodomy law[298] have promoted the public perception that Kennedy is a different type of conservative than, say, Scalia and Thomas, or Chief Justice Roberts. But his voting record as a justice (as opposed to his comment in *Hudson*) indisputably indicates that he is very much opposed to the exclusionary rule. In contrast to other so-called "moderate" justices who have sat on the Court in recent years, Kennedy has *never* voted to impose the Fourth Amendment exclusionary rule. By comparison, O'Connor and Souter, neither of whom championed the exclusionary rule, voted to impose the rule at least once during their tenure. O'Connor voted for the defendant in *Illinois v. Krull*[299] and in *Murray v. United States*,[300] while Souter voted for the defendant in *Pennsylvania Board of Probation & Parole v. Scott*.[301] According to the *New York Times*, O'Connor was also prepared to vote for the defendant in *Hudson*, but she resigned before the Court decided the case.[302] And as chapter 6 revealed, in the 1983 Term, O'Connor voted to apply the exclusionary rule in juvenile delinquency proceedings to bar the admission of evidence obtained from an illegal search by a school official.[303]

While Kennedy's influence and votes have been crucial, it would be folly to believe his moderate views in other areas of constitutional law indicate uncertainty surrounding the future of the exclusionary rule. Five justices have already made their move, although they are not yet marching in lockstep together. Kennedy's statement in *Hudson* on the continued viability of the rule tends to mislead rather than inform the public about the Roberts Court's objectives for the rule. Professor Craig Bradley takes the view that a majority of the Court has decided "that the exclusionary rule must be reconsidered."[304]

One could go further and say that the Roberts Court has already made its intentions known. Abrogation of the exclusionary rule appears to be the ultimate goal of the Court. Even if outright repeal of suppression is unattainable, however, then the other objectives

---

296 *See* Bradley, *Red* Herring, *supra* note 257, at 53 (describing Kennedy as a "judicial moderate").

297 Planned Parenthood of Se. Pa. v. Casey, 505 U.S. 833 (1992).

298 Lawrence v. Texas, 539 U.S. 558 (2003).

299 480 U.S. 340 (1987).

300 487 U.S. 533 (1988) (O'Connor joined Marshall's dissent).

301 524 U.S. 357 (1998).

302 *See* David A. Moran, *Waiting for the Other Shoe:* Hudson *and the Precarious State of* Mapp, 93 IOWA L. REV. 1725, 1731 (2008); Linda Greenhouse, *Court Limits Protection Against Improper Entry*, N.Y. TIMES, June 16, 2006, at A28; Charles Lane, *Court Eases "No Knock" Search Ban Illegally Collected Evidence Allowed*, WASH. POST, June 16, 2006, at A1.

303 Sandra Day O'Connor, First Draft of Dissenting opinion in *New Jersey v. T.L.O.* (June 12, 1984), Blackmun Papers, Box 414.

304 Craig M. Bradley, *Reconceiving the Fourth Amendment and the Exclusionary Rule*, LAW & CONTEMP. PROBS., Winter 2010, at 211, 217; *see id.* at 212 (noting that the Court is "dissatisfied with the mandatory aspect of the *Mapp* rule," and that in *Hudson* and *Herring*, the "Court has indicated that the rule should be changed but has stopped short of mandating a broad alteration").

of the Court are within reach. The Court will continue to eliminate the exclusionary remedy from entire categories of violations, as was done for knock-and-announce violations in *Hudson*. An additional objective of the Roberts Court is to confine invocation of the exclusionary rule to cases of culpable police misconduct, as the language and logic of *Herring* and *Davis* require, until the rule is, in effect, of little consequence to Fourth Amendment jurisprudence. Achieving this goal will not require explicitly overruling *Weeks* or *Mapp*. It merely requires the Court to apply the language and logic of *Herring* to run-of-the-mine Fourth Amendment violations.

Conclusion

JUSTICE HOLMES IS often viewed as a paragon of American jurists. According to one study, Holmes is one of the three most cited American legal scholars of the twentieth century.[1] Justice Scalia has described Holmes as of one of the nation's "greatest Justices."[2] Among other things, Holmes has been lauded for his philosophy of judicial restraint and praised for his credo: "The life of the law has not been logic: it has been experience."[3] Despite this widespread admiration of Holmes's judicial and legal contributions, opponents of the exclusionary rule rarely acknowledge, and never praise, Holmes's view of the Fourth Amendment and exclusion. Indeed, the current Court has altogether abandoned it. According to Holmes, "[t]he essence of a provision forbidding the acquisition of evidence in a certain way is that not merely evidence so acquired shall not be used before the Court but that it shall not be used at all."[4] Holmes's view of exclusion did not rest on a deterrence theory, or upon merger of the Fourth and Fifth Amendments. Rather, the constitutional bar on the use of illegally acquired evidence, in Holmes's interpretation, derives from the Fourth Amendment itself.[5]

---

[1] Fred R. Shapiro, *The Most-Cited Legal Scholars*, 29 J. LEGAL STUD. 409, 424, 426 (2000).

[2] Antonin Scalia, *The Rule of Law as a Law of Rules*, 56 U. CHI. L. REV. 1175, 1187 (1989).

[3] OLIVER WENDELL HOLMES, JR., THE COMMON LAW 1 (Boston, Little, Brown and Co. 1881).

[4] Silverthorne Lumber Co. v. United States, 251 U.S. 385, 392 (1920).

[5] Silas Wasserstrom & William J. Mertens, *The Exclusionary Rule on the Scaffold: But Was It a Fair Trial?*, 22 AM. CRIM. L. REV. 85, 138 (1984) (explaining that "[t]he 'no use' requirement was not, to Justice Holmes, a mere remedial protection applied in service of the substantive protection. Rather, it was the essence of the protection itself." (footnote omitted)).

Since the midpoint of the twentieth century when the Court, under the influence of Justice Frankfurter, abandoned Holmes's understanding of exclusion, the Court's treatment of the exclusionary rule has been driven by political motives and preferences of the justices rather than neutral legal principle. Consequently, the role of the exclusionary rule in Fourth Amendment jurisprudence and its impact has evolved over the years to reflect the motives of the most influential justices on the Court at the time. The function of the rule has evolved into a strictly instrumental device diametrically opposed to Holmes's view. The conflict between the current Court's treatment of the exclusionary rule and that of Holmes is not a result of the text or history of the Fourth Amendment; but rather, the politics of crucial justices reflected in their hostility to suppression. Not only has Holmes's view of the Fourth Amendment and exclusion entirely disappeared from Fourth Amendment jurisprudence, the current Court appears positioned to repeal the exclusionary rule altogether, or, at the very least, limit its application to flagrant or egregious Fourth Amendment violations, which will strip the rule of its ability to protect the Fourth Amendment rights of everyone.

Table of Authorities

Amar, Akhil Reed, The Constitution and Criminal Procedure: First Principles (1997) ... 329*n*206

Amar, Akhil Reed, Fourth Amendment First Principles, 107 Harv. L. Rev. 757 (1994) ... 2*n*6, 2*n*9, 18*n*102, 96*n*74

Amsterdam, Anthony G., Perspectives on the Fourth Amendment, 58 Minn. L. Rev. 349 (1974) ... 98*n*88, 225*n*425

Amsterdam, Anthony G., Search, Seizure, and Section 2255: A Comment, 112 U. Pa. L. Rev. 378 (1964) ... 185*n*102, 186*n*103, 216*n*347

Atkinson, Thomas E., Prohibition and the Doctrine of the *Weeks* Case, 23 Mich. L. Rev. 748 (1925) ... 3*n*10

Beale, Sara Sun, Reconsidering Supervisory Power in Criminal Cases: Constitutional and Statutory Limits on the Authority of the Federal Courts, 84 Colum. L. Rev. 1433 (1984) ... 35*n*31

Beisel, Albert R., Jr., Control Over Illegal Enforcement of the Criminal Law: Role of the Supreme Court (1955) ... 66*n*268

Belknap, Michal R., The Supreme Court under Earl Warren 1953–1969 (2005) ... 122*n*263

Biskupic, Joan, American Original: The Life and Constitution of Supreme Court Justice Antonin Scalia (2009) ... 344*n*291

Biskupic, Joan, Sandra Day O'Connor: How the First Woman on the Supreme Court Became Its Most Influential Justice (2005) ... 270*n*300

Black, Hugo, Draft of Concurring Opinion in *Mapp v. Ohio* (June 8, 1961), Clark Papers, Box A115 ... 90*n*40

Black, Hugo, Draft of Concurring Opinion in *Mapp v. Ohio* (June 12, 1961), Clark Papers, Box A115 ... 90*nn*40–42

Black, Hugo, Draft Opinion of *Mapp v. Ohio* (June 6, 1961), Black Papers, Box 349 ... 90*n*37

Black, Hugo, Letter to Warren Burger on *Harris v. New York* (Jan. 5, 1971), Harlan Papers, Box 432 ... 129*n*22

Blackmun, Harry, Conference Notes on *Illinois v. Krull* (Nov. 7, 1986), Blackmun Papers, Box 464 ... 320*n*141

Blackmun, Harry, Conference Notes on *INS v. Lopez-Mendoza* (Apr. 20, 1984), Blackmun Papers, Box 407 ... 256*n*194, 257*n*196, 258*n*211

Blackmun, Harry, Conference Notes on *James v. Illinois* (Oct. 6, 1989), Blackmun Papers, Box 553 ... 306*n*28

Blackmun, Harry, Conference Notes on *Murray v. United States* (undated), Blackmun Papers, Box 496 ... 299*n*186

Blackmun, Harry, Conference Notes on *New York v. Harris* (Jan. 12, 1990), Blackmun Papers, Box 545 ... 310*nn*62–68, 311*nn*73–75

Blackmun, Harry, Handwritten Notes on *James v. Illinois* (Sept. 23, 1989), Blackmun Papers, Box 553 ... 304*n*18

Blackmun, Harry, Handwritten Notes on *New York v. Harris* (Jan. 9, 1990), Blackmun Papers, Box 545 ... 310*nn*69–72

Blackmun, Harry, Internal Memorandum 71-732 on *Schneckloth v. Bustamonte* (Sept. 29, 1972), Blackmun Papers, Box 156 ... 143*n*138, 143*n*140, 144*nn*141–43

Blackmun, Harry, Letter to Hugo Black (June 16, 1971), Black Papers, Box 403 ... 137*nn*98–99

Blackmun, Harry, Letter to Hugo Black (May 4, 1971) Blackmun Papers, Box 128 . . . 137*n*96

Blackmun, Harry, Letter to Sandra Day O'Connor on *INS v. Lopez-Mendoza* (May 29, 1984), Blackmun Papers, Box 407 . . . 259*n*222

Blackmun, Harry, Letter to Warren Burger on *Killough v. United States* (Jan. 24, 1962), Blackmun Papers, Box 50 . . . 275*nn*7–11, 287*n*89

Blackmun, Harry, Letter to Warren Burger on *Killough v. United States* (Jan. 30, 1962), Blackmun Papers, Box 50 . . . 276*nn*16–17

Blackmun, Harry, Letter to William J. Brennan, Jr. on *United States v. Crews* (Feb. 19, 1980), Brennan Papers, Box I: 504 . . . 203*nn*248–49

Blackmun, Harry, Memorandum on *Brown v. Illinois* (Mar. 10, 1975), Blackmun Papers, Box 206 . . . 181*nn*54–55, 182*nn*56–63

Blackmun, Harry, Memorandum on *Rakas v. Illinois* (July 3, 1978), Blackmun Papers, Box 290 . . . 217*nn*357–60, 218*nn*362–64

Blackmun, Harry, Memorandum on *United States v. Janis* (Dec. 5, 1975), Blackmun Papers, Box 219 . . . 160*n*271, 160*nn*273–78, 259*n*219

Blackmun, Harry, Memorandum on *Wolff v. Rice* and *Stone v. Powell* (Feb. 23, 1976), Blackmun Papers, Box 220 . . . 165*nn*317–20, 166*n*321

Blackmun, Harry, Memorandum to the Conference on *New Jersey v. T.L.O.* (June 13, 1984), Blackmun Papers, Box 414 . . . 272*nn*316–18

Black's Law Dictionary 250 (9th ed. 2009) . . . 180*n*50

Bloom, Robert M., Inevitable Discovery: An Exception Beyond the Fruits, 20 Am. J. Crim. L. 79 (1992) . . . 283*n*68, 300*n*194, 330*n*210

Bradley, Craig M., The "Good Faith Exception" Cases: Reasonable Exercises in Futility, 60 Ind. L.J. 287 (1985) . . . 252*n*166

Bradley, Craig M., Mixed Messages on the Exclusionary Rule, Trial, Dec. 2006 . . . 336*n*251

Bradley, Craig M., Reconceiving the Fourth Amendment and the Exclusionary Rule, Law & Contemp. Probs., Winter 2010 . . . 346*n*304

Bradley, Craig M., Red *Herring* or the Death of the Exclusionary Rule?, Trial, Apr. 2009 . . . 337*n*257, 341*n*280, 345*n*295, 346*n*296

Bradley, Gerard V., Present at the Creation? A Critical Guide to *Weeks v. United States* and its Progeny, 30 St. Louis U. L.J. 1031 (1986) . . . 17*n*96, 26*n*144

Brennan, William J., Jr., Case Histories, October Term, 1968 (undated), Brennan Papers, Box II: 6 . . . 118*n*228, 118*n*231

Brennan, William J., Jr., Case Histories, October Term, 1970 (undated), Brennan Papers, Box II: 6 . . . 129*n*20, 132*n*51, 133*nn*58–59, 133*nn*61–62, 134*nn*63–64

Brennan, William J., Jr., Case Histories, October Term, 1973 (undated), Brennan Papers, Box II: 6 . . . 155*n*235, 155*nn*240–43

Brennan, William J., Jr., Case Histories, October Term, 1982 (undated), Brennan Papers, Box II: 7 . . . 235*nn*20–26

Brennan, William J., Jr., Case Histories, October Term, 1983 (undated), Brennan Papers, Box II: 7 . . . 265*n*252, 267*n*276, 270*n*302

Brennan, William J., Jr., Case Histories, October Term, 1989 (undated), Brennan Papers, Box II: 8 . . . 305*n*24, 306*n*34, 307*nn*39–40, 307*n*44, 307*n*47, 308*n*49, 308*nn*52–53, 311*n*76

Brennan, William J., Jr., Conference Notes on *Bivens v. Six Unknown Named Agents of Federal Bureau of Narcotics* (undated), Brennan Papers, Box I: 228 . . . 135*n*78

Douglas, William, Docket Sheet on *Rochin v. California* (assigned on Oct. 23, 1951), Douglas Papers, Box 1121 . . . 50*nn*122–23

Douglas, William, Docket Sheet on *Stefanelli v. Minard* (assigned on Oct. 23, 1951), Douglas Papers, Box 1121 . . . 48*n*105

Douglas, William, Docket Sheet on *Wolf v. Colorado* (voted on Oct. 23, 1948), Douglas Papers, Box 1121 . . . 38*n*53

Douglas, William, Letter to Potter Stewart on *Elkins v. United States* (May 20, 1960), Stewart Papers, Box 5 . . . 74*n*329

Douglas, William, Letter to Warren Burger on *Harris v. New York* (Jan. 5, 1971), Harlan Papers, Box 432 . . . 129*n*22

Dressler, Joshua, A Lesson in Incaution, Overwork, and Fatigue: The Judicial Miscraftsmanship of *Segura v. United States*, 26 Wm. & Mary L. Rev. 375 (1985) . . . 288*n*94, 296*n*166

Dressler, Joshua & Alan C. Michaels, Understanding Criminal Procedure (4th ed. 2006) . . . 124*n*276

Dripps, Donald, The Fourth Amendment, the Exclusionary Rule, and the Roberts Court: Normative and Empirical Dimensions of the Over-Deterrence Hypothesis, 85 Chi.-Kent L. Rev. 209 (2010) . . . 327*n*201, 336*n*250

Dripps, Donald, Living With *Leon*, 95 Yale L.J. 906 (1986) . . . 17*n*96, 98*n*90, 255*n*181

Dripps, Donald A., About Guilt and Innocence: The Origins, Development, and Future of Constitutional Criminal Procedure (2003) . . . 16*n*94

Duke, Steven, Making *Leon* Worse, 95 Yale L.J. 1405 (1986) . . . xiii*n*8, 301*n*201

Edwards, Richard A., Standing to Suppress Unreasonably Seized Evidence, 47 Nw. U. L. Rev. 471 (1952) . . . 216*n*346

Estreicher, Sam, Bench Memorandum to Lewis Powell on *United States v. Ceccolini* (Dec. 2, 1977), Powell Papers, Box 48 . . . 190*n*146, 191*nn*147–49

Estreicher, Sam, Memorandum to Lewis Powell on *United States v. Ceccolini* (Jan. 20, 1978), Powell Papers, Box 48 . . . 190*n*145, 191*nn*150–54

Feldblum, Chai, Memorandum to Harry Blackmun on *Illinois v. Krull* (Oct. 19, 1986), Blackmun Papers, Box 464 . . . 318*nn*114–15, 319*nn*126–27, 320*n*128

Flynn, Martin J., Bench Memorandum on *Bawden v. California* (Mar. 27, 1963), Clark Papers, Box B190 . . . 109*n*150

Fortas, Abe, Draft of Concurring Opinion in *Kaufman v. United States* (undated), Brennan Papers, Box I: 187 . . . 120*nn*243–46

Fortas, Abe, Handwritten Letter to Earl Warren (undated), Warren Papers, Box 624 . . . 116*n*215

Fraenkel, Osmond K., Concerning Searches and Seizures, 34 Harv. L. Rev. 361 (1921) . . . 216*n*345

Franck, Matthew J., Hyperventilating About the Exclusionary Rule, Nat'l Rev. Online (Feb. 16, 2009, 11:21 AM), http://www.nationalreview.com/bench-memos/50452/hyperventilating-aboutexclusionary- rule/matthew-j-franck# . . . 338*n*257

Frankfurter, Felix, A Dialogue, (undated) (unpublished essay), Frankfurter Papers, Box 152 . . . 13*n*71, 76*nn*345–46, 77*nn*347–49, 77*n*352, 81*n*374

Frankfurter, Felix, Docket Sheet on *Wolf v. Colorado* (undated), Frankfurter Papers, Box 31 . . . 37*nn*45–46, 38*nn*50–51

Frankfurter, Felix, "Incorporation" of the Fourth into the Fourteenth Amendment?, (unpublished essay), Frankfurter Papers, Box 168 . . . 78*n*353, 81*nn*372–73

Frankfurter, Felix, Letter to Anthony Amsterdam (undated), Frankfurter Papers, Box 152, Reel 77, Frames 585-86 . . . 76*n*345

Frankfurter, Felix, Letter to Earl Warren (Apr. 19, 1957), Frankfurter Papers, Box 92 . . . 32*n*13, 78*n*353, 102*n*107

Frankfurter, Felix, Letter to Earl Warren (May 27, 1957), Harlan Papers . . . 94*n*66

Frankfurter, Felix, Letter to Frank Murphy (Feb. 15, 1947), Murphy Papers, Reel 135 . . . 32*n*12

Frankfurter, Felix, Letter to Fred Vinson (Nov. 29, 1951), Frankfurter Papers, Reel 4, Frame 675 . . . 50*n*133

Frankfurter, Felix, Letter to Stanley Reed (Apr. 13, 1939), Frankfurter Papers, Library of Congress . . . xiv*n*10

Frankfurter, Felix, Letter to Tom Clark on *Irvine v. California* (Dec. 29, 1953), Clark Papers, Box A28 . . . 58*nn*207–11

Frankfurter, Felix, Letter to William J. Brennan, Jr., on *Frank v. Maryland* (Apr. 16, 1959), Stewart Papers, Box 163; Frankfurter Papers, Box 109 . . . 80*n*370, 81*n*371

Frankfurter, Felix, Memorandum on *Irvine v. California* (circulated Dec. 17, 1953), Clark Papers, Box A28 . . . 57*nn*200–206

Friendly, Henry J., The Bill of Rights as a Code of Criminal Procedure, 53 Calif. L. Rev. 929 (1965) . . . 231*n*1

Garcia, Charles Patrick, Note, The Knock and Announce Rule: A New Approach to the Destruction-of-Evidence Exception, 93 Colum. L. Rev. 685 (1993) . . . 332*n*221

Goldberg, Arthur, Second Draft Opinion of *One 1958 Plymouth Sedan v. Pennsylvania* (Apr. 10, 1965), Clark Papers, Box A177 . . . 108*n*142

Goldstein, Tom, The Surpassing Significance of *Herring*, SCOTUSblog (Jan. 14, 2009, 11:32 AM), http://www.scotusblog.com/2009/01/the-surpassing-significance-of-herring/ . . . 342*n*281

Gosnell, Harold F., Truman's Crises: A Political Biography of Harry S. Truman (1980) . . . 52*n*141

Graham, Fred P., The Self-Inflicted Wound (1970) . . . 30*n*4, 85*nn*11–12

Grant, J.A.C., Circumventing the Fourth Amendment, 14 S. Cal. L. Rev. 359 (1941) . . . 216*n*346

Green, J. Patrick, *Stone v. Powell*: The Hermeneutics of the Burger Court, 10 Creighton L. Rev. 655 (1977) . . . 100*n*97

Greenhouse, Linda, Becoming Justice Blackmun: Harry Blackmun's Supreme Court Journey (2005) . . . 143*n*137

Greenhouse, Linda, Court Limits Protection Against Improper Entry, N.Y. Times, June 16, 2006 . . . 346*n*302

Greenhouse, Linda, Lewis Powell, Crucial Centrist Justice, Dies at 90, N.Y. Times, Aug. 26, 1998 . . . 316*n*107

Greenleaf, Simon, A Treatise on the Law of Evidence (Boston, Charles C. Little & James Brown, 2d ed. 1844) . . . 14*n*79

Haddad, James B., "Retroactivity Should Be Rethought": A Call for the End of the *Linkletter* Doctrine, 60 J. Crim. L. Criminology & Police Sci. 417 (1969) . . . 112*n*183, 113*n*188, 125*n*280

Handler, Emmerich, The Fourth Amendment, Federalism, and Mr. Justice Frankfurter, 8 Syracuse L. Rev. 166 (1957) . . . 16*n*94

Harlan, John, Letter to Tom Clark on *Mapp v. Ohio* (May 1, 1961), Clark Papers, Box A115 . . . 114*n*195, 125*n*281

Harlan, John, Memorandum to the Conference on *Whiteley v. Warden* (Apr. 21, 1970), Harlan Papers, Box 430 . . . 131*n*33

Hauptfuhrer, Cammie, Memorandum to Lewis Powell on *Nix v. Williams* (Mar. 18, 1984), Powell Papers, Box 109 . . . 283*n*67

Heffernan, William C., On Justifying Fourth Amendment Exclusion, 1989 Wis. L. Rev. 1193 . . . 252*n*166

Hessler, Stephen E., Establishing Inevitability Without Active Pursuit: Defining the Inevitable Discovery Exception to the Fourth Amendment Exclusionary Rule, 99 Mich. L. Rev. 238 (2000) . . . 297*n*174

Holmes, Oliver Wendell, Jr., The Common Law (Boston, Little, Brown and Co. 1881) . . . 348*n*3

Horowitz, Donald L., The Courts and Social Policy (1977) . . . 154*n*232

Hughes, Charles Evan, Speech before the Elmira Chamber of Commerce (May 3, 1907), *in* Addresses and Papers of Charles Evans Hughes: Governor of New York, 1906–1908 (1908) . . . xiii*n*9

Hutchinson, Dennis J., The Man Who Once Was Whizzer White: A Portrait of Justice Byron R. White (1998) . . . 132*n*53, 133*nn*54–56

Jackson, Robert, Docket Sheet on *Irvine v. California* (voted on Dec. 5, 1953), Jackson Papers, Box 185 . . . 56*n*192, 57*n*199

Jackson, Robert, Draft of *Irvine v. California* (Jan. 6, 1954), Clark Papers, Box A28 . . . 58*nn*212–15, 59*nn*216–17

Jackson, Robert, Draft Opinion of *Irvine v. California* (re-circulated Feb. 4, 1954), Clark Papers, Box A28 . . . 59*nn*219–21

Jeffries, John C., Jr., Email to author (Apr. 12, 2011) (on file with author) . . . 301*n*199

Jeffries, John C., Jr., Justice Lewis F. Powell, Jr. (1994) . . . 173*n*2, 230*n*472

Jeffries, John C., Jr., Memorandum to Lewis Powell on *United States v. Robinson* (Aug. 15, 1973), Powell Papers, Box 131 . . . 148*n*186, 149*nn*187–90

Jeffries, John C., Jr. & George A. Rutherglen, Structural Reform Revisited, 95 Calif. L. Rev. 1387 (2007) . . . 301*n*200

Jenkins, John A., The Partisan: A Talk With Justice Rehnquist, N.Y. Times Mag., Mar. 3, 1985 . . . 213*nn*326–28

Johnson, Eric A., Causal Relevance in the Law of Search and Seizure, 88 B.U. L. Rev. 113 (2008) . . . 314*n*94, 328*n*203, 329*n*208

Johnson, Phillip E., The Return of the "Christian Burial Speech" Case, 32 Emory L.J. 349 (1983) . . . 279*n*37

Kainen, James L., The Impeachment Exception to the Exclusionary Rules: Policies, Principles, and Politics, 44 Stan. L. Rev. 1301 (1992) . . . 52*n*146, 130*n*28, 212*n*319

Kamisar, Yale, Does (Did) (Should) the Exclusionary Rule Rest on a "Principled Basis" Rather Than an "Empirical Proposition"?, 16 Creighton L. Rev. 565 (1983) . . . 1*n*1, 3*n*11, 9*n*45, 13*n*73,

Lash, Joseph P., From the Diaries of Felix Frankfurter (1975) . . . 32*n*15

Laurin, Jennifer E., Trawling for *Herring*: Lessons in Doctrinal Borrowing and Convergence, 111 Colum. L. Rev. 670 (2011) . . . 337*n*256

Law Clerk, Letter to Harry Blackmun on *New York v. Harris* (Feb. 22, 1990), Blackmun Papers, Box 545 . . . 311*n*77

Law Clerk, Memorandum on *Walder v. United States* (undated), Clark Papers, Box B152 . . . 53*n*148

Law Clerk, Memorandum to Harry Blackmun on *INS v. Lopez-Mendoza* (Apr. 16, 1984), Blackmun Papers, Box 407 . . . 262*n*240

Law Clerk, Memorandum to Harry Blackmun on *INS v. Lopez-Mendoza* (May 23, 1984), Blackmun Papers, Box 407 . . . 259*n*221

Law Clerk, Memorandum to Harry Blackmun on *Murray v. United States* (Dec. 7, 1987), Blackmun Papers, Box 496 . . . 298*n*178

Law Clerk, Memorandum to Tom Clark on *Irvine v. California* (undated), Clark Papers, Box A28 . . . 59*n*218

Law Clerk, Memorandum to Tom Clark on *Walder v. United States* (undated), Clark Papers, Box A30 . . . 55*nn*173–75

Law Clerk, Preliminary Memorandum to Harry Blackmun on *Illinois v. Krull* (Nov. 20, 1985), Blackmun Papers, Box 464 . . . 318*nn*117–18

Law Clerk, Preliminary Memorandum to Harry Blackmun on *James v. Illinois* (Jan. 27, 1989), Blackmun Papers, Box 553 . . . 304*nn*11–12

Law Clerk, Preliminary Memorandum to Lewis Powell on *Dunaway v. New York* (Aug. 29, 1978), Powell Papers, Box 63 . . . 315*n*99

Law Clerk, Preliminary Memorandum to Lewis Powell on *United States v. Ceccolini* (Apr. 18, 1977), Powell Papers, Box 48 . . . 188*nn*115–17

Law Clerk, Preliminary Memorandum to Lewis Powell on *United States v. Havens* (Nov. 6, 1979), Powell Papers, Box 70 . . . 207*n*276

Law Clerk, Supplemental Preliminary Memorandum to Harry Blackmun on *Illinois v. Krull* (Jan. 6, 1986), Blackmun Papers, Box 464 . . . 318*n*119, 319*n*120

Law Clerk Memorandum to Felix Frankfurter on *Elkins v. United States* (undated), Frankfurter Papers, Box 116 . . . 71*n*304

Leibensperger, Edward P., Case Note, Impeachment by Unconstitutionally Obtained Evidence: The Erosion of the Exclusionary Rule, 34 Ohio St. L.J. 706 (1973) . . . 208*n*283

Leo, Richard A., Police Interrogation and American Justice (2008) . . . 308*n*54

Lewis, Anthony, Term of Supreme Court Marked By 2 Blows Dealt to U.S. Reds, N.Y. Times, June 25, 1961 . . . 83*n*2

Liptak, Adam, A Significant Term, With Bigger Cases Ahead, N.Y. Times, June 29, 2011 . . . 345*n*294

Liptak, Adam, Justices Step Closer to Repeal of Evidence Ruling, N.Y. Times, Jan. 30, 2009 . . . 344*n*291

Liptak, Adam, Roberts Court Shifts Right, Tipped by Kennedy, N.Y. Times, July 1, 2009 . . . 345*n*294

Long, Carolyn N., *Mapp v. Ohio*: Guarding Against Unreasonable Searches and Seizures (2006) . . . 30*n*4, 74*n*333, 86*n*14, 89*n*31

MacKenzie, John P., Critics Fight Rule on Illegal Evidence, Wash. Post, July 30, 1972 . . . 141*n*125, 141*n*127

Maguire, Robert F., How to Unpoison the Fruit, The Fourth Amendment and the Exclusionary Rule, 55 J. Crim. L. Criminology & Police Sci. 307 (1964) . . . 277*nn*26–27

Maltz, Earl M., The Chief Justiceship of Warren Burger 1969–1986 (2000) . . . 300*n*197

Mathias, Charles McC., Jr., The Exclusionary Rule Revisited, 28 Loy. L. Rev. 1 (1982) . . . 2*n*6

May, Gregory, Bench Memorandum to Lewis Powell on *United States v. Havens* (Mar. 13, 1980), Powell Papers, Box 70 . . . 208*nn*278–82

May, Gregory, Bench Memorandum to Lewis Powell on *United States v. Payner* (Feb. 12, 1980), Powell Papers, Box 62 . . . 226*nn*434–35, 227*nn*436–44

May, Gregory, Memorandum to Lewis Powell on *United States v. Crews* (Dec. 13, 1979), Powell Papers, Box 65 . . . 197*n*191, 197*n*195, 197*nn*198–99

May, Gregory, Memorandum to Lewis Powell on *United States v. Havens* (Apr. 30, 1980), Powel Papers, Box 70 . . . 211*nn*309–13, 212*n*319

May, Gregory, Note to Lewis Powell on *United States v. Crews* (Jan. 2, 1980), Powell Papers, Box 65 . . . 201*nn*225–26

May, Gregory, Supplemental Memorandum to Lewis Powell on *United States v. Crews* (undated), Powell Papers, Box 65 . . . 197*n*197

McAdams, Richard, Wither the Exclusionary Rule?, U. Chi. L. Sch. Fac. Blog, (Oct. 29, 2008, 5:23 PM), http://uchicagolaw.typepad.com/faculty/2008/10/wither-the-excl.html . . . 342*n*285, 343*n*286

Meltzer, Daniel J., Deterring Constitutional Violations by Law Enforcement Officials: Plaintiffs and Defendants as Private Attorneys General, 88 Colum. L. Rev. 247 (1988) . . . 17*n*96, 125*n*279

Mertens, William J. & Silas Wasserstrom, The Good Faith Exception to the Exclusionary Rule: Deregulating the Police and Derailing the Law, 70 Geo. L.J. 365 (1981) . . . 30*n*5, 41*n*74, 44*n*87, 153*n*226

Monaghan, Henry P., Foreword: Constitutional Common Law, 89 Harv. L. Rev. 1 (1975) . . . 151*n*209, 153*n*225

Moran, David A., The End of the Exclusionary Rule, Among Other Things: The Roberts Court Takes on the Fourth Amendment, 2006 Cato Sup. Ct. Rev. 283 . . . 328*n*202

Moran, David A., Hanging on by a Thread: The Exclusionary Rule (Or What's Left of It) Lives for Another Day, 9 Ohio St. J. Crim. L. 363 (2011) . . . 339*n*267, 341*n*277

Moran, David A., Waiting for the Other Shoe: *Hudson* and the Precarious State of *Mapp*, 93 Iowa L. Rev. 1725 (2008) . . . 346*n*302

Morris, Arval A., The Exclusionary Rule, Deterrence, and Posner's Economic Analysis of Law, 57 Wash. L. Rev. 647 (1982) . . . 13*n*74, 98*n*87

Mulqueen, Matthew S., Note, Rethinking the Role of the Exclusionary Rule in Removal Proceedings, 82 St. John's L. Rev. 1157 (2008) . . . 264*n*248

Murphy, Bruce Allen, The Brandeis/Frankfurter Connection: The Secret Political Activities of Two Supreme Court Justices (1982) . . . 43*n*81

Murphy, Frank, Conference Notes on *Harris v. United States* (undated), Murphy Papers, Reel 135 . . . 32*n*12

Murphy, Frank, Letter to Hugo Black (undated), Murphy Papers, *Wallace & Tiernan Co.* File . . . 39*n*57

Newman, Roger K., Hugo Black: A Biography (1994) . . . 87*n*21, 89*n*35, 101*n*101, 104*n*116

Nixon, Richard, The Memoirs of Richard Nixon (1978) . . . 127*nn*3–5

Note, Formalism, Legal Realism, and Constitutionally Protected Privacy Under the Fourth and Fifth Amendments, 90 Harv. L. Rev. 945 (1977) ... 7*n*36, 8*n*39, 17*n*96

Note, The Life and Times of *Boyd v. United States* (1886–1976), 76 Mich. L. Rev. 184 (1977) ... 7*n*36

Note, Standing to Object to an Unreasonable Search and Seizure, 34 U. Chi. L. Rev. 342 (1967) ... 65*n*259

Note, State Police, Unconstitutionally Obtained Evidence and Section 242 of the Civil Rights Statute, 7 Stan. L. Rev. 76 (1954) ... 64*n*254

Oakes, James L., The Proper Role of the Federal Courts in Enforcing the Bill of Rights, 54 N.Y.U. L. Rev. 911 (1979) ... 13*n*74

Oaks, Dallin H., Studying the Exclusionary Rule in Search and Seizure, 37 U. Chi. L. Rev. 665 (1970) ... 2*nn*4–5, 141*n*126, 141*nn*128–29, 142*n*130, 162

O'Connor, Sandra Day, First Draft of Dissenting Opinion in *New Jersey v. T.L.O.* (June 12, 1984), Blackmun Papers, Box 414 ... 270*n*303, 271*nn*304–10, 346*n*303

O'Connor, Sandra Day, Letter to Harry Blackmun on *INS v. Lopez-Mendoza* (May 22, 1984), Blackmun Papers, Box 407 ... 258*n*216

O'Connor, Sandra Day, Letter to Warren Burger on *Segura v. United States* (June 12, 1984), Powell Papers, Box 110 ... 294*n*155

O'Connor, Sandra Day, Letter to Warren Burger on *Segura v. United States* (May 21, 1984), Powell Papers, Box 110 ... 294*n*150

O'Connor, Sandra Day, Letter to William J. Brennan, Jr., on *James v. Illinois* (Nov. 22, 1989), Brennan Papers, Box I: 8559 ... 308*n*48

O'Connor, Sandra Day, Memorandum to the Conference on *New Jersey v. T.L.O.* (June 26, 1984), Powell Papers, Box 117 ... 272*n*322

Office of Legal Policy, U.S. Dep't of Justice, 'Truth in Criminal Justice' Series, Report No. 2: The Search and Seizure Exclusionary Rule (1986), *reprinted in* 22 U. Mich. J.L. Ref. 573 (1989) ... 344*n*291

Palm, Greg, Memorandum to Lewis Powell on *Stone v. Powell* and *Wolff v. Rice* (Mar. 11, 1976), Powell Papers, Box 30 ... 168*nn*354–57, 169*nn*358–69

Palmer, Jan, The Vinson Court Era: The Supreme Court's Conference Votes (1990) ... 37*n*46, 50*n*132

Patton, Alison L., The Endless Cycle of Abuse: Why 42 U.S.C. § 1983 Is Ineffective in Deterring Police Brutality, 44 Hastings L.J. 753 (1993) ... 290*n*108

Petersen, Henry E., Assistant Attorney General, Dep't of Justice, Address before the Section of Bar Activities Award of Merit Luncheon, American Bar Association Convention (Aug. 13, 1972) ... 140*nn*120–22

Petitioner's Opening Brief, California v. Krivda, 409 U.S. 33 (1972) (No. 71-651) ... 139*n*114, 140*n*115, 140*nn*117–18

Petition for Writ of Certiorari, Colorado v. Quintero, 464 U.S. 1014 (1983) (No. 82-1711) ... 243*n*79

Pfander, James E., The Story of *Bivens v. Six Unknown Named Agents of the Federal Bureau of Narcotics*, *in* Federal Courts Stories (Vicki C. Jackson & Judith Resnik eds., 2010) ... 134*n*70

Pitler, Robert M., "The Fruit of the Poisonous Tree" Revisited and Shepardized, 56 Calif. L. Rev. 579 (1968) ... 277*n*25, 278*nn*28–30, 329*n*209

Powell, Lewis, Handwritten Notes on *Illinois v. Krull* (Nov. 6, 1986), Blackmun Papers, Box 464 . . . 320*n*142

Powell, Lewis, Handwritten Notes on *INS v. Lopez-Mendoza* (undated), Powell Papers, Box 112 . . . 257*n*205, 258*n*209

Powell, Lewis, Handwritten Note to Greg Palm on *Stone v. Powell* and *Wolff v. Rice* (Mar. 11, 1976), Powell Papers, Box 30 . . . 169*n*370

Powell, Lewis, Letter to Byron White on *New Jersey v. T.L.O.* (April 21, 1984), Powell Papers, Box 117 . . . 269*n*290

Powell, Lewis, Letter to Byron White on *New Jersey v. T.L.O.* (Apr. 24, 1984), Blackmun Papers, Box 414 . . . 269*nn*288–89

Powell, Lewis, Letter to Potter Stewart (Mar. 1, 1973), Powell Papers, Box 6 . . . 146*nn*161–69, 147*nn*170–72

Powell, Lewis, Letter to Warren Burger (June 18, 1976), Powell Papers, Box 30 . . . 168*nn*352–53

Powell, Lewis, Letter to Warren Burger (Feb. 11, 1977), Powell Papers, Box 36 . . . 176*nn*18–25, 230*n*473

Powell, Lewis, Letter to Warren Burger on *Illinois v. Krull* (Mar. 19, 1986), Powell Papers, Box 132 . . . 319*n*124

Powell, Lewis, Letter to Warren Burger on *Nix v. Williams* (Apr. 12, 1984), Powell Papers, Box 109 . . . 286*nn*81–82

Powell, Lewis, Letter to Warren Burger on *Segura v. United States* (May 18, 1984), Powell Papers, Box 110 . . . 294*n*147

Powell, Lewis, Letter to Warren Burger on *Segura v. United States* (June 15, 1984), Powell Papers, Box 110 . . . 294*n*154

Powell, Lewis, Letter to Warren Burger on *Stone v. Powell* and *Wolff v. Rice* (June 18, 1976), Powell Papers, Box 30 . . . 170*n*382

Powell, Lewis, Letter to William J. Brennan, Jr. on *United States v. Crews* (Dec. 14, 1979), Brennan Papers, Box I: 504 . . . 199*nn*213–14

Powell, Lewis, Letter to William J. Brennan, Jr. on *United States v. Crews* (Jan. 10, 1980), Brennan Papers, Box I: 504 . . . 203*nn*243–44

Powell, Lewis, Letter to William J. Brennan, Jr. on *United States v. Crews* (Feb. 14, 1980), Brennan Papers, Box I: 504 . . . 203*n*247

Powell, Lewis, Letter to William Rehnquist (Apr. 22, 1975), Powell Papers, Box 24 . . . 158*n*262, 159*nn*263–67

Powell, Lewis, Letter to William Rehnquist on *United States v. Ceccolini* (Jan. 23, 1978), Powell Papers, Box 48 . . . 191*n*157, 192*nn*158–60

Powell, Lewis, Memorandum on *INS v. Mendoza* and *Sandoval Sanchez* (Apr. 13, 1984), Powell Papers, Box 112 . . . 257*nn*203–4

Powell, Lewis, Memorandum on *Rakas v. Illinois* (July 10, 1978), Powell Papers, Box 60 . . . 218*nn*365–67

Powell, Lewis, Memorandum on *Segura v. United States*, Nov. 7, 1983, Powell Papers, Box 110 . . . 291*nn*113–15

Powell, Lewis, Memorandum to Eric Andersen on *Dunaway v. New York* (Mar. 6, 1979), Powell Papers, Box 63 . . . 315*n*100

Powell, Lewis, Memorandum to Eric Andersen on *Payton v. New York* and *Riddick v. New York* (Mar. 6, 1979), Powell Papers, Box 69 . . . 316*nn*104–6

Powell, Lewis, Memorandum to Gregory May on *United States v. Havens* (Mar. 21, 1980), Powell Papers, Box 70 . . . 210*nn*300–301, 210*nn*305–7, 211*n*308

Powell, Lewis, Memorandum to Greg Palm on *Stone v. Powell* and *Wolff v. Rice* (June 24, 1976), Powell Papers, Box 30 . . . 172*n*396

Powell, Lewis, Memorandum to John Calvin Jeffries, Jr. on *United States v. Robinson* (Aug. 31, 1973), Powell Papers, Box 131 . . . 149*nn*191–97, 150*nn*198–207

Powell, Lewis, Memorandum to John J. Buckley on *United States. v. Calandra* (Nov. 8, 1973), Powell Papers, Box 13 . . . 152*nn*214–17

Powell, Lewis, Memorandum to John J. Buckley on *United States v. Calandra* (Nov. 10, 1973), Powell Papers, Box 13 . . . 152*nn*218–21

Powell, Lewis, Memorandum to Rob Couch on *United States v. Leon* and *Massachusetts v. Sheppard* (Jan. 3, 1984), Powell Papers, Box 109 . . . 246*nn*105–7, 246*n*109

Powell, Lewis, Notes on *Stone v. Powell* (Feb. 27, 1976), Powell Papers, Box 30 . . . 166*nn*322–28

Powell, Lewis, Notes on *United States v. Leon*, *Massachusetts v. Sheppard*, and *Colorado v. Quintero* (undated), Powell Papers, Box 109 . . . 244*nn*93–95

Powell, Lewis, Preliminary Memorandum on *Colorado v. Quintero* (June 6, 1983), Powell Papers, Box 109 . . . 245*n*96

Powell, Lewis, Summer Memorandum on *United States v. Calandra* (July 30, 1973), Powell Papers, Box 13 . . . 151*nn*210–13

Powell, Powell, Handwritten Notes on *United States v. Ceccolini* (undated), Powell Papers, Box 48 . . . 189*nn*127–28

Price, Polly J., Judge Richard S. Arnold: A Legacy of Justice on the Federal Bench (2009) . . . 87*n*21

Rehnquist, William, Draft of Concurring Opinion in *United States v. Crews* (Dec. 18, 1979), Powell Papers, Box 65 . . . 200*nn*219–20

Rehnquist, William, Draft of *United States v. Peltier* (circulated Apr. 2, 1975), Powell Papers, Box 24 . . . 157*nn*254–56

Rehnquist, William, First Draft of *United States v. Ceccolini* (Jan. 20, 1978), Powell Papers, Box 48 . . . 189*nn*134–35, 190*nn*136–44, 191*nn*155–56

Rehnquist, William, Letter to Lewis Powell (Nov. 6, 1972), Powell Papers, Box 6 . . . 145*nn*151–58, 146*nn*159–60

Rehnquist, William, Letter to Lewis Powell (Apr. 24, 1975), Powell Papers, Box 24 . . . 159*nn*268–69

Rehnquist, William, Letter to Lewis Powell on *United States v. Ceccolini* 1 (Jan. 25, 1978), Powell Papers, Box 48 . . . 192*nn*164–66

Rehnquist, William, Letter to the Conference on *New Jersey v. T.L.O.* (Mar. 30, 1984), Blackmun Papers, Box 414 . . . 267*n*277, 302*n*1

Rehnquist, William, Letter to Warren Burger on *Segura v. United States* (May 18, 1984), Powell Papers, Box 110 . . . 294*n*148

Rehnquist, William, Letter to Warren Burger on *Segura v. United States* (June 12, 1984), Powell Papers, Box 110 . . . 294*n*153

Rehnquist, William, Letter to William J. Brennan, Jr. on *United States v. Ceccolini* (Jan. 23, 1978), Powell Papers, Box 48 . . . 192*nn*162–63

Rehnquist, William, Letter to William J. Brennan, Jr. on *United States v. Crews* (Dec. 13, 1979), Powell Papers, Box 65 . . . 197*n*196

Rehnquist, William, Letter to William J. Brennan, Jr. on *United States v. Crews* (Dec. 14, 1979), Brennan Papers, Box I: 504 . . . 199*nn*211–12

Rehnquist, William, Letter to William J. Brennan, Jr. on *United States v. Crews* (Feb. 20, 1980), Brennan Papers, Box I: 504 . . . 203*n*250

Rehnquist, William, Memorandum to the Conference on *Colorado v. Quintero* (June 15, 1983), Powell Papers, Box 109 . . . 243*n*81, 244*nn*82–83

Rehnquist, William, Memorandum to the Conference on *United States v. Leon* (June 22, 1982), Powell Papers, Box 109 . . . 244*nn*84–87

Rehnquist, William, Memorandum to Warren Burger, Potter Stewart, Harry Blackmun, and Lewis Powell on *Rakas v. Illinois* (Oct. 17, 1978), Blackmun Papers, Box 290 . . . 219*nn*387–90, 220*n*391

Rehnquist, William H., Memorandum to John W. Dean, III, on Constitutional Decisions Relating to Criminal Law (Apr. 1, 1969) . . . 212*nn*320–22, 213*nn*323–24

Remaking the Supreme Court: Nixon Sets a Pattern, U.S. News & World Rep., Nov. 1, 1971 . . . 139*n*112

Roots, Roger, The Originalist Case for the Fourth Amendment Exclusionary Rule, 45 Gonz. L. Rev. 1 (2010) . . . 3*n*10, 194*n*180

Rossi, Elizabeth, Revisiting *INS v. Lopez-Mendoza*: Why the Fourth Amendment Exclusionary Rule Should Apply in Deportation Proceedings (May 13, 2011) (unpublished manuscript) . . . 264*n*248

Rutledge, Wiley, Assignment Sheet (Oct. 25, 1948), Rutledge Papers, Box 167 . . . 40*n*63

Rutledge, Wiley, Conference Notes on *Wolf v. Colorado* (Oct. 23, 1948), Rutledge Papers, Box 173 . . . 38*nn*52–53, 39*nn*58–60, 40*n*62

Rutledge, Wiley, Unpublished Dissent on *Wolf v. Colorado,* (undated), Rutledge Papers, Box 163 . . . 37*nn*47–48, 38*n*49

Savage, David G., Turning Right: The Making of the Rehnquist Supreme Court (1992) . . . 300*n*195, 319*n*125

Scalia, Antonin, Letter to William J. Brennan, Jr., on *James v. Illinois* (Dec. 7, 1989), Brennan Papers, Box I: 859 . . . 308*n*50

Scalia, Antonin, Memorandum to the Conference on *Murray v. United States* (Mar. 22, 1988), Blackmun Papers, Box 496 . . . 299*n*184

Scalia, Antonin, The Rule of Law as a Law of Rules, 56 U. Chi. L. Rev. 1175 (1989) . . . 348*n*2

Scharf, Irene, The Exclusionary Rule in Immigration Proceedings: Where It Was, Where It Is, Where It May Be Going, 12 San Diego Int'l L.J. 53 (2010) . . . 264*n*248

Schlesinger, Steven R., Exclusionary Injustice: The Problem of Illegally Obtained Evidence (1977) . . . 2*n*5, 2*n*9

Schlesinger, Steven R., It is Time to Abolish the Exclusionary Rule, Wall St. J., Sept. 10, 1981 . . . 2*n*9

Schlesinger, Steven R. & Bradford Wilson, Property, Privacy and Deterrence: The Exclusionary Rule in Search of a Rationale, 18 Duq. L. Rev. 225 (1980) . . . 111*nn*177–78

Schrock, Thomas S. & Robert C. Welsh, Reconsidering the Constitutional Common Law, 91 Harv. L. Rev. 1117 (1978) . . . 153*n*226

Schrock, Thomas S. & Robert C. Welsh, Up from *Calandra*: The Exclusionary Rule as a Constitutional Requirement, 59 Minn. L. Rev. 251 (1974) . . . 11*n*59, 13*nn*75–76, 17*n*96, 93*n*61, 94*n*68, 99*n*92, 99*n*94, 153*n*223

Schwartz, Bernard, The Ascent of Pragmatism: The Burger Court in Action (1990) . . . xiv*n*10, 128*n*18, 300*nn*196–97

Schwartz, Bernard, Super Chief: Earl Warren and His Supreme Court—A Judicial Biography (1983) . . . 31*n*9, 64*n*252, 64*n*255, 80*n*367, 82*nn*375–76, 87*n*21, 94*n*66, 101*n*100, 122*n*263, 178*nn*35–36

Scott, Austin W., Jr., Criminal Jurisdiction of a State Over a Defendant Based Upon Presence Secured by Force or Fraud, 37 Minn. L. Rev. 91, (1953) . . . 194*n*180

Seidman, Louis Michael, Factual Guilt and the Burger Court: An Examination of Continuity and Change in Criminal Procedure, 80 Colum. L. Rev. 436 (1980) . . . 172*n*395, 172*n*397

Semple, Robert B., Jr., Nixon Influenced by Fortas Affair in Court Choices, N.Y. Times, May 23, 1969 . . . 128*n*17

Shapiro, Fred R., The Most-Cited Legal Scholars, 29 J. Legal Stud. 409 (2000) . . . 348*n*1

Silverstein, Mark, Constitutional Faiths: Felix Frankfurter, Hugo Black, and the Process of Judicial Decision Making (1984) . . . 33*nn*19–20, 36*n*43

Simon, James F., The Antagonists: Hugo Black, Felix Frankfurter and Civil Liberties in Modern America (1989) . . . 33*n*17

Sklansky, David A., *Katz v. United States*: The Limits of Aphorism, *in* Criminal Procedure Stories (Carol S. Steiker ed., 2006) . . . 122*n*259

Slobogin, Christopher, Privacy at Risk: The New Government Surveillance and the Fourth Amendment (2007) . . . 290*n*108

Slobogin, Christopher, The Poverty Exception to the Fourth Amendment, 55 Fla. L. Rev. 391 (2003) . . . 263*n*242

Slobogin, Christopher, Why Liberals Should Chuck the Exclusionary Rule, 1999 U. Ill. L. Rev. 363 . . . 2*n*4, 18*n*102, 104*n*116

Souter, David H., Telephone Interview (June 24, 2010) . . . 136*n*90, 137*n*92

Specter, Arlen, *Mapp v. Ohio*: Pandora's Problems for the Prosecutor, 111 U. Pa. L. Rev. 4 (1962) . . . 83*nn*3–4, 84*nn*6–7

Steiker, Carol S., Second Thoughts About First Principles, 107 Harv. L. Rev. 820 (1994) . . . xiii*n*6, 254*n*175

Stern, Seth & Stephen Wermiel, Justice Brennan: Liberal Champion (2010) . . . 179*n*41

Stevas, Alex L., Memorandum to the Conference on *Colorado v. Quintero* (Nov. 30, 1983), Powell Papers, Box 109 . . . 246*n*104

Stevens, John Paul, Draft of Dissenting Opinion in *Illinois v. Gates* (Nov. 15, 1982), Powell Papers, Box 92 . . . 234*n*10

Stevens, John Paul, First Draft of Dissenting Opinion in *New Jersey v. T.L.O.* (June 11, 1984), Blackmun Papers, Box 414 . . . 270*nn*297–99

Stevens, John Paul, Letter to Warren Burger on *Segura v. United States* (Jan. 3, 1984), Powell Papers, Box 110 . . . 292*n*135

Stevens, John Paul, Letter to William J. Brennan, Jr. on *United States v. Crews* (Jan. 9, 1980), Powell Papers, Box 65 . . . 203*n*242

Stevens, John Paul, Letter to William J. Brennan, Jr. on *United States v. Crews* (Feb. 1, 1980), Brennan Papers, Box I: 504 . . . 204*nn*251–53

Stewart, Potter, First Draft of *Brewer v. Williams* (Nov. 24, 1976), Powell Papers, Box 36 . . . 174*n*10, 176*n*27

Stewart, Potter, Letter to William J. Brennan, Jr. on *Elkins v. United States* (May 31, 1960), Stewart Papers, Box 5 . . . 74*n*336

Stewart, Potter, Letter to William J. Brennan, Jr. on *United States v. Crews* (Dec. 13, 1979), Powell Papers, Box 65; . . . 198*n*204

Stewart, Potter, Letter to William J. Brennan, Jr. on *United States v. Crews* (Feb. 21, 1980), Brennan Papers, Box I: 504 . . . 204*n*254

Stewart, Potter, Memorandum to William Douglas, William J. Brennan, Jr., and Thurgood Marshall on *Coolidge v. New Hampshire* (June 2, 1971), Brennan Papers, Box I: 224 . . . 137*n*95

Stewart, Potter, The Road to *Mapp v. Ohio* and Beyond: The Origins, Development and Future of the Exclusionary Rule in Search-and-Seizure Cases, 83 Colum. L. Rev. 1365 (1983) . . . xii*n*4, 18*nn*103–5, 21*n*121, 23*n*129, 30*n*5, 74*n*333, 86*n*16, 87*n*21, 95*n*71, 115*n*202, 120*n*248, 121*n*251, 343*n*287

Stewart, Potter, Second Draft of *Elkins v. United States* (circulated May 20, 1960), Clark Papers, Box A95 . . . 74*n*328

Studdard, Gloria J., Recent Decision, *Miranda* Warnings Do Not Per Se Render Admissible a Confession Following an Arrest Which Violates Fourth Amendment Rights: *Brown v. Illinois*, 25 Emory L.J. 227 (1976) . . . 187*nn*111–12

Stuntz, William J., The Collapse of American Criminal Justice (2011) . . . xiii*n*6

Stuntz, William J., The Substantive Origins of Criminal Procedure, 105 Yale L.J. 393 (1995) . . . 7*n*33

Stuntz, William J., The Virtues and Vices of the Exclusionary Rule, 20 Harv. J.L. & Pub. Pol'y 443 (1997) . . . xiii*n*6, 97*n*80, 254*n*175

Sunderland, Lane V., The Exclusionary Rule: A Requirement of Constitutional Principle, 69 J. Crim. L. & Criminology 141 (1978) . . . 13*n*76

Supplemental Brief for the United States as Amicus Curiae Supporting Reversal, Illinois v. Gates, 462 U.S. 213 (1983) (No. 81-430) . . . 237*n*31

Task Force on Violent Crime: Public Hearing Before the Attorney General (1983) . . . 2*n*6

Taylor, Telford, Two Studies in Constitutional Interpretation: Search, Seizure, and Surveillance and Fair Trial and Free Press (1969) . . . 6*n*29

Thomas, George C., III & Barry S. Pollack, Balancing the Fourth Amendment Scales: The Bad-Faith "Exception" to Exclusionary Rule Limitations, 45 Hastings L.J. 21 (1993) . . . 252*n*166

Tomkovicz, James J., Constitutional Exclusion: The Rules, Rights, and Remedies that Strike the Balance Between Freedom and Order (2011) . . . 2*n*10, 34*n*28, 180*nn*47–48, 253*n*173, 283*n*65, 330*n*214

Tomkovicz, James J., *Hudson v. Michigan* and the Future of Fourth Amendment Exclusion, 93 Iowa L. Rev. 1819 (2008) . . . 325*n*184, 326*n*187, 327*n*197, 327*n*200, 328*n*203, 333*nn*234–36

Toobin, Jeffrey, The Nine: Inside the Secret World of the Supreme Court (2007) . . . 263*n*245, 270*n*300

Totten, Christopher D., The Exclusionary Rule After *Hudson v. Michigan*: Mourning the Death of the Knock and Announce Rule, 46 No. 5 Crim. L. Bull. 843 (2010) . . . 328*n*203

White, Byron, Memorandum to the Conference on *Coolidge v. New Hampshire* (June 17, 1971), Blackmun Papers, Box 128 . . . 138*nn*100–103, 232*n*6

White, Byron, Memorandum to the Conference on *Illinois v. Gates* (Nov. 5, 1982), Powell Papers, Box 92 . . . 235*n*27

White, Byron, Second Draft of *New Jersey v. T.L.O.* (June 12, 1984), Blackmun Papers, Box 414 . . . 271*nn*311–12, 272*nn*313–15

White, Byron, Third Draft of Concurring Opinion in *United States v. Crews* (Feb. 4, 1980), Powell Papers, Box 65 . . . 203*n*246

White, G. Edward, Earl Warren: A Public Life (1982) . . . 64*n*250, 64*n*256

White, James Boyd, Forgotten Points in the "Exclusionary Rule" Debate, 81 Mich. L. Rev. 1273 (1983) . . . 18*n*102

White, Welsh S. & Robert S. Greenspan, Standing to Object to Search and Seizure 118 U. Pa. L. Rev. 333 (1970) . . . 225*n*427

Wigmore, John H., Using Evidence Obtained by Illegal Search and Seizure, 8 A.B.A. J. 479 (1922) . . . 3*n*10, 14*n*80, 16*n*94, 95*n*69

Wigmore, John Henry, Evidence–Fourth Amendment–Documents Illegally Seized, 9 Ill. L. Rev. 43 (1915) . . . 16*n*91

Wigmore, John Henry, A Treatise on the Anglo-American System of Evidence in Trials at Common Law (2d ed. 1923) . . . 2*n*7, 8*n*40

Wilkey, Malcolm Richard, Enforcing the Fourth Amendment by Alternatives to the Exclusionary Rule (1982) . . . 2*n*9

Wilkey, Malcolm Richard, The Exclusionary Rule: Why Suppress Valid Evidence?, 62 Judicature 214 (1978) . . . 2*n*7

Wilson, Bradford P., Enforcing the Fourth Amendment: A Jurisprudential History (1986) . . . 3*n*14, 18*n*101

Wilson, Bradford P., The Fourth Amendment as More Than a Form of Words: The View from the Founding, *in* The Bill of Rights: Original Meaning and Current Understanding (Eugene W. Hickok Jr. ed., 1991) . . . 96*n*74

Wollin, David A., Policing the Police: Should *Miranda* Violations Bear Fruit?, 53 Ohio St. L.J. 805 (1992) . . . 308*n*54

Woodward, Bob & Scott Armstrong, The Brethren: Inside the Supreme Court (1979) . . . 104*n*116, 137*n*94, 138*n*105, 171*n*383

Yackle, Larry, The Burger Court and the Fourth Amendment, 26 U. Kan. L. Rev. 335 (1978) . . . 88*n*23

Yackle, Larry, The Story of *Fay v. Noia*: Another Case About Another Federalism, *in* Federal Courts Stories (Vicki C. Jackson & Judith Resnik eds., 2010) . . . 143*n*139

Yarbrough, Tinsley E., Harry A. Blackmun: The Outsider Justice (2008) . . . 143*n*137

Yarbrough, Tinsley E., John Marshall Harlan: Great Dissenter of the Warren Court (1992) . . . 31*n*8

Zion, Sidney E., Detectives Get a Course in Law, N.Y. Times, Apr. 28, 1965 . . . 84*n*5

Zotti, Priscilla H. Machado, Injustice for All: *Mapp vs. Ohio* and the Fourth Amendment (2005) . . . 86*n*14

Table of Cases

C

D

E

F

G

K

L

M

N

O

P

T

U

V

W

Index

Q

R

Z